Tracklaying 1,000 miles beyond Omaha, as noted by the sign hanging from the tree, in Weber Canyon, Utah. (1868)

UNION PACIFIC COUNTRY

The windmill, water tank, engine, and 20-stall roundhouse (in background) at Laramie were part of the technology employed in developing Union Pacific Country. (1868)

UNION PACIFIC COUNTRY

By Robert G. Athearn

UNIVERSITY OF NEBRASKA PRESS
LINCOLN AND LONDON

PHOTO CREDITS—Union Pacific Railroad Collection: i, iii, xiii, 29, 40–41, 47, 58–59, 64, 72 (bottom), 73 (bottom), 77, 80 (bottom), 80–81 (top), 84, 92–93, 106–107 (top), 110, 134–135, 140–141, 154, 164, 222, 283, 303 (top), 359; Nebraska State Historical Society: 24–25 (top), 81 (bottom); Denver Public Library Western Collection: 24–25 (bottom), 154–155, 178 (bottom); Northwestern Bell Telephone Company: 59 (top); Utah State Historical Society: 72–73 (top), 106 (bottom), 256–257, 277; Nebraska State Historical Society, S. D. Butcher Collection: 161, 178–179 (top); Harper's Weekly: 169; Kansas State Historical Society: 190–191; University of Iowa Library: 243; Oregon Historical Society: 257 (top), 295, 302 (top), 302–303.

Maps by NICHOLAS F. MRAZ

Book Design by MARIO PAGLIAI

Third Bison Book printing: 1982
Most recent printing shown by first digit below:
     4   5   6   7   8   9   10

Bison Book edition reprinted by arrangement with the author.

Manufactured in the United States of America

Library of Congress Cataloging in Publication Data
Athearn, Robert G.
  Union Pacific country.

  Reprint of the 1971 ed. published by Rand McNally, Chicago.
  1. Union Pacific Railroad—History. 2. The West —History. I. Title.
[HE2791.U55A37 1976]   385'.0978   75–11707
ISBN 0–8032–0858–8
ISBN 0–8032–5829–1 pbk.

For Byron and Sally Raney

Contents

List of Illustrations

List of Maps

Interior of the Union Pacific Railroad ticket office at 1000 Main Street, Kansas City, Missouri. (1892)

UNION PACIFIC COUNTRY

Introduction

As the American frontier moved across the Appalachians and approached the Mississippi River, one dominating subject of conversation among settlers was the need for improved transportation facilities. The need was partially remedied, during the 1820s and 1830s, with the construction of canals and turnpikes.

Both the Erie Canal and the National Road were regarded by contemporaries as great engineering projects, achievements that also swelled the national pride and promised accelerated economic development for the West. However, as improved as were these means of transportation and travel, each had its limitations, especially during winter. But a railroad promised speedy, relatively cheap, and all-weather service. During the 1840s and 1850s the "canal craze" gave way to a "railroad mania" and even the smallest villages hoped that they would be connected to the mainstream of the American economy by these magic threads of iron.

The pre-Civil War decade was one of railroad expansion in the West and of consolidation in the more settled parts of the land. Dreamers talked of spanning the continent, of reaching out to the Orient, and of joining the oceans with an iron link. But the great sectional question intervened and confined the effort to planning and surveying, as North and South fought over which region should be the beneficiary of such progress. A panic in 1857 tended to temporarily dry up capital, and by the time this financial distress had been alleviated the Civil War had erupted, diverting national attention for another four years.

Although the war plugged ordinary economic arteries and overloaded others, momentarily setting at rest any talk of rail expansion, the long-range effect was to be beneficial. The isolation of the West now became a matter of national concern, particularly after a Confederate thrust penetrated New Mexico and seriously threatened Colorado. The entire Pacific

Coast, including mineral-rich California, stood in danger of possible foreign intervention. Tethered to the Union by the most fragile of connections, the trans-Missouri West became increasingly the nation's concern. Not unusual, therefore, were Lincoln's efforts to reassure the American people that his administration's intent to protect this domain would include a specific proposal for a railroad to the western sea.

The Pacific Railroad Act of 1862 was enacted because of a wartime emergency, but in congressional minds, it also fulfilled a promise to the nation, a promise underscored by the supplementary Act of 1864, that the government would help to carry out a project which had been talked about for three decades. As the war ended, private enterprise responded to the attractions provided by congressional legislation and at long last rail-laying began.

The war-weary American public, sickened by the destruction wrought during the fratricidal conflict, gladly turned its attention to this constructive enterprise. As the rails reached for each other from Sacramento and Omaha, there developed a mounting excitement among a people who traditionally loved a contest. The drama of crews battling Indians and the elements, of crossing high mountains and dangerous deserts, and roistering far into the night after having labored during heroic days not only intrigued contemporaries, but it would also hold hostage the minds of those who would recount the great event in the decades to come. Writers would invariably label it "A Work of Giants" or "Moguls and Iron Men" to describe the superhuman effort of the builders. The movement toward Utah would be called the "High Road to Promontory" or "Westward to Promontory" to depict that lonely point on a Utah summit as the ultimate goal. And May 10, 1869, would represent not only the climax of the story, but also its conclusion. For a century after that date Americans regarded the event much the same as had those who watched the ceremonial spike-driving: a moment of triumph, the successful and satisfying realization of an American dream.

The story of the Union Pacific's development in the years following that champagne-drenched day at Promontory has never been told. Nelson Trottman's *History of the Union Pacific* (1923) came closest. That work, written by an attorney and subtitled "A Financial and Economic Survey," dealt largely with administrative matters and corporate problems. Because of the vast amount of material available on that aspect alone, the author was able to devote only a single 20-page chapter to the growth of auxiliary and branch lines. Yet the trackage of those feeders was more than four times larger than the core system (including the Kansas Pacific and the Denver Pacific).

The original line served only a relatively narrow strip of land across

Nebraska, while portions of the road in both Wyoming and Utah crossed country that even today is hardly regarded as a garden spot. If the UP's managers hoped to own anything but a carrier of through traffic they had to expand the road far beyond the confines of the granted lands. Company officials recognized this at an early date and began at once to think in terms of feeders that would augment main line traffic. As that policy was put into effect, piece by piece, there developed a large segment of the West that might properly be called "Union Pacific Country."

Executives of the modern Union Pacific recognize that the spread of the system and the development of the country through which the road and its many branches ran comprise the real history of the road. As the centennial year approached, and as the flow of "Dash to Promontory" books began, these officials looked with increasing interest at the prospect of telling the story that might well be entitled "Promontory Epilogue." After long discussions with Arthur Z. Gray, President of the Union Pacific Foundation, it was agreed that I should undertake such a study. The conferences were the result of a deep interest in the subject expressed to Mr. Gray by E. Roland Harriman, son of E. H. Harriman and then Chairman of the Union Pacific's Executive Committee.

The principal concern of these men was that the book be written independently and with as much objectivity as possible. Although they offered to support my efforts during summers, when I might otherwise have engaged in teaching, they stressed that all points of view, attitudes, and conclusions were to be mine and mine alone. They further promised that no company doors would remain closed in my search for materials pertinent to the study. I am happy to say that this agreement was carried out to the letter. Even better, company employees who had knowledge of the whereabouts of material that might be useful came forward and volunteered their help in making it available to me.

The principal problem I faced was that of recounting the growth of a railroad empire made up of a great many lines, large and small. The country they served stretched from the Missouri River to the Pacific Northwest and from Texas to Montana. By the early 1900s it would involve Nevada and California, when the Los Angeles to Salt Lake City line was included, and for a brief moment would include the whole Southern Pacific system. In an effort to make the story as manageable as possible I decided to concern myself principally with what might be thought of as the pioneering period of the company's history, or, to put it another way, the pre-Harriman era. Even within that scope, choices had to be made. I elected not to dwell heavily upon the original construction aspects, since that has been done many times, but rather to take the point of view of those contemporaries who waited patiently in the West for the coming of the railroad. Using that background I then made an effort to tell the story of the road's penetration of a virgin land and to make some assessment of both the problems encountered and the successes or failures in solving them. So voluminous is the material available for a work of this kind that a great many things had to be left out or merely touched upon if a readable and understandable result were to be reached. This then is not intended to be the history of a railroad company, but rather one chapter in the larger story of how the American West was penetrated, settled, and developed with the aid of steam and iron.

"There Lies a Desert Land"

It was late June 1862, and the emigrants in the wagon train that crawled westward along the Platte River Valley already had begun to feel the isolation of the plains. Here and there they came upon small farms whose drought-stunted crops had taken on the tawny color of the buffalo grass that dominated the landscape of this great, unclaimed land. These lonely agricultural efforts stood as brave, but pitiful, attempts to settle a country that the Maker apparently had designated as off limits, and their wilted appearance suggested that the penalty for trespass already had been invoked. Young Randall Hewitt eyed the scene thoughtfully from his wagon perch and then made a note for his diary. The evidence at hand, he decided, made it clear that the party was now well into the Great American Desert he had seen described in classroom geographies. It was decidedly impressive.

The country struck the travelers as being different. To those accustomed to more humid areas, particularly the neatly fenced and cultivated sections, the sandy stretches of cactus, sagebrush, and greasewood looked wild and desolated. The word "desert" had been used loosely to define unsettled, barren areas, and the word came easily to the minds of those who approached the high plains. The fact that the organized area of Nebraska lay behind this group, and before it stretched an unpeopled empire yet to be domesticated, did much to blend the words "desert" and "isolated" in men's minds. Randall Hewitt felt this when he wrote: "To the westward civil authority practically ceased; everything was in unsettled condition, and where emigrant parties had joined for security and combined for their own protection, each company was a law unto itself."

The title of this chapter comes from Henry Wadsworth Longfellow's *Evangeline:* "Far to the West there lies a desert land, where the mountains lift through perpetual snows, their lofty and luminous summits."

As the wagon train approached the forks of the Platte, ascending the imperceptible yet steady rise toward the Rockies, its members felt even more the loneliness of their situation. "The plains all around are bleak and desolate, barren enough to all intents and almost, one can readily believe, under the ban of the Creator; forbidding in every conceivable aspect," wrote the young emigrant. He was impressed, as were all other newcomers, by the great sweep of western distances, the apparent endlessness of the vistas gained as each rise was topped, and by the lack of foliage that dotted the landscapes of childhood memory. The country seemed to defy man and beast to live from it. The wagon train's work animals fared well enough, the buffalo grass being still in adequate supply; however, the human passersby felt the parsimoniousness of the land when they were obliged to pay ten cents for each stick of wood purchased for fuel.

Although the Platte Valley had been used by westbound wagon trains for almost a generation, and numberless thousands had passed that way, the notion of its general sterility had undergone little or no change. After the early explorers had come the Oregon pioneers, followed by the Argonauts of 1849 and the Pikes Peakers of 1859, all of whom had regarded this part of America as a place to be utilized as a crossing to a better land. By 1862 much of Nebraska was still unsurveyed, its organized counties extending westward from the Missouri River only four tiers deep. Beyond lay country little changed from the time it was purchased from France some six decades earlier; for, as Randall Hewitt wrote, "It was always understood that all the country one hundred miles west of Omaha was desert, hopeless and irreclaimable." There was almost nothing that lay between this line of demarcation and the Sierras that could provide westbound travelers with a more optimistic point of view.

In retrospect one would imagine that these people, moving westward at an average daily rate of between 15 and 20 miles, would have dreamed of a time when some better means of passage would be developed. Statesmen, planners, and visionaries had long talked of a continent spanned by rails, and of a day when the transit would be made by the magic power of steam. The emigrants themselves, however, either were shortsighted, disinterested, pessimistic, or downright practical, if the comments of Randall Hewitt may be taken as typical. During the hot, dry days of his westering experience he watched his people struggle across unfriendly country and commented: "None of that band of travel-worn emigrants paid much attention to railroad problems or possibilities. . . ." He did not criticize them for this, but instead explained: "It would have been but the dream of an enthusiast, colored as dreams always are, and dismissed to the realm of impossibility."[1] These were ordinary people. They knew how to go West, for their predecessors had shown them the way, and now they were carrying out their desire to move in the accepted manner of the day. As they crossed the country so long designated as desert, they accepted it as such, and looked for little that was agriculturally promising. They might have admitted that a railroad was perhaps possible, as an exercise in engineering, but few would have regarded the intervening country as a source of local business.

Still, during June of 1862, as Randall Hewitt and his people followed that well-worn path westward along the Platte and watched prairie dogs scurry through patches of sagebrush, Congress passed a Pacific railroad bill that proposed the building of an iron road through this desolate part of America. A few days later President Lincoln took his eyes off the map of Virginia—where Gen. George McClellan was so busily engaged with the Confederacy—long enough to sign the bill into law. The memorable event was little noticed, with the nation in a deep convulsion of civil war. Nebraska was far away, both in distance and in degree of importance. The idea was meritorious, if propounded for no better reason than national defense; but practical men knew that a law was not an operating railroad, and the next few years would show that such a creation could not be merely legislated into existence. As a government project, financed wholly by the federal treasury, the scheme was not out of the question; but when the legislators tried to sell the American businessman a piece of national "desert" as sufficient enticement to undertake the work, there was little response. These men had not attained their present positions by engaging in chimerical financial enterprises; even more, they had studied geography in school. The ensuing reluctance of investors to participate in the great national enterprise probably came as no surprise to those who went west by wagon in 1862.

By the time the Pacific Railroad Act of 1862 was passed, the Great American Desert had been a part of national thinking for over half a century, most of which time it was of concern primarily to geographers, scientists, explorers, and writers. The average frontiersman, who was a farmer, saw little reason to consider seriously an area reported to be so infertile, and so lacking in transportation, when other land lay ready for the taking. During the decade of the 1850s, however, the question became less academic, for by now the nation's borders had been pushed to the Pacific Coast and two new states had been created in that area. In this process America's greatest mining boom had begun in California, soon spread to Nevada, Oregon, Idaho, Colorado, and Montana, and created demands for improved transportation. Meanwhile, the farmers' frontier had crept westward, gingerly feeling its way across the Missouri River, reaching out toward markets in the western mining country, and testing the edges of the desert. Then came the great railroad surveys of the decade, lending the strongest evidence to date that the construction of a transcontinental line was not far off.

As sectional issues intervened and heated the argument, the still un-decided potential of America's mid-continent came to public debate. More conservative Americans maintained that the desert theory was correct and that time had done nothing to show it to be fallacious. An unsigned article published in the *North American Review* for January 1856 reiterated the old arguments: that for two or three hundred miles beyond the Missouri River the soil had agricultural possibilities, but after that, and until one reached the Rockies, there was nothing but buffalo grass, soil of hard clay, and little water. "Our rich possessions west of the 99th meridian have turned out to be worthless, so far as agriculture is concerned," said the magazine. "They never can entice a rural population to inhabit them, nor sustain one if so enticed." Calling Kansas and Nebraska, except for a small strip along their eastern borders, "perfect deserts," the writer concluded that whatever railroad route was selected "it must wind the greater part of its length through a country destined to remain forever an uninhabited and dreary waste."[2]

Army explorers, dating back to Maj. Stephen H. Long in 1820, clung to the view that the country beyond the 100th meridian would be primarily useful for grazing, but not for agriculture as it was normally practiced. As late as 1858 Lt. Gouverneur K. Warren, well known for his explorations of the American West, was sure that much of the great plains, without irriga-tion, "must remain incapable of agriculture." Westward from the banks of the Missouri, said the officer, the soil grew steadily thinner until at last it degenerated "into a cold and desolate moor, on which no vegetation can live." It seemed obvious to him that the pioneers recognized this condition, for little settlement had developed in Kansas or Nebraska. This great barrier had, he thought, dammed the stream of American emigration, and if the westward pressure grew irresistible, pioneers would rather go north by way of the Missouri River, or southwest toward New Mexico, than attack the desert frontally.[3]

Politicians, publicists, and dreamers placed their arguments on a higher plane, supporting the idea of a transcontinental railroad in general and even in philosophical terms. They refused to accept traditional findings and placed their faith in the resistlessness of the land to the westward thrust, certain that American determination, ingenuity, and perseverance would overcome all obstacles. Senator Thomas Hart Benton, Missouri's great champion of the West, took this stance in January 1855 when he addressed his colleagues on his favorite subject, expansion. In eloquent terms he com-pared eastern Kansas to Egypt, contending that for 200 miles beyond the Missouri River lay one continuous cornfield, beyond which awaited an

empire somewhat less humid, but well supplied with grass. The valley of
the Kansas he portrayed as the bucolic region of America, describing it as
a diversified region well supplied with springs, streams, and wood, while
beneath the surface lay building stone, coal, and iron. The senator argued
that a country possessed of all these natural resources could easily provide
ample local business to a railroad. It was only necessary to build such a line
to prove his point; and then, he said, "emigrants of our America would
flock upon it as pigeons to their roosts, tear open the bosom of the virgin soil,
and spring into existence the long line of farms and houses, of towns and
villages, of orchards, fields, and gardens, of churches and schoolhouses, of
noisy shops, clattering mills, and thundering forges, and all that civilization
affords to enliven the wild domain from the Mississippi to the Pacific; to give
protection and employment to the road, and to balance the populous communities in the eastern half of the Union by equal populations on its western
half." The road would soon be started, Benton predicted, and the work
would be carried out by private enterprise, because this was a progressive,
utilitarian age in which capital seeking investment would find this particular
temptation to be irresistible. Once these enterprising businessmen took the
necessary step, their work would be rewarded by a westward flood of emigrants, and the land between the Missouri River and California would feel
the pressure of the most rapid expansion of the human race ever yet witnessed.[4]

Horace Greeley, the New York editor whose name is so thoroughly etched
in the pattern of westward expansion, was equally enthusiastic, but somewhat more specific in his arguments. In 1859 he made a stagecoach trip to
the Pacific Coast, the purpose of which, he said, was to study the possibility
of a railroad and to assist in bringing it about. One of the results of his tour
was a book entitled *An Overland Journey,* in which he concluded that although much of the land to be crossed was indeed barren, the railroad was
a national necessity. The journalist wrote freely of the desert when he
reached western Kansas, calling the sands along the Republican River "as
pure as Sahara can boast," and he admitted "the dearth of water is fearful."
As he approached Denver, Greeley looked behind him and entitled the
chapter describing the country through which he had passed "Goodbye to
the Desert."

Despite the difficulties of drought and distance Greeley felt that the
road could be built and that there were economic arguments in its favor.
Playing heavily upon the growing population of California, he wrote of
the thousands who had gone there by sea or by wagon train, and he guessed
that nine-tenths of them would have used a railroad if one had existed. The
journalist estimated that not less than $50 million worth of gold was shipped

TOP—*A lonely dirt shanty, an ox-drawn wagon, and the family cow were this family's armament in the battle to subdue the desert. Thoughtful easterners must have wondered if the great giveaway of western lands was overly generous once they had seen pictures such as this.*

BOTTOM—*Westward by steam was the preferred way to travel, but the persistence of the covered wagon was great, as evidenced in its use by this group of settlers in Wyoming in 1882.*

out of San Francisco annually, and that the federal post office was paying $1.25 million a year to carry mail to the West Coast. In addition, the writer said, the government then paid about $6 million a year to transport its men, munitions, and matériel to the vast western country, and that its total cost of maintaining the army in this region was at least $25 million.[5] Surely, he said, half of this could be saved by the construction of a railway, if one considered the increased mobility of troops in such a situation. Moving from the material to a higher plane, he described the benefits of sending letters, literature, and other forms of communication to California and, best of all, the supplying of that state with "intelligent, capable, virtuous women," a commodity bound to raise the moral level of the whole community.

All of this, said Greeley, could be achieved by the construction of a road that could be built for as little as $5,000 a mile and perhaps in the most difficult spots, for $100,000 a mile. In any event, the total cost would run into the millions—$100 million or $150 million—and even to Greeley, who was often regarded as somewhat visionary, this was far too large a figure for private capital to consider. "The amount is too vast; the enterprise too formidable; the returns too remote and uncertain," he wrote. He called it madness to try to raise that kind of money, and even if it were done, "what assurance could an association of private citizens have that, having devoted their means and energies to the construction of such a road, it could not be rivaled and destroyed by a similar work on some other route?" Considering all these hazards, Greeley concluded that the government would have to come forward with part of the cost—he suggested $50 million—in the form of a bonus to the winning bidder. He was certain that the services offered by such a road and the resultant benefits to the nation would repay the government within five years.

Few who had traveled across the high plains and beyond the Rockies could honestly say that the country promised much in the way of local traffic and that it had any particular attractions as an investment. John W. Dawson, who made the crossing in late 1861 to take up his duties as Governor of Utah Territory, told his legislative assembly that as badly as the road was needed, and as little as he doubted the constitutional power of Congress to authorize the project, the character of the intervening country was such that private capital could not undertake the work. To this staunch Unionist the railroad was a national undertaking, and "it is right that it should be made by the nation."[6]

The feeling that the desert challenge would be too great for even the boldest of investors persisted, and found its supporters in Congress when the matter came up for formal debate. Representative Justin S. Morrill, of Vermont, assured his colleagues that no capitalist would invest a single dollar in a project that ran for any distance across the plains. He was convinced that speculators would avail themselves of the provisions of the bill only to the extent of "seizing the land at either end, but the gap that will remain before any through connection can be made will remain unfilled so far as they are concerned." Representative James Campbell, of Pennsylvania, agreed. As chairman of the committee that reported favorably on the bill for the road he asserted that every member of the House knew it was "to be constructed through almost impassable mountains, deep ravines, cañons, gulfs, and over sandy plains." Therefore, he argued, it was not reasonable to "apply ordinary rules concerning roads in the Western States to this great enterprise."[7]

The spring of 1862 was no time for contemplation or prolonged debate. Not only had the dramatic events of the Civil War taken command of congressional attention, but there was a disposition on the part of many legislators to activate some national programs long blocked by their Southern colleagues, who were no longer in Washington, D.C. In May the much-debated and once-vetoed Homestead bill was passed and signed into law. The proposal for a transcontinental railroad, which also had been bandied about the halls of Congress for years, appeared to be a natural counterpart to this land legislation when viewed from the vantage point of some who backed the measure. Their enthusiasm for it temporarily wiped away the desert, or perhaps materialized for them a mirage that bespoke of locomotives steaming across Senator Benton's bucolic portion of America. If not that, then they agreed with Representative Campbell that ordinary rules of rail-roading did not apply to the western reaches of the country.

The notion that private enterprise would not, in the foreseeable future, be enticed very deeply into the West was old and ingrained in congressional minds. In 1858 Sen. Alfred Iverson, of Georgia, predicted that "When the country between the present uninhabited portions of the United States on the east and west . . . shall be settled up by whites, and shall furnish travel and minerals or agricultural products for transportation, then, and not until then, will individual wealth and enterprise be bold enough to run the iron horse between the Atlantic and Pacific over any route within the United States." Even then, he doubted the venture's feasibility: "If it should cost only a hundred millions, would it ever pay? Would the stock ever draw a dividend?" he asked his colleagues. "What shrewd, intelligent Yankee will ever invest his money, his labor, or his time in such an undertaking?"[8]

Arguments of this congressional faction rested upon the ground of public necessity, as it would later on, and upon the more general demands of civilization and progress. New York's Sen. William H. Seward, well known as an expansionist, contended "that a railroad is necessary, and ought to be built; and I think it has been scientifically demonstrated . . . that not only one such road is feasible, but that at least three, four, or five routes offer the necessary facilities for the security of this great object."[9] A few years earlier Sen. Augustus C. Dodge, of Iowa, had appealed to the Senate for aid, "so far as the Government can give it, in doling out its miserable acres for the construction of such a road as this." He felt that the sufferings of the men, women, and children who had "crossed that desert prairie" by older and more arduous modes of travel could be alleviated by the legislators.[10] As the debate proceeded over the years government aid, to an indeterminate degree, became a presupposed condition for the construction of the road, and legislators found it increasingly hard to protest against so worthy a national project. Many of them were convinced, even in 1862, that they were giving away nothing more than some "miserable acres."[11]

Supporters of government aid to the Pacific railroads need not have felt apologetic, for there were precedents. Government aid had been given to those who undertook the first transportation breakthrough to the West, earlier in that century, when the Cumberland Road reached out for the headwaters of the Ohio River, and again when the National Road was pushed through to the Mississippi River. State and local governments had invested heavily in a network of canals that served the lower states of the old Northwest Territory. When the westward sweep of empire reached the Missouri River, there was an entirely accountable hesitation, for those who looked beyond confessed that they had never faced anything like the American Desert in their long, migratory history. The land that became Nebraska, and the country to the west, possessed resources; but there was no way to tap these without a railroad. The next step westward was to be a giant step, and its execution called for a return to the earlier practice of seeking aid more powerful than that afforded by private enterprise. It was not unnatural that men of the time should turn to Congress for this help.

The Act of (May) 1862 was one of compromises. To satisfy the clamors of various economic interests along the Missouri River it was stipulated that the single span of road should begin at the 100th meridian (near Fort Kearny, Nebraska), to be served by five rail fingers reaching out from the river towns. Thus Kansas City (Mo.), Leavenworth, Saint Joseph, Sioux City, and some unnamed municipality would be given railroad connections. By presidential designation Omaha became the terminus of the fifth branch, to be constructed by the Union Pacific Company as a continuation of the main line. As it developed, this was the only branch built according to plan.

This serpentine swath across Nebraska represents the Union Pacific's land grant, as of the 1864 revision. The company owned the odd sections, the federal government the even.

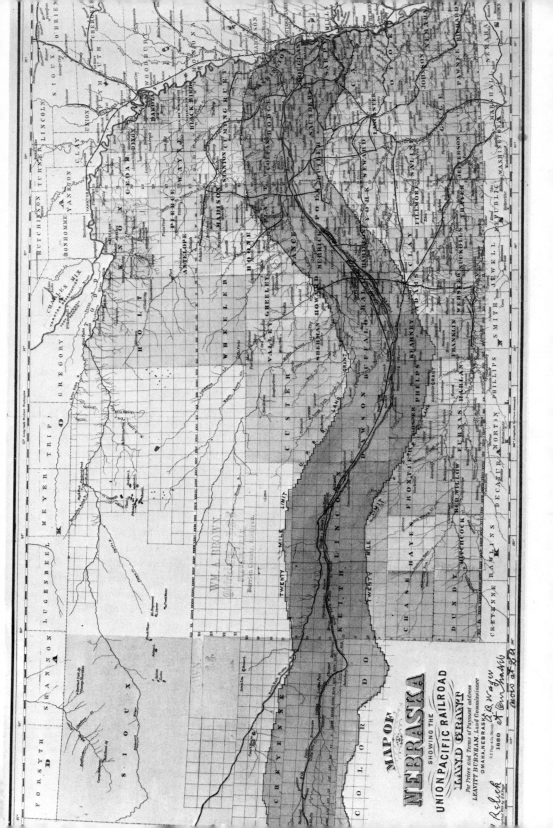

MAP OF NEBRASKA

SHOWING THE

UNION PACIFIC RAILROAD

LAND GRANT

For Prices and Terms of Payment address
LEAVITT BURNHAM, Land Commissioner
OMAHA, NEBRASKA
1880

The second compromise of the act was in finance. To provide a partial subsidy, while leaving construction in private hands, Congress offered the Union Pacific a land grant of ten sections (6,400 acres) for every mile of road built, and a 30-year loan of government bonds that were scaled at $16,000, $32,000, and $48,000 per mile, depending upon the difficulty of the terrain through which the road passed. In return, the government was to hold a first mortgage on the property and was to withhold payment until government commissioners approved each succeeding 40 miles of construction. As a further guarantee of compliance Congress ordained that one-fourth of all bonds duly earned were to be withheld until the work was completed. The stock issue was apportioned in shares of $1,000 denominations, to the extent of 100,000, and no one would be permitted to hold more than 200.

Supporters of the proposed road did not feel that the government's offer would excite the investing class, but circumstances allowed only one course. Without much enthusiasm a group of congressionally designated commissioners, including two who represented the government, met at Chicago in early September, elected a temporary set of officers, and then launched a subscription drive.[12] Their goal was temporary and aimed at raising $2 million, which represented the sale of 2,000 shares, a necessity before a permanent management could be legally elected. Rather than trying to convince investors of their project's great potential, they appealed to the citizens' patriotism, and asked for money to keep the charter from lapsing on the ground that the government was bound to make its offer more attractive to private enterprise. Six months of such advertising generated only about $300,000 worth of enthusiasm, most of which came out of the West. In a booming wartime economy few eastern investors were interested in a proposal that could promise no appreciable returns for years.[13]

For a year after the September 1862 meeting, subscription books for Union Pacific stock lay waiting for a public response that never came. In the latter part of this period a former New York medical man named Thomas C. Durant staged a one-man campaign of persuasion that committed subscribers to $2,177,000 worth of stock, although he was obliged to supply three-fourths of the necessary ten percent down payment himself. The law complied with, the stockholders met on October 29 and 30, 1863, and elected directors, adopted a set of bylaws, set up an executive committee, and provided the stripling corporation with its first official management.[14]

John A. Dix, well known in public life and in railroad circles and a man who at the time wore major general's stars, accepted the presidency, although it was obvious to most, and particularly to Durant, that he would have little time to devote to his new duties. "The Doctor," as his friends called him, became vice president and general manager, which, along with a directorship, gave him all the control of the road he felt was necessary. John J. Cisco, an attorney who had recently served as assistant secretary of the United States Treasury, accepted the post of treasurer. The office of secretary went to Henry V. Poor, well known for his editorship of the *American Railroad Journal,* but who would shortly be much more widely recognized for his *Manual of Railroads,* issued annually for many years. In time he would become one of the Union Pacific's great critics. Important at the time, however, was the fact that Poor was a familiar figure in Washington circles, as were Dix and Cisco. It was another of the details that had not escaped the watchful eye of the cunning doctor, who was about to mastermind a financial medicine show that would dazzle the nation.[15]

Formal organization of the company did not mean that rails would soon be laid west of the Missouri River. Money was still the principal problem that faced management, and while there seemed to be little prospect that it would be forthcoming under existing conditions, the effort to procure it had to be carried forward. At a board of directors meeting on November 5, 1863, a seven-member finance committee was appointed and directed to "devise plans for the raising of money to prosecute the work."[16] Theirs was a dismal task, for wartime financial developments were rapidly increasing the difficulties they faced. The government bonds, to be made available upon completion of each section of the road, promised a yield of six percent in currency; but in a period of sharp inflation, currency was not stable. By the spring of 1864, for example, the price of gold was advancing so rapidly that no one knew from day to day what currency was worth. Gold that sold at $180 in May had advanced to $250 by August. Thus the value of the bonds depended upon the success of the project they supported, and the public had not yet shown any confidence in building a railroad across what was still regarded as a desert.[17]

Even Durant, the promoter of the century, recognized the impossibility of enticing players into the game unless the odds were appreciably improved. With this in mind he turned to congressional connections, hopeful of persuading the legislators to follow a good turn with one that was even better. During the winter of 1863-64 Durant, assisted by two influential businessmen, Henry S. McComb and Cornelius S. Bushnell, preached the railroad's cause among members of Congress so effectively that by spring they had a revised act upon Lincoln's desk. The act's provisions considerably liberalized the original law. The legislation that the president signed into being on July 2, 1864, authorized the Pacific railroads to issue bonds in an amount equal to the government bonds already provided, an action that reduced the government to the rank of a second mortgage holder. Both types of bonds were henceforth to be released after the completion of each 20 miles of road, instead of the earlier figure of 40, and in the mountain regions there was a conditional provision for release of part of the government bonds in advance of construction. Further liberalization came in the doubling of the land grant—from 6,400 acres to 12,800 acres per mile—and the increase of shares to one million, with no limitation on the amount to which any individual might subscribe.

While it is frequently said that bribery was employed in Congress, and this may well have been true, there is room for argument that it was not needed.[18] Rowland G. Hazard, intimately associated with Union Pacific financial matters, later referred to this charge, and he admitted that while Durant was not above such practices, the doctor was not a man to bribe when bribery was unnecessary. Congressmen generally favored granting terms attractive to individuals who would build the road. They had put out their bait in 1862, but had felt no strikes for two years. Now they recognized that they had to make their offer more attractive to financiers. Hazard denied there was any organized body of capitalists asking Congress for better terms. "On the contrary," he wrote, "in consequence of the indifference with which capital regarded the enterprise, it was dragging along in the hands of men of little pecuniary responsibility."[19]

The months that followed passage of the Act of 1864 bore out Hazard's contention. The most aggressive efforts to raise capital through stock subscriptions utterly failed to attract investors.[20] The nation was caught up in its bloodiest war, and the outcome was yet in doubt. Most investors looked to sources of quick profit in the highly inflationary economy of the day, sources that promised a much faster return than a western railroad could offer. The Homestead Act, only two years old, neither drew farmers westward onto free lands nor excited them about the possibilities of railroad land that as yet had no rails. Nor were land promoters yet interested in subdividing the West. When a railroad was assured, or when one was actually built, they would take another look. In the meantime, nothing had altered the myth of the desert. The principal barrier in the minds of potential investors, large or small, continued to be psychological. As late as 1866, when Union Pacific rails were being laid across Nebraska, Horace F. Clark was invited to invest in the venture. "I gave some attention to the subject . . . and I came to the conclusion that the whole enterprise, except as a Government measure, was beyond the range of ordinary prudence," confessed the man who later accepted the presidency of the road.[21]

This attitude of caution was widespread in 1864. In the autumn of that year a leading magazine published an article about the proposed railroad construction in which the author, Fitz-hugh Ludlow, argued that the project was unique in American railroad history. And because no road of any length yet had been built in advance of settlement, he believed that this one could not be undertaken by traditional methods. Contending that the Great Plains "have no natural fascination for the white man which can induce him to take up his residence there," he assumed that no settler would venture forth out of pure quixotism, and he concluded that only a railroad could elevate the plains farmer beyond a condition of mere self-subsistence. Thus it seemed apparent to him that "the Pacific Road is the absolutely essential stimulus to such settlement."

Ludlow simply reiterated the attitude of the business world when he admitted that although New York City or the state of California probably contained enough capital to accomplish the task, no money would be forthcoming without a satisfactory guarantee behind it. "We feel it imperative upon the National Government to endorse its position as . . . capital's trustee," he wrote, for "no ordinary business-organization of citizens will accomplish it alone."

The journalist's evaluation of the plains country's economic potential indicated that in 1864 no fresh knowledge of the area had been contributed since the *Pacific Railroad Reports* of the previous decade. He supported William Gilpin's contention, made nearly 20 years earlier, that these western reaches were primarily a continental pasture, valuable only for raising livestock. However, because Ludlow appeared to have a special interest in Kansas, he excepted it from his charges of sterility and spoke of a fertile land whose climate was of Mediterranean mildness. Along the Republican River, he predicted, vineyards rivaling anything east of California would dot the land, while cattle would graze unsheltered on nearby slopes all the year around. In this land of soft breezes, "haymaking and building of barns are works of supererogation." It was quite apparent to him that here was the chosen land for railroad builders.[22]

This now-pessimistic, now-optimistic view of the Great Plains that so sharply underscored the American public's suspicion and ignorance of the country deeply concerned supporters of the Union Pacific project. Fearful that the opportunity to cash in on a large governmental offer of bonds and land would be lost through hesitancy of investors, Durant and his associates turned to a moneymaking device that was to be used rather commonly in western railroad building: they formed a construction company of their own and thereby suggested to the financially timid that not only was the project going to be pushed, but that it would bring quick returns from railroad building contracts. He and seven others, who were either stockholders or directors, put down 25 percent cash toward a subscription of $1,600,000 as an initial investment. When the same amount of money was asked, as payment of the next installment, some of the speculators became frightened and began to balk.[23]

The doctor, who was to show his ingenuity many times, produced for his colleagues the Pennsylvania Fiscal Agency, quickly renamed the Crédit Mobilier of America, at the suggestion of the eccentric George Francis Train, and offered those gentlemen who wanted early profits at a minimum of risk, a device that provided limited personal liability. With this instrument, and from aid given by a syndicate of New York banks, which proposed to loan the Union Pacific $1 million, the management was ready to proceed with construction.[24] It is very doubtful that any of them had a sincere interest in developing the West, or in a long-range return on their money. What they wanted was a large and immediate profit from what they continued to regard as a very risky investment, even after Durant had provided them with the Crédit Mobilier.[25] That they succeeded beyond their expectations became the subject of a congressional investigation less than a decade later. Unfortunately, their spectacular financial gains and the methods by which these were made left a birthmark upon the Union Pacific that has never completely disappeared.[26]

"Let Us . . . Not Despise the Plains"

By the spring of 1865 the military aspects of Southern rebellion had been concluded and the nation could again turn its attention to western development. A member of the British Parliament, who toured America in the early postwar period, said that although the war had been fought at a frightful cost in blood, he believed Southern opposition would have continued to impede the admission of western states until the political convulsion had run its course. He pointed out that even during the war the Oregon, Washington, Idaho, Dakota, Utah, Colorado, New Mexico, and Arizona territories had "all been more or less opened out of settlement and enterprize," and that in addition to their known mineral riches they contained 800 million acres of land "through which it is only needed that railroads should be constructed, in order to induce cultivation."[1] It was an opinion with which the American public generally agreed, and as the armies disbanded, the country that lay beyond the Missouri River became a place of increasing interest.

By 1865 the West had shown a considerable potential in mineral wealth. California, Nevada, and Colorado had produced heavily and had attracted sufficient population, with the result that the first two had become states and the third was clamoring for that status. At this time Montana's gold fields were pouring their riches down the Missouri River toward "the States," sometimes in single shipments that amounted to a million dollars. These mineral deposits already had attracted many people, and as the war came to a close there were clear indications of the renewed westward movement that was to come.

Because of the stirrings in the West, the War Department was faced with defending a frontier bigger than it had ever known. Thousands of miles separated remote settlements, and these required protection against Indian depredations. Furnishing manpower was only one of the necessities; an enormous amount of supplies was required to keep army posts functioning.

Military transportation in the West had posed problems in the antebellum period, but after the war they were to be greatly increased as the mining frontier fanned out across the land. Costs soared as more wagons were needed to supply distant posts. War Department officials looked forward to the day when rails would serve this endless country where there was little water transportation and overland wagon transportation was so slow and expensive.[2] Western communities, whose prices were governed by the high costs of haulage, shared this enthusiasm for cheaper transportation.

In time, the man on the street, so anxious for work to begin and to progress, would come to regard the enterprise as one carried out hastily and wastefully. However, in those exciting days after Appomattox a sense of urgency prevailed that seemed to call for speed, without regard to cost. Durant shared the feeling, but for other reasons than public need. His road was about to divide up the West with the Central Pacific Company, then building eastward from California, and every mile of Union Pacific "captured ground" meant more land and more bonds under the subsidy program. When the rails should join, the rush for contract riches would be over, and since construction profits were his principal target the doctor laid on the lash and tried to drive his men westward as fast as possible.

Despite all pleas and threats, the work at Omaha progressed with agonizing slowness. Although the eastern journalist Samuel Bowles called the construction of railroads east of Omaha "mere baby work," it was July 10 before tracklaying commenced. The construction department, as yet inefficient and fumbling, was unable to organize itself into any kind of effective instrument. Workmen, whose pay was over two months in arrears by the time the first rail was laid, were uninspired by coaxing; they wanted their money. During these hectic months Durant made frantic efforts to find sufficient funds to keep the men at their jobs, offering various contractors stock in return for work on the first hundred miles, while at the same time he appealed to his finance committee for greater efforts in the East.[3]

Fortunately, the floundering corporation was momentarily saved by the entry, during August 1865, of a wealthy New England shovel manufacturer and member of Congress by the name of Oakes Ames.[4] He, and his brother Oliver, bought $1 million worth of Crédit Mobilier stock at a time when Durant could show no more than several miles of track in return for an original investment of about $2 million.[5] This demonstration of confidence, reinforced by a loan of $600,000 by Oakes Ames himself, brought forth other New Englanders whose contributions shortly swelled the total of new money to $2.5 million.

Although the newcomers were to spell trouble for Durant, he was in no position at that time to quibble over the source of his funds. Rowland

Hazard later said that the Ames group—or Boston Party, as it was called—believed the road could be made to pay, and the stock would become valuable. Durant, on the other hand, "was determined to make all that was possible out of the building of the road."[6] At the moment, what he wanted most was to lay tracks across the Nebraska countryside as fast as possible to qualify for some of the government money that awaited him in Washington.

While the high cost of railroad building would not become a matter of national concern until 1873, when the Crédit Mobilier scandals erupted, it certainly was recognized long before that time. In 1865 the government directors of the Union Pacific openly admitted that the amount of cash necessary to complete the first hundred miles, in order to qualify for government bonds, would be hard to come by. "Capitalists could not be expected to make such advances in a frontier undertaking like this, so distant from commercial centers, and the entire completion of which to the Pacific was so remote in point of time, and its immediate profits, therefore, so problematical, without a large margin in the contract." They did not favor the building of the road by large contracts which led to large profits, but they justified it on the ground of public necessity. "Such necessity," explained the government's representatives, "frequently arises in new countries, and we believe exists in respect to this work as the law now stands." The directors estimated that costs could be reduced as much as 20 to 30 percent by putting the work out to small contractors, payable in cash, "but the method in which government aid is furnished the company, and which is according to the usage of the Government in aiding public works, the adoption of any such plan is impossible." Thanks to the Ames brothers and their friends, whether in or out of Congress, the cash advance was forthcoming and the work went forward.[7]

By mid-October Durant was ready to display about 15 miles of track, and he took advantage of a visit to Omaha by Maj. Gen. William Tecumseh Sherman to publicize the road's progress. The general was treated to the first of many inspection trips that would characterize each major step westward until the road was completed. Sherman, who was earlier reputed to have said, "I should be unwilling to buy a ticket over it for my grandchildren," was now much more favorably impressed by the project, for which an Omaha paper labeled him a man of "superior views."

Encouraged by the tangible results of his efforts, and by a brighter financial picture, Durant redoubled his efforts, stressing the need for speed as opposed to patient workmanship or attention to detail. "You are doing too much in masonry this year," he complained to one of his subordinates at Omaha. "Substitute tressel [*sic*] and wooden culverts for masonry wherever you can for the present." In another urgent communication he asked: "What is the matter that you can't lay track faster?" Two days later he demanded: "Telegraph me daily," a request that was followed by his telegraphic snarl: "I insist upon being fully advised." As the first winter of construction approached, the irascible vice-president announced that he intended to keep his crews at work during the cold months; he was determined to drive his iron wedge as deeply into the West as the blizzards would allow. This might cause complaint, he admitted, but he warned his men in Omaha that his personal orders were to be followed strictly, "let the consequences be what they may."[8] By mid-December 100 miles of roadbed lay graded and waiting for iron, of which the company had on hand at Omaha enough for 65 miles. The crews by now were better organized, and they were laying one mile of track a day. Shortly, Durant would ask the government to accept the first 40 miles of completed work.[9]

The American public was fascinated by the construction of what was to be the first of the so-called "transcontinental" railroads, partly because of the national implications of the project and partly by the magnitude of the undertaking. As men of the trans-Missouri West watched the first rails of the Union Pacific creep away from the Missouri River, their excitement was more than that arising from fascinated interest; it was one born of anticipation that a new day was at hand, one which promised great and significant changes in their lives, and they gave it their closest scrutiny.

Omaha was the first of many western towns to experience the benefits of the Union Pacific Railroad.[10] In autumn of 1865 the city's press anticipated the great effect the road would have upon the small community, and it talked in large terms about the good things the rails would bring, essaying at length upon the mineral wealth of the Rocky Mountains and the fabled trade of the Orient, both of which would pass through Nebraska's great entrepôt of trade, with the result that "into the coffers of our bankers and business-men must unnumbered millions annually fall." The railroad was called "the great almoner of our prosperity," and "the grand lever" that was to raise the entire Territory "to the pinnacle of fortune and expand her population into tens of thousands."[11]

In spring of 1866 the money supplied by the men of Boston began to be felt. Now the editorial focus of Omaha turned to the more immediate benefits bestowed by eastern capital, as opposed to earlier generalities that spoke of Oriental traffic and world trade. With great enthusiasm the press reported a sudden spurt in municipal growth, noting the appearance of each new structure and the arrival of additional boatloads of supplies. The Union Pacific was very much in the news, as its employees began to build a base from which to advance upon the plains. Shop buildings were erected, a brick roundhouse with ten locomotive pits was begun, and around this cluster of buildings appeared dwellings for railroad workers and their families, making the whole complex "a little city of themselves," as a local newspaper described it.[12] George Francis Train, the erstwhile capitalist and promoter, had promised in late 1865 to build a hundred cottages at Omaha, if Chicago businessmen would participate in the project. "This shows that some capitalists at least know where to invest their money," commented an Omaha paper, hopeful that Train would carry out his promise.[13]

Despite more living quarters, the influx of railroad men created a housing problem that was typical of boomtowns. John S. Casement, one of the brothers to become famous in the road's construction, despaired of finding anything suitable enough that he could send for his wife. He told her that there were no good boardinghouses in Omaha and that the hotel in which he was obliged to stay was "cram full and kept very poorly." The food was plentiful enough, but nothing was served that "a white man wanted"; therefore, he began to collect furniture in the hope that somehow he could find a house for rent and return to the enjoyment of home-cooked meals.[14] The booming river town, which claimed 7,000 residents at that time, would double its population within a year, and strangers looking for lodging would continue to walk the streets.

During the summer and autumn of 1865 small mountains of materials piled up at Omaha. The company assigned five of its seven river steamboats to the exclusive task of hauling ties, wheels, rolling stock of all types, as well as an endless miscellany necessary to carry the work forward.[15] Other vessels brought more workers and additional quantities of supplies. Aboard one of these was a youngster who would later work for the railroad, and many years afterward he vividly recalled the vessel's name because of the raucous laughter that accompanied its pronunciation by riverfront roughs. Despite hoots of derision the *Jacob Sass* deposited its cargo at Omaha and contributed to building a railroad that one day would help to retire it and the other riverboats from the trade.

During the busy months that followed, more shop buildings were constructed and equipped with machinery capable of building railroad cars. One of them had ways for the simultaneous building of nine cars, and these were soon pressed into use as the demand for freight cars mounted. By October a great cluster of stores, hauled in by river steamer, had grown around the freight depot where harried railroaders worked overtime. "The benefits of a railroad to the interior, as well as to our city, begin to show themselves plainly," observed the Omaha *Republican.*[16]

The benefits were seen on all sides. "Wanted: Carpenters to work on the U.P.R.R., who understand building, to whom good wages will be given," read one advertisement. Another stated: "Wanted immediately! One hun-

Top—*Horses and men preceded the rails while soldiers guarded the westward path. Here the artist depicts the invasion into Indian country, one (seated) of whose residents seems more resigned than warlike.*

Right—*The iron rails were relatively light, compared with those of later years, and the ties were uneven and the grading primitive. But these Union Pacific track-layers were hurrying westward; refinements would come later.*

dred and fifty choppers, to get out cedar ties, telegraph poles and logs, in the vicinity of Cottonwood." There were calls for brickmakers, with the admission that the city's bricklayers were falling behind in their efforts to fill the demands made upon them by builders. On another occasion, 150 teamsters were asked for, to haul railroad ties. Good wages and prompt pay were promised.[17]

The feverish pace is reflected in Durant's correspondence during these months. He ordered thousands of tons of rails, fittings, and various other necessities, constantly urging his suppliers to work faster and to produce more. In June he notified Glidden & Williams, of Boston, that the *City of Memphis* had blown up, carrying 2,500 bars of iron to the bottom of the river. "Notify insurance companies," he ordered, and then asked for more iron. In June he told G. W. Frost, his purchasing agent at Omaha, that he had ordered three ready-made houses, directing that "the small house with the kitchen is to be placed at some station on the road where there is no other house." Then, turning his attention to the tracklayers, he worried about the fact that they had on hand only a six-day supply of spikes. "How much track laid Monday, how much Tuesday, and Wednesday?" he asked Samuel B. Reed. As the pace quickened, he said to Reed: "Can't you get more men?"[18]

As the tracklayers picked up speed and began to penetrate the fabled desert, attitudes at Omaha underwent a gradual change. In the early days of 1865, before any rails had been laid, the press of that city had talked in very general terms of tapping the mineral wealth of the Rockies and of sharing the China trade, but now the potential of interior Nebraska became a matter of growing interest. Local railroad enthusiasts had supposed the project would bring settlers to their part of the West, but the numbers that came in the spring of 1866 provided a surprise. By August an Omaha editor predicted that with "the great U.P.R.R. stretching westward and opening to settlers the fertile interior of our Territory, we shall have an emigration another season compared to which the past has been but the advance guard of a grand army."[19] Even as he wrote, the construction crews, themselves an advance guard of sorts, were 180 miles west of the river.

During these exciting months, as the nation watched the tiny thread of iron appear along the Platte River, a reassessment of the Great Plains country began. Samuel Bowles, the famed Massachusetts editor, suggested modification of earlier judgments when he saw the country in the summer of 1865. He spoke in long-accepted terms when he referred to an area 400 miles wide as the great central desert of the continent; yet, he said, it was not really a desert, "not worthless, by any means." It was, to him as it was to many others, the nation's pasture, capable of growing grass that fattened animals. He foresaw a day when a railroad would carry eastward beef, mutton, wool, and hides. "Let us, then, not despise the Plains; but turn their capacities to best account," he counseled.[20]

By 1866 the desert had begun to show signs of even greater promise. Moses Thatcher, who crossed central Nebraska in June, remarked that "the country is one vast green ocean." But there was something new in the national pasture. "There are some fine farms recently located here," he noticed. "The small grain such as wheat, oats, barley & corn are looking finely." Although building timber was sparse, the soil was rich and black, and he could not resist the remark that if his fellow Mormons lived there the place "would rapidly assume a much improved appearance."[21]

Bayard Taylor, a well-known traveler, author, and lecturer, viewed the same countryside a month later and concluded that it was the most beautiful he had ever seen. The gently rolling slopes had the smooth finish of land that had been long cultivated, as had the fields of Europe, and it struck him that the region resembled one from which war had swept away the inhabitants. He had read of the desert, but he searched for it in vain on his trip westward to the Rocky Mountains. At best, he thought, "Mr. Greeley's 'vanishing scale of civilization' has been pushed much further west since his overland trip in 1859." This land beyond the Missouri, said the traveler, combined with the western parts of Iowa and Missouri, constituted the largest unbroken area of excellent farming land in the world.[22] Although the Union Pacific had reached only central Nebraska, a prediction made by the Secretary of the Interior was already beginning to be realized. He had said, in 1865, that the influence of the road in promoting settlement and opening new regions "will be more and more appreciated as it approaches completion."[23] The enthusiasm of both Thatcher and Taylor for the rich lands of central Nebraska suggested that such an appreciation already had been realized.

To the settlers of the Platte Valley the coming of the Union Pacific was a mixed blessing. With its arrival, as one of them put it, "conditions changed rapidly." He referred to the hordes of tie-cutters who invaded the area in search of what timber there was and promptly harvested all they could lay hands on. They contended that since the lands were unsurveyed, and held only under squatters' rights, no laws were being violated. On one occasion an emigrant named Friedrich Moeller, who had a hundred acres of likely looking trees, was obliged to stand by while the invaders deforested his land. Carl Miller, who lived near the confluence of the Wood and Platte rivers, took a stronger stand; armed with revolver and shotgun, he drove off the cutters. This, said a local farmer, caused the Union Pacific to forward Henry rifles and ammunition to the clerk of one of the railroad contractors, who passed them on to the woodchoppers with the suggestion: "Now, shoot the God damn black Dutchmen!" A resident of Merrick County accused Nebraska's governor, Alvin Saunders, of furnishing similar groups of men with arms belonging to the territory, a charge he promptly denied. The governor lamented the difficulty and said he had talked about the matter to Durant, who "admitted that it was not good policy to take all the timber from the settlers in that county." Free transportation, free board, wages of $49 a month, and a 29-cent bonus for each tie cut over the number of 15 per day, was sufficient incentive to attract enterprising young men who were not particularly interested in selective cutting or in legal niceties.[24]

Durant, now working with all possible speed, was not, in all probability, particularly troubled about the commotion over the ties. The unruly conduct of those employed by the various contractors was to become a part of the legend of the building of the road, and already it was making itself felt in Nebraska. As early as August 1866, the little railroad town of Columbus experienced some of the disorder that was to be common in railroad camps all the way to Ogden. The bad feeling that persisted among local residents and construction workers erupted into what the local editor deplored as a "disgraceful fight" on a Sunday afternoon, in which the visitors took a severe beating. Several of the victors were brought before the law, and each was assessed five dollars and costs for shattering the Lord's day. "All the parties were under the influence of liquor," lamented the editor.[25] Nebraska, so anxious for the benefits of improved transportation, was beginning to discover that it could not be delivered without some birth pangs.

For those who watched the progress of the road from their remote locations in the Rocky Mountain mining camps, its approach was a matter of mounting anticipation and of daily excitement. So great was the anxiety of these people for it that they probably would have tolerated the boisterous conduct of the builders, and perhaps even have offered to supply the liquor which so disturbed the Columbus editor, for strong drink was no stranger to the miners. Colorado, the oldest and most populous of the mountain mineral regions, was very hopeful that the line would pass through that territory and thereby assure not only its membership in the sisterhood of states, but also its commercial future. Distance and the high cost of wagon transportation were held to be the major obstacles to economic development.

Happily, said the mining men, their day of salvation was at hand; but as certain as they were that the road must pass their way, they cautioned each other about complacency and resolved to offer help to any cities farther east whose leaders were working toward similar transportation improvements across the plains.[26] Denver's oldest newspaper preached such caution to its readers and fussed uneasily over the possibility—the remote possibility

—that the rails might take another westward course. Surely, said editor William Byers, himself a great railroad enthusiast, Congress could not be so blind as to overlook the importance of sending the road through Colorado, to the south of what he called a "sterile and barren country," and thus bypass the large and growing trade of the mountain community. He cited the trade out of Plattsmouth, Nebraska, as evidence of the obvious advantages railroad stockholders would inherit by furnishing better facilities to the mountain trade. During 1865, he said, that place forwarded over the plains to Colorado nearly 44 million pounds of freight in more than 7,000 wagons. Taken all together, the commerce of this and various other river towns ultimately must provide so much business that a single railroad track would be unable to carry it all.[27]

Admittedly, all the good things to come from railroad construction would not accrue to the road alone; Colorado would benefit enormously. It was estimated that the average cost of plains freight haulage during the preceding three years was ten cents a pound, making a total of $10,400,000 paid by the federal government and by people of the territory for such service. By this time "pick and pan" mining had played out and the days of surface-skimming were nearly over. The remaining gold, and much was left, would have to be blasted from the earth, and only heavy machinery could sufficiently reduce the chunks of quartz to make extraction of the metal possible. The *Rocky Mountain News,* of Denver, argued that under existing transportation facilities the cost of bringing in provisions, labor, and especially heavy machinery was so high as to make mining unprofitable. Nine-tenths of the miners were said to have suspended operations, awaiting better and cheaper freight-hauling facilities. While this was without doubt something of an exaggeration, there is no question that rails would make quartz mining much more feasible, particularly in low-grade areas. Editor Byers estimated that with such service ore production in Colorado would jump threefold, thus benefiting not only the territory but also the railroad.[28] A local mining man asserted that the advance of the Union Pacific during the summer of 1866 alone had shortened wagon haulage enough to reduce freight costs by 50 percent.[29] Colorado's governor, Alexander Cummings, agreed that even now the road's influence was apparent and he stated that emigration to Colorado in the travel season alone had increased noticeably because of it.[30]

The mineral wealth of the Rocky Mountains loomed large in western talk about railroad building because it was the most obvious and most tangible source of business for such an enterprise. Although some Union Pacific founders entertained doubts about the road's ability to develop much local traffic, the average railroad enthusiast—easterners and westerners alike—used this as one of the important arguments for such a venture. Colorado was now famous for its mines, and its boosters promised to share this wealth with the world once better means of transportation were available. "Give us the Pacific Railroad," exclaimed Byers, "and in five years Colorado in point of population and power, will stand second to no State in the Union." The *News* expressed pleasure when the famed traveler and journalist Albert D. Richardson wrote that until such a road came into being no man could know the magnitude of the West's riches. He called it the immediate and vital need for western territories.[31]

Official sanction for such talk was suggested in the comments of government director Jesse L. Williams. He told Durant that mountain communities would provide a railroad with both traffic in ore shipments and the importation of groceries, general merchandise, and heavy machinery. The Union Pacific was, he asserted, being built "for the development of our interior resources as well as for through commerce."

Lest Coloradans take such an endorsement with too much enthusiasm and infer it meant sending the main line through such an invaluable country, Williams hastened to add that this particular portion of the Rockies was too rugged for a rail passage.[32] That such an explanation was untrue was later demonstrated by other railroads. The real reason for avoiding the Colorado mountains lay in the national urge for an early connection with the Pacific Coast and in the Union Pacific's desire to build as much road as it could in the shortest time. The Union Pacific had no desire to dig expensive tunnels while the Central Pacific moved across the flatland of Nevada and increased its grant money with every finished mile.

Williams did not intend to suggest that Colorado should be overlooked. In the interest of the company, of Colorado, and of the nation—in that order—he believed branches into the mountain valleys were of great importance.[33] Coloradans had difficulty in understanding why the richest and best-developed area of the Central Rockies should be thus bypassed, but they did their best to hide their chagrin and to watch the main line pass through neighboring Wyoming. They offered generous contributions if the road would change its mind, but to no avail, and the bitter pill of defeat went down hard. "Our time of triumph will surely come," wrote a deeply disappointed Byers, "and the day is not distant when the old fogy capitalists of the East will see with shame and remorse how much they have lost by ignoring the resources of this rich and though now struggling Territory."[34]

In its hour of disappointment Denver found a new source of hope. On February 21, 1866, managers of the branch being built from Kansas City to a junction with the main line near Fort Kearny, asked the Department of the Interior to withdraw public lands along a westerly route that ran

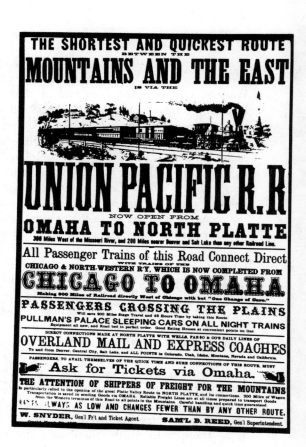

TOP—*This poster, dated March 8, 1867, announced the opening of rail service westward from the Missouri River to North Platte, Nebraska.*

BOTTOM—*Beyond the 100th meridian was said to lay the Great American Desert. This group of excursionists (circa 1867) were literally "following the flag" westward. Note the firewood in the "coal tender."*

beyond Fort Riley, up the Smoky Hill branch of the Republican River, and to Denver. Originally chartered in 1855 as the Leavenworth, Pawnee and Western, this road had been sold in 1864 and renamed the Union Pacific Eastern Division to suggest its association with the main Pacific route, although it was not then owned by the Union Pacific Railroad Company. The confusion in terms would end in 1869 when the line took on yet another name—Kansas Pacific. On July 3, 1866, Congress provided the necessary legislation to authorize the change in route but stipulated that any connection with the Union Pacific must be at a point more than 50 miles west of Denver, and that no more bonds would be issued than if the road had made the connection called for in the original act.[35] The change of route occurred at a time when Coloradans had begun to realize they had lost their bid for a place on the main line, and this helped considerably to soothe their injured feelings.

In the autumn of 1866, however, Denver civic and business leaders remained optimistic. The *News* accepted the idea of a Union Pacific branch line from Cheyenne, for which it said, "we shall be duly thankful," and it predicted that the new service would be of great importance to the area's commercial interests; but, said editor Byers, "when the competing line of the eastern division reaches us we may reasonably expect cheaper transportation than while a single road has the monopoly." He then essayed upon the superiority of the Kansas route, showing it provided a more accessible connection with the Missouri River and had the added advantage of "passing through a country improved and densely populated" which would supply local trade.[36] In truth, there was practically no population in eastern Colorado or in western Kansas at that time; and even years later, when the Union Pacific owned that portion of the road, settlement would come slowly. But in 1866 optimism was the order of the day, and Byers called the coming of the Kansas line "the next best thing to our being admitted as a State."[37] When the *Chicago Republican* stated that "the locomotive headlight is about as good a symbol of the star of empire as we can ask," Byers quickly reproduced the sentiment as one to which all his readers could subscribe.[38]

Although Coloradans were disappointed at being "side-tracked," and time would show their arguments for the road to be better than were believed at the time, other western communities no doubt felt the mountaineers were lucky to have the prospect of any kind of rail service at that early date. Transportation was the key to economic development, which in turn meant political, social, cultural, and other advances. After the Civil War the desire to develop the West was rekindled and burned with a new brightness. "This *furor Americanus* has ever possessed those who have turned their thoughts westward," wrote an observer in 1867, and he added that one need only go beyond the Mississippi River to understand why the feeling persisted. Here was a land where "the very air of the prairies, as it sweeps across those vast and fertile valleys, fills one with the inspiration of a new life; and the soul expands with such conceptions of the future of this country, that reason trembles for its own sobriety."[39] To many a westerner these high-flown phrases could be capsulized in a single word: railroads.

In January 1865, Gov. John Hutchinson of the Dakota Territory gave his approval to a legislative memorial asking that a branch of the Union Pacific Railroad be commenced somewhere beyond the 100th meridian and built across Dakota toward the Great Lakes region in order to develop his territory and to shorten Missouri River navigation by 300 miles. Such a road, he said, would tap the rich resources of the Upper Missouri and would be of great mutual benefit. On February 2 the Minnesota legislature passed a joint resolution expressing the same sentiments.[40] In March 1866 a Texas convention passed a resolution asking for a similar branch, on the ground that the state had over 175 million acres adapted to agriculture and pasturage, and only 460 miles of railroads, with no connections to those of any other state. The convention, assembled at Austin, argued that a connecting line through Indian Territory (present-day Oklahoma) was imperative to the economic development of Texas.[41]

The northwestern mining communities of Idaho looked longingly at the oncoming railroad and nursed a hope that its projectors would find their economic prospects too inviting to overlook. In his annual message of 1865 Gov. Caleb Lyon reflected the sentiment of his territory's press when he referred to the great need for a branch line from Salt Lake City. The *Idaho Statesman,* of Boise, sounded much like the Colorado press with its references to inexhaustible mineral resources and untold acres of arable land that waited only for rail service to realize their potential. Idaho, "our gem of Territories soon to be a State," was on a natural route to the Columbia River and the Northwest, said the journal. It also recommended a second branch, one that would serve the Montana communities of Virginia City and Fort Benton, the latter being the head of Missouri River navigation.[42] In time the requests of both Montana and Idaho would be answered by the Union Pacific.

By the autumn of 1866 Idaho had begun to feel the first pulsations of the main line, then creeping through eastern Nebraska, and its excitement mounted. Already, said a Boise paper, local people were receiving mail from the Atlantic Coast two to four days earlier than before the era of construction. Within two or three years the road would reach Utah, and then Idaho would feel the shock waves of its appearance: An increased population would appropriate valley farmlands, and dormant mines would spring to life as cheap labor began to "unlock the rocks," as the *Statesman* put it, making "each quartz ledge an underground hive of profitable industry." All this would occur, of course, when the inevitable branch line felt its way along Idaho's verdant valleys to meet a proposed line projected southward from Umatilla, on the Columbia River, to a point on the Snake River in Idaho.[43]

Before long the Idaho press began to talk about a "through line" that would cross the territory on its way to the Pacific. The *Statesman* explained that since the Union Pacific could not go much farther west than Salt Lake City, it would turn north to reach the ocean and to tap the Puget Sound trade. The Boise paper argued that not only was this the cheapest route, but it passed through a mining country rich in local business. The move also would serve "as a check to any extortion that may be attempted by the Pacific Central [*sic*] Company," explained the editor.[44] Time would prove the prediction accurate in a number of ways. Meanwhile, Idaho would cry out continuously for rail service, now pleading with the Union Pacific, now petulantly angry with Portland businessmen who seemed more interested in a California connection, always militantly defensive over its remote location, and ever ready to encourage rail extension toward it—from any direction.

Utah, destined to be served by the Union Pacific, watched the progress of construction crews in Nebraska as anxiously as did any other western territory. Governor Charles Durkee spoke of some progress in developing Utah's mineral resources, but he frankly admitted that it would continue to be slow until the "Pacific Railroad shall inaugurate the era of cheap transportation and supplies."[45] Utah farmers also felt the need for cheaper transportation, for by now they were raising large crops. While much of this produce was consumed by the Mormon community, there remained a sizable surplus for which a market was wanted. The mining camps of Idaho and Montana furnished such a demand, as did mineral areas lying both to the east and west of Utah. Rail service would make them much more accessible.

As the Mountain West waited and counted the days until they would be served by modern transportation, the tracklayers pushed westward along the Platte River. Behind them came the excursionists and the curious, riding the new rails, drinking toasts to progress and American ingenuity, marveling at the speed with which the work progressed. Early in July 1866 assorted dignitaries, including army generals, federal railroad commissioners, and representatives of the stockholders, were taken to Columbus to view the work, after which they returned pleased and gratified by what they had seen. The Nebraska legislature publicly thanked Durant, and promised that it would "ever kindly regard Mr. Durant and the Union Pacific R.R.," a vow that it would break within a few years.[46]

Shortly after the excursion the company announced that it would connect to one of its construction trains a passenger car by which the public
could be conveyed out to Lone Tree Station, 41 miles beyond Columbus,
and shortly thereafter regular daily service to Grand Island was announced.[47]
By late August the railroad advertised "Open to Kearney," a well-known
stop along the old California Trail near the military post of Fort Kearny,
where travelers were told they might take one of Ben Holladay's stagecoaches
to points farther west.[48]

The initial service offered the public was sometimes irregular, and the
passage sometimes problematical, but it was a start, and the American public
was gratified to see steam locomotives crossing what had once been called a
desert. The first trains burned cottonwood poles which often were so green
that the firemen insisted they sprouted when placed in the firebox. Still,
enough steam was somehow generated to haul a small train of cars across
the countryside at 20 miles per hour. It was a crude beginning, in the manner
of earlier railroading much farther east, yet it was such an improvement
over travel by jolting, wearying prairie schooners that to the postwar traveler
it must have seemed he was moving through another world, in another age.

Into the Virgin West

Anxious to keep the Union Pacific in the public view, and to encourage timid investors in the East, Durant offered another of his motive extravaganzas in late October 1866. Two engines, sporting flags and bearing appropriate mottoes, pulled a train made up of the famous Lincoln car, the directors' car, four passenger cars, an express car fitted to serve refreshments, a mess car, and a baggage car. Aboard the train were all the important road officials (except Dix, who had left the presidency to accept diplomatic appointment abroad) and a number of influential military, political, and business figures. Among those present were Benjamin Wade and J. W. Patterson, both United States senators; Gov. Alvin Saunders, of Nebraska; Gen. Philip St. George Cooke, commanding the Department of the Platte; Gen. Grenville M. Dodge, now chief engineer to the Union Pacific; and Gen. Samuel R. Curtis, who was to die suddenly at the conclusion of the trip. Other guests were Robert T. Lincoln, son of President Lincoln and a future secretary of war; Rutherford B. Hayes, the Ohioan who would be president; several foreign visitors; and many less important personages.

The officials were carried 275 miles beyond Omaha, stopping at Columbus long enough to watch a group of Pawnees put on a war dance, and then on to the end of track, near Fort Cottonwood. Here a detachment of the Second Cavalry waited to greet the visitors. The soldiers had dragged from the fort an artillery piece that provided an appropriate salute, after which they served supper in a large dining tent erected for the occasion. Before the easterners went home they were treated to a buffalo hunt, conducted by one of the army officers. The West had turned out for the occasion: howling Indians, rampaging buffalo, an army feed, cannonading, and fanfare. Happy that the star of empire was on course, the excursionists made their way back home.[1]

Before long the money spent upon the excursion began to bring returns in national publicity. The eastern press showed an increased enthusiasm for the project, especially after it had been demonstrated that passengers could be conveyed into the wilds of Nebraska in what amounted to luxury and then returned safely to the waiting arms of civilization. In December a Boston paper explained to its readers that quite understandably not much attention had been given to the proposed road during the recent war, and that even in the early postwar years the American people had been slow to accept the reality of its construction since "so vast a project cannot be forced upon the public in a day"; but now success seemed assured, and before five more years had elapsed, travel by rail from Bangor, Maine, to San Francisco would become a reality. "Though New England will only indirectly reap advantage from its completion," said the paper, "we are sure the people will sustain our representatives in Congress in voting for measures which will expedite the completion of the great enterprise."[2] This was just the kind of journalistic talk that managers of the road had hoped would follow the latest westward excursion.

New York also accepted the early completion of the Pacific roads as a foregone conclusion. It seemed clear to the *Commercial Advertiser* that an ocean to ocean rail line, once regarded as no more than a dream, was about to be realized. By the spring of 1867 some 400 miles of road lay completed; obviously this was a serious project, not an experimentation. With his eye on the Orient, and the prospect of connecting international markets to New York by rail, the editor labeled the work the greatest undertaking of Western civilization.[3] Agreed, said the *World*. This "grand highway of all nations" promised to transfer the earth's financial center from London to New York and "give to San Francisco the keys of all the treasures of the distant Orient." This road, the "most magnificent sensation of the age," would propel America to the forefront of global commerce.[4]

Not to be overlooked in a view that portrayed exotic Asia, was the country in the foreground: the American West. The advance of the Union Pacific "has virtually annexed, for business purposes, our mountain states and territories, hitherto almost isolated by six hundred miles of wagon communication—a territory worth a score of Alaskas," commented an eastern journal. These westering rails, mused the editor, surely would develop a local traffic of their own and this in turn would spawn villages, cities, even states.[5] Or, in somewhat different terms, copies of Illinois, Iowa, and Missouri would crop out on the western map "and the entire land will join in the benefits therefrom."[6] Pursuing this thought, a contemporary noted that historically the western population had multiplied fivefold every 20 years, thanks to improved transportation; by projection this promised a population of some 10 million beyond the Missouri River not later than 1880.[7]

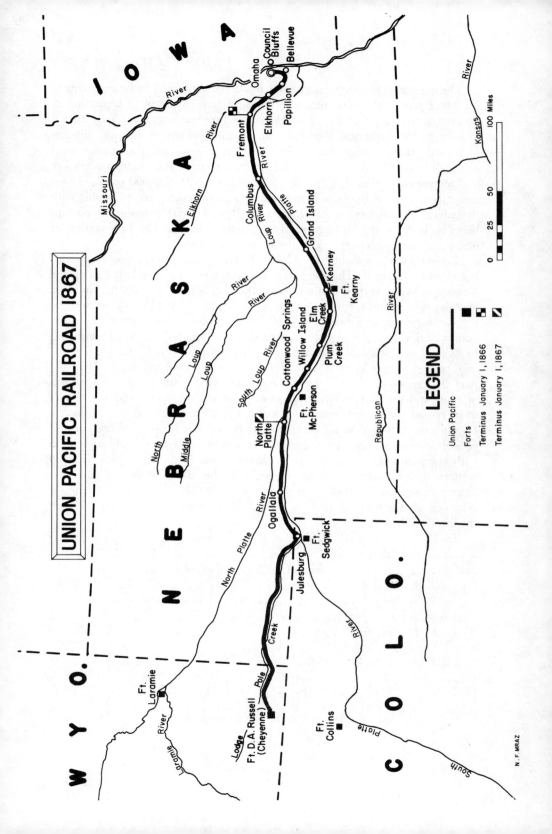

During the 1860s western mineral resources continued to be regarded as the great potential of the road; agricultural possibilities were beginning to be recognized, but not as an immediate source of business. Coal, known to exist in Colorado and Wyoming, now became a matter of more interest since rail transportation would make its extraction and distribution economically possible. Although precious metals dazzled the contemporary eye and temporarily blinded it, by 1867 an estimated $100,000,000 worth of coal came from western mines, a figure that was predicted as able to double with the advent of rail service. All extractive industries were promised important benefits, both in the haulage of their products and in the importation of heavy mining machinery—with the coming of steam.[8]

Easterners who watched the Union Pacific's progress experienced mounting enthusiasm for it. The road was variously termed a new Erie Canal, the Mississippi River turned east and west, the backbone of the United States, a seedling that would sprout other lines. This, and other railroads, were to be the harbingers of civilization with all its trappings—schools, churches, mills, and factories. One journalist enthusiastically compared the advancing rails to "a long and irresistible arm, with which the powerful East embraces the mighty and virgin West."[9] It was an interesting analogy, particularly the part that spoke of the West as an economic virgin, for while the residents of that land thought in terms of commercial marriage they did not expect to surrender their virginity without certain guarantees of reciprocal benefits. In the next hundred years much would be written about exploitation and economic rape in the West. Some of it would be true. Closely associated with complaints concerning eastern financial manipulations which affected western development would be charges that the railroads were a part of a large plot against the West, and, since the roads furnished the most tangible evidence of big business in many small plains communities, they received the brunt of the attack.

In 1867, however, the story was just beginning. The railroad then was a pair of rails that crawled westward along the Platte River of Nebraska, and this was a time of celebration, of high hopes, of soaring progress; in the East and the West alike there were few knockers and many boosters. From the national viewpoint the work was one of public necessity, one that would bind together a nation that only recently had been torn asunder in another direction. During those postwar days, as the nation licked its wounds, to criticize or oppose the road was regarded almost as an unpatriotic act. The Union Pacific Company, unlike others, said the New York *Evening Mail,* was a thoroughly national company, one that derived its charter directly from Congress, was governed in part by five government directors, and was subject to inspection by three government commissioners.[10] In other words, this was a project to benefit all, presumably spearheaded by a group of wealthy, farsighted, public-spirited Americans whose efforts deserved the unstinted support and approval of their countrymen.

The glowing accounts of good things to come from the great enterprise were accompanied by pieces of editorial advice for the investor. Various eastern papers carried comments about the road's great potential, the handsome dividends it was bound to pay, the limited amount of first mortgage six percent bonds that would be available to those who bought promptly, the soundness of those bonds and where they might be purchased, plus other encouraging pieces of financial information.[11] The similarity of argument, the concentration of the appeal in point of time, and the coincidence of advertising by the company in the issues that spoke well of its future, suggest a concerted publicity campaign by its managers to raise funds.

While the press lauded the fiscal soundness of the organization, those within its ranks knew that a crisis was at hand. Early in 1867 Durant warned the executive committee that "The Company is greatly embarrassed in its operations and cannot sustain its credit much longer unless some means are adopted at once to raise money for its present necessities and the prosecution of work for the ensuing year will have to be abandoned."[12] A few days later C. W. Tuttle, the assistant treasurer, informed President Oliver Ames that two notes of $100,000 each were due within two days and that he did not know how the obligation was to be met. "I cannot see how the money can be raised here," Tuttle confessed. "We are not receiving anything on our stock."[13]

Involved in the financial crisis was a struggle for power from within. Banker John Pondir later testified that from the time the "Boston people" entered the picture there had been a fight for supremacy with Durant. Matters came to a head in mid-May when the doctor was evicted from control of the Crédit Mobilier, with Sidney Dillon taking his place. Rowland Hazard, who was offered but declined the agency's presidency, later maintained that its management "from that time onward was in able and honest hands." At a Union Pacific board meeting on May 23 a committee of three was appointed to terminate existing agreements between the Crédit Mobilier and the railroad for the further construction of the road. Technically, the relationship between the two ended at this point, the Crédit Mobilier having built the first 247 miles, after which Durant, as an individual, took the next contract.[14]

In a desperate effort to raise money, the directors voted to give each shareholder who would increase his stock by 50 percent $1,000 in first mortgage bonds for each $1,000 paid in. Although some of the larger stockholders were not attracted by the offer, the increase was made, and there

TOP—*As the artist shows, prior to the bridging of the Missouri River rail cars were transferred from Council Bluffs to Omaha by steamer. These arrived at Omaha in 1871, the year the bridge was completed.*

BOTTOM—*Excursionists who wanted to ride to the "end of track" often came to Omaha by boat. These steamers brought some of them from Saint Louis for a trip during the summer of 1866.*

was sufficient acceptance of the offer by others to produce more money.[15] Meanwhile, without any success, Durant tried to enlist Jay Cooke in disposing of between $6 and $10 million worth of the bonds through the house of that well-known financier.[16] Another effort at moneyraising was made when, on the motion of board member Cyrus H. McCormick, $10,000 was voted on March 1 to be used for distributing information at the forthcoming Paris Exposition "with respect to the magnitude and importance of the Union Pacific Railroad, and its effects upon the wealth and credit of the United States." By late June this plan was abandoned, and the agent who had been appointed to carry out the work was paid off.[17] Apparently, through the publicity program launched in this country, enough money was raised by late October so that auditor Benjamin F. Ham of the Crédit Mobilier could tell Oliver Ames, "Finances are in good condition though money is somewhat tight."[18]

During the months in which financial experts toiled with their problems in the East, the railhead moved across Nebraska and into the territory of Wyoming, leaving infant municipalities in its trail. Omaha, not much over a decade old, served as the main supply base for the assault, and as the road grew longer, the river port and rail terminus boomed. The place was so busy, and its face changed so rapidly, that travelers thought they were in a city larger than was the case. Colonel Philippe R. de Trobriand, who passed through Omaha on his way to Fort Stevenson, Dakota Territory, in July 1867, confessed that "in such a devil of a country as this, things change so rapidly that they cannot be recognized from one year to the next." The place was no longer a village, he said, but it was not yet a city. Boosters told him that the place had a population of 10,000 and local newspapers claimed 12,000, but the colonel did not think the figure exceeded 5,000 or 6,000. Two or three blocks of business houses, connected to the river by Farnham Street, comprised the heart of the city's commercial center. Some of the buildings were brick, others frame, and in addition to the dispensers of merchandise were "as many bars and eating houses of low quality."[19] It was largely a male town, and the men's needs were attended to in the fashion of a typical frontier boomtown. While there were 20 churches whose pastors had attracted perhaps 3,000 members of the population, there were 127 bars, 25 "temples of vice," as the *Herald* called them, about 10 full-fledged gambling establishments, and an indefinite number of back-room card tables in full operation.[20] As Jack Casement put it, "This country is flooded with men, the town is full."[21] Colonel de Trobriand predicted that when Omaha became a way station on the route from Chicago, and such rival cities as Saint Louis were connected to the West, Omaha's growth would drop sharply. Yet, he said with some truth, cities in the United States might stop going forward, but they never go backward.[22]

Nearly 300 miles beyond Omaha was North Platte, to become one of the more important Nebraska towns along the Union Pacific. In late December 1866, Gen. J. H. Simpson passed through on an inspection tour and remarked that where nothing but prairie had been three weeks earlier, there now stood some 20 buildings that included a brick roundhouse capable of serving 40 engines. Near it were a frame depot "of the usual beautiful design" and a frame hotel that cost $18,000.[23] Within a few months the town could claim 15 business houses, nine of which served either food or strong drink.

Dr. Henry C. Parry, who stopped at the small city on his way west, remarked that a number of traders and miners there "were having a good time, gambling, drinking, and shooting each other." In such a boisterous social scene the welfare of saloon employees was looked after; those who dispensed the goods carried revolvers loaded and set at half cock, ready for instant use. "Law is unknown here," said Parry.[24] The doctor referred to formal law, for North Platte was governed in the manner of many other new western communities: by the code of the West. One of the patrons described the principal gambling saloon as a rude structure made of logs and lumber that housed four card tables where, he said, both lives and dollars were staked. Placed in a prominent place on two of the walls were placards showing a knife and revolver design, with the printed explanation: "All disputes will be settled with this code of law."[25] Questioned about the character of the infant community by one of the emigrants passing through, an Irish resident answered: "Well, Sir, I would say that North Platte is a place where people suffer for a time before going to hell."[26]

As the weather warmed, entertainment moved outside. Five hundred Mormons were camped at North Platte on their way to Utah in the spring of 1867, and they became the victims of pranks played by those construction workers who looked for a less violent brand of recreation. "One that nearly always worked well was to fill an old pocket book with Southern scrip, twenty dollars on top, nailed fast to the walk," wrote one of the Union Pacific men. "As they passed, many stopped, tried to yank it loose, but failed, while we enjoyed a good laugh out of sight."[27]

As with many other rail camps, there were also soldiers in the neighborhood. During the winter of 1866-67 a company of them was stationed at North Platte to protect construction crews. Obliged to live in tents during bitterly cold weather, the men found military life far from attractive. One night nine of them deserted, only to be captured and incarcerated in a homemade guardhouse constructed of railroad rails piled into a 12-foot-high triangle and covered. Here they suffered through the coldest kind of weather.[28] In March 1867 Gen. Christopher C. Augur offered Frank North, of the Pawnee Agency, a major's commission if he would enlist some Indian scouts to support the troops already assigned to the protection of the line. North agreed. He organized 200 Indians into four companies, one group of which he put under the command of his brother Luther. Frank, who was then only 27 years old, had three years earlier led a group of scouts in aid of Gen. S. R. Curtis. In accomplishing this latest assignment, however, Frank placed himself in the ranks of important plainsmen.[29]

By the spring of 1867 the Union Pacific had established a regular schedule of two trains daily each way between Omaha and North Platte.[30] Travelers who formerly had bounced by stagecoach or wagon now rode in comparative luxury. Not only did they speed across a land formerly designated as desert, but they were afforded amusements that in all probability were more engrossing than those provided by airlines in a later age. As a contemporary described the recreational aspects of rail passenger travel of the time, it was "the daily practice of some passengers, and railroad employees, to carry sixteen-shooter rifles, and when a drove of wolves or antelopes appears in the distance, to up with the window and fire round upon round after their retreating steps." So anxious were the men to shoot at something that they opened fire on smaller animals, such as prairie dogs, but with little effect except that of annoying the female passengers who objected to their enforced membership in a roving rifle range.[31]

Emigrants bound for new homes in the West paid much lower fares and received only the simplest kind of accommodations. A young Danish girl later recalled the train trip from Omaha to North Platte in 1867, for which her father paid $10 each to carry his family to the end of the line. Obliged to sit on benches without backs and to be jolted by the movement of a springless car over new track was a tiring experience for the family, and one that the girl remembered years later as having been quite unpleasant.[32] Beyond North Platte lay Julesburg, Fort Sedgwick, Sidney, and Cheyenne. In June Dr. Parry stopped at Fort Sedgwick, where he wrote that the railroad was then rapidly approaching that place. He and his friends watched with fascination as one of the engines steamed in, its whistle shrieking and its stack belching skyward. "Every cloud of its white smoke seemed to bring with it peace and civilization over the plains of the Far West," he commented. It brought even more. Every nearby ranch on the south side of the Platte had moved its quarters to the railroad side, and even a town was drawn forth, as if the iron were magnetized. "Old Julesburg is no more," said Parry, "and a new Julesburg has been established." There was little else that might attract interest, for not a tree, not a bush or even a stick of wood was evident on the vast carpet of grass that stretched out of sight. "I like to see things level," a soldier remarked grimly to Parry, "but I'll be hanged if I want to see any more of it."[33]

By early autumn the rails had reached Lodge Pole Creek, within 50 miles of the modern Wyoming line, and here the town of Sidney was founded. Shortly there appeared a scattering of buildings—a water tank, roundhouse, depot, section house, and other evidences of railroad life. A company of troops arrived, with instructions to hold back small freighting outfits until enough manpower was collected to send well-protected groups into Indian country. The sutler's store, there to serve military men, plus a few assorted shacks that included a saloon, made up the remainder of what was labeled a town.[34]

Progress across Nebraska was not made without objection on the part of the Indians. All during the spring and summer of 1867 Nebraska newspapers carried accounts of attacks upon working parties and of losses suffered by the railroaders. Small bands of Indians harassed surveyors at the western end of the line and sniped at crew members working in more settled parts. In May Durant warned General Grant that unless more military protection could be supplied work would have to stop.[35] Despite efforts to answer this and other requests, the raids continued. In July government director T. J. Carter told Secretary of the Interior Orville H. Browning that drastic moves would have to be made to keep the work going; a still larger military force was requested.[36]

General Sherman, in command of the country westward to the mountains, assured his superiors that he would lend all the protection possible to the railroad because, as he said, not only was the government interested pecuniarily in this private enterprise, but the road itself was vital to military operations against the Plains Indians.[37]

Delays caused by Indian raids were minor annoyances that did not materially affect progress across Nebraska. Swarms of workers surveyed, graded, and laid track with increasing momentum that propelled the little army of civilians toward the Rocky Mountains. Working in advance of the construction crews Union Pacific officials laid out townsites and encouraged the political organization of those municipalities it was spawning on its way westward.

Grenville Dodge platted Cheyenne in late July 1867, and during the first week of August residents held a mass meeting to talk about the formation of a government. Three days later an election was held in which a mayor and councilmen were elected, with 350 votes having been cast. Quickly the officials appointed a chief of police and instructed him to hold any prisoners

Top–*Prominent in the technology of post-Civil War America were the products of the iron and steel industry. Here are two of its representatives, prepared to invade the plains country west of the Missouri River.*

Bottom–*Engine No. 2, weighing only 28 tons, was shipped via Saint Louis to Omaha and put into service in August, 1865. Nicknamed "Grasshopper," it was one of the engines used to haul cars from the Missouri River transfer boats after crossing to the Nebraska side. The Chicago and North Western Railway had a track to the levee on the east side of the river.*

in irons, since the stripling city had no jail. In the interest of community safety an ordinance was passed that prohibited the carrying of firearms in town, and a jail, 20 feet square, was hastily erected. Neither of these actions halted the periodic shootings. As the railroad approached, the city fathers expressed their intention to achieve order by increasing the police force to 14 and hiring additional special officers in anticipation of increased commotion.[38]

As the day of the first locomotive neared, excitement and activity at Cheyenne reached a fever pitch. Louis Simonin, a French traveler who was there in October, wrote that quantities of portable houses were being shipped in from Chicago, prefabricated and designed to satisfy individual need, just as ready-made clothes were produced. Buildings were going up so fast that residents did not even have time to name their streets, merely calling them A, B, C, or D; or 1, 2, 3, or 4. Simonin put up at the Dodge House where, to his surprise, he was billeted in a room containing 30 beds, most of them occupied by two sleepers. "The democratic customs of the Far West permit this nocturnal fraternity, and the American endures it with very good grace," commented the Frenchman, who added that he did not care to share his bed. Nor was he pleased to find that in the common washroom everyone used the same brushes, combs, and towels. Bravely he hauled at the roller towel until he found a relatively clean spot with which to wipe his face. As he made ready to leave, he speculated as to whether Cheyenne's excitement would depopulate Colorado. Local boosters no doubt promised him that such would be the case, especially after the great day—the day the Union Pacific came to town.[39]

Late in the afternoon of November 13, rails were laid into the city of Cheyenne, followed shortly by a whistle-blowing locomotive that brought people rushing to the newly laid tracks. Homes, shops, and saloons were emptied only briefly, for there was little time for celebration; the tracklayers moved through town, and by nightfall "Hell on Wheels," as the construction train was called, was left a half mile in the rear of the railhead.[40] The impact of the road quickly made itself felt upon Cheyenne. Before November was out the town's residents were agitating for the formation of a new territory, which some thought should be called Lincoln, and the city that expected to become the capital already boasted 200 buildings and 2,000 residents.[41] In typical boomtown fashion, reminiscent of Denver in an earlier day, dry-goods boxes were dumped from wagons and torn open for display on the spot. The local paper explained that this evidence of temporary residence by the merchants was misleading and that it occurred only because those businessmen had not yet had time to erect the large and commodious stores planned for the community. Around the edge of the downtown district appeared a scattering of shanties, thrown together in great haste for living quarters. In fact, so popular was Cheyenne that newcomers moved onto lots claimed as railroad property and, calling themselves law-abiding American citizens, defied anyone to move them. They argued that the railroad had no right to the land upon which the city rested, except for a right-of-way, depot grounds, and room for switches, sidetracks, and other necessities. Their claims were answered with a visitation by troops from nearby Fort D. A. Russell, who tore down the shanties and ran off the indignant residents.[42] The Union Pacific's problem was that Dodge had completed platting toward the end of July, after which lots were offered for sale, but the results were not filed until September 21, 1870.[43]

In the spring of 1868 Union Pacific construction crews resumed their westward push, hoping to reach Salt Lake before the year was out. Jack Casement admitted to his wife that Durant and Dillon, who were "driving the work to their utmost capacity," thought such a goal was feasible. With 500 teams and more than 1,000 men at work, management expected to see at least three miles of track go down each day. Casement complained that he had "never been more harried" in his life, but agreed that if the men were pushed hard enough the working force might see the neighborhood of Salt Lake by year's end. Early in August the railhead reached Benton, described by Casement as "certainly the meanest place I have ever been in," and with rails only halfway across Wyoming it was apparent that even superhuman efforts would not put rails into Mormondom that year.[44]

However, as the road reached that midpoint, Wyoming was removed from Dakota and given a territorial status of its own. Fourteen months earlier it had not contained a thousand white inhabitants, not counting troops, but by now the coming of the railroad had produced a population estimated at 40,000. The route west was old, but the means of travel was new, and those who followed the rails had high hopes of exploiting Wyoming resources hitherto denied them because of transportation costs. That year the commissioner of the General Land Office spoke of iron, coal, gold, forests, grazing lands, soda deposits, and medicinal springs in his annual report. All these resources were now more promising because of their sudden nearness to more populated portions of the nation. Before it had penetrated Wyoming even halfway, the Union Pacific had spawned a new western territory and had changed the political map of the United States.[45]

Between August and November crews graded and laid track between Benton and Granger, not far from the Wyoming-Utah line. The Casement brothers drove their men and drafted moonlit nights and Sundays into service to gain extra hours, as one newspaper correspondent described it. But as the cold deepened and winter storms appeared, the work was brought to a halt. Jack Casement complained that in addition to the onset of cold weather, crews were idled by a lack of materials and by Durant, who was creating delays in his efforts to speed up the work. "We are straining every nerve to get into the Salt Lake valley before the heavy snows fall," he wrote in early November, predicting at the same time that another 30 days of good weather would put tracks near the Mormon capital.[46] By the end of the year, however, the work had progressed only as far as the head of Echo Canyon. Utah had been reached, but the Great Salt Lake was not yet in view.

As the track was laid across Wyoming the company platted towns, sold lots, and moved on. It was said to have disposed of $17,000 worth of lots in Benton during the first few weeks of that village's existence.[47] At the crossing of the Green River another city was platted and given the river's name. Cheyenne's first mayor, H. M. Hook, became president of a new town company there, one that was owned principally by railroad and stage-coach men. The owners regarded this as the place where demands for sup-plies to Utah, Idaho, and Montana would converge, and it was therefore regarded as a site with a commercial future. There was the usual "lot jumping," accompanied by demands for troops to remove the interlopers, and followed by the establishment of the city cemetery that had two freshly made graves before the city was barely established.[48]

Travelers must have been puzzled over the violent struggle for possession of city lots in so desolate a country. Samuel Bowles rode over rails laid straight as an arrow across what he described as a "high, rolling, desert country . . ., with scarcely any vegetation but the rank, coarse sage bush, and the soil a fine, alkali-laden dust," the view of which, he said, generated a "memorable pain." Every 12 or 15 miles was located a small station that as yet was no more than a water tank and a woodpile. Occasionally there appeared a division point, with shops, back of which an eating house, several stores, saloons, and shops sprawled along a dusty street. Seedy looking loafers, referred to by Bowles as the "fungi indigenous to American railways," leaned against such local emporiums and watched passing trains with de-tached boredom. Every 30 or 40 days, he explained, these perishable board and canvas shanty towns were nearly depopulated as the railhead moved forward, and the local real estate booms faded overnight.[49]

A few individuals, tired of moving or hopeful that this particular loca-tion had some peculiar commercial future, stayed on while the sporting class and the drifters were drawn westward behind the company pay car. Even the most charitable description of the sprawling municipal efforts fell short of the statement, made in an English journal, that across Wyoming "villages are springing into existence, and the habits of civilized communities [are] beginning to be introduced."[50] The view was overly optimistic; however, in a relatively short time the embryonic little cities would shake off the violence of their birth, and, little by little, their community habits would shift in the direction indicated by those who viewed the countryside from afar.

Meanwhile, the work trains continued westward, and the iron tendrils that carried them probed through arid country that sported only sagebrush, edging toward Zion and the completion of the nation's most exciting engineering project since the Erie Canal. By now success was assured, and those who undertook it—both labor and management—became impatient to finish the great work that had attracted the attention of postwar America.

Opening the Gates of Zion

During 1866 and 1867 the American reading public became increasingly engrossed in a contest that was developing in an area still frequently labeled the American Desert. Union Pacific construction crews, off to a slow start in the summer of 1865, now were mounting their attack upon the distances of the plains with a vigor that attracted national attention. With each passing month the army of workers improved its techniques, added manpower, and commenced to set tracklaying records that generated complimentary remarks in an increasing number of newspapers and periodicals.

Utah, the oldest and best-developed region between the Missouri River and the Pacific Coast states, received very little favorable attention in the barrage of publicity that accompanied the building of the Union Pacific. The memory of the Mormon War was less than a decade old, and few observers who had written of their visits to the Great Basin area since that time had found many kind things to say about its people. Polygamy, one of the twin evils referred to in the election of 1856, was not only present, but the elimination of the other evil, slavery, appeared to make the continued existence of this Mormon custom all the more repugnant to American "Gentiles," as non-Mormons were called by the Mormons. Brigham Young's earlier opposition to commercial intercourse with outsiders and his disapproval of efforts to mine precious metals in Utah were interpreted to mean that the Mormons wanted no contact with the eastern business world. The story spread, therefore, that Zion did not look with favor upon the coming of the railroad facilities.[1] Even after the Union Pacific's construction was assured, and despite Brigham Young's words and deeds to the contrary, there remained a stubborn belief as to his presumed opposition.[2]

There are indications that Young had long believed the day would come when Utah would be served by rail, and while he may have thought this circumstance not to be an unmixed blessing, he was not blind to the advantages of such service. Edward W. Tullidge, a contemporary Mormon historian, wrote that during the original Mormon crossing of the plains to the Salt Lake Valley, the church leader had pointed to where railroad tracks one day would run. As early as the meeting of the first Utah territorial legislature, in session during the winter of 1851-52, a memorial, signed by Young, asked Congress for rail service.[3] In his message to that body, December 12, 1853, Young again referred to the prospect of such a road, remarking that "pass where it will, we cannot fail to be benefitted by it."[4] A little over a month later a mass demonstration favoring a Pacific railroad was held at Salt Lake City; obviously such a gathering had the full support of church leadership.[5]

A decade passed, and there was no railroad. However, in his message to the legislature in December 1863, Acting Governor Amos Reed reminded his fellow lawmakers that the time of waiting was nearly over. After describing the national benefits of a Pacific railroad, he spoke of its influence upon Utah, saying that it "draws us closer to our former homes and opens to our vision the near prospect of wealth and prosperity."[6]

By the summer of 1864, with passage of amended legislation that increased the Union Pacific's land subsidy and placed the federal government in the position as second mortgage holder, prospects for the commencement of construction brightened considerably. On July 13 Samuel Reed, a divisional chief engineer of the Union Pacific, conferred with Brigham Young and showed him survey maps of the country between the mouth of Weber Canyon and a point just east of Bear River Mountain, where, he said, a railroad could be built as cheaply as one crossing any point in Iowa. Very shortly Young revealed the conversation to the editor of the *Millennial Star* of Liverpool, England, a city from which the bulk of British Mormon emigrants sailed for the United States.[7] Before long the westward movement of railroad rails was to be an important consideration in Mormon planning of the annual European emigration to Zion, as Young pointed out in his letter.

Early in 1865 the Mormon church leader referred to the survey earlier discussed with Reed and he expressed his pleasure that the Union Pacific Railroad finally had begun its trek to Utah. He spoke of the advantages of the telegraph, already in use, and predicted that when the two "great discoveries of our age," the telegraph and the railroad, were available to the Mormons, the territory would be much benefited.[8] The Mormon leader was willing to do more than say kind things about the approaching road; he subscribed to five shares of stock, par value $1,000 each. In December 1864 Chief Engineer Peter A. Dey referred to Young's payment of the balance of what he owed on the stock and thanked him for this and other assistance to the Union Pacific.[9] General John A. Dix, the company's president, referred in 1866 to the "zealous cooperation" in reconnaissance and surveying that the road received from the Mormons who, he said, were contributing to a work that would bind the states of the Union together with new and indissoluble ties.[10]

In January 1866 Brigham Young once more made reference to the oncoming road when he addressed the legislative body of the State of Deseret. Its progress, he said, was such that during the approaching season rails would reach several hundred miles nearer "our isolated position in the tops of the mountains." To hasten the process he suggested that the brethren lend material aid to the speedy completion of, what he termed, a great national work. Mormon business with the East was increasing yearly, said Young, and the heavy outlay necessary to supply freight outfits made that slow and unreliable method of transportation quite expensive. The legislators, many of whom were businessmen, did not have to be reminded that the want of a railroad was "sensibly felt," to use Brigham Young's words, or that its completion was "to be viewed as very desirable."[11]

Expensive also was the annual convoy of teams and wagons sent east each spring to aid the emigrant parties in their crossing of the plains. As plans were being made for the 1867 migration, Elder Wilford Woodruff advised his colleagues in England that it was possible no teams would be sent forth that year because "we are waiting awhile for the Pacific Railroad to approach nearer to us."[12] Young, when addressing local legislators, referred to the tedious miles that lay between Utah and more populated regions. Travel over what he termed "the unsettled plains and deserts" had for years made the approach to Utah difficult and costly, but now, in 1867, the railroad was approaching at a rate that promised an early end to that annoying problem. Rather than fearing its approach, he welcomed it, saying, "this gigantic work will increase intercourse, and it is to be hoped, soften prejudices, and bind the country together."[13] While the road might increase the westward flow of Gentiles, it would also make much easier the importation of Mormons whose presence in larger numbers would tend to maintain numerical superiority.

Although no teams were sent in 1867, there was such a demand for immigrant transportation in 1868 that a record number of wagons—534— were sent forth that year to bring in the newcomers.[14] On March 18 Brigham Young wrote to Edward Hunter, the presiding bishop of the church, that "it is deemed necessary to send five hundred teams to the terminus of the U.P.R.R. each team to consist of one wagon and four yoke of oxen, or their equivalent strength, in either mules or horses." Pointing out that the railroad was now prepared to convey passengers over 500 miles beyond Omaha, team-

Top—*Corinne, Utah, became a great supply base for Montana-bound traffic, as suggested by the names of business firms on several buildings.*

Left—*Bear River City, Wyoming, a "hell on wheels" town 965 miles west of Omaha, boasted of 200 inhabitants when this Main Street view was taken.*

Bottom—*Main Street, Salt Lake City, presented a quiet and almost pastoral scene in 1865. A few years later it became much busier as the iron horse with its great iron "cow catcher" snorted into town.*

sters could leave Salt Lake City as late as June 15 to meet their passengers at the rail terminus.

Even with the modern convenience of rail service, there were many plans to be made. Young recommended the location of a temporary depot near the end of track, where provisions—such as dried fruit, because it was "an excellent substitute for vegetables"—could be stored and where there were adequate camping facilities for a large number of people. He estimated that not less than 5,000 adults bound for Zion would cross the plains that season.[15]

In February 1867 Brigham, Jr., eastbound on an errand for his father, went to the Wells, Fargo & Company office at Salt Lake City, where he picked up his ticket and paid $210. Two days later, in a driving snowstorm, he was aboard a stagecoach bound for the railhead. Alternating between coach and sleigh, the stage company took its passengers eastward across present-day Wyoming and to Denver, where those who were going farther east transferred to the North Platte run. Although the weather was bad, and deep snowdrifts undoubtedly made the road hard to follow, the young man from Salt Lake City explained that the wandering propensities of the vehicle were caused by the driver, who nursed a bottle steadily across those desolate, cold miles.

Beyond Denver the roads were rough and the drivers "ungentlemanly," but by the time the party neared Fort Sedgwick the situation seemed to improve. "The drivers do not get drunk along this part of the road, for they are bullet proof," wrote the younger Brigham, who added, "but they are constantly pouring down the liquor, and it is only their great power . . . of endurance that keeps them sober." Early on the morning of February 13 the coach crossed the solidly frozen Platte River and arrived at the railroad station at ten o'clock. There was no train in sight. It was supposed to have arrived from Omaha two hours earlier, but the storm's snowdrifts covered the tracks. Hopeful rail passengers had to sleep that night in the depot waiting room because the unfinished hotels could do no better than supply what Young called "the commonest kind of food." At one o'clock on the morning of the fourteenth the train pulled into North Platte, 17 hours late. The return trip did not begin until noon, and by then it was a thoroughly angry party of travelers who boarded the cars for Omaha.

Among the group was the son of the Mormon leader, who bitterly expressed his displeasure at the inefficiency of the train's crew. "I firmly believe that the characters referred to," he wrote, "are paid by Restaurant proprietors to detain passengers if possible a few days at their miserable hovels." As the train got under way things looked brighter. The road was smooth, and the train slid along at 25 miles an hour, carrying its load comfortably across a frosted countryside. At Kearney, Nebraska, the conductor announced there would be a short stop of 20 minutes for supper before resuming the journey. Instead, the passengers stayed there all night. "The wind is fearful and drifting the snow in the car covering our beds," wrote Young. "The cold is intense and the provisions miserable."

The next day the train moved out, its engine bucking snowdrifts six to eight feet high. "The concussions were sometimes terrific and then we would become stationary, powerless to retreat or advance until the road was cleared by shoveling," the Mormon wrote in his diary. By the sixteenth the train had worked its way to Grand Island, but progress was so slow that some passengers got off and walked on ahead to the depot, "being very hungry and disgusted with the railway officials." At eleven that night the party reached Omaha, where young Brigham gratefully checked in at the Herndon House, glad to have a warm room and a good meal, after a trip that left him with far less enthusiasm for rail travel than that expressed by his noted father.[16]

Travel during the warmer months was much more comfortable. The Scotsman A. N. MacFarlane, of Dundee, called the Union Pacific "decidedly the finest railroad over which we passed," stating that its cars far surpassed the first-class carriages in his own country. "The trains on this line of railway ran so smoothly," he recalled, "that when I passed over it I could, with the greatest of ease, take my shorthand notes of all that was going on around me."[17] By the time the Scotsman made his run across the plains the snows had melted, and what he saw was quite another world than that viewed by the younger Brigham.

The relative degree of ease with which Union Pacific trains passed westward was of incidental interest to the Mormons, who eagerly awaited the arrival of any vehicle that rode the rails. Upon reaching Cheyenne Engineer Samuel B. Reed notified Brigham Young of the accomplishment, noting that his crews were then just 16 miles beyond a point half way between the Missouri River and Salt Lake City. The Mormon leader responded at once, congratulating Reed and expressing a wish to see the engineer "on one of those elegant western cars" before long. "God bless you in your good labor," he concluded.[18] By the spring of 1868 the rails were deep into Wyoming Territory, feeling their way to Mormondom, and there was talk that Zion would be served as early as that autumn. Even if that happy day did not take place until the next year, Mormons conceded that a construction record would be set.[19]

Not only were the Mormons enthusiastic about the prospect of having a railroad, but they were also increasingly defensive over accusations that their people wanted to be shut out from the rest of mankind. Referring to the long and dusty miles that stretched westward from the Missouri River, across which most Mormons had traveled in jolting wagons, the *Deseret News* wrote of the day when passage to Zion could be made under less trying circumstances. Nor were the brethren blind to the effect rail service would have upon the price of all imported goods, especially heavy machinery so long freighted in at exorbitant rates. Instead of viewing Salt Lake City as a place of religious refuge, the local press now spoke of it as a stopping place on an international highway—even a large and influential seaport— that would carry passengers from London to Bombay in half the time formerly required.[20]

One reason that Americans generally believed the Mormons were clannish and hostile to outsiders was the persistence of that group's feeling against mining and mining people. Brigham Young had long emphasized the value of a community that combined agriculture with manufacturing, one that worked toward economic independence as opposed to the traditional dependence upon the East experienced by many western settlements. As the railroad came nearer, there was reiteration of this sentiment among the Mormons. Pointing out that the territory had increased steadily in wealth from its earliest days, the *Deseret News,* the voice of the Mormons, argued that such would not have been the case if mining had been encouraged. The paper's management claimed that mining did not produce real wealth or prosperity; rather it brought a floating, impermanent population. California was used as an example of a state that would have been depopulated after the mining boom but for its agricultural potential. That state would "today be among the least prosperous and possibly the most wretched communities in the world," said the editor, in support of his argument that only agriculture had saved the place.[21]

Utah leaders admitted that mining was not prospering. Governor Charles Durkee argued that some progress had been made in mining, but he conceded that no real success was likely until cheap transportation was available.[22] So far as official Mormon policy was concerned, railroad service might indeed aid mining, but it was not one of the benefits that the church looked forward to with pleasure.

On the contrary, stress was laid upon Utah's agricultural advance, and how rail service would help to sell its farm products throughout the West.

Echo City, a small and peaceful Mormon community, became a very active place when construction crews arrived. Here, in 1868, are three Mormon women from that farming community posing for the famed photographer A. J. Russell.

In 1867, for example, over 80,000 acres of cereal crops were harvested, not to mention nearly 2,000 acres of sorghum, about 7,000 acres of root crops, a small amount of cotton, and over 1,000 acres of orchard produce. In addition nearly 30,000 acres of meadowland fed local livestock.[23] It was the farmer and the craftsman the Mormons wanted, classes apt to settle into the already established community, and not those who came to get and get out, taking from the land but leaving nothing.

When Brigham Young addressed the State of Deseret's legislature in February 1868, he spoke once more of the Union Pacific's progress, expressing the hope that within two years "the solitude of our mountain fastnesses will be broken by the shrill snort of the iron horse," and he again referred to the many benefits it would bring. At that time Young did not know on which side of the lake the Union Pacific proposed to build; and although he thought the south side promised a more direct route and one that would accumulate a heavier local business, he did not appear to be deeply concerned over the choice. He felt that if the road passed to the north a branch line could be built to Salt Lake City at a relatively small outlay.[24] In any case Young was willing to speed the work and to lend any assistance he could. He advised Thomas Durant that Mormon workers could be hired for $1 to $2.25 a day, according to their talents, provided their board was furnished.[25]

Brigham Young and his followers were keenly aware of what the Union Pacific could do for them, and as early as December 1867, Brigham Young, Jr., discussed with Elder Franklin Richards of Liverpool the possibility of making transportation contracts that would enable Mormon immigrants to travel all the way from New York to Cheyenne with only one or two changes of cars. He estimated rates of $25 in greenbacks from New York to Omaha and $10 for each adult from there to North Platte.[26] Brigham Young also utilized the rails to haul hardware and other necessities part of the way to Zion. During 1868 the amount of freight passing westward over the line toward Utah reached such proportions that it drew criticism from Washington. Referring to a clause that permitted supplies for Young's employees to pass over the road free because the church leader had contracted to build a section of it, government director C. H. Snow commented that the freight consigned to Young was "so largely in excess of what is for the use of his men [that it] suggests mismanagement, if nothing else."[27] On the contrary, argued Young, large amounts of Mormon goods were lying at Omaha and other points on the line due to the unwillingness or inability of the company to furnish transportation. "Some little has," he wrote, "however been forwarded at my earnest request, to supply the men working on the railroad with blankets, boots, &c."[28] Union Pacific officials were to discover, before long, that they were dealing with a shrewd and hardheaded businessman when they associated themselves with the Mormon leader. The relationship had its advantages, however, because it continued for years.

In 1868, as the Union Pacific neared Utah, Mormon excitement grew. Salt Lake City papers gave increasing space to new commercial possibilities that would appear with the rails, most of which were verified later by a local historian who attributed the birth of Utah's important Zion's Co-operative Mercantile Institution to railroad stimulation of the economy.[29] The assiduous Mormons overlooked no possibilities for the future economic growth of Zion. In August 1868 Brigham Young wrote to Seth Green of New York, saying that "we fully expect when the Railroad comes through to plant the oyster, lobster and other salt water fish in suitable places in our lakes and rivers."[30]

To reassure readers that the incoming flow of goods was largely beneficial, the *Deseret News* quoted an Iowa paper whose editor warned that gamblers and fancy ladies would find no haven in the new business metropolis of the West. "I have been told," he wrote, "that as soon as such persons enter this quiet abode, the President dispatches a messenger, intimating gently that the climate is not healthy for them and that they should select a more salubrious locality. A hint from such a power will go a great way." He had a further warning for those who thought that boomtown social life had accompanied the new prosperity when he said: "Drinking saloons are very scarce and there are but one or two lager beer [establishments]."[31]

As the railroad net spread across the American West, many a small town envisaged itself as the commercial capital of its region and talked of achieving the title "Great Railroad Center." Salt Lake City businessmen saw this as a distinct possibility for their town. In 1868 Joseph S. Wilson, commissioner of the General Land Office, wrote from Washington, D.C., that the Mormon capital was sure to become a radiating point for other roads, one of which would lead to the Columbia River and then to Portland, while another would connect Utah with Arizona and California and run clear to San Diego Bay.[32] The *Deseret News* announced that the Union Pacific already had plans to connect Salt Lake City with both Portland and Los Angeles, a prediction that would come true a good many years later.[33] Much sooner, however, small Mormon lines were to be built in several directions from the City of the Saints, binding the religious and the commercial lives of Utah to its capital.

Anxious to build Zion into a strong economic unit, Mormon leadership continued to insist that it did not fear the coming of the railroad. The *News* in May 1868 outlined the past history of persecution suffered by the Mormon people and admitted to the widespread belief in the United States that penetration of Zion by the Union Pacific would end Mormonism. Those who

TOP—*A westbound construction crew in the late 1860s.*

BOTTOM—*Important to the railroad, and to the communities it served, was the telegraph. These men are at work in Weber Canyon, setting up communications with "the front" as the army of construction workers moved toward Promontory, Utah.*

BOTTOM, RIGHT—*A work train, in the vicinity of Promontory, Utah, 1869.*

retailed such stories, said the editor, supposed that the Mormons had a similar belief and would therefore oppose the coming of the rails. He asked if the large force of Brigham Young's people, working at top speed all that summer to complete a grading contract made by their leader, did not sufficiently deny these rumors. "The railroad is coming," said the *News*. "It is a fixed fact. We intend, as a community, to do all in our power to push it through . . . . We need it."[34] In praise of the project the *News* of June 5, 1868, exclaimed: "We live in a wonderful age." Admittedly, the railroad would bring in Gentiles; but it also would carry them out, said the Mormons. Nor would the presence of those who stayed sway the "confidence in our system and its great author" or cause the faithful to waver, the *Deseret News* had promised earlier.[35]

While the *News* editor was confident that his people could cope with ideas foreign or antagonistic to them, he warned that material changes inherent in railroading might be more disruptive. The Mormons, who had worked so hard to develop home manufactures, might be threatened by importation of such items as fine tables, wagons, and other products. Should this happen, the coarser local manufacture might suffer from eastern competition. To ward off such a development the editor pointed out that a better grade of raw materials should be imported. Rather than suffer from the coming of the railroad, highly skilled Mormon artisans ought to redouble their efforts to compete with the imports it would bring to Utah. Editor George Cannon was one of those who foresaw the necessity of tightening Mormon business lines to meet a new and potent threat.[36]

Samuel Bowles, an eastern journalist who visited Salt Lake City during this period of change, commented upon the prospect of Gentile competition in a growing commercial community and the church's probable reaction to such danger. He guessed that before the coming of the rails there were not more than 3,000 or 4,000 Gentiles in a territorial population of between 100,000 and 125,000, but this ratio appeared likely to change in the near future. Bowles therefore predicted a tightening of the practice, already in partial use, whereby Mormons bought only from Mormons in order to prevent any further breakdown of their rule "growing out of the revolutionary influences of the railroad."[37] Intercourse with Gentiles was to be limited to absolute necessities, and those who grew careless in their purchases were promised stern punishment.

Brigham Young reiterated his views regarding the advantages of the railroad several times during 1868. At a mass meeting held on June 10, he told over 3,000 assembled listeners that rumors about Mormon antipathy to the project were false and that, on the contrary, the church strongly desired to have it. With the typical Young directness he suggested that even he might become less disliked by his detractors when he became better and more widely known; the railroad would help spread his name.[38] Writing to one of the foreign missionaries early in November, Young remarked that "we want the railroad, [and] we are not afraid of its results." Once again he suggested that the new means of transportation would make it easier for strangers to come to Zion and to see for themselves the good order, the peace, and the freedom from crime enjoyed by the Mormons.[39] He felt that by comparison with other American communities his was an outstanding example of civic advance.

During the summer of 1868, as Mormon boys worked on the railroad grade and their people prepared for the coming of the rails, the church used the partially constructed facilities to expedite and to enlarge the annual emigration from Great Britain. The first group of westbound Mormons to sail from Liverpool that season came on the *John Bright,* hoping to reach the Union Pacific rail terminus by July 10.[40] Between them, that vessel and the *Minnesota* brought 1,250 emigrants to the United States, all of whom had reached Laramie before the end of July, where they were met by the usual wagon trains. By that time the *Colorado* had delivered another 600 who also came west by rail.[41] The total emigration from Europe that year amounted to 3,232 persons, most of whom came from the British Isles.[42]

Brigham Young was pleased by the dispatch with which the converts made their way, commenting that they arrived looking well thanks to a rail ride of 650 miles beyond the Missouri that made the journey across the plains far less dangerous and wearing than in years gone by.[43] One of the Mormons who accompanied the travelers gave a less glowing picture, remarking that "It cost us much trouble to get the saints in the crowded cars [at Omaha], as these were poor and uncomfortable." On arriving at Laramie, he said, "Some of the saints were very sick on account of the heat and the ride."[44]

Although it was uncomfortable, the trip was cheaper and quicker than before. Brigham Young estimated that it cost about $65 a person to bring his people from Liverpool to the rail terminus, a figure that was quite reasonable considering what the road charged other customers. The regular fare from Omaha to the terminus was ten cents a mile, a figure that equaled what the British emigrants had to pay for the entire trip to the end of the rails.[45]

By the time the road was in full running order, conditions seem to have improved, even for the cheap-fare passengers. In August 1869 Elder David M. Stewart reported to Young that employees all along the route "are disposed to do what is right by our emigrants." The rail superintendents, he said, "are doing all in their power to make our people comfortable, and to speed them on their journey to Utah."[46]

After the road's completion the church no longer had to deal with the

While the railroad promised year-round travel across the plains, there were delays during inclement weather. Here a train is having slow going across the Laramie plains.

plains-wagon travel season; now the people could be brought in at the season of most favorable rates. In May 1869 Brigham Young wrote to Albert Carrington, head of the European Mission, and directed that the next group be held until August or early September. "The chances are that the rates will then be lower," he explained.[47] Even so, church records show a receipt of $25,826.16 for the haulage of passengers and baggage during a period covering August 20 to October 25, 1869.[48]

During the final months that preceded the union of the rails at Promontory Summit, the entire Utah community began to feel the excitement of anticipation. In January 1869 Acting Governor Edwin Higgins spoke of the approaching railroad in his address to the legislative assembly, as had Utah chief executives for more than a decade and a half. Once more the many advantages to immigration, to the exportation of local products, and to the importation of necessities were outlined. He made special mention of mining, a subject that the church had played down for years, commenting that Utah's subsurface riches now could be extracted profitably and to the great benefit of the entire community. As he looked into the future, Higgins saw a Utah connected to the world by a modern transportation system, and he quite correctly predicted that "every branch of our social and political life must consequently feel the influence of its existence."[49]

To the average resident of Utah, both Mormon and Gentile, the prospect of rail service had a more immediate appeal. Not only was transportation becoming easier, but it was also cheaper. Speaking of the yet-uncompleted road, Elder George A. Smith remarked that already it had reduced the price of merchandise, and when the demands of construction crews had been satisfied he thought the additional available cars would mean a further reduction in the price of freight. Smith called the million dollars already injected into the Mormon community, through construction contracts and employment, "very opportune," especially so because grasshoppers had caused heavy damage to crops, thereby sharply reducing the territory's income. "There is about another million due us," he said, in reference to the Mormon grading contracts, and its receipt promised further to aid the local economy.[50]

While the Mormon community was happy to acquire railroad facilities and to have its supply of cash replenished as a fringe benefit, there began to be some misgivings about the price to be paid by the outside world for these endowments. It was anticipated that the employment of local men would diminish the influence of the roistering element which accompanied construction, but such a hope was in vain. As the railroad approached Utah it continued to produce the rough and ready towns it had strewn across the countryside all the way from Omaha. Bear River City (just outside Utah's border) was described by a dismayed Mormon elder as "several hundred tents, wagons and shanties ... erected for the sale of whiskey and for gambling and dance houses." It was governed by a vigilance committee that seemed bent upon hanging half the population. The next mushroom municipality was Wahsatch, a temporary village that existed primarily for the large crews called in to cut a long tunnel nearby and to build a temporary track around it while the bore was being made. The life of Wahsatch was so short that no serious disorder had a chance to mount before the town faded away.[51] "Terminopolis," as each new railhead community was dubbed, moved on as inevitably as before.

Echo City was more orderly, but it also felt the impact of the railroad. Suddenly town lots began to sell rapidly. Prices soared, and temporary business houses did a thriving trade. Late in 1868 a Salt Lake City newspaper correspondent counted 50 flimsy structures, exclusive of Union Pacific buildings, most of which, he said, were "mere duck tenements ... as frail as the erring humans in some cases sheltered by them." The occupants to to whom he referred, known to his colleagues as "nymphs du grade," recently had been imported from what was called an "Emporium of Fashion" at Bear River City. The reinforcements, noted a newsman, "place ... Echo in direct 'communication' with all the gilded enticements with which wanton pleasure decks herself to charm her votaries." While reporters talked lightly of the sporting element that accompanied construction crews, the Mormon press generally showed open concern over what it called "the brutalization ... setting so strongly westward." One of its representatives confessed that he did not see how local authorities could condone a situation where "unblushing depravity, gross intemperance, gambling hells and kindred places are allowed full swing."[52]

In more ordinary commercial transactions, Echo City displayed the confusion typical of other western boomtowns. Sheltered by what one observer described as "a vigorous spread of cotton," was a wide array of groceries, dry goods, clothing, hardware, and general merchandise. With lumber selling as high as $250 a thousand and termed "non-come-atable" even at that price, the stores, bakeries, blacksmith shops, restaurants, saloons, and other businesses became a part of a canvas world which had crept across the continent to Utah.[53] The excitement was brief, the commotion passing westward with the rails, and before long the transient population had departed, leaving the place with not much more than an appropriate name: Echo.

Uintah, located at the mouth of Weber Canyon and about seven miles from Ogden, served as depot for Salt Lake City passengers during 1869. To Elder John Jaques, who passed through it that summer on his way to Liverpool, it seemed that every building in the place was either a grog shop, a gambling den, or what might loosely be termed a restaurant. "Uintah, in fact," he concluded, "is one of the most repulsive looking places I ever saw."[54] Non-Mormon sources attest to the violence in the construction camp. "There was a man shot and hung at Wasatch tonight," noted Paymaster O. C. Smith in his diary. "Reason given: He is a Dammed Nigger."[55] Nearby Ogden was described as "a changed place," where hotels, boardinghouses, restaurants, and "meals at all hours" chophouses were jammed to overflowing.[56] The city, which had been incorporated for many years, was now growing rapidly and real estate prices soared. Again, prosperity was not without its price. "Until the advance of the railroad drunkenness and crime were almost unknown," wrote one of the Mormon elders. Here, however, municipal leaders were able to exercise better control than that attempted in newer towns, and lawless elements tended to move on to greener pastures.[57] Beyond Ogden lay Brigham City, another Mormon community that experienced a crush of humanity bigger than it could handle. So many businessmen and travelers demanded lodging that rooms could be had only by telegraphing to hotels a day or two in advance.[58]

At Corinne, near where the Union Pacific and Central Pacific would join, disorder and chaos ruled. One of the Mormons called the place a "headquarters for libertines." A Mormon newspaper reporter in the early spring of 1869 commented that the railroad already was developing the resources of the territory, for dance houses and saloons were springing up in all directions. Venturing a guess that there were no less than 300 whiskey shops between Corinne and Brigham City, the journalist sarcastically remarked that newcomers were indeed showing the Saints "what is necessary to build up a country and make it self-supporting and permanent."[59] A Nebraska journal, scorning the Mormon alarm at the influx of wickedness, stated that "Brigham Young's paper advises that a whistle be kept hanging up in every house, to be sounded in case robbers or murderers break in."[60] The quiet agricultural community that had grown up in the Great Basin during the preceding two decades was understandably disturbed by the sudden injection of rowdyism, and it is not surprising that some of its members thought it was time literally to blow the whistle and cool the proceedings.

As it was with the many other western railroads that were built later, the commotion caused by construction in Utah passed away when the pay car no longer supported the workmen and their followers. As early as July 1869, a local observer who visited Echo could write: "Everything is so still and quiet that the wonder arises how those who profess to do business here contrive to pass the time . . . . Store doors stand open with their usual dispensers of goods lounging around, while saloons boast each a couple or three occupants stretched full length on benches adorning the canvas sides. . . ."[61]

Already the social wounds caused by the gash cut through Utah during railroad construction days were beginning to heal. Sensible Mormons realized that disorder was only part of the birth pangs, and that the benefits promised by rail service would emerge in due time. Long before "See America First" became a promotional slogan, Mormon leaders thought of selling the region's scenery, trout fishing, and hunting to easterners. In the early spring of 1869, Salt Lake City boosters were already calling for a "Grand National Hotel" to accommodate the many visitors who were expected.[62] During the first summer of regular service, the prediction of a heavy tourist season was realized; more visitors stopped at Salt Lake City during those travel months than at any time since its founding. They were welcomed by the local press, with the comment that Mormondom had nothing to fear from being examined by intelligent minds, for only through such exposure could the prevailing ignorance about the church be fought.[63]

Equally welcome were commercial men of the East and Midwest. Hardly had the road been opened before a large delegation from Chicago arrived at Salt Lake City to talk business. Brigham Young greeted them with enthusiasm and listened with interest to their comments about the mutual advantages of rail service. He agreed with such sentiments and sagely reminded them that the Mormons had built part of the Union Pacific.[64] The *Salt Lake City Directory* of 1869 made much of the new economic union with the Midwest, giving considerable space to a section entitled "Chicago: Its Growth and Trade," in which it described places of interest, theaters, museums, hotels, and the leading business houses of Chicago.[65]

As the work ended on the great construction project, the Mormon community looked back upon an earlier day of isolation and regarded it as the true period of pioneering. Ahead lay a physical connection with the commercial vigor of postwar America, out of which could grow a strong and economically integrated Utah. In 1869 these people stood upon the threshold of great change, and the more thoughtful of them recognized that the days ahead might bring problems as well as advancements. They understood that progress in the form of improved transportation facilities was not always an unmixed blessing. Nevertheless the new link introduced them to a whole new world, and the progressive elements of the community were anxious to take advantage of its benefits while endeavoring to cope with any spiritual dangers inherent in the change.

"Brother Brigham Holds the Whip"

By 1867 the Mormon settlements in Utah were approximately two decades old. They had prospered through energetic application of muscle to the land, and through trade carried on with passersby and with mining camps, particularly those of Montana. By now the Montana placer boom was tapering off, its floating population was moving on, and there was a general decline in the war-born prosperity that had affected American business in general. The Mormons, faced with declining agricultural exports and the ravages of grasshoppers to their crops, were beginning to experience economic distress. Therefore, the coming of the Union Pacific promised not only to reduce high transportation costs for their imports, and thus reduce prices, but it also offered the Mormons a chance to earn cash by working on the construction crews of that project.

During the summer of 1867, at a time when the Union Pacific terminus had progressed no farther west than North Platte, Nebraska, there came the first hints that perhaps Mormon boys would be able to find employment with the railroad. On July 26 Brigham Young, Jr., and his family arrived at Chicago, en route to Salt Lake City from Europe, and while visiting a newspaper office he learned that a number of important Union Pacific figures were about to leave for the end of track in a car described as being "most elegantly fitted up." Sidney Dillon, whom Young identified as a man "who seemed to be one of the chief directors," invited the Youngs to share the accommodations and provided them "with one of their magnificent compartments." On the way to Omaha, Dillon, government director Springer Harbaugh, Sen. John Sherman, brother of the famous general, and Gov. Jacob Cox of Ohio "conversed freely" with the son of Utah's spiritual leader. Before long the reason behind the elaborate courtesies was revealed by Dillon, who, as Young wrote in his diary, "wants our assistance in laying out the U.P.R.R. and building the road." Those with whom he traveled assured him that they wished to show the son of Brigham every possible courtesy because "they were anxious to awaken a real interest in the minds of our people to push this railroad through our Territory." Upon arriving at Omaha, Young found that he had no difficulty in borrowing $1,500 from a local bank, which ran his indebtedness there to $3,500. Happy over the shower of compliments and cash, he proceeded to the railhead at North Platte.[1]

No specific request for assistance was presented to the Mormon leadership until May 6, 1868, at which time Durant telegraphed Brigham Young from Fort Sanders (near Laramie) and asked him if he would take a contract to prepare a road grade from the head of Echo Canyon toward Salt Lake. Apparently there was to be no haggling over price; Durant simply asked Young to name the figure—per cubic yard and depending upon the character of the material to be worked—for which he was willing to assume the task. No time was lost in contemplation at Salt Lake City; Durant had an affirmative answer to his telegram the same day he made his request.[2]

Within two weeks a contract was signed at Salt Lake City between Samuel B. Reed, Union Pacific superintendent of construction, and Brigham Young. It provided that the Mormons would grade the road from the head of Echo Canyon toward the Salt Lake Valley for 54 miles, and if it was determined that the tracks were to be laid around the north end of the lake, Young was to have the contract as far as the lake. Work was to commence within ten days and was to be completed by November 1. The railroad agreed to carry men, teams, and tools from Omaha free and to provide powder, steel, shovels, picks, sledges, wheelbarrows, scrapers, crowbars, and other necessary tools at cost plus freight charges no higher than those paid by other contractors. For their work the Mormons were to receive 30 cents a cubic yard for excavations where earth was hauled less than 200 feet away and 50 cents for greater distances. Cuts made through harder materials were scaled at higher prices, depending upon the nature of the terrain, and the cost of tunneling was fixed at $15 a yard. Estimates of work costs were to be made monthly, with 80 percent of such figures to be paid on the twentieth of each month.[3]

At the time of the Young contract there was a widely held impression that the Mormon leader was to undertake all the Union Pacific grading in Utah. Actually, the work east of Echo Canyon, for about 50 miles in the direction of Bridger, was awarded to Joseph F. Nounnan and Company, a non-Mormon organization.[4] In both cases, Mormon and non-Mormon, misunderstandings and miscalculations on the part of bidders resulted in considerable acrimony between contractors and the railroad. Hasty negotiations for bids were not, however, unusual in the construction of the road, and the recriminations heard later in Utah would not be unique.

Brigham Young was happy to have a contract for even part of the Utah portion of the road. Commenting upon the extent of indebtedness among his people, and the possibility of turning a surplus of labor into money, he called the opportunity a godsend.[5]

According to Jack Casement, some 4,000 Mormons responded to the initial call.[6] Others would follow during the summer.[7] The *Deseret News* reflected the church's further satisfaction over such an arrangement when it stressed the fact that Mormon boys now would not have to range very far from home to find work.[8] On the other side of the coin was an equally attractive picture. As one of the local churchmen explained it, the contract would "obviate the necessity of some few thousand strangers being brought here, to mix and interfere with the settlers, of that class of men who take pleasure in making disturbance wherever they go."[9]

But at the same time Brigham Young was worried that Union Pacific needs might require more men than could be spared from Utah fields. Accordingly, he wrote to Franklin D. Richards, at Liverpool, requesting that the annual migration be dispatched early enough to have it arrive at the rail terminus no later than the middle of July. Anxious that no able-bodied man remain idle for a moment, he directed that if the wagon trains sent forth to get the immigrants should reach the terminus first, their members should work for the railroad until their passengers arrive. If the immigrants arrived first, they were to hire on as construction workers while waiting for the wagon trains to come up. Under an arrangement made with the Union Pacific all Mormon immigrants able to work would be passed free from Omaha to the terminus. This, said Young, meant that a larger migration than normal could be sent forth because the mission money would go farther. The contract was used by the Mormons to benefit themselves in a number of ways.[10]

By early June Salt Lake City newspapers carried notices calling for anyone who wanted employment to report to Joseph A. Young, Brigham Young, Jr., or to John W. Young, all sons of Brigham, who were now ready to let subcontracts. It was rumored that as many as 10,000 men might be wanted. By mid-June Bishop John Sharp had a crew of 80 men at work in Weber Canyon, but already he had been obliged to refuse employment to others because the defile in which the men were working was too narrow to accommodate any more. Once that point was passed, the bishop said, he could use as many as 500 men. Meanwhile, Joseph Young forwarded lumber for temporary shacks to house the additional crews.[11]

While a number of prominent Mormons took grading contracts in varying amounts, four men stood out as important participants in the work.

Top–*Supply train for construction crews in Echo Canyon, 1869.*

Bottom–*Promontory, Utah, as it appeared in May, 1869.*

They were Brigham's three sons and Bishop John Sharp. The latter, who was close to the spiritual leader and also was his attorney, would remain a major Utah railroad figure for two decades. Joseph A. Young associated himself with Sharp in a firm known as Sharp & Young, in which the pair undertook large grading contracts and the boring of several tunnels. The younger Brigham was assigned the role of superintending and coordinating all the subcontracts by his father "as my representative." Before the end of 1868 the firm of Sharp & Young alone had 1,400 men at work in Echo Canyon. By then, said the elder Young, the men were working together well and accomplishing much more than at first. As he said, "they have got used to the labor."[12]

As the work got under way that spring, Mormon leaders at Salt Lake City began to publicize the part their people were to play in the great national project. Early in June a mass meeting was held in the new Tabernacle at which Brigham Young made the principal address. He told his people that he had always wanted the railroad and that he would help to build it, provided he was well paid. One of his followers wrote: "We felt much better after he did that; we feared he might not be willing and we'd never have a road." Even at this late date Young professed to believe that the line would be built around the south end of the lake, thus serving the Mormon capital, for in his speech he spoke of the coming of rail service to Salt Lake City. A Wyoming newspaper criticized him for it, saying that a more northerly route was 60 or 70 miles shorter, but it admitted that Brigham Young probably would have his way because "There is more political strength and influence united in him than in any other one person in America."[13]

His enemies overestimated the Mormon leader's influence. General Grenville Dodge, chief engineer of the Union Pacific, later wrote that Young exerted great pressure to have the road built through Salt Lake City, but that in his judgment, and that of other engineers, the northerly route was superior. According to Dodge, Brigham Young then tried to get the Central Pacific to use the south end of the lake as its approach and thus force the Union Pacific to alter its decision, but here again he failed. "He even went so far as to deliver in the Tabernacle a great sermon denouncing me, and stating a road could not be built or run without the aid of the Mormons," wrote the general. The decision having been made, Young accepted it, and he "returned to his first love, the Union Pacific."[14] The association between the Mormons and the Union Pacific generated a jealousy in other sections of the country that was to continue for some time to come. A correspondent from the *Cincinnati Commercial* charged that while Young had taken the contract for 30 cents a yard, he paid his subcontractors only 27 cents, "and the Prophet pockets the odd million."[15]

In neighboring Wyoming the feeling was so strong that a Cheyenne paper openly called the contract outright slavery. Each Mormon ward, said the journal, was called upon to furnish manpower in accordance with its population, and the draftees were obliged to work at prices set by the leader. Workers were said to be given store orders, in lieu of cash, these being good at either the tithing stores or with Salt Lake City merchants with whom Young had made previous arrangements. "To make the settlement final, and completely Mormon," said the editor in deep scorn, "ten per cent of the entire earnings of the laborer is deducted for tithing to 'the church' which is another name for Brigham Young." The Wyoming newspaper's real complaint was suggested in its charge that the Union Pacific was pampering the Mormons, and that it was "the settled policy of the railroad company to give large contracts to Brigham" despite the fact that Gentiles allegedly had offered to work for less.[16] Outsiders, jealous of such apparent favoritism, contented themselves by saying that the Mormons were, in effect, digging their own graves, for ultimately the Union Pacific would serve as an instrument which would one day extinguish Brigham Young and Mormonism itself.[17]

The Mormon leader may have returned to his first love, as General Dodge said, but before Young's part of the work was completed he was sometimes disenchanted with the company. After three months of effort, during the summer of 1868, many of the men had not been paid, although Young himself advanced sizable sums of money to keep them at their work. "The men are exceedingly anxious to get their pay for day work performed last June and since," he wrote to Samuel B. Reed in September.[18] Part of the money was forthcoming, but it was not enough to cover Young's advances. By early October the Union Pacific had paid him $243,478.76, all of which was turned over to the subcontractors; however, the church leader still had $46,860 of his own money invested in wages to the men.

Some of the workers did go home in disgust, partly because of time lost in waiting for necessary supplies and partly because the monthly estimates were thought to be about a third to a half of the value of work performed. To hold the rest, subcontractors had borrowed money at two percent a month to meet their payrolls.[19] The dissatisfaction, said a Cheyenne paper sneeringly, arose from the fact that some of the workers were "weak in the faith," or were, perhaps, of "Gentile independence," but in the main they tended to stay at their posts because "Brother Brigham holds the whip as well as the reins, and whither he would drive they go, although it may be in unwilling silence."[20] An additional annoyance to Mormon contractors was the tendency of the Union Pacific engineers to change their minds about what they wanted the graders to accomplish.

Despite various hindrances, the Mormon crews continued to work for the Union Pacific. Although some of the problems were solved, that of finance continued to plague the railroad and, in turn, the various contractors working for it. By January 1869 Brigham Young was pressing the railroad for back payments. In asking about the amount due for November, Young's chief clerk, T. W. Ellerbeck, admitted: "We are pretty well cornered and hope that you will be able to do something for us without delay, as the men are not to be appeased without money."[21] When Durant responded by placing $100,000 to Young's credit in New York, the Mormon leader said that since he had already drawn checks for nearly that amount, and he was still $130,000 in arrears, the deposit granted only a temporary relief. "I have expended all my available funds in forwarding the work," wrote the worried contractor, "and if I had the means to continue would not now ask for any assistance. These explanations must be my apology for troubling you in the matter."[22] A further complication was indicated in a request he made that the estimates be paid in currency. This commodity was in such short supply that Utah banks were paying a one percent premium for it, "making it almost impossible for me to procure the amounts necessary to pay the men."[23] The difficulty persisted, giving Young "a good deal of extra trouble," as his clerk expressed it.[24]

Jack Casement was equally aware that the railroad company was experiencing a good deal of financial difficulty. "I am afraid the Union Pacific is in a bad way, they owe an awfull [sic] amount and as we are running a big machine that would run us out of money and in debt besides," he wrote to his wife. But, he added reassuringly, "don't be alarmed, for I don't think we will go to the Poor house." He admitted that "Dan had been quite as scared as I had been, but I hope things will work out right." His brother, however, was able to collect more money from the railroad than Jack thought he could and, as the latter said, "if the company don't quarrell [sic] too hard amongst themselves we will come out right." By March 1869, Jack himself had been paid to such an extent that he told his wife he hoped to send home $50,000 if the company honored the drafts it had given him.[25]

As the Union Pacific construction phase neared completion, the financial situation became critical. "Things look awfull bad and I can't hear a word from New York," wrote Jack Casement. "I can close up the work now and have some money left if the Banks don't burst. We owe our men about $90,000 and have $160,000 in the banks at Omaha and Cheyenne." As the contractor looked to the future, he worried about the railroad's condition. "The banks are loaded with UPRR paper," he commented, "and if the Company don't send some money here soon they will burst up the whole country. The Company owe us over $100,000, but we can wait on them if there is any show of helping them out." Worry about money increased in

Utah when the contractors, Mormon and Gentile alike, failed to get any response from New York. "I have telegraphed Dillon," Casement explained, "but got no answer.... The men on many of the jobs are striking and things look very blue." He admitted that the road owed "millions of dollars," and worse, he was convinced that the government favored the Central Pacific to the detriment of the company for which he worked.[26]

Brigham Young grew increasingly concerned. In January he had praised Durant, saying that the nation was deeply indebted to the doctor for his "energy & go-ahead-itiveness," but by April he was writing that the time had come for final settlement of the grading debt. Complaining that some of the contracts adjacent to his had brought sums up to 40 percent higher for the same work, the church leader said that he had done his best, under the circumstances, and now he wanted his money. No remittances had been forthcoming for the months of January and February, and "as the men are very clamorous for their pay, ... I am exceedingly anxious to settle up the business."[27] While Young strove for a settlement, he counseled patience to his people. Some of the Mormon workers, desperately in need of money, were exchanging their due bills for merchandise at discounts up to 50 percent. On one occasion Young wrote to two of them, advising that they hold their paper, for it would be worth more when the railroad remitted the rest of the amounts due.[28] Meanwhile, railroad officials made every effort to find the money necessary to pay off outstanding obligations.

During the final weeks of construction the great speed with which the work was driven forward, combined with a deepening concern over financial matters, began to wear on the nerves of those involved. Early in March Jack Casement wrote his wife that his tracklaying crews had just reached the Salt Lake Valley proper, having passed through some "very wild looking country" during the approach. The earlier excitement of construction was fading away, and Casement looked forward to the day his work would be finished. "I wish we were done now," he said. "I am homesick. ... I have not been to Salt Lake City and don't know as I will. I have no desire to toady Brigham."[29] Casement's annoyance derived from the Mormon's suggestion that he lay track even faster. "I sent him word [that] all he would have to do would be to come where we were at work and open His Eye," growled the Ohio contractor. Brigham accepted the invitation, but Casement ignored him. "I think so little of him and his pretensions that I did not stay to receive him," he admitted to his wife.[30]

Ogden was reached just before noon on March 8, when the tracklayers "hove in sight of this city," as a newspaperman recorded the event. By 2:30 P.M. an engine steamed into town, its moaning whistle answered by the blare of a brass band and the cheers of onlookers. Its appearance was doubly welcome, for during the three weeks prior to that date the road had been blockaded by heavy snow and no mail had been received from the East during the period. Such delays later would cause sharp complaints from westerners.[31]

The tracklayers moved beyond Ogden with high hopes of completing their work as soon as possible, but uncertain as to their goal. "Durant has not made his appearance here as yet, there is no meeting point fixed yet," wrote Casement in mid-March. The "California people," as he referred to the eastbound Central Pacific crews, were grading miles to the east of him by then, and as he viewed the parallel lines across the countryside he commented: "I am afraid we will have trouble in agreeing upon a meeting point." Gloomily he concluded that "There is neither pleasure, glory nor much proffit [sic] left in the concern."[32]

A Cheyenne paper said that Brigham Young wanted the connection to be made at Ogden, but that the Gentiles of Utah and the miners and traders to the north preferred Corinne, where the stagecoaches and wagon freighters left for Idaho and Montana. The newspaper, whose editor viewed Brigham Young with suspicion and hostility, accused the Mormon leader of wanting a junction point that he could control.[33] As the time for making a rail connection with the Central Pacific neared, the question of its location drew national attention. Congress was aware of the problem and by a joint resolution of April 10, 1869, the meeting point was fixed at Promontory Summit, a barren spot north of Great Salt Lake.[34] By the end of April Union Pacific crews were hard at work, completing the last 15 miles of grading and tracklaying to the site where, within a few days, the official junction was to take place.[35]

The prospect of a celebration excited a nation that always had set great store by the commencement or completion of such great enterprises. Various cities did participate in the event, but the center of the stage was not located in any of them, not even at Salt Lake City or Ogden, but rather at Promontory Summit. On May 10, 1869, the Central Pacific and Union Pacific elements of the first "transcontinental" railroad were joined as engines of the two companies stood "facing on a single track, half a world behind each back," to borrow a line from Bret Harte's description of the scene. It was a busy day for the participants, each of whom saw the events from a different vantage point. The climax of the event was the driving of the last, symbolic spikes. Central Pacific President Leland Stanford, with a silver maul, stood on the south side of the track, while Durant took an opposite position, each tapping their respective targets. Thomas O'Donnell, a Union Pacific worker who was a witness, said the privilege of striking the first blow was "given to some lady, whose name I don't know, but she

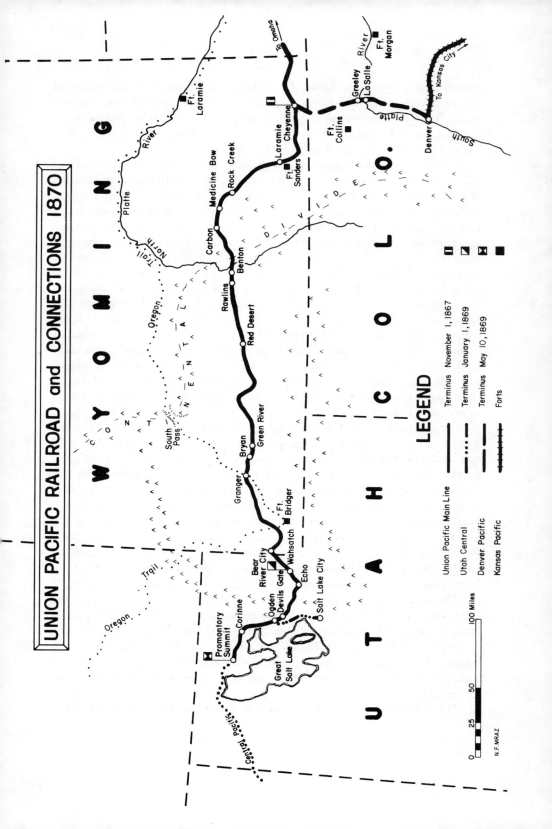

UNION PACIFIC RAILROAD and CONNECTIONS 1870

LEGEND

Union Pacific Main Line	Terminus November 1, 1867
Utah Central	Terminus January 1, 1869
Denver Pacific	Terminus May 10, 1869
Kansas Pacific	Forts

N. F. MRAZ

0 25 50 100 Miles

WYOMING

UTAH

COLO.

To Omaha

To Kansas City

To Kansas City

Promontory Summit
Corinne
Ogden
Devils Gate
Echo
Wahsatch
Bear River City
Ft. Bridger
Granger
Bryan
Green River
Red Desert
Rawlins
Benton
Carbon
Medicine Bow
Rock Creek
Laramie
Cheyenne
Ft. Sanders
Ft. Laramie
Ft. Collins
Denver
Greeley
LaSalle
Ft. Morgan

Salt Lake City
Great Salt Lake

Central Pacific

Oregon Trail

South Pass

North Platte River

Platte River

South Platte

Greeley River

WIND RIVER MOUNTAINS
UINTA MOUNTAINS

proved a poor 'Spiker' and missed it." Durant and Stanford then completed the ceremony, after which the two engines edged forward and touched noses. "Both engines were crowded with people and they exchanged greetings by exchanging bottles of champagne or wine, I could not tell which as I did not taste it," O'Donnell wistfully recalled.[36]

Several ceremonial spikes were provided. California sent one made of gold. Nevada's was appropriately silver, while Arizona offered a combination of iron, silver, and gold. They were driven into a tie made of highly polished California laurel on which a silver plate bearing a dedicatory inscription had been placed. To the last spike driven was attached a wire that carried a telegraphic message to both coasts. The one leading west not only communicated the completion of the road through its pulsations, but it also set off cannons in Sacramento and San Francisco. The other, provided to spread the good news throughout the East, was received with particular interest in Washington, D.C. There, in the War Office, sat Gen. W. T. Sherman and his staff, listening to the signals emanating from Promontory. Shortly his old friend Grenville Dodge sent a personal message that read: "As a steadfast earnest friend of the Pacific Rail Road, I send you greetings." Now, said Dodge, the General of the Army could visit his old friends in California by rail. After the ceremonies came refreshments, served in Durant's car, where champagne flowed and the fun-loving Casement brothers joked and entertained their listeners.[37]

For the residents of Salt Lake City, who had so eagerly anticipated the completion of the railroad, there was only moderate excitement. At 12:32 P.M. a signal was received that the rails had been joined, after which the national flag was unfurled in several places, brass bands around the city blared their approval, artillery salutes were fired, and the governor, Charles Durkee, made a speech. To further honor the occasion most of the city's important business houses closed their doors. The *Deseret News* spoke of the wedding of the West to the commercial East, using the Mormon term "seal" to describe the long-desired consummation. The Mormon press called the completion of the railroad project "of more significance and interest [to Mormons] than to any other portion of their fellow citizens of the Union."[38]

The chief Mormon, however, was not at Promontory, or even at the celebrations in Salt Lake City. As oratorical salutes sent their echoes rolling from the place where metal touched metal, Brigham Young spent the day at Nephi, driving over to Payson for dinner, quietly conducting church business and seemingly oblivious to the celebrations that were under way.[39] Bishop Sharp, his right-hand man in railroad affairs, represented Young at Promontory.

Those who witnessed the ceremonies appear to have taken the day's events in their stride. The Union Pacific paymaster, O. C. Smith, noted that on this "clear, cool beautiful day," he and his wife rode up to Promontory Summit to "see the last rail laid that connects the Union Pacific and Central Pacific RRds. A large crowd was there." They stayed until 2:00 P.M., returning on the first train back to Echo.[40] A local photographer who was also a member of the Salt Lake City delegation, C. R. Savage was too engrossed with his duties to reflect upon the importance of the occasion. "I worked like a nigger all day and secured some nice views of the scenes connected with laying the last rail," he wrote in his diary. "Everything passed lively and the weather was delightful. Saw but little of the actual driving of the gold spike, and laying of the laurel tie, as I was very busy."[41] Samuel Reed, who had shouldered so much responsibility as construction engineer, was simply glad that the job was finished. He made only brief mention of the celebration, and remarked that he intended to stay around only long enough to close accounts and go home.[42] Nor was there much excitement generated at nearby Ogden. Charles F. Middleton, who spent the red-letter day as a temporary policeman in that city, seemed to be more concerned about a prisoner in his custody, who had been charged with indecent exposure before females, than with events of national interest. Much of his diary for that day concerned the culprit, who, incidentally, paid a $75 fine for the indiscretion, and only at the end of the entry does one find the laconic comment: "Today the last tie & the last rail was laid on the P. R. Road."[43]

To Brigham Young and other church leaders, the event at Promontory was significant but it did not solve all their problems. Utah businessmen were happy that the two companies had met somewhere within their territory, for they had earlier feared that if the Union Pacific were built a hundred miles beyond Salt Lake City, as a rumor once had it, Mormon merchants would have no choice between western and eastern markets because the Union Pacific surely would put such prohibitive rates on freight to the West that traffic in that direction would be throttled.[44] Now that this potential danger had been averted, there were other suspicions about the Union Pacific, probably arising out of the ill feeling generated by the railroad's apparent unwillingness to pay its debts in Utah.

Had the Mormons seen a letter written about this time by Henry W. Moulton, U.S. marshal at Boise, Idaho, their uncertainty as to the role of the Union Pacific in Utah might have increased. The ceremonies at Promontory were barely a month old when Moulton wrote to Oliver Ames, telling him that a secret movement was afoot in Idaho to obtain from the next Congress legislation which would appropriate for Idaho the northern part of Utah. He assured Ames that this was in the best interest of the railroad, for "The Mormons will give you unjust and *severe* taxation; they will in every way annoy you. No towns of any importance will spring up on your road in Utah." Assuring Ames that the whole nation "demands of Congress to *strike* at Utah and her Mormons," the writer asked for the support of the Union Pacific's friends in Congress. He promised that, if the move were successful, "Corinne and all the towns of Utah on the line of your road would rejoice at the deliverance."[45] Ames responded cautiously, telling the marshal that he could not answer decisively without consulting other officers, that the matter would be duly considered at the appropriate time, that Congress was not to meet until December, and that any action taken would be in the best interests of all parties concerned. Clearly the president was treading carefully, anxious to avoid involvement by the company in a territorial situation that might backfire.[46] While the railroad was to enter local politics in other states and territories, its friendship with the Mormons was to be demonstrated by a long period of cooperation with them. This was no time to take any risks with Brigham Young.

Even so, in the days that followed the Union Pacific's completion there was friction between the company and the Mormon church leadership over money due from grading contracts, and this gave the impression that the road's public relations in Utah were off to a bad start. As John Sharp told one of his fellow churchmen, "The U.P.R.R. is finished, but . . . the worst part of it is to be done yet, that is getting our pay."[47]

Determined to have a showdown, Brigham Young sent John Sharp and clerk T. W. Ellerbeck to Ogden where, on July 19, they intercepted Cornelius Bushnell, a member of the Union Pacific's board of directors, on his return trip, "but he paid nothing," alleging that such an important matter must be considered by the entire board.[48] "To say the least, it is strange treatment of my Account," wrote Young, in bitter complaint. "It is not for myself that I urge, but for the thousands that have done the work, and have been waiting from half to three quarters of a year for their pay."[49]

The failure of the Ogden conference left Brigham Young in a pessimistic mood. It was decided that the best alternative was to accept iron and rolling stock for the proposed extension from Ogden to Salt Lake City in partial payment. Bishop Sharp was dispatched to Boston where he was instructed to do his mightiest, first pressing for badly needed cash and accepting equipment only after he had obtained every dollar he could wring from the railroad company. Young gave his representative an additional bargaining card: permission to accept transportation for Mormon immigrants over the Union Pacific tracks—or even from New York City if the road could make the appropriate arrangements—in lieu of cash. However, cautioned Young, under no circumstances was the railroad company to be given any control, directly or indirectly, over the Utah Central, as the line south of Ogden was to be known.[50]

Toward mid-August Young wrote to Sharp, assuring him that although alternative settlements were offered to the Union Pacific, there was no need to retreat an inch for "they *will* pay us, and have got plenty of means to do it." If money could not be obtained, he repeated, "get the Iron and Rolling Stock at advantageous figures, and then we will rest awhile, but make no compromise to reduce our claim."[51] Meanwhile, the *Deseret News* declared editorial war on the Union Pacific in an effort to strengthen the hand of Utah claimants. It recalled the road's earlier need for laborers, the speed with which Young had responded to the request, and the work that had been accomplished despite delays and broken promises by the railroad. Pointing out that local bankers and merchants were out of pocket for advances made to contractors, the newspaper charged that the railroad's unwillingness to settle up was hurting the entire Mormon community, and that this was very foolish conduct in a territory where the road would for years to come solicit traffic and business.[52] To underscore the Mormon feeling, mass indignation meetings were scheduled throughout the territory.[53] Church leaders were prepared to make it plain to the men of Boston that there was much unhappiness among the Saints, and if the Union Pacific wanted to thrive in their midst there was no time like the present to square accounts and set sail for the future together.

In the discussions held at Boston, Union Pacific representatives fought a stubborn rearguard action. They agreed to furnish 4,000 tons of rails, but when $150 a ton was demanded Young called the figure "extravagantly high," and he alleged that on the rails alone the inflation of price amounted to $120,000 more than the going market rate. While prices asked for other materials were padded to a lesser degree, he felt that such demands amounted to a surcharge. However, said Young, he would submit to such conditions provided that there followed a speedy and equitable settlement of all other claims and that the materials purchased were delivered without delay. Fearful that the Union Pacific would try further to improve its position by ridding itself of worn-out equipment at inflated prices, the wily church leader stipulated that no locomotives were to be accepted until his son Joseph had determined that they were in good working order.[54] Finally, Young asked that the Union Pacific grant to the proposed Utah Central branch free use of its tracks between Echo Station and Ogden for a period of five years. This would provide the Mormons with the exclusive right to haul fuel from their own coal beds without interference or outside control of rates.[55]

Time was important to the Youngs. If they had to settle, in part, for equipment, they wanted to put it into operation as quickly as possible.

Further delays occasioned by haggling over amounts of money could prove costly.

By a memorandum agreement of August 31 between Sharp and the Union Pacific authorities at Boston, it was agreed that the company would pay $940,138.15 of Young's claim. Since he had asked for $1,139,081.89, there remained nearly $200,000 in dispute. It was agreed that each of the two parties would choose a disinterested person as a referee, and that they should meet at Omaha within 30 days to adjudicate the claims. Young chose Judge Elias Smith, of Salt Lake City, as his referee. Meanwhile, Ames directed Col. C. G. Hammond, the road's general superintendent at Omaha, to deliver to Young at Ogden 4,000 tons of rails, plus a sufficient number of spikes, splices, bolts, frogs, and switches. Apparently complaints about the proposed overcharge on rails had their effect, for in this memorandum rates were scaled down to the market price. The rolling stock included four passenger cars (first class), four passenger cars (second class), three mail and express cars, ten flatcars, 20 boxcars, and seven handcars. The total value of the track equipment and rolling stock was set at $599,460.[56] On September 4 Brigham Young acknowledged that he had received word from Bishop Sharp of a favorable settlement and that equipment for the Utah Central would be started for Utah very shortly. The mass indignation meeting at Salt Lake City, called for the sixth, was indefinitely postponed.[57]

The controversy between the Union Pacific and the Mormons over the grading contracts was not evidence of disagreeableness by either party, but rather it pointed to the difficulty of concluding a construction campaign whose magnitude was then unsurpassed in American history. Similar to the American experience in warfare, all efforts had been directed toward an early conclusion, and in the process money was spent recklessly. There were misunderstandings, delays, and a lack of communication that inevitably led to difficulties between the railroad and several of its contractors. Joseph Nounnan and J. M. Orr, Gentile contractors, sued the railroad for over $175,000 in unpaid bills, and for delays that cost them money in wages. Captain Thomas H. Bates sued for nearly $40,000 for ties furnished and money disbursed while he was employed as a division engineer.[58]

The root of the difficulty was money. Colonel Hammond, general superintendent at Omaha, found himself in the eye of the financial hurricane when he assumed that office in the summer of 1869. Unpaid payrolls for March, April, May, and June totaled $770,090, and another $320,000 would be due at the end of July. As he explained, this arrearage of more than a million dollars made life difficult for him because "a moiety of labor is secured from men distressed and harrassed for want of their pay." Even worse, violence might erupt if the situation were not corrected. "In this frontier world which abounds in adventures and where municipal, state or territorial justice is to a great extent deficient or unknown, many fear a stoppage if not injury to our trains from those disaffected by delay of payment," he cautioned Oliver Ames.[59] The president took this warning seriously, and when he learned of a wreck that occurred at the western end of the line, he asked: "Do you think the train run off by [a] misplaced switch was done by discharged employees or by Mormons who have lost cattle and want to be settled with for Land Damages?"[60]

Union Pacific officials were painfully aware that the termination of contractual relationships associated with completion of the work was a matter fraught with difficulties. Almost overnight the flow of construction money dried up, and this was bound to affect those who had flocked to the new "diggin's" in the West. Bushnell, who visited Utah in July 1869, estimated that various subcontractors had made $750,000, most of which he thought was legitimate. "I do not think there has been but a very small proportion of dishonesty practised on us of what I had expected to unearth," he commented. The greatest loss, he thought, came from "our crazy attempt" to send men far in advance of the road's probable terminus to capture territory that might produce land grant bonds. In Bushnell's eyes, a concentration on the work at hand, in Utah, would have been much the wiser course.[61] It also would have led to much less criticism of the company in the years that lay just ahead.

Members of President Ame's staff were aware that liquidation of the construction effort in 1869 was to be troublesome. Benjamin Ham argued that if an agent had been sent to Utah with orders to stay six months, if necessary, to investigate each claim, a great amount of money would have been saved. Instead, the matter was so loosely handled that a great speculation developed in drafts, and many a discouraged claimant sold his at a disastrous discount. "I have talked with a person who has just returned from there," wrote Ham, "and who will make $250,000 out of the drafts he has purchased."[62] His comment suggests that part of the vast sums alleged to have been made by the "insiders" at Boston were spilled around the western countryside.

Another problem was the vast amount of stores and supplies left over from the work. It was almost as though a war had suddenly terminated, leaving mountains of matériel stranded in a foreign land. Contractors who had stockpiled unused timber and ties now insisted upon payment. Not only did the company worry about finding money to honor such obligations, but it wondered how to protect such accumulations in the West where the property of large corporations was, and would be for years to come, considered fair game for anyone who thought he had need for it. Samuel Reed

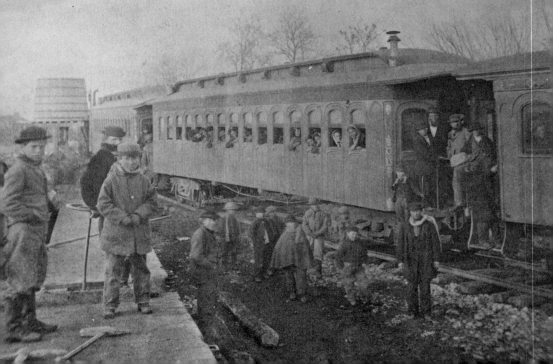

TOP–*Laying the last rail between the Union Pacific and the Central Pacific, at Promontory, May 10, 1869. A number of photographers were at work that day; this picture was taken by A. J. Russell, who did a great deal of work for the Union Pacific.*

LEFT–*The Mormon population readily accepted the railroad, as this view of the first train of the Utah Central (1870) suggests.*

told Colonel Hammond that he had been obliged to put a guard over collected stores "because the material would have been stolen unless some person was in charge of it until it was hauled out."[63]

During the days that followed the road's completion, the people of Utah sought to accommodate themselves to the changes in their lives wrought by the new transportation, and to accept the attendant financial difficulties as best they could. A Denver paper sympathized with them, saying that "the people of Utah were caught badly at the close [of the work] and have been sweating over it a good deal." It quoted a Salt Lake City newspaper whose editor advised his readers to be patient and "to banish from their tongues the hateful conversation" they had practiced with regard to the unsettled debts. The Utah editor offered the advice that "Neither U.P. nor C.P. nor any other P. can damn us and it should bother us no longer. It has been a lesson—a severe one but wholesome—and there let it rest."[64]

Brigham Young was not quite ready to let the matter rest, however. Early in October 1869 he wrote to Bishop Sharp, who was then at Omaha, charging that the railroad had failed to comply with the spirit of the recent agreement. He wondered if there were some undiscovered loophole in the document by which the company hoped to escape its obligations; if so, there was good cause for concern at Salt Lake City. His disillusionment grew out of the fact that the proposed arbitration was stalled when the railroad's representative failed to appear at the Nebraska terminus. Gloomily Young directed Sharp to wait only a reasonable time and then get affidavits showing that he had been on the ground, ready to negotiate, as stipulated in the Boston agreement.[65] The railroad's reluctance to settle the matter was explained by Samuel Reed, who told Oliver Ames that in his view all claims for delays and damages had been properly adjusted, and that even though Durant had made some promises, the company had paid fairly and liberally for Young's work.[66]

Unable to obtain an adjustment of the disputed portion of the debt or to get any of the money claimed in the case, Young continued his efforts to effect a settlement by barter. In late September he asked for a 30-ton locomotive for use on the Utah Central, and Colonel Hammond sent one to him along with a bill for $13,000. When Hammond learned that the Mormons proposed to deduct the sum from the railroad indebtedness he asked Boston: "Is this all right?"[67] In another instance, when the company submitted a $15,826.16 bill for Mormon transportation, the formidable church leader responded by saying he would subtract it from a Union Pacific promissory note he held for a similar amount, one that was a year overdue.[68] Hammond agreed to the request. Next, Young asked if amounts his people owed for freight on coal and railroad ties could be deducted from monies owed by the Union Pacific. Hammond in this instance demanded cash, but he said that if other arrangements could be made with Boston it was all right with him.[69] If money was short in the Union Pacific coffers, so was it short in Zion.[70] Young complained that because he had been obliged to pay out of his own funds for labor performed on the grading contract near Echo, he was hard pressed to finish the Utah Central. Worse, the Union Pacific had compounded the difficulty by not forwarding the material agreed upon at Boston. In one instance, he wrote, there had been but a half day's work on the Utah Central that week, due to the lack of iron, at a cost of some $1,000 a day to pay 225 idle men. The people of Utah were depending upon this branch to bring in their winter coal, he said. Unless the Union Pacific lived up to its promises, Mormon families would suffer.[71]

The Utah Central branch, completed to Salt Lake City in January 1870, provided the much-desired connection with the Union Pacific tracks at Ogden. Inauguration of service occasioned a good deal of local satisfaction, with much being made of the fact that the grading, tying, and tracklaying was done by Mormon workers. But even in their hour of triumph church leaders remained bitter over the delays that originated in Boston. The line, about 40 miles in length, would have been completed two months earlier, said one of them, had it not been for the failure of Union Pacific officials to live up to their agreement.[72] The annoyance was compounded by the continued inability of Young's representatives to get a final settlement of the railroad grading contract. Despite the coming of the main line, and the completion of a branch to Salt Lake City, Utah's commercial life lagged. Wheat sold for 90 cents a bushel, beef at 12½ cents, coal at $12 a ton, and trout could be had for 15 to 20 cents a pound. "Business is very dull, money is scarce, and the usual number of men, under such circumstances, are out of work," complained Elder George Teasdale. Unable to find employment, and disappointed at not getting the money due from Union Pacific grading work, laborers were in an unhappy mood. "Some are apt to get the blues," Teasdale admitted.[73]

Determined to get a satisfactory settlement from the Union Pacific, Young once more sent Bishop Sharp to Boston with orders to stay with railroad officials until they paid up. The bishop arrived there on May 5, 1870, and went at once to the railroad's offices, where he was well received. Oliver Ames professed a willingness to negotiate, at which Sharp said that he had been ready to do so for some time, but nothing encouraging had transpired. The board of directors, having just met, was in the process of dispersing, and while Ames and Sharp were talking Bushnell and Durant came into the room. They both greeted the bishop warmly "and laughed heartily at the idea of me coming hear [*sic*] for more money, and after some considerable

LEFT—*Grenville M. Dodge, prominent in the early affairs of the Union Pacific, maintained his connection with the company for two decades.*

RIGHT—*Oliver Ames, third president of the Union Pacific Railroad.*

BOTTOM—*The road's directors frequently met in one of the ornate private cars. Here, seated at table, left to right, are Colonel Silas Seymour (a consulting engineer), Sidney Dillon, T. C. Durant, and John Duff. Samuel B. Reed stands behind Durant.*

talk, Mr. Bushnell offered me ten thousand Dollers [*sic*] and call it even and I might turn arond [*sic*] and go home tonight, but I told him I would stay over night, and perhaps he would be more liberal in a day or two." Durant remarked that the Union Pacific people had allowed "all that they considered right in the first place and did not expect to hear from us again. He wanted a proposition from me as Bushnell had made and I made one for $198,942.68 which was another grand laugh, and after a great deal of talk and gas the Doctor wanted to act as referee for the Co. and myself for Brigham Young, and wherein we could not agree Mr. Bushnell would decide." When the bishop promptly called the bluff, Durant backed down, which Sharp found "rather amusing, it being his own proposition."

The Utah emissary took up the negotiations again the following day, urging Ames and John Duff to pay the debt, but they insisted they had paid the Mormons all that was due them. The railroad officers agreed, however, to call the directors together again in a day or so. On May 12 Sharp reported that he was still waiting, but that Ames and Duff would not do anything without the other board members, or Durant, who was now out of town. The determined bill collector then went to New York City in search of Durant, only to learn that the doctor had gone to Saratoga. Back in Boston again, he talked with Sidney Dillon, but with no result. "So you see," he told Brigham Young, "that although the Doctor holds no office of the Co. he holds a mighty influence over them, so will have to wait patiently until he returns." During the early days of June the bishop stubbornly sat in the Union Pacific offices, waiting, and commenting grimly to those present that Durant was purposely avoiding him. Ames denied this, and promised that in a few days the missing doctor would turn up, but the discouraged Sharp left for the West, resolved to return and to fight another day.[74]

By early July Sharp, apparently armed with new instructions, was back in Boston. On the seventh of July, he reported to Young that he had made a settlement. "They decided to pay $35,000 in cash and $35,000 in notes payable in 3 months which I accepted," he told Brigham Young. "The notes I have had made out in $5,000 each, payable to your order." The compromise was made for a good deal less than Young had wanted, but this was not for lack of persistence on his part, or that of John Sharp. Accepting less than he had sought did not relax the bishop's vigilance. He assured Brigham Young that he planned to stay on after the negotiations "to labor with the committee in relation to your claims for reduction on Iron . . . ." At the time of the Utah Central's completion the Union Pacific had failed to deliver all the iron and equipment agreed upon in August 1869, but Young was not ready to give up in his efforts to get it. Nor was he ready to accept the inflated prices the sellers were endeavoring to obtain for their goods. He and his sons were interested in building more Utah branches, and in the Union Pacific they had found a source of supply. The Mormon boys would grade and tie; the Union Pacific would find rails and cars to complete the job.[75]

The Mormon contract with the Union Pacific was mutually beneficial. Although the railroad had great difficulty in finding money to pay off its contractual agreements with the men of Zion, matters were settled in a generally amicable manner. Both Brigham Young and his attorney, John Sharp, were persistent in their efforts to gain a settlement satisfactory to them, but in the lengthy negotiations that developed they conducted themselves well, never antagonizing the Bostonians unduly, yet pursuing their quest with a doggedness that generated more admiration than annoyance among railroad executives. The Youngs used their railroad money well, spreading an iron network outward from their religious capital. In so doing, they generally benefited the Union Pacific Company. John Sharp, whose rustic ways often amused officials of the larger road, became a trusted friend, and his relationship with the company lasted for years. In contrast with other western communities, whose leaders later entered into bitter controversies with the Union Pacific, the Mormons accepted the coming of the road and used it to every advantage, countering any moves that might be viewed in the business world as shrewd with homegrown financial maneuvers that brought applause from the sophisticates of the financial East.

CHAPTER

6

"We Need Only to Stand Together"

During the months in which Brigham Young figuratively wrestled with Union Pacific officials over the issue of compensation for his contribution to the great national effort, the American public experienced an emotional letdown that put it in much the same mood as the Mormon leader. Suddenly, the exciting climax of the project, so long anticipated and so joyously celebrated, was over; all that remained was to pay the bill. In the quiet that followed Promontory the man on the street began to feel some remorse for the recent spending spree.

The Union Pacific was somewhat unfortunate in the timing of its birth. At its completion the nation had entered a normal postwar period of dejection over the great debt engendered by the conflict, and of revelations of fraud—or at least unduly high profits—originating in wartime contracts. At a time when many an American was complaining of high taxes and calling for retrenchment, enormous sums of money were being spent to drive a railroad westward at top speed. Those who foresaw no direct benefit took issue with the apparent extravagance of the construction. For example, during 1868, when the Casements were accelerating their efforts and mobilizing an army of workmen for the final drive to Utah, the eastern press began to express doubts about the quality of the work being performed. Not only did most Americans expect the work to proceed rapidly but, considering its cost, they also demanded the result be first-class. In June of that year a representative of the *New York Herald* inspected the work and rated it as decidedly third-class, one that a European engineer would barely accept as a slow freight line for the conveyance of cattle. He criticized the use of cottonwood ties, the inadequacy of culverts, the flimsiness of bridges, and the lack of proper ballasting, calling the line no more than a temporary ribbon over which cars might be run.[1]

Oliver Ames at once came to the defense of his road, explaining that at the time of construction cottonwood ties were the best available, the Chicago and North Western Railroad not yet having reached the Missouri River, and the river itself being useful for only part of the year. When transportation became available the company had brought oak ties from Wisconsin and Michigan, with the result that by 1868 only on a third of the road did one find cottonwood ties, and these were rapidly being replaced. He defended the use of wood in bridging, saying that only the best pine had been used and that the Howe truss was considered an excellent support for railroad trains. Railroad commissioners had, in accordance with the law, examined each 20-mile section before acceptance and they had pronounced it a first-class road.[2]

Such explanations did not silence criticism. During the summer and early autumn of 1868 eastern papers debated the issue, some of them holding that speed was essential not only to satisfy an eager public, but also because the full utility of the road could not be realized by its owners until completion. The eastern papers understood the consequences of haste, but they expressed confidence that temporary appurtenances would be replaced, of necessity, when the road came into full use. Others argued that the road was being built only for the land-grant bonds offered, and that once it was completed the necessary improvements might not be supplied. Arguments ranged from the *New York Tribune's* assertion that the great railroad project was, and would be for years to come, "the great absorbing fact of the West" to a charge made by the *National Intelligencer,* of Washington, that the road was "simply a speculation, nothing more or less."[3]

In the face of mounting criticism, Secretary of the Interior Orville H. Browning appointed a special commission to examine the road and to determine its quality. On October 29, about three weeks after their appointment, Gen. Gouverneur K. Warren, well known for his topographical examinations of the West, and Jacob Blickensderfer and James Barnes, both civil engineers, left Omaha to commence their study. Although they concluded that the road was generally well constructed, they maintained that certain deficiencies existed, the correction of which they estimated would cost about $6.5 million.[4] Those associated with the Union Pacific objected, holding that "the General has been quite hard on the road and [has] taken good care of the interests of the government." The general was inclined to take extreme views, said another, demanding unreasonably high standards and overestimating the amount of business the road would do.[5]

The criticism was just beginning. In January 1869 Charles Francis Adams, Jr., who would one day be president of the Union Pacific Company, published an article in the *North American Review* in which he charged that the "Pacific Railroad," whose retainers were said to be represented in both houses of Congress, was destined to be "the most powerful corporation in the world; it will probably also be the most corrupt." Admitting that the men who undertook to build the road assumed great risks, that they invested in a lottery from which they well might have drawn blanks, he argued that the new country was so in need of railroads it was willing to pay anything to get them. So anxious were potential users to have railroads that "every expedient which the mind of man can devise has been brought into play to secure to the capitalist the largest possible profit, with the least possible risk."[6]

Chauncey H. Snow, appointed government director the same month Adams's article appeared, was even harsher in his judgment. After a trip over the Union Pacific he charged that because of painful mismanagement the line was littered with rusty, dead locomotives, abandoned trains, and freight cargoes which had been delayed up to two months. He accused the road's managers of trying to make the project cost as much as possible and of representing its cost "at as high figures as the facts will admit." When Snow tried to ascertain the correct figures, he could only learn what the road had been charged, and not what construction actually had cost the contractors.[7]

When board member Cornelius Bushnell publicly attacked Snow's report and suggested that the director had attempted to blackmail the railroad, Snow promptly sued for libel, asking $100,000 in damages. Snow accused the company of previously having paid for favorable reports, a charge that brought no countersuits from the firm. Oliver Ames responded to Snow's opinion that it would take millions to put the road in a first-class condition by suggesting to Secretary of the Interior Jacob D. Cox that the government grant an additional $5 million to cover the extra cost involved in speedy construction. He argued that early completion had saved the government at least a million dollars a year in its own transportation bills, and that the nation probably received $100 million of value through the opening of a vast tract of country in such a short time.[8] While Ames's proposal caused no objections in the West, residents of the older states had begun to ask if the government's generosity had not gone too far. In March 1869 the Wisconsin legislature's lower house adopted a resolution opposing the policy, contending that already it had "resulted in the creation of numerous and powerful corporations" whose managers had gained control of a western empire.[9]

As criticism grew, President Grant appointed a special commissioner to make a new examination of the unaccepted parts of the Union Pacific. Isaac N. Morris, who made the inspection, reported that the road had been built too rapidly because the temptations in lands and subsidies had been "too great for poor, avaricious human nature to resist." He called the road the worst over which he had ever traveled and condemned it as dangerous. He was highly critical of the practice of laying ties over frozen ground because in the spring the road looked "like a succession of small waves." The ties themselves, he said, were put down so unevenly that it looked as if they had been thrown into position and the rails nailed to them regardless of where they fell. Morris was further disturbed when upon returning to Omaha railroad officials handed him a report already drawn up as a convenience to the inspector; he declined the courtesy and wrote his own version of conditions.[10]

Union Pacific officials were much annoyed at this latest blast of criticism. Secretary Edward H. Rollins thought it was "as bad as it can well be for the road" and that it had done the line a "great injustice." He suggested that "something should be done at Washington to counteract the influence of this stock-jobbing operation of Morris," and, following his own suggestion, he went there to speak for the road. Rollins was pleased at his reception, reporting to John Duff that the various department heads there felt kindly toward the road and were not at all disposed to take the Morris report too seriously. His visit convinced him that the matter would not cause any great harm; however, he suggested, "the case needs a little care and it seems to be all will come out all right."[11]

Despite the efforts of Rollins, public demand for a thorough inspection of the work reached such proportions that Congress was obliged to heed the clamor. By the terms of a joint resolution, passed April 10, a committee of "Eminent Citizens" was appointed to make the examination. Although the railroad apparently made suggestions, its recommendations were not followed. Officials hoped their friend Sen. Benjamin F. Wade would be one of the appointees; he was not. Neither was Horace Greeley, who was invited, but declined. Those appointed were: Hiram Walbridge, S. M. Fenton, C. B. Comstock, E. F. Winslow, and J. F. Boyd. Somewhat disappointed in the selection, Union Pacific lobbyist William E. Chandler described Winslow as an Iowa railroad contractor, Fenton as a man whose mind was said to be impaired, and Walbridge as one who "has the reputation of looking after his own interests pretty sharply." However, he advised, it was better not to interfere at the present time, but rather to go along with those "men whose influence may be used to injure us far beyond the amount which we would pay them." Once the road was able to "get free of the Government, we can afford to defy these shysters." Resigned to the selection, road officials tried hard to get the road in shape before the newly appointed inspectors made their trip in August.[12]

Much to the relief of those at Boston, the "Eminent Citizens" gave the work a satisfactory mark. While they found the rails west of Omaha quite worn after four years of use, they detected no substantial errors in location or serious deficiencies in the bridges, trestles, or culverts. With understanding, they showed concern as to the meaning of the term "first-class road." They had been asked to determine if this was what the public had received for its money; yet, as they pointed out, roads in the older part of America which deserved such rating were far from that when they opened for business. Moreover, this was a road built rapidly, through new country, and under unprecedented conditions. Under the circumstances, the committee members concluded, the Union Pacific should be classified as first class. This, however, presupposed that $1,586,100 more would be spent in perfecting it before receiving governmental approval. Since the commissioners estimated that the road had on hand surplus and materials worth $1,800,000, they felt such a requirement would not be an undue burden.[13]

In May 1869 the Union Pacific officially opened for business. Calling the inauguration of service a "grand event," lobbyist William Chandler remarked that already public opinion had begun to shift in favor of "the men who have perilled their fortunes & it seems their reputations! to build it [the railroad]."[14] One of the reasons for such a shift was the road's assiduous efforts to create it. Those individuals who had "perilled their fortunes" were not men who would stand by and watch their efforts suffer from criticism; rather, they were perfectly willing to counteract such detractions in any way they could. Cornelius Bushnell, who traveled over the newly completed line in July 1869, indicated the hope management had for returns from future business, as opposed to construction profits, when he told Ames: "None of us, not even the over-sanguine Bushnell, have heretofore begun to comprehend the vast returns we are to secure from our property when we get it into such shape as we will in a few months."[15]

If the road was to prosper and grow, if the country through which it ran was to develop, favorable public opinion was important. Therefore, as the applicant for a position seeks favorable recommendations, so the managers of the Union Pacific sought endorsements from prominent political figures. Benjamin Wade, president pro tempore of the Senate during Andrew Johnson's recent administration, was regarded as an important friend of the road. In the spring of 1869 he made a western trip, as a guest of the company, and reported that he found it in good condition. He went further. "I am more than ever persuaded of the great injustice that has been done to the builders of that road, as well as the detriment to the country, by the untruthfulness and it appears to me malicious representations made by several of the agents the government has sent out to inspect and report upon it."[16] Oliver Ames was more than anxious that Wade reveal his findings to the appropriate cabinet officers, and he asked the Ohio senator if he would "represent to the various Departments the actual condition of the Union Pacific Rail Road."[17] Wade agreed, saying he would attempt to "obtain justice for the company and the public" at the capital. Apparently his efforts were satisfactory, for within a few days another of the company's lobbyists reported that he had made a "splendid impression" upon the secretaries of the interior and treasury.[18] Those interested in the road were delighted by his performance. "Honest Ben seems all sound," wrote a member of a Philadelphia banking firm that was then selling Union Pacific securities.[19]

Anxious to overlook no possibility of favorable publicity the railroad solicited other important figures. Rollins sent passes to James G. Blaine, for the use of two friends, and urged the Maine politician to go west himself. "You must go out yourself and visit the Pacific Coast if you expect to be President or even Vice President," he urged.[20] From a friend in Missouri came the suggestion that Gen. Winfield Scott Hancock might be willing to say a kind word. This well-known officer had passed over the road and it was believed that he would express a favorable opinion.[21] Company employees were urged to testify in their company's behalf. After Treasurer John M. S. Williams returned from the West Coast a company lobbyist suggested that he come to Washington "& tell some of our Congressional friends about his trip & help fix a few matters?"[22]

Meantime, the company encouraged the publication of favorable articles in the press. On one occasion Treasurer Williams made bitter complaint when one of the firm's paid agents failed to answer attacks in the New York press with "the right kind of articles" about the road.[23] When Williams complained that another of the company's publicists, Sidney Andrews, was falling down on the job, Andrews said that the product of his work was to be found "in all of our five western papers."[24] The DeHavens, of Philadelphia, used their influence as bankers to spread favorable words in various newspapers. Said a member of the firm, "We have been singularly successful in getting articles in the interest of the Union Pacific R R inserted in the *money* columns of the leading papers . . . ."[25] While Williams was more than anxious to put his company's efforts before the public he did, on occasion, complain as to the cost. When New York papers, the *Times* and the *Tribune,* charged $200 and $344 respectively for printing an article by Edward Atkinson, Williams said "their bills look *large.*" Considering the *Tribune's* normal charges, he thought in this instance there must be a mistake.[26]

While easterners fussed about excessive costs and unusually large profits that developed as the Union Pacific's westward drive accelerated to its climax of May 1869, westerners showed less concern about financial aspects. Cheyenne's only criticism arose from the fact that so much high priority construction material was being sent to the West that merchants could not get their goods aboard trains at Omaha. It was a complaint that Brigham Young's followers also voiced. So urgent was the railroad's need for transportation that at one point Durant issued an order to the effect that the iron must go forward even if all business, other than passengers and mail, had to be suspended.

He even threatened to put the trains under the direct control of the contractors.[27] In August 1868, as the work progressed across Wyoming, business houses at Green River, Benton, and South Pass were warned that they must lay in their winter supplies early, because the railroad had requisitioned most of the available space for its own needs. Meanwhile, Omaha complained that its wholesalers could not deliver goods ordered by western merchants due to activity along the line and a lack of freight cars.[28] During such periods there was little disposition in the West to complain about the high cost of railroad building. Teased by the appearance of improved facilities, but rationed as to their use, these businessmen regarded the road as a water tap turned on to a slight dribble before a crowd of thirsty men. They wanted a full flow, and no talk about the cost.

Eastern criticisms of the line gained little currency in the Mountain West. Denver, once remote on its perch at the edge of the Rockies, welcomed the sound of steam and celebrated the fact that "distance is no longer distance; years are reduced to weeks."[29] Cheyenne lauded the Union Pacific as being a corporation that "is giving money value to almost half of this continent which had long been considered almost worthless." The railroad promoted commerce, created jobs, built up communities, and brought civilization. Progress always generated some opposition, but it was hard for western people to believe such opposition would injure the road. Why, said a Wyoming paper in a satiric thrust at critics, the opening of the road meant that a man might kiss his wife good-bye at the eastern terminus of the road on Monday morning and kiss some other man's wife in San Francisco the following Saturday night. "Eureka! we can't have too many Pacific Railroads!" exclaimed the editor.[30] Denver also made fun of those who quibbled about quality in times such as these. Inspection parties had not averaged more than one a month, said the *News,* but such trips provided entertainment for gentlemen who had not yet seen the West. Their travels also benefited the public, now furnished with "the widest possible variety of entertaining reading." Even though the junkets were said to accomplish nothing, "surely no harm is done, and it helps to increase travel and make business lively." The newspaper suggested, however, that the outpouring of reports should be numbered or lettered so that western readers might be able "to distinguish the latest and most reliable."[31] When Chauncey Snow's harsh report was received, the *News* lost its light touch and angrily called the work "manifestly ill-tempered," badly organized, and so hastily written that it appeared to have been put together on the spur of the moment "for some special purpose."[32]

In the earliest days that followed the ceremonies at Promontory, those who supported the road based their attitudes on hope. Edward Bliss, formerly of the *Rocky Mountain News,* asserted that even without its projected branches the Union Pacific was a success, that it had earned $5 million in 1868, and now that the road was finished this amount would increase.[33] The country through which the road passed was beginning to be recognized as having a great potential value. One day great profits would be realized from land sales, but even so, said one observer, the prospective gain by individuals in the company was a mere trifle in the light of benefits to be conferred upon the country.[34] The commissioner of the General Land Office did not deny that there had been large profits to the builders. If the capitalists had been fortunate, he contended, it was because they gambled their money "against the imposing front of untried difficulties that then beset the enterprise." Big risks implied big rewards.

There would be even greater rewards to the American people, said western rail enthusiasts. The residents of western mining communities who had staged wild demonstrations of joy at the completion of the main line reflected a general hope for future development of their communities. The land commissioner foresaw a great immigration into a West which had hitherto stagnated because of a lack of transportation, even going so far as to predict that the desert would be planted with trees which would prevent excessive evaporation and would ameliorate a harsh climate.[35] Senator William M. Stewart, chairman of the Senate Committee on the Pacific Railroads, also showed great optimism. He felt that there was no better use for federal money than for developing the American hinterland. The Nevada solon was particularly interested in the welfare of the Central Pacific. Stewart, rather than recoiling from the enormous expense involved in building across the mid-continent, argued that one road would not be sufficient to carry the traffic that was bound to develop. The senator also understood the force of the frontier movement, the relentless pressure that had for generations pushed back agricultural frontiers. "It is not the nature of the American to abstain from new and unoccupied soils; he will have them," was his accurate judgment. To him these roads appeared to be national in the scope of their length and cost, by their passage through the public domain, as avenues to far-off states, territories, and foreign commerce, and as necessities for his country's defense.[36] Senator Stewart was a loyal supporter of western American railroads.

That the trans-Mississippi West had grown during the decade of the sixties was easily demonstrated; how much of it was due to the railroads was not so easy to discern. One report showed that in 1860 the states and territories along the line of the Pacific Railroads had embraced a population of just over a half million; by 1870 this figure had almost doubled. Investment capital had grown accordingly. During this decade the population of

Colorado had increased by 400 percent; Nebraska, 300 percent; and Wyoming, 250 percent.[37] From 1869 to 1870 the number of steamboats ascending the Missouri River had declined from 40 to 8, owing to the completion of the Union Pacific.[38] Other adjustments accompanied the coming of the rails. Stage travel, wagon freight, and prairie schooner emigration so declined that the little communities established to serve them were nearly abandoned. While trail travel did not disappear as rapidly as was commonly believed, the effect of the railroad was such that those operating stage stops and supply ranches felt its presence severely; many of them answered the call of the locomotive whistle and moved closer to the new westward passage.[39]

The burning question in those days was: Would the railroad pay? While the Senate Committee on the Pacific Railroads was convinced that every dollar invested in American railroads created $5 yearly, minority members doubted the assumption when applied to western roads. Senators Henry Wilson and E. D. Morgan thought income from such lines would not be sufficient to carry the interest owed the government. They called the right to take over roads failing to pay interest "a barren right," the exercise of which would only involve the government in additional losses. With regard to land grants, the minority agreed, the policy had enabled thousands to obtain farms and it "has cost the nation nothing whatever."[40]

President Oliver Ames would not have presented any spirited arguments against the views of the minority members, at least in private. By mid-1870 he confided to Superintendent C. G. Hammond that his colleagues were disappointed in the net returns of the road and did not feel "that buoyant confidence in its ultimate success that they did last year." However, with rigid economy and an honest administration, he wrote, "we shall come out right and the Road will yet be a brilliant success." If the company should fail to meet its interest payments, all parties concerned would be much mortified, because these people had put their money into the project with the confident expectation that the investment would yield dividends on both its coupons and its stock. "If it fails here we are all great losers ourselves, but disgraced before the public," Ames concluded.[41] In search of an explanation for the road's financial condition, the head office pointed to the expensive supplies furnished Brigham Young's Utah Central, to the small amount of coal taken by the Central Pacific—as opposed to the 500 to 700 tons a day that road had said it would take—to Indian difficulties on the plains, to rumors that influential stockholders were unloading, and to the falling off of bond sales in Europe due to war on the Continent.[42]

Faced by public criticism in the West and the East, plus congressional suspicions, the Union Pacific was confronted by internal problems that were of a more pressing and immediate nature. From the outset the company had faced one financial crisis after another, a problem that was to persist throughout its early years. Government bonds, promised as a part of congressional assistance, frequently were held up, pending inspection of the work completed. The various study commissions of 1868 and 1869 not only generated public suspicion of the road, but the circumstances of their appointment prevented the delivery of government bonds until the work they recommended had been completed. Such delay brought bitter complaint from Ames.[43]

In order to meet its obligations the company turned for money to some of its wealthy directors and important stockholders. First-mortgage bonds, land-grant bonds, and ten percent income bonds, each issue in the amount of $10 million, were pledged by these influential figures who, in turn, borrowed money against such securities. A steady decline in prices erased the margins for the loans, resulting in heavy losses to the investors.[44]

Cyrus H. McCormick, who was one of the trustees for the land-grant bonds, complained that the refinancing was not working as advantageously as he had been led to believe. "We all feel that there has been large steelings [sic] in this business, while *I* have had not an *equal chance* at that!" he told Treasurer Williams.[45] When Williams asked him for $50,000 to pay coupons, McCormick at first refused, but within a few days he signed a note in that amount. He did not want to sell the bonds he held because their price was too low.[46] "I am really getting somewhat concerned about the situation of the Road," McCormick admitted. "I have been induced to think our Bonds wd certainly go up after 1st July; but the agony is being piled on thicker & still thicker. Bonds down to 87½ or 88!"[47] A little over a month later he criticized Bushnell, saying that while he had dutifully held his bonds, expecting them to rise, Bushnell and others "kept the market glutted & stuffed to the throat" with the result that their value had sunk to 86. "I find myself entirely too slow for this game," said the industrialist. Complaining that he had already borrowed $200,000, personally, he said he had no more money to send.[48] Jay Cooke & Company found itself in a similar situation. "We are still obliged to carry your Company for nearly a million of currency," he told Ames in the summer of 1869. He was very hopeful that the government would soon deliver its next batch of bonds.[49] Ames assured the international financier that the commission was then examining the road, and bonds should be forthcoming shortly. Next Ames heard from an investor named Frances L. Thomas, of West Point, New York, who asked if it were true that the first-mortgage bonds were depreciating very rapidly and that their interest would not be paid.[50] Such requests usually were answered by assurances that the road was in good condition and had a promising future.

To keep public confidence from falling further, annual reports were made to look as optimistic as possible. As Benjamin F. Ham prepared the September 1869 report, he commented to Rollins, "There is also the statement of the Debt which is not filled out as it may need some doctoring."[51] Desperate over the road's deepening financial plight, its officers made every effort to keep bad news from the investing public.

Despite brave words, the financial weather worsened. In the dying days of 1869 the DeHavens averred that they, too, had hoped for better times but "Union Pacific R. R. Co. bonds keep moving straight down."[52] Oakes Ames, Oliver's brother, felt that it was time to try artificial resuscitation. He talked of floating a loan to try to shore up the bonds, and the DeHavens agreed, saying to Williams, "If you & Oakes Ames & the other copartners & ourselves would tie up our bonds & make up a purse of $500,000 we could put the price to 75 or 80."[53] A. H. DeHaven regarded the land-grant bonds as the best prospect among the railroad's securities; public confidence seemed greater in this area.[54]

In the face of growing financial strictures the Boston office was doing all it could to improve the situation. It called for extreme economy at Omaha, asking why the road could not be operated as cheaply as eastern lines. Superintendent Hammond promised his very best efforts but, he explained to Ames, western conditions were unique, and, while economy was highly desirable, the facts of life on the high plains did not promise results such as those in the East.[55] Economy measures and desperate efforts to bolster the company's securities were insufficient. By the end of 1870 there was serious doubt that the January coupons on the first-mortgage bonds could be met, a crisis that was once again averted by frantic borrowing. The respite was only temporary; before long there was talk of receivership.

At the suggestion of interested business figures that included Andrew Carnegie and George Pullman, a change of Union Pacific management was brought about. Thomas A. Scott, a prominent Pennsylvania railroad executive, was persuaded to take the presidency. He served only a year, until February 1872, leaving the road to participate in southwestern railroading, but in that brief time he was able to bring the Union Pacific's decline to a momentary halt. The control then passed to a group of New Yorkers and Horace F. Clark, Cornelius Vanderbilt's son-in-law, assumed the presidency. His regime returned the road to its former condition of mounting debt and renewed financial complications.[56] It was during this period that the nagging criticism of the company, apparent even before it reached Promontory, finally culminated in the Crédit Mobilier investigation, an affair that was to leave a nearly ineffaceable stain upon the railroad's reputation.[57]

The question of large profits during construction days is found in the early reports of the government directors. In 1868 a suit against the Union Pacific was undertaken by Jim Fisk, whose motives apparently originated in his desire to influence the market value of securities as opposed to a defense of the citizenry, for no national indignation over excessive profits was generated in this litigation. Charles Francis Adams also made open charges of profiteering by the Crédit Mobilier in his *North American Review* articles published in 1869 and 1870.[58] Still, the echoes of corruption and unduly high profits seemed to die in the public jubilance occasioned by the project's much-publicized completion.

The Union Pacific's managers at Boston were not unacquainted with charges of fraud in connection with construction of their road. In August 1869 W. R. Story, of Salt Lake City, wrote to Oliver Ames, alleging that Davis, Sprague & Company had bilked the company out of considerable money in a timber and tie contract. He spoke of one $18,000 transaction in which ties paid for were never delivered. In another instance he said supplies of sugar, coffee, tea, bacon, etc. were hauled into the Salt Lake Valley and sold for private gain. Learning that Davis and Sprague were suing the railroad for payment of materials, Story volunteered to testify that the lumbermen had been highly overpaid.[59] A month later D. Harding, of Lincoln, Nebraska, told Ames that H. E. Brown and Associates had swindled the railroad out of thousands of dollars. Specifically, he said, the firm had falsified vouchers regarding purchases of hay and lumber. The results were so profitable that Brown told Harding he expected to clear $100,000 above expenses for four months of work.[60] When lobbyist Uriah Painter warned Congressman Oakes Ames that stories coming from the road indicated "robbery & scoundrelism," he inferred collusion, or at least carelessness, in the higher echelons. If "your friends are not willing to join you & put in a nearly new board of live men, men of honor, Bankruptcy is inevitable," predicted Painter.[61]

Nor were threats to unmask the Crédit Mobilier any novelty before the final exposé made national headlines. As early as July 1869 James W. Davis, who had been awarded a contract for about 125 miles of the road, demanded overdue payments at once. He accused Bushnell of trying to bribe one of his associates in relation to the attachment of some construction materials. This, and the story of the division of profits among the trustees of his contract "and *certain* shareholders of the 'Credit Mobilier,'" would appear in the New York papers, promised Davis.[62] Later that summer Uriah Painter warned Rollins that a former employee of Peasley & Company, advertising agents, had threatened to expose the directorate at Boston for dividing up construction profits. Further, said Painter, it was being whispered around Wall Street that the railroad owed $4 million more than it could pay and that the worried management was secretly selling off equipment "preparatory to a smash." The lobbyist answered these rumors with the statement that such stories were deliberately set afoot "to depreciate the road so the Erie crowd could get in at a low figure."[63] That the directors were fully aware of the problem they had on their hands is seen in a letter of Sidney Dillon's, written late in June 1869, in which he admitted to Treasurer Williams: "I am in trouble daily about the Credit Mobilier, takes all my time to try and get it in shape, it looks rather bad."[64] Dillon was then president of the Crédit Mobilier of America.

Of the various threats lodged against the railroad it was the one made by Henry S. McComb, of Wilmington, Delaware, that finally brought matters fully into the public view. In March 1866 McComb, who was one of the seven trustees of the Hoxie Contract, had agreed to purchase 250 shares of Crédit Mobilier of America stock for a friend named H. G. Fant. When Fant did not pick up the stock McComb asserted that he understood the company would reserve the shares for him. There were no discussions about the matter until December 1867, when a healthy stock dividend appeared in the offing. By then, through accretion, the number of shares had grown to 375. McComb tried to get possession of the stock he thought had been reserved for him, but the board of directors would not support his contention. In an effort to force the matter he appealed to the courts and it was during this litigation that several compromising letters passed between McComb and Oakes Ames, who was a trustee of the stock in question.[65]

McComb's unrelenting persistence brought trouble. In addition to his resort to suit, he hounded the Union Pacific officers for his money, engaging in bitter arguments with them. In January 1870, for example, he told John Williams that "if you had been as particular and careful with the Company's assets hitherto, I take it for granted Mr. Bushnell would not have been so well off, nor would you have gotten so much pay for your services."[66] Late in the following year he challenged the railroad to sue him over a disputed sum involving some grading scrapers, saying: "I would like to make a little test before the Courts of some of the tergiversations, and dishonesties, as I call them, practiced by some of your people."[67] Rollins, to whom the letter had been directed, was furious. He charged McComb with spoiling for a fight and reminded him about the vulnerability of people who lived in glass houses.[68] McComb came back, a few days later, with more accusations. He spoke to a prominent company director who bought between $2 and $3 million worth of bonds, and when he could not pay for them the company carried him, paying as much as 18 to 20 percent interest per annum while charging the director only 6.[69] McComb, described by John Pondir as a "perfect plunderer and thief," would not give up.[70] Taking advantage of election-year emotions, he offered his correspondence with Oakes Ames to the *New York Sun* which, on September 6, 1872, published it. Now, in the heat of political battle, rumors that had persisted for several years took on added meaning: Not only had a great deal of money been realized from the Union Pacific Railroad's construction, but it also appeared to have been used for the corruption of congressional members. Set in the scene of post-Civil War revelations of political corruption the whole affair now assumed the proportions of a national scandal.[71]

Early western reactions to the charges tended to defend the Union Pacific people. The *Rocky Mountain News* quickly took the position that the accusations were a part of campaign lies, and that the Crédit Mobilier "slander" originated in the offices of the *New York Sun,* "the most disreputable paper in America." Although men of prominence who were accused made prompt denials, the *News* said only McComb's side of the story was published, the scandal being perpetuated "in all the Greeley organs" around the country.[72] Before the year was out the Denver paper had modified its stand. By then the *News* thought no Republican member of Congress would be hurt except, perhaps, Oakes Ames, who was so closely associated with the Crédit Mobilier of America. A few months later it concluded that the notorious construction company had made off with $45 million, or more than that paper's estimate of the road's entire cost.[73] Meanwhile, the *Herald,* of Omaha, made enough uncomplimentary remarks to bring complaints from the Union Pacific. The railroad did not, however, complain about Omaha's *Daily Republican,* whose editor defended the Crédit Mobilier on the ground that without this organization, and the genius of Durant, the road would not have been finished so quickly.[74]

The charges made by the *Sun* resulted in investigations by two congressional committees headed by Reps. Jeremiah M. Wilson, of Indiana, and Luke P. Poland, of Vermont. Both groups had finished their work by February 1873. The Wilson committee found that the railroad company, in acting as its own contractor, had put the road so deeply in debt there was a question whether it could ever pay off its obligations or, carrying such a heavy load, could long remain solvent. The Poland committee stressed the alleged graft among congressmen and it recommended, but did not get, the expulsion of Ames and Director James Brooks from Congress.

The government next attempted to recover money said to have been made fraudulently, but the Union Pacific took the position that since the Crédit Mobilier was so closely intertwined in its own organization the railroad would be put in the position of being both a plaintiff and a codefendant in the case. In January 1879 the Supreme Court upheld this contention, also holding that until the railroad's subsidy bonds matured the government, being merely another creditor, had no ground for action.

In addition to the embarrassment afforded those associated with the Union Pacific, the most important outcome of the Crédit Mobilier scandal and investigation was the thoroughly antagonistic attitude toward it and other railroads that lingered in the public and the congressional minds. This strong feeling was also reflected in state legislatures during the years that followed. Popular antipathy toward the further granting of any lands, money, bonds, or any kind of subsidies, was so deeply ingrained that it not only curtailed future railroad expansion and resulted in a number of regulatory acts, but it so marred the reputation of the Union Pacific, in particular, that textbooks nearly a century later associated the company with a taint of corruption and subterfuge that was presumably unique in American railroad history.[75]

In the days when the road was new, however, those who lived in the country through which it ran or who anticipated that one of its iron tendrils would reach out to their community, were more inclined to gloss over the details of its birth. They hungered for rail service, knowing that it would give the undeveloped West an enormous injection of economic strength, and if the price tag caused more conservative easterners to have second thoughts, the matter was not serious enough to result in any loss of sleep in the more primitive parts of America.

"The Gossamer Throws Its Delicate Lines"

Easterners might write to local editors, or perhaps to their congressmen, complaining of the way the road to Promontory was being laid, but those who lived hundreds of arid miles beyond the Missouri River had other problems. Colorado, for example, was not happy with the projectors of the Union Pacific, but hardly for the same reasons. In the manner of a spurned suitor the mountain territory watched the treasured rails bypass it to the north and tried to rationalize the lost opportunity by taking the position that its attractiveness was sufficient to win such rewards in the near future.

In the earliest days of its realization that the Union Pacific intended to pass some hundred miles to the north, Denver had displayed momentary pique. William Byers, editor of the *Rocky Mountain News,* asked why his people should make any effort to attract the Chicago trade when the business interests of that city, and of Omaha, allegedly had used their influence to send the main line on a more direct westerly route. "If this is all the importance that those cities attach to the securing of our trade, why it follows as a matter of course that they do not think us worthy of their notice," he complained. Therefore, concluded Byers, he found it hard to agree with Denver businessmen who were willing to support a Union Pacific branch by subsidy bonds.[1] The editor gained little satisfaction from the railroad company's advertisement in his own paper, during the spring of 1867, that told of direct stage connections between Denver and North Platte, and how 48 hours, or 200 miles of staging, would be saved by taking the Nebraska route east.[2] Even when that line had completed its westward sweep, residents of his city would have to travel a hundred miles by stage to reach rail service.

Despite their disappointment at being bypassed, Denverites did not discount the necessity of gaining a branch railroad that would connect them to the main line. They assumed that if it were built the Union Pacific—rich, powerful, and only a hundred miles away—would provide the money. Early in July Samuel B. Reed and Gen. John Casement, by now widely known for their construction efforts across Nebraska and Wyoming, visited Colorado's capital city. Rumor had it that they had come to lay out the needed extension.[3] A few days later a big railroad meeting was held, at which T. J. Carter, government director of the Union Pacific, and a director of a proposed subsidiary known as the Colorado Central, was the principal speaker. There was talk that a branch would be built through Denver, and on to the mines of Gilpin and Clear Creek counties. The Union Pacific appeared willing to furnish iron and rolling stock if local money amounting to $600,000 could be raised for gradework and ties. While the proposition was not as generous as some had anticipated, the suggestion that the new road would not only connect Denver with the main line, but that it would also penetrate the Rockies and reach the rich mining camps, generated new enthusiasm. Even Byers was inclined to emerge from his position of aloofness. The *News* now gave its approval to such an investment. It would, said that paper, insure Denver's role as an important rail center, and it would guarantee future prosperity to the community. Encouraged by Carter's presence, the meeting adjourned with three cheers for the speaker "and the iron horse in Denver within a year."[4]

Such interest by the Union Pacific precipitated even more railroad talk in the mountain mining camps. The *News* published figures stating that 23 Denver merchants had paid $1,200,000 in freight bills during the past year, from which it deduced that had railroad service been available those businessmen would have saved at least $400,000. Further rationalizations made inescapable the conclusion that a railroad to Denver and to the mines would indeed be a paying proposition.[5]

In 1867 Ovando J. Hollister, a well-known Coloradan, published *The Mines of Colorado,* in which he reiterated much of the argument found in contemporary newspapers. Speaking of the Union Pacific and the Union Pacific Eastern Division (Kansas Pacific), he predicted that when these lines touched Colorado new life would be infused into the entire community. Lower transportation rates, said Hollister, would mean cheaper supplies and a wider availability of labor, both of which would tend to increase the value of minerals extracted. To bolster and diversify the economy would come farmers, businessmen, and tourists. Colorado's climate, its unparalleled scenery and forests teeming with game, promised to draw sportsmen, health-seekers, and travelers from all over the world. Even better, said the enthusiastic author, rails would bring women. Reminiscent of Horace Greeley's earlier statement about importations of the opposite sex, Hollister pointed out that not only would the new service save time, for miners were too busy to go East for raiding purposes, but it would bring girls westward more easily

and with greater safety. In the expanded economy they could find employment and thus take more time in their selections, relieving themselves of the
necessity of marrying virtually upon arrival. The argument was seemingly
designed for eastern readership, part of which was made up of girls of a
marriageable age, or fathers of daughters who now might allow their off-
spring to chance it in the West, once the dangers of travel were moderated.[6]

Persistent railroad rumors generated and regenerated excitement among
the businessmen of Denver during the summer and early autumn of 1867.
On November 19 a climax was reached as the Denver Pacific Railway was
incorporated under the laws of Colorado. Led by former governor Dr. John
Evans and David H. Moffat, later to be so famous as a Colorado railroader,
the company proposed to build the 106-mile link between Denver and
Cheyenne.[7] A mixture of excitement and concern at being isolated prompted
Denverites to subscribe to $300,000 worth of bonds and for the voters of
Arapahoe County to vote a $500,000 bond issue with practically no dissent.[8]

Not only did Denver look forward to a physical connection with the
Union Pacific Railroad, but it felt sure the larger road would participate
actively in construction of the branch. Such expectations appeared to have
been realized when, in 1868, a contract was signed between the two parties
in which the Union Pacific agreed to lay the iron in exchange for $3.5 million
worth of Denver Pacific stock, or seven-eighths of its total issue, and the
right to operate the line when it was completed. Further encouragement
came in the spring of 1869 when, on March 3, Congress authorized the
Kansas Pacific to transfer its land grant between Denver and Cheyenne to
the Denver Pacific in return for an additional $800,000 in subsidy bonds to
the Kansas road.[9]

Despite high hopes and the apparent realization of an early rail connection to the north, a lingering apprehension hung over Denver during 1868.
Samuel Bowles, who visited the West again that year, thought the city's
pace had slowed considerably since he saw it in 1865. Businessmen, he
noticed, wore a "fixed fact sort of air" as they resolutely waited for better
times, and things were so quiet that there was only a single street fight during
the time the visiting journalist was there.[10] The *News* put up a brave front,
asserting that merchants owed less to the banks than in former years and
that they were generally better off; but it had to admit conditions were
something less than desirable. While an Indian war disrupted traffic directly
to the east, merchants and miners north of Denver were trading at Cheyenne,
both of which factors adversely affected the struggling businessmen in the
mile-high city. Cheyenne businessmen, happy to have the northern Colorado
mining trade, had mixed feelings about the possibility of a railroad, many
of them asserting that more business would come their way under existing

conditions. When John Evans visited the Wyoming city during the spring of 1868, he plied his neighbors with enthusiastic railroad talk, and let it be known that they had an opportunity to buy $100,000 worth of Denver Pacific stock. Lack of response to the offer suggested that the stripling city felt no need to lean upon the older Colorado community. This bitter realization brought out jealousies and recriminations. The *News* admitted that Cheyenne now had a population of about 2,500, but added this was more than "the rest of the Territory has or ever will have." Why did not the "habitable belt" of Wyoming join Colorado and abandon the rest of its sterile countryside?[11] The invitation, framed as a boast about Colorado's multiple resources, was an admission of its own economic stagnation.

To make matters worse, work on the Denver Pacific lagged. The Union Pacific was so pressed for money to complete its main line that it was unable to carry out its agreement with the Denver Pacific. With the branch line $180,000 in debt, and another $100,000 worth of grading to be done before rails could be laid, John Evans found his project stranded. Denver's gloom, now more than justified, deepened.[12]

Early in June 1869 Evans undertook to finish the road himself. To do this he received $3.5 million in stock and $2.5 million in bonds to be issued against a land-grant mortgage, the Arapahoe County bonds, and a small amount of cash. After a brief attempt to again interest the Union Pacific and, failing that, an unsuccessful effort to attract eastern money, he turned to the Kansas Pacific as his last best hope. Three weeks of negotiations yielded an agreement, the terms of which provided that Evans was to retain control of the Denver Pacific for five years and then surrender it to those controlling the Kansas Pacific. In return for their part in building the branch, managers of the Kansas road not only gained a westerly outlet, via the Union Pacific, but they also were to receive half of the Denver Pacific's traffic receipts. The significance of the latter arrangement lay in the fact that the region north of Denver was much more populated than that lying to the east.[13]

Resumption of railroad construction between Denver and Cheyenne produced new predictions by the Colorado press. Exulting over the Kansas Pacific's "remarkable liberality" in giving up their Colorado land claims, and glowing with pleasure at the efforts of John Evans and his associates, the *News* of Denver repeated its belief that Colorado's economic future was assured. Now the subsurface treasures—coal, copper, iron, silver, and gold—could be developed as never before. With timber resources in its mountains and fertile farmlands in both the mountain valleys and on the plains, the territory was possessed of versatile resources. There was no reason, said the *News,* why flour, brewing barley, vegetables, and dairy products could not be sold in competition with those of other regions, the local offerings being of fine quality and much closer to potential customers. Such growth would make possible further rail construction into the mountains, where lay an untold fortune in undeveloped resources. Every available man, therefore, should be called out to hasten completion of the line to Cheyenne.[14]

Union Pacific supporters saw a great potential in Colorado. Engineer F. M. Case, who had earlier surveyed passes west of Denver in the hope of finding a suitable route for the main line, and later was first chief engineer of the Denver Pacific, now lamented that the Union Pacific had been unable to build the Denver Pacific. "According to the present arrangement we are monopolized by the Kansas Pacific, sold out to them 'body and breeches,' " he complained in a letter to Oliver Ames late in 1869. He strongly urged the construction of a branch from Julesburg, along the South Platte, to Denver. Not only could such a line compete successfully for the Colorado trade, but it would run through the most valuable land-grant country in Colorado. Case assured Ames that he presently had no connection with any railroad and was "simply a citizen of Denver."[15] Although it was a personal letter, the suggestion it carried must have been current talk on the Denver streets, for the *News* admitted that the idea had "produced considerable excitement among our business men."[16]

To forestall possible isolation and to gain the much-desired rail connection with "the States," Denverites gave Evans wholehearted cooperation in his efforts to connect with Cheyenne. Although the work was attended by the usual delays, frustrations, and financial problems, it was completed in the spring of 1870, and on June 23 the line was opened to traffic. The *News,* of Denver, called this the end of isolation and the harbinger of a new era of progress. Now Coloradans could press forward into the mountains and open their treasure-house to the nation. Editor Byers offered cheers for all involved, but especially for the local men who had pursued their goal to a successful completion; for them he suggested "three times three and a tiger," or the heartiest thanks of all.[17]

Less than a year after the completion of the Cheyenne connection, Colorado felt the effect. In April 1871 the *News* asserted that already the flow of immigration had increased sharply, which, in turn, had commenced to influence every branch of industry and commerce. Real estate prices were rising, the building trade reported a sharp demand, business houses hummed with activity, and travel was heavy, all of which sent the commercial community into flights of hope for the future. There was no argument as to the source of this newfound stimulus. The Denver Pacific had arrived the previous June, followed by the Kansas Pacific in August. No one should forget, said the *News,* how much Colorado owed these roads; they were

RIGHT—*Judge W. A. Carter, the post trader at Fort Bridger, engaged in a number of enterprises, including the sale of cattle. During the 1870s he was said to have owned a herd of 2,000 head.*

BOTTOM—*Sixteenth Street, Cheyenne, in 1868.*

CATTLE MEN READ THIS!
Great Inducements to those who wish to
Ship Cattle on the U. P. Railroad!!

Having entered into special arrangements with the U. P. R. R. Company, by which I can ship Cattle East at greatly reduced rates, and having selected a point between Carter and Church Buttes Stations some ten miles East of the former place, near the junction of the Big and Little Muddies, and having Constructed Commodious Lots and Extensive Enclosures, and the Company having put in a Switch capable of holding 40 Cars, I will be Prepared to Commence Shipping on or before the 15th of the Present Month, and will be able to promptly ship any Number of cattle that may be Offered.

Persons driving Cattle from Montana and Idaho, and passing by Soda Springs and the Bear Lake Settlements, will cross over from Bear River to the head of Little Muddy and follow down that stream, over a good road, to within a mile and a half of the junction of the Little with the Big Muddy, where they will cross a bridge and find a rich pasture, extending many miles; good water & perfect security for their stock, within convenient distance of the stock yards.

The cattle yards are in an enclosure of some 400 acres, and stock scales and all conveniences for shipping will be furnished. If parties do not wish to ship themselves, I will purchase, at good prices, all shipping cattle that may be offered. As cattle are now bearing excellent prices East, it would be well for persons to bring their Cattle forward as soon as possible.

For further particulars, address

W. A. CARTER,
Fort Bridger, Wyo. Ter.

Fort Bridger, July 2, 1877.

directly responsible for "the reigning prosperity, and the future commercial and industrial greatness which they assure." Admittedly Arapahoe County had been obliged to encumber itself with $500,000 worth of bonds, thereby increasing taxes, but already the returns on the investment were said to be so obvious that "taxes were never so easily, so promptly, so generally paid."[18] In contrast, the mining business westward in the mountains remained slow. A correspondent from Central City said that only the richer mines were being worked, due to the high cost of transportation, and until rail service reached his neighborhood, hundreds of other mines would lie dormant or would be operated at little profit.[19]

Cheyenne, at the other end of the Denver Pacific, stood in sharp contrast to Denver. While the latter had enjoyed steady growth and had brick buildings and the Mint, Cheyenne was almost an overnight city, clearly a railroad creation, and one whose boosters boomed it loudly but uncertainly. The city's largest newspaper, the *Cheyenne Leader,* reflected community views in the best of frontier traditions, losing no opportunity to extol the climate, the natural resources, and the fine people who had been granted the good sense to settle there. It warred incessantly upon what it termed "croakers"; that is, anyone, anywhere who had words less than complimentary to say about the West's newest "Queen City." Upon the croakers was laid the blame for predictions that Cheyenne would be another temporary railhead such as Julesburg; or that the population figure, the very heart of community pride in young western municipalities, would suffer as fresh towns sprang up in the wake of future mainline construction. The paper joyfully quoted the response of a local Irishman who, while visiting Saint Louis, was asked if he thought that city had any future. No, he said, it would never amount to much; it was too far from Cheyenne.

Perhaps most galling of all were behind-the-hand remarks that the city had not been situated in the right place. This was heresy, suggested the *Leader;* common sense should have told doubters that the Union Pacific needed a halfway point between Omaha and Salt Lake City for its shops, warehouses, and other maintenance facilities, and also for its strategic location at the western edge of the plains where feeder lines would be run south to Colorado and north to Montana.

During the dog days of 1868, as the Denver Pacific faltered and as the Union Pacific's directors discussed the matter of making Cheyenne an important base, there were moments of doubt and hesitation among its residents that brought forth the bitterness born of apprehension. In an editorial entitled "The Hour of Trial," the *Leader* confessed that at no time since the city's founding had there been deeper gloom in the streets. Admitting that the place was "a creation of the U.P.R.R., and by the acts of that corporation does she stand or fall," the editor suggested that the railroad had an obligation to all those businessmen it had encouraged by advertising the new place as one it expected to be the most important between Omaha and Salt Lake City. Should the company fall short of its commitments to Cheyenne it would stand forever branded for its faithlessness. Those who had invested heavily in city real estate or business ventures breathed easier when President Oliver Ames visited them in June 1868 and assured them that his road did indeed plan to make Cheyenne a main base for Mountain West operations.[20]

Visitors generally regarded Cheyenne as a permanent locality, although they found it difficult to predict its unlimited growth. Samuel Bowles thought the place well situated, with a degree of agricultural wealth surrounding it, and in 1868 he called it a first-class western town, the progress of which had made Denver jealous.[21] Others who saw it that year estimated its population to be between 4,000 and 5,000. With three daily and four weekly newspapers, a roundhouse with a capacity for 24 locomotives, and a branch line to Denver, there seemed to be ample evidence that Cheyenne was there to stay. Fort D. A. Russell, only four miles away, provided a payroll that was always considered an economic resource by western towns, and there was talk in 1868 that a government arsenal was to be located in the vicinity of the fort.[22] By 1869 the population was said to have fallen from a onetime high of 6,000 to 3,000, but this was explained as evidence that the days of construction were over, and that the "scum of the population has moved off to other pastures," leaving the streets of Cheyenne "as quiet as the streets of other Western cities in which law has conquered license."[23] When an outside newspaper alleged that the town had, among other things, 8 lawyers and 400 abandoned women, the *Leader* made heated denials. While the paper did not offer corrective figures, it stated that "the number of lawyers and abandoned women is about equal," leaving the reader to judge the actual number. In defense of his community the editor asserted that there was not half the wickedness, there was twice the morality, and there was ten times the business estimated by other correspondents. Again, he did not offer specific figures.[24] If Cheyenne had declined, suggested a visitor, the change was in the nature of an adjustment, the correct interpretation of which was that those who had stayed on were "settling down into soberness and permanent work."[25] However, even the most optimistic of observers had to admit that Cheyenne was not located in the agricultural garden of the world, and if there was any hope of profit from its "oppressively monotonous" scenery that met the horizon in all directions, it would be from grazing.

Nor was Wyoming itself regarded as anything but a place of potential value. The *News,* of Denver, declared that it was decidedly a railroad territory, "made by the railroad, because but for the railroad there was not the

faintest shadow of a necessity for it," and except for which it would not have
had more than a thousand white residents by 1870.[26] Visitors who gained
only a fleeting look at Wyoming from the car window as the sagebrush flowed
past, tended to agree with such an assessment, one of them remarking that
part of the route was so "hopelessly barren that I doubt if it will ever do
more than carry the track."[27]

The coming of the Union Pacific to Wyoming increased interest in cattle
raising, one that was pursued by the railroad for years to come as the territory
developed into one of the West's important grazing areas and one that
contributed heavily to Wyoming's image as the Cowboy State. As early as
1870 Dr. Hiram Latham, who had worked for the railroad as a surgeon,
and who was now interested in Wyoming's emerging cattle business, began
to promote the grazing prospects of the young territory. During 1869 he had
solicited the opinion of men who had gained earlier experience in the business and publicized his findings in a pamphlet called *Guide to the Union
Pacific Railroad Lands,* published by the Union Pacific's land department.

Other men also saw possibilities in the great pasture of the plains. Church
Howe, U.S. marshal for the Wyoming Territory, wrote to E. H. Rollins,
the Union Pacific's secretary-treasurer, at Boston, suggesting that Oliver
Ames, John Duff, and some of the other railroad officers, might be interested
in investing about $10,000 in a stock raising venture. He enclosed a letter
from Judge John W. Kingman, Wyoming supreme court associate justice,
who stated that there were enormous profits to be made in such a business,
100 percent not being at all unusual. Edward Creighton, a prominent Omaha
banker, was then (1871) grazing about $500,000 worth of cattle on the
plains. Creighton was said recently to have sold some $50,000 worth of
animals that had cost him only $10 to $25 a head. The judge also noted
that yearling Texas cattle could be bought in Kansas for $5 or $6 a head
and that 150,000 head of livestock were presently for sale at Abilene. It
was a sound investment, he felt, one in which the loss was "hardly one in a
thousand," and one whose growth was "almost beyond belief."[28]

President Oliver Ames passed on such information to his stockholders.
In his report of 1870 he told them that stock raising in the Platte Valley
and on the Laramie Plains promised to be an excellent source of railroad
business. On these virtually unlimited open spaces, he said, cattle could be
raised cheaply and safely, the cost of raising a three-year-old steer being only
$5 to $8, and with a good eastern market all that remained was the necessity
of getting the product to the consumer's table. Here the railroad stood ready
to serve the cattleman's needs. And the new beef bonanza promised to be
more than a flash in the pan, said the president, because "these plains cannot
be settled up for many years."[29] Ames had advanced to stage two of the

American Desert theory: that the arid portion of the West would never suit the needs of the plowman, but it would serve as a vast grazing ground for the use of herdsmen.

It is understandable that the Massachusetts industrialist took this point of view about Wyoming. His neighbor from Springfield, Samuel Bowles, had written that west of Cheyenne "the eye has no joy, the lips no comfort through it; the sun burns by day, the cold chills at night; the fine, impalpable, poisonous dust chokes and chafes and chaps you everywhere."[30] Judge W. A. Carter, who did some trading and stock raising at Fort Bridger, was less harsh in his judgment. Admitting that there were few religious or educational advantages to be found in his part of the West, since the population was largely native American Indian, he argued that the land was not completely sterile. The valleys already yielded good crops, and, in addition, timber and coal resources held the promise of future development.[31]

The discovery of coal in quantity in Wyoming had been of great interest to the Union Pacific's managers; it helped to solve the motive fuel problem in a distant country and it also suggested that the barren land concealed something of commercial value. As construction crews worked their way beyond Cheyenne in 1868 they began to find evidences of coal close to the surface. In June 1868, while grading near Rock Creek, a cut was made through a bituminous vein eight feet thick. More coal was found near Benton, this time by an Irishman who sold his claim to Edward Creighton, the Omaha banker, for $200. Creighton at once contracted with the railroad to sell several thousand tons at $8 a ton, the operation costing him about $2 a ton. Not far away he opened up an anthracite mine that also showed considerable promise.[32]

Union Pacific officials did not take long to realize they could do better. After preliminary explorations, sponsored by the road, the company entered into an agreement with a pair of Missourians, Cyrus O. Godfrey and Thomas Wardell, to prospect and mine coal along the entire length of the road. The agreement, dated July 16, 1868, provided that the men would make the extraction at their own expense and that for two years the road would buy coal at $6 a ton, the price then dropping progressively until it reached $3. The railroad agreed to furnish spurs, switches, sidetracks, and all facilities for loading the cars at the mines. The 15-year contract guaranteed the producers a minimum profit of 10 percent. In addition, Godfrey and Wardell could send their coal over the line, for general sale, at the same rate charged others, but they were to receive a 25 percent rebate. They, in turn, agreed to pay the road a royalty of 25 cents a ton for nine years, and none after that, provided the coal they sold to the road came to no more than $3 a ton.[33]

Before the year was out the railroad company apparently had reason to

TOP—*Much of the labor in the Union Pacific's coal mines was done by Chinese. They were also hired to supply fuel for the trains.*

RIGHT—*Artist's drawing of the Union Pacific depot at Omaha, September, 1868. Either he, or the sign painter, experienced some difficulty with the word "Union."*

regret its generosity. Late in that autumn a new organization called the Wyoming Coal and Mining Company was formed, and in January 1869 it was incorporated under the laws of Nebraska. Its capital stock, of $500,000, was divided into $100 shares, nine-tenths of which were held by six directors of the railroad. By now Godfrey had turned over his interest to Wardell, and with the formation of the new company the latter assigned to it his contract. He became the superintendent, secretary, and general manager in return. At a Union Pacific board meeting held in November 1869, it was resolved that the old Wardell contract was "contrary to public policy, tends to retard the development of the country along the line of the Road and tributary thereto," and it established discriminatory rates over the line. Therefore the superintendent at Omaha was instructed to "disregard the said contract in his department." The new arrangement stood until March 13, 1874, when the railroad terminated Wardell's association by forcibly taking over management of the coal company. A lengthy lawsuit followed that was finally settled in favor of the railroad. The "men of Boston" had made an initial mistake; in correcting it they regained full possession of a valuable resource, but at the price of considerable criticism from the public.[34]

In addition to coal, which early became a valuable economic asset, Wyoming showed indications of petroleum deposits. In the spring of 1869 western newspapers began to talk about such deposits in "that much abused country" of western Wyoming. At this time hope lay in the mountain country, on both sides of the Union Pacific's holdings, but most particularly in the area of Evanston. Early in the next year Oscar F. Davis, head of the road's land department, told Oliver Ames that a group called H. Dillingham and Associates, of Chicago, wanted to prospect in the Evanston area and were willing to spend $10,000 in their search. If results were favorable the group wanted to buy railroad land at the same price the government charged within the grant—$2.50 an acre—and since the land was not yet surveyed they asked for an agreement to such terms. Davis urged Ames to accept the proposal on the ground that any and all of Wyoming's resources should be developed whenever possible.[35]

In the late sixties and early seventies, as the Union Pacific passed beyond the days of construction excitement and settled down to developing an expensive road cut through the desert into a paying corporation, it watched with interest that part of the line thought by many to be worthless. Officials were encouraged when any sources of business showed themselves. Word came from Omaha that Cheyenne was giving the railroad a third more business than any other town along the line.[36] In short, those of the Union Pacific management who had looked for something more than immediate gain from construction profits took cautious hope that there remained a long-range reward which time and patience would reveal.

Meanwhile, it seemed logical to the railroad's managers that the development of Nebraska held the greatest immediate promise of substantial business for the road. Although the mining frontier tended to leapfrog forward, the older and more traditional frontier of the farmer had advanced more slowly and had remained contiguous to settled regions. This, coupled with the view that the agricultural mind was still imbued to a degree with the notion of the desert, suggested that the westward movement of small farmers would continue, as it had in the past, only after more easterly areas were sufficiently filled to force settlement deeper into the interior.

Nebraskans assigned a significant place to transportation in the development of their state when they designed a seal for the new commonwealth. In addition to a hammer and anvil, sheaves of wheat and shocks of corn, all of which attested to the importance of industry and agriculture, they included the figure of a steamboat ascending the Missouri River and, in the background, a train of cars headed for the Rocky Mountains.[37] The railroad's first circular, issued in the initial year of statehood (1867), estimated an annual business of a million dollars over the 305 miles of road then completed. When the gross earnings for the last eight months of that year came to more than double this figure, the committee which had designed the state seal realized the appropriateness of including a railroad train in its design.[38]

Stripling Nebraska communities along the new railroad looked at Omaha and foresaw the future. Samuel Bowles spoke for many of them when he noted in 1868 that when he had seen the city three years earlier it was just another river town, fighting for supremacy among such other places as Atchison, Leavenworth, and Nebraska City, but now it had rocketed into importance as the leading railroad center of the Missouri and Mississippi valleys.[39] In that brief period the city's population had grown from about 3,000 to 16,500. Other estimates held that the total was closer to 20,000, a figure accepted as valid by the commissioner of the General Land Office.[40] These people operated manufactories, breweries, and distilleries; were served by 2 newspapers, one representing each major party; had a choice of 15 different churches; put up their guests in 11 hotels, one or two of which were said to be first rate; and did business at 5 banks. The Omaha Smelting and Refining Works, established in 1870 with a capital of $60,000, was to grow so steadily that within 15 years its annual output was in the neighborhood of 20 million. By then the city would be the largest manufacturing point on the Missouri River and west of Chicago and Saint Louis.[41] That this thriving community should lose its position as the capital city and surrender the honor to a small place some 50 miles westward named Lincoln was beyond the comprehension of a traveler who visited Omaha in the late sixties.[42]

So successful was Omaha that other cities in the West showed their jealousies. Denver, for example, watched the growth with envy and lost no opportunity to build itself up by criticizing the river town. Gleefully it watched Omaha's concern over the development of other railroads in its neighborhood, fearful that they would drain away its trade, and remarked that the place really was not on the most direct line of travel westward. "The growth of Omaha has been false and exotic," said the *Rocky Mountain News,* contending that military disbursements and construction profits in the early phases of Union Pacific construction had allowed the city to grow far out of proportion to the needs of the country around it.[43]

The facts belied such charges. West of Omaha the country developed early and in considerable density. "As mile after mile is left behind, ... the surrounding country, instead of being wild and desolate, is rich and filled with settlers. Farm houses and tilled fields are seen on both sides of the line, and this spectacle is a common one throughout a large tract of the State of Nebraska." These comments, made by a contemporary observer, supported the railroad's contention that the Platte Valley was rich in arable soil, well watered, and subject to immediate tillage. In the words of another observer, the railroad had helped to develop the resources "of a country more extensive than many of the Kingdoms of Europe, and whose riches cannot be estimated; has made a new market for manufactures, and a new source of supplies."[44]

In 1869 Gov. David Butler told his people that to discuss the influence of the roads upon securing rapid settlement was a waste of time; the answer was too obvious. He could think of no community without a road that was not making a serious effort to get one. America, he said "is emphatically a land of railroads." If the government had encouraged roads, as in the case of the Union Pacific, he thought the state and the communities within it should do the same.[45] The press, and the men on the street generally, supported such sentiments. Local papers sometimes surpassed the enthusiasm of railroad propagandists, promising prospective settlers that their lands would multiply five times in value within a ten-year period; that Nebraska, being a new state, was free of war and bounty debts and therefore tax burdens would be light; and that town lots were available at the very lowest figures. One paper put its town's attractions in verse: "Behind the Squaw's light birch canoe, / The Steamboat rocks and raves, / And City lots are staked for sale / Above old Indian graves."[46]

As communities not served by rail watched the railroad towns burgeon, their people gave wholehearted support to town leaders who sought to obtain the coveted rails. They floated bond issues, pledged themselves to stock purchases, made donations of townsites, and offered any other inducements they could. Even though bond donations were restricted under 1869 legislation, Nebraskans without railroads continued to show their unstinted enthusiasm for such transportation facilities.[47]

Railroad towns, in turn, vied with each other for commercial supremacy, hopeful of gaining an advantage that would assure growth and permanency. A Union Pacific employee, involved in town-lot sales, reported that building along the line was very active. "I hope to see 2,000 buildings put up during 1872," he wrote.[48] The completion of the line by no means ended the day of the boomtown or the proliferation of fresh communities along the road. In 1869, three years after the road had passed through eastern Nebraska, the little town of Schuyler appeared, 75 miles west of Omaha. In less than a year it claimed a population of 400, two hotels, several stores, and a steam ferry. Town lots had soared in value from about $25 to $300 and even up to $500. The appearance of Texas cattle in large numbers accounted for Schuyler's sudden growth. In August 1870, 20,000 animals stood waiting there for transportation to eastern markets.[49] Nearby Columbus, only several years older, boasted of its 800 citizens, brick buildings, a waterpower site that suggested the possibility of manufacturing, and a strategic location—at the confluence of the Loup and Platte rivers. When it indicated jealousy over Schuyler's rise as a shipping point, Union Pacific officials pointed out that if Columbus would provide stockyards, as had the younger city, the railroad would supply track and other facilities necessary to make it another cattle emporium.[50]

So great was the railroad mania, so extensive was uncritical participation in it, that measures of control were incorporated in a Nebraska constitutional convention held in 1871. Under the proposed revisions there was to be a prohibition against municipal subscription to railroad stock, or to aid construction, unless three-fifths of the qualified voters approved. To further restrict speculative investment, stockholders of corporations were to be made liable, as individuals, for all debts contracted, up to the full par value of their holdings. Finally, the convention document provided for legislative control over rates and the power to prevent unjust discrimination.[51] The voters' answer to the prohibitions was to reject the new constitution.[52] They would feel differently at a later date; but now, in the first flush of railroad excitement, they wanted no tampering with the goose that was laying golden eggs.

To outsiders, the growth of western railroads and their towns was astonishing. As a British editor stated, in later years, these roads were "flung out over boundless wastes, inhabited by wild beasts and Red Indians, much as the gossamer throws its delicate lines upon the summer air." They were built upon faith that people would follow, a faith that time fully justified, but in the day of their conception there was so little evidence they would succeed, suggested the British editor, that knowledge of the truth would have given investors a thorough fright.[53] When an Englishman questioned such highly speculative efforts in a barren land, a westerner answered him with a whimsy that became a part of the frontiersman's armor against such odds. "We commence building a line and send an engine with a barrel of lager beer ahead as far as it will go," he solemnly explained. "Then we deposit the barrel somewhere in the prairie. A bar and some Germans gather around it, and soon there is a small colony, with a church and a schoolhouse. Meanwhile, we push our line ahead for five or six miles and repeat the beer-barrel business; and by the time the whole road is ready we have quite a nice little population."[54]

The frontier folk who pushed out into the desert, as it had appeared in their childhood geographies, could laugh at the beer-barrel story and create new versions of it, but their willingness to move westward found its origins in stronger stuff. They recognized that the mineral frontier was capable of yielding a product sufficiently rich to warrant the high-cost transportation afforded by wagons; agricultural endeavor, on the other hand, never could offer such a promise. The advance of the farmers' frontier was predicated upon the existence of rail service, or the most solemn assurances that it soon would be available. Those who ventured away from the Union Pacific during the late sixties, to probe attractive Nebraska valleys in search of farmsites, supposed that they were near the future route of at least a branch line. In their search for cheaper and perhaps more desirable lands, these settlers were willing to sacrifice rail service only temporarily. If it did not appear within a reasonable time they were willing to lend every personal inducement to make their desires come true. To them the iron rails were the arteries through which the lifeblood of the new agricultural economy would flow; without them that age-old method of subsistence could not exist in this land of distances.

"The Garden of the West"

That the Great Plains country would be attractive to farmers once it was served by a railroad was one of the assumptions under which the projectors of the Union Pacific had engaged in the enterprise. They did not suppose that more than 1,700 miles of road between Omaha and Sacramento, almost all of which ran through uninhabited country, could be supported by through traffic alone.

Dreamers who had talked of linking the Orient to the industrial portions of the United States by such a thread had thought in terms of international trade. To many of them it was inconsequential whether or not the road ran through a portion of the nation long regarded as a desert; if this barren stretch could be crossed, to reach the sea, the question would be answered. More practical men held that local traffic was necessary to support such a venture, and to assure such a development every effort to people the route òf the road would be necessary.

The principal investors who put their money and their faith into the Union Pacific, especially those whose motives were founded upon the belief in rewards from a profitable business as opposed to quick returns from construction only, took a great interest in the land grant received from Congress. As time passed, these investors reached the conclusion, as had the government in an earlier day when it modified its land policy, that the important end to be achieved was settlement, as opposed to that of profit. Although the Union Pacific never was to reach the point of giving away lands, as had the federal government, it was obliged to meet the competition, and thousands of acres were sold at figures that would be regarded as extremely small in later years.

Thoughts of formulating a workable land policy took firm shape as early as the spring of 1867. Faced with selling nearly 12 million acres of land— a serpentine tract stretching westward more than a thousand miles beyond the Missouri—to be received from the government, management realized the necessity of devising a method for its disposition. The corridor that pierced the West clear to central Utah was 40 miles in width, and its ownership was divided equally between the road and the government, the odd-numbered sections being intended for the company's use. The railroad was free to get as much as it could for each acre; as for the government, it promptly doubled the price it customarily asked, raising the figure from $1.25 to $2.50 an acre within the granted area.

The railroad lands first to be considered lay in Nebraska, for it was here that the initial trackage was laid. In that state alone the road's holdings finally would amount to 4,857,744 acres, or slightly less than one-tenth of Nebraska's entire area. As construction crews completed their work on each section of road, and received governmental approval of it, adjacent lands were qualified for sale. That the company understood the importance of developing a population in the country through which it ran was expressed by the passenger agent at Omaha at an early date. The Union Pacific, he said, could not expect to be the only railroad line to the Pacific; ultimately it would have to share the traffic with other roads. To build a solid foundation for future prosperity it was necessary to populate what was to be Union Pacific country, even if the company had to entice settlers away from competing roads.[1]

At a board of directors meeting, held on March 28, 1867, it was resolved that the committee on land grants be instructed to formulate a plan for organizing a land department and to submit a proposal at the next meeting.[2] Two months later the board assigned to Grenville M. Dodge the task of locating and laying out towns and townsites along the line "at such places as shall be deemed most practicable," after which he was authorized to sell lots in the company's name.[3]

There was a ready market for farmland along the completed line, a fact which was reflected in a contemporary journal when it commented: "Throughout the vast plains heretofore occupied by savages or lying vacant in solitary grandeur a new and attractive expanse will now be opened, presenting the advantages of safety, fertility, and ready access which will make it inviting and remunerative to the immigrant." In this great belt of land, continued the editor, the entire population of Europe could be sustained. He suggested that those interested should make early application, for the rise in price of such attractive land would be very sharp once the road was finished.[4]

Early in 1868 General Dodge announced that 200 miles of country beyond Omaha was ready for immediate settlement. Here were 2 million acres, ready for the plow. Another vast tract of land, nearly as great in extent, lay to the West; Dodge thought this would have to be irrigated, and he suggested the Platte River as a source. Near the base of the Rockies was another section that could be supplied from the mountain watersheds. He estimated that 6,752,000 acres were then ready for the market.[5] Late in 1868 Oscar F. Davis, an experienced government surveyor, was appointed head of the Union Pacific's newly organized land department and charged with disposal of agricultural tracts. He at once began to organize his staff, to make surveys, and to prepare for the anticipated rush of business.[6] His office opened on July 28, 1869.

During the first year of operation, sales were restricted to an area ten miles wide on either side of the track for 200 miles beyond Omaha. Initial sales, on prime farmland in eastern Nebraska, yielded between $5 and $6 an acre. Within two years Davis had sold approximately 480,000 acres, for somewhat over $4 an acre, which put more than $2 million into the company's treasury.[7]

The rapidity with which buyers came forth caused the railroad some problems. Both Davis and Dodge were concerned at how slowly the government surveyed lands along the line. Until the survey was done the road could not gain title to the land it claimed or make any of its own surveys. Davis thought that at the rate government surveyors were working it would be eight to ten years before they reached Salt Lake City.[8] In addition to delays occasioned by the surveyors there was difficulty in persuading federal authorities to turn over to the railroad the lands previously promised. The Department of the Interior was unwilling to issue land-grant patents until there was proof that a first-class road had been built, one that was acceptable to examining commissioners. During 1868 the Union Pacific was able to gain title to lands within the 20-by-200-mile strip in Nebraska, previously mentioned, but it was unable to deliver to prospective buyers the lands lying between the 10- and 20-mile boundaries. In January 1869, the company's executive committee resolved to allow those who wanted lands in this section the right of preemption—that is, to give notice in writing to Davis of their intention to buy when the lands were brought into the market.[9]

Dr. Hiram Latham, of Laramie, complained bitterly about the lack of surveys in Wyoming. Since there was no means of distinguishing railroad land from public land a double harm was worked: Squatters took advantage of the situation, while law-abiding citizens, who wanted to be sure of a clear title, refused to buy lands under existing circumstances. In effect, he said, across 450 miles of Wyoming people were prevented from settling within 20 miles of the railroad.[10] In the fall of 1869 Davis had submitted a map of lands claimed by the railroad north of the surveyed portion of Colorado, recommending that Oliver Ames forward it to the commissioner of the General Land Office with the request that sections claimed by the road be withdrawn from the market. There was need for haste, he said, for lands already filed upon would be lost to the road.[11]

Accordingly, the railroad company urged Joseph Wilson, commissioner of the General Land Office, to withdraw lands from the public domain, in order to prevent settlers from claiming lands destined to come under its control.[12] By 1869 there were four land offices in Nebraska and two in Colorado dispensing lands to homesteaders, most of whom wanted to be as near the railroad as possible.[13] That they were getting too close was suggested by Dodge when he complained to Oliver Ames that the surveyor general of Wyoming was accepting preemption filings on (odd-numbered) railroad sections, although it was in direct violation of the law of 1862. Even residents of Cheyenne, located on section 31, had ignored railroad claims.[14] Ames made an official protest to Secretary of the Interior Jacob Cox, stating that unless the railroad received protection it stood to lose a good deal of land to these unauthorized claimants. The secretary replied that Commissioner Wilson had orders to warn the public, in a series of newspaper advertisements, that those who settled on lands reserved to the railroad did so at their own risk. The surveyor general of Wyoming, said Cox, could not legitimately receive filings before land offices were opened, and as soon as that happened railroad lands would be withdrawn immediately.[15]

The opening of the Union Pacific's land office at Omaha brought numerous inquiries from land promoters and hopeful colony founders. William H. Martin, of Baltimore, wrote in the name of the International Emigrant Protective Union, asking for a "definite and permanent arrangement" with the railroad whereby he would act as an agent for immigrants arriving at that port. He felt that if the newcomers were not accommodated upon arrival "they are liable to be stopped on the way by the numerous Land sharks at Chicago and elsewhere in the West, and perhaps never get as far as Omaha." His plan involved receipt of a down payment at Baltimore and through tickets to Omaha to insure sale to the Union Pacific. He explained that since the North German Lloyd steamers arrived every fortnight, bringing between seven and eight hundred emigrants per trip, there were plenty of prospective buyers. "We all know that the Germans are the best class to sell our lands to," he told Oliver Ames, "for in almost every instance, by their thrift and enterprise, they add greatly to the value of the lands in the vicinity of the sections they purchase."[16] From Washington, D.C., came a request for free transportation from a writer who claimed to have an influential connection with German newspapers. He wanted to make the trip for the benefit of those "who seek to better their deplorable conditions in Europe," by finding what he was sure would be "a free and happy home, adapted to their habits and nature," along the line of the new railroad.[17]

Some of the agents made large promises. The representative of the European agency of the American Line of Railways, W. F. Gray, said he would send the Union Pacific 100,000 settlers. He was then at Hull, England, bound for Germany. At Hamburg he went to work immediately, readying thousands of circulars for distribution throughout Germany, Denmark, Norway, and Sweden. Assuring Oliver Ames that he was sending all possible emigrants via the Union Pacific route, Gray suggested that $50 would be of great assistance in furthering the work. By October 1869 he was back in New York with 210 passengers bound for California. Since he vowed to direct "the largest Emigration ever known to this country," he thought it appropriate that he should be awarded a free travel pass.[18]

Rather than scour Europe in person, searching for families ready to emigrate, a few of the agents established themselves at gateways to the West, hoping to attract both Europeans and Americans from such vantage points. One of these representatives, C. R. Schaller of the European Emigration Agency, located on Omaha's Farnham Street, said he had left England three months earlier for the purpose of directing families to America. He proposed to issue at London, Manchester, Liverpool, and some large continental cities contract tickets that would bring emigrants to Nebraska, "which State I find in every way suitable, where lands can be selected from some of the very best in the world with a climate unequalled and in every way adapted to this class of emigrant." He wanted reduced rates for his groups.[19]

Dr. H. Wiesecke, general director of the Workingmen's Emancipation Institution, wrote from Saint Louis, asking the location of the Union Pacific's most productive lands, the best places to lay out villages, and for other particulars about the western country. He told Oliver Ames that there were at least 5,000 workingmen of that city who would go west if they could have free transportation. Another 50,000 living in Europe felt the same way, said the doctor. The institution which he represented sought to give workers "the means to liberate themselves from the oppression of capital, from being dependent upon the employers, and to accumulate, in the course of ten years, an independent living."[20] One might well speculate upon the reaction of Oliver Ames—manufacturer, employer, and capitalist—to such methods of freeing laborers from their existing chains, especially since it was proposed that his railroad foot the bill. Nor were the downtrodden workingmen the only ones seeking emancipation. Mrs. George W. Moore, a widow who was "not yet very old . . . and have the western fever," was anxious "to see some way opened for many of the overworked and underpaid women of this country to get where they can be, and will be appreciated and probably appropriated into better spheres and more congenial circumstances." As for herself, Mrs. Moore wanted to go forth "to make money and get health"; the others, she hoped, would procure husbands.[21]

Union Pacific officials did more than negotiate with various agents seeking to cooperate with them in developing the great land grant. They encouraged Davis in his efforts to appoint representatives abroad who would actively seek immigrants from various European nations. Board member John Duff, for example, spoke approvingly when Davis secured the services of a Scandinavian who agreed to circulate land and railroad information in his native country.[22] In another instance Oliver Ames wrote to C. G. Hammond, superintendent at Omaha, endorsing an agent Hammond had recommended. Ames spoke of the desirability of having a man "to write and talk us up in Europe." Hire him, said the president, but at a modest salary if this were possible.[23] Management at Boston was anxious to have any and all settlers; as individuals or as members of organized colonies they were the catalyst that would stir into activity the great latent economic potential of the West.

During the spring and summer of 1869 inquiries from prospective colony organizers flowed into Union Pacific offices. A Philadelphian, who asked for the usual pass, said he was on his way west to find a suitable location along the road for a group of farmers from his state. Another organizer from the same city, who was getting up a party of 10 to 25 to settle near Omaha, wanted to learn all he could about land prices, terms of payment, rail fares, and other pertinent facts useful to the group.[24] Late in 1869 the Greeley Colony was organized in New York City, and an executive committee was appointed to investigate the advantages and inducements to be found in several western states.[25] Northeastern Colorado was its ultimate choice.

In its *Guide to the Union Pacific Railroad Lands,* first published in 1870, the Union Pacific provided a lengthy description of its available lands and how to acquire them. Quite correctly the pamphlet located the property in the vicinity of the forty-first parallel, but then literary license got the upper hand, the region being described as one "removed from the severe cold and long winters of the north and the hot, relaxing influences of the south." Highly misleading also was the contention that fuel was easily available and that timber grew with great rapidity. Those who wanted to go and see for themselves, said the brochure, had only to buy an exploration ticket which permitted the holder to stop at any and all stations where lands were offered for sale. Those who purchased 160 acres were credited with the full amount of the ticket; buyers of 80 acres were returned half the fare price.

Even though the railroad painted an extremely vivid picture of opportunities for settlers, its hues were no brighter than those offered by the promoters of many towns throughout the West. While one might take exception to the claim that in Nebraska "the heat of summer is tempered by the prairie winds, and the nights are cool and comfortable," or that the Platte Valley was a "flowery meadow of great fertility clothed in nutritious grasses, and watered by numerous streams, the margins of which are skirted with timber," time has shown that large portions of the state were highly productive. Less creditable was the assertion that the atmosphere was so dry it was peculiarly adapted to "persons predisposed to pulmonary diseases, many of whom rapidly recover under its influence and become hale and robust." Claims that their country was one large sanatorium might better have been reserved to the mountain communities where they were used extensively.

Despite great exaggerations as to the climate and certain resources, for which this and other railroads later were severely criticized, the Union Pacific's promoters showed restraint by not advising all to come. Destitute families were warned against making the move, for even after a farm was secured two to three hundred dollars would be necessary to sustain them until crops were harvested. Fifty dollars would be required to complete a small cabin; a one-story frame house of two to four rooms could be built for between two and six hundred dollars. A Chicago firm offered ready-made houses, knocked down and prepared for quick assembly, at prices of two hundred dollars and up, delivered.[26]

Realistic, also, was the land department's advice to capitalists that holdings near the railroad would grow rapidly in value and that real estate was the key to wealth in a newly developed country. A great many people who bought large tracts of land for speculative purposes realized generous profits. Friends of the road were permitted to invest in land at very favorable rates, on the assumption that values were bound to increase sharply in the vicinity of the rails. In the summer of 1869, for example, Oscar Davis informed General Sherman that he had set aside an entire section within a hundred miles of Omaha. Although the appraised value was $8 an acre, Davis said it had been agreed that the general would pay only $2.50. He promised to withhold the parcel from sale until Sherman confirmed his desire to have the property. Shortly the general answered, saying he was ready to buy at the agreed price, because to purchase at $8 "would put me to some trouble."[27]

In addition to the many small buyers, and the colony founders who

FARMS AND HOMES IN KANSAS.

EMIGRANTS
LOOK TO YOUR

INTEREST

FARMS AT $3. PER ACRE!
AND NOT A FOOT OF WASTE LAND.

FARMS ON TEN YEAR'S CREDIT!
And on purchase no portion of the principal required ! !

Lands not Taxable for Six Years!

FARMING LANDS IN
EASTERN KANSAS
BUT ONE HOUR'S RIDE FROM THE CITY OF ATCHISON AND THE MISSOURI RIVER, ARE OFFERED ON TERMS WHICH GUARANTEE TO THE ACTUAL SETTLER LARGER BENEFITS THAN CAN BE SECURED UNDER THE HOMESTEAD ACT.

THE CENTRAL BRANCH
UNION PACIFIC RAIL ROAD CO.,
Offer for sale their lands in the celebrated
KICKAPOO INDIAN RESERVATION,
Situated in the counties of Atchison, Brown and Jackson, in the State of Kansas, on the line of the CENTRAL BRANCH UNION PACIFIC R. R. This tract is 24 miles in length and 12½ miles in width and contains
152,417 ACRES.

This tract of land is situated just twenty miles west of Atchison and is distant from Leavenworth and St. Joseph but thirty-five miles. It is interested by all the old lines of communication between the east and the far west, to-wit:—The Great Military Road from Ft. Leavenworth to Ft. Kearney, the Overland Rail Route to California and Colorado, the Emigrant Road from St. Joseph, and now the C. B. U. P. R. R. passes through the tract in a northwest course, on the line of which, within its limits, arrangements have been made for the building up of three enterprising towns. At MUSCOTAH and NETAWAKA neat and commodious depot buildings have been erected, and other substantial improvements are in progress. The establishing of

SCHOOLS AND CHURCHES
At convenient points on the Company's lands, will be encouraged and generously assisted. It is stipulated in the treaty with the Kickapoo Tribe of Indians, by which the Railroad Company acquire title to these lands, that they shall be and remain

FREE FROM TAXATION FOR SIX YEARS!
or until patents are issued by the U. S. Government. These peculiar advantages are applicable to and can only be obtained by settlers on the Kickapoo Indian Reservation, who, in addition, have all the advantages which are offered to settlers upon lands in any other locality in Kansas and the west.

The Walnut, Grasshopper, Wolf and Nemeha rivers have their source in the Northern portion of this body of land. The two former traverse the entire length in a South-easterly course, and flow into the Kansas River. The two latter flow North-West into the Missouri River. These several water courses and their tributaries within the limits of this tract of land are upwards of 200 miles in length. The banks of which are skirted with a variety of timber, principally of Oak, Walnut, Hickory, Maple, Hackberry and Elm, making this the

BEST WATERED AND TIMBERED TRACT OF LAND IN NORTHERN KANSAS.

AGRICULTURAL & STOCK-RAISING PURPOSES
are unsurpassed. The Country surrounding this tract of land has been settled for many years, and numerous Towns and Villages have grown up on its border, the largest of which is the enterprising town of Hiawatha, in Brown Co. The other places are Grenada, Kinnekuk, Claytonville and Eureka. The fact that the C. B. U. P. R. R. is the most constructed road west of the Mississippi river, is in part attributable to the character of the country, the material for which, was obtained from the numerous Fine Quarries of Stone which have been opened on the Company's lands. The presence of COAL in various localities on the land gives promise of an abundant supply for domestic and mechanical purposes. The attention of those arranging for Emigration to the West and

SETTLEMENT IN COLONIES
is especially invited to the advantages which are here offered. The subscriber is authorized to offer
EXTRAORDINARY INDUCEMENTS
To persons applying to purchase homes for immediate improvement. To such, FROM FOUR TO TEN YEARS CREDIT The land has been appraised mostly from $3.00 to $10.00 per acre, average price less than $7.00 per acre.
EMIGRANTS STOP AT ATCHISON CITY,
And confer with the subscriber, who will grant you every facility to acquaint yourselves with the R. R. Co. offer to settlers on their lands. Remember that this Kickapoo Reserve tract is
1,000,000 ACRES
On the line of this road which the Company are preparing to offer for sale.
For full information, Maps, Circulars, &c., address,

Atchison, Kan., May 1867.　　[4]　　Land Commissioner C. B. U. P. R. R. CO.

"Daily Champion" Print, Atchison, Kan.

LEFT—*The railroads competed actively with the federal government in selling land near the tracks. The government price was $2.50 per acre within the granted strip.*

BOTTOM—*Before the day of the automobile westerners sought out their recreational spots by team and wagon. Here is a group camped near Colorado Springs.*

wanted to purchase larger tracts for joint enterprises, there were some who were willing to purchase sizable tracts of land far out along the line in what was yet considered desert country. In the autumn of 1869 the DeHaven financial house informed Treasurer Williams that it had a party willing to buy 100,000 acres of land somewhere between a point 900 miles beyond Omaha and east of Promontory provided it could be had for 50 cents an acre. While the DeHavens did not say these were cattlemen, the size of the tract and its location suggested that it was desired for range use. Since the buyers were said to have as much as $300,000 to put into the land within the span of a few years, they were obviously men of means, and if they were willing to invest that much in Wyoming, at that time, livestock undoubtedly was the investment they had in mind.[28]

As settlement along the road began in earnest, the company undertook an active advertising program. Before the end of 1869 Davis had prepared brochures, complete with maps, that he proposed to distribute throughout the country. Newspaper advertisements told of 12 million acres of the best farmland in America now opened for settlement at prices of $2.50 to $10 an acre.[29] During that winter the land department spent approximately $12,000 in advertising and printing, a figure Davis raised to $20,000 the following winter.[30] Treasurer Williams agreed, reporting sales for June 1870 of more than 14,000 acres for almost $69,000, or just under $5 per acre.[31]

Land along the first 200 miles of the road sold well, but those opened in western Nebraska and in Wyoming were hard to move. One way to break down mental barriers about the desert was to advertise in depth and as far afield as possible. Aside from the efforts of Davis, the Union Pacific entertained proposals from others who could spread the word about its western lands. In the spring of 1870 Oliver Ames corresponded with Henry Villard, then the secretary of the American Social Science Association of Boston. Villard at that time proposed to compile a handbook for immigrants— written in English, German, and Swedish—and to distribute 100,000 copies of it in Europe. He asserted that European immigration to the United States in 1869 had exceeded 350,000, and that 1870 promised to be even bigger.[32]

Another outside source of advertising came through the DeHavens of Philadelphia. Anxious that the company's securities rise in value, these financiers fed any and all good news about it to a large number of newspapers. For example, in the spring of 1870 they circulated in 125 newspapers a story that described a land sale near Columbus, Nebraska, where the company recently had disposed of 4,000 acres for $14,260, and they added the comment that the Platte Valley was settling up rapidly and it would soon be thickly settled. "You see we are working for the road all the time," said a representative of the financial house.[33] Individual land speculators carried on their own advertising campaigns. In 1870 Andrew J. Stevens, of Columbus, Nebraska, offered 400,000 acres of choice land in the Platte Valley "at prices within the reach of all, and on terms to suit every variety of purchaser."[34]

Indirect support was lent by newspapermen who toured the West, often at railroad expense, and then wrote of their findings. In 1870 Joseph B. Lyman, agricultural editor of the *New York Tribune*, spoke of a proposed western expedition by a party of journalists, the purpose of which was "to advise our readers of the quality of lands, wholesomeness, scenery & prices." He thought such a report would promote immigration. His group, numbering between 20 and 30, proposed to charter a railroad car. All he asked of the Union Pacific was that the car be attached to regular trains and shunted into sidings at various points of interest so members of the group could have time to examine the various cities.[35]

Response to such requests apparently was favorable, for there is evidence that Davis took an active part in escorting agricultural editors through his domain. In August 1873 such a group was given a conducted tour in a special train. Buggies awaited members at train stations to take them on tours of inspection in cities along the line.[36] An Omaha paper praised Davis and his employers for their part in settling the country between the Missouri River and the Rocky Mountains, acknowledging that liberal inducements to immigrants and generous travel facilities had brought many such people to the West.[37] By October 1, 1873, the railroad had sold 799,748.71 acres of its lands at an average price of $4.50 per acre. By then $1,389,000 of the original $10,400,000 of land-grant bonds had been retired. The government directors predicted that the present rate of sale promised ultimately to pay off the entire sum and still leave a considerable surplus to the railroad company.[38]

Business in the land department continued to be brisk, even in the "grasshopper year" of 1874. Davis reported that June sales amounted to 44,000 acres, sold for $202,000. Another 16 land-grant bonds now could be canceled, he told Frederick L. Ames, trustee for the bonds.[39] Despite crop failures that year, activity continued along the line. During the summer the land department commenced publication of a handout sheet known as *The Pioneer,* the purpose of which was to furnish information to homeseekers who wanted to settle in the West. A free copy could be obtained by writing to Oscar F. Davis at Omaha. In an early issue the paper gave a general description of available lands, a short history of Nebraska, testimonials regarding the fertility of railroad lands, an estimate of industrial possibilities, descriptions of conditions in various Nebraska cities and counties, and a number of miscellaneous items of interest. Five years after sales had begun there still remained over 4 million acres for sale in Nebraska, much of which was in the eastern and central part of the state, or "the Garden of the West," as Davis termed it. Prices ranged from $2 to $10 per acre, with plots as small as 40 acres available. Agents at the principal stations along the road were ready to take parties into the country to make their selections, after which a $360 down payment would put the settler on his new farm. Those who wanted to send for relatives or their families could buy through tickets from principal European ports directly to Omaha, from the Union Pacific offices at Omaha.[40]

While there is no gauge to measure the effectiveness of such promotional efforts, it is probable that in themselves they did not induce an unusual number of people to settle in Nebraska, if one takes into account the historic pressure of the westward movement and the apparently insatiable desire for fresh land. The fact that a high percentage of lands settled were sold, as opposed to homesteaded, gives rise to the contention that these people were "promoted" westward. For example, by 1870 only 11,454 homestead claims were filed in the state. If the average family numbered only four this represented but 38 percent of the total population, a figure that diminishes the stimulus furnished by the Homestead Act.[41] However, the fact that the lands first taken up lay near transportation, so vital a factor west of the Missouri River, and that their settlement was facilitated by relatively low prices, time payments, and railroad cooperation in getting to one's new farm, must account to a large degree for the willingness to purchase.

As railroad lands were occupied and settlement was forced to spread out on either side of the land-grant strip, more homesteads were taken up. In Nebraska the speculators and various land companies, including those of the railroads, dominated the picture until about 1872. In that year an estimated 75,000 settlers arrived, followed by an equal if not larger number the next year. In 1872 a solid block of western counties between the Kansas line and the Platte River, representing an area 100 miles long and 100 miles wide, had only a scattering of settlers along its streams. By the end of 1873 almost all the area open to homesteading was occupied, leaving only some unsold railroad lands, school sections, and some odd parcels of land. Farmers, forced away from the land-grant areas and from the railroads, took up farms under the Homestead Act because they had no other choice except to move deeper into what many still regarded as the desert.[42]

Anxious as were the directors of the railroad to sell their western lands, they objected to the expense involved. Sidney Dillon agreed, and E. H. Rollins relayed Dillon's attitude to Davis: "We must come down to the hard pan all around." Davis had no recourse but to follow orders; however, he argued fervently that the Chicago office must not be closed, holding that it was more important than even New York in the business of enticing emigrants. His wish was granted.[43]

By the end of August 1874 the company had sold another 269,292 acres, principally in Nebraska, at an average of slightly over $4.91 per acre.[44] Davis contended that such favorable sales were derived in a large part from the efforts of his department, an organization that was doing yeoman work at a relatively small cost. In November 1874 he made a report showing that agencies were maintained at Omaha, Lincoln, Chicago, Saint Louis, Indianapolis, Cincinnati, and Washington. The Chicago agent drew a salary of $125 a month, while the local representative at Omaha was paid $75. The multitude of agents at smaller places drew no salaries, but worked on a commission basis and were furnished stationery and other supplies. Advertising costs for a month came to $500; the printing of German books, to $250; of Scandinavian books, $125; of English folders, $200; and of German folders, $50. The account sheet that Davis presented totaled $6,207.01.[45] It was expenses such as these to which the Boston office objected. The directory now seemed to feel that government lands on alternate sections would attract settlers who would not only furnish the road with local business, but would at the same time attract buyers to the adjacent railroad lands.

The spring of 1875 was a time of frustration for Davis. Passenger travel boomed, but land sales lagged. The demand for tickets was so heavy during April that at one point over 200 passengers were obliged to lay over at Omaha. Families of all nationalities jammed the station platform, where they waited for new trains to be made up. First-class passengers preempted available facilities, leaving the immigrants to wait until equipment could be found to accommodate them. A Union Pacific representative at Omaha called the westbound passenger traffic "immense," especially that of the immigrant class, and only by keeping all rolling stock moving could the delays be held to an average of 36 hours. At one point immigrants were arriving at an estimated rate of from 300 to 500 per day, causing momentary concern among railroad officials over how these people could be cared for if the "blockade" were not quickly broken.[46]

Lamentably, from Omaha's point of view, most of these people were on their way to California, "attracted thither by bright dreams of wealth and plenty in that golden state." Having suffered from the Panic of 1873, they seemed to be bound for the farthest point from the scenes of their recent troubles. Some of the more sensible of these dreamers, said a Nebraska editor, had saved themselves bitter disappointment by electing to settle along the Platte River Valley, where they were bound to be much better off.[47]

Davis and his staff shared the concern about through traffic. "We are having a hard time with land sales and collections," he admitted to Rollins. Prospects were good—as they always seemed to be in the spring—and the signing up for land was great. If the coming season brought a crop, business was bound to pick up; but, at the moment, the fear of another grasshopper invasion was uppermost in the minds of the farmers.[48]

Meanwhile, during the waiting period, the land department pursued the retrenchment policy ordered by the Boston office. In April Davis reported that he had cut his office force to the bone, had reduced expenditures at Chicago, and shortly he would close the Saint Louis office. However, he said, "we must advertise and circulate books and papers, and make extraordinary efforts to overcome the bad reputation we obtained last summer from the scourge of grasshoppers." He predicted that soon his department would be selling town lots all along the line, as well as opening new lands in Wyoming and Utah, but he had to admit that for the moment, "the prospect in Nebraska lands is not now very bright."[49] Hopeful of better times he proceeded, appointing new local agents to work on a commission basis and pressing forward his advertising campaign. Nebraska newspapers carried advertisements that bravely continued to describe the Platte Valley as the "Garden of the West," where one could buy land on credit at six percent interest.[50]

By late summer and autumn excursions of land hunters appeared in larger numbers at Omaha, and their presence generated purrs of pleasure in the columns of the local press. These visitors were consistently accorded low rail rates, a policy that "greatly assists in the interests of Nebraska," noted one journal. In addition, remarked another, this renewed interest helped to dispel the notion that Nebraska had been "grasshoppered" beyond redemption, and it squelched rumors spread by unfriendly parties in the East. An ever-enthusiastic editor said he hoped prospective settlers would take advantage of the Union Pacific's excursion rates to view cornstalks so high that one almost had to use a stepladder to reach the lowest ears.[51]

Despite the mightiest and most enthusiastic efforts on the part of Davis, the Boston office continued to show a deepening disenchantment with the progress of land sales. By the spring of 1876 Sidney Dillon was ready to turn over to the government all or a large part of the granted lands at $2.50 per acre, the price that the government charged on its sections within the grant area. Holding that the opening of millions of acres of government homestead and preemption lands along the road "cannot fail to gratify the

Emigrants entering the Loup Valley, Nebraska, in 1886.

people of the country," he was ready to get out of the real estate business. Although the Union Pacific had by this time realized an average price of $4.47 per acre, it had sold only about 1,200,000 acres of its original 12-million-acre grant. Dillon was increasingly discouraged by the tendency of the states and territories to "impose very unreasonable and exorbitant taxes upon the railroad lands in advance of either surveys, sales or settlements," which tended to reduce the value of the lands to the company. He did not deny that such property ultimately would be valuable, but so far it had not produced cash returns as rapidly as had been expected. He proposed that the company sell 6 or 8 million acres to the government, the proceeds to be applied to the company's debt which was to mature by 1897. To the amount thus raised the Union Pacific annually would place in a sinking fund enough money to retire the debt on schedule.[52]

Davis had to admit that things were slow. In the summer of 1877 he confessed to Vice-President Elisha Atkins that he had bought for himself four sections of land in Hall County, paying $6 an acre for it, and he could not dispose of it for half this amount. He had also acquired 440 acres near Columbus, Nebraska, which he now wanted to surrender and apply the money he had paid down on it against the land he wanted to keep. His request was referred to the executive committee, but when he heard nothing more about it Davis surrendered lands upon which he had already paid over $2,700. The same land later sold for $8 an acre.[53]

The discouragement expressed by the Union Pacific leaders during the mid-1870s was not theirs alone. These were years of mixed feelings, a time of returning doubts about the fertility of the soil beyond the 100th meridian, a period of reassessment of the desert. Some still spoke bravely of the future and of the great potential of the country, discounting momentary setbacks. Those who had settled in the Platte Valley jeered at the trainloads of emigrants bound for California, warning that the golden sands of the Pacific shores were now overcrowded and that the frugal Chinese soon would make life difficult for the average laborer. Let the foolish ones go forth and find out the truth, warned the prairie press.[54] A British traveler who passed through Nebraska at this time called the countryside west of Omaha one of "perfectly wonderful fertility," a region of rich farms and prosperous cities. Grand Island, a city of about 1,200, boasted of two newspapers and a prosperous economy. North Platte was described as one of the most promising cities of Nebraska, even though its population had dropped from 2,000 in 1867 to about 800 eight years later.[55] When cities experienced such declines they always were described as being promising, as places that were characterized by steady growth, in contrast to the artificial, boomtown crowding of construction days. Even the boosters were now beginning to issue more qualified predictions.

Charles Francis Adams, Jr., widely known for his writings about railroad problems, made the flat statement in the spring of 1875 that the westerners simply had gone too far west. He blamed the people for the trouble in which they found themselves, but sharing the responsibility for their predicament was "that wretched land-grant and subsidy policy which did so much to stimulate the mania for railroad construction." The western mind, he maintained, for years had been ruled by the idea of bringing "remote acres, and ever acres more remote, under cultivation." Now, thanks to their own foolish optimism, and encouragement by the railroads, they had overstepped reasonable bounds of agricultural possibility.[56]

General William B. Hazen, a man of considerable western experience, publicly announced that the nation was rapidly approaching the time when the landless and the homeless no longer could satisfy their ambitions for property merely by settling on empty lands. He did not think that more than one acre in a hundred lying between the 100th meridian and the Sierra Nevadas had any real value for agricultural purposes or would "for the next hundred years sell for any appreciable sum." He noted that the government had sent forth many scientific expeditions to gather information about the flora and the fauna of the western country, but he could think of none that had been charged with the task of learning anything about the most important question of all: whether it was suitable for agriculture. He agreed with others, such as Adams, that a 200-mile belt of country beyond Omaha was arable, but west of the 100th meridian the agricultural potential dropped off drastically. At that point, he warned, "a very perceptible change takes place." He doubted that even stock raising could be carried on successfully unless shelter and food were provided for livestock during the rigorous winters. Hazen's opinion, published in a leading periodical, undoubtedly was widely read among members of the investing class. It is unlikely that very many prospective settlers ever saw it.[57]

Further evidence of a recurrence of "desert fever" on the high plains was shown by increased settlement in communities that lay beyond. From Washington Territory came word that 1876 was a good year there for immigration, many families from Kansas and Nebraska having been "grasshoppered" out of those states. Colorado reported a growth in population and business, particularly in mining communities. Montana, still remote and without rail service, took hope as inquiries about its resources began to appear.[58] Both of these mountain states were objects of interest to farmers who felt that rather than having gone too far west, they had stopped too soon.

By 1877 the annual disposal of land by the government had fallen to less than 5 million acres, a decline of over 6.5 million from the previous year.[59] Anxious to dispose of as much railroad land as possible, and by the cheapest

THE
UNION PACIFIC RAILROAD COMPANY

Proclaims to

FARMERS

Who have spent years grubbing stumps or picking stones, or who pay annually as much rent as will purchase a farm in Nebraska; to

Mechanics

Who find it hard work to make both ends meet at the end of a year's toil, and to EVERYBODY wishing a comfortable home in a healthy, fertile State:

NEBRASKA!

Is destined to be one of the leading Agricultural States in the Union, and greatest beyond the Mississippi; Because,

1st. The land does not have to be cleared of stumps and stones, but is ready for the plow, and yields a crop the first year.
2d. The soil is a deep loam of inexhausible fertility.
3d. Water is abundant, clear and pure.
4th. The productions are those common to the Eastern and Middle States.
5th. Fruits, both wild and cultivated, do remarkably well.
6th. Stock Raising is extensively carried on and is very profitable.
7th Market facilities are the best in the West. The great mining regions of Wyoming, Colorado, Utah and Nevada are supplied by farmers of Nebraska.
8th. Coal of excellent quality is found in vast quantities on the line of the road in Wyoming, and is furnished to settlers at cheap rates.
9th. Timber is found on all streams and grows rapidly.
10th. No fencing is required by law.
11th. The climate is mild and healthful; malarial diseases are unknown.
12th. Education is Free.

TICKETS By way of Columbus and Chicago and St. Louis will be furnished at reduced rates for persons desiring to prospect and select lands in Nebraska.

☞ To those who purchase 160 Acres of the Company on Cash or Five Years' Terms, a rebate not to exceed Twenty Dollars, will be allwoed on price paid for Ticket.

FREIGHT : Reduced Rates given on Household Goods, Live Stock, Farming Tools, Trees and Shrubbery, in Car Loads, for Settlers' use.

LEAVITT BURNHAM, Land Commissioner U. P. R. R.

The Union Pacific Railroad and Branches.

Best Equipped, Most Direct and Popular Route to the Rich Mineral Districts, Grazing and Farming Regions and to the Famous Pleasure Resorts and Hunting Grounds of the Rocky Mountain Country.

THE COLORADO CITIES AND RESORTS are best reached via the UNION PACIFIC RAILROAD, Colorado Division. By far the most direct, pleasant and popular route to Ft. Collins, Estes Park, Boulder, Golden, Denver. Central, Georgetown, Idaho Springs and Leadville. Best Hunting, Fishing and Pleasure Resorts in sight of the Union Pacific.
THE BLACK HILLS.—The Sidney Stage Line, in connection with the Union Pacific Railroad, affords the shortest, quickest, and the only safe and pleasant stage journey to Rapid City, Custer, Rochford, Deadwood, Crook City. and other prominent points in the Hills, being the only line passing along the entire length of the Hills.
UTAH, IDAHO AND MONTANA.—The UNION PACIFIC, connecting with the UTAH CENTRAL at Ogden, for Salt Lake City, Frisco, Leeds, and all points in Utah, and with the UTAH & NORTHERN, for the Snake and Salmon River Mines, as well as Helena, Deer Lodge, Virginia, Butte City, Glendale, Bozeman, and all the best mining and Agricultural regions in Montana.
CALIFORNIA, ARIZONA, OREGON AND WASHINGTON.—The UNION and CENTRAL PACIFIC RAILROADS form the only line across the continent, to all points in Nevada, California, Oregon, Washington; and in connection with the Southern Pacific, affords a through rail route to the heart of Arizona; or in connection with the finest Steamship lines, to China, Japan and India.

For information concerning the Resources, Climate, and other attractions of the Great West, address **THOS. L. KIMBALL,** General Passenger and Ticket Agent U. P. R. R., Omaha, Neb.

Reproduced full page advertisement (printed in 1879) appearing in booklet

The Commerce of Two Cities, the Present and Future of Council Bluffs and Omaha

Railroads were among the leading land-boomers of the West. In this advertisement the Union Pacific enumerated a dozen virtues that Nebraska held out to the prospective settler.

means, Oscar Davis recommended that company property be sold in large blocks wherever feasible. Dillon assented to this, but said that to do so would be very difficult if a maximum amount of money was to be realized. Jay Gould, now prominent in Union Pacific affairs, took a short-range point of view. He wanted to sell grazing lands for any price to any and all stockmen who wanted to locate along the road. Never one to miss a current opportunity, Gould noted the Black Hills gold rush, citing that wagon freighting between the mines and the railroad had experienced a sharp upturn.[60] He suggested that the company's town-lot department might profit from this new mineral excitement. Company officials, alarmed at the lag in western growth, were doing their best to compensate for a decline in land sales to farmers.

Despite loud praise by the Nebraska press for the railroad's generosity to prospective settlers, Davis blamed the parsimonious policy of the company for its failures to attract immigrants. Early in 1878 he looked back upon the preceding three years and called them disastrous. He felt that he had been shackled by miserly managers at a time when rival roads were competing fiercely for a dwindling flow of European immigrants. Davis argued that emigrant rates, said to be cheap, were far too high. He wrote that the carload rate from Davenport to Council Bluffs, Iowa, a distance of about 300 miles, was $40. To haul the same car westward from Omaha to Clarks, Nebraska, only 121 miles, the Union Pacific asked $35. His company charged more than any other road leading to Omaha, said the land commissioner. Nor was the Boston office thought to be very generous about issuing exploring tickets or free passes. Not only did such a policy drive away prospective settlers, he argued, but it was very hard on those who had already established themselves along the line and were now desperately in need of lower freight rates. By the time he wrote, some half million acres of Nebraska land, within the first 200 miles beyond Omaha, lay unsold. Davis confessed that he had not pushed the sale of this land with particular vigor, for even without artificial stimulation it brought $5 per acre, and he thought before long it would easily sell for $7.50. The reason for the agent's bitterly defensive attitude was that he had been fired.[61]

Davis requested that he be allowed to stay on for a little longer, but Superintendent Silas H. H. Clark, at Omaha, would have none of it. Clark wanted to hire Albert E. Touzalin away from the Burlington and Missouri road, but he was already drawing a salary higher than the Union Pacific was willing to pay. Editor J. Sterling Morton, well known in Nebraska politics, was a willing candidate for the job, but Clark had some doubts that he would "suit us in some other directions." Morton was an able writer, and he was willing to work for $4,000 a year, but he was "more or less a politician and this is quite objectionable," said Clark.[62] The choice fell to Leavitt Burnham, who began his duties on February 1, 1878. Since Dillon's plan to sell most of the Union Pacific's lands to the government, at $2.50 an acre, had not met favorable response, the road's chief executive now decided to make a new effort at disposing of them to settlers. He advised Clark to encourage Burnham in his efforts to increase land sales. Dillon now agreed to buy more advertising, to offer the lowest possible emigrant rates, and possibly to offer settlers free transportation after they had made a down payment only on land. "I think we should give publicity to all our matters and put new life into our land department," wrote the president.[63]

One of the reasons why settlement along the Union Pacific was disappointing to management arose from continual disputes with the government over issuing patents on the granted lands. The Act of 1862 provided that when the Pacific roads were completed patents would be issued and title given to those lands set aside for the railroads. Because of the government's continued reluctance to accept the Union Pacific as a completed first-class road, Secretary of the Interior Jacob Cox had withheld these patents. In 1872 his successor, Secretary Columbus Delano, relaxed the suspension and granted patents on the first 200 miles beyond Omaha. However, as late as 1874 patents to half of all granted lands were still withheld, the question of completion not yet having been settled. In that year, by presidential order, the Interior Department lifted the ban; the president had decided that the railroad had complied with the recommendations of the earlier Committee of Eminent Citizens and that the road was completed. This did not completely solve the railroad's problem, because much of the land had not yet been surveyed. While this delayed disposal of railroad lands, it had a compensating effect, for until the patents were issued to the railroad such property was not taxable.

The taxation issue immediately caused another furor, the states involved becoming highly excited over the prospective loss of revenue. In 1879 the Supreme Court affirmed the road's contention that its lands were not taxable until patented. Although the company took refuge in the court's decision, it could not shield itself from the wrath of local residents. As late as 1887 the Union Pacific was charged with having allowed 11 years to elapse before selecting almost 2 million acres of its lands in Nebraska that had been surveyed ever since 1876. The record was not much better in other western states and territories through which the road ran. It was the doubt cast upon the validity of title for lands sold under these conditions that frightened away some prospective buyers and, in turn, brought complaints from Boston that the Union Pacific part of the West was not being settled as fast as was desirable.[64]

The Boston office also worried about the volume of land sales made by competing roads. Dillon complained that the Burlington and Missouri, the Kansas Pacific, and the Atchison, Topeka and Santa Fe were selling large quantities of land in the spring of 1878. It was far better than the Union Pacific was doing, he said to his new land agent, Burnham. "You must strain every point to sell our lands by judicious advertising and any other way you can."[65] The Kansas Pacific, rather than surrendering to the desert, had undertaken an aggressive policy of furnishing seeds to settlers and of breaking land where no one else would, to see if it would yield crops. By 1878 that company had rolled back the desert's edge in Kansas another hundred miles.[66]

Although the government directors of the Union Pacific publicly stated that scarcely a quarter of the road's lands were arable, that another quarter was pure wasteland, and that the remainder was useful only for grazing, settlers had no difficulty in finding suitable farms along the eastern portion of the line before the 1880s. Not until then would there be much pressure upon the land beyond the 100th meridian. Meanwhile, immigrants continued to arrive. Their numbers increased rapidly as memories of the grasshopper years faded. The surveyor general of Nebraska reported more than 100,000 newcomers in his state during 1878, some of whom settled upon railroad lands, the others taking homesteads from the public domain.[67]

Recognizing that it must gain a share of the increasing flow of immigrants the Union Pacific reassessed its settlement policies. With over 10 million acres yet to be disposed of, Dillon pressed his program of enticing farmers to Union Pacific country with renewed diligence. A general European agent was appointed, salaried at $125 a month, and by mid-1879 he was hard at work, distributing literature printed in German, Swedish, and Danish that told of new homes in America. So heavy were the demands for information that the representative feared the $300 a month limitation on his expenses would curtail his efforts.[68] During that time, as of November 1, the railroad company sold more than 200,000 acres of land for just under a million dollars.

The presence of agents throughout Europe, particularly in Norway and Sweden, was advanced as one of the reasons for the upturn in immigration to lands of the Union Pacific.[69] During the spring of 1879 sales continued to be favorable, with 150,000 acres being sold for nearly $.5 million.[70] By the end of that year, land-department officials could look back upon a decade of sales and report that nearly 2 million acres had been sold at an average price of $4.42 per acre. Forfeited sales and canceled contracts reduced the total sales to a little over 1,600,000 acres, most of which had been sold in tracts averaging 100 acres to each purchaser. This had brought 15,000 to 16,000 farmers into the country adjacent to the road.[71]

Prosperity seemed to be returning to the United States by 1879, evidence of which was shown in part by a greater flow of westwardbound settlers. The auditor of railroad accounts wrote that the development and growth of what he called permanent towns, as opposed to construction camps, was proof that a solid expansion was taking place. "To a certain extent these rising towns are the result of an energetic and liberal effort on the part of railroad companies to obtain more business, and show what is possible when harmonious relations are established between the railroads and the people," he commented. "The railroad is the great civilizer of modern times."[72]

Residents of towns along the Union Pacific took issue with the notion of liberality from the company. In 1874 a Cheyenne paper sharply criticized the road and called its town-lot policy "suicidal." Until 1874, when the government released patents to western lands, it was understandable that sales of city property were delayed; but, said the paper, now that this question was cleared up the road had no excuse for its unwillingness to sell town lots. If such land had been sold to residents of Cheyenne who wanted to buy it, more than $25,000 worth of buildings would have been built in the preceding year, ran one lament.[73] The road's reluctance to sell city lots at the going price did not arise solely from difficulties in issuing clear title. Members of a government commission later charged that these delays originated in the speculative desires of the company to make more money from such property by waiting for its value to appreciate. It was the practice of the railroad to demand a proportion of the lots in a proposed city as a reward for so favoring that particular location when selecting stopping points.[74] When such building sites were held for higher prices, townsmen complained loudly. Even when the lots were sold, there was unhappiness. "They keep an agent here ostensibly to sell lots," said the *Cheyenne Leader* in the autumn of 1875, "but he really does nothing but receive the people's money and receipt for the same." He referred to the practice of issuing only receipts, but giving no clear title to the property in question.[75] Rather than aiding town growth, Cheyenne accused the Union Pacific of hindering it.[76]

There was a difference of opinion between Omaha and Boston regarding disposition of city property. A general town-lot agent, J. M. Eddy, who worked under Grenville Dodge, told his superior that a number of railroad company lots in Cheyenne, earlier "donated in Washington," had been jumped, fenced, and built upon. Some of the jumpers had offered to buy,

HARPER'S WEEKLY.

A JOURNAL OF CIVILIZATION.

Vol. XVIII.—No. 915.]   NEW YORK, SATURDAY, JULY 11, 1874.   [WITH A SUPPLEMENT PRICE TEN CENTS

Entered according to Act of Congress, in the Year 1874, by Harper & Brothers, in the Office of the Librarian of Congress, at Washington.

Optimistic westerners found the land office an ever-fascinating place, a center of their projected hopes and dreams. This one was in Kansas.

and Eddy said: "I would sell them if they were mine. They will never bring more & there is but a faint shadow of forcing them off by any legal process."[77] Eddy's doubts about running off interlopers were strengthened because the company itself was not sure of such land titles. General Dodge had been put in charge of town-lot sales in 1867, on the assumption that he was to act in the name of the railroad, but apparently he considered himself "legally and morally responsible to parties to whom he has given contracts or deeds," as one of the firm's counselors expressed it. "I infer that Genl. Dodge's proceedings have been irregular, and are invalid," said the attorney.[78]

In 1873 the board of directors relieved the general of his duties and placed the sale of town lots in the land department, then headed by Oscar Davis. Although some city property was held for better prices, the money realized from sales already made had "never been idle," to use the words of J. M. Eddy. It was used to help pay for the Missouri River bridge, for obtaining rights of way, for purchasing operating department supplies, for erecting housing, and for covering part of the surveying costs along the line.[79] At best there was confusion in disposing of property held within the towns along the line. It generated another criticism of the road's methods, one that did little to help the company at a time when Congress was growing increasingly hostile to its management.

By 1880 the American economic scene indicated a continued improvement from the ravages of the postpanic years. A good many settlers, however, still wary of drought and grasshoppers, were now investigating possible homesites in the Rocky Mountain region and farther west. Colorado claimed 100,000 new residents in 1879, the largest immigration in its history, and Oregon asserted that a large westward flow had turned in its direction. Idaho boosters talked of 12 million acres awaiting the plow in that territory, plus 25 million acres of pasturage and another 10 million of timberland. No less an authority than Ferdinand V. Hayden, the renowned western surveyor, described Kansas as "bewitchingly inviting to all of small means, whose only hope for a farm and home of their own is government land."[80] Only Utah, where a drought had severely damaged crops, did not sound the clarion for newcomers.[81] Although Nebraska's population grew from 122,993 in 1870 to 452,402 in 1880, and 5 million acres of public domain were homesteaded in the West during the 1879 fiscal year, there were still lingering doubts as to the fertility of that state's western reaches.[82] Publicists began to warn that the outer boundaries of arable land had been passed and that the adventurous farmer now had moved into the real American desert.

The plains country had its defenders. In 1880 Samuel G. Aughey,

Professor of Natural Sciences at the University of Nebraska, published his *Sketches of the Physical Geography and Geology of Nebraska,* in which he asserted that rainfall in his state had increased during the decade of the seventies. He and C. D. Wilber, who also wrote on the subject, held that the apparent aridity was only a temporary condition. They discounted contrary evidence as being offered by ignorant persons. Aughey deemed the increased rainfall due to natural cyclical changes. He mentioned also the existence of rail and telegraph lines as a possible, but not very probable, additional source of moisture.[83] The presence of rails as rain inducers, however, was seriously believed by some of his contemporaries.

The government directors of the Union Pacific came to the West's defense. The railroad itself was no longer an experiment, they stated in their report for 1881, for it was now an established thoroughfare of nations that carried a growing volume of traffic from ocean to ocean. But equally significant was another and important function performed by the Union Pacific. It was fast changing "what was formerly supposed to be the 'Great American Desert' into civilized homes, and opening up to settlers the vast wealth of the extensive and rich mineral and farming and stock-raising regions along the line." From this steel spine that stretched across the land there had begun to grow a series of ribs extending north and south of it, probing new country, opening up new areas to miners, ranchmen and herders that were "once profitably given up to the Indian and the buffalo and the wild beasts." The railroad had become a pioneer among pioneers, one that not only opened the way, but also provided a population which would develop the country. Its projectors had taken large risks, said the directors, but they had won the gamble and had created business where there had been no business. They called the road "a pecuniary success."[84]

CHAPTER

9

Beyond the Magic Meridian

By the early 1880s the western farmer had reached the 100th meridian, or at what was then regarded as the eastern edge of the Great American Desert. His plow had cut the land much farther west than his forefathers had believed possible, and those who had warned against such a move admitted they had misjudged the outer boundaries of arability. Now, they said, surely the absolute limit had been reached and any further penetration would be foolish. The momentum, however, had been maintained all the way from the slopes of the Appalachians, and it was not to be stopped by warnings now any more than it had been in the past. Armed with railroads, barbed wire, patented windmills, and other forgings of a rising industrial nation, the new frontiersman believed himself to be ready for the new challenge.

To the railroad went much of the credit for revising former estimates of the mid-continent's desirability. Charles Nordhoff, writing for *Harper's,* assured his readers that the Great American Desert had "disappeared at the snort of the iron horse." After he had toured the western country he concluded that "on the plains and on the mountains the railroad is the one great fact."[1] That the road was accorded the role of an economic savior, of a corporate medicine man endowed with mystic powers, of the eighth wonder of the world, was not entirely due to the unbounded enthusiasm of its promoters. There existed a general public feeling that steam and steel would provide the ultimate weapon for the conquest of America's last West, and no claim for its power seemed to be too great.

Horace Greeley, who had passed through the land only a few years back, was now discredited, and his views were called "most ludicrously erroneous."[2] Those who were willing to forgive the New York journalist for his pessimism as to the agricultural potential of the plains held that times had changed since he saw the West. The coming of the rails had not only solved transportation problems, they argued, but the event had even altered the climate. The new bands of iron, reported the *Army and Navy Journal,* had so affected the electrical conditions of the atmosphere of the desert "as to increase the fall of rain."[3] The theory was not passed off as nineteenth-century science fiction. Over a decade later a leading Montana newspaper discussed the influence of the rails in detail, asserting that the American nation as a whole had experienced greater rainfall since the rail network had been built. Even England, a humid country, was said to have experienced increasing rainfall since its railroads were constructed; in fact, the country was reported to be receiving so much rain that crops were being damaged rather than helped.[4] A Laramie paper asserted that railroad building, plus cultivation of the soil and the planting of trees, had accomplished the increase of natural moisture in the American West.[5] Dr. William A. Bell, who accompanied the Kansas Pacific surveying party in 1867–68, addressed himself to the question: "As the settlers advance from the East; as they sow corn, plant trees, and open up the soil, will the rainfall increase to any considerable extent?" His answer was affirmative.[6] The theory that "rain follows the plow" was thus introduced, and for nearly two decades it was seriously advanced by homegrown scientists and those who merely wanted to believe.

After completion of the Union Pacific between Omaha and Ogden, the mental advance of the agricultural frontier moved steadily westward from the river in the direction of the 100th meridian. It was usually agreed, at least during the decade of the 1870s, that one hundred was the magic number, beyond which line the land was primarily grazing country. The rule applied to both Kansas and Nebraska. During that decade, as settlement crawled forward, and as settlers furnished proof that crops could be grown successfully, the region of agrarian acceptability west of the river steadily expanded. In 1872 Gen. Randolph B. Marcy fixed the 99th meridian as the desert's border, asserting that when one reached that point "a sudden transformation takes place." Beyond it lay bad water, a treeless plain, and an occasional patch of cultivable ground.[7]

In later years, when farmers on the high plains, particularly those beyond the 100th meridian, found themselves in distress, they lashed out at all possible causes for their plight. One of the reasons given for their difficulty was that they had been enticed westward by railroad advertising, lured beyond the realm of reasonable agricultural possibility, misled by assurances that this was the promised land. In fact, many of them were victims of their own talk, of their own homemade propaganda. The little villages, planted bravely in the lonely land, shouted loudly of their merits and of the wisdom demonstrated by their founding fathers, assuring those who had stayed behind that all was well with them. Their self-justifications were justified in terms of municipal growth, of great agricultural resources, and of economic discoveries that they wished to share with all. They attacked their critics with violence, offering proofs of all kinds that stories about dull times were lies and inventions originated by jealous easterners. In December 1879 there appeared in *The Atlantic Monthly* an article written by a Boston visitor in which the author criticized Kansans for encouraging immigrants at a time when destitute residents of western Kansas were asking for aid to take them through the winter. He thought it ironic that these westerners should advertise their lands as places of competence and comfort to every worker, when those who had the means to do so were fleeing eastward.[8] By the autumn of 1880 between 8,000 and 10,000 settlers in western Kansas were obliged to appeal for food and clothing to take them through the winter.[9]

Kansans struck back, calling the magazine's account one of great exaggeration. "For some unexplained reason," said one western newspaper, "New England people are the most unsuccessful immigrants we have. We have seen several colonies where the failure was complete." The editor suggested that there were fewer practical farmers from New England in his neighborhood than from any other section of the nation.[10] Perched at the western edge of settlement, these people answered every criticism with exaggerations of their own, fearful that their experiment in migration might fail, and concerned that such an event would prove their own venturesome spirits to have been in error. They overlooked these assertions later when accusing others of having lured them into economic disaster in a country too far west for agriculture as they knew it.

The eastern portions of Nebraska and Kansas were not densely populated during the 1870s, but they were much more heavily settled than areas farther west. As the push continued into more arid lands, those who by now might be termed "the establishment," in a political and economic sense, had mixed feelings about the continued advance of the settler. Cities in eastern Nebraska and Kansas were anxious to see their respective states grow, but they were also concerned about the bad name overexpansion might bring to each state. The *Daily Bee,* of Omaha, was a "booster" paper, as most western papers were, but at the same time it was sharply anti-Union Pacific. When northern Nebraska failed to settle up as rapidly as the *Bee* thought it should, editor Edward Rosewater accused the Union Pacific of failing to do its part in advertising. The southern portion of the state, he said, had developed well because immigration there was in the hands of energetic and skillful managers of railroad grants "who set about their work in earnest, of selling their lands in that section first." They did this by resorting "to the use of printers' ink ... and by means of active untiring agents to all parts of the eastern states and of Europe."[11]

Kansas watched its western portion grow with a mixture of pride and parental concern. A Topeka paper was critical of those "interested parties" who haunted seaports, waiting for fresh immigrants to whom they might offer inducements in prairie farmlands. It concerned the editor that these promoters were motivated primarily by individual profit and that they generally took "no account whatever the prospective welfare or disappointment of the intending settlers—their only object being to effect the sale." He suggested the establishment of a state authority to direct the immigration and to keep these innocents away from what he called "inferior places," presumably non-Kansas locations.[12] In Nebraska an official immigration organization had functioned since 1870. Officials and business leaders of both states were increasingly interested in receiving newcomers who were financially responsible. Those who arrived in a near-destitute condition frequently appealed for help, or returned east; in either event the publicity for the new country was bad. In the spring of 1880 a Kansas City paper expressed its pleasure over the prosperous appearance of its most recent immigrants. During April a trainload of 275 people from Pennsylvania passed through the city, having sold their eastern farms, some for figures as high as $45,000, and they intended to invest the money in western Kansas. This was good news to those in the more settled portion of the state.[13]

By 1880 the Union Pacific had sold nearly 2 million acres of lands in its original grant, leaving nearly 10 million yet to be disposed of. The Kansas Pacific lands, now a part of the Union Pacific holdings, had amounted to approximately 6 million acres, a little over 1.5 million having been sold by this date. Remaining lands in the Kansas division, located primarily in western Kansas and in eastern Colorado, were estimated to be worth $2 or $3 an acre. While the Nebraska lands already sold had averaged $4.50 an acre, those in Kansas had brought about a dollar an acre less.[14] Henry Copp, in his pamphlet *The American Settler's Guide,* held that in either case the buyer had a bargain. Land near a railroad at $5 an acre was regarded as cheaper than that selling for $1.25 an acre (the government price) farther from transportation.[15] Although the Union Pacific sold less than 17,000 acres of land in its Kansas division during March of 1880, its agents warned that land was going so fast that good lands would not be in the market very long at the rate immigrants were taking them up. Such a warning came at a time when the company advertised "62,500 fine farms for sale in Kansas at prices and on terms within the reach of all, and easily accessible to the great through line."[16]

As the new decade began, settlers responded to the agricultural opportunities in the plains states. Englishmen could read in the *Illustrated London News* that the fertile and arable lands of Kansas were unsurpassed in quality, and that the climate was delightfully mild.[17] American papers carried the same message, as they had done for nearly 15 years. With better times at hand, and the grasshopper years partially forgotten, the response was heavy. Droves of immigrants arrived at both Kansas City and Omaha, clamoring for passage over the Union Pacific to some new and promised land, ready to go beyond the prescribed limits of agricultural endeavor to gain cheaper farms. "New York and Ohio arrived at the Union depot yesterday en route for suffering Kansas," said the *Kansas City Daily Journal* in a thrust at that state's detractors. "Wednesday was the day for Indiana and Illinois, and today New England arrives." Excursion tickets had been placed on sale for one day in the autumn of 1880 and the crowds that turned up swamped the sellers.[18]

As the advance beyond the 100th meridian continued, a more conservative attitude developed on the part of those who had boomed the westward push. When a correspondent for the *New York Tribune* charged that the difficulties had commenced in 1879, with the "glaring railroad advertisements and glowing descriptions of the country" inducing thousands of innocents out to what he called "the Western frontier line," westerners hastened to admit that this was no place for novices. They shared the writer's dismay when he described the arrival of an Iowa man who had only one dollar left after paying his fees; one dollar, a wife, four little children, and a span of horses with which to start a new life. The journalist's further statement that "what added to their misfortune was that they attempted to farm upon the same principles as in Illinois," found agreement in the West.[19] Already those who had settled upon lands afforded only minimal rainfall had concluded that the old methods would not work, and that where crops would not grow readily livestock should be raised.

Defenders of the agricultural frontier would not, however, agree that cultivation of the soil should generally be abandoned in favor of grazing. A western Kansas paper accused its town rival of adopting "the 100th meridian theory" when it held that only cattle raising could be depended upon in that neighborhood. The editor probably felt vindicated when the purveyor of such gloomy assessments went out of business after only 16 months.[20] In an effort to justify their own judgment, agricultural frontiersmen constantly pointed out that times were changing. Two decades earlier Topeka was said to have been the western limit of cultivation, but only a few years later this line had moved westward to Manhattan or Junction City, in Kansas. Heads had been shaken in doubt when the town of Salina was laid out, but by 1880 local boosters were convinced that their city was

TOP—*This combination sod and lumber structure represents the transition that took place in building as supplies became more available. Taken in Custer County, Nebraska, 1888.*

BOTTOM—*The artist, R. F. Zogbaum, entitled this sketch as "The Modern Ship of the Plains," to indicate the relative ease with which families crossed the great western expanse.*

located "almost in the very heart of the agricultural region of the state, and the mythical line of demarcation between the producing region and the 'Great American Desert' of a few years ago has retreated to near the western line of the state."[21] Admittedly those who were now in the forefront of the farming frontier would experience some reverses, but this was held to be a normal condition in newly developed areas. The venturesome, who advanced bravely to the western edge of Kansas, would prevail if they were patient, promised one newspaper editor. "He who comes and stays will win."[22] Even as he wrote, the rush from Europe continued and Atlantic seaports were kept busy, receiving the newcomers.

In March 1879, approximately 6,000 immigrants passed through the port of New York; in March 1880, the figure soared to over 21,000.[23] Some of these immigrants, mixed with a large number of native Americans, accounted for the sharp increase in rail traffic at Kansas City and Omaha. To accommodate the increased human flow the Union Pacific tried to improve its service. More emigrant cars were built, and sleeping cars, designed to carry this class of travel, were introduced. The ordinary day cars contained benches, without cushions, and were heated by flat-topped stoves with which the passengers also heated their food and drink. At night boards were improvised into bunks upon which the passengers placed their own coats, shawls, or blankets and obtained minimal comfort. The trains moved slowly, yielding the right-of-way to passenger trains, and as a rule nine or ten days travel were required to get from Omaha or Kansas City to the Pacific Coast. In 1879 these people could go from Omaha to Portland for $80, from Kansas City to Denver for $25, and from Omaha to Salt Lake City for $42. One observer called them "fairly comfortable, about equal to the third-class cars in Europe," or about the same accommodation offered steerage passengers aboard ships. The new sleeping cars were equipped with two tiers of double berths on each side of the car, giving a capacity of 48, the passengers to furnish their own bedding. No extra fare was asked for this service. In addition, the road constructed a building known as "the Emigrant House" at Omaha, whose 60 rooms would accommodate up to 200 people. For a small sum the waiting traveler could spend the night; plain but substantial meals were furnished at 25 cents each.[24]

Although such travel facilities were relatively inexpensive and much faster than those of prerailroad days, a considerable number of settlers continued to migrate by wagon. Train passengers often were surprised to look out the windows of their cars and see the familiar covered wagons moving slowly along old and established trails. In the spring of 1881 the editor of a small western Kansas newspaper counted 21 such wagons passing through his town, bound for Oregon. They were muledrawn and well equipped for the long journey; about 75 persons were in the party. In that same period James H. Kyner, a contractor for the Union Pacific, watched such a caravan as it moved along the Oregon Trail in Idaho. "I could see an almost unbroken stream of emigrants from horizon to horizon," he recalled. "Teams and covered wagons, horsemen, little bunches of cows, more wagons, some drawn by cows, men walking, women and children riding— an endless stream of hardy, optimistic folk, going west to seek their fortunes and to settle an empire."[25]

In the early eighties the westward drive continued, as the force of the frontier movement sustained itself and farmers poured onto the high plains, determined to find new homes while the land was yet open to settlement. Despite the recent warning of Maj. John Wesley Powell that the land beyond the 100th meridian was good only for grazing or irrigated farming, the army of plowmen plunged onward.[26] For those who preferred more optimistic reading than the arid prose of Major Powell, there were other writers who spoke in more humid terms. In *Our Western Empire*, L. P. Brockett stated that the Union Pacific and other roads had reconnoitered the plains country and had "made the discovery that these lands were not really a desert, but were capable of yielding excellent crops, and of furnishing superior pasturage to cattle and sheep."[27] Orange Judd, editor of Chicago's widely read *Prairie Farmer,* told his subscribers that all of this was the gospel truth.

A popular Nebraskan, C. D. Wilber, carried his message to western farmers in even stronger and more optimistic terms. In his book *The Great Valleys and Prairies of Nebraska and the Northwest,* he held that "by the repeated process of sowing and planting with diligence the desert line is driven back, not only in Africa and Arabia, but in all regions where man has been aggressive, so that in reality there is no desert anywhere except by man's permission or neglect." Then came the heart of his thesis: "To be more concise. *Rain follows the plow*."[28] So enthusiastic were his followers that a newspaper in Ellis, Kansas, demanded a $2.5 million appropriation from Congress to plow up the entire western end of Kansas. This, said the editor, would put an end to prairie fires, hot winds, and irregular seasons; it would also cause a natural growth of trees, creating a whole forest within a decade.[29]

The spring of 1881 brought a new rush of immigrants to Atlantic ports. Baltimore papers reported new records, with thousands replacing former hundreds; individual ships now commonly brought between 1,000 and 1,500 people per trip.[30] The government directors of the Union Pacific mentioned the human surge across the Missouri River, and commented that it was sufficiently large to cause concern among some of the European governments.[31] Western railroads responded to the situation with widespread advertising. "Are you going West?" asked the Union Pacific. Anyone contemplating a move to western states or territories was advised to correspond with the general passenger agent at Omaha before purchasing tickets from any other railroad. All the inducements and advantages of this line were itemized for prospective settlers.[32] The road's president himself lost no opportunity to help people get to Union Pacific country. When the developer of a proposed colony for Negroes visited Sidney Dillon in July 1881, the executive responded favorably, instructing his representative at Omaha to "take especial pains with him," and if a large tract were sold, it ought to be at a low rate, and the lands should be suitable for cultivation. These blacks may have been part of the "Exodus," as it was called, that had taken them in great numbers up the Mississippi and Missouri rivers, particularly into Kansas, during this period. However, far from representing the impoverished "exodusters," to use the expression of the time, they had plenty of money with which to purchase lands if the colony promoter's word may be taken.[33]

Although immigration into Nebraska continued unabated, Kansas complained that it was not getting its fair share of the immigrant trade. The land commissioner for the Union Pacific's Kansas division, S. J. Gilmore, charged that agents in other states were creating prejudice against that state to entice foreigners to areas of their own interests. Stories of drought, grasshoppers, famine, hail, and tornadoes were used to prejudice prospective settlers. The *Kansas City Daily Journal* denied all, except tornadoes and hail, and of these, said the editor, there were just enough "to remind sinners that there's a day of judgment in store for them."[34] To add insult to injury, the state's new prohibition law was being used among Germans to convince them of the absolute aridity of the Jayhawker country. Coming at a time when whole villages were said to be migrating from Posen, Prussia, and Schleswig to avoid military conscription of their young men, such prejudice against Kansas was regarded as deplorable.[35] The result was a redoubled effort among local boosters.

The desire for an increase in population arose from more practical origins than mere self-justification on the part of those who had come first. Every newcomer shared the expenses of the district school; of state, county, and township taxes; and other municipal costs. So anxious were the small communities for this aid that they tended to frown upon those who were inclined to leapfrog beyond such settlements to the new and unpeopled parts of the West. Editor W. S. Tilton of a WaKeeney, Kansas, newspaper called upon his readers to unite in preventing settlement of the country beyond their town. While he defended western Kansas faithfully, he admitted that there had been destitution in the frontier counties, and to eliminate such difficulty and such bad advertising, he thought the westward movement should pause for regrouping.[36]

Despite warnings by people in more settled communities, the westward push continued. In the autumn of 1881, Colorado's Las Animas *Leader* drew attention to the new railroad town of Coolidge, Kansas, located near the Kansas-Colorado line. With the encouragement of the Union Pacific, a townsite recently had been surveyed, and very shortly lots were bringing favorable prices. The railroad had built a good eating house, and was making other improvements to attract residents.[37]

Other parts of the West now competed with the unsettled portions of Kansas and Nebraska. Both Idaho and Montana boasted of rail service, the Union Pacific's Utah and Northern having been completed in the early eighties. Robert Strahorn, a leading publicist who wrote a great deal for the Omaha office, said that 10 million acres of arable land lay waiting in Idaho's valleys, only one-twentieth of which was occupied. Here, he said, all kinds of fruits and vegetables, as well as such cereal crops as wheat, oats, and barley, could be raised. He spoke also of the great promise for potatoes, of yields up to 200 bushels per acre, and of prices from $2 to $5 per hundred pounds, depending upon the time of year. Beyond the valleys lay mountain rangeland, federal domain that was free from taxes, a new home for thousands of cattle.[38]

Montana newspapers reported on the large immigrant business experienced by railroads running out of Chicago in the spring of 1881, but they complained that the movement seemed to stop short of their territory.[39] The Salt Lake City press, however, stated that all northbound passenger trains of the Utah and Northern were heavily loaded, mainly with settlers bound for new homes in Idaho and Montana.[40] The Union Pacific did its best to encourage such traffic. Round-trip excursion tickets from Omaha to Silver Bow Junction, near Butte, could be had for $108, a sharp reduction in the usual rates. Bona fide settlers could obtain passage for even less, depending upon the size of the group traveling, and they could bring along entire freight carloads of their livestock, machinery, and household goods for $350 per car.[41]

Despite copious and sometimes exaggerated advertising issued by railroads, land promoters, and western newspapers, caution was often urged for those who planned to emigrate from their homes. The grasshopper scourge of the midseventies, and the dry years experienced in western Kansas and Nebraska toward the end of that decade, resulted in calls for aid from the stricken communities. Help was given, but it involved unfavorable publicity for such places. After such experiences western newspapers frequently qualified their assertions by warning the unprepared of the dangers that lay ahead. In L. P. Brockett's descriptive work about the West, published in 1881, the author laid down five basic rules for prospective settlers to consider: No one should come who (1) was beyond 45 years of age; (2) was in poor health; (3) was averse to work or expected an easy life; (4) would give up easily at the first rebuff; or (5) had no capital. He recommended that the immigrant have at least two or three hundred dollars over and above the price of his land. In the West, said Brockett, the stranger would find hard beds, poor cooking (from the want of proper utensils), clothing he would have disdained at home, and a lack of all the conveniences of life he had known. There would be at first no church, school, or post office; and home was apt to consist of a sod hut. After about five years of such Spartan existence the settler could expect improved conditions and at least an approach to the comforts known to other Americans.[42]

During 1882 and 1883 immigration into the Mountain West continued to show an increase, many of the settlers choosing to leapfrog over the "desert" section that lay beyond the 100th meridian. In June 1882 a Montana newspaper reported the arrival of 250 immigrants in a single party, bound for eastern Washington by way of the Utah and Northern road. Most of them came from Iowa, Nebraska, and Kansas, bringing their families, livestock, and farm equipment. Taking advantage of a special emigrant fare of $25 for passage to the end of the Union Pacific's line, and of a charge of only $35 a pair for draft animals, settlers estimated that they had saved at least two months of travel by older methods. In this period they could earn more than the cost of transportation, while their neighbors who chose to come by covered wagon toiled across the plains.[43] Others moved into Colorado, seeking lands along the Union Pacific's Julesburg branch, which had been completed from the main line to Denver in 1881. A contemporary admitted there had been little settlement along the South Platte River until the spring of 1882, but now that a railroad served the region it was beginning to gain attention. While some of this land could be classified as desert, its more westerly reaches were in an area of available irrigation water, and here began an endeavor that would later become widely known for its sugar beet culture.[44]

While the tendency of the homeseekers to take up land beyond the "desert" in the early 1880s was acceptable to the managers of the Union Pacific, provided they settled in what might be termed Union Pacific country, the men of Boston were somewhat disturbed that the region immediately beyond the 100th meridian was not being populated very rapidly. When the Omaha office was asked for details, land commissioner Leavitt Burnham admitted that up to the latter part of 1883 almost no sales had been made west of North Platte, Nebraska, "at which place was the imaginary line dividing the agricultural lands on the East from the grazing lands on the West." There were signs of hope in 1884, when some large tracts were sold in western Nebraska. In a burst of optimism typical of land agents Burnham predicted that this part of the country "by climatic changes—by the operations and experiments of settlers who are entering upon both R.R. and Gov't lands in large numbers—will undoubtedly be soon developed as agricultural lands."[45]

Sidney Dillon, who was soon to give up the presidency of the road, did not share Burnham's opinion that the rainbelt was marching westward. Although his report for 1882 showed that the company had sold nearly 400,000 acres that year, and while his estimation as to the value of remaining lands was phrased in terms designed to please the stockholders, he never had been happy with the land-sale program. The main difficulty in disposing of the road's pastoral lands lay in the checkerboard system under which the company held the alternate sections. Cattlemen wanted large, contiguous holdings where they could run up to 50,000 head of livestock. Unable to buy the government sections as cheaply as they could those of the railroad, the ranchers elected not to buy any. Instead, they simply ran their stock on the holdings of both, paying nothing. The railroad suggested to the government that a trade be made, by which it would hold all the land on one side of the road, the government to receive all of it on the opposite side. Contending that such a transfer would cause endless confusion because titles were already established in some portions, and to deal with each of these owners would be nearly impossible, the road's government directors turned down the idea. As an alternative, it was suggested that the existing laws might be modified to provide for the sale of large tracts of federal land, at low prices, to be used for grazing. Another possibility was that of long-term leases by stockmen. However, either of these courses would tend to shut out those who wanted to take up land under the Homestead, Preemption, Desert Land, or Timber Culture acts.[46]

As the railroad waited for some solution to the problem, it tended to delay large sales in the arid country. Dillon remarked in 1883: "It is a grave question in my mind whether we want to sell any of our desert lands until we know whether the Government will not make some arrangement with us."[47] In the meantime there were decisions to be made, for cattlemen continued to show an interest in expanding their already vast holdings. When his company received an offer for a large tract, at ten cents per acre, Dillon admitted that although such grazing lands were to be disposed of under the best terms possible, "we should hesitate about giving them away entirely."[48]

By this time the railroad had 600,000 acres left for sale in Nebraska "where agriculture is deemed practical," to use the words of the government directors, from which the company hoped to realize an average price of at least $3 an acre. Beyond this lay nearly 8 million acres of grazing land, valued at an average of a dollar an acre. The government directors admitted that although thousands of cattle grazed upon this untilled empire, it yielded almost no returns to the road except in the transportation of beef to market. While these men believed that "there is yearly an undoubted gradual westward extension of the moisture belt, and other climatic changes which must in time include within the agricultural area many of the above designated lands," they admitted freely that "their present and immediate use is only for grazing purposes."[49]

The main hope for a realization of better prices for the railroad's holdings lay in the farmers' age-old desire for more land. By this time a good deal of the company's grant in the first 200 miles beyond Omaha had been sold. A Grand Island newspaper said such property was no longer available in that vicinity and it was diminishing rapidly in nearby counties. The editor advised prospective settlers to buy at once, for "soon the excellent bargains they have afforded will be things of the past, and he who gets a farm will pay well for it."[50] By now land sales were being made in Kansas some 350 miles west of the Missouri River, but no one knew how much deeper farmers could penetrate the desert. Certainly the westward movement would continue, said the government directors of the railroad. It would advance until the character of the soil and the absence of moisture precluded successful cultivation. When that point was reached, irrigation appeared to be the only solution to western aridity. Considering the degree of settlement already effected, these representatives of the government felt that regardless of future developments the nation had benefited greatly from its liberal land grants. "If the corporation has profited by them the country also has been an enormous gainer," they concluded.[51]

Benjamin A. McAllaster, the new land commissioner for the railroad's Kansas division, reported in 1883 that over 10 million acres of government land lay waiting beyond the 100th meridian, but he said it was relatively useless for the farmer who wanted to raise corn or grain on the typical 160-acre homestead. Those who tried often were driven back to their old homes, and from them had come the frightening stories about the desert. It was not the fault of Kansas, he said, but of those who had so foolishly ventured forth.[52] Dillon had agreed that the railroad's real estate in western reaches of the state was of questionable value. In the summer of 1883 he authorized McAllaster to sell 10,000 acres of land near Grinnell at $2 an acre.[53]

Part of the difficulty faced by the Union Pacific in disposing of land in Kansas was its association with the National Land Company, inherited in the consolidation of 1880. This organization was formed in 1867 by the officers of the Kansas Pacific road, and it stayed under their control until 1879. During 1868 the company made a contract with the Kansas Pacific for 200,000 acres of land "to make money for a few," as a Union Pacific official later expressed it. By 1870 its listings had increased to 6,400,000 acres.[54] Allowed to purchase large tracts at a low price, for only ten percent down, the land company was to pay the balance as sales were made. All property unsold after a period of five years was to revert to the Kansas Pacific. As this date drew near, however, the land company conveyed its unsold holdings to Charles B. Lamborn, one of its officers, who in turn disposed of it to prevent forfeiture. At the annual meeting of the National Land Company, in 1882, the Union Pacific gained control by virtue of its majority holdings. The road then refused to distribute cash held by the company which, by 1884, amounted to $131,000.[55] Charles Francis Adams, who was by then president of the Union Pacific, asked his counsel, John F. Dillon, to give him more information about Lamborn's operations. "Who knows anything about the National Land Company, its history, its officers, and methods of procedure?" he asked. "I want to make an investigation of the concern, but do not know where to begin."[56] Dillon assigned the task to Artemus H. Holmes, who reported that "the Land Company was a great fraud upon the Railway Company and that the Railway Company should long since have brought the perpetrators of it to account."[57]

By September 1884, 5.5 million acres of the Union Pacific's original grant had been sold. The sales realized just over $18 million, or an average price of $3.31 per acre. At that time the patented lands were principally in Nebraska and included practically the entire grant for 250 miles beyond the Missouri River.[58] Earlier in the year Burnham had informed the Boston office that sales were "working well westward," and that he was mapping and preparing ranges as far out as Sidney, Nebraska. Shortly, he said, his office would be obliged to deal with the cattle ranges of extreme western Nebraska and eastern Wyoming, at which time the railroad company would have to redefine its policies of disposal. As an indication of the westward pressure, Burnham reported that he was selling lands in western Nebraska at nearly double the price realized a year earlier when many of the buyers were cattlemen. This marginal farmland was averaging $2.40 an acre, but beyond it lay the grazing areas where no more than $1 to $1.50 could be expected.

That the favorable prices were the result of railroad promotion, as well as the natural inclination of farmers to move deeper into the West, was readily admitted by the Union Pacific's land commissioner at Omaha. "The prices we are now receiving for lands from North Platte west can

hardly be said to be justified by anything but *expectations*," he confessed
to Fred Ames, trustee for the land department. In a burst of praise for his
own efforts Burnham explained that "by a system of agencies and advertising,
more effective than I have ever before been able to control, we have worked
up an interest and excitement concerning this part of our territory producing results beyond anything known in this part of the West."[59] However,
whether these "excitements" accounted for great population movements
to the West has been a matter of debate.

In 1884 the Union Pacific actively put its far-western Nebraska lands on
the market, selling to small farmers for prices that ranged from $1.25
to $4 an acre. Within three years an Ogallala newspaper reported that
most of the real estate in that neighborhood had passed into the hands of
actual settlers, some of whom had already realized handsome profits by
resale. By then tracts near the town were bringing $6 to $10 an acre, while
tracts along the line of the road commanded between $4 and $7 an acre.

Prices fell in proportion to the distance from the road. At the inception
of these sales the town was a cattle trail stop, with one hotel, a post office,
two stores, and two saloons. When the railroad offered its lands for sale,
settlers came not only to buy these, but also to take up claims under the
Homestead and Timber Culture acts. The result was a leap in the county's
population from 500 to 7,000 within two years, Ogallala itself having grown
to 800.[60] Of approximately 600,000 people in the state, land commissioner
Burnham estimated that 250,000 were there because of land and emigration
agencies.[61]

Meanwhile, the Kansas agricultural frontier edged forward. A Colby
newspaper noted that the railroad had temporarily withdrawn its lands
from sale so that it might reappraise them at a higher value. The editor
showed no objection, but merely expressed the hope that these farms did
not fall into the hands of speculators.[62] Colby, organized as a town in the
spring of 1885, lay close to the 101st meridian. Although Kansas crops
were poor that year, it was reported that about 1,500 homeseekers per day
arrived in the state during the summer months.[63] By this time land around
Hays, situated less than a hundred miles to the east, was being offered at
between $6 and $9 per acre where, asserted that city's newspaper, there
was plenty of rainfall.[64]

Those who sought justification for the movement deeper into the high
plains country continued to receive verbal support from all manner of
"experts." Major Powell had disagreed with the optimists, or with those
who thought the climate was changing, but many westerners had regarded
his study as merely another government project, one whose findings could
be ignored in the face of burgeoning progress in the West. If one wanted

to find another view in the federal documents, he could examine the report of Joseph Nimmo, made to the Treasury Department in 1885. "It appears to be a well-established fact that in the States of Kansas and Nebraska the limits of the area sufficiently watered by natural rainfall for agricultural purposes has during the last twenty years moved westward from 150 to 200 miles," he told the secretary of that department. As a result of this change the mean annual rainfall was much greater than at the time when the area "was erroneously called the Great American Desert." While he did not say he agreed with it, Nimmo published the statement that there were those who believed railroad and telegraph line construction in the dry area "has tended to increase the amount of rainfall in that region."[65] Readers could reach their own conclusions.

In addition to their efforts in the field of agricultural sales during 1884, Union Pacific land agents made great progress in disposing of large tracts to cattlemen. During February Burnham negotiated with the Ogallala Cattle Company, through A. H. Swan, for the sale of 94,000 acres at $1.50 an acre and for another 125,000 acres with Bratt & Company.[66] During May he was at Cheyenne, ready to open additional large grazing tracts. Here he found some resistance on the part of the cattlemen, but "by positive but courteous action I was able to overcome this and opened sales of some 100,000 acres at $1.00 to $1.50 per acre. . . ." With great optimism he predicted that "I think we shall be able to pretty much sweep the range East of the mountains within 90 days, and I am arranging to move on the west side of Sherman, across Laramie plains etc. as soon as practicable." Burnham promised to keep the average price as near $1.50 an acre as possible, "but some of the poorest and roughest will be well sold in the opinion of local appraisers at $1.00."[67] Before the month was out he reported closing a deal to sell the remaining lands in Lincoln County, Nebraska—some 300,000 acres—at $1.50. If his plans worked out he promised that "we shall be able to practically dispose of everything in Neb. and Col. west to the Wyoming line. . . ." The land agent foresaw sales of $300,000 to $500,000 in the very near future. Sales for May, in round numbers, promised to total $1,200,000. He expected to sell $3,235,000 during the year 1884.[68] In June the Bay State Livestock Company offered to buy 350,000 acres at $1 an acre, but the superintendent at Omaha suggested to Burnham that he hold out for more money. The land commissioner agreed to try. He hoped for a compromise price of $1.25, but if this failed he suggested that the road sell at the offered price.[69] In the end Bay State compromised and offered $1.25.

The country in central and western Wyoming could not always command even $1 an acre. When an offer of 50 cents an acre was made on a tract

Top–*Corn harvest in Norton County, Kansas, during the 1890s. This northwestern county, near the Nebraska line, was once a part of the Great American Desert.*

Bottom–*These farmers are threshing wheat in Ford County, Kansas, about 1894. The famed Dodge City, once a cattle capital, is in the same county. By the 1890s the farmers had taken over.*

of 425,000 acres near Fort Steele, in south central Wyoming, by the Swan
Land and Cattle Company, Burnham called it "a good sale for reasons
that it brings a fair price for a very large quantity of poor lands" that
could not otherwise be easily sold.[70] It was recommended that the railroad
accept an offer of $1 an acre on 575,000 acres of land in the vicinity of
Rock Creek, Wyoming. Admittedly some 100,000 acres of this tract were
worth more, but the rest were rough and barren; therefore the sale, he
thought, would be "a most excellent thing for us."[71]

By the spring of 1885 the Union Pacific had sold a large area in extreme
western Nebraska and eastern Wyoming. Burnham reported, in April, that
the great bulk of the property as far west as Fort Steele, Wyoming, was
"practically disposed of." Lands in the North Platte area, once thought
to be virtually unsalable, were disposed of for $2 an acre, while cattlemen
in Wyoming and northern Colorado had purchased large blocks for prices
ranging downward from $1.25 an acre to 50 cents.[72] Within a year the
principal body of unsold land was confined to an area between Fort Steele
and Evanston, in arid, sagebrush country where only grazing was feasible,
and even this use was doubtful in some parts of this district. Most of it
would sell for $1 an acre or less. By now the original Union Pacific grant
of approximately 11,150,000 acres had been reduced to 3,309,842 acres,
some 800,000 of which were unsurveyed. Thus a little over 2.5 million acres
were available for sale by January 1886, and nearly all of this appeared
to be low-priced land. Burnham recommended a price of 50 cents an acre.[73]

Although railroad officials wanted to dispose of the "desert" lands on
the best terms, how it was done generated complaint at Boston. "My
suspicions have been excited in regard to land transactions in Wyoming,"
wrote Charles Francis Adams in January 1885. While he had no specific
charges, the president was convinced that recent transactions had greatly
sacrificed the interests of the company he represented. Sales of 456,778
acres to the Swan Land and Cattle Company, and of 219,476 acres to
Laramie attorney Stephen W. Downey, trustee, were of particular interest.
"To say the least they were not well considered," Adams commented.[74]
Upon investigation it was reported to the president's office that the
company's land agent at Cheyenne had boasted of a $17,000 personal
profit in the year 1884 alone. Although witnesses said the local representative
was a liar, and one in whom no faith could be placed, there was no concrete
evidence of fraud. Burnham himself was under suspicion for having sold
lands at very low figures, parcels that later realized a great deal of money
from resale. But again, the worst that could be said of him was that he was
guilty of bad judgment.[75]

Burnham was ready to defend his position. Writing to Gardiner M.

Lane, assistant to President Adams, the land commissioner explained that sales in the arid areas, particularly in western Wyoming, were made in large blocks and at low rates to various cattlemen. He saw no other course that might have been pursued, if the company wanted to dispose of its granted acres. Agricultural development in much of this region was in the experimental stage, he asserted, and under the circumstances he had necessarily taken "a more lenient attitude and informal indulgence than would otherwise have been permitted."[76] As he explained in a letter to company attorney Andrew J. Poppleton: "The policy as laid down repeatedly, is as you are aware, that these cheap, rough, waste lands must be sold in large bodies *only* . . . . The Company has never advertised for, or invited, and scarcely *permitted* (except at their own risk) settlers upon this class of lands . . . ."[77] Lane, who investigated the situation personally for Adams, admitted that there was no way to tell from examining Burnham's books if the commissioner had been dishonest. The only way for him to cheat was to recommend a lower price than the market value of the land and take a bribe for doing it. Bribe money obviously would not be entered in the books. He concluded that Burnham was honest, but lacking in both ability and judgment.[78] This did not save the land commissioner. He was replaced by George M. Cumming who took over the land department at Omaha on June 1, 1886.[79]

In 1886 the Union Pacific's efforts to solicit immigration slowed almost to a halt. Since remaining lands were in areas regarded as unsuitable for one-family agriculture there seemed to be no point in spending large sums to induce settlers. As early as the autumn of 1884 Charles Francis Adams had told a Canadian inquirer that his company had no intention of opening an emigration office in Europe because "The lands the Company now has for sale are, as a rule, unfit for agricultural purposes."[80] By this time the movement of westbound settlers through Omaha had slackened. Burnham had kept track of these people during 1885 and reported that 1,230 emigrant teams and 1,030 cars of household goods passed through the city in 1884, a considerable decline from the previous year's figures.[81] Competition by other lines accounted for some of the loss. Superintendent S. R. Callaway advised Adams that if the company was interested in the trade it should upgrade its equipment. "The emigrant business is all leaving us in consequence of the luxurious cars run over the Santa Fe and Northern Pacific roads," he wrote in November 1885.[82]

The new land commissioner did not favor spending money on further promotional efforts. There had been talk in company circles of hiring a commissioner of immigration at $5,000 a year with a budget of $25,000, but Cumming discounted the value of such an investment. He did not believe there was much profit in supporting European emigration offices. "The only desirable and available European settlers are the Scandinavians and Germans," he told Adams. The Mennonites did not appeal to him for they were, he thought, as clannish and repellent to other settlers as were the Mormons, and as "difficult to assimilate as so many Chinese." There was some missionary work to be done in the Midwest, however. The commissioner proposed to send a man into southern Illinois, "where I hear that there is a great deal of discontent and where I hope he will be able to secure a good number of settlers for this company's territory." One of the difficulties in the past, as he saw it, was the inclination of buyers to speculate rather than to settle on the lands themselves. These people tended to gobble up the farmsites before the bona fide settlers discovered their availability.[83] Benjamin McAllaster's methods, on the Kansas division, involved the awarding of a commission ranging from two and a half to five percent. This, said Cumming, ought to be done away with, for it merely encouraged further speculation and a constant turnover of land that never saw the plow.[84] Cumming also opposed the establishment of a company literary bureau. He thought his department could provide midwestern newspapers with sufficient information and effect a program that might be augmented by giving passes to the leading men of key towns.[85]

Henry W. Rothert, who made an investigation of the land department for Adams in 1886, tended to agree with Cumming. Rothert said there were two distinct classes of purchasers: (1) parties who bought lands for their own use whether they were small farmers or large cattle ranchers; and (2) those who bought for speculation only. Cattlemen, he said, sometimes represented both classes; they used the land and occasionally speculated with it, selling off tracts at opportune times. Promoters admittedly sold to people who actually settled, but since they worked on a commission basis they tried to make large sales. Rothert thought more recognition ought to be given to the man who brought in large numbers of settlers on smaller pieces of land.[86]

Despite poor crops in 1887 settlers continued to press westward. During a three-month period 83,000 acres of government land were taken up in a single Nebraska county. As one writer put it, the rush was so heavy that land-office statistics sounded like fables.[87] The newcomers were greeted by weather so unfavorable that by the following spring the businessmen of Ogallala, Nebraska, were obliged to raise a fund of $200 to buy seeds for those who had experienced a complete crop failure.[88] In Kansas the Union Pacific offered to forego the collection of debt principal on lands sold if the purchaser would pay his interest and taxes.[89] Two weeks of unusually dry weather in August had so damaged the corn crop of Nebraska that prospects for the line's branches in the hard-hit areas were called very poor. Adams confessed that the drought was expensive. "This is the case with all Kansas and Nebraska properties," he commented.[90]

As always, the outlook early in the new year was better, but in July 1888 the hot winds returned and foliage withered. The resulting unfavorable publicity cost the company dearly, said C. J. Smith, who had replaced Cumming in the land office. Sales that had reached 30,000 acres a month dropped to 5,000 or less. Good crops prior to 1887 had paved the way for land agents who had been obliged to use very little advertising. "Now it requires good advertising, a great deal of it," he admitted, "and hard work on the part of our agents to arouse any interest in Kansas lands. . . ." During 1887 the total sales for all the railroad's divisions amounted to 573,864 acres; in 1888 the figure plummeted to 145,899.[91] Meanwhile, Smith advised that the more arid and yet unsettled lands in far western Kansas and in Colorado be leased to cattlemen until such time as the property could be sold for better prices. He thought a wait of at least three years would be necessary. His argument was supported by the fact that the land sales of 1888, although much lower in terms of acres, brought better average prices. Part of the reason was that much of the land sold lay in the agricultural districts of Nebraska, and that in Kansas was what Smith called "picked lands," or farms sold to actual settlers, as opposed to speculators.[92] Smith approved of picked land sales, for they tended to settle the country more rapidly. He recommended a liberal rebate for actual settlement and proof of cultivation. The railroad's executive committee had passed a resolution in November 1888 allowing the land commissioner to grant a rebate of 20 percent of the purchase price for every acre broken and cultivated within two years of the sale. Smith agreed this was a good thing, but he thought it did not go far enough. He estimated that it cost about $2.50 an acre to break land, and to induce settlers to spend such money he recommended rebates on the second and third payments made by the farmers so that they might more quickly recover money they had invested.[93] Where the lands were useful only for grazing he was willing to sell at low prices, provided the property had been thoroughly examined first for mineral resources. His sensitivity about mineral deposits arose from the fact that the Union Pacific had been obliged to buy back from the Swan Land and Cattle Company some Wyoming coal land it had so readily disposed of at 50 cents an acre.[94]

By the early summer of 1888 agent Smith concluded that lands in extreme western Kansas had been placed on sale too soon. Settlers, in search of cheaper farms, tended to bypass more easterly areas, with the result that over 100,000 acres lay vacant in Ellis and Russell counties.[95] Western

Kansans agreed with him that the road had pushed too far, too fast. The resultant boom, said one newspaper, "violated Nature's laws by seeking to build up this region too rapidly." This abuse of nature, and the work of "dishonest land agents," were regarded as being detrimental to those who lived in more arable parts of the state. The editor called for a newspaper crusade against "fool booming," a program he termed a holy war waged to save the populated part of the West.[96] Nebraskans agreed, arguing that much of the land was controlled by absentee owners who did not cultivate it, but instead they waited for it to rise in price so that they could profit from their investment. An Ogallala newspaper editor held that but one acre in ten in his county was owned by actual settlers and perhaps one in a hundred was under cultivation. His city, a place of about 1,000 people, wanted farmers who would make the neighboring lands productive and profitable.[97]

The railroad's land department took the same view as that of westerners: Better years would solve the problem. Agent Smith expressed this hope in a letter to Charles Francis Adams, admitting that if the situation did not improve a good many of those people who had arrived recently would give up their contracts and return to the East.[98] That the wait for better times would be longer than anyone expected is seen in a comment made by an Ogallala, Nebraska, editor two years later, in the spring of 1891. He said that the state board of relief had exhausted its resources and would not be able to send farmers any more immediate aid. However, that agency would furnish what seed it could—about $5 worth per person—so that farmers could plant a crop and make another try at surviving in western country.[99]

As the decade of the nineties neared, the Union Pacific realized that the active years of its land disposal program were ending. Most of the granted lands in Nebraska and Kansas were by now in the hands of farmers or owned by land companies which hoped to sell to such people. Colorado lands that lay along the base of the mountains also had sold well, but the more arid country to the east as well as the western fringes of Kansas were as yet unsettled. A little more than half the company's offerings in Wyoming had been disposed of, in most cases to cattlemen, and about three-quarters of its property in Utah was still available to purchasers.[100]

The availability of moisture, through natural or artificial means, generally accounted for the spread of agricultural settlement throughout Union Pacific country. Farmers penetrated the country as deeply as they dared, and in some cases they even ventured beyond that limit. Cattlemen utilized regions regarded as marginal for purposes of cultivation and thus accounted for many sales that otherwise would not have been made. The reluctance to move into Utah, despite its activity in railroad building, apparently arose from the agricultural undesirability of company lands as well as the difficulties posed by the so-called "Mormon question." However, despite various difficulties the road managed to sell a large percentage of its arable acres; a great deal of that remaining continued to be regarded as marginal for farming purposes in the year that lay ahead. By June 30, 1889, some 13 million acres of a total grant amounting to 19 million had been sold for $31,325,294 in cash and $11,661,676 yet outstanding. The average price per acre on the Union division was $2.54; for the Kansas division, $3.78; and for the Denver division, $4.26.[101]

Although the Union Pacific still had farmsites for disposal to settlers, the main force of its agricultural advance into the American desert was spent by 1890. Three years later, as Frederick Jackson Turner was telling his colleagues about the closing of the American frontier, a brief history of Nebraska appeared on the market in which the author said of that portion of the West: "In the midst of this seemingly hopeless sterility Nebraska . . . sprang up and put to shame the ancient desert myth, forever casting out the grim specter from her fruitful borders."[102] The state, said another, "so recently on the frontier of the 'Far West' is now quite central."[103] Through its settlement policy the Union Pacific had played a prominent role in peopling a country long believed to be useless for tillers of the soil. It led the way in rolling back the "desert" in its part of the West and was one of the major contributors to the destruction of an American myth.

Picket Line of Civilization

During the two decades that followed the building of the Union Pacific, the American public watched the further growth of this and other roads with continued fascination. Over the main lines rolled thousands of passengers and untold tons of freight; along the spreading branches filtered settlers, bound for freshly opened lands and a new life. In consequence of the westward movement by rail, cities sprang up, states were created, and maps of the West underwent constant alteration.

These were dramatic and tangible changes that could be translated into impressive statistics. But often obscured by the clouds of steam, the shrieks of whistles, and the rush to subdivide the virgin prairie was the enormous change that occurred on what has been termed the Indian-military frontier. The "old" army, scattered across a land of giant distances, and fragmented into ineffectual units, was transformed by the introduction of modern transportation. The very frontiers that it had formerly guarded were at once made more accessible to troops and less dangerous to settlers by this connection with the outside world. The same railroad that shuttled soldiers back and forth and supplied their needs also brought in hordes of settlers whose very numbers forced the Indians to relinquish their lands.

Lack of an efficient and inexpensive form of transportation had barred the way to earlier settlements in the trans-Missouri West. So had it complicated the role of the military in "subduing" that region. Army men were among the first to discover the high cost of supplying a population in remote areas, a discovery that was accentuated by the acquisition of the Southwest following the Mexican War. Then, a few years later, with the development of mining in the West, came new demands for "protection" against the Indians. Within a few years military requirements in the West soared, and along with them came unheard-of demands for appropriations.

During the early post-Civil War years Congress was asked to furnish more than $5.5 million annually to supply troops in New Mexico and Arizona alone, a figure that did not include the cost of Indian agencies, the transportation of mail, or of supporting territorial government.[1] The quartermaster general reported disbursing $3,314,495 for Colorado military establishments in the year 1866.[2] But change was in the air. Within two years the *Cheyenne Leader* stated that the average cost of government transportation on the completed section of the Union Pacific Railroad was ten and one-half cents per ton-mile, and that in a single year the road had saved the government nearly $2 million. "Goods are now brought from Omaha to this city at a saving of at least two-thirds of the amount formerly paid for wagon rates of transportation," said the journal.[3]

Transportation costs, of course, comprised a substantial portion of western prices. The army, as well as the civilian population, felt this keenly. During the winter of 1865–66, for example, the garrison at Fort Sedgwick, Colorado, and the residents of nearby Julesburg, paid $105 per cord for wood, a price set by a government contract. The wood was purchased in Denver for about $20 a cord; the charge for haulage added some $60 to $75; and the remainder was profit realized by the contractors. Users demanded and got an investigation, but it was the advent of rail service that shattered this price structure. Wood fuel was not only cheaper, but very shortly coal was available from the Wyoming beds.[4] The *Leader* called the railroad one of the best investments ever made by the United States, for it not only reduced prices but provided a key to the development of a country that was destined to remain in its native condition until such facilities were available.

Viewing the newly completed road in 1869 the Committee on the Pacific Railroad studied a compilation of governmental military expenditures for the preceding 37 years and concluded that the Indian wars during that period had cost the nation 20,000 lives and more than $750 million. During 1864 and 1865 the quartermaster's department spent over $28 million for military service against the Indians in the country through which transcontinental service was planned. The chairman of the House Committee on Indian Affairs estimated that current expenses for military campaigns against the natives were running up to a million dollars a week. Nine weeks of such campaigning would cost as much as the interest on a sum necessary to build additional lines to the Pacific Coast. The committee concluded that not only were the roads an economy to be felt immediately, but their existence would replace the buffalo with cattle and grain fields, thus effecting a "final solution" to the problem of the hostile tribes.[5]

In addition to the money that could be saved by the War Department, the railroad promised to greatly simplify the logistical problem of the western army. William Tecumseh Sherman, under whose command the plains country fell, commented in 1867 that the railroads "aid us materially in our military operations by transporting troops and stores rapidly across a belt of land hitherto only passed in summer by slow trains drawn by oxen, dependent on the grass for food; and all the States and Territories west have a direct dependence on these roads for their material supplies." He predicted that when the lines passing westward through Nebraska and Kansas reached the Rockies, and when the Indian title to the country lying between was extinguished, then the problem of Indian hostilities would be comparatively easy, for "this belt of country will naturally fill up with our own people who will permanently separate the hostile Indians of the north from those of the south, and allow us to direct our military forces on one or the other at pleasure . . . ."[6]

Captain Eugene F. Ware, who had campaigned along the Platte River in 1864, later wrote: "Soon the Union Pacific Railroad was built, and the Indian problem was solved."[7] By this overly simplified statement he meant that Sherman's prediction had come true; that the Union Pacific, in Nebraska, and what was later known as the Kansas Pacific, in Kansas, formed a long steel fence which cordoned off a vast belt of land running between the Missouri River and the Rockies. Into it poured settlers who drove off the buffalo, fenced the land, and made life untenable for the tribes. It was as though a huge snowplow had wedged its way west, turning Indians to either side. While this did not occur as easily or as quickly as Ware's comment suggested, it nevertheless proved to be the ultimate course of events.

Those who anticipated the settlement of the West regarded the railroad as a key instrument for cutting away the barriers that blocked the way. As construction began in 1865, a Saint Louis paper foresaw a "settlement of the Indian troubles and difficulties" resulting from the project. In a statement that characterized much of the thinking of the time, the paper argued that the money spent in placating the peaceful Indians and fighting the hostiles would alone be sufficient to build the road. Given easy, safe, and cheap passage, the settlers would flow westward in great numbers, creating new states and diluting the Indian danger as time passed.[8] A Chicago paper took much the same point of view, asserting that the railroad builders were performing a more effective service in preventing Indian depredations than the entire army could accomplish by more direct methods. The editor predicted that an "All conquering civilization will be borne upon the wings of steam to the uttermost parts of the western plains, preparing the way for safe and rapid settlement by white men, and compelling the savages to either adopt civilization or suffer extinction."[9] A contemporary writer used this same theme when he predicted that the locomotive's whistle would announce the coming of an "aggressive civilization" which would force the natives into a last stand for barbarism, a battle they would lose against sheer force of numbers, leaving them no alternatives but submission or death.[10] The Secretary of the Interior, who understood the force of the westward movement, agreed that the railroad had indeed placed Indian-White relations in what he termed "a new and interesting aspect," one that he thought demanded the concentration of Indians upon reservations to save them from annihilation.[11] It was out of this thinking that the great reservations of the northern plains finally were established.

Arguments by the white population of the West, that the railroads would aid the army in "solving" the Indian problem, were not lost upon the natives. Many of them objected to the appearance of the "fire wagon" —their name for the steam locomotive—because they feared its power and were mystified by its noisy functioning. But the more thoughtful Indian leaders foresaw that its ultimate effect would be detrimental to their people.

Even though there were large numbers of Indians on the plains, it was difficult for their leaders to organize a great fighting force to campaign any distance from the home country. The powerful and capable Sioux, who would long resist white encroachments, could have given the rail builders much more trouble than they did had the railroad's threat seemed more immediate. Only small parties, therefore, tended to harass surveyors and later the rail layers as they moved westward along the Platte River. Union Pacific officials objected to such sniping and continually asked for more military protection. In the spring of 1867 Thomas C. Durant told General Grant that such raids were interfering seriously with surveyors who were trying to lay out the line in what is now Wyoming. He warned that unless the Indians could be kept away from these men there was a danger that surveying would have to be suspended.[12] Samuel Reed, one of the railroad's engineers, admitted that the natives were decidedly hostile, and that "some men have been killed and a large amount of stock lost." However, he said, the attacks merely had caused delays, not a work stoppage.[13] A government director of the Union Pacific, T. J. Carter, also spoke of the matter but he, too, used terms no stronger than "embarrassment" as opposed to language that suggested any possibility of abandoning the project.[14]

Most of the attacks were raids executed by roving bands of Indians who frequently picked off isolated individuals or very small groups of workers. For example, Nebraska papers carried a story in May 1867 that described the killing of an engineer from one of the surveying parties at work in Wyoming. Significantly the Indians did not attack the party itself, or its military escort, but swooped down upon two men who had separated them-selves from the group, killing one of them.[15] In another instance, a stage-coach carrying a single passenger was attacked, but there were no casualties.[16]

Occasionally Indians became bolder and fought with working parties, but no great numbers on either side were involved in the incidents. One of the most publicized of these events was the foray near Plum Creek in August 1867, in which several men were killed. In this instance the Indians used tools left by section hands who were preparing track a few miles west of present Lexington, Nebraska, to remove spikes and bend the rails sufficiently to derail any train that made its way along the road. The Indians had cut the telegraph line and half a dozen men had been sent out by handcar to discover why messages had ceased to flow along the line. When their vehicle hit the roadblock and spilled its occupants, 40 Indians came out of the tall grass and launched an attack. At the height of the action a freight train of about 25 cars came along and it, too, was wrecked, killing the engineer and fireman. The conductor, who was injured, ran back to Plum Creek and spread the alarm. The next day a group of armed civilians returned to the scene and found the Indians still celebrating by riding around the site with streamers of calico, taken from the wreckage, tied to the tails of their horses, while others attended to two barrels of whiskey that had been part of the cargo. When the leader of the celebrants was picked off by the first shot fired, his followers promptly fled, and the rescue party set about cleaning up the wreckage. One of the workers lived to tell the tale, even though he had been scalped. Retrieving his hairpiece, he had it tanned and carried it around later to show, and to horrify, his acquaintances.[17]

The Plum Creek affair was more bizarre than most of the raids against the road. But the Union Pacific could not call for additional troops or criticize the government for its lack of protection, because the road itself was at fault for sending out such a small party when Indians were known to be in the area. Andrew J. Poppleton, a company attorney, admitted that this was the case when he later discussed the claims for damages that had arisen out of the event. He told President Oliver Ames that a suit involving $9,000 in claims for property lost by shippers probably would go against the road, due to its own negligence. Laconically he noted that the matter undoubtedly could be settled for 50 cents on the dollar, and he recommended that such a course should be followed.[18]

Complaints concerning Indian harassments increased during 1868. During that year, as the workers moved across western Nebraska and ap-proached Cheyenne, their isolation was more apparent to wandering bands of Indians, who rarely attacked unless the odds were right. The *Cheyenne*

Leader complained periodically, asserting that the government had granted lands for railroad construction for the purpose of opening and developing the western country, and it should protect those who had answered the call. It was perfectly clear to the editor that the railway and Indians could not exist together. "One of them must relinquish," he insisted. "If the railroad is to succeed, the Indian must retire, but if the Indian is to rule, there can be neither railway nor settlements."[19]

Late in April a mass meeting was held at Cheyenne to complain about the government's laxity in protecting the rail route, at which time a committee was appointed to memorialize Congress on the subject. Anticipating the arrival of General Sherman, on one of his inspection tours, residents called for yet another meeting to discuss the matter with him. Without giving any figures, the editor of the *Leader* assured his readers that between their city and North Platte the Indians were said to be thicker than fiddlers in Hell. He bitterly criticized the "feeble, listless opposition offered by the U.S. troops" and predicted that all-out war was an immediate prospect for those unfortunate enough to live in the region.[20] In response to the complaints Sherman promised that Generals Alfred Terry and Christopher C. Augur would protect the Union Pacific "with jealous care," and that they would round up all the roving bands of Sioux in the region, after which these Indians would be herded northward to reservations where they would be fed by the army.[21]

While Sherman's comments were formal and he seemed unconcerned about the situation, nevertheless his interest in the project was real and of long duration. He argued that although the Union Pacific was in private hands it had more than the usual claim for protection because of the government's pecuniary interest in the work. General Christopher Augur reported to his superiors in 1868 that he had placed detachments of troops at every station between Fort Kearny and Cheyenne, plus some at Forts Sanders and Steele in Wyoming.[22] When more soldiers were needed Frank North organized four companies of Pawnee Indian scouts, 50 men to a company, to patrol the line. As his brother, Luther, commented, the tribes knew the road meant the extinction of their way of life and they resented it.[23] However, despite sporadic raids, the Indians were not a major problem or a real deterrent to construction crews. General Augur stated that the precautions taken by the army prevented any serious interference with construction during 1868.[24] Editors and worried residents of towns along the road did not share his viewpoint. To them, even the smallest interruption in this great work could not be tolerated.

Before the Union Pacific reached Promontory it began to influence both the Indians and the disposition of troops in the West. In August 1868 posts were abandoned along the Bozeman Trail, which ran along the Big Horn Mountains and into Montana. The action is still heralded by pro-Indian historians as a great victory for the Sioux and as a great defeat for the army. As Sherman correctly pointed out, those posts—built in 1865 and 1866 for the benefit of travelers to Montana—"had almost ceased to be of any practical use to them by reason of the building of the Union Pacific railroad . . . ." The trail never had been used by any regularly organized freight lines; rather, it was fortified in response to heavy pressure for a shortcut into the mining country. The route north of the Utah communities was much shorter, and along it lived Indians less hostile than the Sioux. While the army was capable of keeping open the Bozeman Trail, the expense of doing so, considering the traffic it bore, was needless.[25] Some of the troops formerly stationed at forts in that area were transferred to Fort Steele, in Wyoming, and the rest were sent back to Omaha. It was here that the economy effected by the road was demonstrated. General Augur reported that it was now cheaper to winter the soldiers at Omaha than to build and supply new quarters in the more remote West.[26] Should the occasion arise, detachments could be sent forth by rail at any time of year.

Upon the completion of the Kansas Pacific to Denver, in 1870, Gen. John Pope remarked: "It becomes practicable, therefore, to conduct military operations with facility over the larger part of this department [of the Missouri], to receive immediate intelligence, and to concentrate troops rapidly." He heartily endorsed the new campaign-by-rail policy.[27]

General Pope's reference to the new mobility afforded the soldiers was not lost upon the Indians, who were impressed by the speed and efficiency of the railroads. In 1879, at the time of the Ute uprising in Colorado, troops were moved in from both east and north to help quell the disturbance, and during that operation a small incident occurred which went almost unnoticed among the more exciting events of the day. Passengers on a southbound Utah and Northern train noticed two rifle-carrying Indians come aboard, and upon inquiry as to their destination the warriors said they were headed for Salt Lake City where they planned to take the Union Pacific eastward to some point in Wyoming, from which place they planned to join the Colorado Utes in their struggle with the bluecoats. Apparently no move was made to halt these reinforcements, and contemporary newsmen expressed amusement at the resourcefulness of the natives in utilizing modern facilities in moving to the front.

General Sheridan reported in 1869 that elements of two cavalry and three infantry regiments were stationed at strategic points on the road from Omaha Barracks to Camp Douglas, near Salt Lake City.[28] During the years that followed, smaller posts continually gave way to larger and more permanent bases. Recognizing that such establishments not only offered protection, and hence encouraged settlement, but were also of economic value, Denver called loudly for consideration. A local editor asked for a large depot to supply the military posts in Colorado and neighboring communities, arguing that it was not only necessary and economical, but also that "our people have a right to some of the patronage of the government."[29]

Although the spread of rail transportation lessened governmental expenses over known routes, it tended to push the frontiers of settlement outward, generating new demands for protection. In 1870 Secretary of War William Belknap admitted that the railroad across the plains had saved the American people much money, but "with the opening to settlement of the wilder portions of the country, army posts are pushed further and further into the wilderness, and as the stations are extended the expenses of transportation are and will remain very great."[30] This, however, was part of America's westward expansion, and the railroad made possible such growth. As new posts were required in more remote areas, older forts nearer the tracks were broken up and abandoned. Troops would continue to be stationed near the Union Pacific for only a few more years. As settlers poured in and towns grew and a white population bulked large in the land, the Indians moved back.

In the autumn of 1872 Gen. Philip Sheridan noted the rapid expansion of rails and said that no additional protection had been necessary for the Union Pacific or the Kansas Pacific during the year. Already the roads had begun to have their effect on the central plains. The deeper thrust into unsettled areas, mentioned by Secretary Belknap, was made possible by the entering wedge driven through Nebraska and Kansas. The frontier movement, which had moved forward for over 200 years, now gathered momentum; soon it would break into a gallop. Before long the Northern Pacific would accelerate its lateral drive through the Dakotas and Montana, bringing many more farmers into Indian country. In 1872 Commissioner of Indian Affairs Francis A. Walker predicted that this development "will of itself completely solve the great Sioux problem, and leave ninety thousand Indians ranging between the two transcontinental lines as incapable of resisting the Government as are the Indians of New York or Massachusetts." He predicted that army columns moving north from the Union Pacific and south from the Northern Pacific would crush the Sioux and their allies "as between the upper and nether millstones."[31] He was correct. However, the theory that such events would completely solve the Sioux problem was true only from the white man's point of view.

During 1877 Union Pacific officials talked of building a branch across Wyoming and into Montana. General George Crook, then commanding the Department of the Platte, with headquarters at Omaha, gave his enthusiastic endorsement. Such a plan would "have a most salutary and positive effect in settling our Indian troubles," said the general.[32] The government directors of the Union Pacific agreed with Crook, holding that wherever railroads went "the Indian question is practically settled."[33]

Among the generals, none seemed to be more impressed by the rapid settlement of the railroad West than Phil Sheridan. In 1878 he called the emigration to Kansas unparalleled, while Nebraska, Colorado, Utah, and Wyoming were "not far behind in acquiring population." He estimated that 2 million settlers had recently spread across the plains and mountain areas from Texas to Montana, where they were busily engaged in farming, mining, and ranching. From their efforts, including that of town-building, had emerged a whole new segment of the American economy, "and the millions obtained by the sweat of their brow adds much more to trade, commerce, and prosperity of the world." His wonderment grew and he concluded that "all this comes from the development of a country which only ten years ago was the land of the Indian, the buffalo, and the elk."[34]

In 1882, as Sheridan watched the Utah and Northern enter Montana he commented that this and similar extensions of main lines not only developed new country, but the process also wrought a change in the western army. He reiterated the conviction that this additional service made more obvious the desirability of abandoning small posts and concentrating the men in larger units. At the large garrisons the discipline was better, as were the daily living conditions. "I have already selected points with a view to such a concentration," he wrote, "as soon as the condition of Indian affairs will admit of the withdrawal of troops from the more remote places."[35]

The general was aware of his own great enthusiasm for railroads in the West, and he was almost apologetic for constant references to it in his reports. But, as he explained in one of them, this new instrument of steel was already a great factor in reshaping military strategy on the high plains, and its use was regarded as being of prime significance in the solution of the army's most urgent current problem—the American Indian.[36]

General Pope also recommended the policy of concentrating troops at larger posts. In 1879 he suggested the elimination of several smaller outposts, as they no longer fulfilled any important military objective. For example, he said, Forts Larned and Hays, in Kansas, and Fort Lyon, in Colorado, had by now outlived their original usefulness because of the coming of the railroad. The country in which they had been located originally as defensive positions was now so well settled that there was little likelihood of any successful Indian uprisings in those parts. Such places were, to use Pope's words, "out of position"; that is, they were so far away from potential Indian trouble it would be difficult to transport their garrisons to areas where trouble was apt to occur.[37] George W. McCrary, Secretary of War, agreed that the revolution of the rails had left the War Department with a large number of useless military reservations. The advance of settlement had converted what were once vital military sites into property that had become "simply a source of expense to the United States."[38]

Sherman, who now held the rank of General of the Army and was its senior officer, read the reports of his subordinates with great interest. Having followed the progress of railroad construction since the laying of the first Union Pacific rails at Omaha, he was perhaps the greatest rail enthusiast among army men. More than once he had recalled with pride that the Union Pacific's first locomotive had borne his name, and he was aware that the little 22-ton engine had made history on the plains of Nebraska. By 1880 the general, who was nearing retirement age, had concluded that western railroads had "completely revolutionized our country in the past few years." He agreed with the findings of his subordinates that these roads had wrought a complete change in the plains military situation. Sherman supported the recommendation that many of the small posts which once had guarded wagon and emigrant routes should be abandoned in favor of larger establishments. He suggested that the new forts might well be located at intersections of railroads, to make them as versatile and ready for trouble as possible, and that some of them be near the nation's borders.

The "revolution" of which Sherman spoke had so thoroughly met the problems of internal protection that future fortifications would fall more into the category of national defense than they had at any other time since the founding of the nation.[39] His beliefs coincided with those of the journalist Albert Richardson, who had earlier talked of the role of the railroads in national defense and had labeled the locomotive as "the true apostle of the Monroe Doctrine."[40]

As Sherman viewed the nation's newer defensive posture and what had taken place since the conclusion of the Civil War, he saw significant changes. In an earlier day the trans-Missouri West was, to use his words, "occupied by wild beasts, buffalo, elk, antelope and deer, and by wilder Indians." But now, as a result of railroad development, this vast region had been reduced to a state of "comparative civilization." "Three great railroads now traverse the continent, with branches innumerable, and a fourth is making rapid progress," he wrote. "States, Territories, cities, and towns have grown up; neat cattle have already displaced the buffalo; sheep and goats have replaced the elk, deer, and antelope; and crops of wheat, rye, barley, and oats are now grown in regions believed hitherto to be desert or inaccessible." This advance of settlement and this taming of the land, he said, "is the real cause of the great prosperity which now blesses our country and swells the coffers of our national Treasury."[41]

Nor was the nation the only beneficiary. The army itself, thought Sherman, faced a new and happier day because of the technological advance provided by rail service. For years western assignments had meant privation and even suffering for both officers and enlisted men. Sherman, himself a hardened campaigner of many years, had seen the conditions under which his troops lived in these remote posts, and he reacted strongly to the situation. During one of his inspections, in 1866, he stopped at Fort Sedgwick, in eastern Colorado, and after examining the men's quarters the general called them "hovels in which a negro would hardly go," adding that if Southern slaveholders had kept their field hands in such quarters "a sample would, ere this, have been carried to Boston and exhibited as illustrative of the cruelty and inhumanity of the masters."[42] But by the early eighties, thanks to rail service, said Sherman, many of these posts were being abandoned and the men were being stationed at places where living conditions were much superior, where schools were available, and where the constant effort merely to keep alive no longer dominated daily life. Gone, too, were many of the long marches across arid stretches. "Now almost every post in the Army has railroad communication near, with mails, and connection by telegraphy to all parts of the world," he wrote. "In my judgment, the condition of the Army, officers and men, is incomparably better and more comfortable than it was twenty years ago." With all these advantages, thought the old general, army life would be sufficiently attractive to encourage enlistments by a larger and better group of men.[43]

From the earliest days of Union Pacific construction the army had looked forward to the development of railroads as an answer to many of its western problems. As construction crews of various roads spread their iron network across the barrenness beyond the Missouri River, there developed a warm relationship between railroaders and military men. Although the land-grant roads were obliged to carry government traffic at half rate—and during the 1870s the Secretary of the Treasury withheld even this amount pending the outcome of litigation over the matter—the roads cooperated with military officials. Not only did they provide transportation on regularly scheduled trains, but special service was available for any emergency. For example, in the autumn of 1879 Sidney Dillon directed his general manager at Omaha to carry soldiers immediately to any point on the line when the situation demanded it. "The resources of the road are at the service of the Government for the protection of the settlers," he wrote.[44]

The War Department went to great lengths to show its appreciation for such ready cooperation on the part of the Union Pacific and other land-grant roads. In 1878, after the government had for several years withheld money due land-grant railroads for transportation, the Secretary of War intervened in behalf of the roads. He argued that Congress had "greatly embarrassed" the operations in his department and he strongly recommended that the legislators rescind their actions, thus allowing the roads to collect money due on military accounts.[45] Although the legislators failed to respond to the request, and the matter was later settled in favor of the roads through court action, the secretary's gesture was appreciated by the companies involved.[46]

For the first seven years of rail service on the Union Pacific alone, beginning in July 1866, the government had spent slightly over $5 million for the haulage of troops and supplies. The cost of wagon transportation over the same routes was estimated at nearly $16 million. Troops were carried by rail at approximately five cents a mile (through rates), compared with 12½ cents by stagecoach. The average rate for through freight, by rail, was 19 cents a hundred pounds per hundred miles; by wagon this would have ranged from $1.45 to $1.99 for the same distance. Here the government had saved an estimated $6 million.[47] Since a number of military posts that existed during the 1870s and 1880s did not have rail service but were served by stagecoach and wagon, the War Department had dramatic comparisons in transportation costs available for each annual report. In 1873, for example, American railroads carried nearly 73,000 military personnel, compared with approximately 2,000 transported by wagon and stagecoach. Most of the military using the older method of travel were in the West, where rail service at that time was in its infancy. In that year the Union Pacific carried just under 6,200 military passengers.[48]

Although the figures rose during the ensuing years, due to new construction, so did the statistics for horsedrawn vehicles. As late as 1880 the quartermaster general reported that the army had 45 contracts for wagon transportation, and this method had been used during the preceding year to carry over 4,000 passengers and nearly 32,000 tons of supplies.[49] Despite such an increase in wagon haulage, the great proportion of military traffic was by rail. In 1882, for example, the Union Pacific alone carried approximately that much army freight, while other roads hauled a proportionate amount. In that year the Union Pacific also transported nearly 12,000 military personnel and over 4,000 animals.[50]

Not only were new areas opened to settlement by the advent of rail service, but a good deal of country was occupied beyond its reach, in anticipation of its arrival. The army, therefore, was obliged to provide protection for an increasing number of communities that grew up in more remote regions; and until railroads reached them, transportation was of the horsedrawn variety.

In 1883 the picture began to change considerably. Both the Northern Pacific and the Santa Fe had completed their main lines, opening vast sections of the West. The Denver and Rio Grande connected Salt Lake City to Denver in the same year, while only months earlier the Utah and Northern had been finished from Salt Lake City to connect with the Northern Pacific in Montana. With the completion of these and other principal western roads, such as the Southern Pacific, the country beyond the Missouri River soon was interlaced with trunk and branch lines that served a large part of what so recently had been a barren land. General Pope called this rapid spread of railroads "one of the wonders of this western country," saying that it seemed to progress without cessation. He predicted that "it will be but a short time before the whole region will be a network of railroads, and all Indian reservations of Indian country will be so easy of access from them that troops can be concentrated so soon that any hostilities on a large scale can be dealt with almost as soon as begun."[51]

By the late 1880s the so-called Indian wars were practically ended, and only the final death struggle of the tribes remained to be enacted during the next few years. Already an era had passed; not only were there no "wild" Indians to be seen along that great swath the Union Pacific and Kansas Pacific had cut westward across the plains, but even the military forts that had once protected the roads were disappearing.

As early as 1871 Forts Kearny and Sedgwick were abandoned. The former, located in central Nebraska, had guarded the old California trail since 1848; the latter, first named Camp Rankin, had been established on the south bank of the Platte River in northeastern Colorado in 1864 to protect wagon travel. A half dozen years later North Platte Station, originally built as Camp Sergeant and intended to protect Union Pacific construction crews working near the junction of the North Platte and South Platte rivers, also was closed. At Fort McPherson, established in 1863 near the present town of North Platte, Nebraska, the last of its troops marched out in the spring of 1880. By then Fort Sidney remained the only important Nebraska post west of Omaha. Established in 1867 along the line of the Union Pacific, it was active until 1894.

Wyoming posts were similarly affected. Fort Sanders, near present-day Laramie, was built in 1866 to protect the stagecoach route, but by 1882 it had outlived its usefulness as a sentinel along the main travel route and it was closed. To the west, in south central Wyoming, lay Fort Steele. Built near the crossing of the North Platte River to protect the railroad workers, in the spring of 1868, it was abandoned in the autumn of 1886. Only Forts Laramie and Bridger remained; both lived on until 1890. Fort Laramie was not on the line of the road, but this old post, occupied by the army in 1849, served as a guardian of the westward passage for over four decades. Bridger, rebuilt as a military post in 1858 at the time of the Mormon War, served in a similar capacity.

The story of the Kansas posts was much the same. West of Forts Leavenworth and Riley, both of which were built in the days before the railroad, lay such posts as Harker, Hays, and Wallace. Harker, built in 1864, guarded both the old stage route to Santa Fe and the Kansas Pacific railroad construction crews; it was the first to go, being abandoned as early as 1873. Wallace, built in western Kansas in the autumn of 1865, was no longer needed in 1882; by then the surrounding countryside was undergoing heavy settlement. Hays, established in west central Kansas during 1865 especially to guard Kansas Pacific workers, lasted until 1889. The editor of a Kansas newspaper, noting that the government had called for the post's abandonment, recalled its importance as a military station, having served there during the early days of its history. Commenting upon the rapid development of western Kansas that had taken place during the intervening years he spoke of the changes which had taken place. "In this brief period the Indians have been sent from this region to stay, and the civilization of the white man shows here in its splendor," was his testimony to the accomplishment of the railroads.[52]

"An Apple Tree Without a Limb"

The agricultural invasion of Nebraska and Kansas was made possible by the coming of railroads. Construction crews, protected by troops, prepared the way for the main army of plowmen that took up positions along the line of the road and established permanent settlements. As the Indians retreated before this final thrust, the country between the two lines was cleared for development by the whites. When that portion was secured, the great wedge of settlement gradually widened.

Since the Union Pacific's real estate holdings extended no more than 20 miles on either side of its tracks, land disposal represented only a part of the company's plan for attracting business to its domain. In order to benefit from western resources more thoroughly, the road had to construct a series of branches along existing lines that would penetrate unsettled country beyond the confines of the original route. Farmers could haul produce to market in their wagons only for limited distances; beyond such points the railroads had to come to them. Similarly, if the Union Pacific expected to profit from the mineral trade of the mountains, longer and more expensive branches into that difficult country would be required.

Even as the Union Pacific made its much publicized connection at Promontory, its more sober projectors had looked into the future and had anticipated the necessity of building feeder lines that would funnel trade into the main system. They foresaw that the monopoly established in 1869 would be relatively short-lived. The availability of land grants was sure to make other promoters anxious to avail themselves of such governmental largess, and the prevalence of the railroad mania, already developing rapidly in postwar America, predicted additional transcontinental efforts. It was questionable that revenue from through traffic would be sufficient to sustain the railroad, even with a monopoly, and the prospect of sharing such a dubious income with others was not inviting. Therefore, local business, garnered from one's own territory and claimed before interlopers could enter the picture, appeared to promise an income that would insure the railroad's future security and prosperity.

As early as 1868 intimations appeared in print. "Along its entire route over the great plains lateral branches will be constructed to tap it, which will pour into their wayside contributions to an extent that cannot today be approximately estimated," said one pamphleteer, in writing about the Union Pacific's future development.[1] At this time the principal source of such revenue was thought to be in mineral wealth, the mines of the West having been developed over the preceding decade; agricultural traffic was regarded as a latent resource. George L. Miller, an Omaha editor, eyed the riches of the Mountain West and commented that Durant "has his plans and maps" to build branches into Montana and along the Snake River in Idaho.[2] Early Union Pacific brochures contained maps on which dotted lines depicted the plans attributed to Durant.[3]

Montana and Oregon, however, were relatively remote, as were the richer parts of Idaho. Closer to the main line lay a more densely populated area from which mineral products had come in quantity for a decade, and it was to Colorado that the thoughts of the Union Pacific's directorate first turned. At a time when they were hard-pressed for money, and before the stockholders had received any dividends, the men of Boston began their financial penetration of that portion of the Rocky Mountains. Although an invasion of the agricultural West would later become a major consideration, precious metals promised to yield the highest immediate dividends.

The Colorado Central Railroad, incorporated in 1865 as the Colorado and Clear Creek Railroad Company, was a narrow-gauge railroad designed for the mining country west of Denver. Its principal promoter, William A. H. Loveland, of Golden, hoped the Union Pacific might be attracted to his project and utilize it as a part of the main line to the Pacific Coast. That destination was suggested when the road's name was changed to the Colorado Central and Pacific Railroad Company in 1866. After it became clear that the westward passage would not be through Colorado, the little road was reorganized and its name was changed once more, this time to the Colorado Central Railroad Company.[4] An agreement dated June 25, 1867, determined that the Central would grade and furnish ties while the Union Pacific would lay rails and furnish rolling stock.[5] The first piece of road, of standard gauge, was laid in the direction of Denver; west of Golden the gauge would be the usual three-foot width used by other narrow-gauge lines in the mountains.

Groundbreaking ceremonies were held at Golden on New Year's Day, 1868. During this year 15.5 miles of grade were prepared and its ties were put in place. By September 1870 a connection with the Denver Pacific had provided service to Denver. Loveland next moved to further accommodate the Union Pacific by extending his road northward toward Cheyenne. During 1870 a standard-gauge line was laid toward Longmont, a small agricultural community a few miles north of Denver. Residents there began to fear that the promoter from Golden would offer Denver no more than branch-line service, and since they were by now assured of a connection with the Kansas Pacific, they withdrew their earlier support of his project.[6]

Under its charter the Union Pacific was not allowed to build branches, but neither was it denied the right to lend support in the form of rails and equipment. While the major road thus made no claims to paternity, or even referred to the Colorado Central as a distant relative, its interest in the Central was great. Colonel C. G. Hammond, superintendent at Omaha, revealed the role that the Union Pacific desired to play in Colorado when he wrote to Oliver Ames: "This misfortune, the losing of the control of the Denver Pacific road, and having no substitute for it provided, is greater than I fear is generally apprehended by the Directors." He suggested a solution when he asked that, "in addition to the building of the Colorado Central such other measures shall be taken as will secure us at least a portion of this Colorado business over one half of our line."[7]

Nathan C. Meeker, of the Greeley colony, was at this time endeavoring to convince the Union Pacific that in addition to the territory's mineral wealth there would be agricultural produce available for shipment. A contemporary described the little Colorado community of Greeley as having about 350 buildings, including 17 stores, 3 lumberyards, 3 blacksmith and wagon shops, and a newspaper.[8] Meeker suggested that if the Union Pacific would enter the picture, neighboring Boulder County would put up $100,000 in bonds. "The trade of Colorado is worth having," he argued. "It can be reached by the Union Pacific and we commend your attention to the above considerations."[9]

Top-level officials of the Union Pacific were aware of Colorado's potential and they studied the situation carefully. President of the Colorado Central T. J. Carter reported regularly to Boston as to the progress of tracklaying, the arrival of equipment, and other news of interest.[10] While Ames was not convinced that the small line would pay any stock dividends, he felt that it would "be of considerable service to U.P.R.R. in turning the business of the mining country over to our Road."[11] If it did no more than that, the feeder line would perform sufficient service to justify its existence, for this was to be the role of most branches to mother lines.

Colorado resources had received wide recognition since the gold strikes of 1859, and during the 1870s the extraction of precious metals commanded national attention. The total gold production of the territory through that decade amounted to approximately $54 million; silver, $40 million; lead, nearly $2 million; and copper, about $750,000. The total value of extraction approached $100 million.[12] Coal also was coming to be regarded as a major subsurface resource. As early as 1867–68 the future yields of the Ralston Creek and Marshall beds, both within 25 miles of Denver, were discussed.[13] In the early seventies large coal veins at Erie, to the east of Boulder, were being mined by the Kansas Pacific.[14]

In response to railroad interest in the mining areas Coloradans voted bonds to aid rail construction. When business leaders of Gilpin County, a major gold area, showed signs of lending their support, Union Pacific President Thomas A. Scott assured Henry M. Teller that if the people of the county voted $250,000 in bonds, work on the Colorado Central's extension would begin at once.[15] The voters responded favorably, but with reservations that caused complaint at Boston. The bonds were approved on the condition that the road be finished to Black Hawk by May 1872. Oliver Ames thought the bonds should have been issued pro rata, as the work progressed, for otherwise the county might try to back down if matters did not work out exactly as they wished.[16] The road did not provide service to Black Hawk until December 1872 and, true to the suspicions of Ames, Gilpin County officials reduced the offer figure to $100,000. It was May 1878 before rails reached the county's major point, Central City.

During the autumn of 1871 engineering crews continued their surveys across the country north of Denver, preparing a route that would connect with the main line at Pine Bluffs, a station 43 miles east of Cheyenne. Before construction began the connecting point was moved farther east, to Julesburg, describing an arc across northeastern Colorado and shortening the distance between Denver and the Missouri River. Since Boulder County had voted $200,000 in bonds and Weld County had promised $150,000, the project had sufficient financial backing to encourage its builders.[17] The route, running from its Union Pacific connection to Golden, became known as the Julesburg branch.

Business leaders in Denver viewed the new line with mixed feelings. Their fear that Golden would become the major beneficiary, as well as the conviction that aiding a rival line was inconsistent with support given to the Denver Pacific, had prompted their withdrawal of financial assistance to the Colorado Central. The latter consideration, however, could be set aside provided the Central would agree to move its headquarters, shops, and focus of attention to Denver. Until that time the Denver press proposed to remain hostile to a line which in any way favored a neighboring rival for the riches of the Colorado community.[18]

Although the Union Pacific was anxious for any and all Colorado trade it could obtain, it chose not to intervene in any local quarrels. Such matters would be adjusted in due time. Meanwhile, work began at Julesburg on a line running in the direction of Greeley and thence to Boulder and Golden. At the same time crews advanced the narrow-gauge section of the Colorado Central westward from Golden in an effort to meet the demands laid down by Gilpin County. It was slow and expensive work, digging in rocky terrain and maneuvering for more suitable grades.

The Panic year, 1873, further slowed Colorado Central construction, although the effect was some time in becoming evident. In that year the surveyor general of Colorado spoke in glowing terms of prosperity in all branches of industry, of increasing population, and of satisfying railroad growth. The tourist business, to become so important later, already was worthy of comment, and its probable future growth was used as a further example of the need for adequate transportation.[19] Union Pacific President Horace F. Clark, who had never been west of the Missouri River, visited Denver during May, and after praising Colorado's resources, predicted that the Julesburg branch would be completed in the autumn, a forecast that missed its target by nearly a decade. When that link in the system was in service, said Clark, Denver would enjoy rates lower than it had ever dreamed possible. His listeners, many of whom were business leaders, received such promises with delight. They were anxious to increase commercial connections with the rest of the nation and were pleased to think that a new and productive portion of Colorado soon would be opened to settlers whose needs could be served by Denver. Hostility to the Union Pacific was set aside, for the moment, as the anticipation of bigger and better things to come from the corporation smoothed ruffled feathers.[20] Such enthusiasm frequently was temporary, as railroad history would bear out, and while Clark's proper diplomatic role was to exude enthusiasm for Colorado the Union Pacific would not, until the Julesburg branch was completed, have what the government directors referred to as a "friendly connection" with the territory's commerce.[21] For the time being it was obliged to depend upon the good nature of the Denver Pacific's management for the privilege of sharing mining country wealth.

The Longmont section was opened to traffic in April of 1873 amidst showers of praise from the Denver press that agricultural communities were at last receiving proper attention. "One trouble of our Colorado railways has been that they have not been constructed through the farming settlements," noted the *News,* in commenting upon the dominant part played by mining roads.[22] From the Union Pacific's point of view arrival at Longmont was merely another step in a long journey. Until the main line was reached the

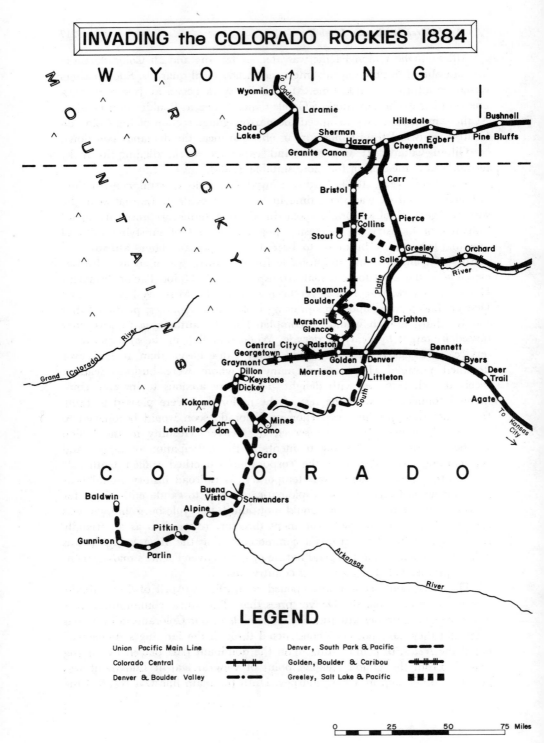

INVADING the COLORADO ROCKIES 1884

W Y O M I N G

MOUNTROCKY

Wyoming
Ogden
Laramie
Soda Lakes
Sherman
Hillsdale
Bushnell
Hazard
Egbert
Pine Bluffs
Granite Canon
Cheyenne
Carr
Bristol
Pierce
Ft Collins
Stout
Greeley
Orchard
La Salle
River
Longmont
Platte
Boulder
Marshall
Brighton
Glencoe
Central City
Ralston
Bennett
Georgetown
Graymont
Golden
Denver
Byers
Dillon
Morrison
Deer Trail
Keystone
Littleton
Dickey
South
Kokomo
Agate
Leadville
Lon-don
Mines
Como
To Kansas City
Garo

C O L O R A D O

Baldwin
Buena Vista
Schwanders
Alpine
Pitkin
Gunnison
Parlin
Grand (Colorado) River
Arkansas River

LEGEND

Union Pacific Main Line	————	Denver, South Park & Pacific	— — —
Colorado Central	—⊢⊢⊢—	Golden, Boulder & Caribou	⊬⊬⊬
Denver & Boulder Valley	—•—•—	Greeley, Salt Lake & Pacific	■ ■ ■

0   25   50   75 Miles

N. F. MRAZ

investment would be hard pressed to pay its own way. Expenses in January had run $800 higher than the Colorado Central's receipts, and although February was better, earnings for the two months came to only $715. "This is a surprising result to us and we are unable to account for it," Rollins wrote to J. W. Gannett, auditor at Omaha. "What does this mean?" he inquired of the Omaha office.[23] It meant, as Rollins was to discover later, that branch building in Colorado was going to be expensive and frequently unrewarding. Willingness to support such ventures, but the inability to control them absolutely, was to cost the Union Pacific a great deal of money, particularly in mining railroads. Meanwhile, strenuous efforts were made to control the main line's latest foster child. Gannett reported on his attempts to cut expenses and to promote efficiency. When he persuaded Colorado Central officers to engage in some judicious firing, Rollins expressed his hope that "all 'bummers' will now be weeded out and the force reduced to the smallest number practicable. We must have economy in Colorado."[24]

Although Oliver Ames was its vice president and Edward H. Rollins its secretary-treasurer, to preserve the fiction of its independence, the Colorado Central was headed by Henry M. Teller. In 1874 Sidney Dillon, who had become president of the Union Pacific, urged that the smaller road be turned over to his company "as I think there can be a larger saving made when it is run as a part of the Union Pacific Rail Road," but despite his desires actual control was not achieved for another five years.[25] Part of his anxiety arose in June of that year when Congress passed a bill requiring the Union Pacific to prorate with the Kansas Pacific, of which the Denver Pacific was recognized as a part, west of Cheyenne. Although the new law required the Kansas Pacific to give its rival equal treatment on the Denver Pacific section and, in theory, obviated the necessity of the Julesburg branch, relationships between the two large lines were not improved through coercive legislation. To force equal treatment on the Denver Pacific, the Union Pacific had gone so far as to establish an ox-line service between Longmont and Cheyenne. As a result of the pro rata ruling, a Cheyenne paper concluded that the Julesburg line was "knocked into a cocked hat and the Longmont and Fort Collins road has vanished into thin air."[26]

Because of the financial condition of the Central, Dillon concluded that the Denver Pacific might provide a more economical approach to Colorado despite the limitations imposed by the arrangement. While this arrangement might bring new trouble, at the time it appeared to be the best short-term solution. A study of the Colorado Central in the autumn of 1875 revealed that its earnings were not sufficient to pay even half the interest on its indebtedness, and the prospect for any dividends lay years in the future. Under these circumstances the Union Pacific moved slowly to increase its involvement in Colorado affairs. When Oliver Ames pointed out the value of the coalfields at Marshall, Dillon recommended that nothing be done in that direction at present. "We will have to connect our U.P. with the Colo. Central before we can make the Colo. Central profitable to us," he told Ames. He had no objection to making all the necessary surveys, and at the propitious moment his company would make a connection with all possible speed.[27] With regard to the proposed Julesburg branch, the president said that plans for its construction had been abandoned for the time being. The Central, having been unable to pay its interest, was about to undergo foreclosure proceedings. The Union Pacific Company stood ready to recommend a receiver.[28] Dillon had approved of the foreclosure because, as he said, the various counties holding stock would not agree to part with it "on satisfactory terms" or approve of consolidation with the Union Pacific.[29] Boulder, Jefferson, and Gilpin counties owned 4,000 shares, private individuals owned another 350, and the Union Pacific held the remaining 9,350.[30]

In May 1876 Loveland and his associates tried to gain a greater control of the Colorado Central's management, a move that Teller thought would be unsuccessful. The move came as the apparent result of Loveland's failure to sell to the Union Pacific earlier that spring. Edward Rollins explained: "His proposition, as I remember it, was substantially to take the Stock of the Counties at about 20 or 25, in Bonds, and have cash for his own stock, if the plan was put through, but it failed, and consequently we are under no obligations to him. Reduced to the simplest terms his proposition was this, that he would *sell* himself and the Counties for about $12,000 in money." Rollins thought that Loveland had "received quite enough from the parties who have furnished all the money to build the Colorado Central Railroad, and ought to be satisfied without further 'blood.' "[31] Unsuccessful in this effort Loveland then tried to prevent the appointment of a receiver, and in so doing he participated in a display of violence that must have made the Bostonians wonder if the West was entirely tamed.

Toward the middle of August the court appointed Denver banker David H. Moffat as receiver and set the fifteenth as the day when it would approve his bonds. En route to Boulder, where the procedure was to take place, federal judge A. W. Stone was taken from his railroad car by 25 armed men who spirited him off into the mountains and held him captive, after cutting the telegraph wires to delay pursuit. Since the limit of the court's term was to expire within a day after the Judge's proposed action, the kidnappers thought they could stop the whole proceeding by removing him from the scene. Although some Colorado papers showed sympathy for local bond-holders, who were presumably to be stripped of their investment by a large eastern corporation, the press generally condemned such violent action and criticized Loveland for his part in the plot. Edward Rollins appealed for federal assistance, through Sen. P. W. Hitchcock, of Nebraska, and on the sixteenth Gov. John Routt called out two companies of militia to enforce the order of the court. That night Judge Stone was placed in a carriage by his captors and after a long ride he was told to get out. When his blindfold was removed he found himself in front of the Alvord House in Denver. On the seventeenth Stone took his seat in court at Boulder, and receiver Moffat filed the necessary bond as uneventfully as if nothing untoward had taken place.[32]

Receivership, however, was not possession. Ten days later Union Pacific attorney Andrew J. Poppleton, who was in Colorado to represent the firm, reported to Dillon that he had a writ of assistance in the hands of an officer who could put the receiver in control of the Colorado Central, but nothing seemed likely to happen. "He has done nothing yet," complained Poppleton, "and I think is surrounded by political influences to such an extent that I don't believe he will do anything. This State is too full of thieves for . . . residents' property to have any chance except in the U.S. Courts. If Oliver Ames or anybody else puts more into this country he ought to lose it."[33] The impasse was complicated by the fact that the road lay in four counties, in which the sheriff of each was thoroughly sympathetic with "the Colorado gang," to use Poppleton's words, and they could not be relied upon to execute the mentioned writ.[34]

Meanwhile, Dillon suggested an accommodation that approached Loveland's earlier unsuccessful proposal. "I would renew the offer to take the stock at 30% and pay in Bonds at par and would give Loveland $20,000 to turn over the road and put in our Board of Directors & to close up all old claims of the parties interested with him and retain to the Company all stock now outstanding," he suggested to Oliver Ames in early September.[35] Despite local criticisms of Loveland's extreme methods, as witnessed in the kidnapping of Judge Stone, he represented the hometown boy who was fighting eastern financial giants and, relying upon popular support, he continued his fight against the Union Pacific. "Loveland controls the Colorado side of this controversy and whatever he agrees to will be done," Poppleton admitted, explaining to attorney Sidney Bartlett that there was extreme hostility toward Dillon and Jay Gould in Colorado.[36] Loveland's supporters took the view that the Central's mortgage indebtedness had been intentionally allowed to reach an unnecessary amount through a conspiracy

Jay Gould, the famed "railroad wrecker." Some western businessmen, however, thought him quite a "bright fellow."

between Oliver Ames and his representatives on the road's directory.[37] Apparently the argument was favorably received by Colorado jurists, for the road remained under local control for several more years.

During 1877, extension of the Colorado Central from Longmont to Cheyenne was finished and put into service. Jay Gould, now powerful in Union Pacific affairs, provided the driving force by aiding the project financially and by cooperating with Loveland. The Denver Pacific stood to lose a great deal by the completion of this parallel route, yet Denverites, who not only had a financial interest in that road and who had therefore opposed the Union Pacific, now saw an opportunity for cheaper rates through such competition. They complained that the Kansas Pacific was using the Denver Pacific in a discriminatory manner, charging more to ship a carload of goods from Kansas City to Denver than it collected for the same service to Cheyenne. In their shortsightedness these businessmen did not appear to realize that Gould's move meant the destruction of the Denver Pacific and removal of the Kansas Pacific's principal weapon used against the Union Pacific in the rivalry for transcontinental traffic. Gould, who appeared to be working in the Union Pacific's interest, was quietly buying Kansas Pacific stock at considerably depressed prices. When that line reached a point of collapse he intended to sell it, at a high price, to the Union Pacific. Meanwhile, the Kansas Pacific fought on, futilely trying to discourage the Longmont extension by every known legal maneuver.

The Colorado Central extension, completed in November, was an unnecessary expense to the Union Pacific, since that road took over both the Kansas Pacific and the Denver Pacific three years later, but this was typical of Gould's methods and it constituted a part of his strategy of persuasion. The fact that the Denver Pacific went into receivership on April 2, 1878, only a few months after the Union Pacific had connected Cheyenne to Longmont, suggests that Gould's move was merely the final blow to a smaller road in the battle of western railroad giants.

Denver now professed happiness at the Colorado Central's growth. In its ignorance of coming events the *News* chortled that the connection with Cheyenne "knocked endways" the Kansas Pacific's discriminatory rate as well as rectifying an eight-year-old blunder the Union Pacific had committed by not absorbing the Denver Pacific when it had a chance to do so. By August 1877 the Central also had sent its narrow-gauge rails into Georgetown, a place the *News* called Colorado's silver mining center. Shortly thereafter the mining town of Central City gained its long-desired rail service. Clear Creek County, which had voted bonds to obtain a railroad, now hoped to recover its money rapidly in reduced rates on ore shipments. Encouraged by Union Pacific support, Loveland determined to press on to Leadville.

In February 1879 the Colorado Central was leased to the Union Pacific for 50 years, at which time its name was changed to the Colorado Division of the Union Pacific Railroad Company.[38] Under the terms of the agreement the Union Pacific was to receive 65 percent of the earnings to cover expenses and apply the remaining 35 percent to payment of interest on the first-mortgage bonds. Less than a year later the Kansas Pacific became part of the Union Pacific, considerably lessening the necessity for recent efforts to extend the Central northward.

The decade of the eighties was to be a period of great railroad expansion throughout the American West, and the Union Pacific was only one of many companies faced by the problem of "expand or die." Despite depression, grasshopper years on the plains, and other adversities, immigration to the new country continued. Quartz mining, the successor of pick and pan methods, boomed during those years thanks to the use of improved technologies that included rail transportation as an important part of their equipment. Faced with expenditures so heavy that they threatened severe financial difficulties, railroad managers chose to stake out country available to them before it was too late, hopeful the risks they ran would prove to be justifiable. In Colorado, for example, the Denver and Rio Grande entered a period of expansion that led to near-disaster; but, literally surrounded by rivals, it felt there was no other choice. The Union Pacific, one of the rivals, also felt that responding to the challenge was the only logical answer in any long-term consideration.

Empire building involved the risk of poorly conceived acquisitions resulting from purely defensive building; however, as expensive as this proved to be, and despite loud recriminations voiced later, it was a part of the process of western railroad expansion. Both Jay Gould and Sidney Dillon advocated expansion. As they watched other major western roads invade the plains and mountains Union Pacific managers realized that unless their line tried to capture the trade of the area it would be taken over by rivals. "We . . . are like an apple tree without a limb," Sidney Dillon told his Board of Directors, and "unless we have branches there will be no fruit." When his listeners reminded him that such a course was prohibited by Congressional acts, he responded: "We cannot stand here and starve if it is or if it is not. I am in favor of building them." He later admitted to a Congressional committee that "if there are any consequences about it I am the father of that trouble." Gould reaffirmed Dillon's stand when he told Congressmen: "I thought that the Union Pacific should occupy the territory tributary to it, and throw out feeders that would bring the business in to the main line, and keep pace with the development of the great West, occupying the country as fast as, or a little faster than, the population went in to sustain it." He denied that any of the Union Pacific directors had made money from the ventures, all of which were aided by the big road, but none of which involved the creation of construction companies in the manner of the Crédit Mobilier.[39]

Both the Union Pacific government directors and the federal auditor of railroad accounts approved of the branch-line policy. The former admitted that some of these feeders were injudiciously located and were unable to pay their own fixed charges, yet "without them the main line would today be a bankrupt property." The auditor called such a policy "undoubtedly the best for insuring a continuance of profitable business for the main line," holding that the federal government, being a major Union Pacific creditor, could not but sanction and confirm this type of investment.[40] By the close of 1884 the government directors estimated that gross income from the branches during the year was about $5 million, or a net of $3.5 million. They maintained that if the net earnings of the Union Pacific were to be reduced by a like amount the road would be unable to meet its own fixed charges, for through traffic from Omaha to Ogden, which only four years earlier had amounted to 28%, by now had fallen to about 9.3% of the line's gross earnings.[41] While the bankruptcy, of which the directors spoke, came about and resulted in the wreckage of the network thus assembled, the difficulty was only partly due to an overly aggressive policy of expansion. The country claimed by this course was to be of vital importance in the success attained later by the reorganized company; without it the way back from bankruptcy would have been much more difficult.

The year 1880 marked a major turning point for the Union Pacific system in several ways. After that came the real branch-line expansion, a development that arose in part from acquisition of the Kansas Pacific system and in part from the Gould-Dillon—and later Adams—program of throwing out feeders wherever potential traffic was believed to be. These expenditures, some of which proved to be unwise investments, as well as the poor buy made in absorbing the Kansas line, and the mounting unpaid debt to the federal government, so burdened the Union Pacific that when times of unusual stress came the whole structure collapsed of its own weight.

The Kansas Pacific purchase, made in 1880, is attributed largely to pressure exerted by Jay Gould. For a decade that road, running between Kansas City and Denver with a connection to Cheyenne over the Denver Pacific, had struggled for existence. Plagued by a lack of Union Pacific cooperation west of Cheyenne, and by competition for Colorado trade by the same road, the Kansas line had slowly withered. When the Union Pacific refused to prorate, on the ground that its rival had not made a direct connection with it, as provided by the charter, the Kansas Pacific bought the Denver Pacific. After the purchase, made in the spring of 1872, lengthy legal action was initiated to force Union Pacific cooperation.[42] As a result of increased indebtedness, poor management, and continued economic warfare with Omaha, the Kansas Pacific defaulted on its first-mortgage bonds in November 1873. The road was then placed in the hands of two receivers, Carlos S. Greeley and Henry Villard, under whose guidance it remained for the next six years.[43] During this period the road's stock at times sold for as low as 9 to 12 cents on the dollar and had no more than a speculative value.[44] Railroads that were literally *in extremis* often had great attraction for Jay Gould, but this one, lying adjacent to the Union Pacific and in rivalry with it, provided additional interesting possibilities. Sometime in 1878 he began to make large purchases of this exceptionally cheap and fluctuating stock and, by early 1879, he was in control of the road. The dominance that Gould and his associates had attained became clear when Sidney Dillon was elected president of both the Kansas Pacific and Denver Pacific roads.

Jay Gould, commonly known in newspaper parlance as a railroad wrecker, and in more sophisticated circles as a "Captain of Industry," now proposed that the natural concomitant of his recent railroad purchases was consolidation of the three roads. In October 1879 Union Pacific officials asked Grenville Dodge to investigate such a possibility and to render a fair plan for the proposed move. His findings apparently were far from satisfactory to Gould, who shortly broke off all negotiations with the "Boston Gentlemen," and he quickly started one of his well-known acts of financial legerdemain. Early in November, and without any appreciable deliberation or investigation on his part, he purchased Commodore Cornelius K. Garrison's Missouri Pacific Railroad, which ran between Saint Louis and Kansas City. As a part of that transaction he also purchased controlling interest in the Kansas Central, a narrow-gauge line which ran westward from Leavenworth, Kansas, parallel to the Kansas Pacific, for 166 miles. Next he bought controlling interest in the old Central Branch of the Union Pacific, located 50 miles north of the Kansas Pacific and running parallel to that road for about a hundred miles.[45] Having gained a connection to eastern roads at Saint Louis and control of outlets on the Missouri River, he then turned upon his colleagues and threatened to extend that system to the Pacific. When he was later asked what such a move would have done to the Union Pacific he answered candidly: "It would have destroyed it."[46]

Dillon and the other "Boston Gentlemen" now discovered the price of their association with "the wrecker." Gould, who had sold most of his Union Pacific stock and had resigned from his offices in the company, had become a competitor, ready to undermine the position of his former colleagues. That he had moved quietly in his maneuver is revealed in a comment made by Dillon to Fred Ames in the spring of 1879: "I was not aware that Mr. Gould had sold so much of his stock until I received your letter this morning. I do not understand it." In his puzzlement he had telegraphed Silas Clark, superintendent at Omaha: "I hardly know what to say. What do you think best to do?"[47]

What Gould now demanded was an exchange of stock between the Union Pacific and a bankrupt, poorly built, and badly managed road. Kansas Pacific shareholders were to receive one share of Union Pacific stock for two of theirs, the price of the Kansas Pacific stock being fixed at $50. A year and a half earlier the same stock had sold for $10. The Bostonians found themselves confronted by a situation in which the Kansas Pacific, in receivership and with no interest charges to pay, not only could cut rates almost to the cost of operation, but also might be extended, as Gould threatened, across Loveland Pass and into Ogden to a connection with the Central Pacific. Doubly embarrassing was that members of the Boston party held some of the Kansas Pacific stock, and if the proposed deal went into effect they would necessarily make money from it. While on the positive side, the Union Pacific, obliged by act of Congress to deliver eastbound traffic to connecting roads at Omaha without partiality, could free itself from this restriction by diverting such traffic at Cheyenne, thereby avoiding the Iowa lines. Another advantage, and one that was used to justify the consolidation, lay in the presumed ability of one company to operate the three lines more economically than they were before. Finally, it would control a vast new area of country in Kansas and Colorado, thereby not only eliminating costly competition but opening new areas of business. These were the rationalizations used in face of the fact that a solvent line, paying dividends and boasting a surplus, was prepared to take over a bankrupt company with a deficit, on equal terms.[48]

At an emotional and historic meeting, held on January 14, 1880, Jay Gould bulldozed the Bostonians into acceding to his demands. The financier, described by a Wyoming paper as "a moral infidel" and "the most powerful conspirator in the world," again had displayed his ability to use force. An agreement, signed the same day, provided that "The Union & Kansas Pacific with all their respective assets and properties and liabilities are to be put together as part of their respective capitals $36,762,300 and $10,000,000 to which is to be added the capital of the Denver Pacific, $4,000,000, making the capital of the Union Pacific Railway Co. as the new line shall be called $51,762,300." By this move the Union Pacific's bonded indebtedness jumped from $88,471,285.23 to $126,818,046.09 and its miscellaneous indebtedness

from $4,072,854 to $9,677,018.[49] While members of a government commission later called Gould's ability to dispose of Kansas Pacific stock so
favorably "a singular feature of this extraordinary transaction," there were
no violent complaints about it at the time. The commission preferred to
confess that the consolidation appeared to have reduced overhead, promoted
efficiency, and solved some of the problems of cutthroat competition. Stockholders ratified the merger without a dissenting vote, as did the government
directors with one exception, and the Secretary of the Interior failed to
challenge an action that involved land-grant railroads.[50] However, as
Edward Harriman's biographer later pointed out, despite the Union Pacific
system's nearly doubling its size by consolidation, it weakened its financial
strength by greatly increasing its capitalization without realizing a pro-
portional increase in earning capacity when it absorbed two unprofitable
railroads. The high price the company paid to free itself of competition
so endangered its own health that insolvency was unavoidable when future
burdens were added to its already heavy load. Taking the Gould roads at far
more than their worth was to play an important part in the financial
problems that lay ahead for the Union Pacific.[51]

In the months that followed consolidation the policy of branch-line
building received new impetus when an additional $10 million of stock was
authorized to pay for the continued expansion. Jay Gould, once again a
force in Union Pacific management as a result of the recent transaction,
joined Dillon in urging conquest of any and all territory that was likely to
provide business. One of the important branches, and one that involved
considerable expense, was the long-deferred link between Julesburg and
Denver. Service on that line began in the autumn of 1881, making it
possible for trains to cover the 568 miles from Omaha to the Colorado
capital in less than 24 hours. "The cut-off is a much better line than that
by way of Cheyenne or the Kansas Division," said the *Railroad Gazette*, in
describing its easier curves and lighter grades.[52]

The new Union Pacific Company now controlled northeastern Colorado
business to such a degree that duplication of service, arising out of earlier
competitive building, could be eliminated. After 1884, for example, the
tracks laid north of Fort Collins were of little use now that the Denver
Pacific was part of the mother system. In 1889 Isaac N. Van Dyke, a Fort
Collins attorney, charged that not a passenger or freight train had run
between his city and Cheyenne since 1884. Alleging that the people of
northern Colorado had suffered a half-million-dollar loss as a result of this
virtual abandonment, Van Dyke charged perfidy on the part of those who
had managed what he termed "this outrage."[53]

During the 1880s Colorado's mineral wealth proved highly attractive

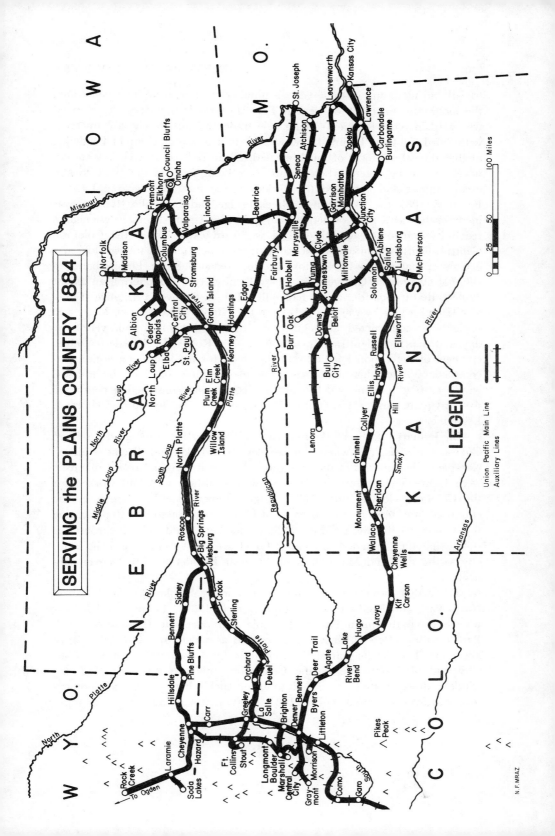

SERVING the PLAINS COUNTRY 1884

LEGEND

——— Union Pacific Main Line
——+—— Auxiliary Lines

0 25 50 100 Miles

N.F.MRAZ

to railroad men, and in those years a number of "bonanza" lines penetrated the mountains in search of wealth. The Rio Grande, for example, plunged westward into the Rockies, seeking new trade and, ultimately, a connection with Salt Lake City. Its first target was the fabled mining camp of Leadville, at that time the subject of much excited talk in railroad circles. Jay Gould, never one to be absent when profits were being handed out, now took a great interest and extended the Union Pacific in that direction. Late in February 1881 the Georgetown, Breckenridge and Leadville Railway was incorporated as a road owned primarily by the Union Pacific, designed to reach its immediate goal through a westward extension of the Colorado Central. Construction across the difficult mountain terrain was so slow and expensive that it was 1884 before the line reached Silver Plume, barely a rifleshot away from Georgetown. The difficulty lay in conquering an ascent so steep that it took four and a half miles of track to cover a distance of only a mile and a half by wagon road. Here the famous "Georgetown loop" and bridge were constructed, an engineering feat that became the marvel of the day and a principal attraction to tourists. To Robert Blickensderfer, chief engineer of the Union Pacific, went the credit for the loop's conception and completion. After this monumental piece of engineering had the railroad winding up to a point 600 feet above Georgetown, construction continued to Graymont, just a few miles distant, only to be halted far short of Leadville.[54]

In January 1881 the Union Pacific had further interested itself in Colorado feeder lines when the Greeley, Salt Lake and Pacific Railway Company filed articles of incorporation. Among its original board members were Henry Teller's brother, Willard; Cyrus Fisher, who had worked for the Colorado Central since 1875; August Egbert, another Union Pacific employee; and several other prominent Colorado businessmen. Representing the Union Pacific were Sidney Dillon and Jay Gould. The incorporators stated that they intended to connect Greeley to Fort Collins, and the latter city to the Erie and Marshall coalfields near Boulder, with a Denver connection.

To further protect their interests in northern Colorado the Laramie, North Park and Pacific road was organized, in 1880. This proposed flanker was to leave the main line at Laramie and penetrate Colorado's North Park country, after which it might be used as a defensive bulwark against any rival. The destination of the mountain lines was said to be Salt Lake City and ultimately the Pacific Coast, but this was no more than the window dressing that decorated most of such charters. An amendment to the articles, executed in July 1881, envisioned a network of roads numbering no less than 19, which, if carried to completion, would have blanketed northern Colorado.

Boulder's *News and Courier* asserted that the Union Pacific's participation in the outbreak of Colorado railroad incorporations was merely an endeavor to protect its through business by laying claim to any possible westward route that might later be used by rivals.[55] A more immediate aim was to capture as much of the mining country as possible before others laid claim to it. One example of such protective methods was the incorporation of the North Park and Grand River Valley Railroad and Telegraph Company in June 1880. Five years later company records showed that a total of $15.25 had been expended, a figure that probably represented the cost of filing articles of incorporation. As one of the president's aides said, "I presume that the company was organized to protect the right to build through the North Park and along the valley of the Grand River."[56] Dillon candidly admitted the defensive nature of his company's moves. "We propose to build these roads up through that country without any regard to what may be done by other parties." He remarked that there were "a good many schemes afloat in Colorado," and that by entering the picture actively "steps will have been taken for the best protection of our interests."[57] "However," he added, "it makes no difference whether they build a road or not. We will not give way even if we have to build a parallel road."[58]

In January 1881, the same month the Greeley, Salt Lake and Pacific was incorporated, the Union Pacific also acquired the Denver, South Park and Pacific. The narrow-gauge road, extending westward from Denver, had originated in the desires of John Evans and some of his business associates to enter the mountain mineral trade. Organized in 1872 and reorganized a year later, the line's proposed route ran through South Park to Del Norte and from there to the San Juan mining district.[59] In 1880 Jay Gould began to buy stock from Evans and shortly thereafter he acquired control. By the end of 1881 the new owners had increased the branch's mileage from 162 miles to 213, reaching into the mining country of central Colorado at Gunnison. In his report to the stockholders for 1882 Dillon said that the move had put his road in a position to tap rich anthracite and bituminous coal and iron ores of "extraordinarily good quality."[60] During the following year a 34-mile branch was built to Leadville, alleviating the necessity of paying what Dillon thought was an exorbitant toll to use the Denver and Rio Grande's tracks.[61] Construction came after Dillon and Gen. William J. Palmer, of the Denver and Rio Grande, had quarreled over trackage rates. "I am much annoyed with that whole institution," Dillon had written about

Palmer's road, "and I feel that unless something definite can be arranged with Palmer we shall have to adopt a very vigorous course." The argument, which he termed a "very vexatious matter," was resolved by building into Leadville.[62]

At the time it was purchased the Denver and South Park appeared to be a reasonably good investment. In August 1880, for example, it paid a four percent dividend. However, beginning in 1883 it lost money steadily, with the result that by May 1886 its first mortgage coupons went unpaid. After some delay, and great reluctance, the Union Pacific arranged to have the May and November coupons honored. But faced with a debt of more than $2 million and a steadily declining income, this mountain branch became a burden to the parent company. While the little road's historian later would assign its difficulties to Union Pacific mismanagement, other factors were involved in its decline. At a time when Colorado mining country was latticed with narrow-gauge roads, the precious metals industry was on the verge of a sharp decline. Within the next few years most of these narrow-gauge lines would suffer heavy losses, and be abandoned one by one. This particular branch came to the Union Pacific as a result of Jay Gould's penchant for acquiring railroads and Dillon's desire to expand. As early as 1885 publicist Isaac Bromley told Charles Francis Adams that its adoption into the family took place under conditions that were "to say the least, very obscure, and made under such circumstances as to arouse a natural suspicion." There was no record of any vote by the directors or executive committee concerning the move. Gould and Dillon, after discussing the matter informally, personally concluded that it would be a good purchase and they proceeded. Bromley felt that they had not made a very careful investigation of the situation, for, as he told Adams, "there was a cooking up of accounts before the sale of the road, by which a very large portion of the indebtedness went over into the year after the transfer was made, which might be an interesting subject of inquiry." He admitted that business depression in Colorado, as well as competition from the Denver and Rio Grande, might have caused net earnings to fall from $1 million in 1880 to slightly over $300,000 in 1881 and down to only $48,000 by 1883, but he thought it an unlikely explanation. He decided that the "shadiness of the original transaction" had to be taken into account.[63]

The years immediately following Bromley's assessment of the situation demonstrated that the investment had been poorly conceived. Income from the 325-mile road sank steadily, and by May 1888 default could no longer be avoided. The Denver, South Park and Pacific, with a good many of its counterparts, went into the hands of a receiver.[64] Although the branch had never paid its parent company a dividend, its acquisition was defended by

Union Pacific management in Colorado. Joseph K. Choate, superintendent at Denver, said that it passed through the finest coal lands in the West, controlled ore shipments from Leadville, and as a feeder had contributed at least $1.5 million worth of business to the main line each year. He contended that if the Denver and South Park had cost the Union Pacific a million dollars a year, as opposed to the fifty to sixty thousand dollars it did cost, it still would have been a valuable possession.[65]

The Union Pacific's first agricultural branch line, built in 1876, forked from the main system 36 miles west of Omaha and ran to Wahoo, a distance of 19 miles.[66] Construction of the Omaha and Republican Valley Railroad was done under a separate organization with funds secured from first-mortgage bonds and bonds voted by Saunders County. It was designed to reach the country south of the Platte River and to open new lands for settlement in an area not yet served by the Union Pacific. Ready for business on January 1, 1877, the road was extended during that year to David City, just over 60 miles from the main line. Dillon reported that response to the project had been immediate, yielding a good quantity of new business to the parent road. During the next two years the road reached Stromsburg, 30 miles farther. Work was then begun on a branch to the capital city, Lincoln, and this was completed by April 1880. By 1883 the Omaha and Republican Valley road, a little rail system in itself, had added 160 miles of feeders to the Union Pacific.[67]

While Dillon and his colleagues sought to induce traffic from the agricultural country lying south of the Platte, they were also attracted by the possibility of business emanating from the recent gold rush in the Black Hills of the Dakota Territory, north of the main line. A line in that direction would not only open up more farming country in northern Nebraska, but it also promised to provide ore haulage. Apparently unsure of the expected life-span of the new mining district, Union Pacific officials proceeded cautiously, making surveys during 1877 and 1878, while fostering business during the period by means of stage and wagon freight subsidiaries. Dillon complained to Silas Clark that the Salisbury Stage Company, operating between Sidney, Nebraska, and the Black Hills, was less efficient than a rival service from Bismarck, Dakota Territory. Because it required 12 hours longer to make the run, he recommended that the Union Pacific sponsor some other and more efficient company or, as an alternative, he suggested giving Salisbury a better financial arrangement in the hope of developing a first-class stage business.[68]

The Omaha, Niobrara and Black Hills Railway, as the Dakota-bound road was named, left the main line 100 miles west of Omaha and went

north to Norfolk, Nebraska, with a small offshoot laid in a westerly direction
to Genoa. Using old iron rails that had been taken from the main line,
construction was completed to Norfolk in 1879. During the planning period
Dillon considered the possibility of building on to Montana, and asked
surveyor James A. Evans to determine if such an extension would be practicable. Although the proposed road did not reach its initial goal, the Black
Hills, it served a rich portion of Nebraska farm country. After making a
slow start, the line picked up business and by 1883 it showed a net profit of
$103,000 which, for a branch, was better than normally expected.[69] Despite
such encouraging returns, progress toward the Black Hills slowed and
finally stopped. Meanwhile, in 1877, another approach to that mining area
was suggested when the Cheyenne, Montana and Black Hills Railroad
Company was incorporated, but within a year the directors decided that,
despite an offer of $400,000 in bonds from Laramie County, business be-
tween Cheyenne and the Black Hills did not warrant construction. They
next pondered the notion of building northward from Sidney but that
idea, too, was abandoned.[70]

   In a further effort to serve the area south of the Platte River, the Union
Pacific constructed the Hastings and Grand Island Railroad in a south-
easterly direction from Grand Island, by way of Hastings, to a connection
with the Saint Joseph and Western road of Saint Joseph, Missouri. The
new service, opened in 1879, formed the southwestern side of a triangle
with the main line and the Omaha and Republican Valley tracks. It opened
the Big Blue River region, a rolling, well-watered section of highly fertile
farming country in southeastern Nebraska.[71] The Saint Joseph and Western,
250 miles long, came into Union Pacific possession in October 1879 at a
time when the little line was in receivership and heavily in debt.[72] In that
same year the Manhattan and Blue Valley Railroad was acquired from
the Atchison, Topeka and Santa Fe for just under $45,000. Organized in
1871 it was sold under foreclosure in June 1879. Comprised of only six miles
of track, then in very poor condition, this road was linked to the Omaha
and Republican Valley road.

   Thus the branch-line construction proceeded, as little metal tendrils
budded out along what might be termed the twin trunks of the Union
Pacific west of Kansas City and of Omaha. By 1883 the road owned 20
branches of various sizes and had what it termed "a large proprietary
interest" in five others, a total of approximately 3,600 miles of railroad.
This was nearly twice the length—1,821 miles—of the three "main" roads
put together in the consolidation of 1880.

   During the quarter century that followed the successful drive toward

Promontory, Union Pacific leaders displayed keen interest in developing the economic empire through which the original thread of iron had been run. It appeared to them that the greatest possibility for future income lay in the fields of agriculture, cattle ranching, and mining. Of the three, the first two promised long-term growth; the third posed problems of high costs and high risks but offered quicker returns. In the manner of a good businessman, the corporation endeavored to spread its risk by building branches in both the agricultural and the mineral West, hopeful that any disappointment in one field might be compensated for in the other. From the day of its birth the railroad had been hampered by a chronic shortage of cash, and to meet the demand for branches it was obliged to make some strenuous—even dangerous—efforts.

Despite the obvious difficulties it faced, the Union Pacific was obliged to plunge ahead, for this was the heyday of western economic expansion, and all America watched with consuming interest as hordes of empire builders invaded the last of the nation's frontiers. Rival railroads, advancing under the banners of many corporate colors, staked their claims with full knowledge that time was running out. They hurled a challenge at the pioneer in the field—the Union Pacific—and implied that it must fight for the country it claimed or yield to more daring entrepreneurs. There was little choice but to join the fray, for, if it did not, the apple tree of which Sidney Dillon spoke would remain a stunted trunk without any limbs, and it would strangle amidst the rival economic overgrowth.

The "Far-Off Country"

The mineral riches of Colorado, so attractive to the Union Pacific, were sufficiently close to the main line that reaching them by rail presented no difficult logistical problem. One hundred miles separated Denver from Cheyenne, and even as the company had debated spanning it, John Evans and his associates had proceeded with the building of the Denver Pacific. The outbreak of narrow-gauge railroad building toward these mining camps demonstrated not only the practicability of penetrating the Colorado mountains but also the necessity of doing so if the Union Pacific were to participate in the latter-day mining rush.

Montana, on the other hand, was much more difficult to reach. The wealth of its placer mines had dazzled the world and had ranked with the successes in Colorado and California. During the 1870s there was promise that quartz mining in Montana would yield returns sufficient to justify considerable expense in reaching that place by rail. Union Pacific management recognized this at a very early date but it did not have the resources to build so long an extension at the time. As the big company eyed the riches of the northern Rockies, a small Mormon narrow gauge cautiously poked its way in that direction, hopeful that someday and in some way it could reach the mines that were so widely heralded in the financial world.

Just as the businessmen of Denver had sought so earnestly to connect their city with both the mining country and the main line of the Union Pacific, so did those of Salt Lake City anticipate the benefits to be derived from feeders that would serve the Great Basin Kingdom, as the area came to be called. Since the Mormon Church, and particularly the Brigham Young family, had great influence in the community, it was not surprising that the impetus for railroad building originated among religious leaders. The involvement of the Youngs in the completion of the main line not only stirred Mormon business interest, but, by the terms of the settlement with the Union Pacific, in which railroad materials were given in lieu of money, the stimulus and means for connecting the capital city with Ogden had been provided.

North of Ogden the country was attractive, for both economic and religious reasons. It lay in the direction of Montana, where a large market for agricultural produce lay waiting, and it represented a part of Mormondom most subject to the inroads of Gentile subversion. A connection with Utah's economic and religious headquarters, by means of rail service, offered several attractive rewards.

Even as the Utah Central was being constructed between Ogden and Salt Lake City there was talk of building a line into northern Utah's Cache Valley in the belief that the little farming communities would justify its existence. In noting the progress of the Utah Central, in 1869, the commissioner of the General Land Office commented: "An early continuation of this latter road is projected, to follow the line of settlements at the western base of the Wahsatch Mountains, northward to the rich mining regions of Idaho and Montana . . . ."[1]

During the summer of 1871 John W. Young went to New York City in search of funds with which to build the next link of the Mormon railroad system. There he talked to Joseph and Benjamin Richardson, wealthy eastern manufacturers, who promised to aid his project. Bishop W. B. Preston, of Logan, who was to be an officer in the new road, questioned the wisdom of accepting such assistance on the ground that it would result in domination by outsiders. He reported that his followers had shown a great willingness to subscribe to stock and prepare the roadbed, but in return they expected Mormon control of the firm. Brigham Young, to whom the question had been directed, assured Preston that "the foreign capitalists in this enterprise do not seek control; this is all understood." Rather, he said, they desired to push the road with all possible speed if the community decided that such facilities were wanted.[2] The spiritual leader had spoken and the matter was put to rest.

On August 23, 1871, the organization of a narrow-gauge line, called the Utah Northern Railroad Company, was completed, with John W. Young and Joseph Richardson as principal incorporers. The capitalist from Connecticut agreed to participate after conferring with the elder Young, who endorsed his son's project. John had made almost $50,000 from his Union Pacific contracts, and he was anxious to invest more money in a business he had found to be so rewarding. His father, who also had an eye for profit, agreed that it was a worthy project.[3] Although the Utah Northern was intended to run northward from Ogden it was decided that a temporary southern terminus would be located at Brigham City, on the Central Pacific road, in order to provide the Cache Valley with rail service as early as possible. Ground was broken at that little village on a moonlit evening late in August as bands played and cannons were fired to celebrate the event. John W. Young, president of the new company, turned the first spadeful of earth.[4]

During the following weeks John Young appeared at gatherings familiar to westerners as "railroad meetings," where he explained to his followers that he had conferred with "men of capital" in the East who were willing to supply iron and rolling stock if the Mormons would grade and tie the road. By using narrow instead of standard gauge Young estimated that as much as 40 percent could be saved.[5] Despite suspicions about outsiders with money, the Mormon farmers responded and grading was commenced that autumn. By March 25, 1872, John Young could inform his father that "We drove the first spike on the Utah Northern R.R. at 11 a.m. Will lay about half a mile this afternoon."[6]

Although the little narrow-gauge road declared itself to be no more than a feeder intended to serve northern Utah agricultural communities, its existence generated much excitement in Idaho and Montana mining circles. Before the first rail was laid a Salt Lake City paper stated that once Soda Springs was reached the people of Idaho proposed to connect it to their principal mining centers. A Boise paper called Mormon management a mere blind to soothe Central Pacific worries, alleging that the road was bound for Montana under Union Pacific auspices. No sane man, said the editor, believed Soda Springs would be the actual terminus, instead it would be much farther north, where mineral riches awaited. "The Union Pacific will push on into Southern Montana," he said, "so as to crowd the Northern Pacific further north, to avoid unhealthy competition."[7]

As speculation continued over the probable terminus, construction proceeded slowly. Logan was not reached until the end of January 1873, and it was almost another year and a half before the little town of Franklin— 77 miles north of Ogden—heard a locomotive whistle. Mormon farmers who volunteered manual labor and teams in exchange for railroad stock worked sporadically, giving such time as they could spare from their other duties. To Moses Thatcher, superintendent of construction, went the rallying of various settlements along the route, and the persuading of local church authorities to the importance of furnishing their quotas of workers.[8] During 1873, while grading crews worked between Logan and Franklin, others undertook to fill in the link between Ogden and Brigham City and to provide a connection with the Utah Central, to give the Mormons a direct line north of Ogden.

In the same year a short narrow-gauge branch was built between Brigham City and Corinne so the Mormon road could profit from a place that for years had served wagon freighters working the Montana trade. The last spike on this portion of the project was driven June 10; but it was not a champagne ceremony, a reporter merely remarking that a half dozen kegs of beer were broached.[9] By February 5, 1874, when a connection with the Utah Central was made, Mormon railroad entrepreneurs had a continuous line of their own running northward from Utah's capital as well as connecting with both the Union Pacific and the Central Pacific roads. Intentions had become reality, as far as narrow-gauge service into northern Utah was concerned, and all who lived beyond that region took encouragement.

News of the Utah Northern's proposed construction excited the communities in southwestern Montana. Connected to "the States" by the winding Missouri River that was useful only part of the year, and by even slower freight-wagon routes, the mountain mining community had long wanted rail service. After the Union Pacific reached Utah, both horsedrawn express and freight service connected Montana to the main line, making Corinne an important commercial point—for awhile. Even though the wagon route north from the railroad was much shorter than before, it remained slow, expensive, and seasonal. Stagecoach passengers paid about 20 cents a mile for an uncomfortable, cramped ride. The railroad remained the ultimate answer.

From the time the Pacific road was begun Montanans had hoped for a connection with it, but not until the Young family started building northward was there evidence that such service might be realized. In the autumn of 1872, as the narrow gauge from Brigham City approached Logan, a Montana banker confessed that "We of the mountains are considerably troubled with railroad on the brain just at the present time . . . ."[10] In September there was formed in Montana a group known as the "Committee of One Hundred." From its deliberations came the creation of a "paper railroad" known as the Montana, National Park and Utah Railroad Company, of which Samuel T. Hauser, president of the First National Bank of Helena, was chief executive officer. Later that autumn Samuel Word, a Virginia City attorney, wrote to John Young and identified himself as chairman of the committee. When he asked about the prospect of a connection with the Utah road, he was told that it was a distinct possibility, provided there was sufficient financial encouragement from Montana communities.[11] The amount mentioned was $1 million.[12]

The vision of railroad service to Montana touched off a number of enthusiastic meetings and excited talk among that territory's residents. "Why is money scarce and hard to get?" asked one of them. "Because we have no railroad—no outer market. Because this Territory loses annually half of the whole tax, for the want of facilities which are enjoyed by almost every other portion of the United States," he answered.[13]

Robert E. Fisk, editor of the *Helena Herald,* argued that his community direly needed better transportation facilities. He was convinced that once capitalists, always a cautious breed, were aware of Montana's potential the territory would come into its own in an economic way. But, said the editor, Montanans could not simply sit and wait for their part of America to be discovered; they must act positively, and they must demonstrate to the financial world a willingness to help in the opening of the country. It was the duty of Montana communities, he suggested, to help build an iron road to their mines.[14]

Business leaders spearheaded a drive for a subsidy to be paid for by the territory. Banker Samuel Hauser, a man whose interest in railroad construction arose from his earlier training as a civil engineer and from railroad experience in Missouri before the Civil War, was also possessed of talents that made him a natural leader in the drive. During 1872 and 1873 he and the Committee of One Hundred conducted a campaign to persuade Gov. Benjamin F. Potts that their problem merited a special session of the legislature. Through newspaper editorials, mass meetings, and personal persuasion—as well as "some misrepresentations, a few Greenbacks & considerable bad whiskey"—petitions suggesting the wisdom of such a move were circulated in various communities. The governor heeded the business world and directed the legislators to assemble at Virginia City in April 1873. Hauser's committee also persuaded Congress to issue a franchise and right-of-way for the proposed road.[15]

While Governor Potts was willing to call a legislative meeting, he did not agree with the committee's proposal. The legislature, argued the governor, who was an able lawyer, had no legal power to encumber the territory with subsidy bonds. Therefore he took a strong antisubsidy stand, in which he found support from members of the Council, or upper house, whose members came from counties all over the territory. However, because of the concentrated nature of Montana's mining population, over half of the 26 members of the lower house came from Deer Lodge, Lewis and Clark, and Madison counties, all of which would benefit directly from the road to Utah.

The debates were fierce, but the Legislative Assembly finally passed a modified subsidy bill that would permit counties along the rail route to invest in capital stock up to 20 percent of assessed valuation. When the governor exercised the right of veto, the bill was passed over it, and then, as a final act, the legislators provided a general incorporation for railroads in the territory.[16] When news of the action reached Helena, there were handshakes, a display of flags, and expressions of joy, accompanied by the blare of Helena's Silver Cornet Band, as the residents of Last Chance Gulch looked forward to a day of economic emancipation from slow and pro- hibitively expensive freight service.[17]

Outlying communities, particularly those not heavily settled or in areas that might not be directly benefited by the Salt Lake connection, continued to oppose the idea of paying for the road in county bonds. Although their representatives had not succeeded in preventing passage of the enabling legislation that permitted counties to raise money by this method, they had kept the territorial government from guaranteeing a fixed subsidy the rail- road builders demanded as a condition to entry into Montana. "Outside of Helena the North and South Railroad project is the most unpopular question that can be suggested," admitted E. S. Wilkinson of the *Rocky Mountain Gazette*.[18] Peter Ronan, one of Montana's prominent men of the day, suggested that more than jealousies directed at the Helena railroad enthusiasts had killed the subsidy in the spring of 1873. He declared that one of the project's detractors had influenced the vote from the outlying counties when he failed to get part of a $30,000 slush fund Sam Hauser was supposed to have brought to Virginia City for the purpose of oiling legislative gears. Opponents, who were not paid off, allegedly took the position that they were insulted by the mere rumor that they were to be approached for their votes, and with self-righteous indignation they stood firm against such manipulations.[19]

Lack of support from those who were not to be directly affected by the road generated considerable ire among its proponents. An angered resident of Bannack had sharp words for James H. Mills, editor of Deer Lodge's *New North-West,* because Mills failed to display proper enthusiasm for the Utah Northern extension. "When a man has been the recipient of a sweet suck at the public titty-bag and obtained a 'fat take' in the shape of public printing," said the critic, "he ought to be grateful enough to the people at large at least to try to promote their interests and welfare."[20] Mills was charged with selfish localism and lack of concern for the general welfare of Montana, a stance that came close to treason in the eyes of those who foresaw

Before the opening of the Utah and Northern, to Montana, freight was carried northward in heavy wagons, such as these. The drivers may have stopped to "fuel up" at the building on the left. Taken at Corinne, Utah.

a new bonanza with the coming of the narrow gauge. The editor was not antirailroad; like many of his Deer Lodge readers, he viewed the standard-gauge Northern Pacific as a better answer to the territory's needs.

Summer and autumn of 1873 was a time of railroad mania in south-western Montana. After the legislature passed its enabling act, Sam Hauser attempted to interest Salt Lake City and San Francisco capitalists, but he found them far from responsive. The failure of Jay Cooke's banking house that year, and the inability of the Northern Pacific to continue construction, made it an obviously poor time to entice outside capital. No one wanted to touch a railroad investment in Montana unless an outright and absolute subsidy by the territorial government was assured. Since it was not, under existing legislation, local boosters embarked upon a campaign to provide a more attractive situation for investors.

George F. Cope, of Virginia City's *Montanian,* spread the good word in his vicinity, as Hauser's paid propagandist. The banker had authorized him to draw up to $100 a month, for services rendered, and in the autumn of 1873 Cope took advantage of the offer, confessing that he was "now in short bunch grass." An indication that railroad enthusiasm was not universal, even in areas to be affected, is seen in Cope's claim that his arguments for a subsidy had cost him 75 subscribers in his own county and perhaps 150 in other sections. However, said the journalist, "[I] know that the railroad feeling is growing in this country."[21] Railroad boosters demonstrated some of that feeling at a rally staged in the streets of Diamond City, near Helena. By the light of torches, and amidst bell ringing and cheers, a procession made its way through town, calling for support. Placards reading "Political death to opponents of railroads," and "We are coming Father Brigham with $2,000,000 more," urged action. From a mass meeting after the parade there came a resolution asking legislators to vote $1 million for the Utah Northern extension.[22]

Newspapers representing the interested communities added their in-fluence to the subsidy campaign by giving a prominent place in their columns to any news items suggesting the importance of railway service. The *Helena Herald* spoke of heavy wagon traffic from Corinne, emphasizing the many days of travel, and lamenting the long delays occasioned by bad roads. When the Corinne *Reporter* described the difficulty Montana-bound passengers were experiencing in securing places aboard the stagecoaches of Gilmer & Salisbury, the Helena paper readily quoted its sister journal, revealing that travelers who came off the trains at Corinne waited up to three days to book passage on the stagecoaches. In some instances premiums as high as $20 were offered for the opportunity to proceed without further delay.[23] Similarly, the Montana paper quoted a story written by a correspondent to the Pittsburgh *Gazette,* who stated that his recent travels had convinced him of the territory's need for a railroad. The long distances to the mines discouraged capitalists from visiting the place to make a personal examination of its potential. Instead, they were drawn to Colorado or Utah, neither of which was as rich in minerals as Montana.[24]

Parades, mass meetings, and newspaper publicity were to no avail. The Panic of 1873 so thoroughly dried up investment money that no further attempts were made to promote a railroad in southern Montana until 1875. Joseph Richardson told Sam Hauser, in the spring of 1874, that "we are heading for Montana as fast as we can," but under existing conditions the Utah Northern could not build any distance without considerable help. "If you want the Road you must secure us a large amount of aid as it is impossible to get eastern capital to go into it without the Territory will offer good inducements," he explained to Hauser.[25] Since the Montana legislature showed little inclination to change its mind, no such subsidy was forthcoming that year. Consequently the Utah Northern crept across the Utah-Idaho line as far as Franklin, where construction ceased for two years.

Despite all discouragements, Montana railroad promoters refused to surrender in the fight to connect the territory with a major transportation facility. They kept up a drumfire of publicity, openly attacking Governor Potts for his steadfast refusal to sanction the subsidy notion. Early in 1875 the *Helena Herald* called the governor "the most shallow and odorous of all the Potts of which we have any record," and it publicly asked him to step down to "make way for his betters."[26] The journal also received the aid of Gen. John Gibbon, who assured readers that property values would double within five years after the completion of a railroad into Montana.[27] Moses Thatcher, general superintendent of the Utah Northern, was quoted as saying that a narrow gauge could be built and put in running order for $5,000 a mile. The road, exclusive of a four-mile branch to Corinne, was 80 miles in length; enough iron had been purchased to extend the line another 80 miles during the coming summer. Should Montana make available $1 million, Thatcher felt sure his company would be able to reach that territory.[28] The publicity campaign was climaxed by a railroad convention, held at Helena, at the end of April.

While his lieutenants were at work on the local scene, Sam Hauser went to New York to interest eastern capitalists in Montana railroading. He told Joseph Richardson and John Young that he was there "to see if you and your friends could be induced to push the U.N.R.R. through to Helena, Montana . . . or join us in a railroad organization to be afterwards consolidated with the U.N. or worked as a separate company." He wanted to know the smallest figure that would be acceptable to them, in the form of a bond subsidy, and also, if he could use their names "or count upon your influence & aid, and that of the U.P. Company." To support his requests, he pointed out that $2.5 million had been paid for freight charges to and from Montana during the previous year, a piece of business that would go to the Utah Northern if it could extend its line only 75 to 100 miles farther north. Wagon transportation facilities, said Hauser, could not accommodate all the products mined in Montana during the year.[29]

Within a few days the Montana banker's fishing expedition produced a nibble. Sidney Dillon of the Union Pacific Company informed Richardson and Young that he would be "pleased to aid your enterprise in any way I can consistently." He agreed to carry railroad iron and other materials necessary for extension of the Utah Northern and to take pay for the charges in bonds of the narrow gauge.[30] While such interest on the part of the Union Pacific was encouraging, it was insufficient to aid the ailing Utah Northern. Richardson and Young conveyed this information to Hauser, and suggested that Montanans promote their own organization on the theory that local participation would not only demonstrate faith in the project, but it would show that "outside capitalists need not fear hostile legislation that might impair their investments in the future." The two entrepreneurs promised that if this were accomplished, and if the territorial legislature would authorize $2.5 million in bonds with liberal laws controlling them, they would be willing to associate themselves in the enterprise as directors.[31]

Hauser's banking associate, Dan C. Corbin, thought a reasonable subsidy was now possible, for never had railroad feeling been more evident in Montana. As tactfully as possible he suggested that when the next move was made Hauser ought to keep his name out of it, and that none of the parties prominent in the earlier campaign should be openly associated with it for fear of accusations that "there is another job put up." If the "old ring" came forward now, he said quite frankly, chances of success surely would be jeopardized.[32]

Hauser passed along the information about railroad enthusiasm in his area to John Young, predicting that when the legislature met in January 1876 it would act favorably upon the subsidy question. To his old arguments in favor of the narrow gauge, he added his impression that many Montanans were by now convinced of the Northern Pacific's hopeless position and that, in turn, they regarded the Utah Northern as their principal salvation.[33]

While Hauser and his friends caucused and corresponded, the Helena press kept the prospect of a railroad constantly before its readers. "The iron key has been found to unlock our golden treasures, and hopeful anticipation of better days are prevalent among the people," said one editorial. "With railroads come population, industry and capital, and with them come the

elements of prosperity and greatness to Montana." That journal optimisti-
cally called the railroad an iron wand, stretched over hidden wealth, and
when the wand was waved the earth would open, allowing the golden
"Cornucopia" to pour forth.[34] But although Helena became the capital
city in 1875, that decade was one of general stagnation among its merchants.
During those years Montana's population nearly doubled, but Helena's
gain was so slight that the city appeared to be standing still.[35]

The prohibitive cost of importing heavy mining machinery used to
extract low-grade ores, and the great difficulty of hauling ore to reduction
plants, appeared to have brought the mineral industry to a standstill.
Freighters charged $30 a ton to transport ores from Helena to the Utah
Northern's railhead, and an average of $60 a ton to bring back merchandise.
If they came back empty, the miner was charged for the round trip, or $90 a
ton for his ore transportation. During the seventies imports into the
territory declined steadily, indicating that more than one wagon must have
returned empty.[36] Meanwhile, placer mining was a dying occupation,
leaving those who pursued it a choice of entering the restrictive quartz
mining enterprises, or some other business. Many chose to leave the territory.
Faced by this situation, local businessmen pinned their hopes on the
coming of the railroad. One of the mining country's earliest pioneers,
Granville Stuart, said: "How to get one at a cost that would not bankrupt
the new and sparsely settled territory engaged the minds of the thoughtful
citizens."[37]

In addition to its promise of succor to Montana's principal industry, the
Utah Northern project was said to have other virtues. It would, asserted
the *Independent,* of Helena, hasten the lagging Northern Pacific which, in
turn, would assist in solving the Indian problem. By the mid-seventies
residents of Montana could view the increasingly heavy settlements along
the Union Pacific line in Nebraska and note that depredations by the tribes
had largely ceased in those areas. They argued that it would be better to
spend money on rails that would bring an influx of people than to continue
the large and often ineffectual expenditures of money on a network of
military posts.[38] In its isolated location, the territory appeared to be
paralyzed by the lack of transportation facilities without which there could
be little or no future economic growth.

By late summer 1875, there was growing impatience among the mining
men of Montana. In a pique, Helena's *Herald* warned the Utah Northern
that if it ever expected aid in its efforts there should be more activity at the
railhead.[39] Joseph Richardson, who by now had invested considerable funds
in the Mormon railroad, was as anxious as anyone to see his road reach the
land of gold and silver. At the moment he was in a deep conflict with

John Young over just that question. The road, originally conceived as an aid to the economic development of northern Utah, appeared to be serving that purpose well enough, but it paid very poor returns on the investment. As one of Hauser's railroad acquaintances put it: "It has always been one of the axioms of Wells, Fargo & Co's agents that 'One Gentile makes as much business as a hundred Mormons' and the Utah Northern has found out that a well settled Mormon community will not furnish business enough to run a railroad."[40] Young and his associates wanted to pursue the original plan of extending the road to Soda Springs to serve more Mormon farmers, but Richardson knew the rails had to reach Montana or he would lose what he had invested.

The outcome of the disagreement was Young's resignation as president, at Richardson's insistence.[41] In a letter dated October 19, 1875, Young informed the Utah Northern board of directors that "for considerations in themselves sufficient to justify me, I hereby tender you my resignation as president of your company." He was succeeded by Royal M. Bassett of Birmingham, Connecticut, who was also president of the Birmingham Iron Foundry of that city.[42] This being done, Richardson now worked hard to increase the interest of the Union Pacific in his project.

The Connecticut investor appears to have been caught between the Mormons on one hand and the financiers associated with the Union Pacific on the other. Desperate for money, Bassett had sold Utah Northern stocks and bonds to the Union Pacific very cheaply. That the Bostonians had driven a hard bargain was revealed by treasurer E. H. Rollins, in the spring of 1875, when he commented to a colleague: "I quite agree with you that the Stocks and Bonds are comparatively worthless and for this reason do not see the propriety of Richardson's 'higgling' about small matters. He ought to deliver Bonds and Stock enough to settle the account squarely, as he gets good hard money from the Company for them."[43]

Rumor in Montana had it that Richardson was willing to put up half the cost of the extension if the larger road would supply the other half, secured by a first-mortgage lien, the entire narrow gauge to be under Union Pacific control. The idea caused no objections in the mining country. "We want a road, and the way it is to be supplied us, we will not stop to consider, in view of the paramount importance of its coming," vowed the *Independent*.[44]

As Sam Hauser had predicted, the legislative session of January 1876 was in a mood to favor a subsidy bill. In its liberality, it passed three of them: one that would support the Northern Pacific to the amount of $3 million (later turned down by voters in the counties) ; a second that provided an outright subsidy of $1.5 million to the Utah Northern; a third that was designed to satisfy the demands of northern and eastern Montana for a Fort Benton connection. The legislative body literally killed the railroad boosters with kindness, for when the Utah Northern backers heard of the action they refused to participate on the ground that Montana's resources were not sufficient to pay for all the subsidies. As Richardson told Hauser, such bonds simply could not be sold in eastern markets; their variety and number, so weakly based, would frighten off prospective buyers.[45]

The Montana legislature's sudden enthusiasm for subsidies, self-defeating as it was, did not extinguish New York interest in the northbound narrow gauge. Martin Maginnis, the territory's congressional delegate, told Hauser that recently he had conferred with Jay Gould, Sidney Dillon, Oliver Ames, Richardson, and Royal Bassett, all of whom expressed interest in the project, making it "evident that the Union Pacific have come up now in earnest to back Richardson." Richardson was "tickled to death" over the developments, said Maginnis, "because it seemed apparent that the U. P. would guarantee the success of the venture." The Montanan was pleased at what he had learned in New York. He was impressed by Bassett, who "is smart, takes his whiskey, and is a generous fellow—business all over." Gould also pleased him when the renowned financier showed such an interest in the future of Montana that he suggested the construction of a broad-gauge line to the territory should Richardson's efforts fail.[46] Maginnis described Gould as "a bright little fellow and who seems to be one of the Directors who has the clearest idea of the advantage of a Montana connection to their road."[47]

Growing involvement by the Union Pacific was revealed in the efforts of Moses Thatcher, of the Utah Northern, to gain a rebate on freight turned over to it at Ogden. He explained that Montana ores that were not shipped down the Missouri River usually were sent to Corinne to be forwarded over the Central Pacific road to San Francisco. To prevent this he suggested a drawback of 15 cents on every hundred pounds of freight delivered at Ogden. If such a practice might cause trouble between the two big roads, the Mormon suggested that the Union Pacific deliver 30 tons of coal a week to the Utah Northern at Ogden, free of charge. The Central Pacific people needed to know nothing of the arrangement. Thatcher admitted that his road already had incurred the Central Pacific's displeasure when it built to Ogden rather than using the Corinne connection, after which the Central Pacific cut its rates from Corinne to Ogden by half.

"The U. P. should help us," said Thatcher. "We are a part of your Company in that you are to some extent our bondholders, and we are a direct feeder to your line. We ought not to be left alone to contend against a power in every respect superior to us, especially when we are constantly

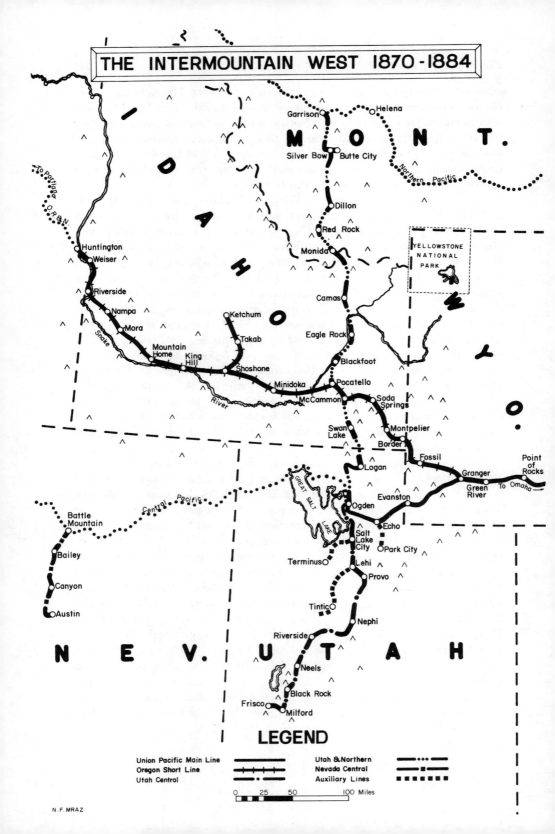

THE INTERMOUNTAIN WEST 1870-1884

Helena

Garrison

M O N T.

Northern Pacific

Silver Bow Butte City

Dillon

Red Rock

Monida

Camas

YELLOWSTONE
NATIONAL
PARK

Eagle Rock

I D A H O

Ketchum

Takab

Blackfoot

Mountain
Home King
Hill Shoshone

Minidoka Pocatello

McCammon Soda
Springs

Swan
Lake Montpelier

Border

Logan Fossil

Point
of
Rocks

Granger

Green
River

To Omaha

Evanston

Ogden

Echo

Salt
Lake
City Park City

Terminus

Lehi

Provo

Tintic

Nephi

Riverside

Neels

Black Rock

Frisco Milford

W Y O.

Huntington
Weiser

Riverside

Nampa
Mora

Snake

River

Central Pacific

Battle
Mountain

Bailey

Canyon

Austin

N E V. U T A H

To Pocatello

O.S.N.

LEGEND

Union Pacific Main Line
Oregon Short Line
Utah Central

Utah & Northern
Nevada Central
Auxiliary Lines

0   25   50   100 Miles

N. F. MRAZ

working for the direct interests of your Company." He promised that in return for more such protection the Utah Northern would not only feed the Union Pacific, but it would make every effort to extend farther north.[48] Dillon instructed his superintendent at Omaha to see what he could do about the request.

When the encouraging words heard from the East, during the early months of 1876, failed to produce any tangible results, Montanans grew despondent. Granville Stuart told his friend Sam Hauser that "Bassette [*sic*] Richardson & Co. don't deserve any help from us, for with all our efforts, we have never succeeded in getting them enough interested in Montana to come, or even send agents to a field we offered to them, & about all they ever have done has been to listen to the misrepresentations of our enemies." Charging that the financiers "don't care a d – – n for Montana," Stuart admitted he was "pretty much disgusted with them & as the Dutchman said to his wife when she played triplets on him, 'I gots nuff mits such foolishness.' "[49]

Newspaper attitudes during this period suggest that Stuart's disillusionment was shared by others. Appearing in print were vague references to a possible railroad north of Denver, through Wyoming, and into Montana; other stories told of a projected road called the Portland, Dalles and Salt Lake Railroad Company whose promoters hoped to build northward from Corinne, into Montana, and thence to Oregon. The old plan of connecting Fort Benton, the head of Missouri River navigation, to the mining country by means of a short railroad was also revived. As these ideas were discussed, the *Butte Miner* quoted a report from Corinne that users of the Utah Northern had found it "hardly as good as a respectable bull-train."[50] Men who once had unstintingly praised the narrow gauge now derisively referred to it as "the wheelbarrow line." In their moment of disappointment, Montanans rejected an enterprise they had earlier regarded as their salvation, and they buried themselves in bitter despair.

Sam Hauser was not one of those who ran up the white flag. All during the summer and autumn of 1876 he busied himself with the details of a new attack. Further conferences with Richardson and Gould produced a syndicate, comprised principally of Union Pacific officials and capitalized at $2 million, the purpose of which was to extend the road north of Franklin, Idaho. Martin Maginnis advised Hauser that he had met with Sidney Dillon and other Union Pacific directors, who wanted Hauser to take charge of matters at Helena. "They mean business now, having gotten a good arrangement out of Richardson," said the congressman.[51] The newly formed group proposed to build at least 100 miles beyond Franklin during 1877, with the aim of completing it within two and a half years.[52] Armed with a concrete proposal, and backed by men of such impressive reputations, Hauser put the matter before Governor Potts, who did not attack its subsidy provisions, to the surprise of many. The legislators responded by passing a $1,700,000 subsidy bill that shortly received the governor's signature.[53]

The New Yorkers seemed pleased with the legislation, Dillon telling Hauser in mid-March that the proposition was acceptable to his group. To the consternation of Hauser and his friends, however, the easterners changed their minds before the month was out. While they could acquiesce to certain modifications of their proposition, the clause that demanded a monthly royalty from revenues of the entire line, to be paid into the territorial treasury, was filled with danger, particularly because it had no date of expiration. In a letter signed by six of the eastern financiers, Governor Potts was informed that the aid offered by the railroad act was declined.[54]

Dillon, however, was not willing to close the door to further negotiations. Several days later, he told Potts that he believed in Montana's resources and recognized that not only would a road bring prosperity to the territory but it would also largely increase the Union Pacific's business. Therefore, he intended to have a competent engineer make further studies and report his findings in detail. Should the result be favorable, the Union Pacific was prepared to make a new proposition, provided "you can give us sufficient inducements by subsidy or otherwise."[55]

Perhaps the decision prevented further turmoil in Montana, at least for the time being. James Mills, of Deer Lodge's *New North-West,* openly opposed extension of the road to Helena, holding out for a line that came closer to the Butte and Deer Lodge area. Or so he said. Northern Pacific influence was heavy in west central Montana at this time, and its proponents were trying to gain a subsidy for its extension. Samuel Word, an attorney who represented the Utah Northern, warned Hauser in February that if the narrow-gauge proposition were accepted by both the railroad and the territory, the Northern Pacific people would spare no effort to defeat it before the people. "You know that the N. P. Co. desire to bottle this Territory up like *chow chow* and save it for its own future use," he said. "It cannot build a road itself now and it desires none built to the Territory until it gets ready. Above all things it does not desire to see this Territory tributary to the U.P." Accusing the Northern Pacific of not being above bribery, Word took the practical view that "the judicious expenditure of ten to twenty thousand dolls" would put the Utah Northern across so effectively that "there will be no one found afterwards to raise his voice against it . . . ."[56] While the lack of a railroad was said to hurt Montana's economy, efforts to gain one apparently were keeping the territory's monies in motion.

The most recent breakdown in negotiations launched territorial residents into new despair. "That a railroad would ever be built to Montana seemed a thing so far in the future that no one gave it a serious thought," recalled one of them a decade later.[57] Newspaper stories reflected disappointment, and perhaps a decline of hope, for now readers were assured that the quartz mines were sufficiently rich to be worked without rail benefits. Accounts of wagon freight shipments out of Corinne appeared in the papers with great frequency, often with the comment that the trip would be made in 30 days if the good weather held.[58] As a consolation, Montanans were told that service on the narrow gauge between Ogden and Franklin was so slow and so costly that the bull teams paralleling its route offered competitive service. The Utah Northern's engines and other equipment were said to be so primitive and inefficient that they were the laughingstock of those who used them.[59]

Then, in the autumn of 1877, came the same tantalizing news that had so excited people in the mining country on earlier occasions. A dispatch dated New York, October 24, and addressed to engineer Washington Dunn, commanded, "Let a contract in my name for 10 or 20 miles, by the Marsh valley route at once." It was signed by Jay Gould. The determination to push northward was generated by a belief in the Union Pacific offices that the mining country's potential was about to be realized. "The business of Montana is growing very fast, and we are getting but a small part of it as there was [*sic*] nearly 100 Steam Boats went up the Missouri this past summer with freight for the territory," Dillon told his fellow board member, Elisha Atkins. He said that if the road were extended even a hundred miles north of Franklin "I think we could get the great part of the Montana business."[60]

Dunn, who was to be prominent in the road's construction all the way to Montana, at once arranged with Moses Thatcher and other Mormons to grade 12 miles of road north of Franklin. Gould, said the account, intended to get as far as Eagle Rock (Idaho Falls) within a year.[61] The Montana press responded with enthusiasm, again predicting that such service would mean lower grocery prices, without any drop in miners' wages, or, in other words, a rise in real wages. Moreover, Montana's rich agricultural potential would be realized, which, in turn, would broaden the territorial tax base. All criticisms of the narrow gauge were forgotten, and once more the little thread of iron pointed north had a magnetic attraction for those who awaited it.[62]

Activity in Idaho was generated by Gould, who, Martin Maginnis said, was "full of schemes." On April 3, 1878, the Utah Northern was sold at a foreclosure sale held in Salt Lake City, and its property was conveyed to a new corporation known as the Utah and Northern Railway Company.

Gould, who had purchased Richardson's holdings for $400,000—about 40 cents on the dollar—and had acquired common stock held locally for $80,000, or 10 cents on the dollar, became the dominating figure in the reorganized road.[63] Operations under new management commenced on May 1.[64]

During the spring months engineer Dunn pushed the road 40 miles north of Franklin, Idaho. Sidney Dillon promised Hauser that both stage and wagon freight service from the end of track would serve Montana's needs with increased efficiency. Goods could be billed directly to Helena from eastern points, by rail, and thence by the Union Pacific's newly organized Diamond R freight line, thus eliminating delays and complications.[65]

As the reorganized company continued the earlier drive to reach Montana, it also renewed efforts to gain help from the territory. Dillon told Hauser that he and his associates intended again to request assistance in the form of bonds, and once more he asked the banker to manage things for him at Helena. Jay Gould also wrote to Hauser, explaining that his group wanted more than permission to "build into & through the Territory." They wanted $1,200,000 in bonds and exemption from taxes for 25 years. He doubted that the road could reach Helena by the fall of 1879, but he believed that "we could come pretty close to it." The proposed main line, he said, would touch Helena, but there would be branches to Butte, Deer Lodge, Virginia City, and other mining communities. The ultimate goal of the road was Puget Sound. Gould asked for Hauser's views on such matters and also the opinions of leading newspapers and businessmen in the north country.[66]

Gould's name was an important addition to an already impressive list of eastern financiers now interested in Montana railroads. Not only was he a familiar figure, and a man of considerable means, but his ability to manipulate public opinion was well known. In September he asked Hauser for a subscription to "the best weekly paper in Helena," because "I like to keep posted as to the developments in the mineral & other resources of Montana."[67] It was more than that. In addition to keeping "posted," he was not unacquainted with means of manufacturing opinion. Editor Chauncey Barbour, of Missoula's *Weekly Missoulian,* told Hauser that some of his friends had suggested he start a paper in Butte. "If anything should come of it," he said, "there should exist between us some such a silent partnership as was suggested last spring." Revealing the source of his interest, he continued: "It has occurred to me that you could manipulate the thing and have a say in such a projected paper without the investment of a cent. I am persuaded from our former conferences, that you can induce Jay Gould to place $5,000 in a vigorous railroad paper at Butte; that he can be persuaded to pass me back and forth for the purchase of such an office as may be needed . . . ."[68]

The Montana press already had resumed its earlier railroad enthusiasm. Editor Fisk of the *Helena Herald* now held the warmest of feelings toward the Utah and Northern. Referring to a recent trip from Ogden to Franklin, he told how the train moved along steadily at 14 to 18 miles an hour, and on one section, as the engineer opened his throttle, the cars covered 14 miles in 28 minutes. "I had never been over the narrow gauge before," the editor admitted, and added that he had sided with those who had referred to it as the wheelbarrow line, "but I have changed my views radically." It was a fine road, he said glowingly, one that would ably take care of Montana's business for many years to come.[69]

From Salt Lake City came reports that were encouraging to Montanans. Business was said to have picked up astonishingly, to a degree that surpassed even the fondest hopes of the recent purchasers. Forty Union Pacific carloads of freight consigned to Montana were reported to be waiting shipment along the narrow gauge. Ten to 20 boxcars were being run over the little line every day.[70] Such exciting news was eagerly read in the mining camps and it appeared to augur well for future rail development.

To the great disappointment of Hauser and his eastern friends the legislature in January 1879 declined to provide the desired subsidy. Jay Gould, who was in the process of selling his interest to the Union Pacific, angrily threatened to stop work unless financial aid was forthcoming. Dillon also applied pressure. He wrote to Potts, saying that he and his associates regarded legislative assistance as imperative, and unless money was forthcoming the Union Pacific was disposed to build into the Black Hills, where a subsidy had been promised. He also said he was opposed to such a shift in direction, and if Montana could offer aid the Utah and Northern would press on.[71] Both he and Gould were bluffing. The investment in the narrow gauge through Idaho was at such a stage that the line had to go forward in order to save the investment.

As before, those parts of Montana not apt to benefit by the narrow gauge showed little enthusiasm for putting up money to enhance the prosperity of Butte and Helena. A Missoula banker, C. P. Higgins, openly opposed the subsidy, charging that the mining towns would be favored over his city. Passengers bound for Missoula, he said, would be "transferred from the tail end of the narrow gauge to the Jerkies of a narrow minded stage Co.," and charged excessive rates. "What's the fare to Missoula?" he asked. "Oh, we have to go thro [*sic*] a hell of a place to get there and we will charge you a hell of a price, $56.00." The Missoula banker argued that the only emigration his part of the territory enjoyed came from Washington

RIGHT–*A Utah and Northern freight train preparing to leave Logan, Utah, in 1885. One of the onlookers has come down to visit the crew on a penny-farthing bicycle.*

BOTTOM–*This engine, manufactured by the Baldwin Company, was used on both the Utah and Northern and the Oregon Short Line. After the engine was scrapped, in 1931, its boiler was used in a laundry at Astoria, Oregon.*

Territory. He did not blame residents of Helena for wanting a road, or for favoring any tax exemptions to get one, but he did not live there and therefore he opposed the idea.[72]

In the face of such opposition Hauser continued his efforts, telegraphing to Gould that he could get at least a 12- or 15-year tax exemption and at least a $200,000 subsidy from Lewis and Clark County, of which Helena was the county seat. Gould was not enthusiastic, but before long Dillon wrote to Governor Potts saying that his group would build into Montana for a 15-year exemption. He also asked those members of the legislature from Lewis and Clark County for a $300,000 bond subsidy, in the event that the legislature agreed to a tax exemption, promising to put a road into Helena during the year 1881.[73]

Benjamin Potts, who was now associated with Hauser in business, asked for, and received, permission to call a special session of the legislature in July 1879. The governor was now much more enthusiastic about the Utah and Northern. In his annual report of 1878 he had spoken of the territory's extensive mines, whose output amounted to $7 million that year. This figure, said Potts, would be steadily augmented "by the early completion of the Utah Northern Railroad, now in the course of construction from Ogden, Utah, to Helena, Mont."[74] The territorial surveyor general stated that emigrants were now entering Montana in great numbers, and the steady approach of the railroad was certain to send these figures to new heights.[75]

Although Hauser did his mightiest, sending agents around the territory to "make sure that the legislature will do what is right after they get together," his efforts again failed and the subsidy bill was defeated by a narrow margin in the special session.[76] George Wilson, a Cheyenne banker, had advised Hauser in 1875 that the Union Pacific would build into Montana, regardless of subsidy action, and some of his friends had come to believe this. Martin Maginnis now refused his support, arguing that such financial aid was unnecessary and that the community was in no position to take on such debts.[77]

Those who opposed the subsidy on the ground that the road would enter Montana anyway were right. On March 15, 1880, the Utah and Northern reached the territorial line, an event described in Butte as the most important occurrence in Montana's history. Those of the copper city who could not witness the event gathered at Owsley Hall, where a telegraph operator stood ready to relay news of the ceremonies being held at the track's terminus. Mayor Henry Jacobs, a clothing merchant, spoke to the gathering, assuring his listeners that the road would bring not only population, progress, and prosperity, but also produce statehood. Amid cheers and the popping of champagne corks, the residents of Butte hailed the approach of what Mayor Jacobs described as a steam instrument that would shortly melt the frosts of isolation which had for so long locked up the Territory's boundless resources.[78] That spring, excitement mounted to new heights in Montana. In June, Washington Dunn, superintendent of construction, and George Wolcott, chief engineer of the Utah and Northern, visited Butte and Deer Lodge to examine mines and mineral prospects in detail. William Andrews Clark, who was to become so prominent in copper mining and so infamous in politics, accompanied the men, showing them the resources that would make a railroad pay.[79]

The long-awaited railroad appeared to be a reality; one question remained—the terminus. Helena had been the strongest supporter, but there was talk that Butte might be the lucky suitor. As that prospect grew stronger, Butte became more vocal. "The trouble is that Helena thinks she is New York or Boston," said the *Miner,* "whereas she is an unimportant village separated from the natural terminus of the road, which is Butte, by a distance of seventy miles and a range of mountains." In a moment of whimsy the editor suggested that a branch might be built to Helena as well as to "San Francisco and other insignificant villages on the Pacific coast."[80]

Sam Hauser and his Helena friends would have been astonished and dismayed had they viewed Dillon's correspondence of this period. In a letter to Washington Dunn, the Union Pacific president commented: "I have no special line in view beyond Butte City, but want to go in the direction which will be the most advantageous to the company...."[81] Dillon was interested primarily in the transportation of ores; he proposed to extend in the direction that held the brightest mineral prospects.[82] During those days he spoke of construction by way of Virginia City, provided the grade was easy, and of building from Boulder Creek to the Missouri River, both of which plans looked toward capturing all the business possible in the area.[83]

Even the road's temporary terminus was decided by the existence of mines. In October Dillon instructed Dunn to stop for the winter opposite Glen Dale, "where the Hecla Consolidated mines and works are situated."[84] Dillon's narrow gauge was following the pattern established by that of Gen. William Jackson Palmer, builder of the Denver and Rio Grande: it was prospecting the country as it proceeded.

Dillon and his associates by now had concluded that failure of repeated efforts to gain a subsidy had sufficiently established a pattern of thought in Montana that would be hard to alter. Moreover, they felt that having built into the territory independently, it would be better to finish the road without interference from government officials enforcing restrictions that might be written into such legislation. As Dillon said, such a development might "be a hindrance to our independent action, and thus perhaps injure us more than benefit us."[85]

Even in the autumn of 1880, at a time when the road had penetrated southern Montana, the Union Pacific president was not concerned about staking out land for depot sites, because he was not yet sure where the road would run. He had little or no fear that such land would be unavailable or would even be expensive because the territory was so thinly settled. "It is a far-off country," he told Samuel Word, "and property in that section cannot enhance very largely." Therefore, Word's suggested aid in procuring depot sites was politely declined.[86]

Although Dillon was not as optimistic as Montanans were about the inevitable rise in property values upon the approach of a railroad, he believed the produce of the country would provide ample business for a narrow gauge and that such a road would make a good feeder for the main line. Placer mining was in a sharp decline, yet pick and pan mining still produced $1 million a year. Quartz and silver mining, however, were increasing. Copper was not yet a valuable source of business, unless it contained a high percentage of silver, but it had potential value.[87]

The territory also had, at this time, about 275,000 cattle and close to 250,000 sheep. In 1880 it exported 30,000 head of cattle and 1.3 million pounds of wool. Forty sawmills turned out 6 million feet of lumber that year. During the mid-seventies Montana had lost population, but by 1880 it was just under 40,000, a figure that had nearly doubled during the decade. Most of the increase occurred late in the decade.[88]

It was in recognition of such growth, and because of the Union Pacific's policy of feeder lines, that the push to Montana had been undertaken. By 1880 the road's government directors reported large orders for rails, passenger coaches, boxcars, Pullman sleepers, express cars, cattle cars, and engines, to be used on the Utah and Northern.[89] The Union Pacific's treasurer revealed that between January 1879 and August 1880 the company had expended $1,182,871.51 for work north of Blackfoot, Idaho. The road south of Blackfoot was built by the Mormons and the Richardsons, with Jay Gould participating in the latter portion of the work. "We paid Mr. Gould seven hundred and fifty thousand dollars for the bonds & stocks," said the treasurer, and he admitted that he did not know what the southern section of the road had cost Gould.[90] The "bright little fellow" apparently had not shared the details of his shrewd investment with Union Pacific officials.

As the Utah and Northern managers studied potential routes into Montana, construction crews suspended all but routine work and prepared to winter in the Beaverhead Valley. The traditional railhead town sprang up in the autumn of 1880 when a promoter named B. F. White bought a 430-

acre ranch from Dick Deacon for $10,500 and divided it into small lots. Having first determined that the railhead would halt there for the winter, provided the company be given a free right-of-way and the usual depot site, White named the place Dillon and commenced operations. His receipts for the first day amounted to $14,000. By 1883 about $50,000 worth of lots had been sold, some of them bringing as much as $3,000 each, and the stripling town boasted a population of one thousand.[91]

The spring of 1881 produced anxiety as well as anticipation in the mining country. Butte continued to be deeply concerned that it might be by-passed in favor of Helena, a place that presumably offered much less business to a railroad. "One single company now operating here will during the present year ship between three and four thousand tons of milling and mining machinery to this camp," said the *Miner*. "This amount of freight is in excess of all the merchandise received in Helena during any twelve months of its existence." Butte claimed to be the home base of at least 50 big mine owners, all of whom would import quantities of heavy machinery. The very fact that Helena's merchants were ready to offer the Union Pacific money for coming their way was submitted as proof that Butte's potential was greater.[92]

The spring of 1881 brought sprouting rails and the germination of new municipalities. Melrose, located 30 miles north of Dillon, had 300 to 400 residents by the time it had reached the lusty age of seven weeks. Lots sold for between $25 and $80, commercial houses appeared, and dispensers of food and lodging opened for business. Meals were three for a dollar, with board and room available at nine dollars a week. Already the railroad had brought down prices in a mining country long known for its high cost of living.[93] Such progress delighted the residents of Butte, who now counted the days until the locomotive reached what they asserted was Montana's principal city and, as the pace of railroad construction picked up in the spring, there were predictions that the copper city would be attached to the outside world sometime in June.

Summer came, but it did not bring the sound of steam. As surveyors made ready to enter Butte by way of Silver Bow, a few miles to the west, difficulties over a right-of-way developed. The proposed route ran over some old placer mining claims, the owners of which decided they might yet be made to pay. The Utah and Northern's charter authorized it to build through Idaho and into Montana, for the purpose of making a connection with the Northern Pacific; but since Butte was not on a direct line, land for the desired branch could not be condemned. The narrow gauge reached Silver Bow in October 1881, and there it stopped as the argument over entry into Butte raged. Each time a settlement seemed to be near, new claimants appeared and the obstacle race had to be started all over again. Despairing of an early solution to the problem, Union Pacific officials decided to make winter camp at Silver Bow, hopeful that time would bring around the more obstinate landowners. To give them something to think about, the New York office ordered grading crews to work toward Deer Lodge, "to which point we shall proceed to build as rapidly as we can procure material."[94]

Such tactics did not take long to halt the uproar at Butte. At the behest of important businessmen a study committee was formed, the members of which determined that $8,400 could buy the old claims. As efforts were launched to raise the money, the Union Pacific authorized Samuel Word to say that it would contribute $5,000 of the necessary amount. By October 10 the local contributions reached $2,750, and on that evening another $750 was pledged at a public rally. With the Union Pacific's contribution, the necessary amount had been raised; the railroad could proceed.[95]

On the bitterly cold night of December 26, a train bearing 50 passengers entered Butte and came to a halt at precisely 11:10. Since no one wanted to stand outside in freezing weather to hear Mayor George W. Irvin announce Butte's newest historic happening, speeches and formal ceremonies were postponed. The city had fervently hoped for a railroad by 1881. It had its wish, with nearly a week to spare.[96]

With the line into Butte secured, Union Pacific crews continued construction toward Deer Lodge and beyond, anticipating a connection with the Northern Pacific, then building into Montana from the east. In February 1882 Dillon ordered his men to build as economically as possible, and to stop at Deer Lodge for the present, there being no reason for haste.[97] By November the extension was completed to Garrison, where, in the following autumn, the Northern Pacific would celebrate the completion of its line.[98]

In 1884 a branch was built to Anaconda to serve Marcus Daly's smelter. By this time 400 men were at work at the reduction plant and a little town had sprung up.[99] With rail service to Butte and to Anaconda, and a connection with the Northern Pacific, the Union Pacific had completed a branch that would become an important mainline feeder. As Dillon said, the extensions were necessary for the acquisition of fresh business and for the protection of territory from rivals. "In the case of the Utah and Northern," he commented to one of his associates, "the Northern Pacific was ready to build into our territory, and we had either to extend the road or give the country up to them . . . ."[100]

Montana, remote and relatively undeveloped, had looked longingly to the East and to the South during the first two decades of its territorial history, ever hopeful that economic salvation in the form of rail transportation was near at hand. Sparse population, great distances, a major financial panic during the 1870s, and local jealousies had delayed the desired development. But a resurgence of general prosperity and a fresh supply of capital that stimulated rail building throughout the Mountain West during the early 1880s sent pulsations deep into the "far-off country." Instead of gaining one road, Montanans were delighted with the appearance of two, and men of the mountain communities could only rejoice over the happy turn in circumstances. Before the decade of the 1880s was finished, statehood was achieved. Despite arguments that political considerations dictated this development, a good many westerners were convinced that rail service had sparked the growth that made such recognition necessary.

To "Lace and Interlace the Valleys"

While others readied themselves for the great celebration at Promontory in the spring of 1869, Brigham Young turned his attention to the matter of a Utah rail system that would connect with the main road and serve the populated areas lying to the south. "We contemplate building a line of Railroad from Ogden to this City," he wrote to one of his members in mid-April. "A company has been formed, stock subscribed and we expect that before long the work will be in active operation and probably be consummated early in the Fall."[1] Within a month a meeting of church leaders was held in Salt Lake City at which final plans for the 37-mile road were completed. That they were serious in their intent was suggested when Wells, Fargo & Company quickly reduced its rates between Ogden and Salt Lake to $3 and offered three daily stagecoach runs.[2] The days of horsedrawn service, however, were numbered; on May 17 groundbreaking ceremonies for the Utah Central Railroad were held at Ogden.

In contrast to the traditional celebration that characterized such ventures, the event occasioned little stir. "There was no great display, no speech making, though somewhat unexpectedly a large concourse of people assembled to witness the ceremony," wrote Brigham Young. "I merely cut out a sod, using a spade for the occasion, which I considered more appropriate than a pick as being the right tool in the right place."[3] By his comments the church leader meant that the spade symbolized the future agricultural development of his territory, as opposed to the pick, a characteristic mining implement. It was his hope that the railroad would bring farmers, not miners, to Mormon country.

As he had done many times before, Young revealed his practical nature, not only by moving quickly to take advantage of the new rail service to Utah, but in his candid confession that he knew very little about such ventures. "As the business of Railroading is new to us, we must move with great caution," he told his son Joseph. "I fully realize the extreme necessity of this, & the importance of being perfectly sure of our position, & of the safety of all our movements." The best approach, he decided, was to "procure *everything* we require to equip the road from the U. P. Co. (provided they will sell at fair rates) & get the road in operation with the least possible delay." A first-class road, fully equipped to provide excellent service, thought the churchman, ought to bring sufficient returns to protect the investment and to insure local control.[4]

Brigham Young's view that to deal with the Union Pacific was the safest course for him was perfectly logical. Since the road owed him a large sum of money for grading near Echo he had an opportunity to convert the debt into construction equipment; to borrow money elsewhere, presumably from the Central Pacific, would involve a probable surrender of local control. The Union Pacific also was in a position to do a heavier business in Utah than its California rival, as commercial statistics later indicated. So the Mormons proceeded, attaching themselves to the road from Omaha. The Union Pacific promised to deed any of its lands necessary to the Utah Central's construction and to furnish iron and rolling stock.[5] Labor was furnished locally, as it had been on the Union Pacific contract, with Mormons who wanted to work off their emigration subsidies. John W. Young, another son of Brigham, organized the working force. "Don't forget, Brethren, it is the Kingdom we are laboring for," he enjoined his father's following, "and that the building of this Railroad is one of the greatest achievements ever accomplished by Latter Day Saints and will really do more good in giving us influence with the World than anything we have ever done." Those who owed the church nothing were asked to work on credit, for $2 a day. Others, who wanted quicker returns, but who "expect to get a little occasionally," were offered $1.50 a day.[6]

Despite the necessity of exerting a certain amount of pressure upon "volunteer" laborers, and annoying delays caused by the nonarrival of materials from the East, the Utah Central was completed early in January 1870. The celebration, held on the tenth, was a gala occasion. Despite Elder George A. Smith's remark that the branch would have been finished two months earlier had the Union Pacific lived up to its promises, hard feelings against the larger road were short-lived. In assessing the role of his eastern associates in the work, Brigham Young pointed out that their sins also included the failure to pay for Mormon labor on the Echo Canyon contract, but in the end all had worked out for the best. As he viewed the newly completed Utah Central he remarked that "if they had paid us according to agreement this road would not have been graded, and this track would not have been laid today. It is all right."[7] And when the leader said it was all right, the matter was closed. His son Joseph, who also spoke at the ceremonies, fixed his eyes upon southern Utah's "Dixie," and expressed the hope that the rails would not only penetrate the region but "every nook and place in this Territory" as well.[8] Acting Governor S. A. Mann agreed, telling the territorial legislature that from such a branch would spring "others which will lace and interlace the valleys of the Territory," releasing it from isolation and revolutionizing Utah life.[9] Mayor Daniel H. Wells capsulized the feeling of the Mormons when he referred to "our railroad."[10]

The speeches and ceremonies concluded, a grand ball was held that evening. Over a thousand people attended, including army officers from nearby Camp Douglas, representatives of the Union Pacific and Central Pacific railroads, church bishops and elders, federal appointees living in Utah, as well as some "outside merchants and apostates," who danced until four o'clock in the morning. "The music was excellent; and the vast hall was beautifully decorated, the national flag predominating," remarked Elder George A. Smith. His mention of the nation's ensign presumably was made in defense of charges that his people were subversive, for he also commented upon the presence of the federal assessor, "who it is reported sets up nights to hate the people of Utah." The assessor apparently found a better occupation that night, for Smith remarked dourly that he "danced lustily with Mormon women."[11]

During the days that followed, excursionists gladly paid $2 each for round-trip tickets between Salt Lake City and Ogden to ride on the bright, new passenger cars pulled along by one of the company's four engines. Travelers expressed pleasure, and even surprise, that they could enter Salt Lake City aboard modern equipment which matched eastern roads in its quality. "It seemed strange that the cars of the Utah Central Railroad should be just like all other cars," later commented authoress Helen Hunt Jackson. "We expected to find 'Holiness to the Lord' inscribed on the panels, and portraits of the Mormon elders above the doors. In fact, I am not sure that we did not expect to see even the trees and shrubs along the track bearing the magic initials of the 'Zion Co-operative Mercantile Association.' "[12]

The excursion trips were highlighted by group singing and numerous speeches, some of which included such subjects as the qualifications of females to vote. These were happy days and the people of Utah were in a gay mood, willing to listen to almost anyone overcome by the desire to take the floor and deliver an oration on railroads or anything else that seemed important. One of the church elders remarked that it was "amusing to see the people running to be in time for the train, for they have learnt a lesson already, that the iron team will not wait as the old fashioned ox team did."[13]

If the residents of Salt Lake City were delighted by the new train service, so was Brigham Young. In June the 70-year-old leader wrote to Albert Carrington, in England, that he had just received a visit from a party of influential Bostonians representing their city's board of trade. While they were interested in the City of the Saints, Young showed an equal fascination for what he called their "city on wheels," as he dined as guest of the travelers. The visit represented the first time passengers had traveled from coast to coast in the same cars, and the unit was as close to being self-sufficient as anything Young had ever seen. Aboard were two well-stocked libraries, two organs, even a small printing press that published a sheet called the "Transcontinental," its first issue being dated Niagara Falls, May 24, and its fourth, Ogden, May 28. "At night the train is ingeniously lighted with gas," wrote the old man, perhaps unconsciously comparing the journey these people had made with his own crossing of the plains nearly a quarter of a century earlier.[14] It would have been hard, in any case, to have imagined a sharper contrast in western travel.

Whatever the disadvantages of wagon-train travel, however, it did not involve the financial complications presented by the introduction of more modern methods of transportation. In addition to his inability to collect cash from the Union Pacific, in return for contract work completed, Brigham found himself financially involved in the Utah Central, the building of which cost about $1.25 million.[15] In August 1870 he issued a circular letter to all bishops, saying that committees would visit them shortly to discuss cooperation in the sale of Utah Central bonds, "this being the means adopted to enable that Company to liquidate its indebtedness to myself, which will thus enable me to pay those of my Creditors, for work done on my Contract on the Union Pacific Railroad, whose accounts still remain unsettled." Young expressed a willingness to accept livestock, grain, or labor or anything else that "can readily be turned into cash."[16]

A few days later the School of the Prophets discussed at its regular meeting "the propriety of the Saints holding up the hands of the servants of God; and especially in liberating the hands of President Brigham Young on the U.P.R.R. indebtedness."[17] Apparently there was no immediate rush to buy bonds, a circumstance that called for sterner measures, for early in October a meeting of the Priesthood was held at which the leader announced a revelation. One of the Mormons summarized it in his journal: "It is the mind and will of God, that the Elders of Israel should take the Utah Central Railroad bonds, and own the road by paying for it; so that he could pay the debt of the Union Pacific, which we owe to the brethren."[18]

Unable to discharge his debts, Brigham Young considered an alternative: sale of the Utah Central. Collis P. Huntington offered him $1.5 million for the road and the Mormon countered, asking $1.6 million. The difference between the two figures was small enough to suggest that Young was ready to sell. Grenville Dodge and Sidney Dillon both urged Oliver Ames to come to some agreement with Joseph A. Young, who represented his father, arguing that if this were not done the Mormons would be forced to relinquish control of their road. Dodge and Dillon assured Ames that the Youngs would "give you any amount of their own Bonds as collateral which we consider perfectly good." Failure to act, they said, could cause serious consequences. "The C.P. expect to force Young to sell to them by refusing to loan [to] him and in that we get the first link in the new combination of the K.P. and C.P. which, if consummated would be a very bad blow to us . . .," was their argument. On the other hand, said the pair, "If we help Young he will agree to favor us and go into writing to offer us the first option on any bid for lease or sale of the Road that they may ever receive if they should ever want to sell."[19]

When Bishop John Sharp, attorney for Brigham Young, confirmed the possibility of a sale to the Central Pacific, Ames responded: "Do not part with your railroad. The arrangement you proposed we will carry out at once, or give you cash."[20] The reference was to the earlier application for a loan, made by John and Joseph Young, to which the Union Pacific officials had responded by saying they had no cash. As a possible delaying tactic the easterners suggested the possibility of trying to raise some money by asking Congress to pay their road what the government owed it for transportation, a request they admitted had little chance of favorable action. When it became apparent that there was real danger of losing their interest in the Utah Central the company's managers proposed to let the Mormons withhold up to $50,000 from collections made at Ogden for eastbound travel over the main line. It was to be in the nature of an advance, to run for two years at nine percent interest. Part of the agreement involved the understanding that the Union Pacific had an option to buy, subject to 60 days' notice.[21]

On January 23, 1871, Oliver Ames reaffirmed his position, telling John Young that he was ready to carry out the proposal made to Joseph A. Young. When Ames asked Joseph if the rumors of sale were really true he was told: "Our road is not for sale. When so we will talk it over with you before selling." While the statement was not entirely true, it suggested that negotiations were still open. In writing to John Young about the matter, Ames advised against letting go the Utah Central. "My impression is," he explained, "with the very large amt. of business you must have from the valuable Silver mines recently opened in Utah your road must be a very paying investment and too valuable to pass out of your control."[22] By the end of February the Mormons had a confirmed agreement with the Union Pacific, and once more they had demonstrated for them the value the railroad attached to the commerce of Utah. As hard-pressed as his administration was for money, Oliver Ames simply could not let a potential trade area go by default.

Although Brigham Young was willing to admit that he knew little about railroad building, and that he intended to proceed with great caution, his precarious financial involvement with the Utah Central failed to dampen his enthusiasm for the new enterprise. Response to the Central was favorable, not only from the joyous Mormons who rode it for recreation, but also from the business community. With the availability of cheaper coal and rail transportation a number of smelters were built in the Salt Lake Valley at this time. Between the summer of 1869 and autumn of 1871 ores valued at $2,500,000 and bullion worth $1,237,000 were shipped from the territory. Significantly, about $6,000 worth of copper was produced; in the years to come this infant industry would grow into one of the most important in Utah.[23] Nearby mining communities in Nevada watched Utah railroad development with interest and hoped that the Central would reach out to serve their needs. "The continuation of the road south from the Mormon city is a matter that every man in White Pine is interested in," wrote the editor of one Nevada mining camp newspaper.[24]

Brigham Young professed disinterest in the business of mining because of the type of people it attracted and the distractions it produced. Yet, since the industry promised to be an important contributor to railroads, he found his position increasingly difficult to defend. His sons, who also interested themselves in railroads, but who did not have to share the burden of their father's religious leadership, were free of any such strictures. While the elder Young chose not to participate personally in further railroad building, he not only permitted his sons to engage in it, but he encouraged them. "I think it would be a good idea to get up a company for a narrow gauge railroad through the Territory," he telegraphed to Joseph while on a visit to Saint George, in southwestern Utah, during January 1871. Such an organization, which could "include a few Gentiles," if Joseph chose to have them, should petition Congress for a land grant of odd sections for five miles on either side of the proposed route and should ask for subsidies of from five to eight thousand dollars a mile, advised father Brigham. However, he enjoined Joseph, "I do not want my name to appear in the Company."[25]

To further encourage local railroad expansion Brigham Young authorized Bishop John Sharp to borrow $300,000, secured by Utah Central bonds. The Union Pacific, good to its promise, participated in such refinancing.[26] During February Sen. John Sherman, brother of General Sherman, introduced the necessary legislation into Congress to obtain rights-of-way for an extension of the Utah Central. Contrary to Young's desires, the Utah Southern received neither land grants nor subsidies from the federal government. Undaunted, he fell back upon Union Pacific aid, and proceeded. By May 1, with preliminary details disposed of, the project got under way with a 40-mile stretch of road south of Salt Lake City contracted for, and with the new superintendent, William Jennings, ready to push construction. The extension, organized as the Utah Southern, and of standard gauge, was headed by Brigham Young, who had said he wanted no public association with it. John Sharp was its vice president.[27]

The Salt Lake City press spoke for the community's business interests when it praised additional railroad efforts in the territory. The *Herald* sharply criticized "all the stuff that has been uttered by unscrupulous, irresponsible, bigoted or prejudiced persons about the Mormons preventing mining," and stated flatly that without the overland railroad there "would have been no profitable mining in Utah today." Rich as was the fabled Emma mine, said that journal, it could not have successfully shipped ore under the old facilities. Now, with the prospect of service to southern Utah, a whole new area of comparatively valueless mining property would become profitable.[28]

At the annual Fourth of July celebration in 1871, there were suggestions of an early revival in mining. Charles F. Middleton, of Ogden, visited the capital city to enjoy the festivities and commented, upon returning home, "There were [*sic*] a great deal of drunkenness & fighting around the saloons among the miners & roughs. A good many arrests were made by the City Police."[29] From far across the country, at Boston, came more sober evidence that Utah mining business held great promise. In commenting that five-sixths of the business into Salt Lake City moved over the Union Pacific, as opposed to one-sixth over the Central Pacific, Oakes Ames listed 4,500 tons of ore haulage in Union Pacific receipts, compared with 500 for its California rival.[30] Utah's governor added his voice to the chorus, urging construction of multiple short lines into the mining districts, and praising the industry as being important to the growth and prosperity of his part of the West. He urged the legislators to do all in their power to encourage rail development in the territory.[31]

Late in 1871 a Salt Lake City newspaper reported upon the Utah Southern's progress and gave an indication of its future ambitions. The standard-gauge road, at that time completed 15 miles from Salt Lake City, was being pushed another 35 miles to Provo, "and as soon as practicable will be extended to the Arizona line."[32] By spring, however, such a destination seemed to be far away, as financial difficulties once again beset the Mormons.

At this point Bishop Sharp made one of his frequent pilgrimages to the Union Pacific offices, seeking further aid. The new president, Horace F. Clark, was reluctant to make any commitments without his board's permission, but was willing to call a special session to consider the request. Sharp offered 5,000 shares of the Utah Central's capital stock, the only collateral available, and while doing so he showed concern at the growing strength of the Union Pacific in Utah. "Although I could see that they would prefer a controlling interest of the road they would be perfectly willing that we should operate the road, yet they would like to dictate," he reported to Brigham Young. The bishop also revealed that he had called upon Collis Huntington, who was unwilling to loan money but indicated a willingness to buy out the Mormons. Faced by a tight money market in New York, one that pinched seriously the Union Pacific, and yet unwilling to relinquish Mormon control of Utah railroads, Sharp was pessimistic about future expansion of the Utah Southern.[33]

As Union Pacific officials were beginning to learn, the irrepressible bishop from Utah was a hard man to turn away. On April 9, a few days after his first meeting with Horace Clark, Sharp addressed a formal letter to the president, again outlining the importance of gaining his assistance. He reminded Clark that the Utah Southern, of which 20 miles now were completed, had been built under contract with the Union Pacific, but that this only partially solved Utah's problem. Beyond the end of track lay a number of mining companies whose managers expected to receive rail service. There was danger that some other railroad would take advantage of the situation, continued Sharp, for even now a bill to grant a right-of-way to such a company was before Congress. It was obvious, therefore, that the money already invested might be wasted unless more was forthcoming to make the original outlay of any worth. "I am authorized on behalf of the Utah Southern," said Sharp, "to propose that if the Union Pacific R.R. Co. will furnish the iron rails, fish plates, bolts, spikes and rolling stock for the construction and equipment of the Utah Southern from its present terminus to the town of Payson, a distance of fifty five (55) miles, the Utah Southern will pay for this material delivered to it at Ogden in first mortgage bonds at eighty (80) per cent of their value, and in addition thereto one third (1/3) of the capital stock, these being the terms of the contract made with the Union Pacific R.R. Co. for the twenty miles already built."[34]

Union Pacific board members tried to get an arrangement more favorable to their road, arguing that it was unreasonable for them to put up more than half of the necessary money and not get even half of the Utah Southern's stock. Clark said that he had never yet made such a deal without gaining control. "I told him the parties with whom he had been dealing were generally of sharp practice and demanded of him such a precaution, but we were working men and had not turned speculators yet, and our interest with theirs in the U.S. was one interest," was the bishop's response. Despite all the arguments against him, Sharp stood fast, assuring Brigham Young that he was prepared to stand by his original proposition and "would not change it one Iota." He apologized for not getting iron and other equipment on its way west, but he advised Young: "I think it will pay us to go sure if not so fast." The bishop, who was known in Utah as "the canny Scot," jokingly admitted that he was tempted to "play them a little Sharp, but I cannot do it. A square transaction always wins."[35]

Matters now settled down to a game of patience. While Sharp waited for a decision from what he termed "that *everlasting board*," he did some sight-seeing, and bought a locomotive for $14,000 to be used on the Utah Central.[36] During these days the eastern press, and that of Utah, commented upon the possibility that the Utah Southern would connect with a transcontinental railroad across the Southwest, a speculation the Mormons always kept before the Union Pacific to suggest interest by other major lines.[37] By early autumn the "stand pat" tactic yielded results.

In September the Union Pacific's executive committee recalled Sharp and again listened to his arguments. It was a difficult assignment for, as he said, the big railroad was "very poor indeed." However, the bishop persisted, playing the role of the western rustic, homespun and honest, but ever unswayable. "They tried very hard to get me to go home and not get the Iron until spring," he wrote, "used a good many arguments such as the winter being bad weather to lay Iron and the scarcity of Iron and hard to get and no money to get it with, but I told them I was sent to get the Iron and I must get it before I went home." Unable to move the Mormon from his position, and secretly admiring his tenacity, the committee appointed Sidney Dillon to find the necessary iron, on credit, with Sharp's assistance.[38]

The bishop found no grounds for optimism in the committee's action; he recognized it as a delaying tactic. He wrote to Young several days later, telling him that there were vague promises for two locomotives, but he held little hope for any immediate delivery. His conferences with Collis Huntington were no more promising, that veteran railroader saying only that "he could do nothing now, but in a little while might." Sharp called the Union Pacific reaction "quite a back out," and swore that if he could get anyone else to help him he would never ask anything of that firm again.[39] Money was very tight in the East, he reported to Brigham Young, but there were still "other parties" who might be interested. He referred to the Kansas Pacific people and their desire for an independent connection with Salt Lake City.[40] The Union Pacific directorate understood that it was caught in the middle, with other roads threatening from both East and West; there was nothing else to do but find the money. It did.

Threats from rivals generated defensive buying and building; it was a negative or at least a premature reason for taking over undeveloped country. Such a move, however, usually involved the possibility of future traffic for the road that captured the territory, and in the case of Utah a trade potential existed. As the *Salt Lake Herald* commented, the Mormon church had ceased to dominate the economic structure of Utah to the degree that it once had, and Brigham Young no longer "sealed up the mines."[41] The Mormons themselves recognized the probability of the territory's economic growth, including that of mining, and they were wise enough to participate in it, rather than to fight it. The Utah Southern was organized principally to take advantage of the mineral trade in both Utah and eastern Nevada. By 1873 there were 11 ore-reduction furnaces within a dozen miles of the Mormon capital, and over 30 in the territory itself. The entire business had been developed since the construction of the Union Pacific Railroad.[42] In that year six lines of varying lengths, totaling 366 miles of track, were in operation; two small roads, totaling 36 miles, were under construction. Also in 1873, the Utah Central carried into Salt Lake City over 93 million pounds of coal, at a cost of $302,341, and nearly 15 million pounds of coke, at a cost of $246,466. Most of it came from Coalville, about 40 miles distant.[43] As the territorial surveyor pointed out, no special effort was being made to force Utah into prominence nationally; its mineral wealth simply was attracting the attention of investors both here and abroad. The population of 110,000 was principally Mormon, yet nine-tenths of the mining property was owned by Gentiles. As a counterpoise, five of the six local railroads were Mormon owned or controlled, and they were the key to the Gentile mines.[44]

As the Mormons watched their mining roads grow, and showed impatience at the slowness of the process, they continued to press the Union Pacific for cooperation. "I find that the C.P. has sent over our Road in the month of Nov. 350 cars and the U.P. 950 cars, which shows that we received almost three times more from the U.P. than from the C.P.," wrote John Sharp late in 1872. He urged his eastern friends to join in a further extension of the Utah Southern, "for I know it to be a safe investment."[45] When the bishop returned to New York to plead his case further, during September 1873, he arrived in time to see Wall Street reeling from the effects of a nationwide financial panic. While passing through Omaha, Sharp learned of the failure of Jay Cooke & Company, and the news worried him during the rest of his trip. "I wish to state that your teachings have always been correct," he admitted to Brigham Young upon arrival at

New York, "viz., never work beyond your means, but it is not the practice of this country, for I think we are all working beyond our means." Too many roads were being built where they were not needed, thought the bishop, the Northern Pacific being one of them. A general tendency to overexpansion, accompanied by widespread financial panic, promised little outside help for Utah. The Mormons, Sharp concluded, must now depend upon their own resources to build in Utah.[46] Already, in fact, local investors had begun to buy Utah Southern stock in return for grading, tie-laying, and even the construction of station houses along the route. Each community was called upon to contribute, as was the practice along the Utah Northern in Idaho.[47]

John Young, for one, saw a great future in Utah railroad building. He advised his father to buy up Union Pacific stock in the Utah Southern, but not the bonds, "as that would require too much," and if the larger railroad declined to sell, then "I would next try & buy out the Brethren & control the road." John suggested that he and Joseph "carry on the road for you, for one or two years, & get the profits of building." He suggested that his father then sell or transfer his personal interests "and have the satisfaction of clearing at least one million to add to your estate, that will, unless you take hold of it, go to others and probably to outsiders."[48]

The Union Pacific, meantime, showed reluctance to spend any more money to help the Youngs. Bishop Sharp lamented over the situation, and remarked that he did not want to solicit aid from other corporations, "for that would complicate our mutual interests." He suggested that the Union Pacific take Utah Southern first mortgage bonds at 80 percent of par value for payment of freight charges on rails shipped over the main line.[49] The executive committee, noting that it had already furnished over $400,000 in money, labor performed, and freight service, refused the request.[50] The Union Pacific, loaded with Utah Southern bonds, desired only to sell some of that plentiful product if possible. "Could a market be made for them? If so, at what price?" Rollins inquired of a New York banking house.[51]

While Rollins was trying to unload Utah Southern bonds, if at all possible, Joseph Young presented the Union Pacific's board of directors with a new request. He wanted it to take bonds of his little Summit County Railroad, that he proposed to run from Echo for 32 miles toward Parley's Park and its silver mines, at 65 percent of par to satisfy debts he owed the Union Pacific. The feeder, he said, serving coal mines on the Weber River, promised to furnish heavy traffic in coal, silver, lead, hay, grain, and lumber.[52] The Union Pacific was faced by an epidemic of railroad building among the Mormons and by now had so much invested in these ventures that it seemed unable to free itself. Like the indulgent father, it continued to say no to further requests but in the end it said maybe, and then yes. When the company moved to assist Joseph Young in building his narrow gauge to Parley's Park the *Salt Lake Herald* declared that the action was taken as a result of "the grasping spirit and exertions of the Union Pacific."[53] The big road next turned its attention once more to the Utah Southern and, in October and November of 1874, made two new contracts designed to help the Mormons along their rail trek to Utah's Dixie.[54]

On February 16, 1875, the last rail of the Utah Southern was laid at York, which was described by a Salt Lake City newspaper as "a small ranche in Juab county." The 75-mile road ran through what was further described as "the wealthiest and most populous in the Territory," to the Juab mines, and so great was its acceptance that journalists publicly wondered how the people south of Salt Lake City had gotten along so many years without rail service. And now, said the press, on to Nephi (the county seat), and beyond, until the road intersected with "the second transcontinental railroad."[55] Union Pacific officials showed little enthusiasm for the move on Nephi and beyond.

Thoughts now turned to the other small lines in which the Youngs had involved themselves. For some years the Union Pacific had been interested in the mines of Coalville, and its desire to tap them was understandable. In 1872 Joseph Young, who owned three-fifths of the Coalville mining property, offered to sell for $40,000, but the Union Pacific was cautious. John Duff asked T. E. Sickels, of the Omaha office, and Thomas Wardell, who was for a time associated with the railroad's Wyoming coal mines, to survey the situation. He wanted to know if the lands were government or railroad lands, if they had been surveyed, and, in short, if Young had a clear title.[56] During the next few years the Union Pacific lent a minimum of assistance to the Summit County road (toward Parley's Park), which it was trying to buy. In February 1876, Brigham Young said he was ready to sell his interest in the road. For $60,000 he offered all his first mortgage bonds of the company except one of par value $5,000 and all the capital stock he held. On the understanding that the road was substantially free from floating debt, Dillon accepted the proposition.[57] By the autumn of 1880 the Union Pacific had complete control of the feeder line to the coalfields.

It was about this time that the Youngs began another of their railroad enterprises. Incorporated in June 1874 as the Utah Western, this latest line

One of the engines on the Utah Central line, being oiled in preparation for a run.

was designed to complete the Salt Lake, Sevier Valley and Pioche Railroad. The latter road had been organized in May 1872 with the hope of connecting Salt Lake City and the Pioche mines in Nevada, some 300 miles distant, but for two years it lay dormant.[58] Through the efforts of the Western's president, John Young, 20 miles of track, to the shores of Salt Lake, were laid by early January 1875. From Black Rock, later to become a famous bathing resort, the road then moved toward Stockton, a small settlement just north of Rush Valley that had been founded in 1864 by prospectors.[59]

This newest branch on the Mormon railroad tree struggled for existence in the manner of the others as financial drought stunted its growth. By autumn of 1875 the road's secretary, John Pike, was complaining to John Young that unless he gave some help, current bills could not be paid. He advised Young that father Brigham was about to order his son home and that there was a debt of $3,000 now due the church leader that might be called for collection any day.[60] Early in 1878 the Western defaulted on its bond interest payment, and by the autumn of 1880 it was purchased at a foreclosure sale by a Union Pacific subsidiary known as the Utah and Nevada. Motivation for such a move by the Union Pacific was that the Denver and Rio Grande by then was pushing into Utah and its managers already were looking at the mines of eastern Nevada. Another reason was the constantly recurring talk in Union Pacific circles of reaching out to California from Utah, either by way of the Utah Southern or by a more northerly route through Nevada.[61] Dillon had no desire to acquire the Utah Western, but he felt there was no other choice. "I purchased the road and we have now all the bonds but about $100,000," he told John Sharp. "I would have preferred not to have bought the road, but it was absolutely necessary in self-defense." Not only was Dillon obliged to adopt a weak narrow-gauge company, but even worse, he felt that he had to extend it. "If it is not done," he concluded, "the other parties will cover the country by paralleling us."[62]

The decade of the seventies was one of railroad development in Utah, a period of expansion that the Union Pacific found expensive and very hard to control. The completion of the Utah Southern, in the early spring of 1875, far from satisfied the Young family. Hardly had the last rail been laid before the clamor to move forward was heard at Union Pacific headquarters. The patience of that road's management was wearing thin, for in the autumn of 1874 it had loaned the Mormons $200,000 to complete the Southern under circumstances it found trying. Treasurer Rollins had informed Dillon that enough money was available from receipts at Omaha to furnish the funds; but, he cautioned, "if we use up our funds in this way we shall have to borrow for our January coupons."[63] During 1876 Jay Gould took an active interest in the Mormon roads, as was evidenced by his investment in the Utah Northern, then building through Idaho, and in him the Mormons found new hope, for here was a man who believed in expansion. Late in the year Bishop Sharp told Brigham Young of a talk he had with Gould, who said that "just as soon as the contract was signed he would pay over the money for your Stock, Bonds and Coal land . . . ."[64] Sharp did not make specific reference to any particular Utah road, but his comment indicated Gould's interest and the availability of a new source of money.

During the next two years the Utah Southern lived upon hope, but prospects for an immediate extension were problematical in face of its financial difficulties. In the spring of 1877 the road's directors laid an assessment of three percent upon its capital stock, to which the Union Pacific promptly objected on the ground that 5,000 of the shares it held were non-assessable. Seventy percent had been paid on 2,850 other shares, and the road finally agreed to accept an assessment on these.[65] Actually, business on the Southern was good, but its parent road, the Utah Central, showed falling receipts. Sharp admitted that because of the poor price for lead, and because of strikes on eastern roads, traffic was light. Some of the Utah smelters had shut down and others were cutting back on production.[66]

But a happy turn of events soon took place. In late June a Salt Lake City newspaper reported that "Jay Gould and party spent yesterday in driving about the city . . . . We understand Mr. Gould has concluded to proceed with the Utah Southern sixteen miles, which will take the road to Nephi."[67] Not only was Gould in the West, ready to invest eastern money, but so was another well-known financier. Jay Cooke, the banker, remembered as the financier of the Civil War, had acquired the famous Horn Silver mine at Frisco. It lay 150 miles beyond the Utah Southern, and so interested was Cooke in obtaining rail service that he offered to finance part of the cost. In December 1878 Cooke conferred with Dillon and proposed that if the Union Pacific furnished half the money, he and the Mormons would each contribute a quarter. Gould agreed that it was a good idea, and he encouraged Dillon to accept.[68]

In January 1879 the Utah Southern Railroad Extension was organized with Sidney Dillon, Jay Gould, John Sharp, and Silas H. Clark among those serving as officers; Dillon was president. In writing to Jay Gould about his plans to push forward to Frisco, John Sharp said that the road, including a small branch, would be about 160 miles long. Its capital stock was $1.3 million, half of which was owned by the Union Pacific, and its bonds were not to exceed $15,000 a mile.[69] Although the Horn Silver mine was an important incentive to the construction, renewed interest in mining, in general, contributed heavily. The Horn mine itself showed exciting possibilities if reports of geologists are taken into account. Professor J. S. Newberry, who examined the property in autumn of 1879, estimated that not less than $15 million worth of ore was in sight, with the possibility of much more when the mine was fully developed.[70]

At a meeting of the directors of the Utah Southern Extension, held February 18, 1879, John Sharp subscribed 5,850 shares for the Union Pacific Company. In the previous month Jay Gould had taken 217 shares; Sidney Dillon, 217; and Silas H. Clark, 216; the total, 6,500 shares, comprised one-half of the extension's capital stock. At the time of the February meeting Sharp announced he was ready to immediately let a contract for the first 30 miles, and he told Dillon that tracklayers would be ready for iron by the middle of March.[71] Backed with sufficient funds to carry out the work, Sharp proceeded, and by June 23, 1880, the Utah Southern was completed to Milford with a branch to Frisco.[72] A year later, in June 1881, the Utah Southern and the Utah Extension companies were consolidated with the Utah Central, forming a continuous line 280 miles south of Ogden.[73] The new corporation, named the Utah Central Railway Company, with a capital stock of $4,225,000, had a heavy representation of the Union Pacific on its board.[74] One of the directors, John Sharp, also was a member of the Union Pacific's directorate.

Formation of the consolidated Utah Central Railway Company was not the only evidence of the Union Pacific's move toward control of Utah's railroads. In the autumn of 1881 the Utah and Pleasant Valley Railroad became a branch of the Utah Central, confirming rumors printed in local newspapers for more than a year to the effect that Jay Gould was steadily buying into that company. The branch, as it was incorporated in October 1881, was directed by a board made up of Mormon leaders and Union Pacific officials. Sidney Dillon recommended the purchase when he saw that the Denver and Rio Grande would connect with it. Rather than have the opposition control the 60 miles of traffic between Spanish Fork and the Pleasant Valley mines, and instead of paralleling the line with new construction—although he thought this a cheaper alternative—Dillon chose to buy the line.[75]

The emergence of the Denver and Rio Grande as a threat to the Utah trade also generated further thoughts about protective building in both Utah and Nevada. The Union Pacific owned a small mining road called the Salt Lake and Western that ran 57 miles southwest of Lehi Junction (in Utah County) to the mining district of Tintic. Built during 1874 and 1875, the line was intended to do more than serve the rich Tintic mines—there was talk of crossing Nevada to a California connection, tapping various mining districts of central Nevada along the way. During 1881 and 1882 Sidney Dillon talked seriously of building westward in a manner that would claim country south of the Central Pacific's line and yet avoid taking trade from that line.

As the Union Pacific contemplated a possible penetration of Nevada, it was obliged to consider the role of a small line it owned. Called the Nevada Central, this little piece of railroad, running between Austin and Battle Mountain, had no physical connection with the Union Pacific; instead, it touched the Central Pacific at the latter city. Sidney Dillon later explained that he bought the line in 1881 to keep it away from competitors. "The Denver and Rio Grande people had a corps of twenty-five engineers in the Salt Lake Valley, in their prosperous times, surveying across, and they were going to make a connection with the Central Pacific at that point and cut us off," he said. "I was induced to buy it to keep it out of their hands, whether it was good for anything or not." As it turned out, the purchase was useless and Dillon admitted it. "I was mistaken," he confessed. "Every one is mistaken some time."[76]

The Nevada Central was purchased from a man identified as Brydges, who boasted that he had made $50,000 on the sale and would have made more, but he was obliged to divide up the profits with Silas H. Clark and Sidney Dillon. An acquaintance of Brydges said he was an awful liar, but that he may have told the truth this time, for "no honest railroad man would have paid the price for so worthless a property." A former Union Pacific official estimated that by 1884 the Union Pacific had sunk $456,000 into this isolated piece of track.[77] Joseph K. Choate, the Union Pacific superintendent who ran the Nevada Central, said employees freely admitted signing vouchers for material they had never seen; he called the road's financial system "the worst possible."[78] The outspoken Charles Francis Adams left no doubt as to his feeling about the investment. "I regard this property as absolutely worthless," he told one of his associates. "I do not think that I, on the part of the Union Pacific, would accept it as a gift accompanied with the condition that we should operate the road and keep it in repair."[79] He later explained that "about the first thing I did when I became president was to throw it overboard, and I have never regretted so doing since."[80]

Despite reluctance to spend funds badly needed elsewhere, the Union Pacific had been coaxed into Utah railroading by leading Mormons who were highly desirous of having both local rail service and feeders from Nevada that would bring them prosperity. By constant threat of turning elsewhere, and through repeated reference to an old friendship, they maintained a steady pressure upon Union Pacific management, with the result that by the early eighties the big road was thoroughly committed to Utah. Even after the disastrous investment in the Nevada Central, and at a time when the Union Pacific was trying to extricate itself from other unwise ventures,

Bishop Sharp continued to press for more building. Pointing to the rich mines of Nevada and the logic of proceeding on to California, he urged continued expansion as late as 1886. "The Union Pacific system by right of position ought to control that country," he told Adams, "and I consider the construction of a line into that territory a matter worthy of careful consideration."[81] Adams may well have recalled Sidney Dillon's reaction to one of the bishop's earlier proposals when he commented: "I think his ideas are very high."[82]

Yet, when the people of Utah had gained the rail service they had so long sought, they were frequently critical of the company that had been instrumental in providing it. The attitude changed most markedly in the early eighties, at a time when Jay Gould's active entrance on the scene spelled the end of Mormon autonomy in Utah railroading. The *Salt Lake Herald*, a Gentile newspaper, was decidedly hostile. "At present, the Union Pacific has this territory completely at its mercy," wrote the editor in the autumn of 1880. "We are all under the monster thumb, which bears lightly or heavily as the managers feel disposed to manipulate it." He spoke of the coming of the Denver and Rio Grande, and predicted that "the heartless course being pursued by the Union Pacific" would be nullified when that happy circumstance released a community "sorely oppressed for these many years."[83] On another occasion, when Union Pacific officials talked of building a large resort hotel on the shores of Salt Lake, the Mormon press commented: "If this kind of thing goes on it will only be necessary to change the name of this section of the country to U.P. instead of U.T."[84]

A principal source of the cry of "great monopoly" originated in the control the Union Pacific exercised over coal rates into Salt Lake City. As complaints increased about fuel prices, some of the prominent businessmen sought to build a line between the coalfields and their city. Late in December 1879 articles of incorporation for the Utah Eastern Railway Company were filed, and within a year narrow-gauge rails had been laid between Coalville and Park City, where silver and lead mines recently had been opened. With this additional stimulus it was hoped that the road could be completed to Salt Lake City, giving the town a local source of transportation for minerals and fuel. To insure themselves against Union Pacific intervention the incorporators had placed a majority of the stock in the hands of three trustees who were prohibited from relinquishing it for 15 years.[85]

The effort to build a line of their own, free from possible absorption

Frisco, Utah, at the end of the Utah Southern (later incorporated into the Utah Central) track.

by another company, created something of a dilemma for Mormon leadership. Public opinion tended to charge the Union Pacific with arbitrarily creating a high price for coal, and of responsibility for periodic shortages during cold weather. The prospect of independence from such control was accompanied by criticism of the big company that was somewhat embarrassing to the church officials, who had worked so closely with it in the past. The *Deseret News,* a Mormon organ, decried the street talk of "war" with the Union Pacific, arguing that there was room for more than one coal road to the heart of Zion and nothing more than a friendly competition ought to arise from such a development. In an effort to tone down public hostility editor Charles W. Penrose warned his readers that such an attitude "will do no good, and may do some harm."[86]

The Mormons could talk of conciliation, but the Union Pacific had no intention of relinquishing its coal traffic. Whether or not it used political influence is speculation, but when a bill passed the territorial legislature authorizing certain counties to issue bonds in aid of the Utah Eastern, it was vetoed by Gov. George W. Emery. As the road floundered, in the manner of other small western ventures, the Union Pacific began to build a parallel standard-gauge line between Echo and Park City, while at the same time quietly acquiring stock in the narrow-gauge company. Before long the Eastern was under Union Pacific domination, and after operating it until 1883 the managers closed down the small and unprofitable line. In the spring of 1887 a bankruptcy sale was held at which the Union Pacific bid $25,000 for the roadbed, locomotives, cars, and other properties of the Utah Eastern.[87] Its real investment, however, had been the $186,000 sunk into first-mortgage bonds of the Mormon road. The foreclosure also resulted in losses for some prominent Utah businessmen and a fresh outcry against eastern monopolists.[88]

Union Pacific management was aware of the criticism leveled against it in Utah, and it was far from insensitive to the situation. In numerous instances efforts were made to satisfy Mormon complaints or to be helpful in other ways. It carried Mormon missionaries at half rate, but this was no special favor since the Denver and Rio Grande did the same thing. Both roads offered such rates to all clergymen. On one occasion there appeared to be a difference of opinion over freight rates on sugar; and apparently the Union Pacific was accused of using discriminatory tactics, for Dillon, advising his general freight agent at Omaha, said: "I do not think we should get into a fight with the Zions Cooperative Institution. You had better harmonize the matter if you can. If they can buy sugar in California cheaper than in the East, I think they should have the right to do so."[89] When Bishop Sharp found himself $178,000 behind in his payments for steel, Dillon refused to press him, asking only that interest charges be paid.[90] Union Pacific officials showed no hesitancy in using political influence to aid the Mormon cause. In 1882 Dillon advised his representatives at Washington, D.C., to intervene with congressmen considered friendly to the road, urging them to be of assistance in what he termed "the Mormon question." He underscored the railroad's feeling toward Zion when he added: "The Mormons are our friends; they ask nothing but justice, and I think the American people should be willing to accord them that."[91]

Charles Francis Adams took much the same attitude. Late in 1885 he wrote to President Grover Cleveland, saying that his road had nothing to do with the burning question of polygamy, or, what he termed the "moral and criminal side of the situation" in that territory, but on the material side it had great interest. He praised the Mormons for their business acumen and management, and deplored the prospect of saddling them with political carpetbaggers. Time would settle the matter, he suggested, for even then "the railroads are preparing to carry into the territory a tide of immigration which would definitely settle the question of polygamy." Meantime, Adams proposed to avoid offending the Mormons if at all possible. In reading over advance copy of a publicity piece prepared for the road Adams objected to a passage he thought derogatory. He asked the author to omit it, arguing that "no good tradesman has a right to offend any customer, no matter what his opinions may be, provided he is civil and pays his bills. To us the Mormons have always been civil, and they have always paid their bills."[92]

Adams showed concern over charges that the Union Pacific was discriminating against Utah in the matter of rates. "There seems to be a general impression in Salt Lake that I lie awake nights meddling with the freight tariffs of the Company," he wrote to a resident of that city. He denied the charge, and instructed his general manager at Omaha to investigate, commenting that "it is especially desirable that we should be civil to the Mormon Church." Be kind to Bishop Sharp, he ordered, and try to fulfill his requests when possible.[93] On another occasion he asked a congressman to aid the Mormons, because his railroad had "a very direct business interest in the affairs of the Territory of Utah," and demoralization among those people would hurt business. "There is in the territory a considerable Gentile interest, so-called," he added, "which is anxious to drive out the Mormon population, for the obvious reason that they covet the Mormon farms."[94]

While the Gentile population of Utah during the eighties was not large, it was growing. As of 1880 the territory's total population stood at just under 144,000, of which nearly 112,000 persons were Mormons, but the Gentiles had nearly trebled their numbers in the preceding decade.[95] In the mid-eighties the anti-Mormon *Salt Lake Tribune* accused the Union Pacific of

discrimination against Gentile business interests and of entering into a plot
with the church leaders to destroy them.[96] P. P. Shelby, of the railroad's
Salt Lake City office, admitted that "it is useless to attempt to disguise the
fact that there is some feeling of hostility toward our company in Utah on
account of our supposed connection with the Mormon Church." The
Denver and Rio Grande people, he added, were assiduously retailing that
rumor to gain more Gentile trade. "About a year ago," he went on, "I was
told by a prominent anti-Mormon that the Union Pacific Company should
not receive any of his patronage until it severed its relations with the Mormon Church. Only a few days ago an ultra-Mormon, who is a large shipper,
said to me . . . that the Union Pacific Company should as a matter of reciprocity, instruct its agents throughout the East to disabuse the public
mind of the prejudice against the Mormon people." Shelby explained to
both parties that the Union Pacific was a common carrier, open to all, and
that it had no feelings about the religious convictions of any of its users.
When Utah's governor suggested that the railroad should use its influence
in Congress, in behalf of the Mormons, Shelby told him that it should not
interfere in legislative matters.[97] Both the church leaders in Utah and high-
level Union Pacific management knew that the company had acted otherwise.

Added to what Bishop Sharp called the "religio-political turmoil" in
Utah, other events combined to diminish the hopes of those who had promoted railroad development so earnestly in the territory. Much construction
had been predicated upon potential traffic from the rich silver mines, but
results proved disappointing. Besides the decline in production there were
a number of questionable sales of mines to Europeans where the owners paid
only to see the bottom of the well. In one instance a mine valued at between $700,000 and $1 million was sold to a French company for $3 million,
after which it never paid a dividend or operated at a profit. Fraudulent
sales, including that of the notorious Emma mine, shattered public confidence and frightened away capital.[98] By the mid-eighties the well-known
Horn Silver mine, the potential traffic from which had done much to spur
on the extension of the Utah Southern, closed down. Adams estimated that
the resultant loss of revenues amounted to a million dollars a year. In another instance an important smelter was destroyed by fire. Declining traffic,
and competition by the Denver and Rio Grande—Bishop Sharp called it a
bankrupt road—cut deeply into the Utah Central's profits.[99] During 1884
passenger receipts for the Utah Central fell off by more than $61,000 and
freight income was down nearly $93,000. Superintendent John Sharp at-
tributed the decline to competition and bad times. Although the harvest
of that year was big, farmers tended to hold their produce for better prices.[100]

When the Zions Cooperative Mercantile Institution refused to receive freight over the Denver and Rio Grande, and other Mormon enterprises discriminated similarly, the commissioner of the Utah Traffic Association lodged a complaint with Charles Francis Adams.[101]

The year 1885 was equally discouraging, the Horn Silver mine still being inoperative. Although 60 tons of ore went from Park City to Denver every day, and during the year 3,075 tons of bullion and 270 tons of sulfur were shipped out of Utah, traffic did not increase satisfactorily. Cattle raisers in southern Utah were beginning to move their herds into Montana and Wyoming for better grazing, but it was hoped that the loss of this business would be compensated for by an increase in sheep raising, grain growing, and potato raising. "There are many people now in Omaha and Kansas City who will not buy any other potatoes at any price," said P. P. Shelby hopefully.[102]

A downturn in traffic did not mean that Utah was not developing or that it had reached the peak of its economic potential. In 1875 the surveyor general for the territory reported that Utah's various industries had produced nearly $3 million worth of goods in that fiscal year.[103] The output of minerals was valued at $7 million.[104] The census of 1880 revealed that Utah had 640 manufacturing establishments, with a capitalization of $2,500,000, and in a year these had produced $4,324,992 worth of goods.[105] In 1881 a Salt Lake City paper reported that three to ten carloads of agricultural produce were leaving Ogden daily for eastern points. Nearly $100,000 worth of salt had been sold, while one merchandising firm had shipped 250 carloads of flour to Montana, averaging nine tons to the car.[106] By the end of that decade Salt Lake City was growing rapidly, having increased in population from 27,000 to 40,000 in a three-year period. Real estate prices had risen from 50 to 200 percent, and new businesses were appearing daily.[107]

In view of this steady growth Mormon leaders continued to press for more railroad development. John Young's correspondence for 1885 contains a letter from an employee of one of the steamship lines that brought Mormon emigrants across the Atlantic, in which the writer called for an extension of road beyond Frisco. The writer, A. M. Gibson, described a trip he had made into northern Arizona from which he came away satisfied that a country so rich in resources would at once make such a road profitable. Salt Lake City, he said, occupied a strategic position, one that could command most of the trade in a vast tributary area.[108] Newspapers carried rumors to the effect that the Union Pacific was considering such a move, although road officials denied it.[109] John Sharp admitted to Charles Francis Adams that there was much local talk about a line from Salt Lake City to Los Angeles and that an organization called the Salt Lake and Los Angeles Railway Company had been set up during 1887. He pointed out that the

Utah Central was already 280 miles along the way to Los Angeles from Ogden and that another 450 miles of track would reach the Atlantic and Pacific Railway at Barstow Junction. The Union Pacific, remarked the bishop, was entitled to the Southwest territory, and it ought to claim it.[110]

President Adams requested Gen. James F. Curtis to survey the country in question to determine the feasibility of such a move. Accompanied by Sharp's son John, the general did so and reported that south of Milford the country was well settled for about a hundred miles, but beyond this point it appeared sterile. Mining, once a prime attraction, now showed little promise. The once-booming camp of Pioche had shipped $29 million worth of silver between 1864 and 1879, but now the place was almost dead. Once boasting 9,000 residents, the city had dwindled in size to 300, and many of its buildings were abandoned. However, concluded Curtis, despite the decline of mining a route to San Diego and Los Angeles was worthy of consideration.[111]

Adams read the report thoughtfully and concluded that 450 miles of new road would cost about $25,000 a mile, or a total of $12 million. "In my judgment," he told Sharp, "it would be quite impracticable to bring out any scheme for raising this amount of money under existing financial conditions. There is no market whatever for securities of new railroad companies, nor is there likely to be any for the immediate present." Since there was no danger of rivals getting into the territory in the near future, Adams decided that "We have, therefore, sufficient time to look about us."[112]

In 1884 the *Utah Gazetteer* concluded that "So far as the people of Utah are concerned, in a financial way, railroad building has been a decidedly unprofitable enterprise." Editor Robert W. Sloan stated that, except for the Utah Central, all the Mormon lines had passed entirely into other hands and now belonged to "one or the other of the large trunk lines that have found their way into Utah." Not only had the circumstances under which the roads had been built proved to be trying, he said, but "possession has departed from the original owners almost for a song." He concluded that "There is much that is lamentable connected with the history of railroad building in Utah . . . ."[113] By 1889 the Utah Central itself had fallen under control of the Union Pacific.

Looking back on the Mormons' efforts to light the path for these larger lines, and on their long and healthy association with the Union Pacific, those who examined the situation after the gloomy year of 1884 may have disagreed with Sloan. By the admission of Brigham Young's sons there was money to be made in railroad building, and they eagerly took advantage of each situation that presented itself. Almost all labor involved was local, and the wages went into the Utah economy. In case after case the Union

Pacific was called upon for aid, frequently at times when such assistance was difficult to provide, and without the partnership that existed between the Mormons and the Union Pacific rail service might never have materialized. That the railroad development of Utah, as it evolved, was beneficial to the community is hard to deny in view of the economic growth which took place in the land of the Saints during the latter years of the nineteenth century and in the following decades.

The Mission of the Railroad

During the years in which the Union Pacific encouraged Mormons to develop a rail system in their country, it continued the effort to develop the economic empire it claimed on the high plains. Faced by competition for a share of both through and local traffic, the road's managers realized that merely to capture territory was not enough; towns and surrounding agricultural communities had to be nourished and served if they were to grow. Unless these customers were reasonably satisfied with the service offered, railroad rivals would be encouraged to offer something better.

One of the first permanent forms of business available to the railroad was the livestock trade. The appearance of the road in Nebraska suggested to drovers the possibility of moving herds from Texas north to the open ranges of the high plains, where the cattle could multiply and be marketed through the new means of transportation. Some of the old-time freighters, though long familiar with oxen and the ability of those beasts to survive on the plains, lost little time in converting from bullwhacking to stock raising. Convinced that a new day was at hand, they sold their wagon outfits and took up grazing land near the railroad.

As early as 1868 a herd of 800 Texas cattle trailed into the vicinity of North Platte, and a Nebraska cow town was born. In the following autumn another 1,700 head arrived, most of which were purchased by the firm of Keith & Barton, and put out to graze upon the nearby prairie. Soon small outfits sprang up all along that section of the railroad and by 1870 it was estimated that 7,000 head of cattle, and a smaller number of sheep, could be found between Plum Creek and Sidney.[1] One of the stockmen later recalled that this was just the beginning; during the following decade thousands of animals were herded northward from Texas to the various Nebraska ranches along the railroad. "These cattle grew fat and multiplied," he wrote, "and the Union Pacific Railroad did an enormous business hauling the fatted, grass-feds to the Chicago Markets."[2]

Word of the successful cattle ranching ventures spread rapidly, and those who wanted to make a fortune in the "beef bonanza" began to move into western Nebraska and eastern Wyoming. In 1873 the surveyor general of Wyoming reported that public confidence in the safety and profitability of such ventures was by then well established. At that time John W. Iliff had 15,000 cattle grazing along the South Platte River in eastern Colorado.[3] The coming of the railroad, with the consequent increase of settlement, resulted in such pressure that the Oglala and Brulé Sioux were moved from their Platte River agency, on the Wyoming-Nebraska line, to new locations in what is now South Dakota. The vacuum thus created was shortly filled by cattlemen who had eyed enviously the rich grazing country once held by these tribesmen.

By 1874 the westward surge of farmers into eastern Kansas and Nebraska had effectively closed some of the earlier cattle trails and forced the herds coming out of Texas to take a more westerly course. This provided a second attraction to the new country of western Nebraska, and from it grew a small municipality that quickly rose to eminence as a cattle emporium. Ogallala, named after the recently departed residents of the area, had only a handful of residents in the early seventies, but with the opening of the country to stockmen and the construction of cattle yards by the railroad, the stripling village entered a boom period that brought it fame as a cowboy capital.[4]

So rapid was the growth of the cattle business west of Kearney that the government directors of the Union Pacific called it "fabulous" in 1875. To document their prediction that this region soon would become a major source of beef for eastern markets, they noted that in July and August 517 cars of cattle were picked up along the line for shipment to Omaha. During the entire year 3,000 cars of cattle, sheep, mules, and horses were hauled over the road, most of the draft animals moving westward to supply the growing agricultural community. In 1876 over a thousand cars carried 20,000 cattle to market. This was a season that saw 122,000 longhorns arrive from Texas to swell the rapidly growing livestock population along the line.[5]

Sidney Dillon, who owned a Nebraska ranch operated by his nephews, assured Oliver Ames that this phase of the company's business was one of great promise.[6] His contention was strengthened by the Union Pacific's government directors who, in 1877, reported that the company was obliged to lease large numbers of cattle cars from roads east of Council Bluffs to meet the demands of cattle shippers along the line. They also noted that the "dead meat" trade, as the British referred to it, was promising. Exports of both live and slaughtered animals grew rapidly in the mid-seventies, as improved transoceanic shipping encouraged trade with the British Isles. "The source of supply for this cheap meat will be largely and mainly the region traversed by . . . the Union Pacific Railroad," concluded the government directors.[7]

Hopes for increased traffic were realized as the cattle boom grew. So favorable was the outlook in the spring of 1878 that Dillon predicted a shipment of at least 100,000 head that year. He later reported a record 5,663 carloads of livestock received in Omaha and Council Bluffs, a figure that proved his estimate to have been no exaggeration.[8] Some of this haulage was in sheep, an industry that was getting a start in Wyoming.[9] The cattle business, of which Dillon had spoken, continued to draw attention in 1879, when it increased another 40 percent. In that year over 8,500 carloads of cattle, horses, hogs, and sheep were transported by the railroad; most of these were beef animals.[10]

In answer to demands of stockmen the Union Pacific constructed cattle yards at appropriate places along the line—it built five of them during 1880 —and otherwise encouraged private operators to erect facilities of their own, for which sidings were provided. A well-known trader at Fort Bridger, Wyoming, W. A. Carter, reflected the growing interest in this new business when he circulated a poster among cattlemen which told of the yards he had built and of the special arrangements he had effected with the railroad whereby livestock could be shipped at greatly reduced costs.[11]

The railroad's government directors encouraged those who contemplated entering the trade by announcing that there was no portion of the United States better adapted to raising cattle than the territory lying adjacent to the Union Pacific between Evanston, Wyoming, and North Platte, Nebraska. They quoted the major dealers as saying that the animals could thrive in this region the year around at a maximum five percent loss from inclement weather. Young Texas cattle could be delivered for about $9.50 a head, and their value when grazed on free range grass increased about $6 a year. Investors who did not want to tend their own livestock could place them in the hands of large dealers who charged a dollar per head annually for their services. Dealers also were willing to select beeves fit for market and put them on railroad cars bound for eastern markets or the feeding areas of eastern Nebraska. During a single day in October 1879, it required 241 cars to ship cattle destined for such markets.[12]

So great was the response to these enticements that by 1880 over 90,000 cattle, 85,000 sheep, and 3,000 horses and mules were said to be grazing within 40 miles of Laramie. These animals, valued at more than $2 million, were on some of the best grasslands in North America, an area in which, in 1867, perhaps not more than a total of 500 head could have been found.[13] That this development had its effect upon stripling western communities was seen in the comment of a Nebraska editor who said that Ogallala was "quite lively and full of stock dealers." In fact, he continued, local authorities had been obliged to ask all cowboys entering the city to leave their revolvers with police officers to prevent a further increase in the quarrels and bloodshed that had accompanied the town's rapid growth.[14] General Phil Sheridan, who commanded the military forces along the line, confessed that it was impossible to understand or appreciate the importance of the cattle boom in the region unless one had seen it for himself.[15] As was true of many other observers, the general found it hard to believe that the core of the desert could spurt into prominence in so short a period of time.

While Union Pacific leaders were pleased that the more arid parts of their domain could be profitably utilized, the boom in beef did present some problems. Leavitt Burnham, land agent at Omaha, reported that many tracts scattered along the line were valuable for their hay or water resources. He had constant applications from stockmen for their purchase. To sell off these segregated pieces would be to render adjoining and less desirable lands almost worthless. He suggested that, since in a good many instances cattlemen had simply squatted on such railroad lands, perhaps the best course would be to leave them undisturbed. A healthy cattle trade would provide a profitable source of business for the road in an area apparently not suited to any other means of livelihood.[16] Sidney Dillon agreed that, for the time being, it was better not to press the matter. "I feel that we will make more out of them by allowing herders to occupy them," he wrote in reference to these lands, "than we would to have a small amount sold and so give the few a monopoly of the business."[17]

That there was some danger of monopoly was evident from the outcries of small landholders. Early in the 1880s a Wyoming farmer—one of the few at this time—complained that the cattle baron "owns no lands and makes no improvements, is opposed to the settling up of the country, [and] is in fact a bitter enemy to the homesteader." He asserted that every foot of Wyoming was then claimed by the large cattle companies.[18] While Dillon could profess concern, his company was partly responsible for such a development. Most of the railroad's land sales in Wyoming had been to stockmen, to whom tracts were sold in blocks of thousands of acres. Nor did the commitment to those businessmen end there. When bitter winter weather threatened livestock the Union Pacific was quick to send help at a cut rate. "If herdsmen want hay up the road to keep cattle from starving you had better ship it at about cost rather than lose the cattle," Dillon instructed

Along the Columbia River, near the Celilo Rapids.

his Omaha subordinates early in 1881.[19] Vice President Elisha Atkins subscribed to this policy, even to one of favoritism. As he remarked to Dillon,
the general freight agent at Omaha "should not be too arbitrary with our
large shippers."[20]

By the decade of the eighties there were many important customers along
the line. Colorado was then shipping over 100,000 head a year. It was estimated that the state had 2 million sheep; a decade earlier it had only
20,000.[21] Wyoming, regarded as a cattle kingdom, was now grazing 300,000
sheep.[22] Meanwhile, the flow of Texas cattle continued. During the summer
of 1880 a Kansas newspaper noted that 170,000 head of cattle had passed
through the vicinity, bound for points along the Union Pacific road.[23]
The cattle were to be shipped to one of the two great markets serving the
railroad—Omaha and Kansas City—the latter then leading in receipts by
four to one.[24] The cattle trade provided the railroad with a business that was
welcome in a country yet to be proved as the breadbasket of the nation,
especially in dry years, when crops fell short of expectations.

Important as the cattle business was to shipping points along the road, it
had its limitations. Various little cities proudly claimed the title "Cowboy
Capital," and the busy exchange of money that took place when the herds arrived was a great boost to the local economy; yet the commerce was seasonal,
possessing the same boom aspect that made mining towns soar and then fall.

Cheyenne, for example, saved itself from the doom of many a railhead
construction town by taking advantage of its location as a shipping point for
livestock. As early as 1872 a newspaper correspondent could reminisce about
the lustier days of Cheyenne. He recalled the construction era when men
lived in tents and "rude cabins [were] hastily improvised to serve for store-
rooms where grasping men assembled to vend their goods for the fleeting
dollars that were so generously floating around them." This was when gamblers plied their professions on street corners for the want of a place to
operate, when dissipation was the order of the day and "lawlessness was
master of the situation." The population soared to nearly 7,000 and then
dwindled to 1,900 as the "railroad went on to its destination and left the
wayside places to sink or survive as circumstances might direct."[25]

Then came another momentary boom and by 1876 Cheyenne claimed
3,000 people, thanks to the Black Hills mineral rush and the renewed
interest in mining throughout the region.[26] The city's new role as a
connecting point with the railroads of Colorado and as an outfitting point
for the mines moved the *Leader* to comment that the place resembled
Rome—all roads led to it. As in the beginning, the town's continued
importance lay in its location, and not the natural attractions of its neighborhood. When Rabbi Isaac M. Wise saw the place in 1877 he found it hard

to explain its existence. As he viewed the surrounding countryside the Rabbi concluded that "I was in the heart of the most dreary alkaline desert that the eye of man can behold. Here Neptune has removed the veil from Pluto's terrible work, and here lies open to your inspection the volcanic eruption of ages unaccountable. Dreary conic hills stare at you in their naked ugliness. . . . You see dreariness itself outdone."[27] Helen Hunt Jackson, to become so famous for her writings about the American Indian, passed through Cheyenne about this time and stayed only long enough to complain about the food.[28]

By 1880 Cheyenne had recovered a good part of its lost population, and by then it was a city of 5,000 with a half dozen churches, two brick hotels, a brick high school, several wholesale houses and factories that turned out items ranging from wagons and carriages to jewelry. In addition to its trade with cattlemen, miners, and wagon freighters, the city drew business from nearby Camp Carlin and Fort D. A. Russell. As a division point on the railroad, the place enjoyed a large and steady payroll from the Union Pacific.[29] The importance of a diversified income was apparent to city fathers and to achieve it they maintained a constant search for new industries.

While Cheyenne searched for increased economic resources a neighboring rival city was achieving some success in this field. During 1874 the railroad erected a rolling mill at Laramie designed to restore wornout or defective rails at about one-third the cost of replacing them. Within a few years the plant employed approximately 230 men, bearing out a prediction that the new industry would increase Laramie's population by 500 or more persons. Cheyenne, whose civic leaders had fought for the mill and had lost, rationalized that it was all for the best. "Rolling mills don't add to the beauty of the place, no how!" said the *Leader*. "They make a great deal of thundering noise and rattle, which is disagreeable to persons of a nervous temperament. Then too, they cover everything with soot, and the smoke is offensive to sensitive olfactories. Pshaugh! We never did like rolling mills." Having done its part in an early crusade against air pollution, the *Leader* then accused Laramie of having made a deal with the railroad whereby assessments on the roadbed and other railroad property in Albany County were reduced by a third, the mill property itself was exempted from city and county taxes for ten years, and a $24,000 donation of bonds was made to the railroad for its cooperation.[30]

When the mill went into operation, early in 1875, it had a capacity to reroll 70 tons of rail a day and to produce another 15 tons of bar iron. One and a third tons of coal were required to process each ton of rails, but that commodity was available at the nearby Union Pacific mines at a relatively low cost. By the mid-eighties the output of the mill slackened because by this time eastern competitors had shown they could deliver new steel rails at prices so attractive that rerolled rails were being used principally on spurs and side tracks. By now, however, Laramie boasted a population of some 3,000, of substantial brick buildings, and of the other attributes associated with modern cities. The mill had contributed to this development.[31]

Westerners, in general, were great advocates of railroads, and those who lived in Wyoming were no exception. Cheyenne, Laramie, Rawlins, and other towns along the line in the territory admittedly were creations of the Union Pacific, and to it they owed their continued prosperity. Governor John W. Hoyt reflected this view when he spoke of the role the Union Pacific had played in the creation and growth of the territory. "Without it," he stated in 1878, "Wyoming would have been as wild and unproductive today as it was one hundred years ago."[32] In another instance he compared the road and its towns to a string of beads, each of the little municipalities and their outlying neighborhoods drawing their strength and sustenance from the steel bands that linked them together.[33]

As one looked at the map and saw that the populated counties were railroad counties, the notion that railroads induced settlement appeared to be reaffirmed. Accordingly, the demand for service in undeveloped northern Wyoming arose shortly after the completion of the main line. In 1873 Silas Reed, territorial surveyor general, suggested the construction of a branch from Cheyenne up the old Bozeman Trail and into Montana or from Fort Fred Steele, through the Wind River country and into Yellowstone Park. In the latter case he thought tourism and gold mining would justify the investment, both of which enterprises would be protected by a fort which he assumed the government would build.[34]

By the early eighties northern Wyoming, east of the Big Horn Mountains, had become "the garden spot" of the territory, where potatoes, wheat, oats, and corn were said to be raised without the necessity of irrigation. "Coal oil flows spontaneously from springs tributary to the Cheyenne River, is dipped out, and sold at $4 per gallon for lubricating purposes," wrote the commissioner of the general land office.[35] Professor Samuel Aughey, of Nebraska, also talked of oil in the region and correctly predicted that in time that product would provide a large traffic for a railroad.[36]

Cheyenne, anxious for a connection with Montana, pressed for a road to the north all during the seventies and eighties. The *Leader* readily acknowledged that this part of Wyoming had a great potential and that it ought to be served. Such construction would make it "as accessible to the white settler within a few years as now is any portion of the Territory along the line of the Union Pacific railroad, and in that portion of the Territory lies our prosperous future as a people," the editor predicted.[37]

As usual in the West, there was more enthusiasm than money available for such projects, but since incorporation was inexpensive that step could be taken without much financial risk. In the spring of 1875 a company was organized to build a line from Cheyenne to Helena, Montana, where a large mining community awaited rail service. Added to financial obstacles was the problem of the Sioux Indians and the Treaty of 1868 that had set aside a portion of the north country for its tribes. However, the Black Hills mining boom had put so much pressure on the Sioux that by 1876 they were obliged to vacate a large section of country, much of which was in Wyoming. When it became obvious that such a course was inevitable the *Leader* anticipated the outcome with the cry: "Northw'rd Empire Takes its Way!"[38]

As far as the Union Pacific was concerned there was no immediate need to spend money on a line north of Cheyenne. The desirability of reaching Montana and its mines was not denied, but already the Mormons had commenced the Utah Northern and it was that endeavor upon which the Union Pacific focused its attention. However, by the mid-eighties the Chicago and North Western was on the move in Nebraska and by 1886 one of its subsidiaries, named the Wyoming Central, had entered eastern Wyoming. The Union Pacific, reluctant to build into an area of questionable potential, now was faced with a line running out of Chicago that had elected to pioneer the new land. Cheyenne businessmen were equally concerned. In that very year, said Gov. Francis E. Warren, cattle shipments over the North Western had amounted to $300,000, much of which had formerly gone by way of Cheyenne. He lamented the fact that most supplies for northern Wyoming ranchers came from the East by the new route, further diminishing the capital city's trade.[39] The Union Pacific, he said, had induced millions of dollars in capital into the territory through its encouragement of stock-raising business. Urging the legislators to aid future rail expansion in any way, he pointed to Colorado, Kansas, and Nebraska as living proof of the benefits to be derived from better transportation. "In no way can our vast resources be developed more rapidly than by the extension of railroads through this Territory," he contended.[40] The governor, who was also a cattleman, had a particular interest in the country north of Cheyenne.

Thomas Sturgis, another prominent cattleman and a leader in the Wyoming Stock Growers Association, wrote to President Charles Francis Adams about the branch line. He said the people of Cheyenne were anxious to have such a feeder and that they usually controlled the county when they were united in any given desire. He warned, however, that a certain prejudice against the Union Pacific had existed since the late seventies, when Cheyenne's hopes for a northbound extension of the Colorado Central had been dashed. Sturgis therefore suggested the formation of an independent local company, the control of which could be turned over to the larger road after a bond issue had been passed.[41] Adams apparently agreed to the strategy for, during the first week of March 1886, the Cheyenne and Northern Railway was incorporated and in a few days a countywide $400,000 bond issue was approved.[42] Two months later the Union Pacific agreed to subscribe to a majority of the new road's capital stock. Within a year and a half a standard-gauge road had been constructed to Wendover, 125 miles north of Cheyenne.[43]

The Cheyenne and Northern was presumably aimed at a connection with the Northern Pacific, in southern Montana, and possibly a projection beyond, to the Canadian border.[44] However, once it touched the Wyoming Central line, it showed no disposition to build farther north. By November 1, 1887, the branch, constructed at a cost of $1.5 million, was turned over to the operating department of the parent company.[45] Apparently this answered the Chicago and North Western's threat, and, much to the disappointment of residents in northern Wyoming, the drive to capture their country ceased, each of the contestants seemingly ready to call off the fight.

The decision not to build into Montana resulted from an examination of northern Wyoming by Union Pacific engineers. The study was made by F. G. Wheeler, who concluded that the region beyond Casper was primarily useful for grazing. He thought Montana possibly might be reached at a later date, but the only justification for it, in the meantime, would be to transport Texas cattle to Canada, where new rangelands were being opened.[46] William Courtenay, a Miles City cattleman, argued that to complete the 200-mile link between Wendover and his city was justifiable because of developments in the livestock business. "The southern cattle trail is practically closed, and cattle cannot any longer be driven from Texas to Montana," he wrote, early in 1889. "They must be shipped by rail. Leading stockmen in Texas and New Mexico tell me that if the Union Pacific would complete a through road to Montana by building from Wendover, Wyo., to Miles City, M.T., a very large number of three and four year old steers would be shipped early in the spring, put on our ranges in May, and allowed to remain until late in the fall, when they could be shipped for beef." Custer County itself, said Courtenay, was larger than the state of Pennsylvania, and was situated in the finest grazing lands in the West. He was convinced that if cattle, formerly driven up the trail from Texas, could be shipped by modern methods there would be great profit to all concerned.[47]

Engineer Jacob Blickensderfer, who also studied northern Wyoming, confirmed Wheeler's opinion. "There is nothing upon which to base a prospect of remunerative business south of Buffalo [Wyoming], and even Buffalo and the country north of it I fear do not afford a prospect of sufficient business to warrant the construction of so long a line . . .," he reported.[48] The day of the open range had passed and the cattle interests, once so powerful, no longer could beckon the rail builders with any measure of success.

By this time the branch policy was under fire by the Union Pacific's directors, and where once such prairie prospecting would have been undertaken the company now showed increasing reluctance to gamble on developing a new part of the West. Although Joseph M. Carey, a congressional delegate from Wyoming and a cattleman himself, urged the Union Pacific to continue to Buffalo, no more road was graded. Even Carey's prediction that the Burlington road soon would enter Wyoming and threaten railroads already there did not move the management at Boston.[49] Apparently there was some fear among the directors that Wyoming, about to become a state, intended to include restrictive or even punitive clauses in its new constitution. Carey, however, did not think any inclusions detrimental to undeveloped portions of Wyoming would find their way into the new document.

The point raised by Adams may have been an excuse rather than a reason. In any event, the Union Pacific refused to invest any more money, even though the Northern Pacific and the Chicago and North Western both were in easy reach of the country. Wyoming was changing, as Gov. Thomas Moonlight pointed out, and the emphasis on open-range cattle raising had been diluted by the great losses suffered in the bitter winters of 1886–87. That, however, did not mean a sudden transformation of the land into an agricultural area. The Union Pacific itself felt severely the "big die" of those winters and the pangs of overexpansion in troublous times. It was in no position to answer the demands of Wyoming boosters who continued to praise the resources of their domain, despite the losses in revenue suffered by its major industry.

A decline in cattle-raising added an incentive for Wyoming towns to seek more sources of income. In 1888 Francis Warren, who was then president of the Cheyenne Board of Trade, sought such assistance from the Union Pacific. In this instance he was interested in the mineral potential of the territory, particularly in reported copper deposits in the Platte Cañon Mining District of the North Platte River country, and in the Silver Crown District, about 20 miles from Cheyenne. Iron ore and sandrock, for making glass, also were said to be available locally. Warren wanted the railroad to cooperate in obtaining reduction works for these ores, and to build a spur from the Cheyenne and Northern to serve such plants.[50] A few days after Adams received his request, a Wyoming journalist wrote to him on the same subject and asked that the road lend its influence in obtaining a copper ore treatment plant for Cheyenne. Noting the increased production of that

LEFT—*The snowfall during the winter of 1884–85—the first year the Oregon Short Line was in use—was very heavy. Here workers are clearing tracks along the O. R. & N. tracks that connected with the O. S. L. at Huntington, Oregon.*

RIGHT—*Some of the contractors for the Oregon Short Line lost money on the work they undertook. One of them was quite bitter about it.*

BOTTOM—*An O. R. & N. train at a portage on the Columbia River.*

"THREE YEARS
on the
OREGON SHORT LINE."

We are writing a work for publication, entitled
"Three Years on the Oregon Short Line."
Contractors and others who have been victimized on
this line, are invited to send us a clear succient
statement of their wrongs, duly sworn to, which we
will publish in our work. Having ourselves experienced from this concern much gross injustice, we
are determined to place the facts before the public,
and question whether a more dishonorable or repre-
hensive record can be found than that of the unscrupulous creatures who had the building of that
badly located road. No act of duplicity or chicanery
do we consider them incapable of, and honestly believe for fraud imbicility, mismanagement, misrepresentation, and general rascality, finds no parallel
in railroad history.

Eastern and Western papers please insert this
notice, and Oblige

DALLIN & CO.,
Contractors O. S. L, Ry.

Address: 39 Clark Street, Chicago, Ill,

ore in Montana, and that much of it was sent East for processing, the writer suggested that since Cheyenne was the geographical center of Union Pacific holdings it would be a logical place for such an industry. "I am sure the Union Pacific management will work on the line of this proposition and will not be behind any road in fostering legitimate enterprises based upon the actual available resources which nature has given to its territory," he said.[51] Adams, however, was not inclined to invest his company's money in such enterprises. He so stated to Fred Ames, who responded: "I agree with you in the general principle that it is not our business, as a railroad company, to put money into these manufacturing and mining interests along the line of the road. If they cannot stand on their own bottom they certainly are not worth undertaking."[52]

While Cheyenne's businessmen were disappointed in the Union Pacific's lack of interest in joint enterprises, they did get tangible benefits from projects more closely associated with the road's immediate interests. During 1889 the company agreed to build extensive car-repair shops, a decision that brought expressions of satisfaction from Rep. Joseph M. Carey.[53] To further encourage such enterprises Cheyenne offered to furnish the road with a free water supply and to vacate some land for the company's use. In return, the road agreed to provide free transportation for all materials used in building a municipal waterworks, including viaducts and sewers, and to provide building stone from its quarries at cost.[54] Before the end of the year the railroad company had spent more than $228,000 on its new Cheyenne shops.

Other points in Wyoming were the beneficiaries of railroad company improvements in 1889. In that year the firm spent $222,000 on the Carbon cutoff, in central Wyoming, and another $341,000 in developing its coal mines in that area. Work was pushed to develop further the mines at Alma, Dana, and Rock Springs in the hope of increasing production. Hanna, to be reached by the Carbon cutoff, promised a profitable business when that source could be reached by rail. "We shall be in shape to move much more coal this Fall than ever before and [we] will have the coal to move," predicted Assistant General Manager William H. Holcomb in the spring of 1889.[55]

By this time the Union Pacific had operated in Wyoming for only a little more than two decades; yet in that time it had developed a thriving business and had contributed heavily to the growth of the territory. The federal census for 1870 had shown that less than 10,000 people (excluding Indians) lived there; 20 years later the figure exceeded 60,000.[56] While such numbers were small in terms of settlements elsewhere, they represented the peopling of a land that was once considered to be a part of the American

Desert, and even the Union Pacific itself had held little hope for the early utilization of its lands in the area. By 1890, however, one of the road's officials had to admit that "an enormous business is doing," to use his words, over the Wyoming and Idaho divisions of the line. Double crews were necessary to keep the trains moving, and traffic flowing into the main line at Granger had increased by 50 percent over the previous year.[57]

The Utah and Northern, begun by the Mormons and completed to a junction with the Northern Pacific in Montana by the Union Pacific, represented the first attempt by the latter company to draw on the vast resources of the Northwest. During this period Wyoming exhibited its great desire for a road to Montana along the eastern slopes of the Big Horn Mountains, but the Union Pacific saw greater opportunities in the Idaho route. The proposed penetration of the old Oregon country by the Northern Pacific merely reaffirmed the belief that this economic empire was of value and was worth fighting for. Spurred by this conviction, and anxious to capture Montana's mineral trade, the Union Pacific concentrated its early efforts on getting to Butte. Later it would build its Oregon Short Line to effect a connection with Portland and then extend its tracks to Washington, but for the moment such plans had to be held in abeyance.

Montana, in the seventies, was a remote treasure-house known principally for its mineral deposits, but during these years this was enough to attract railroad builders. For this prize the Union Pacific had penetrated the mountains of Colorado and had moved southward in Utah. The move upon Butte, therefore, was natural. That mining town, called by Union Pacific publicist Robert Strahorn "the pride of Montana, and, indeed, a youthful marvel in the mining world," had 5,000 residents. Approximately 4,000 quartz mines, ranging widely in value, were located in the general vicinity. In the early eighties, before the coming of rail service, Butte's annual production of silver was valued at $1.5 million. About 3 million pounds of ore were sent east for reduction each year, despite the high cost of transportation.[58] In 1880 the Territory of Montana was producing $3.5 million in silver. By then more than $150 million in gold had been extracted.

Even before the Utah and Northern reached Montana there was evidence that its value to the western mining community was more than a matter of mere anticipation. An Idaho resident, who watched the road progress through his part of the West, testified to its importance when he said that with the appearance of rails a new era in quartz mining had commenced. Now, he said, there were "scores of paying quartz mines being worked in Lemhi and Custer counties alone, with a daily yield of about $10,000. These mines are both gold and silver and pay from $1,500 to $3,000 to the ton." Not only did the railroad provide cheaper means of transportation, but it also brought capitalists. These men, said the writer, were able to get more out of the mines than had the original prospectors, who were not always as industrious or as ingenious as they might have been.[59] The railroad had revitalized a segment of the Idaho economy that had begun to wither for the want of cheaper methods and low cost machinery.

Rail service itself in the frontier economy provided a new industry, one that brought employment and cash into the region, although historically its appearance produced mixed feelings as older means of transportation suffered. Decades earlier, as the rails had swept across the Appalachians and had displaced wagon and stagecoach transportation, small communities—whose residents had made a living by selling livestock feed and by offering travelers lodging—objected to what later would be termed technological unemployment. This feeling was evident during the early 1880s in Idaho, where complaints were heard that the iron horse required no grain or hay, as had the oxteams, and that the change was not for the better.

When the Utah and Northern penetrated southern Montana its presence sent reverberations through the economy of that territory. Pick and pan mining, once so very profitable, had required little capital, but all during the 1870s this mode of extraction had steadily declined. Quartz mining, on the other hand, required capital and heavy machinery. Robert Strahorn estimated that without rail service "quartz needed to be pretty much all metal to pay." The appearance of the railroad, he added, changed "the whole face of the mining field as well as the agricultural." The mineral industry sprang back into activity to an extent that "the frenzied gulch miner of 1862 could hardly have dreamed of."[60] Ore, heavy and bulky, could be sent to reduction plants at a price that allowed the working of some of the lower grade mines.

By 1885 it was estimated that Union Pacific receipts for outgoing and incoming freight amounted to more than $6 million a year. Some 250 million pounds of ore was shipped from Butte, yielding to the railroad company an income that approached one-tenth of that for the whole system.[61] General Manager S. R. Callaway reported, in 1885, that the Anaconda company was doing "an enormous business," and was preparing to double its capacity through new construction. "We have taken twenty seven engines and two hundred cars there [to Butte] from the South Park system, and have all we can do to keep the business moving," he wrote to Charles Francis Adams.[62] Assistant general traffic manager P. P. Shelby estimated that the white population of Montana had risen to 125,000, and the value of the territory's mineral production was approximately $26 million. However, he warned, the output of local smelting works perhaps had peaked, due to the declining quality of ore then being processed. He hoped that receipts from wool and cattle shipments would compensate for any future decline in mineral shipments.[63]

By 1886 predictions of a downturn in mining began to be realized. Governor Samuel Hauser reported that low prices for silver and copper had slowed production in the existing mines and had discouraged the opening of new ventures. Although the value of mineral output at the end of that fiscal year was over $22 million, silver prices were falling and the slump had begun to affect the mining industry.[64] Adams himself admitted the slackening of pace, commenting that "The Northern Pacific has an idea that we have a perfect bonanza at Butte, which they cannot get access to." Gloomily he deemed the business at Butte as hardly worth doing, and he predicted that the city ultimately would share the fate of such mining cities as Virginia City, Leadville, and others.[65] His reference to Leadville grew out of a deepening disillusionment with mining as an income for the Union Pacific. The Denver and South Park, purchased by Jay Gould for the Union Pacific, was in severe financial straits. Adams bitterly charged that "The chief source of revenue of the road was in carrying men and material into Colorado to dig holes in the ground called mines, and until it was discovered that there was nothing in those mines the business was immense. That was the famous mining boom of Colorado . . . when every one was crazy."[66] Adams was beginning to suspect that the same fate was in store for the Union Pacific in Montana. However, despite a doubtful future for gold and silver extraction, copper showed an increasing potential, and although the Union Pacific had experienced some disappointments in the western mining industry, it displayed faith in Montana by laying plans, late in 1888, for standard-gauging the Utah and Northern. William H. Holcomb, of the Omaha office, reported that the smelter at Anaconda was expanding rapidly. So brisk was business, he wrote, that both the freight and passenger depots were hard-pressed to accommodate the business at hand. "They have just erected a large hotel there, finer than any at either Omaha or Denver, and everything indicates very rapid growth," said Holcomb. "It is an entirely different town from Butte and being more pleasantly located and free from smoke, very many Butte people are arranging to make their homes at Anaconda." The young city was, he thought, "one of the most promising mining camps in the United States . . . . Now is our time to secure friendly relations with these people and secure the business."[67] The Anaconda smelter processed some 1,500 tons of ore per day, which required between 500 and 800 tons of coal. The Union Pacific also brought in 5,000 cords of wood a month. Because storage facilities were limited the mining company was absolutely dependent upon the railroad for a daily supply of both coal and ore, and any delays threatened to stop the furnaces.[68] Rail service, a prerequisite to industrial development of an isolated part of the country, was vital to its continued operation and to its very existence.

The Union Pacific's government directors also displayed faith in the future of mineral traffic throughout the Mountain West. In 1890 they called that business "immense," but held it was only a foretaste of things to come, believing that the area's greatest deposits were as yet undeveloped. The key that would unlock these treasures was said to be the railroad. To substantiate that argument the directors looked back over the past two decades. Viewing the Union Pacific as one of the leaders in providing such a vital service, the directors called upon it for even greater efforts. "To penetrate into the mountain ranges of the West and keep pace with the restless activity of the people, who are abstracting their hidden wealth, as well as to be ready to assist in the development of the country generally, should be the mission of the Union Pacific Railway," concluded the directors.[69] Charles Francis Adams agreed that such was the role of his company. It had been, he said, a large factor in the development of the states and territories through which it ran, and this had been accomplished largely through the policy of throwing out branches and feeders as far and as fast as possible.[70]

Gardiner M. Lane, son of a Harvard professor and an assistant to Adams, saw the rapid development of western communities as one that emphasized the material aspects of life. When a young man wrote from Lausanne, Switzerland, and expressed interest in a western railroad career, Lane gave him a Bostonian's assessment of that part of America. "The western country and civilization are absolutely new," he explained. "There are no old buildings, no works of art, but few theaters, no music, no interest in literature and study, and in fact, almost none of those things which make life worth living in European countries and in the seaboard states of this country." Westerners, he believed, lacked an appreciation for the niceties of life, and although undoubtedly many of them were gentlemen at heart, they were without the "refinement and education to which the inhabitants of older communities are accustomed." To Lane a definition of "the living" in western states was confined to food and shelter, both of which he thought were generally poor, and beyond that there was little to nourish the soul. The railroad man was obliged to live where his job took him, and this, said the young executive from Massachusetts, might well be "in the desert with nothing to be seen for miles. . . ."[71] Despite warnings that a cultural desert lay beyond the Missouri, applicants continued to press Lane for information about employment in that country. As one of them said, "I am anxious to go farther west, for the reason that I think a young man with energy can get a better chance to make a home."[72]

The West still exhibited its historic attraction, and the belief that it was a land of opportunity persisted. The railroad had played a large part in sustaining the idea; however, such expansion and search for new business were not undertaken without a price to the company. Growing rail competition in what remained of the frontier, a sharp decline in the mining industry, poor crops and, above all, continued pressure by the federal government for a settlement of the Union Pacific's indebtedness to it, placed the corporation in a deepening dilemma. As it was with other western railroads of the era, the battle for traffic forced Union Pacific managers to adhere to the "expand or die" theory and to compensate for such losses by seeking more territory. Cut off from the east at Omaha, and flanked all across its westward passage by rivals, the "men of Boston" looked to the undeveloped country north and west of Ogden as the natural avenue of expansion. Adams remarked in 1885 that it was better to invest money farther west "where we have a fifteen hundred mile haul" than to compete with other lines nearer to the Missouri River where the company had only two or three hundred miles worth of business for which to fight."[73] With this as the only apparent alternative to their dilemma the road's managers struck off for the Northwest, hopeful that yet another traffic bonanza would be their salvation in an ever-growing railroad war.

Northwest Passage

Residents of the West's farthest reaches observed the approach of railroads and looked forward to a day when their area would be served. In 1868 an Oregonian who had recently served his state as surveyor general, told members of Congress that a branch line to his state not only would be of great service to its people, but also would help to solve major western problems for the federal government. Asserting that the Pacific Railroad already had demonstrated that "railroads increase population and commerce, and advance civilization, in new countries, more than all other agencies combined," he concluded that "nothing but the advancement of a permanent civilization can settle Indian wars . . . ." Should a road be constructed to Oregon, he predicted, the number of troops in the area could be greatly reduced and the cost of hauling supplies to the remainder would be lowered as much as 80 percent. The government, he contended, would profit even if it granted the bonds necessary for construction—he suggested $13 million worth—for it would annually save as much as $3 million a year. In no time at all the cost of such a road would be thus recovered.[1]

As early as June of 1879 Sidney Dillon had called together his directors to discuss with Henry Villard "the organization of a new enterprise to build a road from the Snake River to Oregon which shall secure to the Union Pacific the trade of the Columbia Valley." Villard, he said, had gained control of the existing transportation lines in that country and he now wanted to submit a project for their consolidation with the proposed road "on such a basis that the money to be invested shall receive a large income at once." Dillon thought the matter very important to his company.[2]

Villard's suggestion came when the Union Pacific was about to acquire the Kansas Pacific, and from there to launch itself into a period of rapid expansion throughout the West. It also provided impetus for a move the Union Pacific had contemplated for almost 15 years. The road along the

Snake River, to be known as the Oregon Short Line, would blaze the way for steam locomotives over the path of those who had plodded westward along the historic Oregon Trail. Its completion would mean, in effect, the appearance of yet another of the so-called transcontinentals.

The people of Idaho had watched the building of the Union Pacific eagerly, hopeful that the company might continue its westward push and finally reach the sea or, if not that, would construct a branch into a country long known for its mineral riches. In 1865 the newspapers of that territory urged such action, and the governor, Caleb Lyon, talked of it in his annual message to the legislators.[3] During the following year, as the Union Pacific pushed across Nebraska, men of Idaho talked of the natural roadway leading to the Northwest and saw it not only as a key that would "unlock the rocks" of mining regions, but also as a lifeline that would speed regional economic growth in general. When they noted that already they were receiving mail from the Atlantic seaboard from two to four days faster than before, their excitement grew. Admittedly the Central Pacific would be of some benefit to the territory, but it was to the Union Pacific and to the Oregon Steam Navigation Company, whose managers talked of expansion into eastern Oregon, that Idaho looked with most interest.[4]

Grenville Dodge, chief engineer for the Union Pacific and a man widely recognized for his work, reported to his employers that a study conducted in 1867 had clearly shown the feasibility of a railroad down the Snake River. Because such a route avoided the high elevations of the Sierras, he predicted that "ere long it will become the great through route from the northwest, and control the trade and traffic of the Indies."[5]

Encouraged by Dodge's findings, Vice President Thomas Durant asked him to run a survey line to the Columbia River and to determine a proper route to the Pacific. General Dodge assigned the task to surveyor J. O. Hudnutt, who carried it out during the autumn of 1868 and the spring of 1869. Hudnutt reported that the economic potential of the area was great. He was impressed that shippers paid $30 a ton to transport goods from Portland to Umatilla, from which point wagons carried them to the mines at even higher rates. Eight to twelve thousand tons of freight were hauled into Boise each season, and that which came up the Columbia by water was also potential rail traffic, for it had to be portaged around falls and was otherwise expensive to ship. Dodge, who had been interested in the country since 1853, when he first examined it for a possible road, commented upon its economic promise. "The whole mercantile traffic of Idaho is about to change its course and seek the eastern markets," he predicted. Not only would the Union Pacific benefit from such a shift, but the rails themselves would revolutionize the territory. Mine owners plagued by high prices of transportation and labor would find relief in these departments, and the Indians who blocked the white man's way would be driven back. Dodge estimated that with rail service available Idaho should produce $25 million a year in mineral and agricultural products. "I shall always think that the mission of the Union Pacific railroad is not fulfilled until it builds this branch to the Pacific Ocean," he concluded.[6]

President Oliver Ames agreed that such a mission was a worthy ideal, but sufficient practical matters intervened to make it a subject for future study. "I am satisfied that the Road to Oregon will be a first rate opperation [*sic*] when the time comes for doing it," he told his engineer. "But with the amt. of other work we have the present year on hand and the probability that all aid by gov't. will be refused to lines of Pacific Railroad until those now in progress have been completed leads me to think the Oregon Road will get the go bye this year." Despite the richness of the country, he thought, the road could not be built without a subsidy, and, if this were not forthcoming, construction would have to wait until "the people on its line shall awake to its importance."[7]

Those people were more than awake to their need for a road, but the scattered nature of Idaho's population—estimated at less than 30,000—and the lack of available capital prevented them from rendering aid at the time. In January 1868, delegates from different counties met at Boise where they deliberated for three days and then memorialized Congress for aid. The gathering climaxed railroad meetings held in various localities in which a widespread awareness of transportational needs existed.[8] All that resulted from the convention was some local dissension over proposed routes; Congress was not yet in the mood to award more land grants. Therefore, a bill to incorporate the Idaho, Oregon and Puget Sound Railroad Company, to be directed by Sidney Dillon, Thomas C. Durant, and Brigham Young, and to be granted alternate sections of land on either side of the track, found little enthusiasm at Washington.[9]

The excitement of May 1869 which marked the joining of the main railroads raised expectations that were short-lived. Soon after these ceremonies were concluded, surveying parties in Idaho disappeared and gloom descended upon the country. "So ends, for years we fear," wrote the editor of the *Idaho World*, "all hope or reasonable expectations of there being a railroad which shall immediately connect Idaho with the roads across the continent and with the Pacific States." "Idahoans will have to continue to perform stage riding for years to come to make the connection with either the Central Pacific or the Union Pacific Railroads."[10] Even the incorporation of the Oregon and Idaho branch of the Union Pacific, later in that year, caused little stir.[11]

Idaho, along with other hopeful western communities, grudgingly took its place in line and waited. For the next decade the popular mood ebbed and flowed, as each optimistic rumor sent forth waves of hope that ultimately ran out of momentum in the face of continued rail inactivity. Neighboring western Montana had much the same experience, but since that entire territory contained less than 40,000 people and only 37 towns at the time the Union Pacific approached Promontory, there was little chance of early rail service in such a remote region. To the people of Idaho, however, a populated country south of them, in Utah, and a growing area to the northwest in Oregon and Washington, seemed to offer much more to any railroad than the mere prospect of mineral traffic. When hard times came, the situation was attributed to a lack of railroads, and as otherwise un- promising communities in such places in Nebraska prospered along the Union Pacific, there was a deepening bitterness in Idaho. "We do not anticipate any large portion of our sagebrush lands will be reduced until we get a railroad," wrote Milton Kelley of the *Statesman* in 1872.[12]

As the people of Idaho waited for Congress to appropriate lands for railroad construction the Crédit Mobilier scandal rocked the nation and generated a widespread demand for a cessation of such appropriations. Westerners, who had hungered for the original line across their land, at almost any price and under any conditions, were not particularly aroused by the uproar in the national capital. Idaho's surveyor general said that Congress could well afford to donate the needed land, and the territory's governor, Thomas W. Bennett, decried the growing public attitude against such moves. "Men talk of this subject as if they imagined land was scarce out West," said the governor, "and that when used for building railroads, the owners of it annihilated it or carried it off to some other planet beyond the reach of the 'actual settlers.' They forget how many millions of acres there are lying idle, and must forever lie idle unless opened to emigration by railroad." By donating land, he continued, the government at once created a market for all its holdings. Otherwise, millions of acres would remain unproductive and unimproved for years, bringing no purchase money or taxes, while the prospective settler was "loafing in the slums and grog shops of Eastern cities . . . ."[13]

The moving force that precipitated action in Sidney Dillon's office arose neither from a sudden change of heart on the government's part nor from an immediate threat of serious competition by a major railroad. In 1878 Henry Villard surveyed both sides of the Columbia River east of Portland in search of a suitable rail route to the mineral districts of northern Idaho. In the following spring he negotiated an agreement with Capt. J. C. Ainsworth, president of the Oregon Steam Navigation Company, for the purchase of a majority of stock in that firm,[14] after which he took an option on the Walla Walla and Columbia River Railroad, a small line owned by Ainsworth's company. In June 1879 Villard incorporated the Oregon Railway and Navigation Company, issuing $6 million in stocks and $6 million in bonds. It was his plan to build a road from Portland to Umatilla, where small branches were to spread out in the manner of a frayed rope end. One of the proposed feeders was pointed toward the Oregon cities of La Grande, Union, and Baker, beyond which lay Boise, Idaho. In the same month that the Oregon Railway was organized Villard asked Dillon for a conference, a request that prompted the call for Union Pacific directors to assemble immediately at New York. Although the meeting did not result in a Union Pacific purchase of half interest in Villard's company, as he had offered, the gesture told Sidney Dillon and his friends that it was time to move out along the trail to Oregon. That country, long dormant, appeared to be coming to life. Even as they made ready for the venture Villard began building sections of his railroad up the Columbia River, completing a portion of it in 1880.[15] Action, as opposed to talk, always impressed Union Pacific leaders, and this evidence of activity in the Northwest hastened their preparations to meet the oncoming thrust.

Sidney Dillon later recalled the circumstances of the decision to invade the Northwest, and explained the origin of the extension's name. "I had that Oregon Short Line built . . . . I gave it that name myself at Omaha, and created it and fixed it up at that time, and telegraphed to Boston that with their concurrence we would build that road." At the time of his remarks, he also mentioned the role the Southern Pacific played in the decision, explaining that if that company's subsidiary, the Central Pacific, "shut down the gate at Ogden, and the traffic all goes around the other way, we can stand it."[16] Confronted by the Central Pacific, the Northern Pacific, and the aggressive Denver and Rio Grande, which talked of building across Nevada (and ultimately would finance the Western Pacific, which did cross that state), Dillon saw that unless he acted his road would dead-end in Utah. The prospect of a connection with the Oregon Railway appeared to be the cheapest and quickest way to the sea.

To finance construction the Union Pacific offered its stockholders a chance to invest in the Oregon Short Line. Each holder of 50 shares of Union Pacific stock was permitted to subscribe for a $1,000 bond and five shares of paid-up Oregon Short Line stock for $1,000 in cash. To maintain control, the Union Pacific kept one half of the capital stock, issuing the rest to these subscribers. A few years later President Adams reported that of the 750 stockholders of the Oregon Short Line only 343, or less than one half, were also stockholders in the Union Pacific.[17]

Another source of financial assistance was through a subsidiary known as the Idaho and Oregon Land Improvement Company, whose officers were notified in advance as to the exact location of stations along the road. The company, in turn, agreed to lay out townsites, reserve land for the stations, and promote towns, one-half interest in which was to be conveyed to the railroad. Sensitive to criticism for its past speculations, the Union Pacific insisted that it was to have no direct financial interest in the land company, but that its officials, if they desired, might personally subscribe to its capital stock. United States Senator Alexander Caldwell, of Kansas, was its president; Hugh C. Wallace, later ambassador to France, was secretary; and Sam B. Jones, a Union Pacific passenger agent, was treasurer. Andrew Mellon served on the board of directors. Robert Strahorn, the improvement company's vice president, later wrote that the project was valuable to the railroad because, with other improvements, it also acquired considerable amounts of federal land in which the government had been unable to interest eastern colonists. However, the relationship did not continue as a happy one. Later acrimony between the Union Pacific and officers of the improvement company considerably lessened the value of their arrangement.[18]

Dillon had hoped to begin the Oregon Short Line at Kelton, a Central Pacific station in western Utah, in order to shorten the construction distance, but a favorable arrangement with the rival company could not be made.[19] Instead, the new branch left the main road at Granger, Wyoming, and angled northwestward to its terminus at Huntington, Oregon. The contractors began work in 1881, and after making a slow start, with only 50 miles completed in the first year, the pace quickened. Dillon reported that by the end of 1882, track 321 miles long was ready to carry traffic from Granger Junction to Shoshone, Idaho. Here a branch was built into the Wood River mining district, where tons of ore lay waiting for transportation. Within another year about 420 miles were in service, and the president reported with pleasure that the company had come within $57,000 of paying current interest on construction bonds. He thought this very satisfactory for a new and yet incomplete road.[20] Construction was completed to Huntington by mid-October 1884, adding approximately 600 miles of railroad, including the Wood River branch, to lines owned or controlled by the Union Pacific.

Construction of the Idaho branch generated the same local excitement experienced in other western communities about to get their first railroad. In 1881 Gov. John B. Neil commented that until that time Idaho had only one line, the Utah and Northern, that was then building northward across eastern Idaho, but now the progress of construction crews across the south-central portion of the territory promised to develop another great section of

western country.²¹ Publicists talked of the coming economic diversification—
of farming, stock raising and other activities—and of Idaho's great tourist
attractions.²² One writer even implied that the rails would bring in a hardy,
independent Gentile population that would end the control of the Mormons
who had planted their colonies in the region and had driven off other
immigrants.²³ The Mormons, however, seemed to be thriving under the
new economic stimulus, one firm at Logan having contracted to supply
75,000 ties for the road. The *Deseret News* congratulated them for "sharing
in the results of the present railroad 'boom' of the Territory."²⁴ Portland
watched the progress with equal interest and condemned easterners who
cried out against railroad monopolies. "Are not the railroads the very
instruments through which our Northwest coast is becoming developed?"
asked one journal, in arguing that hostility toward such companies would
be suicidal for western communities.²⁵ The commissioner of the General
Land Office observed the rail penetration of Idaho and reported that a large
emigration was flowing into that country to take up its fertile lands.²⁶
Territorial surveyor general James Tolman thought the boom was just
beginning.²⁷

Construction was not a simple matter, as those who had worked on
earlier sections, such as those of Nebraska, soon discovered. James H. Kyner
later recalled that the terrain was rocky, water was often scarce, and the
contractors found themselves in a high cost situation. "I was told later that
the building of the Oregon Short Line cost three million dollars more than
the construction company paid for it, and I believe it," he wrote. "I know
that I contributed my share on that first contract I had—more than my
share, I thought at the time. Though it didn't quite break me, it broke
many others."²⁸ Another man, who identified himself as "Scraper," charged
that a couple of gentlemen had turned up in the West and, with "no other
capital or virtues to recommend them than that they were Sidney Dillon's
nephews, [had] induced enterprising numbskulls to take contracts, each
having the promise of all he could do." He further stated that the two men's
firm, Collins & Stevens, caused these workers to stand idle because surveys
were not complete and then charged them exorbitant prices at company
stores for food they consumed while waiting. Worse, he said, the contracting
company exploited its subcontractors and made a lot of money as a result
of its relationship to the railroad. "How is that for being U.P. nephews?" he
asked. Tom Jessup, who also had one of the contracts, called the story
exaggerated and said that Collins and Stevens had acted honorably.²⁹

Newspaper stories of this nature worried Dillon, who told Fred Ames,
"I do not wish to have any discredit put upon the building of that road."³⁰
He was understandably sensitive about charges of nepotism, for they inferred

collusion and profit making among Union Pacific managers. However, the majority report of the United States Pacific Railway Commission of 1887 publicly stated that no evidence had been produced tending to show that any officer or director of the railroad was personally interested financially in the Oregon Short Line contracts.[31] Subcontractors who felt they had suffered through delays caused by the railroad company made loud and public complaint about their plight.[32] To silence them Dillon made compromises which, under close study, might not have been necessary or justified. In one case he referred the matter to Chester Collins, with the comment: "If it is a just claim cannot you give them something on it and get it out of the way, and not have them following me around about it."[33] In another instance he suggested settling a $70,000 claim—made by a Mormon contractor by the name of Henry J. Faust—for $5,000, in preference to seeing his nephew take the stand and explain all the details of the Union Pacific's relationship to its contractors.[34]

The commercial interests of both Idaho and Oregon displayed excitement over the connection of Portland to Omaha, and there was much newspaper talk about the economic promise of the union. Yet, the ceremony that formalized the joining of the rails was strangely quiet, passing almost unnoticed in the press. Work was completed by November 10, 1884, but the residents of Huntington waited two weeks for any recognition of the Union Pacific's accomplishment. Finally, on the twenty-fifth, H. P. Rowe, superintendent of the Oregon Railway, and E. C. Smeede, assistant chief engineer of the Union Pacific, along with a few others, including two newspaper reporters, arrived from Portland. The little group gathered around the junction point, where Smeede was accorded the honor of striking the first blow at the symbolic spike. The maul was then handed in turn to other members of the group, including the newsmen, who finished the job, after which they boarded their railroad car and were taken to the Snake River bridge, about three miles away. Here they examined the 740-foot steel span across the river, and then returned home, having formally opened a 1,820-mile rail link between Omaha and Portland. Almost apologetically the *Portland Daily News* explained editorially that intense public interest in the controversial Cleveland-Blaine presidential campaign that month had blotted out coverage of an event of great significance for Oregonians.[35] It might also have mentioned that the completion of the Northern Pacific, which had initiated service to Oregon in 1883, dulled some of the local excitement about transcontinental rail connections.

The last spike driven, regular business began the following week. Omaha passengers now could board a train at eight o'clock Monday evening and reach Portland by eight o'clock on Friday morning. Both Pullman and emigrant sleeping cars were furnished for the long trip, with no extra charge for berths.[36] Union Pacific officials, who had watched the construction of other major western roads with growing concern, intended that their push toward the sea, via the Oregon Railway, would place them among the "transcontinentals" and provide a competitive position in the growing race for through traffic. Unfortunately, the opening of the new service coincided with the arrival of heavy snows and one of the most adverse winters in recent memory. December, the first month in which regular trains were scheduled, was one of blizzards, impassable snowdrifts, and delayed trains. As hand labor slowly removed the blockages, road officials gritted their teeth and prayed that spring would bring the good things promised when the undertaking was conceived.

The Union Pacific's government directors shared the optimism for Idaho. While they admitted that the territory's business had been depressed, as it was in other parts of the West, and although they attributed part of the difficulty to "the prevalence of the Mormon element" in the region, these men saw this part of the country as having a great potential. Admittedly there were parts of Idaho that were "destined to be forever a barren waste," but the valleys gave indications of future agricultural development that would supplement the richness of the known mineral deposits in the surrounding mountains.[37] Charles Francis Adams, new to the road's presidency, had a great interest in the country through which the Oregon Short Line ran. Much of southern Idaho, he said, would have to be irrigated, but here was a part of the West in which there was water for such purposes, and he anticipated rich rewards from reclamation efforts.[38] After inspecting the new road in June 1885, he appointed a special agent to examine the country in greater detail. Agent H. C. Newman, who got the assignment, reported to Adams that the valleys were "remarkably fertile, producing phenomenal crops of wheat, oats and barley, and all the different root crops and potatoes." After viewing the well-watered valleys Newman commented: "I have never seen a more perfect farming country in any of my travels. I consider it far superior to anything I have ever seen in Nebraska, Colorado, Utah, or even Oregon."[39] When Capt. John Codman, of Soda Springs, sent Adams some very large apples, the president said, "If you have, as you say, thousands of acres thereabouts wanting nothing but water to produce millions of bushels of similar fruit, I cannot but think the future of the Oregon Short Line is assured." With the whole Snake River "running to waste," Adams thought it only a matter of time until "the universal Yankee people find out how to avail themselves of it."[40] At the time of construction the Oregon Short Line had one branch—the 70-mile Wood River extension—and Adams now recommended that others be built to reach a country he regarded as being rich in agricultural as well as mineral resources.[41]

While the Oregon Short Line was to have its financial difficulties, and the people it served would have occasion to grumble, this road had two advantages over some of the other Union Pacific branches: its connection with Portland and the sea meant that it "went some place," as opposed to dead-ending in a speculative Rocky Mountain mining camp, and it passed through a country whose resources were not solely mineral. Although it took a long time for the Union Pacific to realize the potential of this undeveloped country, the move into the Northwest was basically sound.

In 1885 one of Idaho's officials spoke of the territory's recent development, saying that six years earlier it had been virtually without railroad service, but in this period 820 miles of road had been built, all of which, except for 90 miles, were controlled by the Union Pacific. The result had been increased immigration, the opening of new lands, and a new prosperity. In a recent four-year period the territorial tax had been reduced from 75 cents to 25 cents on the $100, the treasury had contained a surplus, and indebtedness had been negligible. Such prosperity, bolstered by fresh outside capital seeking to participate in it, was making yet another desert bloom.[42]

While much of the literature printed about new settlement areas was highly optimistic, if not completely biased, railroad officials confirmed the fact that Idaho had possibilities. One official reported to Adams that the total value of products shipped from the territory in 1885 was $4 million. Most of this was bullion, ore, livestock, and wool; the Idaho potato had not yet achieved national fame. Construction of a slaughterhouse at American Falls was suggested because most of the cattle cars returning to the West necessarily traveled empty.[43] Adams agreed, commenting that "there must be a limit to the transportation of animals on the hoof."[44] Live beef, however, provided a profitable business, as the increased traffic of 1885 indicated. By this time the pressure on northern ranges was great, and cattlemen had begun to seek new pasturage in Idaho. For the moment cattle cars were being utilized in both directions, as stockmen used the railroad to place their animals on these new ranges. For example, in the spring of 1885, a single consignment of cattle, comprising 160 cars, moved westward across Wyoming.[45] The search for grazing tracts farther west pleased Union Pacific managers because it promised a longer haul to Omaha.

Although railroad expansion into new areas usually resulted in happy anticipation for the communities, it also brought disappointment to various settlements which supposed that they were about to be awarded the title "Queen City of West." Boise, for example, was bypassed because it lay 600 feet below the Oregon Short Line's tracks, and to have dipped into the valley where it lay would have so increased the grade that helper engines would have been necessary. Rather than force the road's entire traffic over such gradients, the capital city was offered branch service. Publicist Robert Strahorn, who was involved with the Idaho and Oregon Land Improvement Company, later wrote that he was accused of influencing the railroad in favor of Caldwell, and that the residents of Boise became so angry they hanged him in effigy and threatened to commit the act upon his person.[46] Governor Edward A. Stevenson, of Idaho, bitterly criticized the Union Pacific, as did the *Idaho Statesman,* the editor of which accused President Adams of lying to the people of Boise and of sharing in millions made illegitimately in what was called the highly speculative venture known as the Oregon Short Line.[47]

The Oregonians also had complaints, but these were less specific. During the early eighties they attributed their economic boom to the presence of railways and they watched with satisfaction as newcomers poured in to take up new homes. Before long, however, the Portland press began to have second thoughts about the Northwest as a new haven for the poor and the oppressed, and it openly suggested that only men of means or farmers were welcome, there being too few jobs available for the number of mechanics and laboring men afflicted with the westering urge. When immigration declined toward the end of the decade, one editor remarked that the recent flow of newcomers had comprised "an indiscriminate lot of foreigners, good, bad and indifferent," and that the diminution of such arrivals would be "pleasing to the general public."[48]

The immigration machine appeared to be one that did not separate the wheat from the chaff, a limitation that railroad enthusiasts apparently had not foreseen. If, as horns of plenty, they answered a western population famine with something of an unwanted feast, it was not a matter that greatly concerned the roads. As Adams pointed out in 1885, his company was engaged in the task of "working over from the original purpose for which the Union Pacific was built, that is, carrying transcontinental traffic, to the new policy of developing local traffic." The emergence of competing through lines—he called it a "tremendous revolution"—had so divided long-haul profits that they were "comparatively valueless." To counter the trend, the Union Pacific made great efforts to build local business, and in this the road was so successful that by the time Adams made his remark, nine-tenths of the company's haulage was local. To capture this trade it had been necessary to build defensively, and this was, said Adams, "about as hard a game as a man can be called on to play."[49] In such a contest, one that the staid New Englander compared to a poker game, railroads could not be particular about the profession of the immigrant as long as he had the fare. Once the roads staked out new sections of country, they were obliged to fill them with settlers to justify the investment, and to do so they went to great lengths.

Although the Oregon Short Line professed to be an independent road built under an act of Congress, having its own treasury and officers and financed by its own securities, it was clearly a Union Pacific subsidiary. As such, the parent railroad made every effort to develop the country through which ran the smaller road. "In order to increase the traffic of Idaho we must put people into that Territory," urged P. P. Shelby, assistant general traffic manager at Salt Lake City. "The entire white population at present [1886] is not over 70,000." To implement the idea Shelby appointed an immigration agent who, for $125 a month, lectured and distributed pamphlets about the new country. Taking a leaf from the Burlington and Missouri's success story in Nebraska, Shelby bombarded the East with sample potatoes and apples grown along the Oregon Short Line route.[50] The newly appointed agent, M. A. Kurtz, soon reported that he had assembled a group of settlers at Pittsburgh, Pennsylvania, ready to leave for Idaho. But he had not done so without difficulty, for, as he wrote, "You have every agent in the country working against you. They tell me plainly that you pay no commission for Idaho business." Plagued by limited finances, and confronted by an absolute "ignorance of the people as to where Idaho is," the agent called for help.[51] The Union Pacific responded by offering a rate of $150 a carload of 20,000 pounds on emigrant movables and $2 per hundred on less than carload lots on shipments from the Missouri River to the end of Oregon Short Line tracks. Passengers who actually became settlers could travel that distance for $25, half-fare for children.[52]

While Adams, who was financially conservative, entertained doubts about the extent to which the Union Pacific had engaged in defensive building, he was more than willing to promote the country of the existing branches. On one occasion he commented to a fellow Bostonian that he regarded Idaho as the "most promising field for development that the Union Pacific now has."[53] When he was invited to participate financially in developing the Boise and Nampa Canal Company of Idaho, the New Englander declined, saying it would create a conflict of interest and he wanted no part of it.[54] There had been too much of this in the past, he thought, and it had created a bad name for the company. One of the important motives behind the appointment of Adams to the presidency had been to counteract such criticisms, and he was conscious of this role during his entire time in office.

While Adams's administration was aware of increasing public criticism of the road's inclination to participate in local politics when such a course appeared to be necessary, it showed no reluctance to continue the practice where the end seemed legitimate. When Adams learned that there was a movement to detach part of Idaho and annex it to Nevada "in order to bolster up that rotten borough," he directed the company's counsel at Washington, D.C., to investigate at once, stating that "the Union Pacific cannot by any means regard [this] with favor. It would mean for us simply increased taxation and popular odium."[55] In another instance, John Young complained to Fred Ames that the Mormons were not only suffering from new federal legislation that prohibited polygamy, but that the brethren in Idaho were under additional pressure by local legislators who had passed even more severe legislation. Faced by what they regarded as double jeopardy, the Idaho Mormons were thinking about returning to Zion, or of moving even farther south. Young was particularly anxious to see Idaho's chief justice, J. T. Morgan, sent home from the territory. Ames answered at once, saying that he was about to depart for three months abroad, but had turned the matter over to Adams, urging the president to "secure relief to the Mormons from the injustice which is being done them."[56] The Union Pacific, anxious to build up Idaho, was in no mood to stand by and witness another Mormon exodus.

During the early 1880s, as the Union Pacific penetrated Idaho and made great efforts to create new business by building up that country, developments in Oregon threatened to nullify its expensive efforts made in that direction. The Oregon Railway, a badly managed road, found itself in the middle of a contest for traffic waged between the Northern Pacific and the Union Pacific. The battle for control lasted nearly a decade.

From June of 1879, when Henry Villard had first proposed a partnership with the Union Pacific to develop northwestern trade, the history of the Oregon Railway had been tumultuous. When the Northern Pacific threatened to invade the country along the Columbia River, Villard first attempted to dissuade it. Failing in that, he made the extraordinarily bold move of acquiring control of the potential predator. In 1881 he organized the Oregon and Transcontinental, a holding company that had a controlling interest in both the Oregon Railway and the Northern Pacific.[57] The financier explained that the new company was formed to unite control of the two roads and "to supply the Northern Pacific with needed branch lines which the latter Company, owing to the limitations of its Congressional Charter, could not build itself."[58] A member of his staff further revealed that the numerous branch lines proposed in the new articles of incorporation would not be built in the near future, but were included to "anticipate and forestall all future rival corporations, by covering every choice or available location while laws and circumstances are so favorable."[59] Union Pacific officials, who were not unfamiliar with such practices, must have looked on with mounting concern.

By 1883 Villard was in serious difficulty. The Northern Pacific was completed, but the unexpectedly high cost of construction left the Oregon and Transcontinental near bankruptcy. An appeal for help produced additional aid from a syndicate of bankers, two of whom assumed executive control of the two railroads. William J. Endicott became president of the Northern Pacific and T. Jefferson Coolidge headed the Oregon Railway. At a meeting held May 20, 1884, the two men were appointed as a committee empowered to negotiate a lease or traffic contract between the Oregon Railway and the Northern Pacific, the Union Pacific, or any other company willing to participate.[60]

Coolidge, who had once served as president of the Atchison, Topeka and Santa Fe, lasted six months in his office and then disgustedly threw in the sponge. In July 1884 he confessed that he had unwillingly become the president of the Oregon Railway at the request of those largely interested in the road. Endicott had once told Villard that he could not make up his mind whether "it is you, or Barnum ... that has 'the greatest show on earth.' I suppose that you leave no doubts on that point."[61] Coolidge suggested that the Oregon Railway constituted one ring of Villard's circus when he addressed its executive committee on the condition of affairs in the organization. Upon assuming office he had not imagined the state of confusion that confronted him, he said. Not only did the company owe a million dollars in New York, and the same amount in Oregon, but it was also saddled with a contract for 20,000 tons of steel rails, purchased at $40 a ton, none of which had been delivered. His predecessors had not only leased a small and utterly worthless narrow gauge for $193,000 a year, but they also had purchased two unnecessary steamers for $700,000, as well as two useless hulks lying in San Francisco harbor, for another $114,000. "The confusion in everything was so great," said Coolidge, "that 1,400 tons of steel rails which had been shipped by us, *via* Northern Pacific Railroad had been lost without anybody knowing anything about them, and after several months search they were found laid in the track of the Northern Pacific." The result of such chaos was a catastrophic decline in receipts. The only cheerful news Coolidge had for the committee was the possibility of a traffic contract with the Northern Pacific. With that remark he handed in his resignation and the committee at once replaced him with Elijah Smith.[62]

The lease prospects, of which Coolidge had spoken, heightened during the months that followed his resignation. In April 1885 Smith informed President Robert Harris, of the Northern Pacific, that his road favored such a move. When a satisfactory financial arrangement could not be agreed upon, the Oregon Railway board sent a committee to talk with the Union Pacific people, who now had an even greater interest in Smith's company.[63] Adams explained why. Late in May, he said, Northern Pacific forces had attempted to drive Smith from his office, but "an arrangement was effected here, under which the private parties interested in Union Pacific went into the market with Smith and purchased about 40,000 shares of Oregon and Transcontinental," with the result that Union Pacific representatives were placed upon the boards of both the Oregon Railway and the Oregon and Transcontinental. "The significance of this you will see at once," said Adams. "The whole thing changes front. Instead of being in an alliance with the Northern Pacific, it passes into an alliance with the Union Pacific." This meant that the Union Pacific could avail itself of the Transcontinental's charter for the purpose of building branches in western Idaho and in Oregon. "I regard it myself as one of the most significant developments that have taken place since I have been in control," the Bostonian proudly announced.[64] On June 11 he revealed that a tentative lease agreement had been reached.

The terms of the proposed agreement provided that the Oregon Short Line would operate the Oregon Railway property, the Union Pacific to guarantee a six percent dividend on the stock of the leased property and to keep up interest payments on its outstanding bonds. The Northern Pacific had offered five percent, but this had not been acceptable; that road could, however, enter into the arrangement later, if it chose to do so.[65] Franklin MacVeagh, who had studied the Oregon country for Adams, admitted that it had impressive prospects, and he could see why Villard had been attracted to it. Now, he said, the Union Pacific could proceed with its necessary growth in that direction, for it was, to use his words, a road that "seems to neither begin at any beginning nor end at any ending .... The system at present suggests a hand without final joints to the fingers ...."[66] MacVeagh suggested purchasing the Oregon Railway but, as Adams had already said to one of his correspondents, this was not a matter likely to be effected soon, for moves of this magnitude were not a daily occurrence.[67]

Outright acquisition, which was to come eventually, would be achieved only after long and acrimonious negotiation. The lease itself was hard enough to come by. Although Adams spoke of a general agreement in June 1886, not until the following January was the document signed, and not until April 25, 1887, was it executed. The 99-year lease included the terms agreed upon earlier and specified that the Oregon Short Line would pay $1,440,000 per annum, in quarterly installments, to the Oregon Railway.[68] Part of the delay in activating the lease was due to Northern Pacific opposition. This was finally overcome by the passage of state legislation that broke the road's control over the Oregon Railway acquired in an earlier day and permitted the local road to effect the new arrangement.

In pressing for legislative action the Portland press pointed out the benefits to be derived from the emergence of another through line that would serve the community. Idaho's prosperity, said the *News,* dated from the time the Union Pacific sent its branches through the territory. It seemed logical that the road from Omaha would do in Oregon what it had already done in the vast domain it then served.[69]

The Northern Pacific was far from blind to the potential growth in the territory, and it had no desire to admit the interloper without, at least, sharing in the benefits. When Villard demanded admittance to the lease agreement, Adams objected, saying to him: "I fail to see wherein the Union Pacific derives any advantage from it." Not only did Villard want to dominate the trade north of the Snake River in such a partnership, he further asked that he be promised a minimum guaranteed loss, the Union Pacific to cover any deficits beyond a set figure.[70] Since representatives from both the Union Pacific and the Northern Pacific sat upon the Oregon Railway board, there continued to be a certain amount of commotion over the future of rail traffic in the Northwest. When Villard demanded a seat on the Union Pacific's board, strong objections were heard from the East.[71] In January 1888, the Oregon Railway managers finally agreed to admit the Northern Pacific as a joint lessee. Adams reluctantly agreed.[72]

When news of the decision reached Oregon there was an immediate uproar. Although President Elijah Smith had signed the agreement in New York, he needed the approval of the three Portland directors—H. W. Corbett, W. S. Ladd, and C. H. Lewis. Ladd was not only a member of the Oregon Railway board, he headed the Portland board of trade. He and his associates voiced strong objections to the lease, arguing that the Northern Pacific was then charging such high rates on ores from Idaho's Coeur d'Alene mines to Portland that shipments were virtually prohibited. On the other hand, said Ladd, the Union Pacific was Portland's "natural ally." Elijah Smith denied that there were any discriminatory elements in the lease, and asserted that it provided for equal rates to Portland and Tacoma on all business north of the Snake River.[73] He was unable to convince his associates, who thought otherwise. Through Van B. De Lashmutt, mayor of Portland and a man who owned stock in both the Oregon Railway and the Coeur d'Alene mines, a suit was instituted to prevent acceptance of the joint lease.[74]

In June 1888, however, the Union Pacific withdrew from the joint lease agreement that involved the Northern Pacific. Adams explained to Villard that he had advised this move because he did not want to force Portland

and other Oregon communities into arrangements offensive to them, and that his desire to act independently was not to be construed as antagonism toward the Northern Pacific.[75] During the same month, however, Villard regained control of the Oregon and Transcontinental, a corporation that still owned a controlling interest in the Oregon Steam Navigation Company, at which time he announced that he intended to prevent the Union Pacific from leasing the smaller company. Ruefully, Adams took the blame for the turn of events, admitting it was through his own overconfidence that Villard had been allowed to get the upper hand. Now, he said, war with the Northern Pacific was inevitable. Accordingly, the Union Pacific again went into the market and began buying Oregon and Transcontinental stock. It also made plain that a distance of only 250 miles existed between the Utah and Northern, near Butte, and an extension of the Oregon Railway in western Idaho. If such a line were completed it could make a connection with James J. Hill's oncoming St. Paul, Minneapolis and Manitoba (Great Northern) road, and thus parallel the Northern Pacific from Saint Paul to Portland. In 1887 the Northern Pacific had completed its Cascade division, giving it a connection with the Pacific Ocean independent of the Oregon Railway. Should the latter road for any reason fall into the hands of competitors, it could become an important threat to Villard's plans.

By November Adams reported to Grenville Dodge that Villard was ready to make some concessions and to agree to an arrangement whereby the two major railroads would exercise equal control over the Oregon Railway. Pleased by his success, Adams urged his friends to keep up the attack. Early in December he telegraphed to Sidney Dillon, in cipher: "Will not you and your friends buy Transcontinental at present prices? It would be a good thing to have in the house, and small risk of losing. We are buying here." This brought Robert Harris, of the Northern Pacific, to the Union Pacific offices for further negotiations which, said Adams, "were rapidly brought to a satisfactory conclusion." In an almost boastful mood he remarked: "Taken altogether, it was by far the most gratifying experience I have ever had in such matters . . . . I could see plainly enough the effect of the education which has been going on, both general and particular, during the past few weeks. There was no attempt at bragging, and no threats used; no talk of what either company could do by itself, regardless of the other."[76]

Adams, who had remained friendly with Harris of the Northern Pacific, thought an accommodation with that company would be less expensive than a long-term war. He was annoyed by the bickering that continued between minor officers of each company, and it concerned him that the sniping was gradually drawing them into deeper conflict with each other. Adams was convinced both sides were at fault. "Nevertheless," he wrote, "every letter

I receive from my people at the West asseverates before the high Heaven that they are pure as angels, and that their garments are unsullied as the driven snow, but that human flesh and blood cannot endure the long accumulation of wrongs which has been inflicted upon them by the demons of the Northern Pacific."[77]

By May of 1889 the Union Pacific's president was forced to conclude that the olive branch was useless in this deep-seated conflict between two major western railroad powers. On the seventeenth a battle developed in the stock market that was described as the most exciting in Wall Street history, as both sides fought for final control of the Oregon and Transcontinental Company. Elijah Smith, supported by Adams, Sidney Dillon, and Fred Ames, led an unsuccessful attempt to capture the majority of shares.[78] In June the fight shifted to the stockholders' meeting, where Villard, armed with 218,000 votes as opposed to 159,000 for the Union Pacific forces, again triumphed.[79] Control of the Transcontinental however did not solve his problem. Even as he was gaining it, the Union Pacific was on the move, "just as fast as dirt can be thrown," in the words of Adams, to carry out his defensive building threat.[80] Meanwhile, Grenville Dodge appeared in Portland at the time of the stockholders' meeting, apparently armed with authority to make high-level decisions. "When I arrived here and looked the field over I thought we were in a very bad hole," he reported to Adams. But, after conferring with Northern Pacific powers, he gained an agreement whereby Villard would liquidate the Oregon and Transcontinental "down to a small capital," and use the company as a financial institution. The financier further promised to bow out of the Oregon Railway in exchange for the Union Pacific's Transcontinental holdings. The secret of this success, said Dodge, lay in Villard's willingness "to concede anything to get O. & T. in shape," and he advised Adams that "Mr. V. will be in New York July 5th ready to proceed with the exchange."[81]

Adams was particularly pleased at these developments, not only because a very costly fight with the Northern Pacific was halted, but also because he thought highly of the Northwest as a rich and growing region. "To my mind the Oregon Short Line is today the most satisfactory portion of the Union Pacific system," he had written in June. Now that the country beyond Huntington seemed to be safely in his hands he could reaffirm his belief that "the salvation of the Union Pacific lies in development west from Salt Lake City...."[82]

The next move in developing northwestern trade was the reorganization of the branch line system which spread out from the end of the main line in Utah. On August 1, 1889, a consolidation was effected that created the Oregon Short Line and Utah Northern Railway Company. In addition to

these two important branches the new organization included the Utah
Central, the Salt Lake and Western, the Utah and Nevada, the Ogden and
Syracuse, the Nevada Pacific, and the Idaho Central, a total of eight
companies. The new subsystem had over 1,400 miles of track, exclusive of
the Oregon Railway, which still was operated under a lease arrangement.[83]
Adams expressed delight over the development, remarking that it would
"get us out from under the incubus of the government, and put us in a
position to do all the construction necessary, with cheap money, thus putting
the Union Pacific where it never was before."[84] Restricted by terms of the
original charter, the Union Pacific had faced difficulty in building branches
and had, for years, incorporated such lines as independent but controlled
entities. Adams appeared to feel that the consolidation provided for a cluster
of branches, organized into what might be called an "associated" system,
whose management could expand its coverage of the West with less
harassment from Washington, D.C.

There was optimism among Union Pacific leaders that their penetration
of a relatively undeveloped part of the West, one that was many profitable
traffic miles from Omaha, would greatly add to the financial health of their
company. That immigration had fallen off and business showed little signs
of rapid growth, despite the coming of the rails, did not discourage Adams.
He explained to Robert Harris, of the Northern Pacific, that this was the normal course of events on a newly developed frontier. "First, there is the
period of wild speculation and inordinate prices," he wrote, "followed by the
terrible reaction, when it seems as if the country was never going to grow
any more. Meanwhile the process of recuperation is going on." Writing in
1888, he said such a recovery had been going on in Washington and Oregon
for the past four years, and that country was now ready for rapid development. In terms which later would be used by frontier historians, he said:
"The time for the next wave has come."[85] Adams wanted his road to ride
its crest westward.

"In the Hands of the Philistines"

The optimism of Union Pacific managers, the ever-present expectation that "the next wave" was at hand, was prevalent among western railroaders in general. The country through which the roads passed was new and held great promise, to homesteaders and businessmen alike. For the farmers there were dry years, falling prices, and dreams shattered. The railroads suffered, in turn, from these misfortunes, but in addition they had each other for enemies in the fight for riches and finally in the struggle for survival. The Union Pacific had an even greater problem: the federal government itself, whose representatives stayed on its trail, pressing for payment of monies loaned. As the railroad expanded, fighting off its competitors and searching for new business in undeveloped country, the pursuing wolves of Washington slowly closed the gap.

At first glance it would appear that such an enterprise as the Union Pacific, blessed by governmental grants and an apparently generous charter, would have had little trouble surviving, despite having traversed what was at the time a barren land. The profitability of such grants, however, was predicated in part upon the road's having a reasonably lengthy period of "monopoly," or lack of competition. While the undertaking might later have been considered "premature," in the light of risks run in the 1860s it was sufficiently successful to cause others to join the western land rush, and in the squabbling for empire that followed there were costly battles for supremacy. Meanwhile, the public attitude toward western railroad building underwent a change. Where it once had pined for a single line to the Pacific, the American public was shortly dazzled by a proliferation of roads that plunged westward, sprouting branches as they proceeded. The builders of these railroads came to be looked upon as robber barons instead of brave entrepreneurs, and rather than offer them encouragement the man on the street now called for restrictive legislation.

So expensive were the Union Pacific's efforts at expansion, and with such difficulty was this achieved in the new public opinion, that, by the mid-eighties, the road found itself in serious trouble. This led to Sidney Dillon's resignation as president and the installation of Charles Francis Adams, whose assigned role was that of restoring the company's tarnished name and rehabilitating its deteriorated financial position. By late November 1890, Adams, who earlier had attracted national attention through his published criticisms of western railroad building, was obliged to admit defeat and to surrender the office he had held for half a dozen years. Jay Gould, back in power once more, and the one who had forced Adams to retire, returned the presidency to Sidney Dillon. The old man, tired and nervous over conditions on the road, presided over its affairs until his death in June 1892.

Adams, always frank in his appraisals of others, did not hesitate to blame himself for the failure of his administration; but he also rationalized that the company's history was so shot through with mistakes and wrongful deeds that "we would have fallen anyway."[1] Dillon did not offer any explanation for the continued decline in the corporation's fortunes during his last days in office. He knew the ship was sinking, and in the manner of an old captain who had sailed her through many a storm, he was prepared to go down with it.

Considering nineteenth-century railroad history—the difficulties faced by all western roads, and particularly the problems that confronted the Union Pacific—it could be argued that both men had done well enough under the circumstances. The company they managed was a land-grant railroad, one in which the American people exhibited great interest and curiosity during construction days, but one which also involved a partnership with them through their agent, the federal government. As the years went by, transcontinental railroad executives were to discover that the great gift of land involved a figurative passage westward by a public that not only proved to be a noisy passenger, but also an inveterate backseat driver. Had the arrangement resulted in no more than annoyance it might have been tolerable, but when it resulted in restrictions that limited development and posed financial penalties, the affair became much more serious.

In the early days of rail service in the West, its honeymoon period, much praise was heard. During spring of 1870, as the Union Pacific considered the possibility of opening new territory, a Denver paper pointed to Wyoming as an example of the wonders rails could work. "It is emphatically a railroad territory. It was made by the railroad, because but for the railroad there was not the faintest shadow of a necessity for it," said the editor. "But for that it would not have a thousand citizen settlers within its borders today. Nine tenths of all the property, real and personal, belongs to the railroad

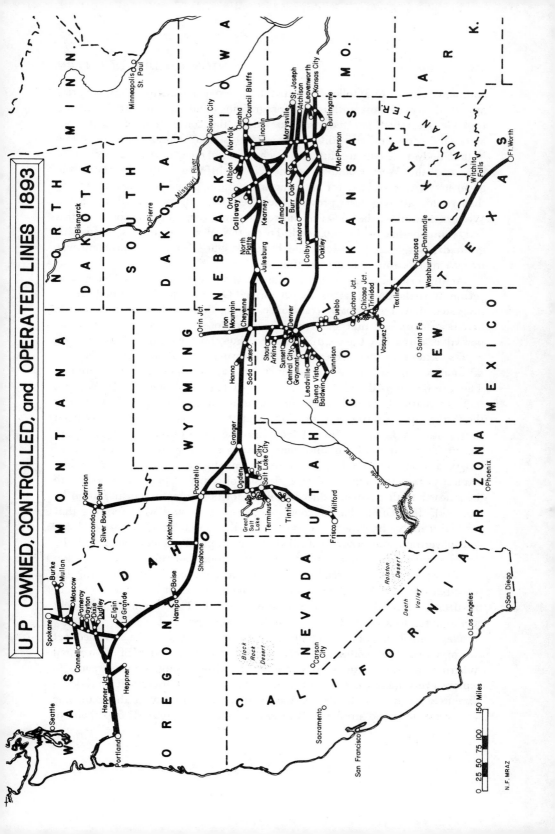

company . . . ."[2] In the following year the same paper lamented that Congress appeared to have lost enthusiasm for granting lands to railroads. Insisting that Congress had pledged itself to aid in the completion of great lines across the continent, the editor spoke of the serious consequences to follow if that body failed in its duty. In such a mistaken course lands would lie idle, and the West would be denied its rightful growth.[3] In short, the government was scolded for slighting a new and promising instrumentality that could, at long last, provide the West with its own road to riches. Westerners wanted their part of the country to grow, and to accomplish this end, railroads had to be extended. To do this in a raw country, even with granted lands, was expensive. The Union Pacific's immediate problem was to find money for such construction.

At this critical moment, at a time when through service to Ogden was yet in a shake-down stage, the Attorney General of the United States suggested that the company commence paying interest due on its bonds. It had been supposed that such money would come from government transportation, carried by the road at reduced rates, but when this traffic did not yield sufficient income, Secretary of the Treasury G. S. Boutwell ordered that all monies expended by the government on rail transportation be withheld. The Pacific railroads objected, and Sen. William M. Stewart, of Nevada, took the matter before his colleagues, arguing, in connection with a rider to the Army Appropriation bill of 1871, that the companies were not obliged to pay interest on their subsidy bonds until the dates of maturity.[4] The rider passed, in a modified form, and there matters rested for the next two years.[5]

As a result of the Crédit Mobilier investigation of 1873 the public clamored for restrictive railroad legislation, and Congress acceded to demands that all payments due these lines for government transportation be withheld. The Union Pacific took its case to court and won a ruling that entitled it to one-half the money so withheld, as specified in the Act of 1864. The government attorneys appealed to the Supreme Court, which, in the autumn of 1875, not only sustained the lower court but ruled that the Union Pacific could not be forced to pay any interest on its bonds until the principal was due. While the road's management was at the time delighted, the decision proved in the long run to be harmful. The Union Pacific's debt accumulated to a figure so large that bankruptcy resulted.

Next, the Union Pacific challenged the government in the so-called net earnings case. The company, short of cash after completion of its original construction, and anxious to expand into virgin country, was ready to explore every means that might provide funds for the growth it considered absolutely necessary. The Act of 1862 had specified that after the main line was completed, and until the land-grant bonds were retired, 5 percent of the road's annual net earnings was to be applied toward that debt. The company now saw the possibility of deferring part of that payment. Arguing that the road was not completed in 1869 but in 1874, when a special commission examined the recent construction and announced that all stipulations had been met, the railroad again went to court, contending it ought not to have paid the five percent during that period. It also argued that "net earnings" did not mean the sum remaining after operating expenses were subtracted, but that such expenses as interest paid, funds withheld by the government for its transportation, and costs of new construction, should first be deducted. In January 1879 the Supreme Court ruled in favor of the government.[6] It held that the Union Pacific was indeed liable for five percent of net earnings beginning in 1869. By 1874, the amount due was just over a million dollars. The court further ruled that net earnings were to be determined by deducting all ordinary expenses of operation, including bona fide improvements, from gross receipts. Interest on bonded indebtedness could not be included because it fell into the category of a dividend. However, said the court, since the government's lien was in the nature of a second mortgage, first-mortgage demands took precedence, and if net earnings in any given year were such that five percent did not cover both obligations, the government was entitled only to what remaining money was available.

Another matter that brought the Union Pacific into conflict with the government during the seventies was the so-called bridge dispute. As early as November 1865 the road's board of directors declared its intention "to construct a bridge across the Missouri River from its terminus at or near Omaha." In the following year Grenville Dodge submitted an elaborate report, showing various sites where the structure might be built. One of these lay about four miles south of Farnham Street in Omaha. The possibility that this might be the site selected threw the city's businessmen into a great state of apprehension, the result of which was an offer from civic leaders to furnish $250,000 in Douglas County bonds to aid in the construction of a bridge closer to town. Council Bluffs, across the river, made a similar but slightly smaller offer.[7]

Construction began in the spring of 1868 and continued for a little more than a year, at which point Douglas County backed out, demanding that Omaha must be the road's terminus, with all shops, freight and passenger transfers, as well as the general headquarters, to be located there. A majority of the board wanted the terminus at Council Bluffs, where Sidney Dillon had large land holdings, but at the insistence of Vice President John Duff, Omaha's demands were incorporated into a new contract and the work proceeded. The delay irritated Grenville Dodge, who called the

Missouri River the only obstacle to travel between the Atlantic and Pacific oceans. At one time, during the spring of 1870, said Dodge, some 800 passengers waited on the Iowa side for passage across the river. By the end of that year, however, a temporary bridge was completed and the bottleneck was enlarged, if not broken.[8] In February 1871 Congress passed a special act authorizing the railroad company to issue bonds in the amount of $2.5 million for completion of a permanent structure, and a year later that work was finished. Eleven spans, each 250 feet long, were laid across the river, some 50 feet above the high-water mark, and the obstacle of which General Dodge had complained was removed.[9]

Bridging the river generated less happiness than had been anticipated. The project had cost the road $2,866,463.72 when discount on the bonds and all other expenses were considered.[10] Although it had been built under the road's original charter, it remained an independent entity, and tolls were charged to pay off the indebtedness.[11] Management took the view that Omaha was the road's eastern terminus and that the short distance across the river to Council Bluffs constituted an independent piece of trackage—mortgaged, owned, and operated separately. Not only did users complain of the tolls collected—receipts averaged about $15,000 a month in the early days of operation—they objected to the inconvenience of transferring to dummy trains for the short passage over the river.[12] By 1874 company Secretary E. H. Rollins confessed that the sentiment in Congress was "very intense . . . upon the subject of the Bridge transfer," and he suggested that "we must get our house in order" or face a bitter fight in the next legislative session.[13] Congressmen not only were sensitive to the public outcry at having to pay 50 cents a head for passengers and $10 for a carload of freight to make the crossing, but they also argued that the bridge was a part of continuous service westward and therefore the railroad company was obliged to surrender a portion of its earnings toward retirement of the firm's bonded indebtedness.[14]

By 1876 the matter had reached the Supreme Court. The jurists decided that the bridge was a part of the railroad's main line on the grounds that "the Iowa branch of the Union Pacific Railroad was fixed by the act of Congress on the Iowa bank of the Missouri River."[15] While the decision placed the government in a position to withhold part of the bridge earnings, it did not prohibit the tolls. In June 1876 Dillon wrote: "I have been in Washington all winter trying to prevent any adverse legislation on the bridge and I think I have succeeded in preventing them from abolishing the tolls at least for the present. As long as we can collect the tolls the interest will be paid and the bonds redeemed for the Sinking Fund."[16] The government directors did not think the freight toll charge excessive or unjust, but they recommended charging passengers only ten cents. To them the railroad was entitled to something for the additional service and it did not matter if the money came from a special fee or as part of a through rate, the charge being merely a means of allocation.[17]

While the legal decisions regarding the net earnings dispute and the bridge controversy momentarily settled some of the issues between the Union Pacific and the government, they did not resolve the larger conflict that continued between them.[18] The heart of the problem lay in a growing public concern that the Union Pacific's principal owners, already under suspicion, intended to avoid payment of its debt to the government. They, in turn, denied that such was the case. Early in 1875 Dillon and Gould proposed the establishment of a sinking fund into which the company would pay half a million dollars a year for 20 years and then $750,000 annually until the debt was retired. Dillon argued that this was a better method than relying upon the fluctuating payments derived from withholding government transportation moneys. To help finance his program he suggested that the government buy back all the unallotted land it had originally granted the railroad, at $2.50 an acre, or the same price the government asked for its own lands within the grant belt. Dillon pointed out that, by 1876, the company had realized only a little more than half a million dollars in land sales, an amount he thought the government could well afford to donate in return for the completion of more than a thousand miles of railroad and a connection with the Pacific Coast.[19] Clearly he did not feel that the "giveaway," of which so much was later heard, was as large as the public was led to believe.

Carl Schurz, Secretary of the Interior, argued that the Pacific roads had demonstrated their earning capacity and that they were fully able to pay off their indebtedness in regular installments.[20] The western press took a similar point of view. The *Rocky Mountain News* contended that leading journalists, east and west, regarded the Union Pacific as a solvent company, whose resources were sufficient to meet its obligations. Any road that levied such extortionate rates surely must have plenty of money, said the editor. However, he concluded, if a choice had to be made between abandoning the original charter provisions and any possible development that would deprive westerners of the use of the roads, the former course should be taken.[21]

Congress, always sensitive to public clamor, claimed that the roads were able to pay, and in the spring it passed a bill, sponsored by Sen. Allen G. Thurman, of Ohio, the main provision of which was the establishment of a sinking fund.[22] The Union Pacific was required to pay annually 25 percent of its net earnings; this amount was to include the government transportation money and the already established five percent withholding required by existing legislation. All the money due for government transportation was to be retained, one-half of it applied to the interest on government bonds, the other half to go into the sinking fund. As Charles Francis Adams later commented, the act made the government a partner, rather than a creditor of the railroad, and it considerably strengthened federal control over its management. Worse, in the eyes of the railroad, it took away surplus revenue needed to build its branches and buried it in a fund that drew little more than two percent interest. Adams felt that such legislation worked a direct wrong upon the people of Nebraska and Kansas (most of the Kansas Pacific was affected by the act) by depriving them of future rail expansion, of the development of their country, and of a potential tax base.[23]

Thomas Nickerson, president of the Atchison, Topeka and Santa Fe, agreed with Adams as to the harm that would be done to the Union Pacific. It pleased him to think that his rival railroad would have to contribute a portion of its earnings to such a fund, after which it would "not have so much money with which to ruin smaller corporations."[24] Since the law applied to only two of the bond-aided roads, Nickerson regarded it as beneficial to his.[25] Jay Gould was so upset with the law that he threatened to surrender the Union Pacific to the government and build a parallel and competing road.[26] Henry Poor, whose railroad manual was widely read, denounced the move as a "gross and unwarranted assumption of power" and warned that this "is anarchy—is revolution."[27]

The Thurman Act was the result of mounting public complaints about the Union Pacific's apparent lack of interest in meeting its obligations. The company's subsidy bonds, for example, originally amounted to just under $28 million; by the time they reached their 30-year maturity, at six percent interest, the railroad would owe the government nearly $77 million. Unable to collect even the interest, and annoyed that the Union Pacific had begun to pay healthy dividends to its stockholders in 1875, Congress sought means of redress. Gould had hoped the railroad's own plan for a sinking fund would be acceptable, for, as he commented, if the government agreed to such a settlement "it gets the Company out of law & I would not sell my stock for 75 & it will go there too."[28] However, since the road asked freedom from "dues of all kinds from the Company to the Government" as a part of the arrangement, Congress apparently felt it would rather establish its own sinking fund and keep the railroad under its control. Legal forays with the railroad's attorneys already had indicated that the Union Pacific would defer payment of any and all money owed to the government as long as possible.

Determined to hold a tight rein on the land-grant roads, Congress, in the spring of 1878, considered a bill to create a board of Pacific railroad commissioners whose duty would be to supervise the companies, to examine their books periodically, and to report unjust discriminations. The measure passed the Senate but failed to get back to the House before adjournment.[29] In June, however, the legislators did pass a bill that provided for a bureau of railroad accounts. Headed by Theophilus French, the bureau proposed to examine railroad books annually, to investigate irregularities, and to ensure that laws applying to the indebted roads were enforced.[30]

The Union Pacific grudgingly submitted to regulations imposed under the new legislation, but fought a rearguard action on certain contentions it had earlier set forth. Dillon objected strongly that the money surrendered to the government, under the Thurman Act, was being invested at a very low interest rate and that sinking fund bonds were sold at an unreasonably high premium. The commissioner of railroads admitted, in 1883, that so unattractive were such offerings to investors that no new money had been put to work since April of 1881. At one point $400,000 lay idle in the U.S. Treasury, with no takers.[31] The railroad also contested the "net earnings" decision, again insisting that costs of new construction and equipment should be deducted from the annual gross. By the autumn of 1883 it was nearly $2 million in arrears of such money claimed by the government.[32]

Railroad attorneys were anxious to settle this question, if possible, because it was the only major issue in dispute with the government.[33] Public animosity toward western roads was growing, and the Union Pacific realized that dilatoriness on its part would be construed as an attempt to thwart the provisions of the Thurman Act. Efforts to combat proposed legislative restrictions, at national and state levels, brought charges of corruption, vote-buying, and political manipulation. Attempts to evade existing legislation heightened the outcry.

Edward Rosewater, editor of Omaha's *Daily Bee,* led a bitter crusade against the Union Pacific, charging that its "bosses drove their gangs to the polls and boasted of 'their cattle.' "[34] James Kyner, who had done some contracting for the company, said he had been persuaded to run for the Nebraska legislature by U.S. Senator Phineas Hitchcock, who was friendly to the Union Pacific, and, upon his election, combatted all hostile bills "with more than a little success." Proud of his record, he boasted that "Not one adverse act was passed while I was there."[35] Even those politicians who owed nothing to the roads admitted they appreciated any help those corporations could give at election time, and showed no hesitancy in promising reciprocity.[36] But western newspapers were not universally unfriendly toward the railroads. The *Wa-Keeney* (Kansas) *Weekly World,* for example, opposed "midnight scheduling" of freight rates and thought the practice ought to be controlled; yet it did not approve of what it called "grinding

laws enforced against railroads," because the roads had a right to live.[37]
The financial editor of an eastern paper wrote that members of Congress
often were governed "by a desire to make capital out of the Granger
sentiment at the west, and that any attempt to get justice for any of the
subsidized roads will meet with great opposition." He went so far as to
question the honesty of the average congressmen when dealing with railroad
corporations.[38] In 1887, the U.S. Railway Commission looked into the
problem of political control and concluded that money and passes had been
used to influence legislation. The money in question, however, appeared to
have been provided to pay lawyers and lobbyists, there being "no evidence
whatever of actual bribery." As for passes, the practice was so universal
that the commission concluded "it would be impossible to predicate any
guilty motive thereon."[39]

While the Union Pacific was anxious to minimize public complaint about
its conduct, it struggled against the government's insistence that costs of new
construction could not be deducted in determining net earnings. The 25
percent withheld from what the courts had defined as net earnings was
badly needed for reinvestment in the road's building program, and company
officers made every effort to commit money that could be deducted before
the annual net was determined. Charles Francis Adams understood this at
the very beginning of his presidency, and he argued that the Thurman Act
had diverted funds which might have been used to build feeders in Nevada,
Utah, Wyoming, and Idaho; instead, he said, it "was placed where it has, as
the record shows, failed to be of use to any one." In an expanding western
economy where both profits and interest rates were high, he thought money
invested in such extensions could have earned up to 50 percent, as opposed
to the pitifully small two percent it drew in the sinking fund. Adams contended that by locking up necessary growth capital the government injured
itself, for had the road been permitted to put its profits to work in the
manner of other lines[40] it could have yielded a return sufficient to make
possible repayment of the debt.

The road's government directors were sympathetic to this point of view.
While they admitted that past business practices of the company had not
been "carried on upon the basis of heroic virtues," they confessed that
unfortunately "very little of the world's business is." The directors believed
in the wisdom of feeder lines, and reaffirmed that conviction in their reports
made during the 1880s.

By 1884 the subsidized portions of the Union Pacific comprised about
1,830 miles, while its total, either owned or controlled, came to approximately 4,428. Including lines where the company had proprietary interest,
the length of the entire branch system amounted to 5,510 miles. Some of the

extensions were speculative, built either on anticipated business or for protective reasons, and in time they were trimmed off as dead limbs of the tree are pruned.

The government's representatives on the board believed that, despite limitations inherent in the railroad sprawl that covered Union Pacific country, the result was more desirable than it would be should the company have to follow a restrictive policy born of congressional apprehensions. They called the Thurman Act a failure, a conception that was not only harsh, but one that did not yield enough funds to accomplish its purpose. "At present the debtor is hampered both by the partnership and by the cloud upon his credit caused by the attitude of the Government," they reported in 1886. Why not free the road from such bondage and allow its management the freedom of action accorded to others in laissez-faire America? Unfettered, and able to experience growth and profit, the road promised to emerge as a healthy concern, with ample credit in financial centers. To the directors, the government would appear to be the gainer under such conditions. They felt that whether the debt was paid in 50, 60, or 100 years, was not as important as the assurance that the debt would be retired ultimately.[41]

As from the beginning, the financial problems of the Union Pacific were multiple and ever present. Those who stayed with the company after construction profits were taken believed theirs was a long-term investment. During the 1880s Gould, Dillon, and general manager Silas H. Clark discussed the road's future and agreed that the day of steady profits was still far away. Before the entire set of transportation facilities could be set in motion to make the system function it had to be expanded to its fullest limit. Time was running out, for other roads with similar ideas were racing across the West to carve their own empires. Among those managers of the Union Pacific who realized the necessity of competing for new territory, Jay Gould was the most vocal. He insisted upon capturing as much of trans-Missouri West for the Union Pacific as possible.[42] Typically, he approved of any and all methods to find the necessary money, especially if it could be wrested from the federal government's grasp.

Conditions in the West had changed greatly since the Union Pacific was chartered in 1862. At that time the government was paying over $7 million annually for transportation westward to the Pacific Coast. By the mid-eighties lower transportation costs and the dissolution of the military-Indian frontier had reduced the figure to about one million dollars, and this amount was being divided among several major roads.[43] Worse for the Union Pacific, the returns from its share of the traffic were being salted away in a sinking fund by U.S. Treasury officials.

Public confidence had faded and people no longer showed much inclination to invest in the railroad. When Dillon asked director Elisha Atkins for financial help in May 1884, he was told that declining values in stocks and securities had posed serious difficulties in this field. Nor, he learned, could Fred Ames produce money with the same ease as before. "He does not find it so easy today as usual to get money from our banks on Union Pacific collaterals," confessed Atkins.[44]

Charles Francis Adams, who became president of the road in June 1884, inherited the situation that had generated despondency in Dillon and had led to his resignation. In that year the company's gross earnings fell by nearly 15 percent and an eight-year period of dividend payments came to a close.[45] Adams noted the large floating debt that had been incurred through new construction, and he reasoned that the company's earnings were not sufficient to meet government requirements, to continue new construction, and to pay dividends. Since meeting the first two demands was imperative, the third had to be set aside. Adams was convinced that if his firm's financial health was to be improved, branch construction must proceed in order to bring new business.[46] While stockholders would suffer from a dividend drought, perhaps the value of their holdings would rise as a result of increased business. Union Pacific stock, which stood at 28 in 1884, had been 131¾ three years earlier.[47]

As the company struggled against economic depression and sharply increased competition by other roads, Congress threatened it with additional restrictive actions and thus contributed to further erosion of public confidence in Union Pacific securities. The alleged justification for new legislation arose from a controversy between the railroad and the government over compensation for mail haulage, but what the legislators primarily sought to accomplish was some means of making the railroad conform to the Thurman Act. If the company's interpretation of the Thurman Act was accepted, it was due $2 million for services rendered; if not, the government had a like amount coming. In view of the road's financial condition, the $4 million at stake was of vital concern.

When Sen. George F. Edmunds (Vermont) and other members of the Senate Judiciary Committee began to prepare amendments to the Thurman Act that were punitive in nature, railroad officials were obliged to take action. Gould, still a power in company affairs, was deeply concerned about the plummeting value of his stock, and, fearing financial disaster, he and his friends persuaded board member Charles Francis Adams to intervene with influential senators. Senator George F. Hoar, of Massachusetts, who was prepared to bring the matter before the Senate, thought very highly of Adams. As a result of the conferences Adams effected an "arrangement" whereby his company would pay $700,000 to meet its legal obligations for the year 1883 to prevent immediate legislative consideration of the proposed bills. Part of the agreement stipulated that Gould retire from the management and that Dillon resign as president.[48]

The controversy over net earnings was heard before the Court of Claims in January 1885, and it was reaffirmed that only bona fide expenses, paid out of earnings and not charged to construction, were deductible from gross earnings even though they could be construed as permanent improvements. A second point in the case, dealing with the sum to be paid by the government for postal compensation, went against the company. The court held that the railroad owed $917,000, which was promptly paid. Union Pacific officials believed that this had, at last, concluded this part of its controversy with the government. To their dismay they learned, in October of the same year, that the Commissioner of Railroads had raised new questions dealing with the unaided (western) portion of the Kansas Pacific and the whole matter was again thrown into litigation.[49]

Union Pacific officials deplored the constant bickering between the company and the government, for it had severe repercussions in the stock market and frightened away potential investors. But until some solution was found whereby the road could reasonably pay off its indebtedness, the question would remain open. Congressional notions about refunding were highly unacceptable to those men who conducted the company's financial affairs. For example, one of the many proposals considered by Congress in the spring of 1884 was the revision of the Thurman Act to increase the government's monetary requirements to 35 percent of the railroad's net earnings, a figure that was later amended to 45 percent.[50] Adams objected strongly to this bill, and told Sen. George Edmunds that if it became law it would destroy the power of his company to conduct further business and would put an end to its credit. He saw no good to come from legislation that merely perpetuated the bad features of the Thurman Act.[51]

Adams had been brought into the presidency, in part, to improve the company's public image. One of the areas thought to need immediate attention was the relationship with the nation's legislators. Yet, any effort to put the railroad's case before the Congress was regarded by the press and the man on the street as improper interference. One legitimate communication was through the government directors. As Adams told one of them, his company had no specific legislation to propose, and it did not favor any particular bill in Congress. He felt that the Thurman Act had been damaging, but since the clock could not be turned back the railroad would have to live with the existing arrangement.[52] However, it annoyed him to think of the near impossibility of interesting members of Congress in railroad matters "unless it is brought to their notice through some private channel." He knew that in the past, lobbying had hurt his company's cause; yet, he said, "It will not do to depend upon the goodness of your cause or the general rectitude of your intentions. You have got in some way to personally interest influential Senators and Representatives."[53]

Another frustration for Adams was the necessity of hacking through the public animosity that had grown over his company's reputation in the previous two decades. "There is a vague, general impression that we are in contumacy, as it were, that we are under great obligations to the government, that we refuse to do anything to meet those obligations, and that we are generally a disreputable nuisance," he complained. Since no positive moves had ever been made to correct this impression it appeared to him that "more than half the papers in the country take for granted the charges against us, which have not the slightest foundation in fact." To counter this development he proposed to open a publicity campaign of his own, and late in 1884 he asked veteran newspaperman Isaac Bromley, "Could you, for the next three months arrange so as to be here, in New York, Washington, or wherever else your presence might be needed to influence the editorial page?"[54]

Almost from the day the Union Pacific's tracks had reached Promontory there had been public comment about the generosity of the government in aiding its construction. The Crédit Mobilier affair, and the road's apparent unwillingness to pay even the interest on its bonded indebtedness, suggested that another set of robber barons was making off with part of the nation's landed heritage. Then, and later, the average person understood little about the nature of the land grants and thus it was easy to arouse public sentiment on this issue.

Adams told Secretary of the Interior L. Q. C. Lamar that he was tired of listening to the lament. He admitted that the United States had paid a large sum of money in interest on bonds advanced at the time of construction, but this was in accordance with the law, it was a contract, and the Supreme Court sanctioned it. "It was a good bargain for the United States," he argued. "This whole subject has been gone into frequently *ad nauseam,* and why it should be raised now I am at a loss to understand. If the United States never makes a worse bargain than it did with the Pacific Railroads, it will be more fortunate than any other government was on the face of the earth."[55]

Adams, who had in his earlier years written some sharply worded prose about railroad rings, the Crédit Mobilier, and questionable practices followed by the Union Pacific's originators, found that his responsibilities as president of the company had considerably altered his position. When Halsey L. Merriman, a government director from Iowa, made scathing comments about the founding fathers of the railroad, Adams took issue. Quoting Merriman, who had admitted it was not difficult to be wise after the event, Adams went on to say that "it is very easy to speak of those men as thieves and speculators, as men who had committed deliberate acts of fraud," in the light of subsequent developments. He suggested that the matter should be viewed in light of the time when the alleged acts were committed. "There was no human being, when the Union Pacific railroad was proposed, who regarded it as other than a wild-cat venture. The government did not dare to take hold of it. Those men went into the enterprise because the country wanted a transcontinental railroad, and was willing to give almost any sum to those who would build it." It was perfectly well understood, continued the president, that those who put up the money would own all the securities in the project. "They were generally looked upon as crazy adventurers," he reminisced. "The general public refused to put a dollar into the enterprise. Those men took their financial lives in their hands, and went forward with splendid energy and built the road the country called for. They played a great game, and they played for either a complete failure or a brilliant prize." Adams pointed out that no one would undertake such an enterprise for a six percent profit. Although these men ultimately made much more than that they would have been willing to settle for ten percent. He asked how anyone could have predicted that coal, from which large profits could be made, would be found in quantity along the line. This, and other resources, were developed as a result of the road; to insert knowledge of the mid-eighties into the thinking of the mid-sixties seemed to him unfair. In any event, he thought the government had more than recovered its investment in the lowered costs of its own transportation.[56]

Adams made no effort to defend those involved in the Crédit Mobilier, but he was concerned that mistakes made by earlier management should linger to hamper a new generation in its efforts to make the railroad a success. While the proper New Englander did not say so, he might well have compared the situation to some youthful indiscretion taking its toll of the perpetrator in later years. He complained to members of Congress that the company's bad name had placed an undue burden upon him and the people he represented. It was his conviction that "if the Union Pacific were in the position of any of the other large corporations in the country, I should have no shadow of a doubt as to my ability to pull it through." He explained why. "We are practically through all the ordinary troubles of a large railroad company. The only weak spot now is our relations to the government, and the manner in which we are tied up and throttled by existing foolish legislation." So impeded, he continued, the

Union Pacific could not do what its competitors could do or what the road itself needed to do: expand. "We cannot lease; we cannot guarantee, and we cannot make new loans on business principles, for we cannot mortgage or pledge; we cannot build extensions; we cannot contract loans as other people contract them. All these things are inhibited to us; yet all these things are habitually done by our competitors." Worse, it appeared that every effort was being made in Congress to block the Union Pacific, much to the satisfaction of its rivals.[57] To Adams, this additional burden upon his road was more than the legendary straw that broke the camel's back. In one of his gloomier moods he grimly remarked that the firm was "in the hands of the Philistines at Washington."

The legislative attack was two-pronged. Not only was the railroad obliged to fight in the congressional arena, as well as against the bears of Wall Street, but it faced continual attack in western legislatures. John M. Thurston, of Nebraska, the Union Pacific's general solicitor at Omaha, held that the road was "perhaps more at the mercy of adverse legislation than any other corporation in the United States, by reason of its Congressional charter and its indebtedness to the government and the power of Congress over it." He recommended a close watch be kept upon proposed legislation in Washington and "if possible favorably fashioned." To effect such a program he thought the company should create an office titled "Assistant Solicitor General," one who presumably could go before committees freed of the odium associated with lobbyists. Find a man "of extraordinary ability," and one who was "not universally known who should keep himself in the background," advised Thurston.

The Nebraska attorney was even more concerned by the growth of hostility in local legislatures. Members of these bodies, he said, tended to be men "totally unacquainted with railway management, who are more desirous of securing the political favor of their fellow citizens than wise and practical legislation affecting railways interests."[58] Efforts to influence elections proved to be discouraging, as Thurston himself admitted. "The Attorney General of Nebraska is rapidly becoming a crank," he wrote in 1888. "I was myself largely to blame for his nomination, now nearly four years ago; and we fell into the unpardonable blunder of nominating an unknown man and lawyer in order to defeat the nomination of an able man who was opposed to us."[59] Adams sympathized with his representatives at Omaha, whose role, he thought, was a hard one. On one occasion, when writing to S. R. Callaway about matters in general, he commented: "Indeed, I often consider, with due appreciation, the fact that, while I at this end, am surrounded with nothing but friends to encourage and cheer me on, dissatisfied only that I move so slowly, you, at your end, have to hold your own with small encouragement and less sympathy."[60]

Even though the Union Pacific president hoped he could restore some of his company's lost reputation by eliminating lobbyists and back-room politics, he believed the firm was due some kind of representation among the lawmakers. "I hold that the railroads, like every other interest of a community, should be represented in its legislative body," he wrote to Thurston. "They have just as much a right to be represented there as the land interest, the commercial interest, the agricultural interest, or the manufacturing interest." Casting an eye toward the "Granger" legislatures he added: "There is no law written or unwritten which prevents the farmer from sitting in the legislature. On the contrary, he is expected to be there. In the same way, I hoped that it is proper for the railroad, if it by legitimate measures can succeed in getting its representatives elected, to see that they are elected. Without this intelligent legislation is not practicable. The railroad side of the case is an important one and it ought to be fairly represented in debate." He recommended that promising young lawyers, friendly to the company, be encouraged and supported in their candidacies.[61]

Flanking the Union Pacific's legislative enemies stood other groups— men who sought to manipulate its stock through the spread of rumors, and those who merely saw an opportunity for blackmail. Adams recognized them for what they were, and, as he commented to a Denver resident, there was "a very large class of persons who are disposed, as you express it, 'to give the Union Pacific a red hot rattle.'" It was difficult to stop intentional rumor-mongering among speculators, but Adams tried to head off as much future damage as possible by warning congressional members of its existence. The question of payoffs was of easier solution; he simply refused to engage in it, remarking that "I fear too much of it has been done heretofore, and with very unsatisfactory results." Attempted blackmail sometimes came from those who had held key government offices. For example, in 1886, Adams reported to Sidney Dillon that the former auditor of railroad accounts, Theophilus French, was in New York in search of a sop. "Could you contrive to get hold of him and find out what he is after?" he requested of Dillon. Referring to French in a letter to a Southern Pacific official, Adams used the term "deadbeat" and guessed that "Not improbably it may be necessary before long to kill this vermin."[62]

Stockholders, ever concerned about their investments, were understandably worried about the dividend policy and the safety of their holdings. Adams told Moorfield Storey, who represented the company at

Washington, D.C., there was a widespread belief, dating back to construction days, that only a few individuals of great wealth were stockholders and therefore no great harm would come if the stock were wiped
out of existence. In a long letter that detailed how these shares were
distributed, Adams stated that there were 5,145 stockholders in Boston
and New England alone in 1884.[63] When a lady from New Haven asked
Adams if he thought Union Pacific stock was a good buy, he discouraged
any such purchase on the ground that the railroad was heavily involved
with the government, "which is very difficult to deal with in business
matters," and he advised that any such purchase could not be "considered
as an investment devoid of unusual risk."[64]

Adams was greatly concerned by the probable necessity of abandoning
dividends, as a result of government pressure, and he predicted that if
it occurred the little stockholders would be driven out because their
investments brought nothing. Should this happen, he warned, speculators
might well take over the road and then the government would get nothing.
"I do not think that anyone will gravely maintain that the United States
Government can hold its own against the machinations of Wall Street
sharpers," he concluded.[65] His pleas were unavailing. As a result of the
1884 "deal" with Congress that required a large expenditure of money,
and due to other economic factors, dividends were discontinued.

Uncertain as to what Congress might do next, and tired of the constant
public wrangling that was so damaging to the road's financial health, the
Union Pacific management sought some negotiated settlement to the long,
expensive guerilla warfare. As Adams commented, his company's role was
comparable to "continual dancing in fetters and running a close race
with a cannon ball attached to your leg."[66] A possible solution that
appealed to the firm was the renegotiation of its debt and the issuance
of new securities that would extend the time of payment and reduce
the interest. During 1886 Rep. Joseph H. Outhwaite, of Ohio, and Sen.
George Hoar, of Massachusetts, introduced bills to that end, but opposition
killed their efforts.[67] Meanwhile, the notion of once again investigating
the Union Pacific found favor among Congressmen. In 1887 Congress
created the Pacific Railway Commission, which examined the history of
the bond-aided roads. In the following year a Senate committee headed
by Sen. William P. Frye, of Maine, proposed a measure that resembled
the Outhwaite bill, but again obstacles were met. When Adams sought
to ease the animosities of opposing senators, one of them stunned him with
a request for a $50,000 bribe. As it had been with the Outhwaite bill, the
latest legislative proposal also died aborning.[68] Despite the best efforts of

the Union Pacific leadership to obtain a divorce from its original relation-ship with the government, the unhappy marriage continued.

Above all else the railroad had struggled against government control because of the restrictions it imposed on physical expansion. Reputation among users of the facilities, the value of its securities, and the condition of its credit all were a major concern, but in the eyes of the developers these things were subordinated to, and could be improved by, economic growth. That growth, so vital and of continuing importance, was stifled while rivals plunged ahead, unfettered.

In his efforts to convince powerful members of Congress that, if allowed to grow in a healthy, normal way, the Union Pacific would find its own economic salvation, Adams offered details. He explained to Senator Hoar that by branching into Idaho, Utah, and Nevada the road would send feeders into country a thousand miles west of Omaha and thereby funnel much traffic into the main system. "You can see at once, therefore, how absurd the suggestion is that we are arranging our system of branch lines in such a way that hereafter we can abandon the Union Pacific as worthless and have an independent line free of Government charges," he wrote. "Everything we are doing depends upon our control of the main stem of the Union Pacific, and what we are doing...alone gives any value to that main stem." In further defense of the branch system, he argued that except for this network, built by capital over which the government had no financial control, the Union Pacific would be prac-tically worthless within another decade. He admitted that his company could construct a much better main line for a third of the original cost if it chose to do so, and if this were done the government would be left with only the trunk, shorn of its productive limbs.[69] Or, as he said on another occasion, without the branches the road's mainline property would not be worth as much as the first mortgage held against it.[70]

Although it would be difficult to find two business figures more unalike than Charles Francis Adams and Jay Gould, both believed that to pay off the road's government obligations it had to prosper, and the key to that goal was expansion. By 1880 such a plan had been developed to a point where the company owned 600 miles of auxiliary road valued in stocks and bonds at $13 million. In the six years that Adams was president, between 1884 and 1890, the road acquired another 3,000 miles of branch-line trackage. Organized under separate management, and built for about $42 million, these feeders were said to have added some $5 million a year in revenue to the parent company.[71]

Both Gould and Adams spoke frankly about their desire to capture the trans-Missouri trade. At the investigation of 1887, Gould expressed regret that the Union Pacific had not enjoyed the same rights accorded other roads, the same freedom to spread across the land and open up unsettled pockets of the West. Had it been allowed to do so, said the financier, "the stock would have been worth 200 today, but while they hesitated and lacked the credit to go ahead, these stronger companies plunged in; and, of course, the building of competing roads at lower rates is what injured the Union Pacific." His strategy was bold, but was simply expressed: "My plan was that the Union Pacific should go ahead and occupy the whole country west of the river, and bring the business to the roads east." Had he been able to do so, Gould would have employed familiar tactics to protect the Omaha road. He freely admitted that he had once threatened Commodore C. K. Garrison, of the Missouri Pacific, with building eastward if the commodore ventured into Kansas Pacific country. However, when the Chicago and North Western later proposed to invade Nebraska, the Union Pacific was unable in retaliation to penetrate the country east of the Missouri River.[72]

Adams sought to occupy the territory west of Omaha, throwing out branches as fast or even a little faster than the population appeared, creating outer defenses behind which he could build in the future. It was expensive business, and it strained his resources as it did those of others who took part in the race for empire. But he knew that there was one main chance, and if it were lost there would be little opportunity to rectify the mistake in coming years. As late as 1887 he talked of building south from Fort Steele, in Wyoming, to Aspen, Colorado, thus bringing together the rich ores and the best coking coal in the West. It would have cost about $8 million. Another plan was to extend westward from Ogden to San Francisco, as did the Western Pacific nearly a quarter of a century later, and to move southwestward from the Utah Central—at Frisco, Utah—to Los Angeles. Meanwhile, any "vacant" valleys in Kansas or Nebraska were to be appropriated before rivals could anticipate him. The money was to come from the sinking fund held by the government and be put to better use. Adams thought the $7 million then lying virtually idle would be worth $20 million within a decade.[73] A contemporary political figure called such a venturesome approach "railroad gambling," but as Adams or any other entrepreneur of the day might have pointed out, western railroad building had been a gamble since its inception.[74]

The U.S. Pacific Railway Commission of 1887 heard considerable testimony and studied the dilemma of the Union Pacific in detail, but arrived at no helpful solution. The majority of that triumvirate concluded only that if the government foreclosed upon the company it would inherit a rail system "without beginning, end, or connections," and would be obliged to compete against other western roads unless it chose to control all of them equally. Should the government put the Union Pacific property up for sale there was small likelihood, considering its large indebtedness, that any rival road would buy it. Therefore, those who were currently interested in the railroad might well be the high bidders, and if that happened the debt would be effectively canceled, thus "presenting it as a bonus to the company itself, or to its directors." The commission recommended some settlement whereby the whole system, including branches, could be mortgaged anew.[75] To such a proposal the Union Pacific had agreed for some years, provided the life of the mortgage and the interest rate were satisfactory.

The commission having no answers, and the Congress being unwilling or unable to agree upon any means of settlement, matters drifted. "The outlook of the whole railroad situation in the West seems to be bad," wrote Adams in the spring of 1888. "Legislatures are pressing down upon us in every direction; and, in presence of this common danger, the railroad men are demeaning themselves like a parcel of maniacs rather than like reasoning human beings."[76] Charles S. Mellen, who came to the Union Pacific that spring as its traffic manager at Omaha, complained about the effects of vicious competition among rival roads in the area. "Men are sent here to operate such unnecessary roads and the fact stares them in the face that there is no possible chance for their roads to earn a living, or they to maintain their positions but by acting the part of a pirate against all vested interests engaged in like business; hence you find them cutting rates," he reported. Mellen blamed the eastern capitalists' lack of judgment for encouraging the proliferation of duplicating lines, and expressed the opinion that if the government were inclined to regulate, its efforts should be directed toward preventing such corporate jungles on the plains.[77]

Plagued by dwindling receipts and sharper competition in the West, Adams faced growing criticism from his board. The directors were particularly opposed to his expensive program of branch building, apparently unwilling to wait for its long-term results, or perhaps frightened by the amount of money it consumed. "They say I have got the company again entangled in debt by so doing; that they cannot see the branch lines recently constructed have been of any signal service to the main line, that until we get some legislation from Congress we are in no position to construct branch lines at all," he lamented to George Miller, editor of the Omaha *Herald*. Although Adams disagreed with his board on this point, he admitted that he would have been a happier man had he never advocated such building. "Branch roads are all very well," he wrote, "but, in order to be built advantageously, they must be built on a systematic and comprehensive plan." To do this required ample resources and strong credit, something Adams felt never would be achieved until Congress "stops battering at us."[78]

As the end of the eighties came into view, the Union Pacific situation seemed to be deteriorating. "We are practically without any defenders in Omaha," complained Isaac Bromley.[79] The election of 1888 provided the usual opportunity to make friends, and, according to an Adams biographer, each major party received a contribution from the Union Pacific.[80] In October of that year Adams told W. H. Barnum, chairman of the Democratic National Committee, that he had learned from Henry Villard of a proposal by which the land-grant railroad companies were to get up a pot of $300,000 to $400,000 to aid the Republicans in carrying the state of New York. For this they were promised a Secretary of the Interior and other national offices satisfactory to them. Adams indignantly told Barnum that "although I am a railroad president I have not yet so wholly ceased to be an American citizen as to not look with sensations the reverse of pleasurable at any such plot . . . ." He flatly refused to participate.[81]

Barnum swore he could get the Outhwaite funding bill passed if anyone could, but he failed to recognize the power of an opposition that included such a prominent figure as Sen. John Sherman, of Ohio. Adams himself tried to exert pressure by writing to national Republican party boss Mark Hanna, asking him to talk to Senator Sherman. "He is altogether too good a business man to be opposed to a settlement so advantageous to the government, and so burdensome to the company, as that contained in the 'Outhwaite' bill," said Adams of the Ohio senator.[82] Efforts to influence Congress favorably were to no avail; in February 1889, the Outhwaite bill was, in the words of Adams, "thrown out."[83]

By autumn of 1890 Charles Francis Adams had to admit he had been unable to unravel the Union Pacific snarl. Repeated attempts to adjust relationships with the government had failed, the branch-line policy had greatly increased company indebtedness, management reforms along the line were ineffective and, to crown these defeats with a final, crushing blow, traffic receipts had dwindled. Gloomily the New Englander embarked upon yet another trip beyond the Missouri River to see if he could find a shred of hope in a steadily deteriorating situation. But defeat hung heavily in the October air, and the general, as it were, prepared to inspect the thinning ranks of his troops before a final effort that promised only another reverse. "As we pulled out from Omaha and I crossed the Missouri," he wrote, "I looked back on the city,—its smoke rising against the glowing Western sky, and in my bones I felt it was the last time. I was nearing the end."[84] Surrender came toward the end of the following month, when he figuratively handed over his sword to Jay Gould's forces and saw the aged, ill Sidney Dillon again assume command.

The situation in which Dillon found himself was similar to that of Jefferson Davis in the dying days of the Confederacy. The cause was crumbling and there was little left to offer but brave words and one final effort. He admitted to Silas H. Clark at Omaha that "demoralization on the road could not be greater. Even Mr. Adams said that it was thoroughly demoralized." Calling for "heroic measures to bring order out of chaos," Dillon proposed lowering salaries and wages and reducing all expenditures in every possible manner. "I think the tendency all round is to cut and cover," he told Clark. "No man can do it better than you."[85] Heroic measures were to fend off disaster for nearly three years, but in the end the long-rumored receivership of the Union Pacific occurred, just over three decades after the government issued its original charter for that great adventure in transportation beyond the Missouri River.

"Receivership Is Inevitable"

When Sidney Dillon again assumed the presidency of the Union Pacific, on November 26, 1890, he was well aware that the corporative craft was foundering in a heavy financial sea. Immediately he ordered W. H. Holcomb, vice president in charge of operations at Omaha, to examine every possibility of cutting expenses and then to make reductions at every turn "without fear or favor to anybody."[1] All construction was halted except that which had progressed too far to be stopped. The Portland and Puget Sound extension, commenced by Adams, could not be abandoned; however, Dillon resolved to spend as little money on it as possible. "Do not stop the work entirely or give publicity to the curtailment, but quietly see that it goes very slow," wrote the president.[2] Tax collectors along the line were told they would have to wait for their money. "Arrange as pleasantly as possible to stand them off for the time being," was Dillon's advice to the Omaha office.[3] In short, Holcomb, to whom Adams had referred as "Flabbyguts," was told to tighten up.

Meanwhile, officials in New York launched an unprecedented austerity program. Second Vice President Gardiner M. Lane instructed the local treasurer at Omaha to "hoard your cash like a miser, remembering that it is of the greatest importance at the present time to help the eastern office." Terming the situation an emergency, he suggested that all local bills be settled with short-term drafts so that all available cash could be sent to New York.[4] Turning to the financial world, Lane assured banker A. A. H. Boissevain that rumors of receivership were untrue and that "Union Pacific affairs are assuming a much better shape." The size of the floating debt, he continued, was much smaller than that quoted by Boissevain and could easily be handled until funded by the sale of bonds.[5]

Efforts to reduce expenditures reached deep into the Union Pacific organization. A number of minor officials were dropped from the payroll, and even some of higher rank suffered. Albert Woodcock, general land commissioner, was told that expenditures in his department were too high; to reduce them it had been decided to abolish his office. Henceforth land matters would be handled by Benjamin McAllaster, who was the land commissioner.[6] Bishop John Sharp, who had been closely associated with the company for over two decades, also felt the touch of the executive pruning shears. By this time he held the position of second vice president of the Oregon Short Line and Utah Northern. Reluctantly Dillon told him that if he stayed, it would have to be as an honorary officer; his salary was to be terminated. When the Mormon bishop assented, Dillon called 'his response "a noble one."[7]

Every conceivable possibility of economizing was examined. The prime example of the degree to which this was carried out involved a former employee who had been admitted to a private insane asylum during the Adams administration with the agreement that the railroad would contribute ten dollars a week toward his support. At the time of commitment it was understood that his condition was such that he did not have long to live. Lane now asked the asylum about the patient's health and requested an estimate of his probable life expectancy. Upon learning the end might come within a year, Lane suggested to Dillon that, under the circumstances, the railroad should continue its support. Apparently the matter was sufficiently important to call for an alternative solution, and the question was put to director Edwin F. Atkins, who suggested that if he and each of his fellow directors contributed $50 it would put the matter at rest. "This would probably be enough to pay his board until he dies," commented Lane. The problem, which had necessitated an exchange of several letters between Dillon and Lane, was solved by the patient, who shortly passed away and thereby placed an extra ten dollars a week in the company coffers.[8]

During the frantic search for funds from within the firm, there continued the traditional quest for loans among financial houses. Dillon joined in this search for money, literally combing the countryside for assistance. In the spring of 1891 he asked the road's local treasurer, at Omaha, if friendly banks in Denver, Portland, or anywhere else could be persuaded to make further loans. Leaving no stone unturned, he called upon James J. Hill, president of the Great Northern Railway, for "two hundred thousand dollars on account to pay pressing matters."[9] At the time Dillon appealed to his fellow railroader for help, figures for the Union Pacific's financial performance during the first seven months of that year were before him. They revealed receipts of less than $8 million as opposed to outlays of more than $9 million.[10] Despite all efforts to borrow money, and even though the company directors had themselves loaned the firm as much as $4 million, the financial situation continued to deteriorate.[11]

Amid the growing possibility of defeat, Dillon fought a hard rearguard action, aware that his company had combated mighty odds in the past, and hopeful of recovering from yet another financial crisis. His long-range plan, as before, was to effect some settlement with the federal government. Explaining the railroad's dilemma once again, this time to a member of Congress, he said times had changed since the day of a Union Pacific traffic monopoly west of the Missouri River. The Denver and Rio Grande; the Rock Island; the Chicago, Burlington and Quincy; and the Missouri Pacific—all strong lines that had been constructed cheaply—now forced the Union Pacific to divide its business with them. The government debt, conceived in another day and under different circumstances, not only had become a heavier burden as interest accumulation mounted, but the means of paying it off had diminished through competition. Dillon thought that if the due date could be extended for another 75 or 100 years, at two percent interest, there would be a reasonable possibility of his road meeting its obligation to the government. The new mortgage, it was assumed, would cover the entire property, including all branches.[12] Secretary of the Interior John W. Noble, noting that since the road's government debt would mature within a few years, urged Congress to fund the debt. He agreed with Dillon that the time limit should be extended, and he warned that if it were not, the road would have to be sold.[13]

Concerned by an increasing likelihood of receivership, and hopeful of a settlement in Washington, Dillon took his case to the public. In an article entitled "The West and Railroads," published in the *North American Review* for April 1891, he argued that while the Union Pacific had been an aided road, it had "done more to open the vast territory between the Pacific and the Mississippi to civilization and the uses of the nation than any other agency." Admitting that land had been granted to assist construction, he pointed out once more that it was "at the time almost worthless, and but for these railways would have remained so for during a long period . . . ." Arguing that the development of the trans-Appalachian West, during the preceding half century, was not due so much to climate, soil fertility, or free institutions as it was to railroads, he contended that the country beyond the Missouri River would not have been settled to any extent without them. Even in that day Dillon could assert that the railroad's most important function was that of freight carrier, passenger traffic bringing in smaller receipts. Dillon speculated on how much it would cost a man to move a ton of wheat a mile, or on how long it would take a horse to do the job, then pointed out that it could be accomplished by

rail for less than a penny and in much less time. Thanks to the new transportation, wrote Dillon, potatoes, wheat, corn, and other products raised
in faraway Idaho were being sold in the East. They came from land
"where formerly nothing grew except sagebrush, and which was a part of
an alkali desert." The railways, he asserted, had virtually changed the face
of the West.

When Dillon learned that President Benjamin Harrison planned a
western tour, he asked him to look carefully at the country through which
the Union Pacific ran and to recognize the part the road played in its
development. If, he said, some reasonable settlement could be reached
with the government, one that allowed the Union Pacific the same freedom
enjoyed by its competitors, the growth of both the railroad and its adjacent
territory would be still greater.[14]

Available figures indicated that the Union Pacific's part of the West had,
indeed, experienced considerable growth in the previous two decades. That
area, including Nebraska, Kansas, Wyoming, Colorado, Utah, Idaho, Montana, Oregon, and Washington, had a population of 773,632 in 1870.
Twenty years later the figure was 4,046,510. Of the original land grant,
more than 11 million acres in extent, somewhat over 8 million had been
sold. On the Kansas division, including the Denver Pacific grant, nearly
three-quarters of the 4 million acres received from the government were
then being worked by individual owners.[15]

In May 1891 Dillon made a western tour to examine the system once
more and to inspect for himself the conditions along the line. As the
plains country does so often, it looked green and rich that spring, and
from this the president took new hope, as would any individual whose
future lay in the ability of the land to produce. "Have just passed through
Columbus and Grand Island," he telegraphed to Jay Gould. "The corn is up
and is being cultivated, and the barley is at least knee high. Country never
looked finer at this time of year than it does today. The farmers are all
delighted. This means more business for the Union Pacific than it can do
when the crop is harvested." As he passed through Nebraska and approached
Colorado, he sent another enthusiastic report to Gould. "Country looking
fine and well filled with cattle. . . . Every indication that we shall have
good business."[16]

As many western farmers discovered in the nineties, a decade said
to have been so gay, the mere prospect of good crops did not always loosen
the purse strings of mortgage holders. Dillon, who headed a powerful firm
—one that was accused of being a heartless eastern corporation sucking
the lifeblood out of downtrodden tillers of the soil on the lonely plains—
discovered that this economic giant was now in the same situation as the

Top–*Sale of the Union Pacific Railroad, at Omaha, on November 1, 1897. The scene is on the steps of the present Omaha freight house.*

Right–*Charles Francis Adams, Jr., the eighth president of the Union Pacific Railroad.*

farmers. A better turn of events had to come about in the near future, or the dreaded specter of foreclosure would become a reality.

Matters did not improve. The stock market continued to drift downward and Union Pacific creditors called more urgently for the payment of their loans. Admitting to Fred Ames that "Mr. Dillon is extremely nervous and in poor health," Edwin Atkins relayed the information to Gould, advising him that unless aid in the form of $1.5 million was forthcoming the president was headed for a general breakdown. Despite such pleas, including one sent by Gould's own son, George, the old "railroad wrecker" did not respond favorably. He said he was sorry about Dillon's health and, as a matter of fact, feared for his own; but he could not supply that much money. He suggested asking for receivership.[17] Unwilling to make such a move, Dillon turned to J. Pierpont Morgan and asked for help; once again his request was rejected.

While Union Pacific leaders were deeply discouraged, they refused to run up the flag of surrender. Dillon again pressed Gould. This time the answer cheered him considerably, and he responded. "I was half sick, tired and discouraged about the Union Pacific until your last suggestion came to bundle up all our securities and, if we could do no better, make notes to the amount of fifteen millions of one, two and three years . . .," he wrote to Gould. Several parties would be interested in such a proposal, he contended. Financier Russell Sage "is fully alive to it and says it is the true principle to work on"; Grenville Dodge was ready to subscribe $500,000. Such being the case, Dillon pledged himself to match Dodge's offer provided Fred Ames would do the same. There was some evidence that the Equitable Life Assurance Society would take one or even 2 million in subscriptions. "I feel more encouraged today than I have for a long time that we will be able to swim through," Dillon assured Jay Gould in early August. "What a credit and a name it would give us all if it can be done. If not done, and it goes in the hands of a Receiver, I fear the worst as no doubt the Government would lay their hands on [the] Union Pacific and complications would arise which would be almost endless and a detriment to all roads in the West."[18]

The plan suggested by Gould provided for the "bundling up," as Dillon had expressed it, of all the company's bonds, stocks, and other securities and depositing them with Drexel, Morgan & Company, trustees, to secure an issue of $24 million worth of three-year, six percent, promissory notes. Although the securities had a par value of over $100 million, their actual worth stood at just over $41 million. The new notes, offered at 92.5 percent of their face value, were generally accepted by the creditors as payment of their claims, although some of them showed reluctance, believing Union

Pacific loans had been underwritten and that they might therefore get cash. While private financiers thought the creation of a collateral trust was a satisfactory move, and Sage could refer to it as "the true principle," the road's government directors had some reservations. The collateral was sufficient, they admitted, and they did not object to the procedure as a temporary expedient, but there remained the possibility that if things did not go well in the future, the whole system, including its valuable feeders that were a part of the collateral, would be further jeopardized.[19] Union Pacific managers may have well agreed with such reservations, but faced with a $20 million floating debt, and waning public confidence, they sought means to bolster company credit. The Creditors' Plan, as the move was called, appeared to be the best protection against receivership.[20]

The creation of the Creditors' Committee, appointed under an agreement of August 18, 1891, and embodied in a Trust Indenture to Drexel, Morgan & Company on September 18, greatly relieved the mind of Sidney Dillon. "Perhaps you would be interested to learn that Mr. Dillon is really in pretty good condition, everything considered," Comptroller Oliver Mink wrote to Silas H. Clark at Omaha. The president had experienced a trying summer, continued Mink, but the prospect of solving a number of financial problems under the new arrangement had put him in an unusually cheerful frame of mind.[21] Dillon himself expressed his jubilation in a telegram sent to one of his acquaintances about the time the Trust Indenture was effected. "All hail. Everything is right here. Subscription practically filled. Union Pacific is safe. Everybody is feeling happy."[22]

Optimism was difficult to maintain in the face of the fundamental difficulties that confronted the road. While management had demonstrated that it could wriggle out of yet another financial corner, the steady decline of business was not a condition that could be solved by manipulation. Not only were receipts off from agricultural shipments, but mining, in which the road had placed so much faith, showed discouraging returns. Anaconda's shutdown sharply reduced copper shipments from Montana and subtracted approximately $100,000 a month from the Union Pacific's anticipated earnings. A strike at the Omaha & Grant smelter resulted in the loss of about $50,000 more each month. Mining companies, unsure about the length of such strikes, sent their ores to smelters served by other lines. As a further blow, the Denver and Rio Grande opened its new standard-gauge service between Denver and Ogden, thus capturing a larger share of the California trade than had been possible during its narrow-gauge days.[23] To add another dimension to this threat the Rio Grande Western indicated a serious intention to build through to California. Grenville Dodge was convinced that Gen. W. J. Palmer, who then headed Utah's Rio Grande

Western, had sufficient backing to make such a move. Unfortunately for the Union Pacific, it could not afford to put another dollar into a parallel line that would pinch off this proposed thrust to the sea.[24] The best it could do was to retrench, hang on, and hope for better days. Vice President Edwin Atkins expressed a mood, perhaps unconsciously, when he commented: "The trains I am pleased to find are running upon time and there are comparatively few wrecks."[25] The remark bore none of the earlier feeling of expansion, growth, optimism, and hope; rather, it suggested that management had reached an emotional plateau and that its attitude was one of watchful waiting.

The burden Sidney Dillon assumed when Adams was forced out of office was too great for a man of his age and physical condition. On numerous occasions, during 1891, he complained of being tired and weak. Early in the year he told Silas Clark: "I have never worked so hard in my life as since I was elected President of the Union Pacific. . . . Yet [we] must try to row ashore, and not sink." In December he admitted that he was nearly worn out.[26] By February 1892 Comptroller Oliver Mink was concerned, admitting to Edwin Atkins that although Dillon was still working with his accustomed vigor, he did not look well and appeared to be very tired. During April the president was forced to give up his office duties and remain at home under the care of his son-in-law, who was a physician. On the morning of June 9 he died, and Silas Clark, then general manager at Omaha, succeeded him as head of the railroad.[27]

In a sense, company fortunes paralleled those of Dillon's last days: The will to survive was strong, but the burden to be carried grew heavier with each passing day. The responsibilities assumed by Clark were enormous, and as an operating man—as opposed to a man with Dillon's financial acumen and widespread connections—he concentrated his efforts on running the railroad at a profit. By now the company was faced with an indebtedness so large that even the most accomplished of railroad managers probably could not have produced sufficient business to successfully attack the financial problem. The 1,822 miles of road actually owned by the Union Pacific were indebted at $76,000 per mile, while the 5,850 branchline miles were bonded at an average of $24,000 a mile. The debt of the entire system totaled $228 million—about $29,000 a mile.[28] The first of the subsidy bonds would begin to mature in July 1897, and there appeared to be less likelihood than ever that they could be honored. By 1892 it had become apparent to Secretary of the Interior Noble that the government might have to foreclose. Even the government, he thought, could not successfully operate a road so heavily indebted, and therefore it ought to make every effort to avoid such an inheritance. At this time there was in the Senate a proposal to refund the debt for another one hundred years, at two percent, and even though its acceptance might cause some public grumbling, Noble thought it the best solution.[29]

As if these problems were not an overwhelming burden, the Union Pacific was nagged by other demands. Appeal after appeal to the courts on the question of net earnings brought only negative answers. In 1892 Secretary Noble cited the decision of the Supreme Court (138 U.S. S.C., 84), which reaffirmed the government's contention that no deductions were to be made from gross earnings for permanent improvements and betterment. "This restatement," he said, "largely increases the amount due the Government under the Thurman act for past years as well as for the future." The Omaha bridge earnings, so long debated, also were subject to the 25 percent withholding, as were Pullman sleepers and dining cars operated over Union Pacific lines. The company had refused to make any report on such earnings, insisting that the government had no claim upon them, but now it finally was induced to pay these amounts, under protest.[30]

In 1892 another blow fell upon the road. An Army appropriation bill included a provision by which government transportation monies due the lines either owned, controlled, or operated by the Union Pacific, were to be withheld by the U.S. Treasury. Oliver Mink called the provision "vicious and unjust," arguing that the branch lines had derived their charters from the states and that they were therefore under no obligation to the federal government.[31]

The government directors, a group which by now had functioned for three decades, once again strongly urged the government to settle its controversy with the Union Pacific. Pointing out that the growth of the road had been so throttled in the past two years that no additional lines had been built, and, indeed, subsidiaries under construction in both Utah and Oregon literally had been abandoned, they urged some resolution of outstanding differences. Calling the uncertain situation disastrous to the company and to the general public, one that "checks all progress and development so essential to the States through which it passes, and to its own healthy growth," these men called for a cessation of further warfare against the road. The ever-present possibility that the road would be broken up, constantly held before the public, sufficiently impaired the credit of the company to frighten off potential investors and worry the existing security holders.[32] This, then, was the condition of affairs as the Union Pacific entered the fatal year, 1893. In a few months the entire nation was to be plunged into a financial panic of major proportions, when economic giants would fall right and left before its onslaught.

Spring, that time of renewed expectations for happier days, yielded only a crop of rumors in the Union Pacific organization. Jay Gould died in February, and there were rumblings that President Clark would be replaced by Oliver Mink. Accompanying the growing uneasiness was the continuing uncertainty about the government's action. It was hoped that Grover Cleveland, who was to be inaugurated in early March, would attempt to solve the long-standing dispute, and thereby give his party credit for the accomplishment. Until the new administration took office, therefore, the railroad's officials initiated no efforts toward refunding, and for this they were criticized.[33] Matters drifted as summer came. As the road's management marked time, grimly hoping for some sign of improvement, a new alarm came from the West.

In June Fred Ames went out West as Adams and Dillon had done before him, searching for answers. Upon his return he had to admit to Oliver Mink that the land beyond the Missouri River was, for the moment at least, a place without promise. "The shipments of commodities generally show an astonishing falling off," wrote Mink, quoting Ames. "The marked decrease in our earnings is due, therefore, not to any special reduction in rates; but to the slack in business generally." His comment about rate reductions referred to a recent move in that direction made by James Hill, of the Great Northern, a move which had been earlier seized upon as the reason for declining Union Pacific business. Mink also repeated remarks made by Ezra Millard, an Omaha banker long associated with the road, who warned of the extreme stringency of the money market. But bankers traditionally talked in these terms, and Mink was not inclined to believe that "the present noticeable depression will continue for many days. It is too acute." He rationalized that "while violent fluctuations in our earnings are not common, they are on the other hand not unusual."[34]

Despite his brave talk, the comptroller had to admit the situation verged on the unusual. "The falling off in our business is, as you will observe, startling," he wrote to young George J. Gould. His authority was a recent telegram from Silas Clark reading: "Bottom dropped out of West bound transcontinental business. Also decrease in grain and livestock shipments. Situation discouraging."[35] In a personal and confidential letter to D. T. Littler, Mink again used the word "startling" in describing the conditions west of the Missouri River. "At no former period has the financial stringency been so pronounced," he admitted. "Trade and the exchanges to trade have almost ceased. The markets, I am told are almost closed against the wholesale dealers of the East and shipments of merchandise, as well as of ore and its products, will, I believe, soon show a very noticeable falling off." Littler, who apparently inquired about the potential of Union Pacific stock, was told now was not the time to make an investment.[36]

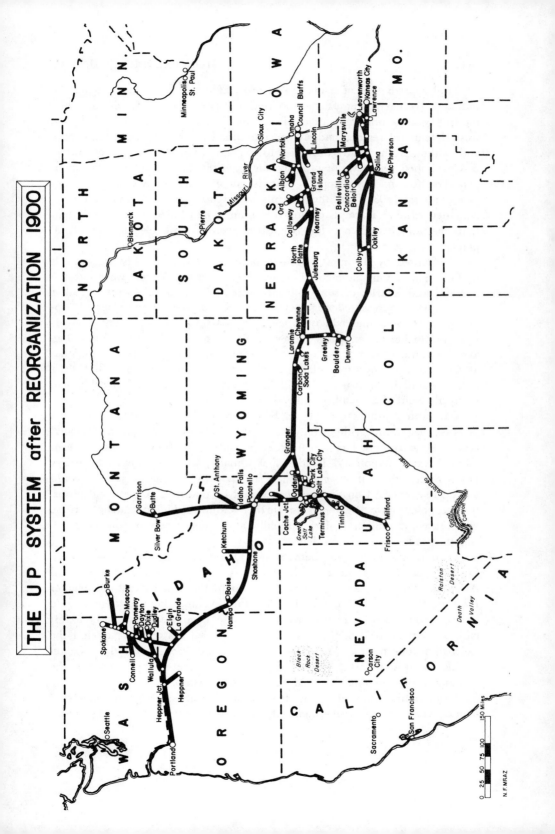

THE UP SYSTEM after REORGANIZATION 1900

MINN.

NORTH DAKOTA

SOUTH DAKOTA

MONTANA

WYOMING

IDAHO

OREGON

WASH.

NEVADA

UTAH

COLO.

NEBRASKA

KANSAS

IOWA

MO.

CALIFORNIA

Minneapolis
St. Paul

Bismarck

Pierre

Missouri River

Sioux City
Omaha
Council Bluffs
Norfolk
Albion
Ord
Callaway
Grand Island
Kearney
North Platte
Julesburg
Lincoln
Marysville
Leavenworth
Kansas City
Lawrence
Belleville
Concordia
Beloit
Salina
McPherson
Oakley
Colby

Cheyenne
Laramie
Carbon
Soda Lakes
Greeley
Boulder
Denver

Granger
Park City
Salt Lake City
Ogden
Cache Jct.
Great Salt Lake
Terminus
Tintic
Frisco
Milford

St. Anthony
Idaho Falls
Pocatello

Garrison
Butte
Silver Bow
Ketchum
Shoshone
Boise
Nampa

Burke
Moscow
Pomeroy
Dayton
Dixie
Dudley
Elgin
La Grande
Spokane
Connell
Wallula
Heppner Jct.
Heppner

Seattle

Portland

Sacramento
San Francisco

Carson City

Black Rock Desert

Ralston Desert

Death Valley

Grand Canyon

Colorado River

0 25 50 75 100   150 Miles

N.F. MRAZ

Mink's prediction of a decline in ore traffic was borne out during the summer. By early August he reported a major cause of falling traffic receipts was the line's extensive mileage in silver producing states. Actually, western mineral regions had shown a decline in production for some time and, although the road continued to depend upon this source of traffic, it was hoped that swelling agricultural output might offer some compensation for the loss. Crops in Kansas, for example, appeared to be very promising in 1893, "but there seems to be no money to handle them," lamented Mink.[37] Receipts during the summer had fallen to such an extent that the anticipated net for August showed a probable decline of 40 percent.[38]

Confronted by the most serious situation in the road's history, officials in Boston and Omaha labored to ward off disaster. Wages were cut ten percent, and salaries of some officials were reduced by 20 percent. Labor leaders, who represented engineers, firemen, trainmen, and telegraph operators, were told the reductions were necessary to help stave off receivership. To further cut expenses, passenger service between Granger, Wyoming, and Portland, Oregon, was reduced by one daily train each way. Officials at Omaha tried every available avenue of economy, hopeful that their efforts would be sufficient. "I still have faith that the old U.P. ship will safely ride out the squall yet ahead of us," wrote one of them.[39]

But even as the crew did its best to save the foundering vessel, the Nebraska legislature, riding the wind of Populist sentiment against "foreign" corporations, proposed new regulatory legislation for freight rates. Government director Joseph W. Paddock, of Omaha, warned Interior Secretary Hoke Smith that, if enacted, such a law would bring disaster, would violate the federal Constitution, and would be punitive. In practical terms, the proposed law threatened to further diminish Union Pacific income by at least a million dollars annually at a time when it was ready to collapse under its other burdens.[40]

By the autumn of 1893 both Sidney Dillon and Jay Gould were dead. On September 12 another of the Union Pacific's leaders was gone. Fred Ames had taken passage for New York aboard the Fall River Line steamer *Pilgrim*. When last seen, on the preceding evening, he had appeared to be in normal health. There was no response from his cabin at breakfast call, and at ten o'clock the ship's captain entered his quarters to find the railroad leader dead.[41] Ames, whose family had been involved in Union Pacific matters almost from its beginning, was spared, by a month, the experience of watching the road go into receivership.

Faced with insolvency, and fearful of separate foreclosure suits that would result in dismemberment of the entire system, the road's major stockholders sought judicial custody. At the request of Edwin Atkins, Peter B. Wyckoff, and the executors of the Fred Ames estate—representing three large stockholders—application was made for receivership and the U.S. Circuit Court for the District of Nebraska took the necessary action on October 13, 1893. George Gould, among others, said this move was good for stockholders because it would prevent the system from being torn apart. It was argued that the company's securities would be in a much stronger position than before receivership. Such reassurances merely delayed the day of evil tidings, for soon applications for separate receiverships of auxiliary roads began to emerge. It was the beginning of the end for the great railroad system. The financial storm of 1893 ruined business firms from coast to coast—6 mortgage companies, 13 loan and trust companies, 554 banks, and 154 railroads, firms with a total capitalization of $2.5 billion. The Union Pacific, its revenues off $2.5 million during the first half of the year, then called upon during the succeeding months to meet a maturing indebtedness of $5.1 million, was too weak to survive.[42]

Even before the main body of the company fell before the onslaught, some of the outlying subsidiaries succumbed. In the summer of 1893 John Evans, the Coloradan who held considerable stock in the Union Pacific's Denver and Gulf, asked for a separate receivership on the ground that the Texas auxiliary line had been misused to benefit the parent company, and on this basis foreclosure followed.[43] That autumn the Fort Worth and Denver City (a part of the "Panhandle" system) went into receivership, as did the Denver, Leadville and Gunnison. Later the same fate befell the St. Joseph and Grand Island.[44] During the summer of 1894 a separate receiver was appointed for the Oregon Railway and Navigation Company. Thus, from Puget Sound to the heart of Texas, and from Utah eastward to the Missouri River, dismemberment of the great rail network that had found its beginnings near Omaha was well under way.

Initially, there were three Union Pacific receivers: Silas Clark, Oliver Mink, and E. Ellery Anderson, the last of whom was to represent the government. Since Clark and Mink were long-time officials of the road, and Anderson was known to be favorable to the company, the government asked and received additional representation: John W. Doane and Frederic R. Coudert.[45] The next step was the selection of a committee representing all classes of securities, the members of which were charged with preparing a plan of reorganization. Appointed were Sen. Calvin S. Brice, of Ohio, J. Pierpont Morgan, Louis Fitzgerald, A. A. H. Boissevain, Grenville M. Dodge, Henry L. Higginson, and Samuel Carr. Fitzgerald, president of the Mercantile Trust Company, represented the Gould interests; Boston capitalist Higginson, the Oregon Railway and Navigation Company; and Dodge, the Union Pacific's Denver and Gulf road. Boissevain, of Amsterdam, represented the foreign security holders, while Carr was appointed in behalf of the Fred Ames estate.

Although the government did not have an official place on the committee, Senator Brice was included to help prepare a plan that would be acceptable to Congress. Financier Morgan's firm was noted for its work in company reorganizations. The group worked on the assumption that a settlement with the government had to be achieved before any sound proposition could be presented to other creditors. The road's government directors took exception to this theory, claiming that Congress, unable to consider the terms offered to other creditors, would be unable to judge the concessions they were willing to make, and hence might well seek a larger settlement than the company was in a position to accept. The committee made no firm recommendations, but offered suggestions to Attorney General Richard Olney, who, in the spring of 1894, sent them on to the House. After considering various alternatives the House Committee on Pacific Railroads, headed by James B. Reilly, of Pennsylvania, set forth a proposal that carried his name.[46]

This latest bill, which did not vary greatly from earlier suggestions, proposed that all monies and securities held in the sinking fund created under the Thurman Act of 1878 be applied as partial payment of the company's first-mortgage bonds, which had priority over the government's lien, and the remnant of that indebtedness paid through an assessment if no other means could be found. The road subsidy debt was then to be refunded, as had been suggested many times, but over a period of only 50 years and at an interest charge of three percent.[47] The bill was debated at length but failed to pass, partially because some congressmen were unable to understand its provisions. Many of them were reluctant to agree to a new long-term arrangement, fearing this merely opened the door to new and more difficult complications.[48]

Prejudice against the road for having so far failed to carry out what were presumed to be the original government stipulations, still lingered in Congress. The popularity of attacking big business, particularly railroads, was then at its height and there seemed to be little disposition among legislators to fight this trend. Criticisms came not only from easterners who believed public domain lands had been misused; residents all across the trans-Missouri West blamed the roads for the economic plight in which they found themselves. Individuals complained about rates, and cities charged prejudice in favor of other rival municipalities.

The reaction of Denver to the Union Pacific receivership is a good example of the mixed feelings held in the West where the road was not the dominant carrier. That mountain city, so bitterly disappointed during the late sixties when the main line bypassed it, had never completely recovered from its original pique. During the three decades that followed the commencement of rail service in 1870, Denver had warmed to the Union Pacific on occasion, even while flirting with other lines; but it always resented the favoritism apparently shown to Omaha. The "Queen City of the Plains" argued that its rival on the banks of the Missouri was merely a station at one end of the line, while the Colorado capital was situated in the center of the entire system.

In 1893 Colorado suffered not only from that year's general depression, but as a mining area it also felt the sharp decline in the price of silver. One Denver paper charged that the Union Pacific receivership was the "result of President Cleveland's foolish and dishonest attempt to force the single gold standard upon the United States."[49] Utah, now heavily dependent upon mining—as Brigham Young had hoped it would not be—also blamed its economic difficulties on Cleveland's handling of the silver crisis. "The appointment of a receiver for the Union Pacific . . . is direct notice to the East that the assault on silver is surely and steadily paralyzing the west . . .," said the *Record,* of Park City.[50] The *Salt Lake Herald* agreed, arguing "it was evident that those who had watched the course of events since the silver fight has caused such depression, were prepared for the news and marveled much that the consummation had been held off so long. That it has is a tribute to the managers of the road."[51]

The Mormon view, represented by the *Deseret News,* held that while there had been some shortsightedness in the road's management, there was a general feeling of kindliness toward the road in the community. "It is the pioneer route," said the editor, "and many of our people's names are associated with its advent and subsequent career. Those who blaze the trail and break the way for others are always associated with a condition of things bordering on the revered to us, and in this light alone, to say nothing of the grand and diversified benefits in the way of opening new fields and general development, do we look upon that road with respect and hope soon to see it emerge from its present difficulties."[52]

More typical of general western animus toward railroads was Denver's bitterness over the effects of financial jugglery at high levels and the influences of "foreign" ownership. One editorial, in condemning "the scheming manipulators who have wrecked great properties and robbed thousands of investors," recommended that the perpetrators of these crimes should be sent to penitentiaries for life.[53] Residents of other parts of the country did not entirely condemn such notions, but they were more disposed

to see the government take over the Union Pacific and retrieve the investment of public money than merely to punish those said to be guilty of
financial manipulations.

Eastern businessmen who saw danger in the idea of government ownership preferred to extend the debt's time limit in the belief that ultimately the
matter could be set at rest by this method. The *Nation* argued that "all
impartial students of this problem" agreed with the desirability of the
government making a fair compromise with the Pacific roads. Even so, said
that journal, serious problems of adjustment could arise. "Let us suppose
for a moment that Farmers' Alliance or private blackmailers defeat any
compromise, and that the Government must foreclose. With the outlying
parts of the system in other hands, the Government could not recover its
sixty millions." The failure of the Reilly bill, which had recommended a
conservative approach, was decried as being tragic. It was "rejected in the
interest of buncombe," said the *Nation*.[54] This comment suggested that
congressional emotions were running high and that these representatives of
the American people had despaired of retiring the second government
mortgage.

The Union Pacific's reorganization committee, aware of the hostility
among legislators, was not totally surprised at the failure of the Reilly bill.
However, its members knew of no practical alternative, and the group
disbanded in the spring of 1895, resolved to await a more favorable political
climate before resuming its efforts.

The government directors concluded there could be no successful reorganization plan without foreclosure of the property. It had been suggested
that such an event might be averted by an assessment of about $10 a share
upon the stock, but the government directors disagreed here, too. They
estimated the current market value of the road's stock to be $8 million, but
the scattered nature of the holders and the almost certain unwillingness of
some to pay the assessment rendered the plan impracticable. Even though
these directors approved of foreclosure, they again rejected the notion that
the government should take over and operate the property in an effort to
collect money due. Such a move was unfeasible to them from a political
standpoint and because of the incomplete nature of the government lien.
Attempting to offer a more positive alternative, they repeated their earlier
proposal that the system be covered by a new mortgage backed by 3
percent 100-year bonds. In estimating the road's net earnings, these men
argued that the figure would come to nearly $5 million for the fiscal year
ending June 30, 1894. Under their plan the company could well contribute
annually an amount larger than that suggested in the Reilly bill.[55]

William J. Coombs, a government director, inspected the Union Pacific during the autumn of 1895 and reported that the property was in good physical condition. The country tributary to the road, he also said, was beginning to recover from the panic, and the receivers were spending money to keep the rail facilities in good working order for the growing trade. Coombs was annoyed by policies of the Central Pacific. Its tracks had been leased to the Southern Pacific for a decade and during that time shippers had been urged to use the more southerly route, thus denying the Union Pacific both passenger and freight traffic. Such pressure, he said, had caused the Union Pacific to seek an alternate—and expensive—route to the Pacific Ocean. While the Oregon Short Line and its various auxiliaries had been helpful to the Union Pacific, Coombs thought this construction added to the worsening financial trouble into which the road had fallen. He suggested that the government force the Central and Union Pacifics into becoming one road, through foreclosure.[56] His colleagues, who earlier had recommended foreclosure, advised that before such action was taken the government should find a purchaser for the property and then fix a minimum price for the settlement of its claims against the road, thus protecting itself against the possible loss of an unreasonably large portion of its investment. In any event, said the directors in 1895, all relations should be terminated between the Union Pacific and the government. Either settle for a fixed sum or agree upon a new long-term bonded indebtedness, they urged.[57]

By 1895 the Union Pacific system had experienced a considerable contraction. Almost half its branches had been lopped off in various foreclosure proceedings, its more than 8,000 miles being reduced to just over 4,400, and in the months to come further reduced to less than 2,000 miles. During that autumn Winslow S. Pierce, representing George Gould, proposed that Kuhn, Loeb & Company, a banking firm, undertake a reorganization of the Union Pacific. Jacob H. Schiff, to whom Pierce talked, became the financial manager of a new group that included Marvin Hughitt, president of the Chicago and North Western Railroad; Chauncey M. Depew, president of the New York Central; T. Jefferson Coolidge, Jr., president of the Old Colony Trust Company; Oliver Ames II, a director of the Union Pacific; and Gen. Louis Fitzgerald. Schiff served on the committee as a representative of Kuhn, Loeb & Company.

The new committee shortly met with discouragements similar to those causing the earlier group to disband. Despite their best efforts committee members came to the conclusion, by late 1896, that some unknown influences were at work against them. Wherever they turned, in or out of Congress, in the business worlds at home and abroad, or among public figures, they met roadblocks. Rumor had it that J. Pierpont Morgan was behind the opposition, and to determine the truth Schiff talked to the financier, who denied complicity. Morgan, perhaps to make his denials convincing, suggested that Edward H. Harriman was the guilty party. Schiff, who had taken a direct approach with Morgan, did the same in Harriman's case, and received the frank response that not only was he the culprit, but that he intended to reorganize the railroad himself. After considerable maneuvering between Harriman and the Schiff forces, it was agreed that Harriman should have a place on the board of the reorganized company if he would join forces with the committee.[58]

During 1896 the Schiff committee sought a final settlement with the government, believing this enduring obstacle to the road's future had to be removed before any proposed reorganization could be successful. A plan was submitted to the Senate Committee on Pacific Railroads, and in April that body presented yet another refunding bill to Congress. After lengthy debate, and the consideration of a House version of the proposal, the effort was defeated, as had all its predecessors. President Grover Cleveland now instructed his attorney general to protect the government's interest, a move that indicated the administration's intention to accept only a cash settlement. The Schiff committee, realizing it now had no alternative, commenced negotiations with the attorney general to determine the best terms it could achieve under these conditions. Since foreclosure suits had been underway since 1895 it was important to learn the conditions under which the government would settle. After further discussion it was agreed that the road should be sold for an amount sufficient to guarantee the original government bonds plus 3 percent interest. The reorganization committee agreed to make a cash bid of over $45 million, but after this proposal was accepted by the government, further doubts were raised among federal officials. Anxious to proceed, the committee raised its guarantee to $50 million, and the foreclosure suits were rapidly concluded.[59]

In anticipation of the upcoming sale, a new corporation, to be known as the Union Pacific Railroad Company, was organized July 1, 1897, at Salt Lake City. The incorporation papers, called "a very important document" by one of the Salt Lake City newspapers, provided a capital stock of $13 million in shares valued at $100 each. Toward the end of that month decrees of sale of the old Union Pacific Railway, under foreclosure proceedings instituted against the road by the federal government, were approved by Judge Walter Sanborn in the U.S. District Court at Omaha.[60] During October rumors were heard throughout New York financial circles to the effect that Coates, Son & Company, a British syndicate, had expressed interest in buying the Union Pacific and the Kansas Pacific "at full price," thereby bringing the federal government $20 million more than it would gain by selling to the American financiers. However, the Britons wanted to give part payment in bonds and asked that the sale be deferred until mid-December to allow more time to negotiate the purchase. Apparently such overtures were not satisfactory to the government and the sale proceeded as scheduled.

Early in November 1897, the syndicate sponsored by Kuhn, Loeb & Company, with Harriman participating, purchased the Union Pacific road lying between Omaha and Ogden at a sale described as "one of the most tame and uninteresting performances possible to imagine."[61] The extensive branch system, already amputated by separate foreclosures, was not included. It required $58,448,223.75 to satisfy the government's claim, after which the first mortgage and other securities had to be purchased. The final price to the reorganization committee came to just over $81.5 million. When one considers the cost of duplicating the road at the time of sale, that figure represented a financial gamble as daring as the one embarked upon by the promoters of 1862.[62] According to an estimate made a decade earlier by engineer Richard P. Morgan, Jr., the road between Omaha and Ogden then could have been replaced and equipped for $44,457,466.23. The value of company lands and other property was not considered in such an estimate.

Shortly before the Union Pacific went under the auctioneer's gavel Sen. William V. Allen, of Nebraska, wrote an article remarking on his region's potential. Despite great distances from market and other limitations, he argued, the West "is the sleeping lion of this country. It has boundless natural resources, and is rapidly increasing in population."[63] Apparently Edward H. Harriman and his associates believed this, for they were willing to risk an amount nearly double the current cost of replacing the Union Pacific to gain use of its facilities and the adjacent lands still owned by the road. If the branches, so valuable as sources of traffic, were to be retrieved, the trunk first must be secured.

On February 1, 1898, the Union Pacific Railroad Company, organized during the previous July, assumed the functions of the corporation formerly known as the Union Pacific Railway Company. It consisted of the road between Council Bluffs and Ogden. The old Kansas Pacific line again came under Union Pacific control on April 1, having been purchased, piecemeal, by the reorganization committee during the early months of 1898. On that date the Denver Pacific, from Denver to Cheyenne, was returned to the mother system along with two smaller pieces of track, one running between Leavenworth and Lawrence, Kansas, and the other from Brighton to Boulder, Colorado.[64] With this acquisition the system totaled 1,850 miles. During the following year some of the other branches, such as the Omaha and Republican Valley Railroad, the Kearney and Black Hills Railway—both in Nebraska—and the Union Pacific, Lincoln and Colorado Railway in Kansas, were recovered, bringing the new total to 2,855 miles. Within another 12 months control of the Oregon Short Line was again acquired so that, before the turn of the century, except for the absence of the Texas lines, the old system was generally recognizable on American railroad maps.[65]

Horace G. Burt, formerly of the Chicago and North Western Railway Company, was the Union Pacific's new president, but it was Edward H. Harriman, chairman of the executive committee, who had firm control of the corporation, and it was he who would be the chief architect in rebuilding a rail empire that had been scattered to the winds by the Panic of 1893.

November 1, 1897, might well be termed emancipation day for the Union Pacific Railroad. For over three decades it had suffered the effects of a difficult birth, followed by the growing pains of corporate adolescence: While its origins had roots in a national desire for a railroad beyond the Missouri, and the West had watched its development with eager eyes, the creature had matured under a cloud. A century after the completion of the original line, men on the street would still speak in pseudo-authoritative tones about the way it and other western roads had violated the national trust and had pocketed millions from unsuspecting taxpayers whose congressional representatives had failed to erect proper safeguards against the robber barons. Even release from parental control in 1897 would not silence such talk, and the old reputation would cling; but after this date the company could proceed under the highly vaunted rules of American free enterprise, relieved from some effects of political warfare at the national level.

In a sense the incorporation of the modern Union Pacific, accomplished at Salt Lake City on that July day of 1897, completed a circle. During that month western newspapers, most of which discussed the event, were filled with stories of an exciting gold rush in the Klondike. A new frontier beckoned, and a new period of inflation appeared to be at hand. There was talk of building a railroad to this latest bonanza, and of what benefits transportation would have serving the region with inexpensive haulage.[66] Such ideas turned back the clock three or more decades to a time when America had excited itself over the great things to come from a railroad across the plains and to the Rockies.

But in 1897 the Union Pacific and its connecting roads were busy hauling tourists, many of whom were bound for California. And when they accomplished this in a manner satisfactory to the public, a western newspaper was moved to remark, "It is a pleasure to be able to find, once in a while, an occasion to say a good word for the railroads...."[67] The comment came from an editor in Utah, a place that was celebrating the fiftieth anniversary of the great trek westward. It coincided with printed recollections of how

Brigham Young had sketched a possible railroad route along that dusty way to a new Zion.

The inferred criticism was not solely a Mormon attitude, or even a western attitude; it simply reflected a characteristic of human nature. The railroad, so cherished before it came, had become commonplace. As an artery, one that pumped commercial lifeblood into the community, it had built the countryside so subtly that those who took no special notice of the part the railroad played in their lives were frequently unaware of its significance. Youngsters who watched the passing trains might well have assumed that these thundering machines always had been there and that they were exciting not because they existed, but because they were big and made loud, steamy noises. A good many adults tended to experience somewhat the same emotions.

Perhaps, in 1897, it was only the ancients in western towns who could recall the day when ox teams toiled westward in a slow and expensive way, with loads of machinery or stocks of merchandise for new communities. If they remembered, they well knew it was the metal strips, threading and criss-crossing an undeveloped land, that accounted for a day in which modern young editors could take the railroad for granted and rather condescendingly find an occasional kind word or so to say about that faithful creature once known as the "Iron Horse."

Retrospect

At a meeting of professional historians held in Chicago during the summer of 1893, Professor Frederick Jackson Turner, of the University of Wisconsin, read a paper entitled "The Significance of the Frontier in American History." Although it occasioned no great stir among his listeners, and did not excite the profession very much during the next few years, the ideas it put forth would occupy considerable space in future American historiography. Noting that the census of 1890 had for the first time mentioned the absence of a definable line between settled and unsettled portions of America, the historian concluded that the frontier, as the nation had known it, was gone. From this postulation Turner moved to the theory that the existence of what he called "free" or unclaimed land, its steady recession, and the advance of settlement westward, explained American development.

By coincidence, the first of the so-called transcontinental railroads to cross the high plains and Rockies declared its insolvency within a matter of weeks after the historian had made reference to the closing of the frontier. While that action did not mean the end of the Union Pacific, it did indicate financial exhaustion, and a consequent reorganization. It also meant the temporary dismemberment of a system that had been assembled under great stress during the post-Civil War years, and the termination of an era in which geographic growth had characterized the road's history.

The Great Plains was the final challenge to frontiersmen who had for generations moved steadily westward. As they encountered new problems, certain modifications in method were called for, certain innovations were necessary. Most of the solutions originated in the ingenuity of the settler, usually with materials at hand. But when the Great American Desert was reached, the farmer-frontiersmen were obliged to seek help from industrial America. This last West was to be subdued only with the aid of new technology, and until the appropriate tools were available, the arid distances beyond the Missouri would stand as an impregnable barrier.

Curiously, Professor Turner, even in his later years, did not dwell at length upon the part railroads played in the advance of the trans-Missouri frontiers or in the final destruction of those frontiers. He did remark that railroads sent increasing tides of emigrants into the West, and that these facilities provided a foundation for economic empires; however, he elaborated very little upon the enormous impact of this, the major transportation utility beyond the Missouri.

In later years the academicians questioned whether or not the venture by the railroads into the Great American Desert was, at the time, premature. As one of them pointed out, the question involved a paradox, for, in the eyes of impatient Americans who had long dreamed of a rail connection with the Pacific Ocean, the project was long overdue; but from the viewpoint of those who were asked to put up private money to build the road, the time for such a venture was not yet ripe. If one takes into account the momentum of the westward thrust in American history and examines earlier economic enterprises in remote areas "out beyond," it becomes apparent that from the cold fact of probable success many a venture could well be called premature. Yet this never had stopped the dreamers from dreaming or public figures from talking in grand terms about the inevitability of eliminating the wilderness that lay beyond, and in the end it usually was the social gain to be accrued that governed the answer. As Robert W. Fogel pointed out in *The Union Pacific Railroad: A Case in Premature Enterprise:* "Clearly then, from a social point of view the Union Pacific was a most profitable venture. There can be little doubt that the government was economically justified in intervening to build a road that would not have been built by unaided private enterprise."

As for government participation in economic development, there is much historical precedent in the notion of subsidy to industry, whether in the form of protective tariffs on the national scale or in state aid to canals and railroads in the Ohio and Mississippi valleys. The latter efforts may have been premature, because they often resulted in financial disaster, at least from the standpoint of immediate or early successes. Nevertheless, internal improvements were viewed as a necessity in opening new sections of the country; and the use of "seed money" from governmental sources was not regarded as bad business.

In the trans-Missouri West, more than in any other of America's many frontiers, the economic endeavors by individuals or even by groups met problems so imposing that some form of initial subsidy was required to induce settlement. Cattlemen used the open range, a kind of subsidy by default in that free grass became the main base of their economy, acquired through the absence of objection from the landlords at Washington, D.C. Farmers and ranchers received subsidization through the Homestead Act and its many modifications. Miners benefited in a similar manner as they staked out claims in an otherwise unclaimed country and predicated possible success upon the fact that labor and equipment, and not land, would involve expenditures of money. Later, those men who made fortunes in lumbering operated in much the same way, assuming that the forests were either free or exceedingly cheap, and in labor lay the greatest cash outlay.

Where the problem of subduing the land was so large as to defeat private enterprise, the government entered the picture. Toward the end of the nineteenth century, when more marginal lands were under assault, a great interest in irrigation developed. The eastern word for this was "reclamation," or the process of retrieving arable land from the desert for conversion into crop-bearing farms. The millions of dollars the government poured into the erection of great dams and other facilities designed to "reclaim" the countryside might also be termed "premature enterprise," even though it was understood that the cost of such projects was to be repaid by water users over many years. If rescuing the lands from the desert through the use of technology and encouragement by the government was "reclamation," then the process might be said to have begun during the summer of 1865 as the first tracks of the Union Pacific were placed on Nebraska sod. It was here that American technology commenced a real penetration of the nation's remaining wilderness.

Whether the final westering was accomplished in a manner that would meet the approval of later generations is not the central question. Men who lived in the post-Civil War era undertook the task in the manner they knew best, and if their method would one day be subject to criticism, there is also to be considered the happier side of the story. The latter part of the nineteenth century was a time of enormous American expansion, the climax of manifest destiny, the realization of the "American dream" as envisioned by men of that early day. This period was not one of territorial expansion only, it was one of great industrial and commercial growth, much of which depended heavily upon the utilization of western resources.

In this, the greatest period of American business growth, the West played a key role by furnishing a large portion of the incentive as well as the materials upon which the economic success of the era rested. It was the system of railroads, built rapidly in answer to the American public's impatient demand, that interlinked a land once regarded as sterile desert. Along these ribs of steel grew the national structure that completed a task begun generations earlier.

ACKNOWLEDGMENTS

The author of a book such as this finds himself in a position similar to that of a railroad locomotive engineer. He is the man who, with a wave of the cap and moan of the whistle, puts the machinery into motion and sends it along the track. However, the engineer is but a small part of the whole operation, from the road's construction to its operation and maintenance. Those who keep him in his job usually go unheralded and unnoticed.

A great many people have been involved in this book. For the many favors they volunteered and for the much needed help they gave, just as a matter of course and with no other motive than their willingness to participate, they are due both acknowledgment and the warmest of thanks.

I have touched upon the part played by Mr. Harriman and Mr. Gray, in my introduction. The latter, who is both an attorney and a man of some experience in the world of publication, stayed in constant touch with the project. His understanding of the problems in such a work, and his genial cooperation in finding solutions, made "construction days" much easier for me. Thanks go also to Frank E. Barnett, who is now chairman of the board, and to Robert A. Lovett, who was chairman of the executive committee when the project was first discussed.

At the company's offices in Omaha are others who lent enthusiastic encouragement and help, foremost among whom are Mr. Edd H. Bailey, the president, and those who manage his public relations department; namely Edwin C. Schafer, Barry B. Combs, and Richard Tincher. Barry, who has done some historical writing of his own, not only dredged up material, but served as a highly responsive sounding board as we frequently argued the pros and cons of western railroad history long into the night. George J. Skorney, of the Portland office, and C. R. "Rocky" Rockwell, at Salt Lake City—both in public relations—also offered enthusiastic assistance. Also to be mentioned are Francis J. Melia (Omaha) and Randall B. Kester

(Portland), of the firm's legal department. The maps were prepared by Nicholas F. Mraz of the U.P. engineering department. And there are others, too numerous for individual mention, who helped that strange fellow, "the Professor," in his excavations carried out in the company's offices.

The state historical societies and other libraries in the region possess much information, all of which came to the top as cream rises in the milk, as the staffs at each institution went to work upon receiving a request for help. Nyle Miller, the affable "old pro" who manages the Kansas Historical Society, is a long-time friend; he and his crew turned the place inside out in an effort to be of assistance. The people at the Missouri Historical Society, particularly Alma Vaughan of the newspaper division, were no less enthusiastic. Richard M. Kolbet, of the University of Iowa Libraries (Iowa City), opened the Leonard Collection to me and made a number of useful suggestions, as did Mrs. Aloys Gilman of the Iowa State Department of History and Archives (Des Moines). Duane Reed, at the Nebraska Historical Society, supplied everything from free coffee, pipe tobacco and matches, to the use of the organization's fine documentary collection. Mary K. Dempsey of the Montana Historical Society and Merle Wells of the Idaho Historical Society did much the same thing. The staffs of the Denver Public Library and the Newberry Library (Chicago) made the author most welcome, as always. The Wyoming Department of Archives and History (Cheyenne) and the University of Wyoming Western History Research Center (Laramie) helped me on numerous occasions. The latter establishment is managed by Gene Gressley, an enterprising and capable Western historian who has contributed much to his field of interest.

The library at home base in Boulder was, as always, cheerfully helpful. Ralph Ellsworth, who captains a delightfully loose ship, put up with my many special requests. His staff, particularly Martha Campbell of the documents division, again earned my gratitude for taking an interest in this latest project. Equally ready to be of help was John Brennan, of the library's Western History Collections.

Special acknowledgment goes to the people of Utah who are, in my eyes, truly "Saints." A. Will Lund and Earl Olson, of the LDS Church library, are old friends who have stood by me in my railroad research for some 15 years. The entire staff of the Utah State Historical Society gave constant assistance, as did Professor Leonard J. Arrington, of Utah State University (Logan).

Some of my graduate students were enslaved and put to work on the project. Craig Miner, Norman Bender, Gordon Chappell, David Rowe, and David Halaas served as academic gandy dancers on the project. Those who had not yet contracted railroad fever fell victim to it before the task was completed. The ladies' auxiliary, Barbara Kirtland and Virginia Grieder, typed the manuscript.

The Huntington Library's Ray Allen Billington, "Dean of Western Historians" and a friend of many years, pointed out sources that had escaped my attention and helped in other ways.

My wife, Claire, who has spent the past 20 years raising two children as well as helping her husband, returned to full-time duty as proofreader and critic. She has not lost her touch.

I would like also to acknowledge permission given by *Montana: The Magazine of Western History, The Utah Historical Quarterly,* and *Idaho Yesterdays,* to reproduce here several chapters earlier published as articles in those journals.

I began my acknowledgments by comparing the author to a locomotive engineer, who is the presiding hero of the moving railroad train. I would like to conclude by saying that he is also the responsible party when the contraption piles up in a spectacular wreck somewhere along the line. So, as the author, I assume full responsibility for all errors of omission and commission and even for driving too fast under existing conditions.

Robert G. Athearn
University of Colorado

NOTES ON SOURCES

Although the diversity of sources used for this book is great, the most important single source is the documentary collection held by the company at Omaha and to a lesser degree its records at Portland, Oregon. Concentrating on this core of materials I worked outward, filling in necessary gaps from holdings in other depositories.

In citing the railroad's collected materials at Omaha and Portland I have used UPA (for the term "Union Pacific Archives") and have added "Portland," to delineate the Oregon-held documents. To use the term archives is an exaggeration because the company has no archivist and the documents remain in nine-inch by eleven-inch volumes frequently used by nineteenth century business firms for the preservation of their correspondence. Some volumes contain incoming correspondence simply glued into the books; in the case of outgoing correspondence the letters have been copied into the familiar letter-press tissue-sheeted volumes formerly used in lieu of carbon copies. The Omaha collection, by far the larger of the two, is arranged in chronological order and occupies approximately 100 lineal feet of shelf space in the firm's museum vault. In time it extends from 1862 to 1893 (receivership) and, with a few exceptions, slightly beyond that date. In all, there are slightly more than 400 volumes. The Portland material is concerned with the predecessors of the Oregon Short Line and the many branches that grew from this principal extension. It is housed in the company's legal department in that city. To the best of my knowledge neither of these collections has ever been used by historians or writers of historical works.

The richest and most revealing information to be found in the railroad's manuscript material is in the correspondence of the company's principal officers. The president's office, for example, usually preserved both incoming and outgoing letters, although this varies with the succeeding administrations. The most complete collections of these letters are from the administrations of Oliver Ames, Sidney Dillon, and Charles Francis Adams, Jr. The letters contain not only descriptions of policy making, but comments relating to a wide variety of miscellaneous matters. There is also correspondence from the office of the vice presidents. The presidents—Adams, in particular—frequently delegated authority to their special assistants who sometimes carried the title of vice president, and bodies of their correspondence were placed in bound volumes under their individual names.

Departmental letters, such as those of the land department, are occasionally segregated, although only enough to frustrate the researcher. These letters are found in correspondence emanating from Omaha, as well as in volumes originally held by the trustees of the land department in the Boston office. Letters from the legal staff are both valuable and highly informative. These also are scattered throughout the collection and often are found under the name of an individual. Sidney Bartlett and John F. Dillon, counsels to the road at New York, and Andrew J. Poppleton, an Omaha attorney who represented the road, are examples.

Of less importance, but still useful, is a large and rather complete collection of correspondence from the secretary and treasurer. Sometimes these letters are found in a single volume under secretary and treasurer; in other instances they are separated into two departments. The assistant treasurer occasionally had a volume of his own correspondence, and here I have used the name of the man to identify the source, because that is the way it was set forth originally. A series of letters from Morton, Bliss and Company, financial representatives of the Union Pacific, contains information about day-to-day transactions. These cover the years 1872 to 1876. The Union Trust Company letters, 1875 to 1880, also are concerned with financial matters and are largely routine.

Although the branches and auxiliary lines of the railroad comprised a much greater mileage than the original trackage, comparatively little is to be found in the company's records dealing with these lines. Something of their history can be learned from the general correspondence, and in isolated instances branch-road records are available. An example of this is the Omaha and Republican Valley Railroad Company letters written between 1877 and 1880 by Silas H. H. Clark, who was both its president and the general manager of the Union Pacific. Available also are the minutes of the boards of directors for the Utah and Northern Railway Company (April 1878 to January 1884) and for the Oregon Short Line Railway Company (June 1881 to May 1889). Another associated company was the Boise and Nampa Canal Company, the correspondence of which

(1887–89) is to be found in the Union Pacific records at Omaha.

There is surprisingly little in the company's archives dealing with the building of the original line and in what there is of it, I found nothing that added materially to the well-known story of construction. Minute books of the directors covering the period from October 1863 to June 1867 were of use, as were copies of engineer Reed's correspondence in the Samuel B. Reed Letter-Press Book (1869). Two letter-press books of Thomas C. Durant's correspondence (1864–66) provided more color than information of significance. Minutes of board meetings, 1864 and 1865, for the Union Pacific Eastern Division (later the Kansas Pacific) contain some material hitherto unavailable for this portion of the system.

Of interest also was a volume labeled "Scrap (Circular) Book of the Kansas Pacific Railway, 1873–1877." Similar to this are bound volumes containing printed circulars of the Union Pacific, most of which contain rules, regulations, rates, and routine items. Factual details concerning the origins of the many branches are collected in a handy volume (mimeographed) entitled "Corporate History of the Union Pacific Railroad Company as of June 30, 1919," prepared in compliance with requirements of Valuation Order No. 20 issued by the Interstate Commerce Commission May 13, 1915.

The Church of Jesus Christ of Latter-day Saints Library in Salt Lake City was a valuable source. In citing letters and other documents held by it, I have used the term "LDS Church Library."

In this very large collection are materials from which several books could be written. I limited myself to that pertaining to the theme of the study at hand: the growth and development of the country through which the road and its branches ran.

BIBLIOGRAPHY

Unpublished Manuscripts

Boise. Idaho State Historical Society. "Ninety Years of Boyhood" [by Robert E. Strahorn]. A reminiscence, typescript.

Cheyenne. Wyoming Archives and Historical Department. "Cheyenne: The Magic City. From the Official Records" [by Louis and LaWanda Ash]. Typescript.

Colorado State Planning Board. "Union Pacific Railroad Land in Wyoming." W.P.A. project, Aug. 1938. Typescript held by Denver Public Library.

Des Moines. Iowa State Department of History and Archives. Grenville Mellen Dodge collection.

Helena. Historical Society of Montana. Samuel T. Hauser papers.

Helena. Historical Society of Montana. Martin Maginnis papers.

Iowa City. University of Iowa Libraries. Thomas C. Durant papers. Leonard collection.

Iowa City. University of Iowa Libraries. Samuel B. Reed letters. Leonard collection. Among these papers are copies of Reed's telegrams from June 11, 1867 to May 1868, and a hand-written manuscript covering period Oct. 1, 1866 to Sept. 1, 1867.

Laramie. University of Wyoming Western History Research Center. J. S. Casement collection.

Lincoln. Nebraska State Historical Society. Robert Wilkinson Furnas papers.

Lincoln. Nebraska State Historical Society. J. Sterling Morton papers.

Lincoln. Nebraska State Historical Society. Frank Joshua North papers.

Lincoln. Nebraska State Historical Society. Luther Heddon North papers.

Omaha, Nebr. UPA. Hoxie Contract. A copy of this much-discussed contract is in the Minute Book of Directors, Oct. 1863–Nov. 1867.

Salt Lake City, Utah. LDS Church Library, Manuscripts Division. John Sharp papers.

Salt Lake City. LDS Church Library, Manuscripts Division. Moses Thatcher papers.

Salt Lake City. LDS Church Library, Manuscripts Division. Brigham Young Letter-books.

Salt Lake City. LDS Church Library, Manuscripts Division. John W. Young letters.

Washington, D.C. National Archives. Record Group 48, Records of the Secretary of the Interior. Lands and Railroads Division: Selected Documents Concerning the Union Pacific Railroad. Film held by Kansas State Historical Society, Topeka.

Diaries

Bamford, John. Omaha, Nebr.: UP Railroad Company. Diary owned by Lloyd B. Horn.

Eldredge, Horace S. Salt Lake City, Utah: LDS Church Library, Manuscripts Division.

Ferguson, A. N. Cheyenne: Wyoming Archives and History Department. Film of typescript.

Middleton, Charles F. Salt Lake City: LDS Church Library, Manuscripts Division.

Smith, O. C. Salt Lake City. Courtesy Ellsworth W. Cardwell.

Thatcher, Moses. Salt Lake City: LDS Church Library, 1866–81. Microfilm.

Unpublished Dissertations and Theses

Anderson, Helen Marie. "The Influence of Railway Advertising Upon the Settle-ment of Nebraska." M.A. thesis, University of Nebraska, 1926.

Crist, William Dale. "The Role of Railroads in the Economic Development of Early Nebraska." M.A. thesis, University of Nebraska, 1962.

Curl, Thelma Jean. "Promotional Efforts of the Kansas Pacific and Santa Fe to Settle Kansas." M.A. thesis, University of Kansas, 1960.

Edrington, L. Kay. "A Study of Early Utah-Montana Trade, Transportation, and Communication, 1847–1881." M.A. thesis, Brigham Young University, 1959.

Emmons, David. "The Boomers Frontier: Land Promotion and Settlement of the Central Plains, 1854–1893." Ph.D. dissertation, University of Colorado, 1969.

Hakola, John W. "Samuel T. Hauser and the Economic Development of Montana: A Case Study in Nineteenth-Century Frontier Capitalism." Ph.D. dissertation, Indiana University, 1961.

Jakl, Mary Ann. "The Immigration and Population of Nebraska to 1870." M.A. thesis, University of Nebraska, 1936.

Jelen, Josephine. "Towns and Townsites in Territorial Nebraska, 1854–1867." M.A. thesis, University of Nebraska, 1934.

Jones, Virginia Bowen. "The Influence of the Railroads on Nebraska State Politics." M.A. thesis, University of Nebraska, 1927.

Knudsen, Rudolph Alvin. "Regulation of Railroad Rates in Nebraska, 1867–1906." M.A. thesis, University of Nebraska, 1937.

Kutzleb, Charles Robert. "Rain Follows the Plow: The History of an Idea." Ph.D. dissertation, University of Colorado, 1968.

Lichty, Kathryne L. "A History of the Settlement of Nebraska Sandhills." M.A. thesis, University of Wyoming, 1960.

Mock, Samuel Donald. "Railroad Development in the Colorado Region to 1880." Ph.D. dissertation, University of Nebraska, 1938.

Petrowski, William Robinson. "The Kansas Pacific: A Study in Railroad Promotion." Ph.D. dissertation, University of Wisconsin, 1966.

Price, Mildred McClellan. "Building the Union Pacific Railway." M.A. thesis, Columbia University, 1929.

Ream, Virginia B. "The Kansas Pacific." M.A. thesis, University of Kansas, 1920.

Sellin, Lloyd Bernard. "The Settlement of Nebraska to 1880." M.A. thesis, University of Southern California, 1940.

Spence, Vernon Gladden. "Colonel Morgan Jones, 1839–1926: Grand Old Man of Texas Railroading." Ph.D. dissertation, University of Colorado, 1968.

Spencer, Morris Nelson. "The Union Pacific Company's Utilization of its Land Grant." Ph.D. dissertation, University of Nebraska, 1950.

Thompson, Leonard W. "The History of Railway Development in Kansas." Ph.D. dissertation, University of Iowa, 1942.

Traxler, Ralph N. "Some Phases of the History of the Colorado Central Railroad, 1865–1885." M.A. thesis, University of Colorado, 1947.

Tubbs, Verna Lee. "Settlement and Development of the Northeast Sandhills." M.A. thesis, University of Nebraska, 1957.

Printed Documents: Federal

Annual Reports of the Commissioner of the General Land Office, 1867–96.

Annual Reports of the Secretary of the Interior, 1865–97.

Annual Reports of the Secretary of War, 1864–84.

Reports of the Auditor of Railroad Accounts, 1878–80. The head of this department later was called "Commissioner of Railroads"; his reports are found in annual report of Secretary of the Interior.

Reports of the Commissioner of Railroads, 1881–89 (see preceding note).

Reports of the Government Directors of the Union Pacific Railroad Company, 1864–86. Sen. Ex. Doc. 69, 47th Cong., 1st sess. (Serial, 2336). During and after this period, individual annual reports are also found in Secretary of the Interior's annual report.

Miscellaneous Printed Documents: Federal

Laws of the United States Affecting Pacific Railroads. Appendix 3, Report of Commissioner of Railroads, 1883. House Ex. Doc. 1, Part 5, 48th Cong., 1st sess. (Serial, 2190).

Pacific Railroad Acts. Appendix 4, Report of Commissioner of Railroads, 1883. House Ex. Doc. 1, Part 5, 48th Cong., 1st sess. (Serial, 2190).

Report of the Committee on the Pacific Railroad, 1869. Sen. Rep. 219, 40th Cong., 3rd sess. (Serial, 1362).

Report of the Committee on the Pacific Railroad, Mar. 1878. House Rep. 430, 45th Cong., 2nd sess. (Serial, 1823).

Report of the Final Completion of the Pacific Railroad. Sen. Ex. Doc. 90, 41st Cong., 2nd sess. (Serial, 1406).

Report of G. M. Dodge, Chief Engineer Union Pacific Railroad, to the President and Board of Directors, Jan. 1, 1868. House Ex. Doc. 331, 40th Cong., 2nd sess. (Serial, 1346).

Reports of the United States Pacific Railway Commission and the Testimony, Vol. 2, 1888. Sen. Ex. Doc. 51, 50th Cong., 1st sess. (Serial, 2505).

Sixth Annual Report of the United States Geological Survey of the Territories (F. V. Hayden). Washington, D.C.: Government Printing Office, 1873.

Statement of the Indebtedness and Liabilities of the Union Pacific Railway Company, Jan. 13, 1897. Sen. Ex. Doc. 62, 54th Cong., 2nd sess. (Serial, 3469).

Transcontinental Railroads. History of Construction. Appendix 1, Report of Commissioner of Railroads, 1883. House Ex. Doc. 1, Part 5, 48th Cong., 1st sess. (Serial, 2190).

Treasury Department Report on the Internal Commerce of the United States (Joseph Nimmo, Jr.). Washington, D.C.: Government Printing Office, 1885.

Miscellaneous Printed Documents: General

Gazetteer and Business Directory of the Union Pacific Railway and Branches for 1890. Omaha, Nebr.: 1890.

Governors' Messages to the Legislative Assembly of Utah. Salt Lake City: LDS Church Library.

Journal History. Indexed. Salt Lake City: LDS Church Library.

Reports to the Stockholders of the Oregon Railway and Navigation Company, 1884, 1885, 1887, 1889, and 1899. Held by the company in its Portland offices.

Reports to the Stockholders of the Union Pacific Railroad (and Railway), 1870–1900.

Sheldon, Addison E., ed. *Nebraska Constitutions of 1866, 1871 & 1875,* Bulletin No. 13, Nebraska History and Political Science Series. Lincoln: 1920.

Pamphlets

Balcombe, St. A. D. *The Union Pacific vs. The People: The Truth of History.* Held by Historical Society of Nebraska. Lincoln.

Bromley, Isaac Hill. 1886. *The Chinese Massacre at Rock Springs, Wyoming Territory, September 2, 1885.* Boston.

————. 1886. *Pacific Railroad Legislation, 1862–1885.* Boston.

Chenoweth, G. D. 1874. *Special Report of a Reconnaissance of the Country for the Proposed Route of the Utah, Idaho and Montana R.R.* Washington, D.C.

Emigrant's Guide to the Kansas Pacific Railway Lands. 1871.

Gray, Carl R. 1935. *The Significance of the Pacific Railroads.* Princeton, N.J.

Guide to the Union Pacific Railroad Lands. 1870. Omaha, Nebr.

History of the Union Pacific Railroad. 1919. Omaha: UP. Held by Kansas State Historical Society.

Kansas: The Golden Belt Lands Along the Line of the Kansas Division of the U.P. R'y. 1883. Kansas City.

Loomis, Nelson Henry. 1923. *Facts About the Railroads.*

Poppleton, Andrew J. 1915. *Reminiscences.* Omaha.

Resources and Attractions of Wyoming. 1893. St. Louis: UP.

Seymour, Silas. 1867. *Incidents of a Trip Through the Great Platte Valley to the Rocky Mountains and Laramie Plains in the Fall of 1866.* New York.

Smart, Stephen F. 1879. *Colorado Tourist and Illustrated Guide via the "Golden Belt Route" etc.* Kansas City: Kansas Pacific Railway.

Union Pacific Railroad Across the Continent West from Omaha, Nebraska. 1868. Omaha: UP.

Union Pacific Railroad: The Great National Highway Between the Missouri River and California. 1868. Chicago. Held by Newberry Library, Chicago.

Union Pacific Tourist. 3rd ed. 1886. Omaha.

Woolfolk, A. M. 1876. *The Helena and Benton Railroad: Letters of Col. A. M. Woolfolk on the Railroad Question.* Helena, Mont.

Zider, H. F. 1869. *Report of the St. Louis Delegation to Omaha and Terminus of the Union Pacific Railroad, September, 1868.* St. Louis.

Newspapers

Anti-Monopolist, Grand Island, Nebr.
Boise Democrat, Idaho.
Butte Miner, Mont.
Central Nebraska Press, Kearney.
Cheyenne Leader, Wyo.
Chicago Tribune.
Colorado Chieftain, Pueblo.
Commonwealth, Topeka, Kans.
Daily Bee, Omaha, Nebr.
Daily Kansas State Journal, Topeka.
Daily State Journal, Lincoln, Nebr.
Denver Post, Colo.
Deseret Evening News, Salt Lake City, Utah.
Ellis County Democrat and Advocate, Hays, Kans. Printed in English and German in 1885.
Enterprise, North Platte, Nebr.
Evening Telegram, Portland, Oreg.
Frontier Index. A "traveling" newspaper printed along route of UP main line during construction period.
Grand Island Daily Independent, Nebr.
Helena Herald, Mont.

Helena Independent, Mont.
Idaho Statesman, Boise.
Junction City Union, Kans.
Kansas City Daily Journal, Mo.
Kansas Daily Tribune, Lawrence.
Keith County News, Ogallala, Nebr.
Lincoln County Advertiser, North Platte.
New North-West, Deer Lodge, Mont.
Platte Journal, Columbus, Nebr.
Platte Valley Independent, North Platte.
Portland Daily News, Oreg.
Railway Pioneer. Published for construction workers; e.g., the Oct. 25, 1866 issue was published at Camp No. 2, U.P.R.R., Buffalo County, Nebr.
Rocky Mountain News, Denver.
Salt Lake Daily Tribune, Utah.
San Francisco Chronicle.
Telegraph, North Platte.
Thomas County Cat, Colby, Kans.
Times, London. American Railway Number, June 28, 1912.
Wa-Keeney Weekly World, Kans.
Wallace County Register, Kans.
Weekly Standard, Portland, Oreg.
Western Kansas Rustler, Wallace.
Western Nebraskian, North Platte.

Articles

Adams, Charles Francis, Jr. "A Chapter of Erie." *North American Review* 109 (1869): 30–107.

————. "The Government and the Railroad Corporations." *North American Review* 112 (1871): 31–62.

————. "The Granger Movement." *North American Review* 120 (1875): 394–424.

————. "Railroad Inflation." *North American Review* 108 (1869): 130–65.

————. "Railway Problems in 1869." *North American Review* 110 (1870): 116–50.

Ager, J. H. "Nebraska Politics and Nebraska Railroads." *Proceedings and Collections of the Nebraska State Historical Society* 15 (series 2, no. 10): 34–44.

Allen, William Vincent. "Western Feeling Towards the East." *North American Review* 162 (1896): 588–93.

Anderson, Davis. "Early Settlements of the Platte Valley." *Nebraska State Historical Society Collections* 16: 193–204.

Arrington, Leonard J. "Utah's Coal Road in the Age of Unregulated Competition." *Utah Historical Quarterly* 23 (1955): 35–63.

Bailey, William Francis. "The Story of the Union Pacific." *The Pacific Monthly,* July 1908, pp. 67–75.

Barrett, Martin. "Holding Up a Territorial Legislature." *Contributions to the Historical Society of Montana* 8 (1917): 91–98.

Beal, Merrill. "The Story of the Utah Northern Railroad." *Idaho Yesterdays* 1, no. 1 (1957), 3–10; and 1, no. 2 (1957), 16–23.

Blackmar, Frank W. "The Mastery of the Desert." *North American Review* 182 (1906): 676–88.

Buchanan, John R. "The Great Railroad Migration into Northern Nebraska." *Proceedings and Collections of the Nebraska Historical Society* 15 (second series, 10) (1907): 25–34.

Church, W. C. "The Pacific Railroad." *The Galaxy* 4 (1867): 482–91.

Combs, Barry B. "The Union Pacific Railroad and the Early Settlement of Nebraska, 1868–1880." *Nebraska History* 50 (1969): 1–21.

Danker, Donald F. "The Influence of Transportation Upon Nebraska Territory." *Nebraska History* 47 (1966): 187–208.

Dillon, Sidney. "The West and the Railroads." *North American Review* 152 (1891): 443–52.

Farmer, Hallie. "The Railroads and Frontier Populism." *Mississippi Valley Historical Review* 13 (1926): 387–97.

Farnham, Wallace D. "The Pacific Railroad Act of 1862." *Nebraska History* 43 (1962): 141–67.

————. "The Weakened Spring of Government: A Study in Nineteenth Century American History." *American Historical Review* 68 (1963): 662–80.

"First Railroad Excursion to Nebraska." *Nebraska History* 1, no. 3 (1918), 6; and 1, no. 4 (1918), 7.

Fuller, E. O. "Cheyenne Looking North." *Annals of Wyoming* 23 (1951): 3–51.

Grey, Alan H. "Denver and the Locating of the Union Pacific Railroad, 1862–1866." *The Rocky Mountain Social Science Journal* 6 (1969): 51–59.

Harrington, Leonard E. "Journal of Leonard E. Harrington." *Utah Historical Quarterly* 8 (1940): 3–64.

Hazen, W. B. "The Great Middle Region of the United States, and Its Limited Space of Arable Land." *North American Review* 120 (1875): 1–34.

"Kansas Farmers and Illinois Dairymen." *The Atlantic Monthly* 44 (1879): 717–25.

Kline, Allen Marshall. "The Attitude of Congress Toward the Pacific Railway, 1856–1862." *Annual Report of the American Historical Association, 1910*, 1912, pp. 191–98.

Knight, Oliver. "Robert E. Strahorn, Propagandist for the West." *Pacific Northwest Quarterly* 59 (1968): 33–45.

"Laramie, Wyoming, and Its Industries." *Camp and Plant* 1, no. 2 (1902).

Larson, Gustive O. "Building of the Utah Central." *Improvement Era* 28 (1925): 217–27.

Leonard, Levi O. "The First Railroad Entering Montana." *The Union Pacific Magazine* 5, no. 6 (1926): 8, 9, 26.

Lewis, Sol H. "A History of the Railroads in Washington." *The Washington Historical Quarterly* 8 (1912): 186–97.

Ludlow, Fitz-hugh. "Through Tickets to San Francisco: a Prophecy." *The Atlantic Monthly* 14 (1864): 604–17.

Mahnken, Norbert R. "Ogallala—Nebraska's Cowboy Capital." *Nebraska History* 28 (1947): 85–109.

Morris, Ralph C. "The Notion of a Great American Desert East of the Rockies." *Mississippi Valley Historical Review* 13 (1926): 190–200.

Nordhoff, Charles. "California. How to Go There, and What to See by the Way." *Harper's New Monthly Magazine* 44 (1872): 865–81.

Pelzer, Louis. "A Cattlemen's Commonwealth on the Western Range." *Mississippi Valley Historical Review* 13 (1926): 30–49.

Poor, Henry V. "The Pacific Railroad." *North American Review* 128 (1879): 664–80.

Pyle, Joseph Gilpin. "Hill on Harriman." *The World's Work* 33 (1917): 368–80.

Roberts, Edward. "Two Montana Cities." *Harper's New Monthly Magazine* 77 (1888): 585–96.

Schmidt, C. B. "Reminiscences of Foreign Immigration Work for Kansas." *Transactions of the Kansas State Historical Society 1905–1906* 9 (1906).

Sheldon, Addison E. "Land Systems and Land Policies in Nebraska." *Publications of the Nebraska State Historical Society* 22 (1936).

Smith, Henry Nash. "Rain Follows the Plow: The Notion of Increased Rainfall for the Great Plains, 1844–1880." *The Huntington Library Quarterly* 10 (1947): 169–93.

Snell, Joseph W., and Richmond, Robert. "When the Union and Kansas Pacific Built Through Kansas." *Kansas Historical Quarterly* 32 (1966): 161–86.

Spearman, Frank H. "The Great American Desert." *Harper's New Monthly Magazine* 77 (1888): 232–45.

Spring, Agnes Wright, ed. "Western Tourism of Samuel Mallory." *Montana: The Magazine of Western History* 15 (1965): 68–79.

Stolley, William. "History of the First Settlement of Hall County, Nebraska." *Nebraska History* 27 (1946): 90 pp.

Utley, Robert M. "The Dash to Promontory." *Utah Historical Quarterly* 29 (1961): 99–117.

Warren, G. K. "Exploration of the Country Between the Missouri and the Platte Rivers etc." *North American Review* 180 (1858): 66–94.

Wise, Isaac Mayer. "Rabbi Wise: By Parlor Car Across the Great American Desert." *The Pacific Historian* 11 (1967): 17–27.

Wrigley, Robert L., Jr. "Utah and Northern Railway Co.: A Brief History." *Oregon Historical Quarterly* 48 (1947): 245–53.

Books

Ames, Charles Edgar. *Pioneering the Union Pacific: A Reappraisal of the Builders of the Railroad.* New York, 1969.

Arrington, Leonard J. *Great Basin Kingdom: An Economic History of the Latter-day Saints, 1830–1900.* Cambridge, Mass., 1958.

Athearn, Robert G. *William Tecumseh Sherman and the Settlement of the West.* Norman, Okla., 1956.

Aughey, Samuel G. *Sketches of the Physical Geography and Geology of Nebraska.* Omaha, 1880.

Bancroft, Hubert H. *History of Utah 1854–1886.* San Francisco, 1889.

Beal, Merrill D. *Intermountain Railroads: Standard and Narrow Gauge.* Caldwell, Idaho, 1962.

Bell, William A. *New Tracks in North America.* London, 1870.

Bowles, Samuel. *Our New West.* Hartford, Conn., 1869.

Boynton, C. B., and Mason, T. B. *Journey Through Kansas with Sketches of Nebraska.* Cincinnati, 1855.

Brockett, Linus P. *Our Western Empire: Or the New West Beyond the Mississippi.* Philadelphia, 1881.

Cafky, Morris. *Colorado Midland.* Denver, 1965.

Cochran, Thomas C. *Railroad Leaders, 1845–1890: The Business Mind in Action.* Cambridge, 1953.

Copp, Henry N. *The American Settler's Guide.* Washington, D.C., 1880.

Crawford, J. B. *The Crédit Mobilier of America.* Boston, 1880.

Crofutt, George A. *Crofutt's New Overland Tourist and Pacific Coast Guide.* Omaha, 1880.

Crossen, Forest. *The Switzerland Trail of America.* Boulder, Colo., 1962.

Curley, Edwin A. *Nebraska, Its Advantages, Resources, and Drawbacks.* New York, 1875.

Davis, John P. *The Union Pacific Railway: A Study in Railway Politics, History, and Economics.* Chicago, 1894.

Decker, Leslie E. *Railroads, Lands, and Politics: The Taxation of the Railroad Land Grants, 1864–1897.* Providence, R.I., 1964.

Derby, E. H. *The Overland Route to the Pacific.* Boston, 1869.

Dilke, Charles Wentworth. *Greater Britain: A Record of Travel in English-Speaking Countries During 1866–1867.* New York, 1869.

Dodge, Grenville M. *How We Built the Union Pacific Railway.* Reprint. Denver, 1965.

Donaldson, Thomas. *The Public Domain.* Washington, D.C., 1884.

Everett, George G. *The Cavalcade of Railroads in Central Colorado.* Denver, 1966.

Fite, Gilbert C. *The Farmer's Frontier: 1865–1900.* New York, 1966.

Fogel, Robert W. *The Union Pacific Railroad: A Case in Premature Enterprise.* Baltimore, 1960.

From Ocean to Ocean, Being a Diary of a Three Months' Expedition from Liverpool to California and Back, from the Atlantic to the Pacific by the Overland Route. London, 1871. Held by Newberry Library, Chicago.

George, Alfred. *Holidays at Home and Abroad.* London, 1877.

Gilpin, William. *Mission of the North American People, Geographical, Social, and Political.* Philadelphia, 1874.

Goddard, Frederick B. *Where to Emigrate and Why.* Philadelphia, 1869.

Greeley, Horace. *An Overland Journey from New York to San Francisco in the Summer of 1859.* Edited by Charles T. Duncan. New York, 1963.

Griswold, Wesley S. *A Work of Giants: Building the First Transcontinental Railroad*. New York, 1962.

Grodinsky, Julius. *Jay Gould: His Business Career, 1867–1892*. Philadelphia, 1957.

_____. *Transcontinental Railway Strategy, 1869–1893: A Study of Businessmen*. Philadelphia, 1962.

Hakola, John W., ed. *Frontier Omnibus: History of the West and Northwest*. Missoula, Mont., 1962.

Haney, Lewis H. *A Congressional History of Railways in the United States*. 2 vols. Madison, Wis., 1908–10.

Hatton, Joseph. *Today in America*. 2 vols. London, 1881.

Hayden, Ferdinand V., et al. *The Great West: Its Attractions and Resources*. Bloomington, Ill., 1880.

Hazard, Rowland. *The Crédit Mobilier of America*. Providence, 1881.

Hewitt, Randall H. *Across the Plains and Over the Divide*. 1906. Reprint. New York, 1964.

Hirshson, Stanley P. *Grenville M. Dodge: Soldier, Politician, Railroad Pioneer*. Bloomington, Ind., 1967.

Hollister, Ovando J. *The Mines of Colorado*. Springfield, Mass., 1867.

Howard, Robert West. *The Great Iron Trail: The Story of the First Transcontinental Railroad*. New York, 1962.

Hughes, Richard B. *Pioneer Years in the Black Hills*. Edited by Agnes Wright Spring. Glendale, Calif., 1957.

Jackson, Helen Maria (Fiske) Hunt. *Bits of Travel at Home*. Boston, 1878.

Kane, Lucile M., ed. *Military Life in Dakota: The Journal of Phillipe Regis de Trobriand*. St. Paul, Minn., 1951.

Kennan, George. *E. H. Harriman: A Biography*. 2 vols. Cambridge, 1922.

Kirkland, Edward Chase. *Charles Francis Adams, Jr., 1835–1915: the Patrician at Bay*. Cambridge, 1965.

Kolko, Gabriel. *Railroads and Regulation 1877–1916*. Princeton, N.J., 1965.

Kyner, James H. *End of Track*. Caldwell, Idaho, 1937. Reprint. Lincoln, Nebr.: University of Nebraska Press, 1960.

Larson, T. A. *History of Wyoming*. Lincoln, Nebr., 1965.

Leonard, Levi O., and Johnson, Jack T. *A Railroad to the Sea*. Iowa City, 1939.

Marcy, Randolph B. *Border Reminiscences*. New York, 1872.

McCague, James. *Moguls and Iron Men: The Story of the First Transcontinental Railroad*. New York, 1964.

Minturn, William. *Travels West*. London, 1877.

Morton, J. Sterling. *Illustrated History of Nebraska*. 3 vols. Lincoln, 1907.

Neff, Andrew L. *History of Utah 1847 to 1869*. Salt Lake City, 1940.

Olson, James C. *J. Sterling Morton*. Lincoln, 1942.

Onderdonk, James L. *Idaho Facts and Statistics*. San Francisco, 1885.

Overton, Richard. *Burlington Route: A History of the Burlington Lines*. New York, 1965.

_____. *Burlington West: a Colonization History of the Burlington Railroad.* Cambridge, 1941.

_____. *Gulf to Rockies: the Heritage of the Fort Worth and Denver-Colorado and Southern Railways, 1861–1898.* Austin, Tex., 1953.

Pabor, William E. *Colorado as an Agricultural State.* New York, 1883.

Park, William Lee. *Pioneer Pathways to the Pacific.* Clare, Mich., 1935.

Peto, Morton. *The Resources and Prospects of America.* London, 1866.

Pine, George. *Beyond the West.* Utica, N.Y., 1871.

Pomeroy, Earl S. *The Pacific Slope.* New York, 1965.

Poor, M. C. *The Denver, South Park and Pacific.* Denver, 1949.

Rae, W. F. *Westward by Rail: The New Route to the East.* New York, 1871.

Richardson, Leon Burr. *William E. Chandler: Republican.* New York, 1940.

Ricks, Joel E., ed. *The History of a Valley: Cache Valley, Utah-Idaho.* Logan, Utah, 1956.

Riegel, Robert E. *The Story of the Western Railroads.* New York, 1926.

Sabin, Edwin L. *Building the Pacific Railway.* Philadelphia, 1919.

Sarnoff, Paul. *Russell Sage: The Money King.* New York, 1965.

Sheldon, Addison E. *Nebraska: The Land and the People.* 3 vols. Chicago, 1931.

Simonin, Louis L. *The Rocky Mountain West in 1867.* Translated by Wilson O. Clough. Lincoln, 1966.

Smith, Joseph Fielding. *Essentials in Church History.* Salt Lake City, 1922.

Stewart, John J. *The Iron Trail to the Golden Spike.* Salt Lake City, 1969.

Strahorn, Robert E. *A Handbook of Wyoming, and Guide to the Black Hills and Big Horn Regions.* Cheyenne, 1877.

_____. *Montana and Yellowstone National Park.* Kansas City, Mo., 1881.

_____. *The Resources and Attractions of Idaho Territory.* Boise, 1881.

_____. *To the Rockies and Beyond, or a Summer on the Union Pacific Railway and Branches.* Omaha, 1878.

Stuart, Granville. *Forty Years on the Frontier.* Edited by Paul C. Phillips. Glendale, 1957.

Taylor, Bayard. *Colorado: A Summer Trip.* New York, 1867.

Thayer, William M. *Marvels of the New West.* Norwich, Conn., 1890.

Tice, John H. *Over the Plains and on the Mountains.* St. Louis, 1872.

Trottman, Nelson. *History of the Union Pacific: A Financial and Economic Survey.* 1923. Reprint. New York, 1966.

Tullidge, Edward W. *History of Salt Lake City.* Salt Lake City, 1886.

Van Oss, S. F. *American Railroads as Investments: A Handbook for Investors in American Railroad Securities.* London, 1893.

Van Tramp, John C. *Prairie and Rocky Mountain Adventures, or Life in the West.* Columbus, Ohio, 1869.

Warrum, Noble, ed. *Utah Since Statehood.* 4 vols. Chicago, 1919.

White, Henry Kirke. *History of the Union Pacific Railway.* Chicago, 1895.

Whitney, Orson F. *History of Utah.* 4 vols. Salt Lake City, 1892–1904.

Wilber, C. D. *The Great Valleys and Prairies of Nebraska and the Northwest.* Omaha, 1881.

Williams, Henry T. *The Pacific Tourist.* New York, 1876.

NOTES AND REFERENCES

CHAPTER ONE

1. Randall H. Hewitt, *Across the Plains and Over the Divide* (1906, 1964), pp. 74, 95, 101, 109, 128, 230.
2. "The Pacific Railroad," *North American Review,* Vol. CLXX (Jan. 1856), pp. 214, 235–36.
3. Gouverneur K. Warren, "Exploration of the Country Between the Missouri and the Platte," *North American Review,* Vol. CLXXX (July 1858), pp. 68, 81, 93. See also Warren's Report in Sen. Ex. Doc. 2, Vol. 2, Part II, 35th Cong., 2nd sess., p. 645.
4. John C. Van Tramp, *Prairie and Rocky Mountain Adventures, or Life in the West* (Columbus, Ohio, 1869), pp. 278–79, 300–1.
5. Greeley's estimate was close. According to Rowland G. Hazard in his book *The Crédit Mobilier* (Providence, R.I., 1881, p. 25) the average amount spent by the government for transporting troops, supplies, and mail to the plains and California in the 5 years before 1862 was $7 million a year. The railroad later cut this by $5 million a year. In 1865 the cost of wagon freight from Omaha to Salt Lake City was $27 per hundred pounds. By the 1880s the railroad was charging one-tenth that amount. See also Henry V. Poor, "The Pacific Railroad," *North American Review,* Vol. CXXVIII (June 1879), pp. 669–70.
6. Message of Gov. John W. Dawson, Dec. 10, 1861. Governor's Messages to the Legislative Assembly of Utah, 1861. Church of Jesus Christ of Latter-day Saints Library, Salt Lake City. Hereafter cited as LDS Church Library.
7. *Congressional Globe,* 37th Cong., 2nd sess. (Apr. 17, 1862), p. 1708; Poor, *op. cit.,* p. 667.
8. *Congressional Globe,* 35th Cong., 1st sess. (Apr. 14, 1858), pp. 1581, 1582.
9. *Ibid.,* p. 1584.
10. *Ibid.,* 32nd Cong., 2nd sess. (Jan. 17, 1853), p. 318.
11. For a fuller discussion of the legislation of 1862 see Wallace D. Farnham, "The Pacific Railroad Act of 1862," *Nebraska History,* Vol. 43, No. 3 (Sept. 1962), pp. 141–67; Robert W. Fogel, *The Union Pacific Railroad: A Case in Premature Enterprise* (Baltimore, 1960), chap. 2; Allen M. Kline, "The Attitude

of Congress Toward the Pacific Railway, 1856–1862," *Annual Report of the American Historical Association, 1910* (Washington, D.C., 1912), pp. 191–98.

12. The temporary officers were William B. Ogden, railroad organizer and former Chicago mayor, president; Henry Varnum Poor, editor of the *American Railroad Journal,* secretary; and Thomas W. Olcutt, of New York, treasurer. Report of Lt. Col. James H. Simpson, in Report of the Secretary of the Interior, 1865. House Ex. Doc. 1, 39th Cong., 1st sess. (Serial, 1248), p. 871.

13. Poor, *op. cit.,* p. 668.

14. Minute Book of Directors, Oct. 1863—June 1867, Union Pacific Archives, Omaha, pp. 7–15. Hereafter cited as UPA.

15. Report of Lt. Col. James H. Simpson, *op. cit.,* p. 872; Wesley S. Griswold, *A Work of Giants* (New York, 1962); James McCague, *Moguls and Iron Men* (New York, 1964); Robert West Howard, *The Great Iron Trail* (New York, 1962); Fogel, *op. cit.*

16. Minute Book of Directors, *op. cit.,* p. 101.

17. Hazard, *op. cit.,* p. 13.

18. For example, see Robert E. Riegel, *The Story of the Western Railroads* (New York, 1926 and Lincoln, Nebr., 1964), pp. 73, 74.

19. Hazard, *op. cit.,* p. 10.

20. Testimony of Charles T. Sherman, Feb. 10, 1873, in Affairs of the Union Pacific Railroad Company, Report No. 78 (Wilson Report). Reports of Committees of the House of Representatives, 1872–73. 42nd Cong., 3rd sess. (Serial, 1577), p. 664. Hereafter cited as Wilson Report.

21. Hazard, *op. cit.,* p. 18.

22. Fitz-hugh Ludlow, "Through Tickets to San Francisco: A Prophecy," *Atlantic Monthly* (Nov. 1864), pp. 606–13.

23. William Lee Park, *Pioneer Pathways to the Pacific* (Clare, Mich., 1935), p. 111.

24. Testimony of Thomas C. Durant, Jan. 15, 1873, Wilson Report, *op. cit.,* p. 64; Hazard, *op. cit.,* pp. 13, 14; Fogel, *op. cit.,* pp. 58, 59; Nelson Trottman, *History of the Union Pacific: A Financial and Economic Survey* (New York, 1923, 1966), p. 30.

25. Park, *op. cit.,* p. 113.

26. Oakes Ames later testified: "Those of us who were willing to aid this great enterprise were under the impression our acts were praiseworthy and patriotic. We certainly hope we would make a profit, but we knew the risk was enormous. To give those who were willing to risk the capital required to avail ourselves of the assistance or reward offered by Congress, it was necessary that we should be our own contractors, and thus receive for building the road what Congress offered to any one who would do so." Testimony of Oakes Ames. Crédit Mobilier Investigation (Poland Report). House Report 77, 42nd Cong., 3rd sess. (Serial, 1577), p. 16. Hereafter cited as Poland Report.

CHAPTER TWO

1. Sir Morton Peto, *The Resources and Prospects of America* (London, 1866), pp. 305–6, 409.

2. In 1865 Secretary of War Stanton called for "the vigorous prosecution of

the work of the railroad to connect the Mississippi Valley with the Pacific coast as a military precaution and as a measure of economy, deserving the fostering care of the government." Report of the Secretary of War, 1865. House Ex. Doc. 1, 39th Cong., 1st sess. (Serial, 1249), p. 40.

3. Durant to O. D. Ashley and to E. Nye, Apr. 3, 1866; to J. J. Crane, Apr. 4, 1866. Durant Letter Press Book No. 2. UPA.

4. Poland Report, *op. cit.*, pp. 19–20. See also George R. Leighton, "Omaha, Nebraska," *Nebraska History,* Vol. XIX, No. 4 (Oct.–Dec., 1938).

5. On one occasion he told Oakes Ames "we need more money," and then advised the financier that he had just drawn upon him for $40,000 "which I will have credited to you on stock or on the notes of the U.P.R.R. Co. you have." Durant to Ames, Sept. 18, 1865. Durant Letter Press Book No. 2. UPA.

6. Hazard, *op. cit.,* p. 19.

7. Reports of the Government Directors of the Union Pacific Railroad Company, 1864 to 1886. Sen. Ex. Doc. 69, 47th Cong., 1st sess. (Serial, 2336), p. 5.

8. Durant to John E. Henry, Mar. 31, Oct. 23, 25, Nov. 13, 1865. Durant Letter Press Book No. 2. UPA.

9. *Nebraska Republican* (Omaha), Dec. 8, 20, 1865.

10. There was a feeling of great optimism over the value of land in the Omaha-Council Bluffs region that had prevailed for several years. Writing to a friend in the East, the commanding officer of Fort Rice, Dakota Territory, remarked: "Did I understand you to say that your father owned land at 'Council Bluffs?' It is very valuable now, a large city and daily increasing. It is the terminus of the Great Pacific Railway. Pres. Lincoln owns a great deal out there." Letter of C. A. R. Dimon, from Fort Rice, Dec. 16, 1864. Dimon Papers, Yale University Americana Library, New Haven, Conn.

11. *Nebraska Republican,* Oct. 23, 26, Dec. 11, 1865; Jan. 10, 1866.

12. *Ibid.,* Feb. 21, 1866; *Omaha Daily Republican* (formerly the *Nebraska Republican*) June 22, Aug. 22, 1866.

13. *Nebraska Republican,* Dec. 11, 1865.

14. J. S. Casement to his wife, Mar. 12, 1866. J. S. Casement Collection, University of Wyoming History Research Center, Laramie.

15. In the spring of 1866 Durant bought a riverboat at Pittsburgh, from Springer Harbaugh, and told the seller to load it with 1,000 kegs of spikes and some iron and send it to Omaha. The boat, named the *Elkhorn,* was registered in the name of T. C. Durant, President of the Crédit Mobilier of America. Durant to Harbaugh, Apr. 14, 1866. Durant Letter Press Book No. 2. UPA. Additional reading about Durant and some of the other leaders of the Union Pacific during this period may be found in John J. Stewart, *The Iron Trail to the Golden Spike* (Salt Lake City, 1969); see chap. 4, "The Men Who Built the Union Pacific."

16. *Omaha Daily Republican,* Oct. 16, 1866.

17. *Nebraska Republican,* Feb. 27, 1866; *Omaha Daily Republican,* Apr. 11, May 18, Aug. 4, 1866.

18. *Nebraska Republican,* Feb. 27, 1866; *Omaha Daily Republican,* Apr. 11, May 18, Aug. 4, 1866. Durant Letter Press Book, 1866, UPA.

19. *Omaha Daily Republican,* Aug. 22, 1866.

20. Samuel Bowles, *Across the Continent: A Summer's Journey to the Rocky Mountains* (Springfield, Mass., 1866), p. 19.

21. Diary of Moses Thatcher, entries of June 11 to June 16. LDS Church
    Library.
22. Bayard Taylor, *Colorado: A Summer Trip* (New York, 1867), pp. 10, 32,
    179–80, 184.
23. Report of the Secretary of the Interior, 1865. House Ex. Doc. 1, 39th Cong.,
    1st sess. (Serial, 1248), p. xii.
24. William Stolley, "History of the First Settlement of Hall County, Nebraska,"
    Nebraska History (Special Issue, 1946), pp. 75–77; *Omaha Daily Republican,*
    May 24, July 17, 1866.
25. *Golden Age* (Columbus, Nebr.), quoted by *Omaha Daily Republican,* Aug. 11,
    1866.
26. *Rocky Mountain News* (Denver), Oct. 4, Nov. 30, 1865.
27. *Ibid.,* Jan. 3, Mar. 21, 1866.
28. *Ibid.,* June 13, 1866.
29. Ovando J. Hollister, *The Mines of Colorado* (Springfield, Mass., 1867),
    p. 441.
30. *Rocky Mountain News,* Dec. 19, 1866.
31. *Ibid.,* May 30, June 6, 1866.
32. Report of Government Director, July 8, 1865 (Serial, 2336), Exhibit B, p. 9;
    Report of Government Director, Feb. 28, 1866 (Serial, 2336), p. 15; *ibid.,*
    Nov. 23, 1866, p. 20; *Omaha Republican,* Sept. 26, Oct. 20, 1866; *Nebraska
    Herald* (Plattsmouth), Aug. 22, 1866.
33. Report of Government Director, Nov. 23, 1866, *op. cit.,* pp. 23, 24.
34. *Rocky Mountain News,* Aug. 29, Sept. 19, Oct. 10, 1866.
35. O. H. Browning to Joseph S. Wilson (Commissioner of the General Land
    Office), Feb. 19, 1867, Report of the Secretary of the Interior, 1867, House
    Ex. Doc. 31, 40th Cong., 2nd sess. (Serial, 1330), p. 4; Minority Report of the
    United States Railway Commission of 1887, Sen. Ex. Doc. 51, 50th Cong.,
    1st sess. (Serial, 2505), p. 133.
36. *Rocky Mountain News,* Oct. 16, 1866.
37. *Ibid.,* July 11, 1866.
38. *Ibid.,* Oct. 31, 1866.
39. W. C. Church, "The Pacific Railroad," *The Galaxy,* Vol. IV (Aug. 1867),
    p. 485.
40. Memorial of the Dakota Legislature, Jan. 16, 1865. Sen. Ex. Doc. 14, 30th
    Cong., 1st sess. (Serial, 1237), pp. 10–12.
41. Resolutions of the Convention of Texas. House Misc. Doc. 88, 39th Cong.,
    1st sess. (Serial, 1271).
42. *The Idaho World* (Idaho City), Dec. 16, 1865; *Idaho Statesman* (Boise),
    Dec. 14, 1865.
43. *Idaho Statesman,* June 2, Nov. 6, 1866.
44. *Ibid.,* Feb. 7, 1867; Mar. 7, 1867, quoting *Reveille* (Reese River, Nev.).
45. Message of Charles Durkee to the Legislative Assembly of Utah, Dec. 10,
    1866. Governors' Messages to the Legislative Assembly of Utah, LDS Church
    Library.
46. Letter of J. H. Brown, July 10, 1866. Typescript, Thomas Clark Durant Manu-
    scripts, Nebraska State Historical Society, Lincoln.
47. *Omaha Daily Republican,* July 14, 28, 1866.
48. Advertisement over the name of Gen. Supt. Samuel B. Reed, *ibid.,* Aug. 23,
    1866.

CHAPTER THREE

1. *Omaha Daily Republican,* Oct. 25, 27, 1866; Silas Seymour, *Incidents of a Trip Through the Great Platte Valley to the Rocky Mountains and Laramie Plains in the Fall of 1866* (New York, 1867), pp. 83–84.
2. Boston *Journal,* Dec. 14, 1866.
3. *Commercial Advertiser* (New York), May 30, 1867.
4. The *World* (New York), May 29, 1867. The New York *Evening Post* of Oct. 31, 1867 called the UP "one of the safest and best investments." So did *The Independent* (New York) on the same date.
5. New York *Evening Post,* Oct. 31, 1867; New York *Evening Express,* Oct. 28, 1867; *The Liberal Christian,* June 8, 1867.
6. *Commercial Advertiser,* Oct. 31, 1867.
7. *The Liberal Christian,* June 8, 1867. The New York *Evening Express,* Oct. 28, 1867, also spoke of carrying the frontier of civilization deep into the wilderness.
8. New York *Daily Tribune,* Oct. 28, 1867; New York *Evening Express,* Oct. 28, 1867.
9. *The Saturday Evening Post* (Philadelphia), Nov. 30, 1867.
10. New York *Evening Mail,* Nov. 12, 1867.
11. For example, see New York *Evangelist,* June 6, 1867; New York *Evening Post,* Oct. 31, 1867; *Commercial Advertiser* (New York), Oct. 31, 1867; New York *Daily Times,* Nov. 1, 1867; New York *Evening Mail,* Nov. 12, 1867; *Home Journal* (New York), Nov. 20, 1867; *The Daily News* (Philadelphia), Dec. 11, 20, 1867.
12. Durant to Executive Committee, Feb. 13, 1867. Minutes of the Executive Committee, Apr. 13, 1865 to Feb. 26, 1869. UPA.
13. Tuttle to Ames, Feb. 19, 1867. Tuttle Correspondence, 1867–69. UPA.
14. Testimony of John Pondir, Reports of the United States Pacific Railway Commission and the Testimony. Sen. Ex. Doc. 51, Vol. II, 50th Cong., 1st sess. (Serial, 2505), p. 441. Hereafter cited as Pacific Railway Commission Reports. United States Pacific Railway Commission Report, 1887 (Serial, 2505).
15. Rowland G. Hazard, *The Crédit Mobilier* (Providence, R.I., 1881), p. 20.
16. Durant to Jay Cooke, Feb. 20, 1867. Tuttle Correspondence, 1867–69. UPA.
17. Copy of Resolution dated Mar. 1, 1867 in Tuttle Correspondence, 1867–69, UPA; Minute Book of Directors, Oct. 1863—June 1867, pp. 205–6, UPA.
18. Ham to Oliver Ames, Oct. 25, 1867. Benjamin Ham Correspondence, Letter Press Copies, 1867–70. UPA.
19. Lucile Kane (ed.), *Military Life in Dakota: The Journal of Philippe Regis de Trobriand* (St. Paul, 1951), pp. 15–17. J. S. Wilson, Commissioner of the General Land Office, accepted the population figure of 12,000 used by the local press. See Report of the Commissioner of the General Land Office, 1867, House Ex. Doc. 1, 40th Cong., 2nd sess. (Serial, 1326), p. 68; Omaha *Daily Herald,* July 21, 1867.
20. *Omaha Daily Herald,* July 21, 1867.
21. Casement to his wife, Apr. 11, 1867. J. S. Casement Collection, University of Wyoming History Research Center, Laramie.
22. De Trobriand, *op. cit.,* p. 17.
23. Silas Seymour, *Incidents of a Trip Through the Great Platte Valley to the*

Rocky Mountains and Laramie Plains in the Fall of 1866 (New York, 1867), p. 124.

24. Edward O. Parry (ed.), "Observations on the Prairies: 1867," *Montana: The Magazine of Western History,* Vol. 9, No. 4 (Autumn 1959), p. 24.

25. "Experiences of Thomas O'Donnell While a Workman in Building the Union Pacific Railroad." Typescript, Nebraska State Historical Society, Lincoln.

26. Richard B. Hughes, *Pioneer Years in the Black Hills* (ed. by Agnes Wright Spring) (Glendale, Calif., 1957), p. 24.

27. O'Donnell, *op. cit.*

28. O'Donnell, *op. cit.*

29. Frank Joshua North Papers, Nebraska State Historical Society, Lincoln.

30. Durant to the Postmaster General, Mar. 19, 1867. Tuttle Correspondence, 1867–69. UPA.

31. *Chicago Times,* Nov. 26, 1867.

32. Maurice Howe, "The Great West: Two Interviews," in John W. Hakola (ed.), *Frontier Omnibus* (Missoula, Mont., 1962), p. 262. The regular passenger rate at this time was 10 cents a mile.

33. Parry, *op. cit.,* pp. 25, 27.

34. O'Donnell, *op. cit.; Nebraska History,* Vol. VII, No. 1 (Jan.–Mar., 1924), p. 14.

35. Durant to Grant, May 23, 1867. Tuttle Correspondence, 1867–69. UPA.

36. T. J. Carter to O. H. Browning, July 23, 1867. Reports of the Government Directors of the Union Pacific Railway Company, 1864 to 1886. Sen. Ex. Doc. 69, 47th Cong., 1st sess. (Serial, 2336), pp. 33, 34.

37. Report of Gen. W. T. Sherman, Oct. 1, 1867. Report of the Secretary of War, 1867. House Ex. Doc. 1, Part I, 40th Cong., 2nd sess. (Serial, 1324), p. 36.

38. Louis and La Wanda Ash, "Cheyenne: The Magic City," typescript, Wyoming State Archives and Historical Department, Cheyenne, pp. 1–11; *Nebraska Herald* (Plattsmouth), Nov. 7, 1867.

39. Louis Laurent Simonin (trans. by Wilson O. Clough), "A Frenchman's View of Cheyenne, Ft. Russell and the Peace Conference of 1867," in John W. Hakola (ed.), *Frontier Omnibus, op. cit.,* pp. 320–21.

40. *The Cheyenne Leader,* Nov. 14, 1867; *The Chicago Tribune,* Nov. 16, 1867.

41. *Ibid.,* Nov. 24, 1867.

42. *Nebraska Herald* (Plattsmouth), Nov. 7, 1867; Report of Grenville M. Dodge, Jan. 1, 1868, House Ex. Doc. 331, 40th Cong., 2nd sess. (Serial, 1346), p. 18.

43. Louis and La Wanda Ash, *op. cit.,* pp. 1–10. Aug. 16 report by the Government Directors stated that the town had been laid off and that at that time the UP was selling lots. Report of the Government Directors, Aug. 16, 1867 (Serial, 2336), p. 35.

44. Jack Casement to his wife, Apr. 21, 22, 26, Aug. 1, 1868. J. S. Casement Collection, *op. cit.*

45. Report of the Commissioner of the General Land Office, 1868. House Ex. Doc. 1, 40th Cong., 3rd sess. (Serial, 1366), pp. 45–49. See also Frederick B. Goddard, *Where to Emigrate and Why* (Philadelphia, 1869), p. 156.

46. Casement to his wife, from Granger, Wyo., Oct. 31 and Nov. 6, 1868. J. S. Casement Collection, *op. cit.* On Aug. 17, he wrote that a succession of excursion trains had visited the end of track. A recent one contained "all

the Professors of Yale College and a lot of Rail Road men with their ladies."
He called the practice "a great nuisance to the work." *Ibid.*

47. *The Cheyenne Leader,* Aug. 14, 1868.
48. *Ibid.,* Aug. 15, 1868.
49. Samuel Bowles, *Our New West,* pp. 50–56; Government Director J. L. Williams, who inspected the UP in 1868, said the region was likely to remain without settlements along the road. Reports of Government Directors of the Union Pacific Railway Company, 1864 to 1886, *op. cit.,* p. 44.
50. *The Illustrated London News,* Aug. 15, 1868.

CHAPTER FOUR

1. For a discussion of this attitude, see Leonard J. Arrington, *Great Basin Kingdom: An Economic History of the Latter-day Saints, 1830–1900* (Cambridge, 1958), pp. 47, 82, 195, 236–40.
2. See Fitz-hugh Ludlow, "Through Tickets to San Francisco: A Prophecy," *Atlantic Monthly,* Vol. XIV (Nov. 1864), p. 615; *Nebraska Republican* (Omaha), Nov. 15, 1865. The *Republican* correspondent predicted that with the coming of the UPRR Brigham Young's "dissolution is inevitable."
3. Edward W. Tullidge, *History of Salt Lake City . . .* (Salt Lake City, 1886), pp. 708–11. See also "Journal History," Dec. 21, 1846. LDS Church Library.
4. Governor's Message, Dec. 12, 1853, "Governors' Messages, 1851–1876." Typescript, Utah State Historical Society.
5. Tullidge, *History of Salt Lake City,* p. 711.
6. Utah Territory, *Governor's Message to the Legislative Assembly of the Territory of Utah* (Salt Lake City, 1863).
7. *Millennial Star,* Vol. XXVI (Liverpool, Eng., 1864), p. 604.
8. *Governor's Message to the General Assembly of the State of Deseret, Fourth Annual Session* (Salt Lake City, 1865). After Brigham Young was replaced as governor of Utah Territory in 1857, the Mormons kept the dream alive of their State of Deseret through a rather novel device. Following each session of the Utah Territorial Legislative Assembly, which had been addressed by the federally appointed Gentile governor, the legislature would form itself into the legislature of the State of Deseret and listen to an address from governor of Deseret, Brigham Young.
9. Arrington, *Great Basin Kingdom,* pp. 236, 237; photostat, UPA; Letter of Dey to Young, Dec. 16, 1864, LDS Church Library.
10. *Millennial Star,* Vol. XXVIII (1866), p. 108.
11. Gov. Brigham Young's Message to the Fifth Annual Session of the State of Deseret, quoted from *Salt Lake Telegraph* in "Journal History," Jan. 22, 1866. LDS Church Library.
12. Letter of Wilford Woodruff in "Journal History," Dec. 12, 1866. LDS Church Library.
13. *Deseret News* (Salt Lake City), Jan. 22, 1867.
14. Arrington, *Great Basin Kingdom,* p. 208. Although the evidence indicates no teams were sent from Salt Lake City to the rail terminus in 1867, there was an emigration that year. Perhaps it was outfitted from eastern sources. The diary of Brigham Young, Jr., relates that he arrived at North Platte

Aug. 1 on his way home from Europe, where immigrants waited, "Impatient to be off, but we have no guns, and must wait for them," as he described it. Brigham Young, Jr., Diary, Vol. VII, *ibid.,* LDS Church Library.

15. Young to Franklin D. Richards, "Journal History," Jan. 25, 1868, LDS Church Library; Young to Edward Hunter, *ibid.,* Mar. 18, 1868; *Deseret Evening News* (Salt Lake City), Feb. 4, 1868; Arrington, *Great Basin Kingdom,* p. 208, estimated that the church teams brought in four thousand people that year. A further account of church wagon trains may be found in William Mulder, *Homeward to Zion: The Mormon Migration from Scandinavia* (Minneapolis, 1957) and P. A. M. Taylor, *Expectations Westward: The Mormons and the Emigration of their British Converts in the Nineteenth Century* (Edinburgh, Scot., 1965).

16. Brigham Young, Jr., Diary, Vol. VII. LDS Church Library.

17. *Millennial Star,* Vol. XXX (1868), p. 818.

18. "Journal History," Nov. 12, 1867. LDS Church Library.

19. *Deseret News,* Aug. 7, 1867.

20. *Ibid.*

21. *Ibid.,* Dec. 17, 1867.

22. Utah Territory, "Governor's Message to the Legislative Assembly of the Territory of Utah, Executive Office, Utah, Great Salt Lake City, Dec. 10, 1866," *Journals of the Legislative Assembly of the Territory of Utah of the Sixteenth Annual Session for the Years 1866–7* (Salt Lake City, 1866), pp. 16–22.

23. Utah Territory, *Journals of the Legislative Assembly for the Years 1866–7,* pp. 159, 161, 166–68.

24. Speech of Brigham Young in "Journal History," Feb. 24, 1868, LDS Church Library; Joseph Fielding Smith, *Essentials in Church History*... (Salt Lake City, 1922), p. 541; *Millennial Star,* Vol. XXX (1868), p. 189.

25. Telegrams, Reed to Young, Apr. 22; Young to Reed, Apr. 23, 24; Young to Durant, Apr. 22. LDS Church Library.

26. Brigham Young, Jr., to Richards in *Millennial Star,* Vol. XXX (1868), p. 27.

27. U.S., Congress, Senate, Government Director C. H. Snow, Reports of the Directors of the Union Pacific Railroad Company 1864 to 1886, Sen. Ex. Doc. 69, 47th Cong., 1st sess. (1881–82) (Serial, 2336), p. 61.

28. "Journal History," Nov. 18, 1868; Young to Joseph Little, Dec. 24, 1868, Letterbooks of Brigham Young, LDS Church Library.

29. Orson F. Whitney, *History of Utah* (Salt Lake City, 1892–1904), Vol. II, p. 277.

30. Letterbooks of Brigham Young, Aug. 28, 1868. LDS Church Library.

31. Correspondent from *True Radical* (Davenport, Iowa), written at Salt Lake City, May 31, 1868. *Deseret Evening News,* July 7, 1868.

32. U.S., Secretary of the Interior, Report of the Commissioner of the General Land Office (1868). House Ex. Doc. 69, 40th Cong., 3rd sess. (1868–69) (Serial, 1366), p. 67.

33. *Deseret News,* Nov. 19, 1868.

34. *Ibid.,* May 20, 1868. Editor George Q. Cannon reiterated this view in an editorial published in the *News,* June 10, 1868.

35. *Ibid.,* May 20, 1868.

36. *Deseret Evening News,* Aug. 10, 1868.

37. Samuel Bowles, *Our New West: Records of Travel Between the Mississippi River and the Pacific Ocean*... (Hartford, 1869), pp. 223, 227.

38. *Cheyenne Leader,* June 15, 17, 1868.
39. Young to George Nebeker, Nov. 4, 1868, Letterbooks of Brigham Young. LDS Church Library.
40. *Deseret Evening News,* June 2, 1868.
41. "Journal History," July 28, 1868. LDS Church Library.
42. *Ibid.,* Sept. 26, 1868.
43. Young to George Nebeker, Sept. 2, 1868, Letterbooks of Brigham Young. LDS Church Library.
44. "Journal History," Sept. 26, 1868. LDS Church Library.
45. *Ibid.,* Oct. 6, 1868; *Deseret Evening News,* Mar. 28, 1868.
46. Stewart to Young, "Journal History," Aug. 18, 1869. LDS Church Library.
47. Young to Carrington, May 22, 1869, *ibid.,* May 22, 1869.
48. Invoice in Union Pacific Railroad Papers (Aug.–Oct., 1869). Manuscript Section, LDS Church Library.
49. Utah Territory, *Governor's Message to the Legislative Assembly of Territory of Utah,* Jan. 11, 1869 (Salt Lake City, 1869).
50. Smith to W. S. Elderkin, Apr. 14, 1869, "Journal History," Apr. 14, 1869. LDS Church Library.
51. *Ibid.*
52. *Deseret Evening News,* Dec. 19, 1868.
53. *Ibid.,* Dec. 20, 1868.
54. Letter of Jaques, Aug. 16, 1869, "Journal History," Aug. 16, 1869. LDS Church Library.
55. O. C. Smith, Diary, June 29, 1869. Held by Ellsworth W. Cardwell, Salt Lake City.
56. *Deseret Evening News,* Mar. 19, 1869.
57. Smith to Elderkin, "Journal History," Apr. 14, 1869. LDS Church Library.
58. *Deseret Evening News,* Mar. 25, 1869.
59. *Ibid.*
60. *Nebraska Herald* (Plattsmouth), June 3, 1869.
61. "Journal History," July 17, 1869. LDS Church Library.
62. *Deseret Evening News,* Mar. 3, 1869.
63. *Ibid.,* Jan. 6, 1870.
64. Whitney, *History of Utah,* Vol. II, pp. 321–23.
65. E. L. Sloan, comp., *The Salt Lake City Directory and Business Guide for 1869* (Salt Lake City, 1869), pp. 189–220.

CHAPTER FIVE

1. Brigham Young, Jr., Diary, Vol. VII, Nov. 23, 1866 to Sept. 30, 1867, LDS Church Library; Brigham Young, Jr., to Franklin D. Richards, in *Millennial Star,* reproduced in "Journal History," Dec. 4, 1867, LDS Church Library.
2. Telegrams from Thomas C. Durant to Brigham Young, and from Young to Durant, May 6, 1868. Union Pacific Railroad Company Account Books File. LDS Church Library.
3. Contract between Brigham Young and Samuel B. Reed, May 21, 1868. LDS Church Library.
4. *The Illustrated London News,* for example, reported that Brigham Young

had taken the contract for "the Utah portion of the Pacific Railroad." *The Illustrated London News,* Aug. 29, 1868, p. 190.

5. Brigham Young to Franklin D. Richards, May 23, 1868. *Millennial Star,* July 4, 1868. LDS Church Library.

6. Casement to his wife, May 8, 1868, *op. cit.*

7. George Pine, in *Beyond the West* (Utica, N.Y., 1871), p. 345, wrote that over 1,000 Mormons had worked off part or all of the money they owed the Church for passage money already advanced by their railroad employment.

8. *Deseret Evening News,* May 21, 1868.

9. Samuel W. Richards to his brother Franklin D. Richards, May 24, 1868. *Millennial Star,* June 27, 1868. LDS Church Library.

10. Brigham Young to Franklin D. Richards, May 23, 1868. "Journal History," LDS Church Library. Mormon dependents were given a special rate, because of the grading contract. Durant told Webster Snyder, superintendent at Omaha, to transport passengers on Young's order at the same rate charged contractors, allowing 100 pounds of baggage to each and collecting half of this fare from children between the ages of 5 and 13. Durant to Snyder, June 8, 1868. Tuttle Correspondence, 1867–69. UPA.

11. *Deseret Evening News,* June 16, 1868.

12. Brigham Young to Heber Young, Oct. 22, 1868. Letterbooks of Brigham Young, LDS Church Library; *Deseret Evening News,* Dec. 15, 1868.

13. *The Cheyenne Leader,* June 17, 18, 1868.

14. Grenville M. Dodge, *How We Built the Union Pacific Railway* (Denver, Sage Books Paperback ed., 1965), p. 34. In an address delivered in the Tabernacle on Aug. 16, 1868 Young said the road might or might not come through Salt Lake City, but either way "it is all right because God rules and He will have things as He pleases. We can act, but He will over-rule." *Deseret Evening News,* Sept. 11, 1868.

15. Quoted in *Deseret Evening News,* Sept. 15, 1868.

16. *The Cheyenne Leader,* June 15, 1868. Mormon records substantiate the charge of paying in kind. A merchant of Gunnison, Utah wrote: "I deem it proper to acquaint you with the fact that people leaving work on the railroad grading at John Reidhead's contract are complaining of not getting their month paiment [*sic*] in cash, according to agreement, but goods is offered, in pretended absence of money. This seems not to be agreeable to the progress of the work on President Young's contract and if there is any improper speculation in it, on the part of John Reidhead I, as his partner in trade . . ., have no part therein." Christian A. Madsen to Bishop A. M. Musser, from Salt Lake City, Oct. 11, 1868. Union Pacific Railroad Account Books, Receipts, Estimates File. LDS Church Library.

17. *Omaha Herald,* quoted in "Journal History," Oct. 25, 1868. LDS Church Library.

18. Young to Samuel B. Reed, Sept. 22, 1868. Letterbooks of Brigham Young, LDS Church Library.

19. Unsigned letter dated Oct. 8, 1868. Letterbooks of Brigham Young, LDS Church Library. The letter appears to be in the handwriting of T. W. Ellerbeck, chief clerk in Young's office. The Church library contains 13 vols. of receipt books showing disbursements to subcontractors, and of monthly estimates for work to be done.

20. *The Cheyenne Leader,* June 15, 1868.
21. T. W. Ellerbeck to C. L. Frost (Assistant Cashier at Echo), Jan. 4, 1869. Letterbooks of Brigham Young, LDS Church Library.
22. Young to Durant, Jan. 16, 1869. *Ibid.*
23. Young to W. P. Kennedy (Cashier at Echo), Jan. 27, 1869. *Ibid.*
24. T. W. Ellerbeck to W. P. Kennedy, Feb. 10, 1869. *Ibid.*
25. John S. Casement to his wife, Feb. 8, 11, Mar. 8, 1869. J. S. Casement Collection, University of Wyoming Western History Center, Laramie.
26. Casement to his wife, Feb. 11, Apr. 6, 1869. *Ibid.*
27. Young to Durant, Apr. 2, 1869. Letterbooks of Brigham Young, LDS Church Library.
28. Young to Jens L. Jensen and Nels Hensen, Apr. 8, 1869. *Ibid.*
29. Casement to his wife, Mar. 3, 1869. J. S. Casement Collection, *op. cit.*
30. Casement to his wife, Mar. 12, 1869. J. S. Casement Collection, *op. cit.*
31. *Deseret Evening News,* Mar. 8, 1869.
32. Casement to his wife, Mar. 12, 16, 1869. J. S. Casement Collection, *op. cit.*
33. *The Cheyenne Leader,* Apr. 8, 1869. See also the issue of Mar. 30, where the charge was made that Young was trying to bribe the UP into making the junction at Ogden.
34. Nelson Trottman, *History of the Union Pacific: A Financial and Economic Survey* (New York, 1923; August M. Kelley Reprint, 1966), p. 64. By an agreement dated Apr. 9, 1869, the UP and the Central Pacific assented to a meeting place at "some point within eight miles west of Ogden to be hereafter mutually agreed on by said companies." The companies were to share any townsite at the junction. The UP was to complete tracklaying to the summit of Promontory, but the CP was to pay the UP the cost of the road from the terminus near Ogden to Promontory, allowing the UP to draw bonds as far as the junction of the roads. Any disagreements were to be put in the hands of three referees, one chosen by each road, the third named by the first two. Dated Apr. 9, 1869 at Washington, D.C.; signed by C. P. Huntington for the CP and by Rowland G. Hazard, Samuel Hooper, and Grenville Dodge for the UP. Copy in Hammond-Rollins Correspondence, Letters Sent, 1868–69. UPA.
35. *Deseret Evening News,* Apr. 23, 1869.
36. Memoir of Thomas O'Donnell, July 26, 1926. Nebraska State Historical Society, Lincoln. See also the recollections of Robert Grewell in *Nebraska History,* Vol. XVIII, No. 1 (Jan.–Mar.), 1937, p. 60.
37. Grenville Dodge to W. T. Sherman, May 10, 1869, William T. Sherman Papers, Vol. 26, Library of Congress, Washington, D.C.; *Deseret Evening News,* May 12, 1869.
38. *Deseret Evening News,* May 11, 14, 1869.
39. "Journal History," May 10, 1869, LDS Church Library; *Deseret Evening News,* May 11, 1869.
40. O. C. Smith, Diary, May 10, 1869. Held by Ellsworth W. Cardwell, Salt Lake City.
41. C. R. Savage, Diary, May 10, 1869. Utah State Historical Society, Salt Lake City.
42. Samuel Reed to H. Canfield, from Echo, May 15, 1869. Samuel B. Reed Letter Press Book, Apr.–Nov., 1869. UPA.

43. Charles F. Middleton Journal, LDS Church Library. For more details on events of May 10 see Robert M. Utley, "The Dash to Promontory," *Utah Historical Quarterly,* Vol. XXIX, No. 2 (Apr. 1961), pp. 99–117 and Bernice Gibbs Anderson, "The Driving of the Golden Spike," *Utah Historical Quarterly,* Vol. XXIV, No. 2 (Apr. 1956), pp. 150–164. The standard works, such as Griswold, *Work of Giants,* McCague, *Moguls and Iron Men,* and Howard, *The Great Iron Trail* also provide colorful details.

44. *Deseret Evening News,* Aug. 18, 1868.

45. Henry W. Moulton to Oliver Ames, June 12, 1869. Misc. Letters to Oliver Ames, Jan.–June, 1869. UPA.

46. Ames to Moulton, June 26, 1869. Misc. Letters from Oliver Ames, June–Aug., 1869. UPA.

47. Sharp to Carrington, Aug. 3, 1869. "Journal History," Aug. 3, 1869. LDS Church Library.

48. D. McKenzie to Joseph A. Young (who was in New York City) July 18, 1869. Letterbooks of Brigham Young, LDS Church Library. McKenzie was a member of Young's office staff.

49. Young to Oliver Ames, Aug. 12, 1869. *Ibid.* LDS Church Library.

50. Brigham Young to Joseph A. Young, July 21, 1869 and Young to John Sharp, July 21, 1869. Letterbooks of Brigham Young, LDS Church Library. In Sept. one of the Mormons commented that cash was so scarce that "we have returned, almost entirely, to barter in our trading." Comments of Joseph Hall, from Ogden, Sept. 7, 1869. "Journal History," Sept. 7, 1869. LDS Church Library.

51. Young to Sharp, Aug. 14, 1869. Letterbooks of Brigham Young, LDS Church Library.

52. *Deseret Evening News,* Aug. 24, 1869. See also a critical story in the issue of Aug. 3.

53. Brigham Young to Joseph A. Young, Aug. 25, 1869. Letterbooks of Brigham Young, LDS Church Library.

54. Brigham Young to John Sharp, Aug. 25, 1869. *Ibid.*

55. The little Coalville and Echo road, 4⅔ miles long in 1869, tapped the Coalville mines. It had a capital stock of $250,000 and was headed by Bishop W. Cluff. "The building of this line was undertaken by the counsel and advice of President Young," said *Deseret News* of Oct. 21, 1869.

56. Memorandum Agreement, Aug. 31, 1869, between John Sharp and the UP, in LDS Church Library; Ames to C. G. Hammond, Sept. 2, 1869, LDS Church Library; in Correspondence, President's Office, Letters Sent, Sept. 1869—June 1870, UPA.

57. "Journal History," Sept. 4, 1869. LDS Church Library.

58. Specifications of the Nounnan and Orr suit. Misc. Letters to Oliver Ames, Aug.–Oct., 1869, UPA; for the Bates suit see account in *Deseret News,* Sept. 16, 1869.

59. Hammond to Oliver Ames, July 27, 1869. President's Office, Misc. Letters Received, 1869. UPA.

60. Ames to Sickels, Nov. 14, 1870. Secretary-Treasurer's Office, Letters Sent, June 1870—Apr. 1871. UPA.

61. C. S. Bushnell to J. M. S. Williams, July 5, 1869. President's Office, Misc. Letters Received, Apr.–July, 1869. UPA.

62. Benjamin Ham to J. M. S. Williams, July 12, 1869. President's Office, Misc. Letters Received, Apr.–July, 1869. UPA.
63. Reed to Hammond, Nov. 3, 1869. Samuel B. Reed Letter Press Book, Apr.–Nov., 1869. UPA.
64. *Rocky Mountain News,* Sept. 14, 1869, quoting the Salt Lake *Telegraph.*
65. Sharp to Young, Sept. 30, 1869, John Sharp Papers, LDS Church Library; Young to Sharp, Oct. 7, 1869, Letterbooks of Brigham Young, LDS Church Library.
66. Reed to Oliver Ames, Oct. 8, 1869. Samuel B. Reed Letter Press Book, Apr.–Nov., 1869. UPA.
67. Young to C. G. Hammond, Sept. 30, Oct. 25, 1869, Letterbooks of Brigham Young, LDS Church Library; Hammond to Oliver Ames, Oct. 11, 1869, Misc. Letters to Oliver Ames, Aug.–Oct., 1869. UPA.
68. Young to Hammond, Nov. 25, 1869. Letterbooks of Brigham Young, LDS Church Library.
69. Young to Hammond, Oct. 20, 1869. Misc. Letters to Oliver Ames, *op. cit.*
70. During these hectic days UP Treasurer John M. S. Williams confessed to one of his colleagues: "My care & anxiety make me sick." John M. S. Williams to Benjamin F. Ham, Oct. 1, 1869. Treasurer's Office, Letters Sent, July–Nov., 1869. UPA.
71. Young to Hammond, Nov. 12, 29, 1869. Letterbooks of Brigham Young, LDS Church Library.
72. George A. Smith to N. S. E. Elderkin, Jan. 8, 1870. "Journal History," LDS Church Library. Smith was a councillor in the First Presidency of the Church.
73. George Teasdale to Albert Carrington in Liverpool, Mar. 21, 1870. "Journal History," LDS Church Library.
74. Sharp to Young, from Boston, May 5, 6, 12, June 1, 3, 1870. John Sharp Correspondence, LDS Church Library.
75. Sharp to Young, July 7, 1870. *Ibid.* In May 1870 Young was still trying to get Hammond to deliver the rest of the iron earlier promised. Hammond sought permission to do so from Ames. Hammond to Ames, May 11, 1870. President's Office, Letters Received, Apr.–Aug., 1870. UPA.

CHAPTER SIX

1. *New York Herald,* June 6, 1868.
2. *Ibid.,* June 10, 1868.
3. *New York Sun,* July 30, 1868; *New York Tribune,* quoted by the *Rocky Mountain News,* Sept. 30, 1868; *National Intelligencer,* Oct. 31, Nov. 6, 1868; the *Daily Chronicle* (Wash.), Nov. 26, 1868.
4. Letter from the Secretary of the Interior, Dec. 18, 1868, House Ex. Doc. 15, 40th Cong., 3rd sess. (Serial, 1374), pp. 15, 16; Report of the Secretary of the Interior, 1868, House Ex. Doc. 1, 40th Cong., 3rd sess. (Serial, 1366), pp. viii–xii.
5. E. H. Rollins to John B. Bloss, June 25, 1869, Hammond-Rollins Correspondence, Letters Sent, 1869, UPA; William E. Chandler to Oliver Ames, May 6, 1869, President's Office, Misc. Letters Received, 1869, UPA.

6. Charles Francis Adams, Jr., "Railroad Inflation," *North American Review* (Jan., 1869), pp. 144–47.

7. Report of Government Director C. H. Snow, Mar. 5, 1869. Reports of the Directors of the Union Pacific Railroad Company, 1864 to 1886. Sen. Ex. Doc. 69, 47th Cong., 1st sess. (Serial, 2336), pp. 59–62.

8. Letter of C. H. Snow in *New York Tribune,* undated issue in May, 1869, President's Office, Misc. Letters Received, Jan.–June, 1869, UPA; Oliver Ames to J. D. Cox, June 14, 1869, President's Office, Letters Sent, June–Aug., 1869, UPA; *Rocky Mountain News,* May 11, 1869.

9. Resolutions of the Legislature of Wisconsin, Mar. 5, 1869. House Misc. Doc. 9, 41st Cong., 1st sess. (Serial, 1402).

10. Report of Isaac N. Morris, May 29, 1869. House Ex. Doc. 180, 44th Cong., 1st sess. (Serial, 1691), pp. 5–18.

11. Rollins to William E. Chandler, June 29, 1869; Rollins to William Gowans, June 29, 1869; Rollins to John Duff, July 12, 1869; all Hammond-Rollins Correspondence, Letters Sent, 1868–69, UPA.

12. Report of the Final Completion of the Pacific Railroad, Sen. Ex. Doc. 90, 41st Cong., 2nd sess. (Serial, 1406); William E. Chandler to Oliver Ames, May 1, 1869, President's Office, Misc. Letters Received, 1869, UPA; John Duff to Oliver Ames, July 23, 1869, *ibid.;* copy of Joint Resolution of Apr. 10, 1869 (16 Stat. 56), in appendix of Report of the Secretary of the Interior, 1883, House Ex. Doc. 1, Vol. 1, Part 5, 48th Cong., 1st sess. (Serial, 2190), pp. 582, 583.

13. Isaac Bromley, *Pacific Railroad Legislation, 1862–1885* (Boston, 1886), pp. 15, 16; Report of the Final Completion, etc., *op. cit;* Report of the Government Directors, Oct. 30, 1869, *op. cit.,* pp. 82, 86; Report of the Secretary of the Interior, 1869, House Ex. Doc. 1, Part 3, 41st Cong., 2nd sess. (Serial, 1414), p. xvi.

14. William E. Chandler to Oliver Ames, May 11, 1869. President's Office, Misc. Letters Received, 1869. UPA. Chandler resigned as Assistant Secretary of the U.S. Treasury in 1867 and took up a law practice at Washington. He represented a number of interests, including the UPRR. In 1868 he was Secretary to the National Republican Committee. Leon B. Richardson, *William E. Chandler: Republican* (New York, 1940), pp. 82, 83.

15. Cornelius S. Bushnell to Oliver Ames, July 13, 1869. President's Office, Misc. Letters Received, 1869. UPA.

16. Benjamin F. Wade to Oliver Ames, July 9, 1869. President's Office, Misc. Letters Received, 1869. UPA.

17. Oliver Ames to Benjamin F. Wade, July 2, 1869. President's Office, Misc. Letters Sent, 1869. UPA.

18. Uriah H. Painter to Oliver Ames. President's Office, Telegrams Received, May–Oct., 1869. UPA.

19. DeHaven and Brothers to John M. S. Williams, July 23, 1869. Treasurer's Office, Letters Received, July–Oct., 1869. UPA.

20. E. H. Rollins to James G. Blaine, June 28, 1869. Hammond-Rollins Correspondence, Letters Sent, 1869. UPA.

21. James S. Rollins to Oliver Ames, Sept. 24, 1869. President's Office, Misc. Letters Received, 1869. UPA.

22. Uriah H. Painter to Rollins, June 8, 1870. Secretary's Office, Letters Received, 1870. UPA.
23. J. M. S. Williams to B. F. Ham, July 10, 1869. Treasurer's Office, Letters Sent, 1869. UPA.
24. Sidney Andrews to Rollins, from Washington, July 3, 1869. Secretary's Office, Misc. Letters Received, 1869–70. UPA.
25. DeHaven and Bro. to J. M. S. Williams, Oct. 25, 1870. Treasurer's Office, Letters Received, Oct. 1870—Jan. 1871. UPA.
26. J. M. S. Williams to the Ham Brothers of New York, Dec. 16, 1870. Treasurer's Office, Letters Sent, Oct. 1870—Mar. 1871. UPA.
27. T. C. Durant to W. Snyder, Dec. 5, 1867. New York Letterbook, 1867–69. UPA.
28. *Cheyenne Leader,* Aug. 29, 1868; *Nebraska Herald* (Plattsmouth), Nov. 26, 1868, quoting *Omaha Herald.*
29. *Rocky Mountain News,* Apr. 30, 1869.
30. *Cheyenne Leader,* Mar. 3, Apr. 15, 1869.
31. *Rocky Mountain News,* Aug. 17, 1869.
32. *Ibid.,* May 8, 1869.
33. Bliss was quoted in Goddard, *Where to Emigrate and Why* (Philadelphia, 1869), p. 544.
34. W. F. Rae, *Westward by Rail* (New York, 1871), p. 75.
35. Report of the Commissioner of the General Land Office, 1869, House Ex. Doc. 1, Part 3, 41st Cong., 2nd sess. (Serial, 1414), pp. 70, 72; Goddard, *op. cit.,* pp. 454–56.
36. Report of the Committee on the Pacific Railroads, 1869. Sen. Report 219, 40th Cong., 3rd sess. (Serial, 1362), pp. 12–15.
37. William M. Thayer, *Marvels of the New West* (Norwich, Conn., 1890), p. 276.
38. Journal of Peter Koch, *Sources of North West History* (Missoula, 1933), p. 8.
39. Samuel Bowles, *Our New West* (Hartford, 1869), p. 50. For example, the *Utah Daily Reporter* (Corinne) stated on July 10, 1869 that 28 emigrant wagons had recently passed through Cheyenne, westward bound. The paper seemed to feel that the situation was the railroad's fault.
40. Views of the Minority of the Committee on the Pacific Railroad, Feb. 9, 1869. Sen. Report 219, 40th Cong., 3rd sess. (Serial, 1362), p. 3.
41. Oliver Ames to C. G. Hammond, July 19, 1870. Secretary-Treasurer's Office, Letters Sent, June 1870—Apr. 1871. UPA.
42. Ames to T. E. Sickles, Dec. 14, 1870, *ibid.;* John M. S. Williams to Cyrus H. McCormick, July 20, 1870, Treasurer's Office, Letters Sent, Mar.–Oct., 1870, UPA.
43. Oliver Ames to Andrew Johnson, Dec. 1868. Letter from the Secretary of the Interior, Feb. 3, 1869. House Ex. Doc. 15, Part 3, 40th Cong., 3rd sess. (Serial, 1372).
44. Julius Grodinsky, *Transcontinental Railway Strategy, 1869–1893: a Study of Businessmen* (Philadelphia, 1962), p. 21. The Land-Grant bonds were purchased at 55; the First-Mortgage bonds at 85 and Income bonds at 80, the latter with a large stock bonus.
45. Cyrus H. McCormick to J. M. S. Williams, June 26, 1869. President's Office, Misc. Letters Received, Apr.–July, 1869. UPA.

46. J. M. S. Williams to C. H. McCormick, June 26, 1869, Treasurer's Office, Letters Sent, 1869, UPA; McCormick to Williams, July 13, President's Office, Letters Received, Apr.–July, 1869, UPA.
47. McCormick to J. M. S. Williams, July 21, 1869. Treasurer's Office, Letters Received, July–Oct., 1869. UPA.
48. C. H. McCormick to J. M. S. Williams, Aug. 30, 1869. Treasurer's Office, Letters Received, July–Oct., 1869. UPA.
49. Jay Cooke & Company to Ames, July 20, 1869. President's Office, Misc. Letters Received, 1869. UPA.
50. Frances L. Thomas to Ames, Sept. 1869. President's Office, Misc. Letters Received, Aug.–Oct., 1869. UPA.
51. Benjamin F. Ham to E. H. Rollins, Sept. 25, 1869. Letter press copies of B. F. Ham Correspondence, 1867–70. UPA.
52. DeHaven and Bro. to Union Pacific Boston Office, Dec. 20, 1869. Boston Offices, Letters Received, Oct. 1869—Jan. 1870. UPA.
53. Oakes Ames to J. M. S. Williams, Jan. 13, 1870, Treasurer's Office, Letters Received, Jan.–Apr., 1870, UPA; DeHaven and Bro. to Williams, Jan. 18, 1870 *Ibid.*
54. A. H. DeHaven to Oliver Ames, Mar. 12, 1870. President's Office, Misc. Letters Received, Oct. 1869—Apr. 1870. UPA.
55. C. G. Hammond to Oliver Ames, Aug. 15, 18, 1870. President's Office, Letters Received, Aug. 1870—Jan. 1871. UPA.
56. Grodinsky, *op. cit.*, p. 22.
57. The story of the Crédit Mobilier scandal has been told many times. It is of interest here primarily for the effect it had upon the future development of the UP. The indisputable result was one of serious detriment to the company and upon the efforts of the road's succeeding managers to work in the climate of opinion created by the affair.

    The basic documents dealing with the investigation are: Crédit Mobilier Investigation, House Report 77 (Poland Report), 42nd Cong., 3rd sess. (Serial, 1577); Affairs of the Union Pacific Railroad Company, House Report 78 (Wilson Report), 42nd Cong., 3rd sess. (Serial, 1577); Report of the U.S. Pacific Railway Commission, Sen. Ex. Doc. 51, 50th Cong., 1st sess. (Serial, 2505).

    See also the following secondary works: Nelson Trottman, *History of the Union Pacific, op. cit.,* has a well-balanced chapter dealing with the problem. J. B. Crawford, *The Crédit Mobilier of America* (Boston 1880); Rowland G. Hazard, *The Crédit Mobilier of America* (Providence, R.I., 1881); John P. Davis, *The Union Pacific Railway: A Study in Railway Politics, History, and Economics* (Chicago, 1894); Henry Kirke White, *History of the Union Pacific Railway* (Chicago, 1895). More recent is Robert W. Fogel, *The Union Pacific Railroad: A Case in Premature Enterprise* (Baltimore, 1960). He concludes that the Congressional investigating committees overestimated the profits alleged to have been made.
58. See *New York Herald,* June 8, 1868; Charles Francis Adams, Jr., "Railroad Inflation," *North American Review,* Jan. 1869; "Railway Problems," *ibid.,* Jan. 1870.
59. W. R. Story to Oliver Ames, Aug. 5, 1869. President's Office, Letters Received, 1869. UPA.

60. D. Harding to Ames, Sept. 13, 1869. President's Office, Misc. Letters Received, Aug.–Oct., 1869. UPA.
61. Uriah H. Painter to Oakes Ames, May 19, 1869. President's Office, Misc. Letters Received, Jan.–June, 1869. UPA.
62. James Davis to Oliver Ames, July 27, 1869. President's Office, Letters Received, 1869. UPA.
63. U. H. Painter to E. H. Rollins, Sept. 6, 1869. Secretary-Treasurer's Office, Misc. Letters Received, 1869–70. UPA.
64. Sidney Dillon to J. M. S. Williams, June 29, 1869. President's Office, Misc. Letters Received, Apr.–July, 1869. UPA.
65. William Lee Park, *Pioneer Pathways to the Pacific* (Clare, Mich., 1935), p. 126. Details of the argument between McComb and Oakes Ames may be found in the Poland Report, *op. cit.,* pp. 2–32. Rowland G. Hazard, *The Crédit Mobilier of America, op. cit.,* p. 33.
66. H. S. McComb to J. M. S. Williams, Jan. 31, 1870. Treasurer's Office, Letters Received, Jan.–Apr., 1870. UPA.
67. McComb to E. H. Rollins, Sept. 22, 1871. Secretary-Treasurer's Office, Letters Received, June–Oct., 1871. UPA.
68. E. H. Rollins to McComb, Oct. 9, 1871. Secretary-Treasurer's Office, Letters Sent, July–Nov., 1871. UPA.
69. McComb to Rollins, Oct. 31, 1871. Secretary-Treasurer's Office, Letters Received, Sept. 1871—Feb. 1872. UPA.
70. Testimony of John Pondir, U.S. Pacific Railway Commission, 1887 (Serial, 2505), p. 439.
71. Trottman, *op. cit.,* p. 73.
72. *Rocky Mountain Daily News,* Sept. 26, 1872.
73. *Ibid.,* Dec. 25, 1872; Feb. 12, 1873.
74. *Omaha Daily Republican,* Feb. 8, 1873.
75. See the comments of Auditor Theos. French in Auditor of Railroad Accounts, 1878, House Ex. Doc. 1, Part 5, 45th Cong., 3rd sess. (Serial, 1850), p. 862; Report of the U.S. Pacific Railway Commission, Sen. Ex. Doc. 51, 50th Cong., 1st sess. (Serial, 2505), p. 21.

CHAPTER SEVEN

1. *Rocky Mountain News,* Mar. 27, 1867.
2. *Ibid.,* May 8, 1867.
3. *Ibid.,* July 10, 1867.
4. *Ibid.,* July 17, 1867.
5. *Ibid.,* Nov. 20, 1867.
6. Ovando J. Hollister, *The Mines of Colorado* (Springfield, Mass., 1867), pp. iii, iv, 448.
7. First Annual Report of the Denver Pacific Railway and Telegraph Company (Chicago, 1869); Report of the Commissioner of Railroads, 1881, House Ex. Doc. 1, Vol. II, Part 5, Appendix 10, 47th Cong., 1st sess. (Serial, 2018), p. 578; *Rocky Mountain News,* Nov. 20, 1867.
8. *Rocky Mountain News,* Jan. 22, 1868; *Cheyenne Leader,* Feb. 29, 1868;

Glenn Chesney Quiett, *They Built the West: An Epic of Rails and Cities* (New York, 1934), pp. 158–60.

9. See chap. 10 in William Robinson Petrowski, "The Kansas Pacific: A Study in Railroad Promotion" (Ph.D. dissertation, University of Wisconsin, 1966). Testimony of Artemas H. Holmes. Reports of the U.S. Pacific Railway Commission, 1888. Sen. Ex. Doc. 51, 50th Cong., 1st sess. (Serial, 2505), pp. 131–32. See also *Cheyenne Leader,* Jan. 15, 1868.

10. Samuel Bowles, *Our New West* (Hartford, 1869), pp. 88, 89.

11. *Rocky Mountain News,* Nov. 4, 11, 18, 1868.

12. Petrowski, *op. cit.,* pp. 197, 198.

13. Petrowski, *op. cit.,* pp. 198–200. For the complicated story of the Denver Pacific's acquisition of the Kansas Pacific's land grant in northern Colorado and the argument about land lying between Fort Collins and Cheyenne see Petrowski, pp. 200–7.

14. *Rocky Mountain News,* May 17, Aug. 5, Oct. 5, 6, Nov. 9, 20, 1869.

15. F. M. Case to Oliver Ames, Nov. 30, 1869. President's Office, Misc. Letters Received, 1869–70. UPA.

16. *Rocky Mountain News,* Apr. 20, 1870.

17. *Ibid.,* June 22, 1870.

18. *Ibid.,* Apr. 6, 13, 21, 1871.

19. *Ibid.,* Aug. 1, 1871.

20. For attitudes expressed by the *Cheyenne Leader* see issues of Jan. 7, 16, Feb. 15, Apr. 13, May 9, June 13, 16, 29, 1868. In his report for 1868 Government Director Jesse Williams confirmed the fact that shops were being built at Cheyenne. Reports of the Directors of the Union Pacific Railroad Company, 1864 to 1886. Sen. Ex. Doc. 69, 47th Cong., 1st sess. (Serial, 2336), pp. 43, 44.

21. Bowles, *op. cit.,* p. 51.

22. H. F. Zider, *Report of the St. Louis Delegation to Omaha and Terminus of the Union Pacific Railroad, September, 1868* (St. Louis, 1869), p. 55; Anon., *Union Pacific Railroad: the Great National Highway Between the Missouri River and California* (Chicago, 1868), p. 9.

23. W. F. Rae, *Westward by Rail* (New York, 1871), p. 84.

24. *Cheyenne Leader,* Feb. 17, 1869.

25. George Pine, *Beyond the West* (Utica, N.Y., 1871), p. 180.

26. *Rocky Mountain News,* May 5, 1870.

27. A London Parson, *To San Francisco and Back* (London, n.d.), p. 49.

28. Church Howe to E. H. Rollins, Oct. 4, 1871. Secretary-Treasurer's Office, Letters Received, June–Oct., 1871. UPA.

29. Report of Oliver Ames, in Report to the Stockholders of the Union Pacific Railroad, 1870 (Boston, 1870), p. 7.

30. Bowles, *Our New West, op. cit.,* p. 54.

31. Letter of W. A. Carter, Aug. 2, 1868, in Frederick B. Goddard, *Where to Emigrate and Why* (Philadelphia, 1869), p. 156.

32. *Cheyenne Leader,* June 29, July 31, 1868; Rae, *Westward By Rail, op. cit.,* p. 92; Report of the Commissioner of the General Land Office, 1870, House Ex. Doc. 1, Part 4, 41st Cong., 3rd sess. (Serial, 1449), p. 128.

33. H. C. Crane to Webster Snyder, May 25, 1868, H. C. Crane Correspondence, 1868, UPA, copy of contract in Thomas Wardell vs. the Union Pacific

Railroad Company, Report of the Commissioner of Railroads, 1881, House Ex. Doc. 1, Vol. II, Part 5, 47th Cong., 1st sess. (Serial, 2018), pp. 593–94; Report of the Government Directors, Dec. 23, 1872, *op. cit.,* pp. 68, 69.

34. Report of the Government Directors, Dec. 23, 1872, copy of Board Resolution of Nov. 19 in President's Office, Letters Sent, Sept. 1869—June 1870, UPA; Oliver Ames to C. G. Hammond, Nov. 20, 1869, *ibid.*

35. *Deseret Evening News* (Salt Lake City), June 9, 1869, quoting the *Omaha Herald;* Oscar F. Davis to Oliver Ames, Feb. 1, 1870, Misc. Letters to Oliver Ames, Oct. 1869—Apr. 1870, UPA.

36. J. M. Eddy to Grenville Dodge, Nov. 27, 1871. J. M. Eddy Letterbook, Aug. 1871—Apr. 1872. UPA.

37. *Omaha World-Herald,* Apr. 23, 1939.

38. *Union Pacific Railroad Across the Continent West from Omaha, Nebraska* (Omaha, 1868), p. 24.

39. Samuel Bowles, *Our New West, op. cit.,* p. 46.

40. *Union Pacific Railroad: the Great National Highway, op. cit.,* pp. 8, 9; Report of the Commissioner of the General Land Office, 1868, House Ex. Doc. 1, 40th Cong., 3rd sess. (Serial, 1366), pp. 36–38. See also W. F. Rae, *Westward by Rail,* pp. 71, 72 and H. F. Zider, *Report of the St. Louis Delegation, op. cit.,* p. 21.

41. Memorandum of Mar. 7, 1885 in T. L. Kimball Correspondence, 1885. UPA.

42. Rae, *op. cit.*

43. *Rocky Mountain News,* Aug. 31, 1869; Feb. 11, 1871.

44. Rae, *op. cit.,* p. 79; Zider, *op. cit.,* p. 56; *Union Pacific Railroad Across the Continent,* etc., *op. cit.,* p. 11.

45. Message of Gov. David Butler, Jan. 6, 1869 in *Omaha Daily Republican,* Jan. 10, 1869.

46. *The Platte Journal* (Columbus), Dec. 14, 1870; *Nebraska City News,* Feb. 12, 1868; *Lincoln County Advertiser* (North Platte), Aug. 14, 1872. The poem is from the *Advertiser.*

47. William Dale Crist, "The Role of Railroads in the Economic Development of Early Nebraska " (M.A. thesis, University of Nebraska, 1962), p. 87.

48. J. M. Eddy to Grenville Dodge, Apr. 1, 1872. J. M. Eddy Letterbook, Aug. 1871—Apr. 1872. UPA.

49. *The Platte Journal* (Columbus), Aug. 17, 1870.

50. *Ibid.,* Sept. 7, Nov. 16, 1870.

51. Virginia Bowen Jones, "The Influence of Railroads on Nebraska State Politics" (M.A. thesis, University of Nebraska, 1927), p. 3.

52. Rudolph Alvin Knudsen, "Regulation of Railroad Rates in Nebraska, 1867–1906" (M.A. thesis, University of Nebraska, 1937), p. 2.

53. *The Times* (London), June 28, 1912.

54. S. F. Van Oss, *American Railroads as Investments* (London, 1893), pp. 7, 8.

CHAPTER EIGHT

1. Frank Colton to Oliver Ames, May 21, 1870. President's Office, Letters Received, 1870. UPA.

2. C. W. Tuttle (Assistant Treasurer) to T. C. Durant, Mar. 28, 1867. Tuttle Correspondence, 1867–69. UPA.

3. Copy of Resolution of the Board of Directors attached to letter from Oliver Ames to Grenville Dodge, May 23, 1867. *Ibid.*

4. *The Round Table* (New York), Nov. 23, 1867.

5. Report of Grenville M. Dodge, Jan. 1, 1868. House Ex. Doc. 331, 40th Cong., 2nd sess. (Serial, 1346), p. 17.

6. Davis was authorized to "select, enter and receive from the United States the lands granted by the United States to said Railroad Company, in the name of the Company, as may be necessary to place the Company in full possession of said lands. And he is authorized to draw upon the Treasurer of the Company for such funds as may be necessary to pay the cost of surveying, selecting, conveying, and also for the Registers' and Reseivers' fees, on so much of said Land as the Company may instruct him to take possession of for them. And he is further authorized to make all the necessary arrangements for the disposition of said lands upon such terms as the Trustees named in the Land Grant Mortgage, and the Company may direct." Quoted in Henry McFarland to Leavitt Burnham, Oct. 10, 1878. Secretary-Treasurer's Office, Letters Sent, Aug.–Dec., 1878. UPA.

7. During his first year in office Davis sold 181,462 acres at an average price of $4.60. Clipping in letter from DeHaven and Bro. to J. M. S. Williams, July 13, 1870, Treasurer's Office, Letters Received, Apr.–June 1870, UPA. *Guide to the Union Pacific Railroad Lands* (4th ed., Omaha, 1871), p. iii.

8. Report of Grenville M. Dodge, Dec. 1, 1869, House Ex. Doc. 132, 41st Cong., 2nd sess. (Serial, 1417), p. 17; Oscar F. Davis to John Duff, Jan. 14, 1869, Minutes of the Executive Committee, Apr. 13, 1865 to Feb. 26, 1869, UPA. See Minutes for Jan. 21.

9. Isaac H. Bromley, *Pacific Railroad Legislation, 1862–1885* (Boston, 1886), p. 16; Minutes of the Executive Committee for Jan. 21 and Feb. 12, 1869, *op. cit.*

10. Dr. Hiram Latham to Oliver Ames, Sept. 18, 1869. President's Office, Letters Received, Aug.–Oct., 1869. UPA.

11. Oscar Davis to Oliver Ames, Oct. 18, 1869. President's Office, Misc. Letters Received, Aug.–Oct., 1869. UPA.

12. Oliver Ames to Joseph Wilson, Oct. 22, 1869. President's Office, Letters Sent, Sept. 1869—June 1870. UPA.

13. Frederick Goddard, *Where to Emigrate and Why* (Philadelphia, 1869), p. 578.

14. Grenville Dodge to Oliver Ames, Aug. 8, 1870. President's Office, Letters Received, Apr.–Aug., 1870. UPA.

15. Oliver Ames to J. D. Cox, Aug. 3, 1870, Secretary-Treasurer's Office, Letters Sent, June 1870—Apr. 1871, UPA; Cox to Ames, Aug. 8, 1870, *ibid.*

16. William H. Martin to Oliver Ames, May 4, 1869. President's Office, Misc. Letters Received, 1869. UPA.

17. Colonel F. Werner to Oliver Ames, June 8, 1869. *Ibid.*

18. Letters from W. F. Gray to Oliver Ames, Sept. 11, 21, Oct. 19, 1869. President's Office, Misc. Letters Received, 1869. UPA.

19. C. R. Schaller to Oliver Ames, Aug. 24, 1869. *Ibid.*

20. Dr. H. Wiesecke to Oliver Ames, June, no day, 1869. *Ibid.*

21. Mrs. George W. Moore to Oliver Ames, June 1, 1869. President's Office, Letters Received, 1869. UPA.
22. John Duff to Oscar Davis, Mar. 8, 1870. President's Office, Letters Sent, Sept. 1869—June 1870. UPA.
23. Oliver Ames to Col. C. G. Hammond, Feb. 16, 1870. Treasurer's Office, Letters Sent, Nov. 1869—Mar. 1870. UPA.
24. W. P. Buck to Oliver Ames, June 7, 1869, President's Office, Misc. Letters Received, 1869, UPA; Richard P. Nichuals to Board of Directors, July 25, 1869, *ibid.*
25. J. H. Tice, *Over the Plains and on the Mountains* (St. Louis, 1872), p. 79.
26. *Guide to the Union Pacific Railroad Lands* (Omaha, 1870), pp. 6–8, 24.
27. Davis to Oliver Ames, Aug. 20, 1869. Copy in President's Office, Misc. Letters Received, 1869. UPA.
28. DeHaven and Bro. to J. M. S. Williams, Oct. 23, 1869. Boston Office, Letters Received, Oct. 1869—Jan. 1870. UPA.
29. Oscar Davis to E. H. Rollins, Dec. 22, 1869. Treasurer's Office, Misc. Letters Received, 1869–70. UPA.
30. Oscar Davis to J. M. S. Williams, Dec. 12, 1870. Treasurer's Office, Letters Received, Oct. 1870—Jan. 1871. UPA.
31. J. M. S. Williams to DeHaven and Bro., July 11, 1870. Treasurer's Office, Letters Sent, 1870. UPA.
32. Henry Villard to Oliver Ames, May 13, 1870; copy of advertisement from the American Social Science Association. Both in President's Office, Letters Received, 1870. UPA.
33. DeHaven and Bro. to J. M. S. Williams, Apr. 6, 1870. Treasurer's Office, Letters Received, 1870. UPA.
34. *The Platte Journal* (Columbus, Nebr.), June 22, 1870.
35. Joseph B. Lyman to Boston Office, June 20, 1870. Secretary's Office, Letters Received, 1870. UPA.
36. *Omaha Daily Republican,* Aug. 14, 1873.
37. *Ibid.,* June 27, 1873.
38. Report of the Government Directors, Dec. 1, 1873. Reports of the Directors of the Union Pacific Railroad Company, 1864 to 1886. Sen. Ex. Doc. 69, 47th Cong., 1st sess. (Serial, 2336), p. 80.
39. Oscar Davis to F. L. Ames, July 2, 1874. Land Department Letters, Jan. 1874—Apr. 1876. UPA.
40. *The Pioneer,* Vol. 1, No. 2 (July 1874).
41. Crist, *op. cit.,* p. 46. Crist attributed much importance to railroad stimulation. See also the comment of the Commissioner of the General Land Office for 1870. House Ex. Doc. 1, Part 4, 41st Cong., 3rd sess. (Serial, 1449), p. 104.
42. Addison Sheldon, *Land Systems and Land Policies in Nebraska,* Publications of the Nebraska State Historical Society, Vol. XXII (Lincoln, 1936), pp. 86, 87; Lloyd Bernard Sellin, "The Settlement of Nebraska to 1880" (M.A. thesis, University of Southern California, 1940), p. 198.
43. Oscar Davis to E. H. Rollins, Nov. 19, 1874, Omaha Letters, Letters Sent, Apr. 1874—Jan. 1875, UPA; Rollins to Davis, Nov. 24, 1874, Secretary-Treasurer's Office, Letters Sent, Oct. 1874—Feb. 1875, UPA.
44. Report of the Government Directors, Dec. 2, 1874, *op. cit.,* p. 92.

45. Land Department Account Sheet. Omaha Letters, Nov. 1874, Letters Sent, Apr. 1874—Jan. 1875. UPA.

46. J. W. Gannett to E. H. Rollins, Apr. 16, 1875. Secretary-Treasurer's Office, Letters Received, 1875. UPA.

47. *Omaha Daily Republican,* Apr. 10, 1875.

48. Oscar Davis to E. H. Rollins, June 14, 1875. Omaha Letters, Jan.–Oct., 1875. UPA.

49. Oscar Davis to E. H. Rollins, Apr. 13, 1875. Secretary-Treasurer's Office, Letters Received, 1875. UPA.

50. *Western Nebraskian* (North Platte), Mar. 12, 1875. An example of advertising in books may be seen in Edwin A. Curley, *Nebraska, Its Advantages, Resources, and Drawbacks* (New York, 1875). The appendix contains a short piece, signed by Davis, that provides the usual description offered by the land department.

51. *Omaha Daily Republican,* Sept. 2, 1875.

52. Sidney Dillon to J. Proctor Knott, May 4, 1876. President's Office, Letters Sent, Mar. 1876—Jan. 1877. UPA.

53. Oscar Davis to Elisha Atkins, July 10, 1877, Omaha Letters, Mar.–Aug., 1877; Davis to Fred L. Ames, June 18, 1879, Land Department Correspondence, Letters Sent, Apr. 1876—Oct. 1882. UPA.

54. In Apr. 1876, a train said to be carrying nearly 600 California-bound passengers passed through North Platte, Nebr. *Western Nebraskian* (North Platte), Apr. 15, 1876.

55. William Minturn, *Travels West* (London, 1877), pp. 79–86.

56. Charles Francis Adams, Jr., "The Granger Movement," *North American Review* (Apr. 1875), pp. 396–421.

57. William B. Hazen, "The Great Middle Region of the United States, and Its Limited Space of Arable Land," *North American Review* (Jan. 1875), pp. 6–27.

58. Report of T. B. Searight, Surveyor General of Colorado, Aug. 25, 1875, Report of the Commissioner of the General Land Office, 1875, House Ex. Doc. 1, Part 5, 44th Cong., 1st sess. (Serial, 1680), pp. 222–23; Reports of W. McMicken, Surveyor General of Washington, Aug. 19, 1876 and Report of Andrew J. Smith, Surveyor General of Montana, in Report of the Commissioner of the General Land Office, House Ex. Doc. 1, Part 5, 44th Cong., 2nd sess. (Serial, 1749), pp. 259, 313.

59. Report of the Commissioner of the General Land Office, 1877. House Ex. Doc. 1, Part 5, 45th Cong., 2nd sess. (Serial, 1800), p. 1.

60. Oscar Davis to Gould, Feb. 7, 1877 with Gould's noted endorsement, Land Department Letters, Apr. 1876—Oct. 1882; Sidney Dillon to Oscar Davis, Apr. 20, 1877, President's Office, Letters Sent, 1877. UPA.

61. Oscar Davis to Fred Ames, Jan. 30, 1878; Oscar Davis to Jay Gould, Feb. 7, 1877, Land Department Letters, Apr. 1876—Oct. 1882. UPA.

62. S. H. H. Clark to Sidney Dillon, Jan. 13, 1878. Dillon-McFarland Correspondence, Nov. 1877—June 1879. UPA.

63. Sidney Dillon to S. H. H. Clark, Jan. 31, 1878. President's Office, Letters Sent, Dec. 1877—Nov. 1878. UPA.

64. O. F. Davis to DeHaven and Bro., Dec. 22, 1870, Secretary-Treasurer's Office,

Letters Sent, June 1870—Apr. 1871, UPA; Davis to E. H. Rollins, Jan. 18, 1872, Omaha Letters Sent, Apr. 1871—Feb. 1872, UPA; Rollins to Morton, Bliss & Co., Nov. 19, 1874, Secretary-Treasurer's Office, Letters Sent, Oct. 1874—Feb. 1875, UPA. See also Report of the Government Directors, Dec. 2, 1874, *op. cit.*, p. 90 and Minority Report of the U.S. Pacific Railway Commission, 1887, Sen. Ex. Doc. 51, Vol. II, 50th Cong., 1st sess. (Serial, 2505), p. 145.

65. Sidney Dillon to Leavitt Burnham, Mar. 26, 1878. President's Office, Letters Sent, Dec. 1877—Mar. 1878. UPA.

66. Testimony of Artemas H. Holmes, U.S. Pacific Railway Commission, 1887, *op. cit.*, p. 139.

67. Report of John R. Clark, Surveyor General of Nebraska and Iowa, 1878. Report of the Commissioner of the General Land Office, 1878. House Ex. Doc. 1, Part 5, 45th Cong., 3rd sess. (Serial, 1850), p. 257.

68. T. Bierck to Leavitt Burnham, from Hamburg, Ger., July 1, 1879. Secretary-Treasurer's Office, Letters Received, Feb.–Aug., 1879. UPA.

69. Report of the Government Directors, 1879, *op. cit.*, p. 157.

70. Report of the Auditor of Railroad Accounts, 1879. House Ex. Doc. 1, Vol. II, Part 5, 46th Cong., 2nd sess. (Serial, 1911), p. 29.

71. Report of the Commissioner of Railroads, 1881. House Ex. Doc. 1, Vol. II, Part 5, Appendix 10, 47th Cong., 1st sess. (Serial, 2018), p. 576.

72. Report of Theophilus French, Auditor of Railroad Accounts, 1879. Report of the Secretary of the Interior, 1879. House Ex. Doc. 1, Vol. II, Part 5, 46th Cong., 2nd sess. (Serial, 1911), p. 5.

73. *Cheyenne Daily Leader,* Oct. 14, 22, 1874.

74. Minority Report of the U.S. Pacific Railway Commission, 1887, *op. cit.,* p. 179.

75. *Cheyenne Daily Leader,* Oct. 20, 1875.

76. *Ibid.,* Jan. 18, 1875.

77. J. M. Eddy to Grenville Dodge, Sept. 13, 1871. J. M. Eddy Letterbook, Aug. 1871—Apr. 1872. UPA.

78. Sidney Bartlett to Oliver Ames, Oct. 25, 1870. Secretary-Treasurer's Office, Letters Sent, June 1870—Apr. 1871. UPA.

79. J. M. Eddy to E. H. Rollins, Aug. 12, 1871. J. M. Eddy Letterbook, *op. cit.*

80. Report of William L. Campbell, Surveyor General of Colorado, Report of the Commissioner of the General Land Office, 1879, House Ex. Doc. 1, Part 5, 46th Cong., 2nd sess. (Serial, 1910), p. 775; William P. Chandler, Surveyor General of Idaho to F. V. Hayden in *The Great West* (Bloomington, Ill., 1880), p. 283. For comments from Hayden on Oregon and Kansas see pp. 270, 271, 346.

81. Report of the Secretary of the Interior, 1879. House Ex. Doc. 1, Part 5, 46th Cong., 2nd sess. (Serial, 1910), p. 60.

82. Report of the Commissioner of the General Land Office, 1879, *op. cit.*, p. 377; and for 1880, House Ex. Doc. 1, Part 5, 46th Cong., 3rd sess. (Serial, 1959), p. 418. See also C. D. Wilber, *The Great Valleys and Prairies of Nebraska and the Northwest* (Omaha, 1881), p. 345.

83. Letter of Aughey in C. D. Wilber, *op. cit.,* pp. 168–72; Henry Nash Smith, "Rain Follows the Plow," *Huntington Library Quarterly,* Vol. 10, No. 2 (Feb. 1947), p. 185.

84. Report of the Government Directors, 1881, *op. cit.,* p. 175.

CHAPTER NINE

1. Charles Nordhoff, "California," *Harper's New Monthly Magazine,* Vol. XLIV (Apr. 1872), p. 877.
2. Report of W. B. Baker, Secretary of the St. Louis Board of Trade, in H. F. Zider, *Report of the St. Louis Delegation* (St. Louis, 1869), p. 68.
3. *Army and Navy Journal,* June 4, 1870.
4. *Butte Weekly Miner,* Apr. 26, 1881.
5. *Laramie Daily Sentinel,* quoted by the *Rocky Mountain News,* July 15, 1870; *Sentinel,* Aug. 2, 1872; *New York Graphic,* quoted by *Rocky Mountain News* (Denver), Aug. 7, 1873.
6. William A. Bell, *New Tracks in North America* (London, 1870), p. 47.
7. Randolph B. Marcy, *Border Reminiscences* (New York, 1872), p. 370.
8. "Kansas Farmers and Illinois Dairymen," *The Atlantic Monthly,* Vol. 44 (Dec. 1879), pp. 717–19.
9. *Junction City Union* (Kans.), Nov. 13, 1880.
10. *Junction City Union,* Jan. 17, 1880.
11. *The Daily Bee* (Omaha), Jan. 24, 1880.
12. *Daily Kansas State Journal* (Topeka), Jan. 2, 1880.
13. *Kansas City Daily Journal* (Mo.), Apr. 9, 1880. See also *The Junction City Union* (Kans.), Mar. 20, 1880.
14. Report of the Commissioner of Railroads, 1881. House Ex. Doc. 1, Part 5, 47th Cong., 1st sess. (Serial, 2018), pp. 575–78.
15. Henry Copp, *The American Settler's Guide* (Washington, D.C., 1880), p. 83.
16. *The Junction City Union* (Kans.), Mar. 20, Apr. 24, 1880.
17. *Illustrated London News,* Apr. 17, 1880, p. 371.
18. *Kansas City Daily Journal,* quoted by the *Junction City Union* (Kans.), Nov. 12, 1880.
19. *Wa-Keeney Weekly World* (Kans.), Feb. 12, 1881.
20. *Wa-Keeney Weekly World,* June 19, 1880. The rival referred to was the *Wa-Keeney Kansas Leader* that expired in Jan. 1881.
21. *Ibid.,* Aug. 21, 1880.
22. *Ibid.,* June 12, 1880; *Kansas City Daily Journal,* Jan. 14, 1880.
23. Figures from *Illustrated London News,* Apr. 17, 1880.
24. L. P. Brockett, *Our Western Empire* (Philadelphia, 1881), p. 253; George A. Crofutt, *New Overland Tourist and Pacific Coast Guide* (Omaha, 1880), p. 20; Report of the Government Directors, 1880, Report of the Directors of the Union Pacific Railroad Company, 1864 to 1886, Sen. Ex. Doc. 69, 47th Cong., 1st sess. (Serial, 2336), p. 164.
25. T. S. Hudson, *A Scamper Through America* (London, 1882), p. 93; *Junction City Union* (Kans.), May 21, 1881; James Kyner, *End of Track* (Caldwell, Idaho, 1937; Lincoln, Nebr., 1960), p. 170.
26. J. W. Powell, *Report on the Lands of the Arid Regions of the United States* (2nd ed., Washington, D.C., 1879).
27. L. P. Brockett, *Our Western Empire, op. cit.,* p. 38.
28. C. D. Wilber, *The Great Valleys and Prairies of Nebraska and the Northwest* (Omaha, 1881), pp. 68, 69.
29. *Kansas City Daily Journal,* June 24, 1880.

30. Wilber, *The Great Valleys, etc.,* quoting the *Baltimore American,* p. 347.
31. Report of the Government Directors, 1881, *op. cit.,* p. 181.
32. Advertisement in *The Junction City Union* (Kans.), Feb. 26, 1881.
33. Sidney Dillon to Leavitt Burnham, July 14, 1881. President's Office, Letters Sent, May–Sept., 1881. UPA.
34. *The Junction City Union* (Kans.), July 9, 1881, quoting the *Journal.*
35. *Ibid.,* Apr. 2, 1881.
36. *Wa-Keeney Weekly World,* Jan. 15, Apr. 30, 1881.
37. *The Leader,* quoted by *Wa-Keeney Weekly World,* Oct. 1, 1881.
38. Robert E. Strahorn, *The Resources and Attractions of Idaho Territory* (Boise, 1881), pp. 64–71. For an interesting article concerning Strahorn's work see Oliver Knight, "Robert E. Strahorn, Propagandist for the West," *Pacific Northwest Quarterly,* Vol. 59, No. 1 (Jan. 1968), pp. 33–45.
39. *Butte Weekly Miner,* June 28, 1881.
40. *Salt Lake Herald,* Apr. 5, 1881.
41. *Butte Weekly Miner,* Nov. 1, 1881; Robert Strahorn, *Montana and Yellowstone National Park* (Kansas City, 1881), pp. 146–47.
42. L. P. Brockett, *Our Western Empire, op. cit.,* pp. 242–47, 380, 1030.
43. *Semi-Weekly Miner* (Butte), June 17, 1882.
44. William Pabor, *Colorado as an Agricultural State* (New York, 1883), pp. 11, 12, 101–3.
45. Leavitt Burnham to Gardiner M. Lane (Assistant to C. F. Adams), Jan. 17, 1885. President's Office, Letters Received, 1885 BC. UPA.
46. Report of the Government Directors, 1879, *op. cit.,* p. 157; Report for 1883, *op. cit.,* p. 214.
47. Dillon to Fred Ames, Aug. 10, 1883. President's Office, Letters Sent, Apr. 1883—Jan. 1884. UPA.
48. Dillon to Leavitt Burnham, Mar. 30, 1883. President's Office, Letters Sent, Oct. 1882—Apr. 1883. UPA.
49. Report of the Government Directors, 1883, *op. cit.,* p. 212.
50. *The Anti-Monopolist* (Grand Island, Nebr.), Oct. 17, 1883.
51. Report of the Government Directors, 1883, *op. cit.,* pp. 211, 212.
52. *Kansas: The Golden Belt Lands Along the Line of the Kansas Division of the U.P. R'y* (Kansas City, 1883), p. 3.
53. Dillon to Benjamin A. McAllaster, July 28, 1883. President's Office, Letters Sent, Apr. 1883—Jan. 1884. UPA.
54. Thelma Jean Curl, "Promotional Efforts of the Kansas Pacific and Santa Fe to Settle Kansas " (M.A. thesis, University of Kansas, 1960), p. 44.
55. Charles B. Lamborn to C. F. Adams, Jan. 1, 1885. President's Office, Letters Received, 1885 KL. UPA. Lamborn was then land commissioner for the Northern Pacific Railroad. See also memo from Gardiner Lane, Dec. 31, 1884. President's Office, Misc. Letters Received, Dec. 1884. UPA.
56. C. F. Adams to John Dillon, Oct. 14, 1884. President's Office, Letters Sent, Oct. 1884—Jan. 1885. UPA.
57. Artemus H. Holmes to Sidney Dillon, June 16, 1885. John F. Dillon Correspondence, 1885. UPA.
58. Leavitt Burnham to C. F. Adams, Sept. 6, 1884. President's Office, Misc. Letters Received, Sept.–Dec., 1884. UPA.

59. Leavitt Burnham to Fred Ames, Apr. 1, 1884. Trustee's Office, Land Department, Letters Received, Oct. 1882—Sept. 1884. UPA.
60. *Keith County News* (Ogallala, Nebr.), Mar. 18, 1887.
61. Leavitt Burnham to Gardiner M. Lane, Oct. 2, 1884. President's Office, Misc. Letters Received, Sept.–Dec., 1884. UPA.
62. *Thomas County Cat* (Colby, Kans.), Mar. 12, 1885.
63. *Kansas City Daily Journal,* July 3, 1885.
64. *Ellis County Democrat and Advocate* (Hays, Kans.), June 6, 1885.
65. Joseph Nimmo, Jr., Treasury Department Report on the Internal Commerce of the United States (Washington, D.C., 1885), Part III, pp. 95, 105.
66. Burnham to Fred Ames, Feb. 22, 1884. Trustee's Office, Land Department, Letters Received, Oct. 1882—Sept. 1884.
67. Burnham to Ames, May 9, 1884. *Ibid.*
68. Burnham to Ames, May 29, 1884. *Ibid.*
69. Burnham to Ames, June 16, 1884. *Ibid.*
70. Burnham to Ames, July 3, 1884. *Ibid.*
71. *Ibid.*
72. Leavitt Burnham to Fred Ames, Apr. 8, 1885. Trustee's Office, Land Department, Letters Received, Oct. 1882—Sept. 1884. UPA.
73. Report of Leavitt Burnham for 1885, President's Office, Misc. Letters Received, 1886, UPA; Burnham to Fred Ames, Apr. 8, 1885, Trustee's Office, Land Department, Letters Received, Oct. 1882—Sept. 1884, UPA.
74. Charles Francis Adams to Charles W. Wright, c/o the Secretary of the Interior, Jan. 20, 1885. President's Office, Letters Sent, Jan.–Feb., 1885. UPA.
75. Copy of a report by an Agent signing himself "C," dated June 22, 1885, President's Office, Letters Received 1885-BC; S. R. Callaway to C. F. Adams, from North Platte, Jan. 16, 1885, Misc. Letters Received, Dec. 1884—Jan. 1885, UPA.
76. Leavitt Burnham to Gardiner Lane, Jan. 9, 1886. President's Office, Misc. Letters Received, 1886. UPA.
77. Burnham to A. J. Poppleton, Apr. 14, 1886. Copy in President's Office, Letters Received, 1886-PR. UPA.
78. Gardiner M. Lane to Adams, Feb. 3, 1886. Lane Correspondence, Letters Sent, Feb.–Mar., 1886. UPA.
79. George M. Cumming to Adams, June 2, 1886. Cumming Letters, 1886. UPA.
80. C. F. Adams to Molyneux St. John, of Montreal, Oct. 24, 1884. President's Office, Letters Sent, Oct. 1884—Jan. 1885. UPA.
81. Report of Leavitt Burnham for 1885. President's Office, Misc. Letters Received, 1886. UPA.
82. S. R. Callaway to Adams, Nov. 20, 1885. S. R. Callaway Correspondence, Letters Sent, Oct.–Dec., 1885. UPA.
83. George Cumming to Adams, July 14, 1886, Cumming Letters, 1886; Cumming to Adams, Sept. 1, 1886, President's Office, Letters Received, 1886-A, UPA.
84. Cumming to Adams, Aug. 12, 1886. Cumming Letters, 1886. UPA.
85. George Cumming to Adams, July 14, 1886. Cumming Letters, 1886. UPA.
86. Report of Henry W. Rothert, received May 8, 1886. President's Office, Letters Received, 1886-RS. UPA.

87. Frank H. Spearman, "The Great American Desert," *Harper's,* Vol. LXXVII (July 1888), p. 245.
88. *Keith County News* (Ogallala, Nebr.), Feb. 3, 1888.
89. Letter of Benjamin McAllaster in *Western Kansas World* (Wa-Keeney), Aug. 27, 1887.
90. Charles Francis Adams to G. M. Williamson, Mar. 3, 1888. President's Office, Letters Sent, Mar.–June, 1888. UPA.
91. C. J. Smith to C. F. Adams, Feb. 15, 1889. President's Office, Letters Received, 1889-S. UPA.
92. C. J. Smith to C. F. Adams, Feb. 15, Oct. 29, 1889. President's Office, Letters Received, 1889-S. UPA.
93. C. J. Smith to C. F. Adams, Feb. 1, 1889. President's Office, Letters Received, 1889-S. UPA.
94. C. J. Smith to C. F. Adams, Feb. 15, 1889, President's Office, Letters Received, 1889-S; W. H. Holcomb to C. F. Adams, Feb. 8, 1889, Adams-Holcomb Correspondence, Jan.–Feb., 1889, UPA.
95. C. J. Smith to C. F. Adams, June 1, 1888. President's Office, Letters Received, 1888-S. UPA.
96. *Western Kansas World* (Wa-Keeney), Dec. 29, 1888.
97. *Keith County News* (Ogallala), Apr. 20, 1888.
98. C. J. Smith to C. F. Adams, Jan. 24, 1889. President's Office, Letters Received, 1889-S. UPA.
99. *Keith County News* (Ogallala), Mar. 12, 1891.
100. C. J. Smith to C. F. Adams, May 22, 1888. President's Office, Letters Received, 1888-S. UPA.
101. Report of the Commissioner of Railroads 1889. House Ex. Doc. 1, Part 5, 50th Cong., 1st sess. (Serial, 2724), p. 464.
102. *Nebraska. A Complete and Comprehensive Description of the Agricultural, Stock-Raising and Mineral Resources of Nebraska* (Omaha, 1893).
103. William M. Thayer, *Marvels of the New West* (Norwich, Conn., 1890), p. 277.

CHAPTER TEN

1. Report of the Committee on the Pacific Railroad, 1869. Sen. Report 219, 40th Cong., 3rd sess. (Serial, 1362), p. 29.
2. Ovando J. Hollister, *The Mines of Colorado* (Springfield, Mass., 1867), p. 443.
3. *Cheyenne Leader,* Sept. 12, 1868. A New York paper thought the saving in freight charges would pay interest on the entire obligation of such a railroad. *New York Evening Express,* Oct. 28, 1867.
4. William M. Thayer, *Marvels of the New West* (Norwich, Conn., 1890), p. 277.
5. Report of the Committee on the Pacific Railroad, 1869, *op. cit.,* pp. 15, 16.
6. Report of W. T. Sherman, Oct. 1, 1867. Report of the Secretary of War, 1867. House Ex. Doc. 1, Part 1, 40th Cong., 2nd sess. (Serial, 1324), p. 36.
7. Eugene F. Ware, *The Indian War of 1864* (1960 ed., Lincoln, Nebr.), p. 405.
8. St. Louis *Democrat,* quoted by the *Rocky Mountain News,* Sept. 27, 1865; Chicago *Journal,* Nov. 18, 1867; New York *Evening Post,* Oct. 31, 1867.
9. Chicago *Journal,* Nov. 18, 1867.

10. W. C. Church, "The Pacific Railroad," *The Galaxy,* Aug., 1867, p. 491. Louis Simonin, a French traveler also predicted that the Indian would have to merge with the white or be destroyed. Simonin, *The Rocky Mountain West in 1867* (1966 ed., Lincoln, Nebr.), p. 142.

11. Report of the Secretary of the Interior, 1867. House Ex. Doc. 1, 40th Cong., 2nd sess. (Serial, 1326), p. 7.

12. Durant to Grant, May 23, 1867. Tuttle Correspondence, 1867–69. UPA.

13. Report of Samuel B. Reed, Sept. 1, 1867. Leonard Collection, University of Iowa Library, Iowa City.

14. T. J. Carter to Orville Browning, July 23, 1867. Report of the Government Directors, Sen. Ex. Doc. 69, 47th Cong., 1st sess. (Serial, 2336), pp. 33–34.

15. *Nebraska Herald* (Plattsmouth), May 29, 1867.

16. *Ibid.,* June 12, 1867.

17. Michael Delahunty, "The Plum Creek Railroad Attack, 1867," *Nebraska History,* Vol. VII, No. 2 (Apr.–June, 1924), pp. 38, 39.

18. Poppleton to Ames, Aug. 26, 1870. President's Office, Letters Received, Aug. 1870—Jan. 1871. UPA.

19. *The Cheyenne Leader,* Apr. 30, 1868.

20. *Ibid.,* June 22, 1868; Aug. 29, 1868.

21. Report of W. T. Sherman, Nov. 1, 1868. Report of the Secretary of War, 1868. House Ex. Doc. 1, 40th Cong., 3rd sess. (Serial, 1367), p. 7.

22. Sherman's Report of Oct. 1, 1867, *op. cit.;* Report of C. C. Augur, Oct. 14, 1868. Report of the Secretary of War, 1868. House Ex. Doc. 1, 40th Cong., 3rd sess. (Serial, 1367), p. 22.

23. Copy of an Address delivered by Captain Luther North at Chadron, Nebr., June 21, 1933. Luther Heddon North Papers, Nebraska State Historical Society, Lincoln.

24. Augur's Report of Oct. 14, 1868, *op. cit.*

25. Report of W. T. Sherman, Nov. 1868. Report of the Secretary of War, 1868. House Ex. Doc. 1, 40th Cong., 3rd sess. (Serial, 1367), p. 3. See also, Robert G. Athearn, *William Tecumseh Sherman and the Settlement of the West* (Norman, Okla., 1956), p. 198.

26. Augur's Report of Oct. 14, 1868, *op. cit.,* p. 23. See also Crofutt's *New Overland Tourist* (Omaha, 1880), p. 88 and W. F. Rae, *Westward by Rail* (New York, 1871), p. 93.

27. Report of Gen. John Pope, Headquarters, Department of Missouri, Oct. 31, 1870. Report of the Secretary of War, 1870. House Ex. Doc. 1, Part 2, 41st Cong., 3rd sess. (Serial, 1446), p. 11.

28. Report of Philip H. Sheridan, Nov. 1, 1869. Report of the Secretary of War, 1869. House Ex. Doc. 1, Part 2, 41st Cong., 2nd sess. (Serial, 1412), p. 36.

29. *Rocky Mountain News,* July 30, 1870.

30. Report of the Secretary of War, 1870. House Ex. Doc. 1, Part 2, 41st Cong., 3rd sess. (Serial, 1446), p. vii.

31. Report of Gen. Philip H. Sheridan, Oct. 12, 1872. Report of the Secretary of War, 1872, House Ex. Doc. 1, Part 2, 42nd Cong., 3rd sess. (Serial, 1558), p. 36; Report of the Commissioner of Indian Affairs, 1872, Report of the Secretary of the Interior, 1872, House Ex. Doc. 1, Part 5, 42nd Cong., 3rd sess. (Serial, 1560), p. 397.

32. George Crook to J. H. Millard (Government Director of the UP), Oct. 9, 1877. Reports of the Directors of the Union Pacific Railroad Company, 1864 to 1886. Sen. Ex. Doc. 69, 47th Cong., 1st sess. (Serial, 2336), p. 136.

33. Reports of the Government Directors (1877), *op. cit.*, p. 128.

34. Report of Gen. P. H. Sheridan, Oct. 25, 1878. Report of the Secretary of War, 1878. House Ex. Doc. 1, Part 2, 45th Cong., 3rd sess. (Serial, 1843), p. 38.

35. Report of Gen. P. H. Sheridan, Oct. 20, 1882. Report of the Secretary of War, 1882. House Ex. Doc. 1, Vol. I, Part 2, 47th Cong., 2nd sess. (Serial, 2091), p. 80.

36. Report of Philip H. Sheridan, Oct. 22, 1880. Report of the Secretary of War, 1880. House Ex. Doc. 1, Part 2, 46th Cong., 3rd sess. (Serial, 1952), p. 56.

37. Report of Gen. John Pope, Oct. 3, 1879. Report of the Secretary of War, 1879. House Ex. Doc. 1, Part 2, 46th Cong., 2nd sess. (Serial, 1903), p. 83.

38. Report of the Secretary of War, 1879. *Ibid.,* p. iv.

39. Report of Gen. W. T. Sherman, Nov. 10, 1880. Report of the Secretary of War, 1880. House Ex. Doc. 1, Part 2, 46th Cong., 3rd sess. (Serial, 1952), p. 4.

40. Richardson, quoted by *Rocky Mountain News,* May 30, 1866. See also New York *Evangelist,* Oct. 31, 1867 and New York *Evening Mail,* Nov. 12, 1867.

41. Report of W. T. Sherman, Nov. 6, 1882. Report of the Secretary of War, 1882. House Ex. Doc. 1, Vol. I, Part 5, 47th Cong., 2nd sess. (Serial, 2091), p. 5.

42. "Protection Across the Continent," House Ex. Doc. 23, 39th Cong., 2nd sess. (Serial, 1288), pp. 6–8.

43. Report of Gen. W. T. Sherman, Nov. 3, 1881. Report of the Secretary of War, 1881. House Ex. Doc. 1, Vol. I, Part 2, 47th Cong., 1st sess. (Serial, 2010), p. 39.

44. Sidney Dillon to S. H. H. Clark and Dillon to Gen. P. H. Sheridan, Oct. 21, 1879. President's Office, Letters Sent, May 1879—Feb. 1880. UPA.

45. Report of the Secretary of War, 1878. House Ex. Doc. 1, Part 2, 45th Cong., 3rd sess. (Serial, 1843), p. x. See also Edward H. Rollins to Lot M. Morrill (Secretary of the Treasury), Sept. 9, 1876. Secretary-Treasurer's Office, Letters Sent, June–Nov., 1876. UPA. The action of which the Secretary complained was a provision in the army appropriation act of June 16, 1874 that prohibited the payment of any money appropriated by the act from being used to pay land-grant roads for services rendered to the government.

46. At the U.S. Pacific Railway Commission hearings in 1887, UP counsel John F. Dillon testified that "with very trifle exceptions, since the act of 1873, the Government has never paid to the Union Pacific Company the half transportation money which by the terms of the contract is due from the Government to the Company for Government services. And this is true not only prior to 1875, when it was expressly judged by the Supreme Court of the United States that this amount was due to the Company in cash, but it is equally true since that time...." Testimony of John F. Dillon, Reports of the United States Pacific Railway Commission, 1887, Vol. II, Sen. Ex. Doc. 51, 50th Cong., 1st sess. (Serial, 2505), p. 824.

47. Report of Quartermaster Gen. M. C. Meigs, Jan. 28, 1873. House Ex. Doc. 169, 42nd Cong., 3rd sess. (Serial, 1567). See also Reports of the Government Directors for 1874 and 1876, *op. cit.*

48. Report of Quartermaster Gen. M. C. Meigs, Oct. 10, 1873. Report of the Secretary of War, 1873. House Ex. Doc. 1, Part 5, 43rd Cong., 1st sess. (Serial, 1597), p. 108.
49. Report of Quartermaster Gen., 1880. House Ex. Doc. 1, Part 2, 46th Cong., 3rd sess. (Serial, 1952), pp. 318–19.
50. Report of Quartermaster Gen., 1882. Report of the Secretary of War, 1882. House Ex. Doc. 1, Vol. I, Part 2, 47th Cong., 2nd sess. (Serial, 2091), p. 259.
51. Report of Gen. John Pope, Oct. 2, 1882. Report of the Secretary of War, 1882. *Ibid.,* p. 101.
52. W. S. Tilton of the *Western Kansas World* (Wa-Keeney, Kans.), Sept. 7, 1889. See also Francis Paul Prucha, *A Guide to the Military Posts of the United States, 1689–1895* (Madison, Wis., 1964).

CHAPTER ELEVEN

1. *Union Pacific Railroad Across the Continent West from Omaha, Nebraska* (Union Pacific publication, Omaha, 1868), p. 25. Quoting editor of *Harper's Weekly.*
2. H. F. Zider, "Report of the St. Louis Delegation to Omaha and Terminus of the Union Pacific Railroad, September, 1868" (St. Louis, 1869), p. 31.
3. *Guide to the Union Pacific Railroad Lands* (Omaha, 1870), frontispiece.
4. Ralph N. Traxler, "Some Phases of the History of the Colorado Central Railroad, 1865–1885" (M.A. thesis, University of Colorado, 1947). The early history of the road is outlined in a letter from Colorado attorneys Teller and Orahood written some twenty years later. Teller and Orahood to C. F. Adams, July 23, 1885. President's Office, Letters Received, 1885-ST. UPA.
5. Agreement between the Colorado Central and Pacific Railroad and the Union Pacific Railroad Company, June 25, 1867. H. M. Teller Papers, University of Colorado Western History Collections, Boulder.
6. Glenn C. Quiett, *They Built the West* (New York, 1934), p. 154.
7. Hammond to Ames, Aug. 15, 1870. President's Office, Letters Received, Aug. 1870—Jan. 1871. UPA.
8. John H. Tice, *Over the Plains and On the Mountains* (St. Louis, 1872), p. 80.
9. Nathan C. Meeker, President of the Union Colony to Hammond, Aug. 14, 1870. President's Office, Letters Received, Aug. 1870—Jan. 1871. UPA.
10. T. J. Carter to John Williams, Sept. 16, 1870. Treasurer's Office, Letters Received, July–Oct. 1870. UPA.
11. Oliver Ames to John Williams, Oct. 9, 1870. *Ibid.*
12. L. P. Brockett, *Our Western Empire* (Philadelphia, 1881), p. 661.
13. Dr. William Bell, *New Tracks in North America* (London, 1870), pp. 112, 113.
14. Tice, *op. cit.,* p. 86.
15. *Cheyenne Leader,* July 15, 1871; Thomas A. Scott to Henry M. Teller, Aug. 2, 1871, Secretary-Treasurer's Office, Letters Sent, July–Nov. 1871, UPA.
16. Oliver Ames to T. E. Sickels, Sept. 19, 1871. *Ibid.*
17. *Omaha Tribune and Republican,* Sept. 2, 1871; Traxler, *op. cit.,* p. 61.
18. *Rocky Mountain News* (Denver), Sept. 14; Oct. 2, 6, 8, 1872.

19. Report of W. H. Lessig, Sept. 1, 1873. Report of the Commissioner of the General Land Office, 1873. House Ex. Doc. 1, Part 5, 43rd Cong., 1st sess. (Serial, 1601), p. 114.

20. *Rocky Mountain News,* May 24, 1873.

21. Report of the Directors of the Union Pacific Railroad Company, 1864 to 1886. Sen. Ex. Doc. 69, 47th Cong., 1st sess. (Serial, 2336), Report of Dec. 1, 1873, p. 78.

22. *Rocky Mountain News,* Apr. 16, 1873.

23. E. H. Rollins to J. W. Gannett, Apr. 14, 1873. Secretary-Treasurer's Office, Letters Sent, Jan.–Apr. 1873. UPA.

24. Rollins to Gannett, Feb. 21, 1874. Secretary-Treasurer's Office, Letters Sent, Jan.–Apr. 1874. UPA.

25. Sidney Dillon to E. H. Rollins, Nov. 14, 1874. President's Office, Letters Sent, Mar.–Dec. 1874. UPA.

26. *Cheyenne Leader,* Oct. 1, 1874.

27. Sidney Dillon to Oliver Ames, Feb. 13, 1875. President's Office, Letters Sent, Jan.–Aug. 1875. UPA.

28. Report of the Government Directors, 1876, *op. cit.,* p. 117.

29. Dillon to Oliver Ames, Dec. 9, 1875. President's Office, Letters Sent, Aug. 1875—Mar. 1876. UPA.

30. E. H. Rollins to Jay Gould, Apr. 29, 1875, Secretary-Treasurer's Office, Letters Sent, Feb.–May 1875; Rollins to H. M. Teller, June 29, 1875, Secretary-Treasurer's Office, May–Sept. 1875, UPA.

31. Rollins to Henry M. Teller, May 26, 1876. Secretary-Treasurer's Office, Letters Sent, Jan.–June 1876. UPA.

32. E. H. Rollins to Sen. P. W. Hitchcock, Aug. 16, 1876, Secretary-Treasurer's Office, Letters Received, June–Nov. 1876, UPA; Andrew J. Poppleton, "Reminiscences" (Omaha, 1915), p. 28; *Rocky Mountain News,* Aug. 13, 16, 17, 18, 1876.

33. A. J. Poppleton to Sidney Dillon (from Denver), Aug. 26, 1876. Secretary-Treasurer's Office, Letters Received, Feb.–June 1876. UPA.

34. Poppleton to Sidney Bartlett (attorney at Boston), Aug. 30, 1876. Sidney Bartlett Correspondence, Letters Received, Sept. 1875—Feb. 1877. UPA.

35. Sidney Dillon to Oliver Ames, Sept. 4, 1876. President's Office, Letters Sent, Mar. 1876—Jan. 1877. UPA.

36. Andrew J. Poppleton to Sidney Bartlett, Jan. 31, 1877. Sidney Bartlett Correspondence, Letters Received, Sept. 1875—Feb. 1877. UPA.

37. Poppleton to Bartlett, Jan. 1, 1877. *Ibid.*

38. Henry McFarland to J. L. French, Aug. 5, 1879, Secretary-Treasurer's Office, Letters Sent, Aug.–Dec. 1879, UPA; Report of the Government Directors, 1879, *op. cit.,* p. 158.

39. Testimony of Sidney Dillon, U.S. Pacific Railway Commission, 1887, Sen. Ex. Doc. 51, 50th Cong., 1st sess. (Serial, 2505), p. 211; Testimony of Jay Gould, *ibid.,* p. 579. See also Dillon's comment to James F. Wilson, Government Director, Dillon to James F. Wilson, Mar. 5, 1878, Secretary-Treasurer's Office, Letters Sent, Dec. 1877—Apr. 1878, UPA.

40. Quoted by Isaac H. Bromley, *Pacific Railroad Legislation, 1862–1885* (Boston, 1886), p. 29.

41. Report of the Government Directors, 1885, *op. cit.,* p. 248.
42. *Rocky Mountain News,* Mar. 3, 1872.
43. Majority Report of the U.S. Pacific Railway Commission, *op. cit.,* p. 55; The Kansas Pacific Railway and Its Relations to the Government of the United States, L. H. Meyer, Chairman, Committee of Nine of First Mortgage Bondholders, Records of the Office of the Secretary of the Interior, Record Group 48, National Archives, Washington, D.C. For a more general discussion of the condition of the Kansas Pacific see Stuart Daggett, *Railroad Reorganization* (Cambridge, Mass., 1908), pp. 225–31.
44. Nelson Trottman, *History of the Union Pacific,* p. 148.
45. After the consolidation, in Sept. 1880, the Central Branch was leased to the Missouri Pacific.
46. Majority Report of the U.S. Pacific Railway Commission, *op. cit.,* pp. 58–60.
47. Sidney Dillon to Frederick L. Ames, June 14, 1879 and Dillon to S. H. H. Clark, June 16, 1879. President's Office, Letters Sent, Nov. 1878—Sept. 1879. UPA.
48. *Kansas City Daily Journal,* Jan. 27, 1880; *The Daily Bee* (Omaha), Jan. 23, 1880; George Kennan, *E. H. Harriman: A Biography* (Cambridge, Mass., 1922), Vol. I, p. 113.
49. Agreement signed Jan. 14, 1880 by Russell Sage, Jay Gould, Fred L. Ames, E. H. Baker, F. G. Dexter, Sidney Dillon and Elisha Atkins, President's Office, Letters Sent, May 1879—Feb. 1880, UPA; Majority Report of the U.S. Pacific Railway Commission, *op. cit.,* p. 64.
50. Majority Report of the U.S. Pacific Railway Commission, *op. cit.,* pp. 62, 64, 110; Report of the Commissioner of Railroads, 1883, House Ex. Doc., Vol. 1, Part 5, 48th Cong., 1st sess. (Serial, 2190), p. 432. For representative western newspaper comment see: *Kansas Daily Tribune* (Lawrence), Jan. 24, 26, 1880; *Junction City Union* (Kans.), Jan. 31, 1880; *The Daily Bee* (Omaha), Oct. 15, 1880; *Kansas City Daily Journal* (Mo.), Feb. 4, 1880, and the *Denver News,* quoted by *Daily Bee,* Feb. 4, 1880.
51. Kennan, Vol. I, *op. cit.,* p. 114.
52. *Railroad Gazette,* Vol. XIII, Nov. 18, 1881, p. 648.
53. Isaac N. Van Dyke to Frederick L. Ames, July 31, 1889. President's Office, Letters Received, 1889-TY. UPA.
54. Elmer O. Davis, "The Famous Georgetown Loop," *Colorado Magazine,* Vol. 24, No. 5 (Sept., 1947).
55. *Boulder News and Courier,* Feb. 25, 1881.
56. Gardiner M. Lane to C. F. Adams, Oct. 22, 1885. Gardiner M. Lane Correspondence, Letters Sent, Sept.–Nov., 1885. UPA.
57. Sidney Dillon to Thomas L. Kimball, Feb. 12, 1881. President's Office, Letters Sent, Jan.–May, 1881. UPA.
58. Dillon to T. L. Kimball (Assistant General Manager), Feb. 9, 1881. President's Office, Letters Sent, Jan.–May, 1881. UPA.
59. M. C. Poor, *Denver South Park & Pacific* (Denver, 1949), pp. 113–19.
60. Report to the Stockholders of the Union Pacific Railway, 1882 (New York, 1883), p. 14.
61. Report to the Stockholders, etc., for 1883 (New York, 1884), p. 13.
62. Dillon to S. H. H. Clark, July 1, 6, 1881. President's Office, Letters Sent, May–Sept. 1881. UPA.

63. Isaac Bromley to Charles Francis Adams, July 2, 1885, Bromley Correspondence, Letters Sent, Jan.–Sept., 1885, UPA; Adams to Board of Directors, June 15, 1887, President's Office, Letters Sent, Mar.–Aug., 1887, UPA; Report of the U.S. Pacific Railway Commission, Majority Report, Sen. Ex. Doc. 51, 50th Cong., 1st sess. (Serial, 2525), p. 65.
64. M. C. Poor, *op. cit.,* pp. 113–19.
65. M. C. Poor, *op. cit.,* p. 274.
66. S. H. H. Clark to Thomas J. Brady (Second Assistant Postmaster General), Jan. 15, 1877. Omaha and Republican Valley Railroad, Letters Sent, Jan. 1877—May 1880. UPA.
67. See Reports to the Stockholders of the Union Pacific Railroad for the years 1877 through 1883; S. H. H. Clark to Thomas J. Brady, Apr. 23, 1880, Omaha and Republican Valley Railroad Company, Letters Sent, Jan. 1877—May 1880, UPA.
68. Sidney Dillon to S. H. H. Clark, Jan. 29, 1879. President's Office, Letters Sent, Nov. 1878—Sept. 1879. UPA.
69. Sidney Dillon to S. H. H. Clark, Apr. 9, 1877 and Dillon to James A. Evans, Aug. 22, 1877, President's Office, Letters Sent, 1877, UPA; Report of the Government Directors, 1879, 1881 and 1883, *op. cit.*
70. Sidney Dillon to Gov. John M. Thayer of Wyoming, Apr. 25, 1877, President's Office, Letters Sent, 1877, UPA; Dillon to Elisha Atkins, Feb. 15, 1879, President's Office, Letters Sent, Nov. 1878—Sept. 1879, UPA.
71. Report of the Government Directors, 1879, *op. cit.,* p. 159.
72. Sidney Dillon to J. I. Wooster, Mar. 11, 1881. President's Office, Letters Sent, Jan.–May, 1881. UPA.

CHAPTER TWELVE

1. Report of the Commissioner of the General Land Office. House Ex. Doc. 1, Part 3, 41st Cong., 2nd sess. (Serial, 1414), p. 171.
2. W. B. Preston to Brigham Young, Aug. 15, 1871; Young to Preston, Aug. 15, 1871, in Orson F. Whitney, *History of Utah* (Salt Lake City, 1892–1904), Vol. II, p. 269. See also Merrill Beal, "The Story of the Utah Northern Railroad," *Idaho Yesterdays,* Vol. I, No. 1 (Apr. 1957), p. 4.
3. Edward W. Tullidge, *History of Salt Lake City* (Salt Lake City, 1886), pp. 719–20; Andrew Jenson to J. Wylie Sessions, Dec. 7, 1933, Letter in Utah Central Railway Company Files, LDS Church Library.
4. "Journal History," Aug. 26, 1871. LDS Church Library.
5. *Ibid.,* Sept. 16, 1871.
6. John W. Young to Brigham Young, Mar. 25, 1872. John W. Young Correspondence, LDS Church Library. Tullidge gives Mar. 29 as the date. For another account of the road's beginning see the *Salt Lake Herald,* Nov. 17, 1877.
7. *Idaho Statesman,* Sept. 23, 1871. According to UP records "The original purpose of the formation of this corporation was to construct a line of railroad between Ogden, Utah Territory, the terminal of the Union Pacific Railroad Company, the Utah Central Railroad Company, and the Central Pacific

Railroad Company, and Soda Springs, Territory of Idaho, a distance of about 125 miles." Corporate History of the Oregon Short Line.

8. Merrill Beal, "The Story of the Utah Northern Railroad," *Idaho Yesterdays,* Vol. 1, No. 1 (Spring 1957), p. 5; Moses Thatcher to John Young, Oct. 31, 1873, Moses Thatcher Papers, LDS Church Library; *Deseret Evening News,* Feb. 10, 1873.

9. *Helena Herald,* June 19, 1873. Merrill D. Beal, *Intermountain Railroads: Standard and Narrow Gauge* (Caldwell, Idaho, 1962) gives a full description of the Utah Northern's origins.

10. Dan C. Corbin to John W. Young, Oct. 18, 1872. John W. Young Correspondence, LDS Church Library. Corbin was cashier of the First National Bank of Helena.

11. Samuel Word to John Young, Dec. 9, 1872. John W. Young Correspondence, LDS Church Library. John W. Hakola, "Samuel T. Hauser and the Economic Development of Montana: A Case Study in Nineteenth-Century Frontier Capitalism " (Ph.D. dissertation, University of Indiana, 1961), discusses this thoroughly, p. 132 ff.

12. This was the amount Samuel Hauser understood was required. S. T. Hauser to John W. Young, Dec. 20, 1872. John W. Young Correspondence, LDS Church Library.

13. Letter of Col. A. G. P. George, Dec. 25, 1872, in *Helena Herald,* Jan. 2, 1873.

14. *Helena Herald,* Apr. 24, 1873.

15. Hakola, "Samuel T. Hauser," *op. cit.,* pp. 131, 133; John F. Dillon to S. H. H. Clark, Oct. 31, 1881, President's Office, Letters Sent, Sept. 1881—Mar. 1882, UPA. (John Dillon, nephew of Sidney Dillon, acted as counsel to the railroad company.)

16. Hakola, *op. cit.,* p. 135.

17. *Helena Herald,* May 15, 1873.

18. E. S. Wilkinson to Martin Maginnis, Apr. 5, 1875. Martin Maginnis Papers, Historical Society of Montana, Helena.

19. Peter Ronan to Martin Maginnis, June 30, 1873. *Ibid.*

20. Letter of J. R. W. of Bannack, in *Helena Herald,* Mar. 13, 1873. In the spring of 1876 O. B. O'Bannon, of Deer Lodge, confessed to Hauser that the Northern Pacific Railroad "has more supporters here than I had any idea of...." O'Bannon to Hauser, Mar. 13, 1876. Samuel T. Hauser Papers, Historical Society of Montana, Helena.

21. G. F. Cope to S. T. Hauser, Sept. 1, 1873. Samuel T. Hauser Papers, *ibid.*

22. *Helena Herald,* Dec. 18, 1873.

23. *Helena Herald,* Apr. 24, 1873, quoting Corinne *Reporter,* and *Herald* of June 19, 1873.

24. *Ibid.,* Oct. 2, 1873.

25. Richardson to Hauser, Mar. 30, 1874. Samuel T. Hauser Papers, *op. cit.*

26. *Helena Herald,* Feb. 4, 1875.

27. *Ibid.,* Feb. 18, 1875.

28. *Ibid.,* Jan. 14, 1875; *Salt Lake Herald,* Jan. 22, 1875.

29. Samuel Hauser to Joseph Richardson, Mar. 17, 1875. Samuel T. Hauser Papers, *op. cit.*

30. Sidney Dillon to John W. Young and Joseph Richardson, Mar. 20, 1875. Samuel T. Hauser Papers, *op. cit.*

31. Richardson and Young to Hauser, Mar. 20, 1875. *Ibid.*

32. Dan C. Corbin to S. T. Hauser, Apr. 4, 1875. *Ibid.*
33. Hauser to John W. Young, May 8, 1875. *Ibid.*
34. *The Helena Independent,* July 17, 20, 22, 1875.
35. Hakola, "Samuel T. Hauser," *op. cit.,* pp. 124–25. During the 1870s Montana grew from 20,595 to 39,159; Helena's increase was from 3,106 to 3,624.
36. *The Butte Miner,* Aug. 31, Oct. 17, 1876; A. M. Woolfolk, *The Helena and Benton Railroad; Letters of Col. A. M. Woolfolk on the Railroad Question* (Helena, 1876), pamphlet.
37. Granville Stuart, *Forty Years on the Frontier* (Phillips ed., Glendale, Calif., 1957), Vol. II, p. 38.
38. *The Helena Independent,* Sept. 8, 9, 1875.
39. *Helena Herald,* Aug. 12, 1875.
40. Unsigned letter attached to a letter from W. R. Wilson to S. T. Hauser, Oct. 18, 1875, written from Cheyenne, Wyo. Samuel T. Hauser Papers, *op. cit.*
41. Account of Judge Hiram Knowles in the *New North-West,* quoted by the *Helena Herald,* Nov. 11, 1875. Young probably was obliged to sell his interests. The Mormon railroad promoter was in financial difficulty, as a letter written to him by the Secretary of the Utah Western Railway Company (in which he was interested) indicates. "We have no money on hand today and have accounts amounting to about $11,000 staring us in the face, and have written you again to let you know how we stand so that if at all possible you will send us some money right away, if you cannot we are gone sure. We will have to go around like other people and say we have lost our money in the Bank of California...." John Pike to John W. Young, Sept. 21, 1875. John W. Young Correspondence, LDS Church Library.
42. John W. Young to Board of Directors, Utah Northern Railroad, Oct. 19, 1875. John W. Young Correspondence, LDS Church Library.
43. E. H. Rollins to James M. Ham, at New York, Mar. 27, 1875. Secretary-Treasurer's Office, Letters Sent, Feb.–May, 1875. UPA.
44. *The Helena Independent,* Aug. 20, 1875.
45. Joseph Richardson to S. T. Hauser, from New York, Mar. 11, 1876. Samuel T. Hauser Papers, *op. cit.* Dillon had promised the Montana legislators that if they provided a suitable subsidy arrangement for the Utah Northern, the UP Co. would support completion of the enterprise. Dillon to Legislative Assembly of Montana, Jan. 21, 1876. President's Office, Letters Sent, Aug. 1875—Mar. 1876. UPA.
46. Martin Maginnis to S. T. Hauser (marked "confidential"), from Washington, D.C., Jan. 14, 1876. Samuel T. Hauser Papers, *op. cit.*
47. Maginnis to Hauser, no month, no day, 1876. *Ibid.*
48. Moses Thatcher to Sidney Dillon, Feb. 13, 1875. Copy in President's Office, Letters Sent, Jan.–Aug., 1875. UPA.
49. Granville Stuart to S. T. Hauser, from Deer Lodge, Mar. 22, 1876. Samuel T. Hauser Papers, *op. cit.*
50. *The Butte Miner,* Sept. 19, 26, Oct. 10, 1876. Corinne obviously was concerned over a loss of trade suffered when the Utah Northern was connected to Ogden.
51. Martin Maginnis to Hauser, from Washington, D.C. Jan. 1, 1877. Samuel T. Hauser Papers, *op. cit.*
52. *The Butte Miner,* Jan. 9, 1877.
53. Hakola, "Samuel T. Hauser," *op. cit.,* pp. 142–43.

54. Letter to B. F. Potts from Gould, Dillon *et al.,* Mar. 24, 1877, in *The Butte Miner,* Mar. 27, 1877; Hakola, "Samuel T. Hauser," *op. cit.,* p. 144. Some objections to the bill are found in the *Miner,* Feb. 27, 1877.

55. Sidney Dillon to B. F. Potts, Mar. 26, 1877. President's Office, Letters Sent, 1877. UPA.

56. Samuel Word to S. T. Hauser, Feb. 21, 1877, Samuel T. Hauser Papers, *op. cit.;* Joseph H. Mills to Hauser, Jan. 22, Feb. 19, 1877, *ibid.*

57. Unsigned reminiscence, Holiday Supplement to *Dillon Tribune,* Jan. 1, 1886.

58. Scattered issues of *The Butte Miner,* Spring 1877. See particularly issues of Apr. 10 and May 15.

59. *Dillon Tribune,* Jan. 1, 1886.

60. Sidney Dillon to Elisha Atkins, Oct. 31, 1877. President's Office, Letters Sent, 1877. UPA.

61. *The Butte Miner,* Nov. 13, 1877.

62. *Ibid.,* Nov. 20, 1877.

63. Beal, *Intermountain Railroads, op. cit.,* pp. 35–38. See also Sidney Dillon to S. H. H. Clark, Mar. 23, 1878, President's Office, Letters Sent, Dec. 1877— Nov. 1878. UPA. Dillon authorized Clark to buy the road under foreclosure.

64. J. W. Gannett to Henry McFarland, July 22, 1878, Omaha Letters, Letters Sent, Mar.–Sept., 1878, UPA; *Deseret News,* Apr. 3, 1878. See also Corporate History of the Oregon Short Line Railroad Company as of June 30, 1916. UPA (Portland). Note: Unless citations are specifically shown as "Portland" all references to Union Pacific Archives are to be found in the Omaha depository.

65. Sidney Dillon to Hauser, Jan. 24, 1878, and Martin Maginnis to Hauser, Jan. 29, 1878, Samuel T. Hauser Papers, *op. cit.; The Butte Miner,* July 9, 1878; Hakola, "Samuel T. Hauser," *op. cit.;* Beal, "The Story of the Utah Northern Railroad," *op. cit.,* p. 8.

66. Jay Gould to Hauser, Aug. 22, 1878. Samuel T. Hauser Papers, *op. cit.*

67. Jay Gould to Hauser, Sept. 1, 1878. *Ibid.*

68. Chauncey Barbour to Hauser (marked "confidential"), Mar. 4, 1878. *Ibid.*

69. Account by Fisk, in *The Butte Miner,* Feb. 19, 1878. See also *Salt Lake Herald,* Mar. 29, 1878.

70. *Deseret News,* Apr. 30, 1878.

71. Sidney Dillon to B. F. Potts, Feb. 7, 1879. President's Office, Letters Sent, Nov. 1878—Sept. 1879. UPA.

72. C. P. Higgins to Hauser, June 11, 1879. Samuel T. Hauser Papers, *op. cit.*

73. Sidney Dillon to Members of the Legislative Assembly from Lewis and Clark County, Apr. 17, 1879, Samuel T. Hauser Papers, *op. cit.;* Dillon to B. F. Potts, Apr. 17, 1879, President's Office, Letters Sent, Nov. 1878—Sept. 1879, UPA.

74. Report of Gov. B. F. Potts, Oct. 17, 1878. Report of the Secretary of the Interior. House Ex. Doc. 1, Part 5, 45th Cong., 3rd sess. (Serial, 1850), p. 1107.

75. Report of Roswell H. Mason, Surveyor General of Montana, Sept. 24, 1879. Report of the Commissioner of the General Land Office, 1879. House Ex. Doc. 1, Part 5, 46th Cong., 2nd sess. (Serial, 1910), p. 794.

76. Hakola, "Samuel T. Hauser," *op. cit.,* pp. 148–50.

77. Beal, *Intermountain Railroads, op. cit.,* p. 82.

78. *Butte Weekly Miner,* Mar. 16, 1880.

79. *Butte Weekly Miner,* June 8, 1880.
80. *Ibid.,* Feb. 17, 1880.
81. Sidney Dillon to Washington Dunn, Sept. 30, 1880. President's Office, Letters Sent, July–Oct., 1880. UPA.
82. Dillon to J. T. Clark, General Superintendent of the Union Pacific, Sept. 30, 1880. *Ibid.*
83. Dillon to J. Blickensderfer, Jr. (Chief Engineer at Omaha), Oct. 11, 1880. *Ibid.*
84. Dillon to Dunn, Oct. 8, 1880. *Ibid.*
85. Sidney Dillon to Samuel Word, Sept. 2, 1880. President's Office, Letters Sent, July–Oct., 1880. UPA.
86. *Ibid.*
87. Report of Roswell H. Mason, Surveyor General of Montana, Sept. 24, 1879, Report of Commissioner of the General Land Office. House Ex. Doc. 1, Part 5, 46th Cong., 2nd sess. (Serial, 1910), p. 793.
88. Report of Roswell H. Mason, Surveyor General of Montana, Sept. 2, 1880, Report of the Commissioner of the General Land Office, House Ex. Doc. 1, Part 5, 46th Cong., 3rd sess. (Serial, 1959), pp. 985–87; Robert Strahorn, *Montana and Yellowstone National Park* (Kansas City, 1881), pp. 27, 36.
89. Report of the Government Directors, 1880, Reports of the Directors of the Union Pacific Railway Company, 1864 to 1886, Sen. Ex. Doc. 69, 47th Cong., 1st sess. (Serial, 2336), p. 166; Dillon to Samuel Word, Jan. 26, 1880, President's Office, Letters Sent, May 1879—Feb. 1880, UPA; *Dillon Tribune,* Jan. 1, 1886.
90. Henry McFarland to James Ham, Nov. 19, 1880. Secretary-Treasurer's Office, Letters Sent, Oct. 1880—Jan. 1881. UPA. See also McFarland to Daniel Chadwick (Government Director), Dec. 24, 1878. Secretary-Treasurer's Office, Letters Sent, Dec. 1878—Mar. 1879. UPA. With regard to the question of Gould's profits in the transaction, Gould said he sold his holdings at cost while New York banker John Pondir contended that the entrepreneur had bought at one price and sold for another. Testimony of John Pondir, U.S. Pacific Railway Commission, 1887. Sen. Ex. Doc. 51, 50th Cong., 1st sess. (Serial, 2505), p. 443.
91. The *New North-West* (Deer Lodge), Oct. 26, 1883.
92. *Butte Weekly Miner,* Apr. 6, 1880.
93. *Ibid.,* July 19, 1881.
94. *Butte Weekly Miner,* Sept. 6, 27, 1881; *Salt Lake Herald,* Oct. 9, 1881; *Deseret Evening News* (Salt Lake City), Sept. 13, Oct. 19, 1881; S. H. H. Clark, from New York City, to T. L. Kimball, Sept. 23, 29, 1881, President's Office, Telegrams Sent, Aug. 1881—Sept. 1883, UPA.
95. *Butte Weekly Miner,* Oct. 11, 1881.
96. *Ibid.,* Dec. 27, 1881.
97. Dillon to T. L. Kimball, Feb. 23, 24, 1882. President's Office, Telegrams Sent, Aug. 1881—Sept. 1883. UPA.
98. Jacob Blickensderfer to Howard Hinckley, Dec. 8, 1884, President's Office, Misc. Letters Received, Sept.–Dec., 1884, UPA; *Semi-Weekly Miner* (Butte), Sept. 12, 1883.
99. *Semi-Weekly Miner* (Butte), July 16, Aug. 20, 1884.
100. Dillon to F. L. Ames, Aug. 15, 1885. President's Office, Letters Sent, Mar.–Sept., 1882. UPA.

CHAPTER THIRTEEN

1. Brigham Young to Albert Carrington, Apr. 13, 1869. Letterbooks of Brigham Young, LDS Church Library. See also "Journal History," same date, LDS Church Library. The road was organized on Mar. 8, 1869, by Brigham Young, his son Joseph A. Young, George Q. Cannon, editor of the *Deseret News,* Daniel H. Wells, Mayor of Salt Lake City and William Jennings, a prominent local merchant.
2. "Journal History," May 12, 15, 1869. LDS Church Library.
3. Brigham Young, in "Journal History," May 22, 1869. LDS Church Library.
4. Brigham Young to Joseph A. Young, Aug. 19, 1869. Letterbooks of Brigham Young, LDS Church Library.
5. Oliver Ames to Brigham Young, June 4, 1869, LDS Church Library; Brigham Young to Joseph A. Young and Brigham Young, Jr., Dec. 22, 1869, Letterbooks of Brigham Young, LDS Church Library.
6. Letter of John W. Young, Dec. 28, 1869. John W. Young Correspondence, LDS Church Library.
7. George A. Smith to N. S. Elderkin, Jan. 8, 1870; Comments of Brigham Young, Jan. 10, 1870, "Journal History," LDS Church Library.
8. Edward W. Tullidge, *History of Salt Lake City* (Salt Lake City, 1886), p. 716.
9. Message of acting Governor S. A. Mann, Jan. 11, 1870. Governors' Messages to the Legislative Assembly of Utah, LDS Church Library.
10. Resolution of Jan. 4, 1870, signed by Daniel H. Wells, Mayor. *Deseret Evening News,* Jan. 7, 1870. See also Report of the Commissioner of the General Land Office, 1870. House Ex. Doc. 1, Part 4, 41st Cong., 3rd sess. (Serial, 1449), p. 144.
11. George A. Smith to William H. Hooper, Jan. 11, 1870. "Journal History," LDS Church Library.
12. Helen Maria (Fiske) Hunt Jackson, *Bits of Travel at Home* (Boston, 1878), p. 17.
13. Letter of Elias Morris to Albert Carrington, Feb. 23, 1870, "Journal History," LDS Church Library; *Deseret News,* Feb. 8, 1870.
14. Brigham Young to Albert Carrington, June 1, 1870. "Journal History," LDS Church Library.
15. Statement of Brigham Young. "Journal History," Aug. 6, 1870. LDS Church Library.
16. Circular letter of Brigham Young, Aug. 18, 1870. "Journal History," LDS Church Library.
17. "Journal History," Aug. 27, 1870. LDS Church Library.
18. Journal of Wilford Woodruff, Oct. 7, 1870. "Journal History," LDS Church Library.
19. Grenville Dodge and Sidney Dillon to Oliver Ames, Dec. 7, 1870. President's Office, Letters Received, Aug. 1870—Jan. 1871. UPA.
20. George Swan, from the Utah Central's offices, to John W. Young, Jan. 20, 1871, John W. Young Correspondence, LDS Church Library; Telegram from Oliver Ames to T. E. Sickels, Jan. 20, 1871, Secretary-Treasurer's Office, Letters Sent, June 1870—Apr. 1871, UPA.
21. Memorandum of Agreement, Feb. 28, 1871. John W. Young Correspondence, LDS Church Library.

22. Oliver Ames to John W. Young, Jan. 23, 1871. John W. Young Correspondence, LDS Church Library.
23. Orson F. Whitney, *History of Utah* (Salt Lake City, 1892–1904), Vol. II, pp. 274–75.
24. *Inland Empire* (White Pine), quoted by *Deseret News,* Jan. 28, 1870.
25. Brigham Young to Joseph A. Young, Jan. 6, 1871. John W. Young Correspondence, LDS Church Library.
26. Power of attorney to borrow $200,000, Feb. 13, 1871 and to borrow $100,000, June 23. Copies of both instruments in LDS Church Library. See also Edward Rollins to John Sharp, July 11, 1871. Treasurer's Office, Letters Sent, Mar.–July, 1871. UPA.
27. "Journal History," May 1, 1871. LDS Church Library.
28. *Salt Lake Herald,* Aug. 22, 1871. See also *Deseret News,* Jan. 6, 1870.
29. Charles F. Middleton Journal, LDS Church Library.
30. Oakes Ames to Thomas A. Scott, July 22, 1871. Secretary-Treasurer's Office, Letters Sent, July–Nov., 1871. UPA.
31. Gov. George L. Woods to the Assembly, Jan. 9, 1872. Governors' Messages to the Legislative Assembly of Utah, LDS Church Library.
32. *Salt Lake Herald,* Dec. 23, 1871.
33. John Sharp to Brigham Young, from New York, Apr. 6, 1872. John Sharp Correspondence, LDS Church Library.
34. John Sharp to Horace F. Clark, from New York, Apr. 9, 1872. John Sharp Correspondence, LDS Church Library.
35. John Sharp to Brigham Young, from New York, Apr. 21, 1872. *Ibid.*
36. Sharp to Young, June 26, 1872. *Ibid.*
37. *Salt Lake Herald,* June 1872, quoting the *Wall Street Journal.*
38. Sharp to Young, Sept. 22, 1872. John Sharp Correspondence, LDS Church Library.
39. Sharp to Young, Sept. 25, 1872. *Ibid.*
40. Sharp to Young, Sept. 29, 1872. *Ibid.*
41. Issue of Dec. 17, 1872.
42. Report of the Government Directors of the Union Pacific, 1864 to 1886. Sen. Ex. Doc. 69, 47th Cong., 1st sess. (Serial, 2336). Report of Dec. 1, 1873, p. 79.
43. Report of Nathan Kimball, Surveyor General of Utah Territory, Aug. 24, 1874. Report of the Commissioner of the General Land Office, 1874. House Ex. Doc. 1, Part 5, 43rd Cong., 2nd sess. (Serial, 1639), p. 158.
44. Report of C. C. Clements, Surveyor General of Utah, Sept. 15, 1873. Report of the Commissioner of the General Land Office. House Ex. Doc. 1, Part 5, 43rd Cong., 1st sess. (Serial, 1601), pp. 149, 151.
45. John Sharp to Edward Rollins, Dec. 18, 1872. Secretary-Treasurer's Office, Letters Received, Dec. 1872—Mar. 1873. UPA.
46. Sharp to Young, Sept. 25, 1873. John Sharp Correspondence, LDS Church Library.
47. *Deseret News,* July 28, 1873.
48. John W. Young to Brigham Young, from Provo, June 3, 1873. John W. Young Correspondence, LDS Church Library.
49. Sharp to John Duff, June 28, 1873. Secretary-Treasurer's Office, Letters Received, Mar.–Oct., 1873. UPA.

50. Edward Rollins to Sharp, Aug. 29, 1873, *ibid.;* Report of the Government Directors, Dec. 1, 1873, *op. cit.,* pp. 77–78.

51. Edward Rollins to Koutz Brothers of New York, Sept. 17, 1873. Secretary-Treasurer's Office, Aug.–Oct., 1873. UPA.

52. Joseph A. Young to Board of Directors, June 23, 1873. Secretary-Treasurer's Office, Letters Received, Mar.–Oct., 1873. UPA.

53. Issue of Aug. 4, 1874. See also Leonard Arrington, *Great Basin Kingdom* (Lincoln, Nebr. ed., 1966), p. 275.

54. Reference in a letter of Edward Rollins to John Sharp, Jan. 26, 1876. Secretary-Treasurer's Office, Sept. 1875—Feb. 1876. UPA.

55. *Salt Lake Herald,* Feb. 17, 1875.

56. John Duff to T. E. Sickels and Thomas Wardell, Aug. 27, 1872. Secretary-Treasurer's Office, Letters Sent, May–Sept., 1872. UPA.

57. Sidney Dillon to John Sharp, Oct. 20, 1876. President's Office, Letters Sent; Mar. 1876—Jan. 1877. UPA.

58. H. S. Jacobs, President of the little railroad, promised UP authorities that it would tap Nevada's mineral deposits and feed them directly to the larger line. H. S. Jacobs to John Duff, Aug. 11, 1873. Secretary-Treasurer's Office, Letters Received, Mar.–Oct., 1873. UPA.

59. Trackage statistics found in memorandum, n. d. John Young Papers, 1874 file, LDS Church Library.

60. John Pike to John Young, Sept. 6, 1875. John Young Correspondence, LDS Church Library.

61. Report of the Surveyor General of Utah, July 20, 1872, Report of the Commissioner of the General Land Office, 1872, House Ex. Doc. 1, Part 5, 42nd Cong., 3rd sess. (Serial, 1560), p. 167; Whitney, *History of Utah, op. cit.,* Vol. II, p. 270; Robert W. Sloan (ed.), *Utah Gazetteer and Directory for 1884* (Salt Lake City, 1884), p. 109; Corporate History of the Oregon Short Line Railroad Company as of June 30th, 1916 (Prepared in accordance with Valuation Order No. 20 of the Interstate Commerce Commission), pp. 15, 16; Testimony of C. F. Adams, U.S. Pacific Railway Commission, 1887, Sen. Ex. Doc. 51, 50th Cong., 1st sess. (Serial, 2505), p. 68; *Salt Lake Daily Tribune,* Mar. 9, May 4, Aug. 6, 1881.

62. Sidney Dillon to John Sharp, Apr. 23, 1881. President's Office, Letters Sent, Jan.–May, 1881. UPA.

63. Edward Rollins to Sidney Dillon, Oct. 28, 1874. Secretary-Treasurer's Office, Letters Sent, Oct. 1874—Feb. 1875. UPA.

64. John Sharp to Brigham Young, Dec. 26, 1876. John Sharp Correspondence, LDS Church Library.

65. Henry McFarland to A. S. Young (Secretary of the Utah Southern), June 6, 1877. Secretary-Treasurer's Office, Aug.–Dec., 1877. UPA.

66. John Sharp to Henry McFarland, Aug. 7, 1877. *Ibid.*

67. *Salt Lake Herald,* June 22, 1878.

68. Sidney Dillon to John Sharp, Dec. 10, 1878. President's Office, Letters Sent, Nov. 1878—Sept. 1879. UPA.

69. John Sharp to Jay Gould, Jan. 16, 1879. Dillon-McFarland Correspondence, Nov. 1877—June 1879. UPA.

70. L. P. Brockett, *Our Western Empire* (Philadelphia, 1881), p. 1178.

71. John Sharp to Sidney Dillon, Feb. 18, 1879. Dillon-McFarland Correspondence, Nov. 1877—June 1879. UPA.

72. Tullidge, *History of Salt Lake City, op. cit.,* p. 718.
73. Sidney Dillon to John Sharp, Feb. 11, 1881. President's Office, Letters Received, Jan.–May, 1881. UPA.
74. *Deseret News,* June 17, 1881.
75. Dillon to John Sharp, Sept. 2, 1880, President's Office, Letters Sent, July–Oct., 1880, UPA; Dillon to S. H. H. Clark, June 30, 1881, President's Office, Letters Sent, May–Sept., 1881, UPA; Dillon to John Sharp, Mar. 25, 1882, President's Office, Letters Sent, Mar.–Sept., 1882, UPA. See also *Deseret Evening News,* Oct. 29, 1880 and *Salt Lake Herald,* Oct. 13, 1881.
76. Testimony of Sidney Dillon, U.S. Pacific Railway Commission, 1887, *op. cit.,* p. 217. For a brief history of the Salt Lake and Western see Robert W. Sloan (ed.), *Utah Gazetteer and Directory for 1884* (Salt Lake City, 1884), p. 110.
77. T. E. Sickels to C. F. Adams, Aug. 15, 1884. President's Office, Misc. Letters Received, Sept.–Dec., 1884. UPA.
78. J. K. Choate to S. R. Callaway, from Battle Mountain, Dec. 21, 1884. President's Office, Letters Received, Dec. 1884—Jan. 1885. UPA.
79. C. F. Adams to John F. Dillon, Jan. 30, 1886. President's Office, Letters Sent, May–Dec., 1886. UPA.
80. Testimony of Charles Francis Adams, U.S. Pacific Railway Commission, 1887, *op. cit.,* p. 52.
81. John Sharp to C. F. Adams, Nov. 17, 1886. President's Office, Letters Received, 1886-RS. UPA.
82. Sidney Dillon to S. H. H. Clark, Nov. 17, 1881. President's Office, Telegrams Sent, Aug. 1881—Sept. 1883. UPA.
83. *Salt Lake Herald,* Oct. 17, 1880.
84. *Deseret News,* Apr. 15, 1882.
85. Arrington, *op. cit.,* p. 347.
86. *Deseret Evening News,* Nov. 17, 1880.
87. Corporate History of the Union Pacific Railroad Company as of June 30, 1919 (Prepared in compliance with requirements of Valuation Order No. 20 issued by the Interstate Commerce Commission, May 13, 1915), p. 144; Leonard J. Arrington, "Utah's Coal Road in the Age of Unregulated Competition," *Utah Historical Quarterly,* Vol. XXIII (1955), pp. 46–63; A. J. Poppleton to G. M. Lane, Mar. 21, 1887, John W. Young Correspondence, LDS Church Library.
88. Report of the Surveyor General of Utah, Aug. 28, 1880, Report of the Commissioner of the General Land Office, House Ex. Doc. 1, Part 5, 46th Cong., 3rd sess. (Serial, 1959), p. 1086; *Deseret News,* Oct. 18, 1880.
89. Sidney Dillon to E. P. Vining, May 23, 1881. President's Office, Letters Sent, May–Sept., 1881. UPA.
90. Dillon to George W. Hall (Assistant Auditor, Omaha), Mar. 31, 1882. President's Office, Letters Sent, Mar.–Sept., 1882. UPA.
91. Sidney Dillon to Shellabarger and Wilson, Mar. 10, 1882. President's Office, Letters Sent, Mar.–Sept., 1882. UPA.
92. Charles Francis Adams to Grover Cleveland, Dec. 1, 1885, President's Office, Letters Sent, Oct. 1885—Jan. 1886, UPA; Adams to Edward Roberts, July 3, 1888, President's Office, Letters Sent, June–Oct., 1888, UPA.
93. Charles Francis Adams to George A. Sanderson, Dec. 15, 1884, President's Office, Letters Sent, Oct. 1884—Jan. 1885, UPA; Adams to S. R. Callaway, Dec. 17, 1884, Adams-Callaway Correspondence, June–Dec., 1884, UPA.

94. Charles Francis Adams to Rep. A. A. Ranney, June 24, 1886. President's Office, Letters Sent, May–July, 1886. UPA.

95. Report of the Surveyor General of Utah for 1880, *op. cit.*, p. 1087.

96. *Salt Lake Tribune,* Dec. 10, 1885.

97. P. P. Shelby to S. R. Callaway, Mar. 27, 1886. Copy in President's Office, Letters Received, 1886-RS, UPA. In the John W. Young Correspondence, LDS Church Library, there is a letter from a man named Seymour, of the Salt Lake and Fort Douglas Railway, in which the writer said that both steamship line and railways should be urged to aid the Mormons because members of Congress, interested in such things, would listen. Letter to F. D. Richards, dated Sept. 11, 1886.

98. L. P. Brockett, *Our Western Empire, op. cit.,* p. 1177.

99. Charles Francis Adams estimated that the closing of the Horn mine cost the Utah Central $1,000 a day in lost revenues. Charles Francis Adams to Joseph Richardson, Aug. 6, 1885, President's Office, Letters Sent, June–Oct., 1885; John Sharp to Adams, Mar. 18, 1885, President's Office, Letters Received, 1885-RS, UPA.

100. John Sharp to Charles Francis Adams, Mar. 2, 1885. President's Office, Letters Received, 1885-RS. UPA.

101. George H. Daniels to Adams, Nov. 21, 1884. President's Office, Misc. Letters Received, Sept.–Dec., 1884. UPA.

102. P. P. Shelby to Adams, Mar. 29, 1886. President's Office, Letters Received, 1886-RS. UPA.

103. Report of Nathan Kimball, Aug. 23, 1875. Report of the Commissioner of the General Land Office, 1875. House Ex. Doc. 1, Part 5, 44th Cong., 1st sess. (Serial, 1680), p. 253.

104. Report of Gov. George W. Emery, Jan. 11, 1876. Governors' Messages to the Legislative Assembly of Utah, p. 28. LDS Church Library.

105. *Salt Lake Herald,* Nov. 29, 1882.

106. *Salt Lake Herald,* Sept. 29, 1881.

107. Caleb W. West to Charles Francis Adams, Sept. 12, 1889. President's Office, Letters Received, 1889-TY. UPA.

108. A. M. Gibson to Anon., from New York, Apr. 11, 1885. Copy in John W. Young Correspondence, LDS Church Library.

109. *Omaha Republican,* Jan. 8, 1886.

110. John Sharp to Adams, Sept. 30, 1887, President's Office, Letters Received, 1887-PS. UPA.

111. J. F. Curtis to Adams, Mar. 1, 1887. President's Office, Letters Received, 1887-CD. UPA.

112. Charles Francis Adams to John Sharp, Oct. 6, 1887. President's Office, Letters Sent, Aug. 1887–Mar. 1888. UPA.

113. Robert W. Sloan (ed.), *Utah Gazetteer, 1884, op. cit.,* p. 106.

CHAPTER FOURTEEN

1. *The Platte Valley Independent* (North Platte), Feb. 19, 1870.

2. Ralph G. Coad, "Irish Pioneers of Nebraska," *Nebraska History Magazine,* Vol. XVII, No. 3 (July–Sept., 1936), p. 175; Report of the Commissioner of

the General Land Office, 1870, House Ex. Doc. 1, Part 4, 41st Cong., 3rd sess. (Serial, 1449), p. 100.

3. Report of Silas Reed, Sept. 25, 1873. Report of the Commissioner of the General Land Office, 1873. House Ex. Doc. 1, Part 5, 43rd Cong., 1st sess. (Serial, 1601), p. 247.
4. Norbert R. Mahnken, "Ogallala—Nebraska's Cowboy Capital," *Nebraska History,* Vol. XXVIII, No. 2 (Apr.–June, 1947), p. 90.
5. Report of the Government Directors of the Union Pacific Railroad Company, 1864–1886, Sen. Ex. Doc. 69, 47th Cong., 1st sess. (Serial, 2336), Report for 1876, p. 112; Report to the Stockholders of the Union Pacific Railroad, 1875, p. 5.
6. Sidney Dillon to Oliver Ames, Oct. 18, 1876. President's Office, Letters Sent, Mar. 1876—Jan. 1877. UPA.
7. Report of the Government Directors, 1877, *op. cit.,* pp. 125, 135.
8. Sidney Dillon to Elisha Atkins, June 25, 1878. Dillon-McFarland Correspondence, Nov. 1877—June 1879. UPA. See also Report to the Stockholders of the Union Pacific Railroad, 1878, p. 7.
9. For example the *Cheyenne Daily Leader* for June 23, 1874 spoke of the herds of Spanish Merino sheep then being grazed by Hay & Thomas and Converse & Warren on their ranches near Lone Tree Creek, but it admitted that as yet the business was not very significant.
10. Report to the Stockholders of the Union Pacific Railway, 1879, p. 7.
11. Copy dated July 2, 1877, University of Wyoming Western History Research Center, Laramie.
12. Report of the Government Directors, 1879, *op. cit.,* p. 156.
13. George Crofutt, *New Overland Tourist* (Omaha, 1880), pp. 83, 84.
14. *Western Nebraskian* (North Platte), July 26, 1879.
15. Report of Lt. Gen. P. H. Sheridan, Oct., 1880. Report of the Secretary of War, 1880. House Ex. Doc. 1, Part 2, 46th Cong., 3rd sess. (Serial, 1952), p. 54.
16. Leavitt Burnham to Henry McFarland, June 14, 1879. Secretary-Treasurer's Office, Letters Received, Feb.–Aug., 1879. UPA.
17. Sidney Dillon to Henry McFarland, June 24, 1879. Dillon-McFarland Correspondence, Nov. 1877—June 1879. UPA.
18. Quoted by Louis Pelzer, "A Cattlemen's Commonwealth on the Western Range," *Mississippi Valley Historical Review,* Vol. XIII, No. 1 (June 1926), p. 37.
19. Sidney Dillon to E. P. Vining, Feb. 19, 21, 1881. President's Office, Telegrams Sent, July 1880—Aug. 1881. UPA.
20. Elisha Atkins to Dillon, Jan. 4, 1882. Secretary-Treasurer's Office, Letters Sent, Nov. 1881—Feb. 1882. UPA.
21. Ferdinand Hayden, et al., *The Great West* (Bloomington, Ill., 1880), p. 136.
22. Report of Gov. John W. Hoyt, Nov. 1881. Report of the Secretary of the Interior, 1881. House Ex. Doc. 1, Vol. II, Part 5, 47th Cong., 1st sess. (Serial, 2018), pp. 1059–61.
23. *The Junction City Union* (Kans.), Aug. 7, 1880.
24. Quoted by Joseph Nimmo, Jr., Treasury Department Report on the Internal Commerce of the United States (Washington, D.C., 1885), Part III, p. 174.
25. Correspondent "H," in *Rocky Mountain Daily News* (Denver), May 17, 1872.

26. Report of Edward C. David, Surveyor General of Wyoming, Aug. 1, 1876. Report of the Commissioner of the General Land Office, 1876. House Ex. Doc. 1, Part 5, 44th Cong., 2nd sess. (Serial, 1749), p. 220.

27. Isaac Mayer Wise, "Rabbi Wise: By Parlor Car Across the Great American Desert," *The Pacific Historian,* Vol. XI, No. 4 (Fall 1967), pp. 20, 21.

28. Helen Hunt Jackson, *Bits of Travel at Home* (Boston, 1878), pp. 10, 11.

29. Report of Edward C. David, Surveyor General of Wyoming, in F. V. Hayden, et al., *The Great West, op. cit.,* p. 207.

30. *Cheyenne Daily Leader,* Sept. 7, 28, 1874; George Crofutt, *New Overland Tourist, op. cit.,* p. 83; Report of Silas Reed, Surveyor General of Wyoming, Sept. 1, 1874, Report of the Commissioner of the General Land Office, 1874, House Ex. Doc. 1, Part 5, 43rd Cong., 2nd sess. (Serial, 1639), p. 259; Report of the Government Directors, 1879, *op. cit.*

31. *Omaha Republican,* Nov. 22, 1874; Silas H. H. Clark to E. H. Rollins, Sept. 9, 1875, Secretary-Treasurer's Office, Misc. Letters Received, 1875, UPA; Report of the Government Directors, 1875, *op. cit.;* Report of the Commissioner of Railroads, 1882, House Ex. Doc. 1, Vol. II, Part 5, 47th Cong., 2nd sess. (Serial, 2100), p. 457; Report of the Commissioner of Railroads, 1884, House Ex. Doc. 1, Part 5, 48th Cong., 2nd sess. (Serial, 2286), p. 308. During 1884 and part of 1885 the mill was shut down, after which it was leased to a private party and continued operations. See *Camp and Plant* (a Colorado Fuel and Iron Company Publication), Vol. 1, No. 2 (Feb. 22, 1902), pp. 1, 2.

32. Report of Gov. John W. Hoyt, Oct. 26, 1878. Report of the Secretary of the Interior, 1878. House Ex. Doc. 1, Part 5, 45th Cong., 3rd sess. (Serial, 1850), pp. 1179–80.

33. Report of Gov. John W. Hoyt, Nov. 1881. Report of the Secretary of the Interior, 1881. House Ex. Doc. 1, Vol. II, Part 5, 47th Cong., 1st sess. (Serial, 2018), p. 1067.

34. Report of Silas Reed, Sept. 25, 1873, *op. cit.,* p. 251.

35. Report of the Commissioner of the General Land Office, 1881. House Ex. Doc. 1, Part 5, 47th Cong., 1st sess. (Serial, 2017), p. 144.

36. In Report of the Government Directors, 1880, *op. cit.,* p. 164.

37. *Cheyenne Daily Leader,* Aug. 1, 1874.

38. *Ibid.,* Mar. 18, 1875.

39. Testimony of Francis E. Warren, July 18, 1887, U.S. Pacific Railway Commission. Sen. Ex. Doc. 51, 50th Cong., 1st sess. (Serial, 2506), p. 2069.

40. Message of F. E. Warren in *The Cheyenne Sun,* Jan. 20, 1886. See also Report of Gov. Francis E. Warren, Sept. 25, 1886. Report of the Secretary of the Interior, 1886. House Ex. Doc. 1, Vol. II, Part 5, 49th Cong., 2nd sess. (Serial, 2467), p. 1005.

41. Thomas Sturgis to C. F. Adams, Feb. 13, 1886. President's Office, Letters Received, 1886-SW. UPA.

42. T. A. Larson, *History of Wyoming* (Lincoln, Nebr., 1965), p. 159.

43. E. O. Fuller, "Cheyenne Looking North," *Annals of Wyoming,* Vol. 23, No. 1 (Jan. 1951), pp. 29, 30; Richard C. Overton, *Gulf to Rockies: the Heritage of the Fort Worth and Denver-Colorado and Southern Railways, 1861–1898* (Austin, 1953), p. 219.

44. Copy of Indenture with American Loan & Trust Company of Boston, 1887.

See N. W. Jordan (of the Trust Company) to Gardiner Lane, May 3, 1887. President's Office, Letters Received, 1887-JL. UPA.

45. Gardiner M. Lane to N. W. Jordan, May 9, 1888. Gardiner M. Lane Correspondence, Letters Sent, Mar.–Aug., 1888. UPA.
46. Report of F. G. Wheeler, Jan. 1, 1887. President's Office, Letters Received, 1887-TW. UPA.
47. William Courtenay to C. F. Adams, Feb. 21, 1889. President's Office, Letters Received, 1889-C. UPA.
48. Report of Jacob Blickensderfer, consulting engineer, to T. J. Potter, Jan. 18, 1888. President's Office, Letters Received, 1888-PS. UPA.
49. J. M. Carey to C. F. Adams, from Cheyenne, Oct. 12, 1888. President's Office, Letters Received, 1888-CD. UPA.
50. Francis E. Warren to Charles Francis Adams, Mar. 26, 1888. President's Office, Letters Received, 1888-WZ. UPA.
51. I. S. Bartlett to C. F. Adams, Mar. 30, 1888. President's Office, Letters Received, 1888-AB. UPA.
52. Frederick L. Ames to C. F. Adams, Oct. 16, 1886. President's Office, Letters Received, 1886-A. UPA.
53. Joseph M. Carey to C. F. Adams, Sept. 3, 1889. President's Office, Letters Received, 1889-C. UPA. See also Report of the Government Directors for 1890. Sen. Ex. Doc. 233, 51st Cong., 1st sess. (Serial, 2689), p. 2.
54. *Wyoming Eagle* (Cheyenne), Oct. 17, 1930.
55. W. H. Holcomb to C. F. Adams, June 18, 1889. Adams-Holcomb Correspondence, May–Sept., 1889. UPA.
56. Report of the Secretary of the Interior, 1890. House Ex. Doc. 1, Part 5, 51st Cong., 2nd sess. (Serial, 2840), p. xciv.
57. L. S. Anderson to C. F. Adams, Apr. 13, 1890. L. S. Anderson Correspondence, Letters Sent, Feb. 1890—Jan. 1891. UPA.
58. Robert Strahorn, *Montana and Yellowstone National Park* (Kansas City, 1881), pp. 46, 152.
59. George L. Shoup of Salmon City, Idaho, to Robert Strahorn, July 20, 1881, quoted in Robert Strahorn, *The Resources and Attractions of Idaho Territory* (Boise, 1881), pp. 76, 77.
60. Strahorn, *Montana and Yellowstone National Park, op. cit.,* p. 43.
61. *Semi-Weekly Miner* (Butte), Aug. 19, 1885.
62. S. R. Callaway to C. F. Adams, Jan. 12, 1885. President's Office, Letters Received, Dec. 1884—Jan. 1885. UPA.
63. P. P. Shelby to C. F. Adams, June 29, 1886. President's Office, Letters Received, 1886-RS. UPA.
64. Report of Gov. Samuel T. Hauser, Sept. 27, 1886. Report of the Secretary of the Interior, 1886. House Ex. Doc. 1, Vol. II, Part 5, 49th Cong., 2nd sess. (Serial, 2467), pp. 831–32.
65. C. F. Adams to John F. Dillon, Jan. 27, 1886. President's Office, Letters Sent, Jan.–May, 1886. UPA.
66. Testimony of C. F. Adams. U.S. Pacific Railway Commission, 1887, *op. cit.,* p. 47.
67. W. H. Holcomb to C. F. Adams, from Salt Lake City, June 4, 1889. Adams-Holcomb Correspondence, May–Sept., 1889. UPA.
68. C. F. Adams to Mark Hanna, Jan. 17, 1890 and Adams to T. F. Oakes

(President of the Northern Pacific), Jan. 16, 1890. President's Office, Letters Sent, Jan.–June, 1890. UPA.
69. Report of the Government Directors, 1890. Sen. Ex. Doc. 233, 51st Cong., 1st sess. (Serial, 2689), p. 5.
70. Charles Francis Adams, Memorandum of May, 1886. President's Office, Letters Sent, May–July, 1886. UPA.
71. Gardiner M. Lane to M. Marc Francillon, Feb. 5, 1889. Gardiner M. Lane Correspondence, Letters Sent, Jan.–May, 1889. UPA.
72. Thomas B. Westron to Gardiner M. Lane, Feb. 1887. President's Office, Letters Received, 1887-TM. UPA.
73. C. F. Adams to Sidney Dillon, Feb. 26, 1885. President's Office, Letters Sent, Feb.–June, 1885. UPA.

CHAPTER FIFTEEN

1. P. J. Pengra, *Oregon Branch of the Pacific Railroad* (Wash., 1868), pp. 1–15.
2. Sidney Dillon to Frederick L. Ames, June 13, 1879. President's Office, Letters Sent, Nov. 1878—Sept. 1879. UPA.
3. *Idaho Statesman* (Boise), Dec. 14, 1865; *The Idaho World* (Idaho City), Dec. 16, 1865.
4. *Idaho Statesman,* June 2, Nov. 6, 1866.
5. Report of G. M. Dodge, Jan. 1, 1868. House Ex. Doc. 331, 40th Cong., 2nd sess. (Serial, 1346), pp. 9, 21.
6. Report of G. M. Dodge, Dec. 1, 1869. House Ex. Doc. 132, 41st Cong., 2nd sess. (Serial, 1417), pp. 14–17. See p. 60 for comments from Hudnutt's report. See also comment in *Cheyenne Leader,* Feb. 19, 1868. In Oct. 1868, when Durant asked Dodge to make the survey, Oliver Ames also urged Dodge to lay UP rails westward from Salt Lake because "It is very important to us to have this line far enough west to take in the Oregon Branch." Ames to Dodge, Oct. 20, 1868. Dodge Collection, Iowa State Department of History and Archives, Des Moines.
7. Oliver Ames to G. M. Dodge, Jan. 7, 1867 [1868?]. Dodge Collection, *op. cit.* While this is dated 1867, it is filed in the 1868 material and from other evidence 1868 would seem to be the correct date.
8. *Idaho Statesman,* Dec. 11, 1867; Jan. 6, 8, 1868. See also issue of Nov. 28, 1868.
9. *Cheyenne Leader,* Feb. 3, 1868; *Idaho Statesman,* Feb. 13, 1869.
10. *Idaho World* (Idaho City), May 20, 1869.
11. *Idaho Statesman* (Boise), Nov. 25, 1869.
12. Issue of Mar. 5, 1872.
13. Gov. Thomas W. Bennett, in *Idaho World,* Sept. 3, 1875; Surveyor General of Idaho, Aug. 20, 1874, Report of the Commissioner of the General Land Office, 1874, House Ex. Doc. 1, Part 5, 43rd Cong., 2nd sess. (Serial, 1639), p. 147.
14. The actual transfer of O. S. N. stock to the O. R. & N. took place Feb. 27, 1880. Minutes of the Executive Committee of the O. R. & N., Feb. 27, 1880, Vol. I, p. 72. UPA (Portland).

15. F. B. Gill, "Railroad Building in the Northwest," *Pacific Semaphore,* Vol. 2, No. 33 (Sept. 10, 1914), pp. 3, 12. The O. R. & N. obtained a foothold in Washington Territory in 1881 by buying up a small road begun in 1871–72 under the direction of Dr. Dorsey S. Baker. The Walla Walla Railroad Company, as it was formally known, was built as cheaply as possible. In lieu of rails, stringers were laid across the ties and covered with strap-iron, in the manner of roads built in the East in the earliest days of construction. Westerners jokingly said the stringers were covered with rawhide which gave rise to the nickname "Rawhide Road." By 1884 the O. R. & N. operated slightly over 200 miles in Washington, principally in the eastern wheat regions. In 1892, the UP controlled this section and had a total of 270 miles of road in Washington. Sol H. Lewis, "A History of the Railroads in Washington," *Washington Historical Quarterly,* Vol. VIII, No. 3 (July 1912), pp. 179–97.

16. Testimony of Sidney Dillon, Majority Report of the U.S. Pacific Railway Commission, 1887, Sen. Ex. Doc. 51, Vol. II, 50th Cong., 1st sess. (Serial, 2505), pp. 211, 212; C. F. Adams to James W. Savage, Peter Dey, George M. Bogue, July 28, 1888, President's Office, Letters Sent, June–Oct., 1888, UPA.

17. C. F. Adams to James W. Savage, Peter A. Dey and George M. Bogue, July 28, 1888, *op. cit.*

18. G. M. Cumming to C. F. Adams, Feb. 3, 1887, Cumming-Adams Correspondence, 1887; G. M. Lane to C. F. Adams, Oct. 27, 1885, G. M. Lane Correspondence, Letters Sent, Sept.–Nov., 1885, UPA; Robert Strahorn, "Ninety Years of Boyhood," Typescript, Idaho State Historical Society, p. 322.

19. Sidney Dillon to Jacob Blickensderfer (Chief Engineer at Omaha), Aug. 12, 1880. President's Office, Letters Sent, July–Oct., 1880. UPA.

20. Reports to the Stockholders of the Union Pacific Railway Company, 1882, 1883 and 1884; *Salt Lake Herald,* Mar. 18, May 29, 1881; *Butte Weekly Miner,* June 21, 1881; *The Weekly Standard* (Portland), Aug. 18, 1882; *Railroad Gazette,* Mar. 18, 1881, p. 163.

21. Report of Gov. John B. Neil, Dec. 31, 1881. Report of the Secretary of the Interior, 1881. House Ex. Doc. 1, Part 5, 47th Cong., 1st sess. (Serial, 2018), pp. 1091–92.

22. Robert Strahorn, *The Resources and Attractions of Idaho Territory* (Boise, 1881), pp. 17, 61, 78, 82.

23. L. P. Brockett, *Our Western Empire* (Philadelphia, 1881), pp. 795–96.

24. *Deseret News,* May 26, 1881. See also "Journal History," June 17, 1882. LDS Church Library.

25. *The Weekly Standard* (Portland), Dec. 22, 1881.

26. Report of the Commissioner of the General Land Office, 1882. House Ex. Doc. 1, Part 5, 47th Cong., 2nd sess. (Serial, 2099), p. 65.

27. Report of James C. Tolman, Aug. 15, 1880. Report of the Commissioner of the General Land Office, 1880. House Ex. Doc. 1, Part 5, 46th Cong., 3rd sess. (Serial, 1959), p. 1069.

28. James H. Kyner, *End of Track* (Caldwell, Idaho, 1937; Lincoln, Nebr., 1960), p. 129.

29. *Deseret News,* Sept. 11, 1881. Edward A. Flint, a civil engineer and a personal friend of Charles Francis Adams, later told Adams that Stevens was "of no account" and that Collins was an "unmitigated scamp." Neither man had any previous contracting experience and it was generally believed, said Flint, that

the two did "what they could to squeeze out of the subs and the latter were certainly victims." Edward A. Flint to Adams, Aug. 21, 1884. President's Office, Misc. Letters Received, Sept.–Dec., 1884. UPA.

30. Sidney Dillon to Fred L. Ames, Apr. 7, 1884. President's Office, Letters Sent, Jan.–Nov., 1884. UPA.

31. Majority Report of the U.S. Pacific Railway Commission, 1887, *op. cit.*, p. 178.

32. A man named William Dallin, for example, published a one-page broadside in which he announced that he was writing a treatise entitled *Three Years on the Oregon Short Line,* in which he proposed to show duplicity, chicanery, imbicility, fraud, mismanagement, misrepresentation and general rascality among UP officials. Later, when C. F. Adams refused Dallin a pass he called the Bostonian "exceedingly superficial minded and utterly incompetent for the position you hold." Chester Collins called Dallin "a crank." Broadside sheet included in S. R. Callaway to Adams, Dec. 1, 1884, Omaha Letters, Letters Sent, Oct.–Dec., 1884, UPA; Dallin to Adams, Nov. 30, 1884; Chester Collins to Sidney Dillon, Nov. 25, 1884, both in President's Office, Misc. Letters Received, Sept.–Dec., 1884, UPA.

33. Sidney Dillon to Chester W. Collins, May 4, 1884. *Ibid.*

34. Sidney Dillon to Fred L. Ames, Nov. 4, 1884. President's Office, Misc. Letters Received, Sept.–Dec., 1884. UPA. Dillon was no longer President at this time.

35. *Portland Daily News,* Nov. 10, 28, 1884; *Omaha Republican,* Nov. 25, 1884; Report of the Government Directors, 1884, *op. cit.,* p. 228; F. B. Gill, "Railroad Building in the Northwest," *Pacific Semaphore,* Vol. 2, No. 36 (Oct. 24, 1914), p. 12.; S. R. Callaway to C. F. Adams, Nov. 14, 1884, Omaha Letters, Letters Sent, Oct.–Dec., 1884, UPA; Joseph Nimmo, Jr., Treasury Department Report on the Internal Commerce of the United States (Washington, D.C., 1885), Part I, p. 53.

36. Circular No. 36, Nov. 26, 1884. Printed Circulars, 1884–86, UPA; *Portland Daily News,* Nov. 26, 1884.

37. Report of Government Directors for 1884. Report of the Government Directors of the Union Pacific Railway Company, 1864 to 1886. Sen. Ex. Doc. 69, 47th Cong., 1st sess. (Serial, 2336), pp. 227–28.

38. Charles Francis Adams to Dr. Emil Deckert, of Morganton, N.C., Jan. 29, 1885. President's Office, Letters Sent, Jan.–Feb., 1885. UPA.

39. H. C. Newman to Thomas L. Kimball (General Traffic Manager at Omaha), Dec. 5, 1885. S. R. Callaway Correspondence, Letters Sent, Oct.–Dec., 1885. UPA.

40. C. F. Adams to Capt. John Codman, Sept. 30, 1884, President's Office, Letters Sent, June–Oct., 1884, UPA; Adams to W. S. Doddridge (Gen. Supt. at Ogden), Oct. 7, 1884, President's Office, Letters Sent, Oct. 1884—Jan. 1885, UPA. In his letter to Doddridge, Adams commented that in addition to the excitement caused in his office by the size of Codman's apples, he also had high praise for Utah potatoes, saying that they had "spoiled me for any others."

41. C. F. Adams to S. R. Callaway, Dec. 24, 1885. Adams-Callaway Correspondence, Nov. 1885—May 1886. UPA.

42. James Onderdonk, *Idaho Facts and Statistics* (San Francisco, 1885), pp. 20, 21. He was the Territorial Controller.

43. P. P. Shelby to Adams, from Salt Lake City, May 19, 1886. President's Office, Letters Received, 1886-RS. UPA.

44. Adams to P. P. Shelby, May 28, 1886. President's Office, Letters Sent, May–July, 1886. UPA.
45. *Omaha Daily Republican,* June 3, 1885.
46. Robert Strahorn, "Ninety Years of Boyhood," *op. cit.,* p. 323; Edward A. Flint to Charles Francis Adams, Aug. 21, 1884, President's Office, Misc. Letters Received, Sept.–Dec., 1884, UPA.
47. Report of the Governor of Idaho, 1880, Report of the Secretary of the Interior, 1880, House Ex. Doc. 1, Vol. III, Part 5, 50th Cong., 2nd sess. (Serial, 1959), p. 766; clipping from *Statesman* in Robert E. Strahorn to S. R. Callaway, Dec. 11, 1886, S. R. Callaway Correspondence, Letters Sent, Nov.–Dec., 1886, UPA.
48. *The Weekly Standard* (Portland), Jan. 5, 1883; Feb. 1, 1884; *The Evening Telegram* (Portland), July 25, 1889; Report of the Commissioner of the General Land Office, House Ex. Doc. 1, Part 5, 47th Cong., 2nd sess. (Serial, 2099), p. 75.
49. Charles Francis Adams to Horace White (of the *New York Evening Post*) (letter marked "private"), Dec. 3, 1885. President's Office, Letters Sent, Oct. 1885—Jan. 1886. UPA.
50. P. P. Shelby to C. F. Adams, May 19, 1886. President's Office, Letters Received, 1886-RS. UPA.
51. M. A. Kurtz to P. P. Shelby, Nov. 1, 1886. S. R. Callaway Correspondence, Letters Sent, July–Nov., 1886. UPA.
52. Samuel R. Callaway to Gen. C. H. Tompkins (President of the Idaho Mining and Irrigation Company), Dec. 14, 1886. Copy in President's Office, Letters Sent, Dec. 1886—Mar. 1887. UPA.
53. C. F. Adams to Luke J. Page, Mar. 22, 1887. President's Office, Letters Sent, Mar.–Aug., 1887. UPA.
54. Adams to Gen. J. F. Curtis, Oct. 6, 1887. President's Office, Letters Sent, Aug. 1887—Mar. 1888, UPA; See also Adams to S. R. Callaway, Nov. 19, 1886. Adams-Callaway Correspondence, May–Dec., 1886. UPA.
55. C. F. Adams to Moorfield Storey, Dec. 15, 1886. President's Office, Letters Sent, Dec. 1886—Mar. 1887. UPA.
56. John W. Young to Fred Ames (copy), May 8, 1885; Fred L. Ames to John Young, May 8, 1885, both in John W. Young Correspondence, LDS Church Library.
57. Henry Villard to William Norris, of San Francisco, June 30, 1881 and Troilus H. Tyndale to C. C. Jackson, Aug. 20, 1881. O. R. & N. Letters, Letters Sent, June 1881—Apr. 1883. UPA (Portland). Tyndale was the Assistant Secretary of the O. R. & N. See also Julius Grodinsky, *Transcontinental Railway Strategy, 1869–1893: A Study of Businessmen* (Philadelphia, 1962), p. 139.
58. Henry Villard to J. H. Halstead, Mar. 2, 1882. O. R. & N. Letters, Letters Sent, June 1881—Apr. 1883. UPA (Portland).
59. Troilus H. Tyndale to Edward S. Moseley, May 24, 1882. *Ibid.*
60. Minutes of the Executive Committee of the O. R. & N., Vol. I, p. 123. UPA (Portland).
61. Quoted by Julius Grodinsky, *Transcontinental Railway Strategy, 1869–1893* (Philadelphia, 1962), p. 206.
62. T. Jefferson Coolidge to Executive Committee of the O. R. & N., July 10, 1884. Minutes of the Executive Committee of the O. R. & N., Vol. I, pp. 16–162. UPA (Portland).

63. *The Weekly Standard* (Portland), Oct. 31, 1884; *The Portland News,* June 4, 1885; *The Omaha Daily Republican,* May 9, 1885; Elijah Smith to Robert Harris, Apr. 10, 1885, Minutes of the Executive Committee, O. R. & N., Vol. I, p. 183 and Minutes of the Executive Committee, O. R. & N., Nov. 1886, Vol. I, p. 242, both in UPA (Portland).

64. Charles Francis Adams to Gardiner Lane (his assistant), June 11, 1886. President's Office, Letters Received, 1886-A. UPA.

65. Memorandum of Charles Francis Adams, Dec. 15, 1886, President's Office, Letters Received, 1886-A, UPA; *Portland Weekly News,* Dec. 9, 1886.

66. Franklin MacVeagh to Adams, Dec. 13, 1886. President's Office, Letters Received, 1886-KM. UPA.

67. Adams to G. P. Bissell, of Hartford, Conn., July 27, 1886. President's Office, Letters Received, July–Nov., 1886. UPA.

68. Minutes of the Executive Committee, O. R. & N., May 10, 1887, Vol. I, pp. 238, 258, 276–95; Testimony of Charles Francis Adams, U.S. Pacific Railway Commission, 1887, *op. cit.,* pp. 91–94, 99.

69. Charles Francis Adams to P. P. Shelby, Jan. 6, 1887, President's Office, Letters Sent, Dec. 1886—Mar. 1887, UPA; *Portland Weekly News,* Feb. 3, 1887.

70. Charles Francis Adams to Henry Villard, Oct. 3, 1887. President's Office, Letters Sent, Aug. 1887—Mar. 1888. UPA.

71. Comments by Villard, quoted in *The Evening Telegram* (Portland), June 15, 1889.

72. Minutes of the Executive Committee, O. R. & N., Jan. 17, 1888, Vol. I, pp. 333–34, 361–62, UPA (Portland); Charles Francis Adams to Sidney Dillon, Jan. 18, 1888, President's Office, Letters Sent, Aug. 1887—Mar. 1888, UPA.

73. Correspondence between Ladd and Smith, Feb. 8, 13; Mar. 5, 1888. Board of Directors, O. R. & N., Meeting of Apr. 23, 1888, Vol. III, pp. 365–66.

74. W. S. Ladd and others to Adams, Jan. 21, 1888, President's Office, Letters Received, 1888-L, UPA; F. B. Gill, "Railroad Building in the Northwest," *Pacific Semaphore,* Vol. 2, No. 38 (Nov. 21, 1914), p. 2.

75. Charles Francis Adams to Henry Villard, Aug. 2, 1888. President's Office, Letters Sent, June–Oct., 1888. UPA.

76. Gardiner M. Lane to Adams, Aug. 22, 27, 1888, President's Office, Letters Received, 1888-L, UPA; C. F. Adams to R. S. Grant, Nov. 20, 23; Dec. 6, 1888; Adams to Grenville M. Dodge, Nov. 30, 1888; Adams to Sidney Dillon, Dec. 4, 1888, all in President's Office, Letters Sent, Oct. 1888—Jan. 1889, UPA.

77. C. F. Adams to R. S. Grant, Apr. 19, 1889. President's Office, Letters Sent, Jan.–May, 1889. UPA.

78. *The Evening Telegram* (Portland), May 18, 1889.

79. *Ibid.,* June 17, 1889.

80. C. F. Adams to G. M. Dodge, June 3, 1889. President's Office, Letters Sent, May–Oct., 1889. UPA.

81. Grenville M. Dodge to C. F. Adams, June 17, 1889, President's Office, Letters Received, 1889-DG, UPA; Edward Chase Kirkland, *Charles Francis Adams, Jr., 1835–1915* (Cambridge, Mass., 1965), p. 121.

82. C. F. Adams to R. S. Grant, June 3, 1889. President's Office, Letters Sent, May–Oct., 1889. UPA.

83. Gardiner Lane to Blake, Boissevain & Co., of London, Sept. 12, 1889 and

Lane to Charles Fairchild, Nov. 19, 1889, Gardiner M. Lane Correspondence, Letters Sent, May–Oct., Oct.–Dec., 1889, UPA; Report to the Stockholders of the Union Pacific Railway Company, 1888, p. 14; Corporate History of the Oregon Short Line Railroad Company as of June 30th, 1916, UPA (Portland).

84. C. F. Adams to F. Gordon Dexter, Aug. 20, 1889. President's Office, Letters Received, 1889-AB. UPA.

85. C. F. Adams to Robert Harris, Jan. 23, 1888. President's Office, Letters Sent, Aug. 1887—Mar. 1888. UPA.

CHAPTER SIXTEEN

1. Quoted to Edward C. Kirkland, *Charles Francis Adams, Jr., 1835–1915* (Cambridge, Mass., 1965), p. 127. For an excellent portrait of Adams in his role as president, see Kirkland's entire chapter, "The Union Pacific Failure, 1883–1890."
2. *Rocky Mountain News* (Denver), May 5, 1870.
3. *Ibid.,* Jan. 20, 1871.
4. Nelson Trottman, *History of the Union Pacific* (New York, 1923, 1966), p. 126.
5. Report of the Secretary of the Interior, 1883. House Ex. Doc. 1, Part 5, Appendix 4, 48th Cong., 1st sess. (Serial, 2190), p. 584.
6. Report of the Directors of the Union Pacific Railroad Company, 1864 to 1886. Sen. Ex. Doc. 69, 47th Cong., 1st sess. (Serial, 2336), pp. 103, 104, 114. Reports of 1875, 1876.
7. Minute Book of Directors, Oct. 1863—June 1867, Union Pacific Railroad, Feb. 27, 1867, UPA; Benjamin F. Ham to Grenville Dodge, Mar. 28, 1868, Grenville M. Dodge Papers, Iowa State Department of History and Archives, Des Moines; Andrew J. Poppleton, "Reminiscences" (Omaha, 1915), pp. 21–23.
8. Report of Grenville M. Dodge, Dec. 1, 1869, House Ex. Doc. 132, 41st Cong., 2nd sess. (Serial, 1417), p. 20; Dodge to Ames, May 5, 1870, President's Office, Letters Received, Apr.–Aug., 1870, UPA; T. E. Sickels to Oliver Ames, President's Office, Letters Received, Aug. 1870—Jan. 1871, UPA.
9. George Crofutt, *New Overland Tourist* (Omaha, 1880), p. 21; Henry T. Williams, *The Pacific Tourist* (New York, 1876), p. 18.
10. E. H. Rollins to William E. Chandler, Feb. 21, 1876. Secretary-Treasurer's Office, Letters Sent, Jan.–June, 1876. UPA.
11. John Duff advised Oakes Ames: "Our U.P. charter gives us the right to build bridge independent of the road, and is all right. Don't let speculators in town lots have a charter to blackmail U.P." John Duff to Oakes Ames, June 23, 1870. Secretary-Treasurer's Office, Letters Sent, June 1870—Apr. 1871. UPA.
12. J. W. Gannett (auditor) to E. H. Rollins, Sept. 17, 1872. Secretary-Treasurer's Office, Telegrams Received, Aug. 1872—Apr. 1873. UPA.
13. E. H. Rollins to A. J. Poppleton, June 18, 1874. Secretary-Treasurer's Office, Letters Sent, Apr.–July, 1874. UPA.
14. For press comments see editor Edward Rosewater's complaints in *The Daily Bee* (Omaha), Dec. 26, 1878.
15. *The Omaha Bridge Case in the United States Courts* (Washington, D.C.,

1878). See also Report of the Government Directors for 1876, *op. cit.*, p. 115. The decision is found in Union Pacific Railroad Company vs. Hall, 91 U.S., p. 343.

16. Sidney Dillon to J. S. (?) Hale, of London, June 13, 1876. President's Office, Letters Sent, Mar. 1876—Jan. 1877. UPA.

17. Report of the Government Directors, 1878, *op. cit.*, p. 149.

18. For a detailed discussion of the net earnings problem, see Trottman, *op. cit.*, pp. 131–36. He also treats the Omaha Bridge dispute briefly on pp. 108, 109.

19. Jay Gould to E. H. Rollins, Feb. 7, 18, 20, 1875, Secretary-Treasurer's Office, Letters Received, Jan.–Apr., 1875, UPA; Sidney Dillon to Sen. George F. Edmunds, Jan. 24, 1876, to Sen. J. Rodman West, Mar. 27, 1876, and to Rep. J. Proctor Knott, May 4, 1876, Dillon to Edmunds, President's Office, Letters Sent, Aug. 1875—Mar. 1876, UPA; Dillon to West and to Knott, President's Office, Letters Sent, Mar. 1876—Jan. 1877. UPA.

20. Report of the Secretary of the Interior, 1877. House Ex. Doc. 1, Part 5, 45th Cong., 2nd sess. (Serial, 1800), pp. xxxiv, xxxv.

21. *Rocky Mountain News* (Denver), Aug. 21, 1877.

22. Report of Theos. French, Auditor of Railroad Accounts, 1878, House Ex. Doc. 1, Part 5, 45th Cong., 3rd sess. (Serial, 1850), p. 866; Report of the Directors of the Union Pacific Railroad Company, 1864 to 1886, *op. cit.*, Report of 1879.

23. Oliver Mink to Board of Railroad Commissioners of Iowa, May 18, 1886, Oliver Mink Correspondence, Apr.–Aug., 1886; C. F. Adams to L. Q. C. Lamar (Secretary of the Interior), Mar. 4, 1886, and Memorandum of May 1886, President's Office, Letters Sent, Jan.–May, 1886. UPA.

24. Thomas Nickerson to J. Sterling Morton, Apr. 8, 1878. Quoted in James Olson, *J. Sterling Morton* (Lincoln, Nebr., 1942), p. 229.

25. As late as 1893 Secretary of the Interior Hoke Smith recommended that the Thurman Act applied to all bond aided roads, instead of two only. Report of the Secretary of the Interior, 1893. House Ex. Doc. 1, Part 5, 53rd Cong., 2nd sess. (Serial, 3209), p. xliii.

26. Testimony of Ezra H. Baker. U.S. Pacific Railway Commission, 1887. Sen. Ex. Doc. 51, 50th Cong., 1st sess. (Serial, 2505), p. 747.

27. Henry Poor, "The Pacific Railroad," *North American Review*, Vol. 128 (June 1879), pp. 679–80.

28. Gould to Rollins, Feb. 20, 1875, *op. cit.*

29. Report of Theos. French, Auditor of Railroad Accounts, 1878. House Ex. Doc. 1, Part 5, 45th Cong., 3rd sess. (Serial, 1850), p. 866.

30. Report of the Secretary of the Interior, 1878. House Ex. Doc. 1, Part 5, 45th Cong., 3rd sess. (Serial, 1850), p. xvii. See also comments by the Secretary of the Interior in his report for 1889, House Ex. Doc. 1, Part 5, 51st Cong., 1st sess. (Serial, 2724).

31. Sidney Dillon to John Sherman (Secretary of the Treasury), Aug. 6, 1880, President's Office, Letters Sent, July–Oct. 1880, UPA; Isaac Bromley, *Pacific Railroad Legislation, 1862–1885* (Boston, 1886), p. 29; Report of the Commissioner of Railroads, 1883, House Ex. Doc. 1, Part 5, 48th Cong., 1st sess. (Serial, 2190), p. 410.

32. Report of the Commissioner of Railroads, 1883, *op. cit.*, p. 402.

33. Sidney Bartlett to John F. Dillon, May 22, 1883. Sidney Bartlett Correspondence, Letters Sent, June 1879—Nov. 1883. UPA.

34. *The Daily Bee* (Omaha), July 8, 27, Aug. 16, 1880. These provide only a few examples of his animosity.
35. James H. Kyner, *End of Track* (Lincoln, Nebr., 1960), pp. 93, 94.
36. J. P. Usher to C. F. Adams, Sept. 25, 1884. President's Office, Letters Received, Oct.–Dec., 1884. UPA.
37. *Wa-Keeney Weekly World,* July 2, 1881.
38. Isaac Bromley to C. F. Adams, Dec. 19, 1884. President's Office, Misc. Letters Received, Sept.–Dec., 1884. UPA. Bromley interviewed a number of editors on this subject in 1884.
39. Majority Report of the U.S. Pacific Railway Commission, 1887. Sen. Ex. Doc. 51, 50th Cong., 1st sess. (Serial, 2505), p. 121.
40. Charles Francis Adams to Government Directors, Dec. 24, 1884. Report of the Government Directors, *op. cit.,* p. 242.
41. Reports of the Government Directors, 1883, 1884, 1885, *op. cit.,* pp. 200, 204, 227, 246, 249; Report of the Government Directors, 1886, Sen. Ex. Doc. 10, 49th Cong., 2nd sess. (Serial, 2448), p. 5. (In 1886 and after the reports are in individual volumes, as opposed to the compilation found in Serial, 2336).
42. William Lee Park, *Pioneer Pathways to the Pacific* (Clare, Mich., 1935), p. 109. Park, a contemporary, recalled conversations among Gould, Dillon and Clark that dealt with such expansion.
43. Bromley, *Pacific Railroad Legislation, op. cit.,* p. 46.
44. Elisha Atkins to Sidney Dillon, May 15, 1884. Secretary-Treasurer's Office, Letters Sent, May–Aug., 1884. UPA.
45. *New York Times,* June 13, 15, 18, 1884; *Omaha Daily Republican,* June 19, 1884.
46. C. F. Adams to Moorfield Storey, Jan. 14, 1887. President's Office, Letters Sent, Dec. 1886—Mar. 1887. UPA.
47. Trottman, *op. cit.,* p. 209.
48. Report of the Directors of the Union Pacific Railroad Company to the Stockholders, 1884; Report of the Secretary of the Interior, 1884, House Ex. Doc. 1, Part 5, 48th Cong., 2nd sess. (Serial, 2286), p. xxvii. See also Julius Grodinsky, *Jay Gould: His Business Career, 1867–1892* (Philadelphia, 1957), pp. 420–23.
49. Report of the Directors of the Union Pacific Railway Company to the Stockholders (1885), pp. 7–16.
50. Bromley, *Pacific Railroad Legislation, op. cit.,* p. 32. For an expression of company attitude toward the legislation see Gardiner M. Lane to Isaac Bromley, Dec. 30, 1884. Gardiner M. Lane Correspondence, Oct. 1884—Apr. 1885. UPA.
51. C. F. Adams to George F. Edmunds, June 27, 1884. President's Office, Letters Sent, June–Oct., 1884. UPA.
52. C. F. Adams to Edward P. Alexander, Dec. 8, 1885. Report of the Government Directors, *op. cit.,* p. 252.
53. C. F. Adams to Government Director Colgate Hoyt, Nov. 19, 1884. President's Office, Letters Sent, Oct. 1884—Jan. 1885. UPA.
54. C. F. Adams to Isaac H. Bromley, Dec. 1884. President's Office, Letters Sent, Oct. 1884—Jan. 1885. UPA.
55. C. F. Adams to L. Q. C. Lamar, Nov. 17, 1886. President's Office, Letters Sent, July–Nov., 1886. UPA.

56. C. F. Adams to H. L. Merriman, Jan. 30, 1885. President's Office, Letters Sent, Jan.–Feb., 1885. UPA.
57. C. F. Adams to Rep. Abram S. Hewitt (Washington, D.C.), Dec. 10, 1886. President's Office, Letters Sent, Dec. 1886—Mar. 1887. UPA.
58. John M. Thurston to C. F. Adams, June 27, 1885. President's Office, Misc. Letters Received, 1885-ST. UPA.
59. John M. Thurston to John Dillon, May 14, 1888. Dillon-Adams Correspondence, 1888. UPA.
60. C. F. Adams to S. R. Callaway, Dec. 31, 1884. Adams-Callaway Correspondence, June–Dec., 1884. UPA.
61. C. F. Adams to John M. Thurston, Oct. 14, 1884. President's Office, Letters Sent, Oct. 1884—Jan. 1885. UPA.
62. C. F. Adams to Col. M. M. Price, of Denver, Oct. 15, 1884, and to John D. Long, Dec. 2, 1884, both in President's Office, Letters Sent, Oct. 1884—Jan. 1885, UPA; Adams to Sidney Dillon, Dec. 22, 1886, President's Office, Telegrams Sent, May 1886—June 1887, UPA; Adams to I. E. Gates (V.P. of Southern Pacific), Dec. 11, 1886, President's Office, Letters Sent, Dec. 1886—Mar. 1887. UPA.
63. C. F. Adams to Moorfield Storey, Dec. 23, 1884. President's Office, Letters Sent, Oct. 1884—Jan. 1885. UPA.
64. C. F. Adams to Mary Hotchkiss, Mar. 19, 1887. President's Office, Letters Sent, Mar.–Aug., 1887. UPA.
65. C. F. Adams to Government Director Colgate Hoyt, Dec. 5, 1884. Report of the Government Directors, *op. cit.,* p. 239.
66. C. F. Adams to Gen. J. H. Wilson, Apr. 19, 1887. President's Office, Letters Sent, Mar.–Aug., 1887. UPA.
67. Bromley, *Pacific Railroad Legislation, op. cit.,* pp. 34–35.
68. For the best discussion of efforts to refund the UP's debt, see Kirkland, *Charles Francis Adams, Jr., op. cit.,* pp. 101–11.
69. C. F. Adams to Sen. George F. Hoar, July 1, 1884. President's Office, Letters Sent, June–Oct., 1884. UPA.
70. C. F. Adams to Colgate Hoyt, Dec. 5, 1885. Report of the Government Directors, *op. cit.,* p. 240.
71. George Kennan, *E. H. Harriman: A Biography* (Cambridge, Mass., 1922), Vol. I, pp. 115, 116.
72. Testimony of Jay Gould, U.S. Pacific Railway Commission, 1887, *op. cit.,* p. 577.
73. Minority Report of the U.S. Pacific Railway Commission, 1887, *op. cit.,* pp. 169, 170.
74. Comment of Robert E. Pattison, *ibid.,* p. 169.
75. Majority Report of the U.S. Pacific Railway Commission, 1887, *op. cit.,* p. 20.
76. C. F. Adams to Frederick L. Ames, Apr. 1, 1888. President's Office, Letters Sent, Mar.–June, 1888. UPA.
77. C. S. Mellen to Isaac H. Bromley, Dec. 18, 1888. Mellen-Adams Correspondence, 1888. UPA.
78. C. F. Adams to Dr. George L. Miller, May 28, 1888. President's Office, Letters Sent, Mar.–June, 1888. UPA.
79. Isaac Bromley to C. F. Adams, from Omaha, July 18, 1887. President's Office, Letters Received, 1887-B. UPA.

80. Kirkland, *Charles Francis Adams, Jr., op. cit.,* p. 108.
81. C. F. Adams to W. H. Barnum, Oct. 29, 1888. President's Office, Letters Sent, Oct. 1888—Jan. 1889. UPA.
82. C. F. Adams to Marcus A. Hanna, Nov. 23, 1888. President's Office, Letters Sent, Oct. 1888—Jan. 1889. UPA.
83. Quoted in Kirkland, *Charles Francis Adams, Jr., op. cit.,* p. 110.
84. Quoted in *ibid.,* p. 125.
85. Sidney Dillon to S. H. H. Clark, Dec. 29, 1890. President's Office, Letters Sent, Nov. 1890—July 1892. UPA.

CHAPTER SEVENTEEN

1. Sidney Dillon to W. H. Holcomb, Nov. 26, 1890. Telegram, President's Office, Letters Sent, Nov. 1890—July 1892. UPA.
2. Sidney Dillon to W. H. Holcomb, Dec. 1, 1890. *Ibid.*
3. Dillon to Holcomb, Dec. 2, 1890. *Ibid.*
4. Gardiner M. Lane to F. D. Brown, Feb. 27, 1891. Gardiner M. Lane Correspondence, Letters Sent, Dec. 1890—Sept. 1891. UPA.
5. Lane to A. A. H. Boissevain, Jan. 31, 1891. *Ibid.*
6. Oliver W. Mink to Albert Woodcock, Mar. 25, 1891. Oliver W. Mink Correspondence, Letters Sent, May 1890—July 1891. UPA.
7. Sidney Dillon to John Sharp, Mar. 17, 1891. President's Office, Letters Sent, Dec. 1890—Aug. 1891. UPA.
8. Gardiner M. Lane to Sidney Dillon, July 3, 10, 15, 28, 1891. Gardiner M. Lane Correspondence, Letters Sent, July–Oct., 1891. UPA.
9. Sidney Dillon to F. D. Brown, June 3, 1891, Oliver W. Mink Correspondence, Letters Sent, May 1890—July 1891, UPA; Sidney Dillon to James J. Hill, July 30, 1891, President's Office, Letters Sent, Dec. 1890—Aug. 1891, UPA.
10. Oliver Mink to S. H. H. Clark, Sept. 19, 1891. Oliver W. Mink Correspondence, Letters Sent, July–Nov., 1891. UPA.
11. Gardiner M. Lane to J. M. Wilson, Aug. 22, 1891. Gardiner M. Lane Correspondence, Letters Sent, Dec. 1890—Sept. 1891. UPA.
12. Sidney Dillon to W. H. Frye, Dec. 4, 1890. President's Office, Letters Sent, Dec. 1890—Aug. 1891, UPA. See also Gardiner M. Lane to John F. Kane, Oct. 13, 1890. Gardiner M. Lane Correspondence, Letters Sent, July–Oct., 1890. UPA.
13. Report of the Secretary of the Interior, 1891. House Ex. Doc. 1, Part 5, 52nd Cong., 1st sess. (Serial, 2933), p. xcvi.
14. Sidney Dillon to Benjamin Harrison, Apr. 14, 1891. President's Office, Letters Sent, Dec. 1890—Aug. 1891. UPA.
15. Oliver W. Mink to J. W. Woolworth, Sept. 18, 1893. Oliver W. Mink Correspondence, Letters Sent, Aug.–Sept., 1893. UPA. See also letter of Mink to W. M. Thompson, bookkeeper in the office of Commissioner of Railroads. Oliver W. Mink Correspondence, Letters Sent, Oct. 1890—Jan. 1891. UPA.
16. Sidney Dillon to Jay Gould, May 22, 23, 1891. Telegrams, Oliver W. Mink Correspondence, Letters Sent, May 1890—July 1891. UPA.

17. Edwin F. Atkins to Frederick L. Ames, Aug. 6, 1891. Oliver W. Mink Correspondence, Letters Sent, July–Nov., 1891. UPA.

18. Sidney Dillon to Jay Gould, Aug. 7, 1891. Copy in Assistant Treasurer's Office, Letters Sent, Aug. 1891—Feb. 1892. UPA.

19. Report of the Secretary of the Interior, 1891. House Ex. Doc. 1, Part 5, 52nd Cong., 1st sess. (Serial, 2933), p. xcv.

20. Gardiner M. Lane to Receiver, United States Rolling Stock Company of New York, Aug. 24, 1891. Gardiner M. Lane Correspondence, Letters Sent, July–Oct., 1891. UPA.

21. Oliver Mink to S. H. H. Clark, Sept. 17, 1891. Oliver W. Mink Correspondence, Letters Sent, July–Nov., 1891. UPA.

22. Sidney Dillon to Henry B. Hyde of Bay Shore, Long Island, Sept. 26, 1891. Assistant Treasurer's Office, Letters Sent, Aug. 1891—Feb. 1892. UPA.

23. C. S. Mellen to Erastus Young, Aug. 22, 1891. Oliver W. Mink Correspondence, Letters Sent, Sept.–Nov., 1891. UPA. Mellen was the new superintendent at Omaha; Young was auditor.

24. Grenville M. Dodge to Frederick L. Ames, Nov. 12, 1891. Copy in Treasurer's Office, Letters Sent, June–Nov., 1891. UPA.

25. Edwin Atkins to Frederick L. Ames, Nov. 14, 1891. Oliver W. Mink Correspondence, Letters Sent, Nov. 1891—Apr. 1892. UPA.

26. Sidney Dillon to S. H. H. Clark, Jan. 13, 1891, President's Office, Letters Sent, Nov. 1890—July 1892, UPA; Dillon to John Gilman, of Gilman, Idaho, Dec. 7, 1891, Assistant Treasurer's Office, Letters Sent, Aug. 1891—Feb. 1892. UPA.

27. Oliver Mink to Edwin Atkins, Feb. 1, 1892, Oliver W. Mink Correspondence, Nov. 1891—Apr. 1892, UPA; Edwin Canfield to S. H. H. Clark, Apr. 6, 1892, President's Office, Letters Sent, Nov. 1890—July 1892, UPA; Oliver Mink to James Sharp (telegram), June 9, 1892, Oliver W. Mink Correspondence, Apr. 1892—Feb. 1893. UPA.

28. Oliver W. Mink to E. Rosewater, Apr. 20, 1893. Oliver W. Mink Correspondence, Letters Sent, Feb.–Oct., 1893. UPA. See also Report of the Secretary of the Interior, 1892. House Ex. Doc. 1, Part 5, 52nd Cong., 2nd sess. (Serial, 3087), p. lxxxviii.

29. Report of the Secretary of the Interior, 1892, op. cit., pp. lxxxiv–lxxxviii.

30. Ibid., p. xvi.

31. Oliver W. Mink to Grenville M. Dodge, May 16, 1892 and Mink to S. H. H. Clark, May 23, 1892, both in Oliver W. Mink Correspondence, Letters Sent, Apr. 1892—Feb. 1893. UPA.

32. Report of the Secretary of the Interior, 1892, op. cit., p. xci.

33. Oliver W. Mink to Gov. Rufus B. Bullock, of Georgia, Feb. 7, 1893, and Oliver Mink to Alexander E. Orr, Mar. 15, both in Oliver W. Mink Correspondence, Letters Sent, Jan.–Mar., 1893. UPA.

34. Oliver Mink to Alexander E. Orr, Chairman of the Board, June 21, 1893. Oliver W. Mink Correspondence, Letters Sent, May–July, 1893. UPA. See also S. H. H. Clark to Gardiner M. Lane (copy), June 16, 1893. Ibid.

35. Oliver W. Mink to George J. Gould, June 16, 1893. Ibid.

36. Oliver W. Mink to D. T. Littler, July 15, 1893. Oliver W. Mink Correspondence, Letters Sent, Feb.–Oct., 1893. UPA.

37. Oliver W. Mink to Edwin F. Atkins, Aug. 6, 1893. *Ibid.*
38. Mink to Atkins, Aug. 10, 1893. *Ibid.*
39. T. L. Kimball to O. W. Mink, Sept. 5, 1893. Copy in Oliver W. Mink Correspondence, Letters Sent, Aug.–Sept., 1893. UPA.
40. Joseph W. Paddock to Hoke Smith, June 27, 1893. Oliver W. Mink Correspondence, Letters Sent, May–July, 1893. UPA.
41. Oliver Mink to a Mr. Barron, Sept. 13, 1893. Oliver W. Mink Correspondence, Letters Sent, Aug.–Sept., 1893. UPA.
42. George Kennan, *E. H. Harriman: A Biography* (Cambridge, Mass., 1922), Vol. I, p. 117.
43. *The Denver Republican,* Oct. 10, 24, 1893. The Denver & Gulf extended to the Texas state line where it connected to the Fort Worth & Denver City. Col. Morgan Jones became receiver for the latter line. These roads had been joined in a consolidation of Apr. 1, 1890 and incorporated into the UP system.
44. Stuart Daggett, *Railroad Reorganization* (Cambridge, Mass., 1908), pp. 248, 249.
45. Frank B. Gill, "Railroad Building in the Northwest," *Pacific Semaphore,* Vol. 3, No. 1 (Jan. 9, 1915), p. 13. See also S. H. H. Clark and Oliver Mink to James G. Harris (Treasurer) and Alexander Millar (Secretary), Oct. 13, 1893. Copy in Treasurer's Office, Letters Sent, Aug.–Dec., 1893. UPA.
46. Report of the Government Directors, 1894. House Ex. Doc. 3, 53rd Cong., 3rd sess. (Serial, 3275), p. 6.
47. Report of the Government Directors, 1894, *ibid.,* p. 7. See also Trottman, *op. cit.,* pp. 256, 257.
48. Report of William J. Coombs (Government Director). Report of the Government Directors, 1895. Sen. Ex. Doc. 1, 54th Cong., 1st sess. (Serial, 3347), p. 14. For some of the debate see *Congressional Records* (Jan. 30–Feb. 2, 1895), 53rd Cong., 3rd sess., pp. 1539, 1554, 1590, 1593, 1629, 1686.
49. *The Denver Republican,* Oct. 14, 1893.
50. *The Park Record,* Oct. 14, 1893.
51. *The Salt Lake Herald,* Oct. 14, 1893.
52. *Deseret Semi-Weekly News* (Salt Lake City), Oct. 17, 1893.
53. *Ibid.,* Dec. 30, 1893.
54. *The Nation,* Vol. 53, No. 1367 (Sept. 10, 1891), pp. 190–91 and Vol. 61, No. 1582 (Oct. 24, 1895), pp. 286–87. Jerry Simpson, the Populist leader, urged that the government take over the UP, commenting: "If we succeed with it, it will be a step toward government control of railways." *Rocky Mountain News* (Denver), Feb. 13, 1894.
55. Report of the Government Directors, 1894, *op. cit.,* pp. 7–11.
56. Report of William J. Coombs, Oct. 11, 1895. Report of the Government Directors, 1895, *op. cit.,* pp. 12–15.
57. *Ibid.,* pp. 9–11.
58. Kennan, *op. cit.,* pp. 123–26.
59. Kennan, *op. cit.,* pp. 127–29; Trottman, *op. cit.,* pp. 264–66. See also Report of Government Directors, 1895, *op. cit.,* pp. 4–8. Stuart Daggett, *Railroad Reorganization* (Cambridge, Mass., 1908), gives a detailed account of reorganization plans for the UP, pp. 241–62.

60. Report of the Union Pacific Railroad Company for the Six Months Ending June 30, 1898, p. 3; *Salt Lake Herald,* July 2, 1897; *Deseret Evening News,* July 2, 1897; *New York Times,* July 3, 1897.
61. *The Denver Republican,* Nov. 2, 1897.
62. For a summation of the UP's indebtedness in 1897 see "Statement of the Indebtedness and Liabilities of the Union Pacific Railway Company" (Jan. 13, 1897), Sen. Ex. Doc. 62, 54th Cong., 2nd sess. (Serial, 3469).
63. William V. Allen, "Western Feeling Toward the East," *North American Review* (May 1896), p. 592.
64. Report of the Union Pacific Railroad Company for Six Months Ending June 30, 1898. Scattered issues of the *Denver Republican* also describe the reassemblage of this portion of the system.
65. Annual Reports of the Union Pacific Railroad Company, 1899 and 1900.
66. *The Salt Lake Herald,* Aug. 1, 1897.
67. *Deseret Evening News,* July 7, 1897.

Index